Atlantic Spain and Portugal

Cabo Ortegal (Galicia) to Gibraltar

Bay of Biscay

I. GALICIA

44°

Cabo Ortegal
Ria de Cedeira
Cabo Prior

See RCCPF
South Biscay

El Ferrol

I. Sisargas
Cabo Villano
Corme
Camariñas

A Coruña

SPAIN

43°

Cabo Finisterre

Santiago de Compostela

Ría de Muros

Ría de Arousa

Vilagarcía

Ría de Pontevedra

Vigo

42°

Cabo Silleiro

Baiona
La Guardia

Río Minho

Viana do Castelo

Atlantic Ocean

Povoa de Varzim
Leixões
Porto

Río Douro

41°

II. PORTUGAL

Aveiro

PORTUGAL

Cabo Mondego

Coimbra
Figueira da Foz

40°N

Nazaré
S. Martinho do Porto

Isla Berlenga

Cabo Carvoeiro
Peniche

Río Tejo

39°

Cascais
Oeiras
Lisbon

Cabo da Roca

Sesimbra
Setúbal

Cabo Espichel

38°

Cabo de Sines
Sines

Vila Nova de Milfontes

Río Guadiana

Cabo Sardão
Baleeira
Lagos
Portimão
Albufeira
Vilamoura
Tavira
Faro

Islas Canela & Cristina
El Rompido
Punta Umbria

Seville

Mazagon

Río Guadalquivir

37°

Cabo de São Vicente

Cabo de Santa María

Vila Real de Santo António

Chipiona
Rota
Cádiz
Puerto Sherry

III. THE ALGARVE AND ANDALUCIA

Sancti Petri
Cabo Trafalgar
Barbate

Algeciras
Tarifa

36°

Strait of Gibraltar **GIBRALTAR**

See RCCPF
North Africa

MOROCCO

10°W   9°   8°   7°   6°

Atlantic Spain and Portugal

Cabo Ortegal (Galicia) to Gibraltar

RCC PILOTAGE FOUNDATION

Henry Buchanan

Imray Laurie Norie & Wilson

Published by
Imray Laurie Norie & Wilson Ltd
Wych House The Broadway St Ives
Cambridgeshire PE27 5BT England
☏ +44 (0)1480 462114
Fax +44 (0) 1480 496109
Email ilnw@imray.com
www.imray.com
2015

First edition 1988
Second edition 1990
Third edition 1995
Fourth edition 2000
Fifth edition 2006
Sixth edition 2010
Seventh edition 2015

ISBN 978 184623 620 4

British Library Cataloguing in Publication Data.
A catalogue record for this title is available from
the British Library.

Printed in Croatia by Zrinski

UPDATES AND SUPPLEMENTS

Any mid-season updates or annual supplements are
published as free downloads available from www.imray.com.
Printed copies are also available on request from the
publishers.

FIND OUT MORE

For a wealth of further information, including passage
planning guides and cruising logs for this area visit the RCC
Pilotage Foundation website at www.rccpf.org.uk

FEEDBACK

The RCC Pilotage Foundation is a voluntary, charitable
organisation. We welcome all feedback for updates and
new information. If you notice any errors or omissions,
please let us know at www.rccpf.org.uk

CAUTION

Whilst the RCC Pilotage Foundation, the author and the
publishers have used reasonable endeavours to ensure the
accuracy of the content of this book, it contains selected
information and thus is not definitive. It does not contain all
known information on the subject in hand and should not
be relied on alone for navigational use: it should only be
used in conjunction with official hydrographical data. This is
particularly relevant to the plans, which should not be used
for navigation. The RCC Pilotage Foundation, the authors
and the publishers believe that the information which they
have included is a useful aid to prudent navigation, but the
safety of a vessel depends ultimately on the judgment of the
skipper, who should assess all information, published or
unpublished. The information provided in this pilot book
may be out of date and may be changed or updated without
notice. The RCC Pilotage Foundation cannot accept any
liability for any error, omission or failure to update such
information. To the extent permitted by law, the RCC
Pilotage Foundation, the author and the publishers do not
accept liability for any loss and/or damage howsoever caused
that may arise from reliance on information contained in
these pages.

Positions and Waypoints

All positions and waypoints are to datum WGS 84. They are
included to help in locating places, features and transits. Do
not rely on them alone for safe navigation.

Bearings and Lights

Any bearings are given as °T and from seaward. The
characteristics of lights may be changed during the lifetime
of this book. They should be checked against the latest
edition of the UK Admiralty *List of Lights*.

Contents

THE RCC PILOTAGE FOUNDATION

The RCC Pilotage Foundation was formed as an independent charity in 1976 supported by a gift and permanent endowment made to the Royal Cruising Club by Dr Fred Ellis. The Foundation's charitable objective is 'to advance the education of the public in the science and practice of navigation'.

The Foundation is privileged to have been given the copyrights to books written by a number of distinguished authors and yachtsmen. These are kept as up to date as possible. New publications are also produced by the Foundation to cover a range of cruising areas. This is only made possible through the dedicated work of our authors and editors, all of whom are experienced sailors, who depend on a valuable supply of information from generous-minded yachtsmen and women from around the world.

Most of the management of the Foundation is done on a voluntary basis. In line with its charitable status, the Foundation distributes no profits. Any surpluses are used to finance new publications and to subsidise publications which cover some of the more remote areas of the world.

The Foundation works in close collaboration with three publishers – Imray Laurie Norie & Wilson, Bloomsbury (Adlard Coles Nautical) and On Board Publications. The Foundation also itself publishes guides and pilots, including web downloads, for areas where limited demand does not justify large print runs. Several books have been translated into French, Spanish, Italian and German and some books are now available in e-versions.

For further details about the RCC Pilotage Foundation and its publications visit:
www.rccpf.org.uk

PUBLICATIONS OF THE RCC PILOTAGE FOUNDATION

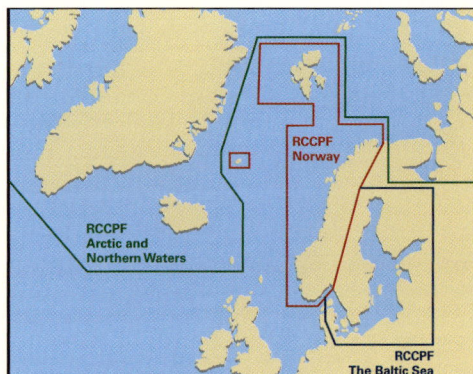

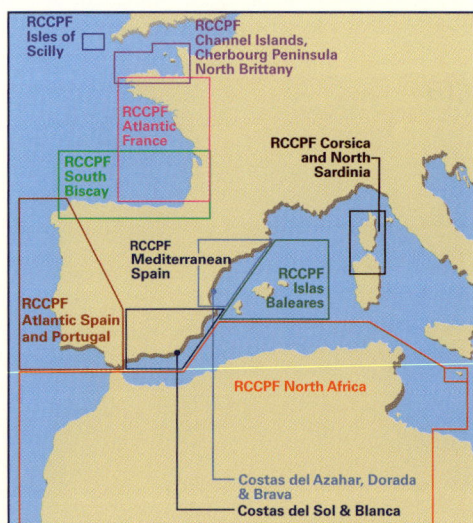

Imray
Arctic and Northern Waters
Norway
The Baltic Sea
Channel Islands, Cherbourg Peninsula & North Brittany
Isles of Scilly
Atlantic France
South Biscay
Atlantic Islands
Atlantic Spain & Portugal
Mediterranean Spain
   Costas del Sol and Blanca
    Costas del Azahar, Dorada & Brava
    Islas Baleares
Corsica and North Sardinia
North Africa
Chile
Black Sea

Imray Nautical app for iPad
Chile North
Chile South
Isles of Scilly

Adlard Coles Nautical
Atlantic Crossing Guide
Pacific Crossing Guide

On Board Publications
South Atlantic Circuit
Havens and Anchorages for the South American Coast

The RCC Pilotage Foundation
Supplement to Falkland Island Shores
Cruising Guide to West Africa
Argentina
Brazil

RCCPF Website www.rccpf.org.uk
Supplements
Support files for books
Passage Planning Guides
ePilots - from the Arctic to the Antarctic Peninsula

Foreword to 7th edition

In recent years I have sailed the full length of the coasts of Atlantic Spain and Portugal between Cabo Ortegal and Gibraltar, both southwards and northwards. On board we had a copy of the 6th edition of The RCC Pilotage Foundation *Atlantic Spain and Portugal* and it became a very well-thumbed reference and an invaluable companion. I join Henry Buchanan in thanking the originators and subsequent authors and editors who have built such a thoroughly useful pilot book.

In this fully revised 7th edition Henry Buchanan has used his own recent experience of cruising these coasts, together with a great deal of useful feedback sent in to the RCC Pilotage Foundation by fellow yachtsmen, to update and extend the information as much as possible. The RCC Pilotage Foundation is sincerely grateful to Henry for taking on the task of editing the whole of this edition, and to all the contributors who have sent in corrections, photographs and additional information.

The Atlantic swell is a very common concern when considering cruising this coastline. As is ever the case, those who do not have deadlines and who are prepared to be patient will be well-rewarded. Others may be lucky to grab a chance in a much shorter time frame. Either way, it is perfectly possible to enjoy favourable conditions whether heading south or north. The trick is to monitor swell forecasts as avidly as you monitor the winds, and to make shorter hops along the coast if patterns are unstable. Every stop off provides something to enjoy. Don't be tempted to pass it all by!

Coastal features do not usually change very much, but harbours and facilities often do. If you find anything which needs updating in this edition please do email us to let us know. An annual supplement will be produced each year after publication and will be available as a free download from both the Imray and RCC Pilotage Foundation websites. Click through to the *Atlantic Spain and Portugal* page of the pilot books section of the websites where you will find any mid-season updates or corrections and links to the annual supplement.

Jane Russell
Executive Director, RCC Pilotage Foundation
February 2015

Preface

This seventh edition of *Atlantic Spain and Portugal* has been written for the mariner either crossing the Bay of Biscay and making landfall off Cabo Ortegal in Galicia, or sailing from the east and south Biscay to join this pilot off the Cape and then turning south. This edition provides more detail than its predecessor on the rías and anchorages north of A Coruña, including the first place of refuge at the anchorage in the Ría de Cedeira some 12M southwest of the Cape. Ría de Cedeira is the only one of the Rías Altas on the northwest coast of Galicia. The others are all east of Cabo Ortegal and any mariner sailing from this

direction should consult RCCPF *South Biscay* for information.

Galicia will be known to many as a delightful cruising area with the Ría de la Coruña in the north, and then the more challenging Costa da Morte and Cabo Finisterre coming south before the Rías Bajas are reached. Here the whole feeling of Galicia changes in the warmer, softer, more sheltered rías of Muros, Arousa, Pontevedra and Vigo. Not to be forgotten are the beautiful Isla Ons and Islas Cíes. But be prepared; because of the huge increase in boats now cruising these waters, the islands have been designated national parks and strict rules covering access are in place and should be planned for, preferably before leaving home (see page 15).

So, sailing on south to ever popular Bayona and then to the rewarding coast of Portugal and the harbours from which the Portuguese explorers set sail. Viana do Costelo known to the Romans; Porto and Figueira da Foz; the Rio Tejo estuary to Lisbon; the Rio Sado and the harbour at Sines where Vasco da Gama was born, before rounding magnificent Cabo de São Vicente. In between are attractive if navigationally more challenging estuaries, harbours and bays, open to the Atlantic, often with shifting sands and strong currents but well worth a visit in the right conditions. Beyond Cabo de São Vicente, the springboard for the great Portuguese explorers, to Lagos and the beautiful Algarve with some interesting lagoons to explore; the Río Guadiana; the Río Guadalquivir to Seville; the Bay of Cádiz and on past Cabo Trafalgar into the Mediterranean to the Bay of Algeciras and Gibraltar.

Good cruising and have fun.

Henry Buchanan

Acknowledgements

Atlantic Spain and Portugal was first published in 1988 using the work of the late Oz Robinson, and has been developed and expanded by Anne Hammick and Martin Walker (for Galicia). It is to these ground breaking authors that grateful thanks are most due, but also to an international cast of sailors, and authorities in Spain and Portugal, who have taken the trouble to send in their suggestions and comments.

These contributors are recognised with thanks in the annual supplement to *Atlantic Spain and Portugal* issued each spring, but as the full list is now so long only those individuals who have helped directly with production of this seventh edition are included here:

Charlotte Watters, Christopher Neil Brown, Christopher and Mo Durnford, David Batten, David E Tucker, Dr Graham Hutt, Filipa Villar, Glenda Neild & Jay Brown, Henning Düerr, James Peto, James Pickford, Jane Russell, Javier Germán Monjas González, Javier Monjas, João Lemos, Joaquín Fernández, John Lancaster-Smith, Lorena Cenamor Fandiño, Luís Fidalgo, María Muriel Clemente, Neil Boot, Niki and Geoff Phillips, Roger Dunstan, Steve Pickard, Steven Anderson, Thierry Renoux.

Finally, thanks go to Willie Wilson and his team at Imray for producing a fine book.

Traditional Nazare fishing boat

Left
Sandeman Port barrels

Centre
Festa dos Maios, Vigo

Right
Galician gaita (bagpipes) are another illustration of Celtic links

Race training at Ría de la Coruña

The old and the new, Muros

Photos
Jane Russell

Introduction

The character of the Atlantic coasts of Spain and Portugal varies widely between the cliffs and rocky shoreline north of Cabo Finisterre in Galicia, and the flat sandy lagoons of the Faro area in the Portuguese Algarve beyond Cabo São Vicente. Their attraction for the cruising yachtsman is equally variable. The aim of this book is to describe the cruising grounds, harbours and facilities of the area and the safety information available in terms of the weather, sea state and navigational hazards. It does not pretend to be a comprehensive guide and should not be used without the appropriate charts. Excellent travel guides are available for crews who wish to explore this intriguing and beautiful coastal region.

Local place names are used except for a few cities and towns, such as Lisbon and Seville, which are widely known by their anglicised form. In Galicia the Gallego form of the name is generally given. Gallego, an ancient language which falls somewhere between Castilian Spanish and Portuguese, remains in everyday use; while away from major routes, road signs rarely use Castilian Spanish. Other non-English words used will be found in the glossary.

Although Gibraltar is included in this book, as it remains an important refuge or staging post for those bound for the Mediterranean or heading south towards the Canaries and beyond, it has offered less to yachtsmen in recent years. Nearby La Línea across the border in Spain offers an attractive alternative.

The cruising grounds

In cruising terms, the Atlantic coast of Spain and Portugal described in this pilot falls naturally into three parts:

Part 1 - Western Galicia: This includes the northwest facing rías and coast of Galicia between Cabo Ortegal and Cabo Finisterre, and the southwest facing rías, known as the Rías Bajas, and their outlying islands from Cabo Finisterre to the Portuguese border at the Rio Miño.

Part II - The west coast of Portugal from the Spanish border south to Cabo de São Vicente.

Part III - The south coast of Portugal and Spanish Andalucia trending eastward from Cabo de São Vicente to the Algarve, Atlantic Andalucia and Gibraltar.

Galicia

Northwest rías and coast

Some 12M southwest of Cabo Ortegal is a secure anchorage in the Ría de Cedeira that provides a welcome refuge after a long haul south across the Bay of Biscay. Sailing on south and west along this dramatic coastline, the rías of Ferrol, Ares and de Betanzos, and Coruña are reached that provide marinas and facilities, and cruising opportunities in their more sheltered waters. This part of Galicia is the most exposed to the Atlantic weather and swell, however, and the aptly named Costa da Morte between A Coruña and Cabo Finisterre should be respected. Cruising this challenging coast is for the adventurous and although good shelter, anchorages and marinas (Camariñas and Muxia) can be found in the Ría de Camariñas, the entrance is fully exposed to winds and seas from the northwest and may be inaccessible in rough weather.

Southwest rías (Rías Bajas) and offlying islands

Some consider this area to be the best cruising area in Galicia and spend weeks pottering about the ports and anchorages, taking advantage of good communications and safe harbours and marinas to explore inland. Less exposed to the Atlantic weather than the coast and rías to the north of Cabo Finisterre, the Rías Bajas have beaches, interesting towns, and opportunities for rock-hopping for those wishing to test their pilotage. There are many restaurants and hotels, while excellent Atlantic fish and local shellfish are readily available.

Offshore are the Isla Ons and Islas Cies, beautiful islands with sandy beaches now part of the National Park and subject to strict access regulations (see page 15-17).

This area suffers more from fog than the north western rías, and the Azores high pressure system in summer can, on occasion, produce a clear weather north easterly blow of Force 5–6 which may last for several days. But there is always shelter to be found within a short distance.

Atlantic Portugal

This coast is not a cruising paradise but it includes some remarkable places to visit, notably Porto and Lisbon for their history and interest, and Aveiro and the Rio Sado for their sandbanks and swamps. The coast itself is, on the whole, low, the hills are inland and in summer may be lost in the haze, and in places there are miles of featureless beach.

The harbours are commercial or fishing in origin, but most are making increasing concessions to yachts. Many have natural hazards of one sort or another in the entrance; Leixões and Sines are notable exceptions. The most common are bars that alter with the winter storms and which, although safe enough for freighters, can be dangerous for the smaller vessel if there is a swell running. The bars are associated with rivers, and conditions are generally worse on the ebb.

Another major feature of this region is the Portuguese trade winds. Many take advantage of these prevailing northerly winds to slide south past the coast as quickly as possible. Making the passage northwards can be tedious, even in summer, but it is possible to day sail north keeping an eye on the weather and, in particular, the swell.

Algarve and Andalucía

The southern coasts of Portugal and Spain offer easier cruising than the west coast. Having rounded the corner at Cabo de São Vicente, the influences of the Mediterranean and the Moors begin to show. Harbours are generally more frequent and better equipped and, with a couple of exceptions, are easier to enter than those on the Atlantic coast.

The Algarve is crowded, both summer and winter, and its harbours busy. The shallow lagoons of Faro and Olhão, the quiet Río Guadiana and the relatively busy Río Guadalquivir, are the best areas for wildlife.

A particular hazard of this coast is the tunny net, which can stretch several miles out to sea at right angles to the shoreline, and is strong enough to foul the propeller of a small coaster. Currently five or six are set annually. Details and locations are given in the text.

Sailing and navigation

Winds and climate
Weather systems
The northern part of the region is influenced by North Atlantic weather systems. In winter, fronts and occasionally secondary depressions may cross the area. Winds are variable but those between southwest and northwest are more common. In summer, land and sea breezes can be expected inshore but the influence of the Azores Highs tends to produce winds from the north; this northerly tendency starts about April and as summer progresses and latitude decreases these winds develop into the Portuguese trades. At the height of summer in the south of the region, the Portuguese trades remain dominant well offshore west of 20°W, while eastwards their influence is felt along the coast from Cabo de São Vicente towards Faro, often reinforced in the afternoons by the land effect. This influence wanes until, by Cádiz, summer afternoons may produce a westerly sea breeze. Cádiz can also be affected by a *levante* coming out of the Mediterranean. Towards the Strait of Gibraltar the winds tend to be either easterly or westerly, the former more common in summer and the latter in winter.

Gales
Gales are rare in the summer. The better known are the *levante* and *poniente*, the easterly and westerly gales of the Strait of Gibraltar, and the *nordeste pardo*, a cloudy northeaster of the Finisterre area. In theory the *vendavale*, a southwesterly blow in Galicia, is unlikely to occur in summer but exceptions do occur. Tarifa, protruding into the Strait of Gibraltar, will frequently experience very strong local winds and yachts should be prepared for this.

Rainfall
Galicia is the wet corner of Spain – it has much the same climatic feel as southwest England. To the south, whilst winters may be like June in the English Channel, in summer rainfall decreases and temperatures rise until, around Cádiz, Mediterranean levels are reached.

Fog
Sea temperatures in summer range from 17°C in Galicia to 21° at Gibraltar, and in winter from 12° to 14°. The chances of coastal fog along the west coast of the Iberian peninsula are greatest in July and August when incidence may rise as high as one day in 10. In the larger rías of southern Galicia it occasionally lasts for a week at a stretch in summer. It is much rarer along the southwest coast.

Swell
Atlantic swell is a factor to consider along the whole of this coast because the edge of the continental plate runs close to the shoreline and so there is not much shelf to dissipate the wave energy. There are seasonal variations, and once you have rounded Cabo de São Vincente (heading south) you are less likely to be plagued. But the swell is generated outside the local weather patterns and therefore your local conditions will not be a good indication of the sea state. For safety and for comfort it is imperative that you monitor swell forecasts. There are several excellent websites which show predicted swell direction and height over several days. Note that in coastal areas you will need to factor in any more locally generated waves and any tidal effects to gain a more complete picture of what the local sea state is likely to be. See 'Weather forecasts on the internet' (page 6) for some useful websites.

Currents and tides
Currents
Currents are much affected by recent winds and may set in any direction. The trend along the Atlantic coast is from north to south, though north of Finisterre there can be an easterly set into the Bay of Biscay. East of Cabo de São Vicente, the upper layers of the sea re-supply the Mediterranean with water lost through evaporation. The current sets towards the Strait at about 0·5kn at the western end, increasing to around 2kn through the Strait itself, to which a tidal element may have to be added – see page 315. However, prolonged easterly winds can produce a reverse current, which is said to set into the bays as far west as Cabo de São Vicente.

Tidal streams

Information on tidal streams is confusing. Off the Rías Bajas the flood is supposed to run north and off Peniche, in Portugal, to the southeast. The only reasonably safe assumption is that the flood tide sets into the Galician rías and the ebb drains them. The same is generally true of a Portuguese rio, but this is less than a certainty and depends on the amount of water coming down the rio itself. The Rio Douro is a particular example of this. In the Strait of Gibraltar, tidal streams can exceed 3kn at springs.

Tide times

The standard ports for the area are A Coruña, Lisbon, Cádiz and Gibraltar and quoted time and height differences for other harbours are related to them. An excellent source of tidal information for those with internet access is the UK Hydrographic Office's user-friendly (and free) Easytide programme at www.ukho.gov.uk/easytide which gives daily tidal data for almost all major harbours and many minor ones.

	A Coruña	Vigo	Lisbon	Faro	Cádiz	Gibraltar
Springs	3·3	2·9	3·3	2·8	2·8	0·9
Neaps	1·3	1·4	1·6	1·2	1·3	0·4

Lights and buoyage

All buoys and lights in this area adhere to the IALA A system, based on the direction of the main flood tide. In Portugal and Spain, heights of lights are measured from mean sea level. They therefore generally appear in Iberian publications as a metre or so higher than in British Admiralty publications.

The four-figure international numbering system has been used to identify lights in text and on plans. In addition to being shown on the plans, details of the main leading lights and, in Galicia, the outer breakwater light are given in the text. All bearings are given from seaward and refer to true north.

Charts

See Appendix I on page 337.

Current British Admiralty information is largely obtained from Spanish and Portuguese sources. The Spanish and Portuguese Hydrographic Offices issue their own charts (often to a much larger scale than Admiralty coverage and corrected by their own *Notices*) but they can be difficult to obtain outside the peninsula. *Notices to Mariners* to update Admiralty charts will be found on www.ukho.gov.uk; the Spanish and Portuguese equivalents – *Avisos* – on www.armada.mde.es/ihm and www.hidrografico.pt/hidrografico respectively.

Before departure Spanish and Portuguese charts (as well as fully corrected Admiralty publications) can be obtained through

Imray Laurie Norie & Wilson Ltd,
Wych House, The Broadway, St Ives,
Cambridgeshire, PE27 5BT, UK
☎ +44 (0)1480 462114
www.imray.com

In Spain Spanish charts can be ordered from
Instituto Hidrográfico de la Marina,
Plaza de San Severiano 3, DP 11007 Cádiz
☎ +34 956 599409 *Fax* +34 956 599396

In Galicia there are Spanish chart agents in A Coruña, Vilagarcía de Arousa and Vigo; in Andalucía in Huelva, Seville, Cádiz and Algeciras. A few marina offices are also willing to order charts for visiting yachts.

In Portugal only two companies, both in Lisbon, sell charts. Full contact details are given in the Facilities section for Lisbon.

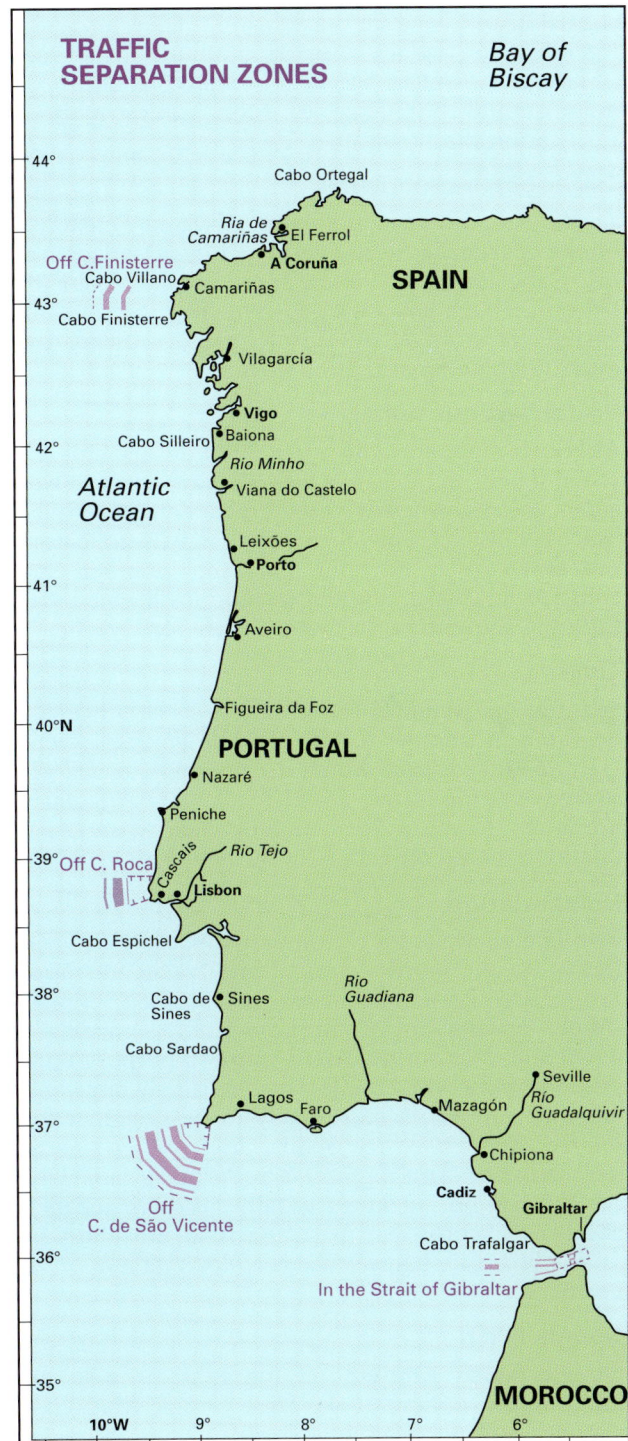

TRAFFIC SEPARATION ZONES — Bay of Biscay / Atlantic Ocean, Spain, Portugal, Morocco

In Gibraltar fully corrected Admiralty charts and other publication are available from the Gibraltar Chart Agency – contact details are given under Gibraltar.

Horizontal chart datum and satellite derived positions

Most charts are now based on WGS84 datum and this is used for all positions in this book. However, some Portuguese charts are still to be converted and navigators are advised to check the chart datum if plotting satellite derived data. GPS positions have been derived from both paper and electronic charts, and observation in harbour. These are offered as an aid to rapid orientation within the book as well as a contribution to safe navigation. They are not intended to replace normal planning or visual observation. Unless specifically stated in the text, none should be linked to form routes without verification that it is safe to do so.

Traffic Separation Zones

Traffic Separation Zones exist off Cabo Finisterre, on the approaches to Ría de Vigo, off Cabo da Roca, off Cabo de São Vicente and in the Strait of Gibraltar. Each has a wide Inshore Traffic Zone and yachts are strongly advised to avoid crossing the main shipping lanes if at all possible.

Visual harbour signals

Although in theory both Spain and Portugal still use visual signals to indicate whether a harbour is safe to enter, in relatively few cases do they appear to be used. It must be remembered that signals indicating the state of a harbour bar are intended for commercial traffic, and that conditions deemed safe for a big ship are not necessarily safe for a yacht.

Time

Spain keeps Standard Euro Time (UT+1), advanced one hour in summer to UT+2, while Portugal keeps UT, advanced one hour in summer to UT+1. (effectively the same as BST). It is particularly important to allow for this difference when using tidal data based on Lisbon in the Spanish *rías bajas*.

Nomenclature

Two likely pitfalls for the unwary English speaker in Iberia are the words 'marina' and 'yacht'. In both Spain and Portugal *marina* or *marinha* implies simply 'marine' (as in *marina mercante* – merchant navy) and does not necessarily imply a purpose-built yacht harbour which, unless it is unusually large and has all facilities, is more likely to be designated a *puerto deportivo* in Spain, and either *porto desportivo* or *doca de recreio* in Portugal. Similarly, the description 'yacht' is usually taken to mean a good-sized motorboat, particularly in the south. A sailing boat of whatever size is a *barco de vela* or, in Portugal, a *barco à vela*.

Google Earth

Google Earth satellite photographs provide an interesting overview of the area. Google Maps can also be useful for planning passages.

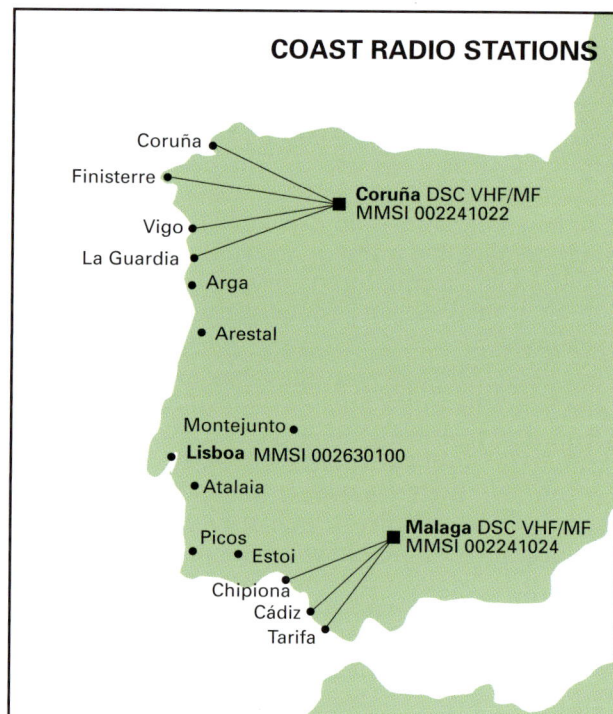

COAST RADIO STATIONS

Coast radio stations

Details of coast radio stations will be found in the Admiralty Leisure publication *NP 289* and in the text. Locations are shown on the plan below, outstations are controlled by A Coruña, Lisboa and Malaga. On receipt of traffic, Spanish coast radio stations will call vessels once on Ch 16; after that the vessel's call-sign will be included in scheduled MF traffic lists.

Weather forecasts

It should be noted that although marinas generally display weather information, yachts may find difficulty receiving official forecasts when in harbour or anchored in quiet bays. Yachts heading for the Mediterranean may later find that reception there can be erratic. Attention is therefore drawn to the use of weatherfax and RTTY messages from DWD and the usefulness of GRIB files.

Fog

Thick fog may descend along this coast with little warning. It may be localised and not mentioned in weather forecasts.

Navtex Stations and forecast areas

(Spanish areas are shown on the diagram opposite) France uses the same forecast areas for the Bay of Biscay plus Alborán.

Portugal uses the same Atlantic areas below 45°N.

Navtex Schedules 518kHz | *** Weather Bulletins**

A	Corsen	0000*, 0400, 0800, 1200*, 1600, 2000
D	Coruña	0030, 0430, 0830*, 1230, 1630, 2030*
R	Monsanto	0250*, 0650*, 1050*, 1450*, 1850*, 2250*
G	Tarifa	0100, 0500, 0900*, 1300, 1700, 2100*
M	Casablanca (proposed)	

Navtex on 490kHz

E	Corsen	in French
W	Coruña	in Spanish
G	Monsanto	in Portuguese

Poor reception may be a problem in the Galician rias or in harbours throughout the area.

GALICIA

Radio Weather Bulletins* and Navigational Warnings

Coruña	1698kHz and	
Finisterre	1764kHz	0703*, 1303*, 1903*
Coruña	VHF Ch 26	0840*, 1240*, 2010*
Coruña MRSC	VHF Ch 10	0005*, 0205, 0405*, 0605 0805*, 1005, 1205*, 1405 1605*, 1805, 2005*, 2205
Finisterre	VHF Ch 22	0840*, 1240*, 2010*
Finisterre MRCC	VHF Ch 11	0033, 0233*, 0433, 0633* 0833, 1033*, 1233, 1433* 1633, 1833*, 2033, 2233*
Vigo	VHF Ch 65	0840*, 1240*, 2010*
Vigo MRSC	VHF Ch 10	0015*, 0215, 0415*, 0615 0815*, 1015, 1215*, 1415 1615*, 1815 2015*, 2215
La Guardia	VHF Ch 21	0840*, 1240*, 2040*

PORTUGAL

Radio Weather Bulletins and Navigational Warnings

Portugal coastal waters up to 20M offshore are in three zones:

Zona Norte	Rio Minho to Cabo Carvoeiro (40°N)
Zona Centro	Cabo Carvoeiro to Cabo São Vicente
Zona Sul	Cabo São Vicente to Rio Guadiana

Forecasts and navigational warnings: in Portuguese and English

RT(MF)	2657kHz	0905, 2105
VHF	Ch 11	0705, 0905, 1905, 2105 Norte & Centro 0805, 0905, 2005, 2105 Centro & Sul

ANDALUCIA

Radio Weather Bulletin* and Navigational Warnings

Huelva MRSC	VHF Ch 10	0315*, 0515*, 0715*, 1115*, 1515*, 1915*, 2315*
Chipiona	1656kHz and	
Tarifa	1704 kHz	0733*, 1233*, 1933*
Cádiz	VHF Ch 26	0833* 1133*, 2003, 2033*
Tarifa	VHF Ch 81	0733*, 0833, 1233* 1933*, 2003*
Tarifa MRCC	VHF Ch 10, 67	Ev Hrs +15* On Receipt
Algeciras MRSC	VHF Ch 74	0315*, 0515*, 0715*, 1115*, 1515*, 1915*, 2314*

FORECAST AREAS (SPANISH) AND NAVTEX STATIONS

France uses the same forecast areas for the Bay of Biscay plus Alborán. Portugal uses the same Atlantic areas below 45°N.

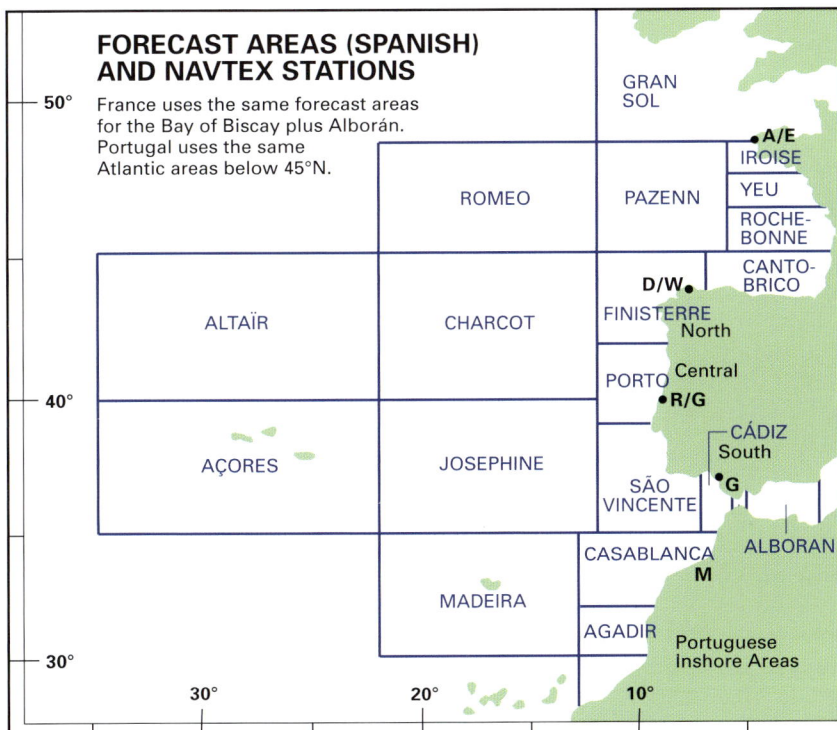

Weatherfax and RTTY

Northwood (RN) broadcasts a full set of UK Met Office charts out to five days ahead on 2618.5,4610,8040 and 11086.5kHz. (Schedule at 0236, surface analysis at three hourly intervals from 0300 to 2100 and 2300.)

Deutscher Wetterdienst broadcasts German weather charts on 3855,7880,13882.5kHz. (Schedule at 1111, surface analysis at 0430, 1050,1600,2200.)

DWD broadcasts forecasts using RTTY on 4583, 7646, and 10001.8kHz (in English at 0955 and 2155) 11039 and 14467.3kHz (in German at 0820, 1429, 2020). Alternatively, a dedicated receiver will record automatically – see 'weatherman' on www.nasamarine.com

Inmarsat

Broadcast times for weather for METAREA III are 1000 and 2200.

GRIB

This service enables arrow diagram forecasts for up to five days ahead, and other information to be obtained in email form (or by marine HF and HAM radio). The data are highly compressed so that a great deal of information can be acquired quickly, even using a mobile phone connected to laptop.

Gibraltar weather forecasts – VHF (FM)

LT	BFBS 1			BFBS2	Gibraltar BC		
	Mon-Fri	Sat	Sun	Mon-Fri	Mon-Fri	Sat	Sun
0530					X	X	
0630					X	X	X
0730					X	X	X
0745	X						
0845	X	X	X				
0945		X	X				
1005	X						
1030					X		
1200				X			
1202		X	X				
1230					X	X	X
1602		X					
1605	X						

Also storm warnings on receipt 1438 AM
93.5 FM   89.4 FM   91.3 FM
97.8 FM   99.5 FM   92.6 FM
Includes high and low water times   100.5 FM

Weather forecasts on the Internet

Excellent weather-related information, including swell forecasts, can be found on the internet.

A guide to marine weather forecasts and how to use them is at

www.weather.mailasail.com/Franks-Weather.

Other useful websites are as follows:

www.metoffice.gov.uk	UK Met Office
www.inm.es/	Spanish Met Office
www.meteo.pt	Portuguese Met Office
www.passageweather.com	
www.windguru.cz	
www.magicseaweed.com	(surf site)

Weather forecasts to be found ashore

Nearly all marina offices display a weather forecast and synoptic chart(s), usually updated daily; although often in the local language, the vocabulary is limited and can easily be deciphered.

For a more general indication of trends try the weather map in a local newspaper e.g. El País, Voz de Galicia or El Correo Galicia (Spain) or Jornal de Notícias or Público (Portugal).

Spanish television shows a useful synoptic chart with its land weather forecast every evening after the news at about 2120 weekdays, 1520 Saturday and 2020 Sunday.

Weather forecasts by radio

A variety of weather forecasts are available by radio, though relatively few in English. It should be noted that all times quoted for weather messages, navigational warnings and traffic lists are in Universal Time (UT) unless otherwise stated. This contrasts with harbour and marina radio schedules, which are generally governed by office hours and are therefore given in Local Time (LT).

BBC Radio 4

Shipping forecasts are broadcast on 198kHz (1515m) at 0048, 0520, 1201 and 1754. They consist of a gale warning summary, general synopsis, and sea-area forecasts on UK local time (BST in summer, UT in winter). The relevant areas are Biscay, Fitzroy and Trafalgar but the latter is only included in the 0048 forecast. While undoubtedly useful, particularly in Galicia, the areas covered are large, reception may be difficult, and forecasts may have little relevance to local conditions.

Radio France International

Weather information is broadcast at 1140 UT daily, (timed to fit the vagaries of programming and therefore not always punctual). The following receiving frequencies vary according to location: English Channel and Bay of Biscay 6175kHz; North Atlantic east of 50°W 11700, 15530, 17575kHz. Although in French, the format is straightforward: gale warnings, synopsis, development and 24 hour area forecasts.

Radio Nacional de España

Weather information is broadcast at 1000 and 1300 LT via from: A Coruña 639kHz; Seville 684kHz.

Sociedad España de Radio

A programme containing information for commercial fishing operations, plus weather forecasts and sea conditions, is broadcast between 0600 and 0700 LT and again in condensed form at 2205 LT from: A Coruña 1080kHz; Vigo 1026kHz; Huelva 100.5MHz; Cádiz 1485kHz; Seville 792kHz.

Radiodifusão Portuguesa

Broadcasts a forecast for the coastal waters of Portugal at 1100 daily on the following frequencies: 650kHz, 666kHz, 720kHz, 1287kHz, 94·7MHz, 96·4MHz, 97·6MHz, 97·9MHz.

Practicalities

Entry and regulations

Under EU regulations, EU registered boats arriving in another EU country are not required to fly the Q flag unless they have come directly from a non-EU country (which could be Gibraltar), have non-EU nationals aboard, or are carrying dutiable goods. Yachts registered outside the EU should always fly the Q flag on arrival. All visiting yachts should fly the relevant national courtesy flag.

Spain

On first arrival in the country check with immigration, most easily done via a yacht club or marina office. Ship's papers, insurance documents and passports should be to hand. It is also a requirement that at least one member of the crew has a VHF radio operator's certificate. At subsequent ports it is not necessary to seek out officialdom, though one may occasionally be approached for information. This relaxed attitude is more noticeable in Galicia than Andalucía, where smuggling is more common and there is greater public awareness of Gibraltar as a political issue. It should be noted that Spain requires all vessels over 6m to carry proof of third party insurance in Spanish. UK marine insurers are aware of this and will provide the appropriate certificate free of charge on request. Skippers should be aware that differing initial length of stay and visa requirements apply according to crew nationalities and also that anyone staying in Spain for more than 183 days in any 12-month period is liable to Spanish tax legislation. A note on this, and VAT, is included in Appendix IV. Officials may not recognize time spent in Gibraltar as being out of Spain.

Portugal

In theory, yachtsmen are still required to notify the authorities on arrival in every harbour, whether entering Portugal for the first time or from elsewhere within it – and to do so immediately upon coming ashore. This should not present problems at one of the increasing number of marinas. In general, produce passports, ship's papers (including proof of VAT status and insurance documents) complete a *Movimento de Embarcacoes de Recreio* form and state an intended departure date. In most harbours there is no requirement for formal outward clearance. Skippers should also carry an International Certificate of Competence or equivalent. In UK this is administered by the Royal Yachting Association www.rya.org.uk/cruising or *Email* cruising@rya.org.uk. At least one crew member must have a VHF operator's certificate. There is no limitation on length of stay for a VAT paid or exempt yacht. However, visiting yachts spending more than 183 days a year in Portugal are liable to tax (see page 338 for details).

Gibraltar

Although Gibraltar is a British Territory, it is not part of the EU. Fly the Q Flag on approach and clear customs at marinas. See page 331 for details.

Day signals / anchor lights

Over the past few years, a number of skippers in both Spanish and Portuguese waters have faced an on the spot fine for not displaying a black ball or white light when at anchor and a cone when motor sailing. Yachts have also been fined for not flying a courtesy flag.

Drugs

Drug running is a serious problem along the entire Iberian coast. The authorities may board yachts at any time, including on passage, though normally this is confined to 'interesting' yachts, with the names of others merely being noted down. In both countries, yachtsmen are asked to inform the authorities of any yacht that merits a particular interest – and presumably of any other goings-on which appear suspicious.

Laying up

Yachts can safely be left afloat, whether laid up or over-wintering, in most of the larger marinas described. It should be clear from the text when this is not the case.

Facilities, chandlery and repairs

In Galicia, the facilities for yachts are extensive and expanding, and travel lifts frequent. The harbour facilities available are included in the text, and a useful publication can be found at major marinas. The following websites are also useful: www.marinasdegalicia.com and www.portosdegalicia.com

In the Portugal and Andalucía sections details are in the text, and for Andalucía the comprehensive website: www.puertosdeandalucia.es can also be consulted.

Chandleries

Well-stocked yachting chandleries are not always easy to find in either Spain or Portugal, and by no means all marinas have one on site. Amongst the best are those at Sada, A Coruña, Vilagarcía de Arousa, Vigo and Baiona (Galicia). Viana do Castelo, Leixões, Cascais and Lisbon (Atlantic Portugal) Lagos, Portimão and Vilamoura (Algarve); Isla Christina, Punta Umbria, Chipiona, Seville, Puerto Sherry and Barbate (Andalucía). Gibraltar's chandleries are some of the best in Iberia, as well as being duty-free. Basic boat tackle is more widely available.

Repairs

There are numerous boatyards throughout all the regions, mainly geared to fishing and other commercial vessels but able to do basic work on yachts. However, for major repairs or other work reportedly good yards are currently located at Sada, Vilagarcía de Arousa and Vigo (Galicia); Lisbon and Seixal (Atlantic Portugal); Lagos, Portimão and Vilamoura (Algarve); El Rompido, Seville (Puerto Gelves) and Puerto Sherry (Andalucía); and, of course, Gibraltar. Note that if taking expensive electrical or mechanical equipment ashore for repair, particularly in Portugal, it is wise to first inform the *GNR–Brigada Fiscal*. Possession of a receipt will confirm that the equipment was bought elsewhere. With the availability of cheap flights it might be preferable to fly back to one's own country.

Fuel

Diesel is widely available (except to yachts visiting fishing harbours); petrol rather less so. In both countries fishermen have access to diesel at a lower rate of tax than do yachtsmen. Fuel supplies are generally clean, but it can do no harm to filter all fuel taken aboard as a matter of course. Credit cards are generally – but not always – accepted when paying for fuel and it is essential to confirm the local situation before going ahead.

Standard grade paraffin (*parafina*) is virtually unobtainable in much of Spain, though the more expensive medicinal grade is stocked by most pharmacies. In Portugal *petróleo para iluminãçao* (lamp oil) is widely available.

Drinking water

Water is available at all marinas and on many fuelling pontoons. It is usually included in the price of berthing. In those harbours where a piped supply is not available for yachts, a public tap can generally be found, when a good supply of five or 10-litre plastic cans will be useful. Though water quality throughout the peninsula is generally good, bottled water is widely available.

Bottled gas

Camping Gaz exchanges are widely available, usually from *ferreterías* (ironmongers), filling stations or supermarkets – in 2·7kg bottles identical to those used in the UK.

Getting other cylinders refilled is much more of a problem, particularly if the cylinder is more than five years old. Boats heading south for extended cruising might consider carrying the appropriate adaptor and regulator and buying local gas on arrival in Spain or elsewhere.

Calor Gas dealers in the UK can advise on installations and supply the necessary parts. Contact Southampton Calor Gas Centre Ltd, Third Avenue, Millbrook Trading Estate, Southampton SO15 0JX
℡ 02380 788155, *Fax* 02380 774768
Email charles@socal.co.uk
www.calorgas.co.uk

Also useful is their free leaflet *LPG (Bottled Gas) for Marine Use.*

Electricity

Electricity is available on nearly all marina pontoons, generally via standard marina sockets, although adaptors should be carried to cope with the European domestic type socket. Mains electricity is 220 volt 50Hz; yachts equipped with 110 volt 60Hz equipment will require a transformer. (These are best bought before arrival; they are readily obtainable from builders merchants in the UK.)

Holding Tanks

Since 2004 it has been compulsory for Spanish flagged vessels to fit holding tanks. Pump-out facilities are increasing and there is a determination to protect the water quality for both the fishing and tourist industries. Skippers should be aware that Spanish legislation on prevention of sewage does not permit sewage to be discharged in port areas, protected zones, rivers, or bays. Crumbled and disinfected sewage may be discharged from four miles off shore by vessels exceeding 4kn.

Marina charges

It is not practicable to list the varying rates at all the different marinas and harbours. Charges will often be based on length x beam and skippers should carry documentation which records both of these (SSR documentation does not).

Marina office hours (local time)

In Spain (both Galicia and Andalucía) it is normal for marina offices to be closed during the siesta period, any time between 1200 and 1700, though seldom for as long as this. In Portugal a shorter lunch break – often from 1230 until 1400 – is the norm. While the majority of marinas have 24-hour security, most offices are closed overnight, sometimes from as early as 1800.

While this latter can cause problems when wishing to leave, a firmly locked office is more likely to disrupt things on first arrival, particularly if an electronic card is needed to open an access gate to the pontoons. In Portugal, where marina offices are increasingly handling clearance procedures, it can also frustrate a quick shopping trip into town or a well-deserved meal ashore.

Sometimes security guards have authority to issue pass cards, often they do not. There is no guarantee that a guard will re-admit an unknown yachtsman to the marina pontoons, particularly if not carrying the yacht's papers and a passport or other identity document.

Security

Crime afloat is not a major problem in most areas. It is sensible to take much the same precautions as at home – to lock up if leaving the yacht unattended, to padlock the outboard to the dinghy, and to secure the dinghy (particularly if an inflatable) with chain or wire rather than line, both to the yacht and when left ashore.

General information

Embassies, consulates and national tourist offices are listed in Appendix III.

Websites relevant to Galicia are: www.turgalicia.es, www.marinasdegalicia.com and www.portosdegalicia.com

Websites relevant to Portugal and Andalucía are listed in Appendix V.

Medical

No inoculations are required before visiting either Spain or Portugal. Minor ailments may best be treated by consulting a *farmacía* (often able to dispense drugs which in some other countries would be on prescription), or by contact with an English-speaking doctor established via the *farmacía*, marina office, tourist office or possibly a hotel. In Spain the emergency telephone number is 091; in Portugal it is 112.

All EU nationals should carry a European Health Insurance Card (EHIC) issued in the UK by the NHS Business Services Authority, www.ehic.org.uk, ℡ 0300 3301350. This entitles one to free medical treatment under reciprocal agreements with the National Health Service. Private medical treatment is likely to be available but may be expensive.

Money

The unit of currency is the Euro. Major credit cards are widely used although it is wise to check this particularly before refuelling. Bank hours are normally 0830 to 1400 Mondays to Fridays with a few also open 0830 to 1300 on Saturdays; most banks have ATMs.

Mail

Nearly all marinas are willing to hold mail for visiting yachts but it is wise to check first. All mail should be clearly labelled with both the name of the recipient and the yacht, but avoiding honorifics such as Esq, which may cause confusion and misfiling. In Portugal it is technically illegal for uncollected mail to be held for more than five days without being returned, though most marinas will stretch this period. Far better to address an outer envelope directly to the marina office, with a short covering note asking for the envelope enclosed to be held pending the yacht's arrival.

Letters also may be sent *Poste Restante* to any post office in either country, though again they are likely to be returned if not collected promptly. In Spain they should be addressed with the surname of the recipient followed by *Lista de Correos* and the town and province. In Portugal, *Posta Restante* is used, and the collection counter labelled *Encomendas*. A passport is likely to be needed on collection. Post Offices are signed: in Spain PTT on a yellow background, in Portugal postal services are indicated by *Correios* on a red background

Telephones
Country code numbers are: Spain +34, Portugal +351, Gibraltar +350 (Gibraltar from Spain 9567).

Email
Internet connection facilities are widespread and marina Wi-Fi is becoming increasingly available. Telephone and Fax numbers as well as email addresses and websites are listed for each harbour or marina.

Transport
In both Spain and Portugal almost every community has some form of public transport, if only one bus a day. Local buses and trains can provide a view of the interior not otherwise available without hiring a car, although the latter offer good value and the road network in Galicia is excellent.

There are rail connections to El Ferrol, A Coruña, Pontevedra, Vigo, Porto, Lisbon, Lagos, Faro, Tavira, Vila Real de Santo António, Huelva, Seville, Cádiz and Algeciras. Other towns may be served by branch lines. Long distance coaches are also popular, and on a par with the railways for cost.

International airports serve A Coruña, Santiago de Compostela, Vigo, Porto, Lisbon, Faro, Seville, Jerez de la Frontera and Gibraltar.

A float in the Romaria Festa parade

National holidays and fiestas
Fiestas are extremely popular throughout both Spain and Portugal, often celebrating the local saint's day or some historical event. Some local *fiestas* occurring during the sailing season are mentioned in the text.

Spain
1 January	New Year's Day
6 January	Epiphany
	Good Friday
	Easter Monday
1 May	May Day/Labour Day
(early/mid June)	Corpus Christi
24 June	Día de San Juan (the King's name saint)
25 July	Día de Santiago (celebrated throughout Northwest Spain as 'Galicia Day')
15 August	Feast of the Assumption
12 October	National Day
1 November	All Saints' Day
6 December	Constitution Day
8 December	Immaculate Conception
25 December	Christmas Day

When a national holiday falls on a Sunday, the autonomous region may either celebrate it the following day or use it to celebrate a regional festival.

Portugal
1 January	New Year's Day
	Good Friday
25 April	National or Liberty Day
1 May	Labour Day
(early/mid June)	Corpus Christi
10 June	Portugal Day (Camões Day)
15 August	Feast of the Assumption
5 October	Republic Day
1 November	All Saints' Day
1 December	Restoration of Independence Day
8 December	Feast of the Immaculate Conception
25 December	Christmas Day

Key to symbols used on the plans
	English	Portuguese	Spanish
⚓	harbourmaster	*diretor do porto/capitania*	*capitán de puerto/capitanía*
	fuel (diesel, petrol)	*gasoleo,gasolina*	*gasoil, gasolina*
(25T)	travel-lift	*pórtico elevador*	*pórtico elevado*
	yacht club	*club náutico,club naval*	*club náutico*
⚓	anchorage	*fundeadouro*	*fondeadero*
Ⓥ	visitors' moorings		*amarradero, ancladero*
	slipway	*carreira*	*varadero*

Depths in Metres

See plan
p.18

Cabo Ortegal
1686·3
Fl(2+1)15s122m18M
AIS

Pta
Estaca de Bares
1686
Fl(2)7·5s99m25M
AIS

Pta
Candelaria
1687
Fl(3+1)24s89m21M

C. Prior
1692
Fl(1+2)15s
105m22M

Cedeira

Pta de la Frouxeira
1690
Fl(5)15s73m20M

Cabo Prioriño Chico
1694
Fl.5s34m23M

El Ferrol

1728
Fl(3)15s108m23M

Is. Sisargas
1729

Torre de Hercules
1704
Fl(4)20s104m23M
AIS

A CORUÑA

Punta Nariga
Fl(3+1)20s
53m22M

Corme

Punta de Laxe
1732
Fl(5)20s64m20M

SPAIN

Cabo Villano
1736
Fl(2)15s102m28M
Racon Mo(M)
AIS

Camariñas

Muxia

C. Toriñana
1740
Fl(2+1)15s63m24M
Racon Mo(T)

I.2

See plan
p.52

Cabo Finisterre
1742
Fl.5s141m23M
Racon Mo(O)

I.1

Ría de Muros

Santiago de
Compostela

Pta Insúa
1782
Fl(3)WR.9s26m
15/14M

Ría de Arousa

C. Corrubedo
Fl(2+3)WR.21s30m15M

1794
Fl(3)R.20s
AIS

Isla de Arousa

1796
Fl(3+1)20s38m21M
Fl(3)20s
AIS

I. Sálvora

Isla Ons
1847.3
Fl(4)24s125m25M

Ría de Pontevedra

Ría de Vigo

VIGO

1884
Fl(2)8s185m22M

Islas Ciés

Cabo Silleiro
1916
Fl(2+1)15s84m24M

I.3

See plan
p.96

BAIONA

42°N

Río Miño

La Guardia

Inshore
Traffic
Zone

43°N

30′

30′

30′

I. GALICIA

2008
Fl(2)9·5s101m22M
Horn Mo(S)25s
Montedor

PORTUGAL

30′   9°   30′   8°W   30′

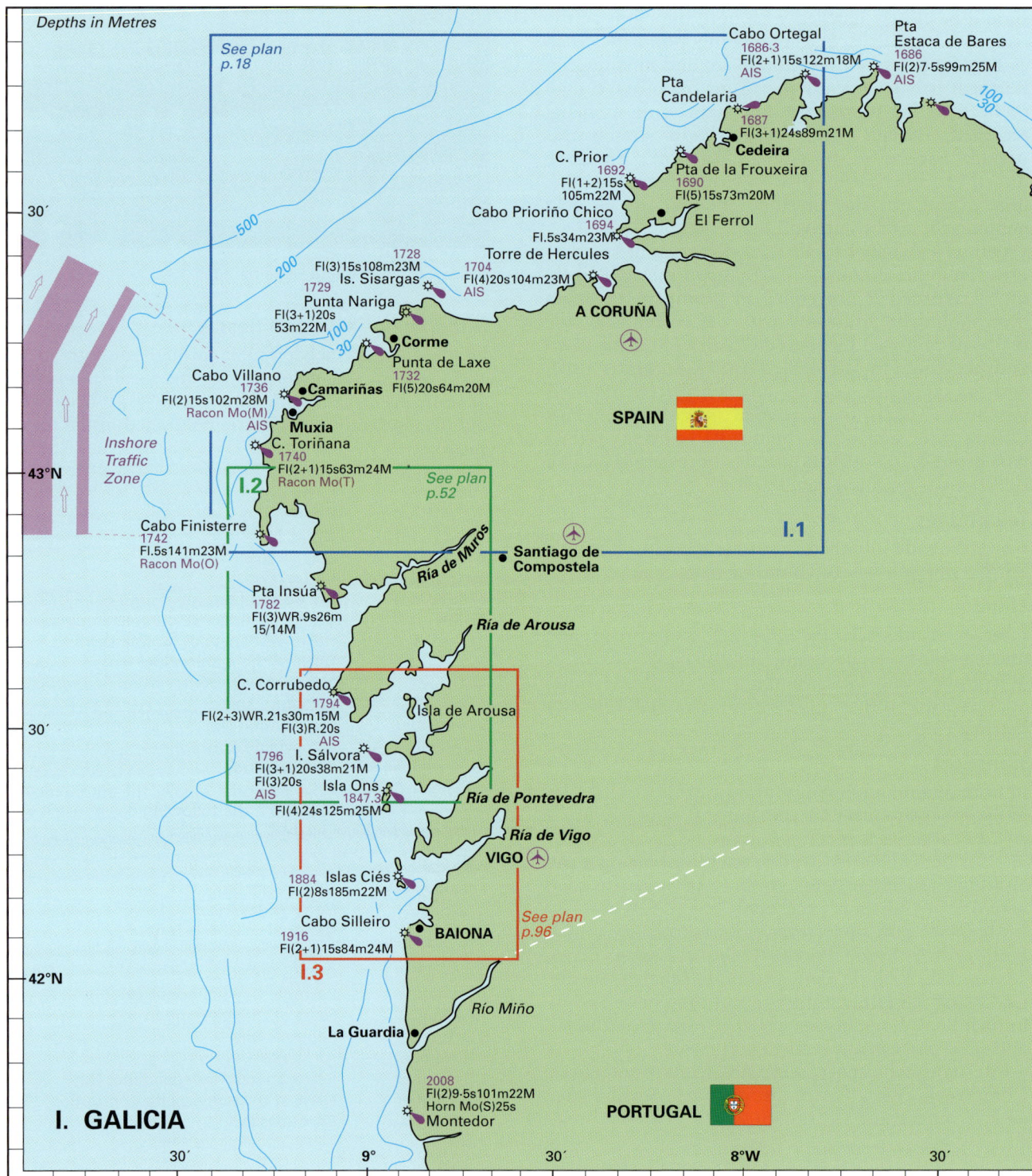

Positions Although a few official charts of this area have yet to be converted from Datum ED50, skippers should note that all positions in this book are to WGS84. All were derived using C-Map electronic charts and Admiralty charts. The waypoints have been included to help with planning and orientation. Much of this coast demands visual pilotage and skippers must satisfy themselves that it is safe to sail directly between any two waypoints.

I. Galicia

Cabo Ortegal to the Portuguese border

Cabo Ortegal to the Portuguese border

This section of the pilot is written for the mariner crossing the Bay of Biscay and making landfall at Cabo Ortegal in Galicia before sailing on southwest and south to the border with Portugal. Cabo Ortegal is one of the highest coastal cliffs in Europe. The 'Aguillons' beneath it strike fear into any sailor. The first place of refuge is the anchorage in the Ría de Cedeira some 12M southwest of the Cape. Ría de Cedeira is the only one of the Rías Altas on the northwest coast of Galicia. The others are all east of Cabo Ortegal and any mariner sailing from this direction should consult RCCPF *South Biscay* for information.

The rías of Galicia offer varied cruising in a most attractive setting. They are well worth visiting in their own right, and changing crew there is straightforward via the airports at A Coruña, Santiago de Compostela and Vigo. The rías also offer a safe haven to yachtsmen on the haul south from northern European waters to the Mediterranean or before heading out into the Atlantic. There is challenging pilotage for those who relish it and there are good anchorages, and many welcoming marinas where boats may be safely secured while the crew explore ashore or leave for extended periods.

Steady development since the mid-1980s has benefitted from the injection of significant EU infrastructure funding. The fishing fleets are of vital importance to the local economy and are well provided for; many now have their own robust, purpose-built marinas in their harbours. Good roads allow rapid travel around the area and, in their wake, have brought major construction of homes and hotels, particularly in the more southern rías. Some beaches are buoyed to protect swimmers, and anchorages are, therefore, moved further offshore.

The stretch of coast between Cabo Ortegal and Cabo Finisterre includes generally small rías with some exposed harbours. The coastline is often high and rugged in between. In the onshore winds and swell for which it is renowned, this coast becomes a dangerous lee shore and the Costa da Morte is aptly named. In settled weather, however, this area provides enjoyable cruising with access to marinas in the A Coruña area and at Camariñas and Muxia some 16·5M north of Cabo Finisterre.

South of Cabo Finisterre are the Rías Bajas and beyond the offshore dangers north of Ría de Muros, the four rías of Muros, Arousa, Pontevedra and Vigo offer more sheltered cruising with a variety of anchorages and harbours to visit. With few exceptions, the rías are wide and deep, and the hazards well marked, although this is not always the case further off the beaten track and, sometimes, close to harbours. Lights, buoys and beacons are generally well maintained.

For general background information on Galicia visit www.galiciaguide.com.

Hazards

Apart from the clearly marked Traffic Separation Zone which lies well off shore, the main hazards are the weather and viveros (a widely-used term to describe the numerous rafts for cultivating mussels and clams in shallow water – although *bateas* is the correct name for the mussel rafts). Weather forecasts are readily obtainable, but local conditions may change rapidly and it is advisable to have a contingency plan when visiting some of the more interesting anchorages. In the summer months, rías, which may start the day in brilliant summer conditions, can be plunged into lingering local mist making passage through the viveros somewhat challenging.

The dramatic 'Aguillons' off Cabo Ortegal, looking E *Jane Russell*

Torre de Hercules, A Coruña

Early season, the main anchorage south of Punta Muxiero Islas Cies *Jane Russell*

The areas on the Plans marked as viveros cannot be definitive; some show up clearly on the air photographs but, although many are well established and remain year after year, some may be removed and others established elsewhere. A few viveros will be found in the more northern rías but the majority are further south, with over 3,000 rafts said to be in Ría de Arousa alone. They are serviced by a large fleet of support vessels and the anchor cables run almost vertically downwards to permit access. It is possible to sail and anchor between them and the shore is generally accessible. However, although the outer perimeters of the rafts are usually marked by yellow buoys and often lit, they do offer a very significant obstacle, particularly at night. An idea of the scale and layout of the viveros may be gleaned using Google Earth.

Shallow waters may include numerous posts, many of these are only visible towards low water. They are dangerous to dinghies. Although their outer edge may be indicated by a solid pole, yellow with an x topmark, care should always be exercised when boating ashore from an anchored yacht.

In addition to the offshore fishing fleet and the viveros support boats, large groups of small fishing boats, some with a clam cage handle stretching up to 20m behind them, may be encountered hard at work or jostling to unload their catch. Life in this area revolves around the fishing fleets and they dominate the harbours. Skippers will wish to respect this when planning their local cruising routes and crews will enjoy the abundant fresh seafood which is obtainable everywhere.

Swell

The exposed coastline is subject to large swells from the Atlantic, sometimes originating in storms hundreds of miles offshore. (See page 2.)

Winds

In summer the dominance of the Azores high pressure area, usually combined with low pressure over the Iberian peninsula, leads to prevailing northeasterlies in the northern part of the area, gaining a more northerly component south of Cabo Finisterre. However, land or sea breeze effects may dictate conditions locally, sometimes leading to a 180° shift in wind direction during the warmer parts of the day.

Gales are infrequent during the summer but may occur, notably the *nordeste pardo*, a cloudy northeaster of the Finisterre area. The southwesterly *vendavale* is also uncommon at this time of year.

In winter, Galicia's weather is largely determined by the passage of North Atlantic frontal systems bringing strong southwesterlies – probably the reason why the Bay of Biscay gained its fearsome reputation in the days of the square-riggers.

Visibility

The chances of coastal mist are greatest in July and August when the incidence may rise as high as one day in 10 or 12 (many yachtsmen would argue that this is conservative), with many more days of early morning mist which then disperses. In the Rías Bajas visibility of less than 2M may occasionally last for a week at a stretch.

Viveros or bateas mussel rafts are a ubiquitous hazard in the rías *Jane Russell*

Currents

Off Cabo Ortegal currents may set easterly into the Bay of Biscay. South of Cabo Finisterre the general trend is southwards, seldom reaching more than 0·5 knot.

Tides

Tidal predictions for north of Cabo Finisterre use A Coruña as the Standard Port; those for the Rías Bajas use Lisbon. When calculating Spanish tides using Lisbon data, note that allowance has already been made for the difference in time zone (Spanish time being UT+1, Portuguese time UT, both advanced one hour in summer – see page 3).

If A Coruña tide tables are not available, as a very rough guide high water occurs at approximately 0510 and 1650 at springs ±20 minutes; and 1045 and 2330 at neaps ±50 minutes. The same figures for Lisbon are approximately 0410 and 1630 ±30 minutes, and 0920 and 2230 ±1 hour 10 minutes.

Ranges are near 3m at springs and 1·4m at neaps, but both time and height may be affected by wind, particularly in the Rías Bajas south of Cabo Finisterre.

The flood stream sets north and northeast around the coast. Unlike some of the rios of Portugal and southern Spain, all Galicia's rías are fully tidal, certainly as far as a yacht is likely to penetrate.

Wonderfully fresh sea food in Galicia *Martin Walker*

The compass rose of Celtic regions, set beneath the Torre de Hercules in A Coruña, highlights the connections between Galicia and the other Celtic nations *Jane Russell*

Flying lessons, Islas Cies

Where no tidal data is given for an individual harbour it will be found under the preliminary notes for the ría as a whole.

Climate

Galicia is the wet corner of Spain – it has much the same climatic feel as southwest England, though on average is rather warmer. Mean air temperature varies from around 20°C in August to 9°C in January, sea temperature from 17°C in summer to 12°C in winter.

Marinas

Marinas are available in Ares, Sada, A Coruña, Camariñas, Muxia, in each of the four southern rías, and in Baiona. Weather information is posted daily and internet facilities are generally available to visiting yachtsmen.

Language

Galicia is a popular holiday area but few foreigners visit the rías. Although English and other languages are spoken in the major marina offices, visiting yachtsmen who do not speak Spanish should arm themselves with the necessary phrasebook.

Berthing costs

Contact details are provided for most ports so that applicable costs can be checked in advance if desired. Joining a *Pasaporte* system may provide discounts.

Facilities

Galicia is no longer a remote cruising area. The large number of fishing fleets means that emergency and basic technical and harbour support is widely available. For normal routine work or chandlery seek advice from the multilingual staff of the major marinas. A Coruña and Sada offer the most comprehensive support in the north: Portosin, Vilagarcia, Sanxenxo, Cangas, Punta Lagoa, Vigo, Baiona in the four southern rías. Easy refuelling places are indicated by * at the start of the sections. Water, food shops and restaurants are widely available.

GALICIA ATLANTIC NATIONAL PARKS

See the following website which provides details of the islands, their bird life, flora and sealife:
www.magrama.gob.es/en/red-parques-nacionales/nuestros-parques/islas-atlanticas/

The mauve dashed lines indicate ferry routes for tourists.

National Park Permits

Experience has shown that the best way to ensure the most trouble- free access to Galician national parks is to apply for a Navigation Permission permit by e-mail before even leaving home. It appears that applying on-line is fraught with difficulty, as is telephone contact. Permits can be obtained through the major marinas and by visiting Park offices but here the issue is time. Through marinas there is normally a processing period of a few weeks, but visiting the actual Park office involves a delay of a few days between applying for and receiving the appropriate permit. However, once a permit has been obtained renewal is reported to be a straightforward process.

The permits last a year but each vessel/skipper combination is only given a cumulative limit of days within that year. For National Park spots it is about 10 full days, but half days are allowed for a lunch stop without staying overnight for example. The system is reliant on having internet access because once the Navigation Permission has been granted it is still necessary to email in advance for an Anchoring Permission when intending to visit a park area and for how long. As boat names and number of people on board are all logged in the application process, the Park wardens will be checking.

Notes from the National Park Authority

Contacts

Parque Nacional Maritimo Terrestre das illas atlanticas de Galicia
Edificio Cetmar (1ª planta), c/o eduardo cabello s/n, 36208 bouzas - vigo
℡ +34 886 21 80 90
Email fondeos.iatlanticas@xunta.es
www.iatlanticas.es

Navigation Permission

The navigation permission, required to get the anchoring permission, is biannual and allows navigating on National Park waters during the current year. In order to apply for it you have to fill in the navigation forms:
 (www.iatlanticas.es/formulario/formulario_ingles.pdf) and send them to the National Park bureau together with the requested documents. You can also find these forms on the National Park website or at the Park bureau, from which the form can be sent to the applicant by email, postal mail or fax.

Renewal of navigation permission is automatic upon expiry. There is no need to send in a renewal application. Any changes in vessel ownership, registration, name and personal data of owner need to be given.

Anchoring Permission

Application for anchoring permission can be done through the internet without any need for sending application through the office. The procedure is as follows:

Anchoring permission (even for the same day) can be applied for through the website www.iatlanticas.es and can be directly downloaded via the anchoring management program. It can be done as follows:

When you connect for the very first time, a User Name will be required. This is the vessel owner ID number (number, space and capital letter). The password is the navigation permission number. After that, the system will suggest that you change your password.

This procedure will also provide you with access to vessel and owner data. The lower part of the screen has a drop-down menu showing the archipelagos. Select one and provide details of the number of passengers. There is another drop-down menu for dates which displays the following seven calendar days, from which you can select three. A thirty day calendar will appear in the drop-down menu if your application is made between the 15th of September and the 14th of June. This allows you to choose up to a maximum of ten days. Permissions are valid on a daily basis and these must therefore be printed and carried onboard the vessel. They can be downloaded from three to ten days prior to date of use.

There are some beautiful walks in the National Parks. This is on Route 1 to Monte Faro on Islas Cies, looking S
Jane Russell

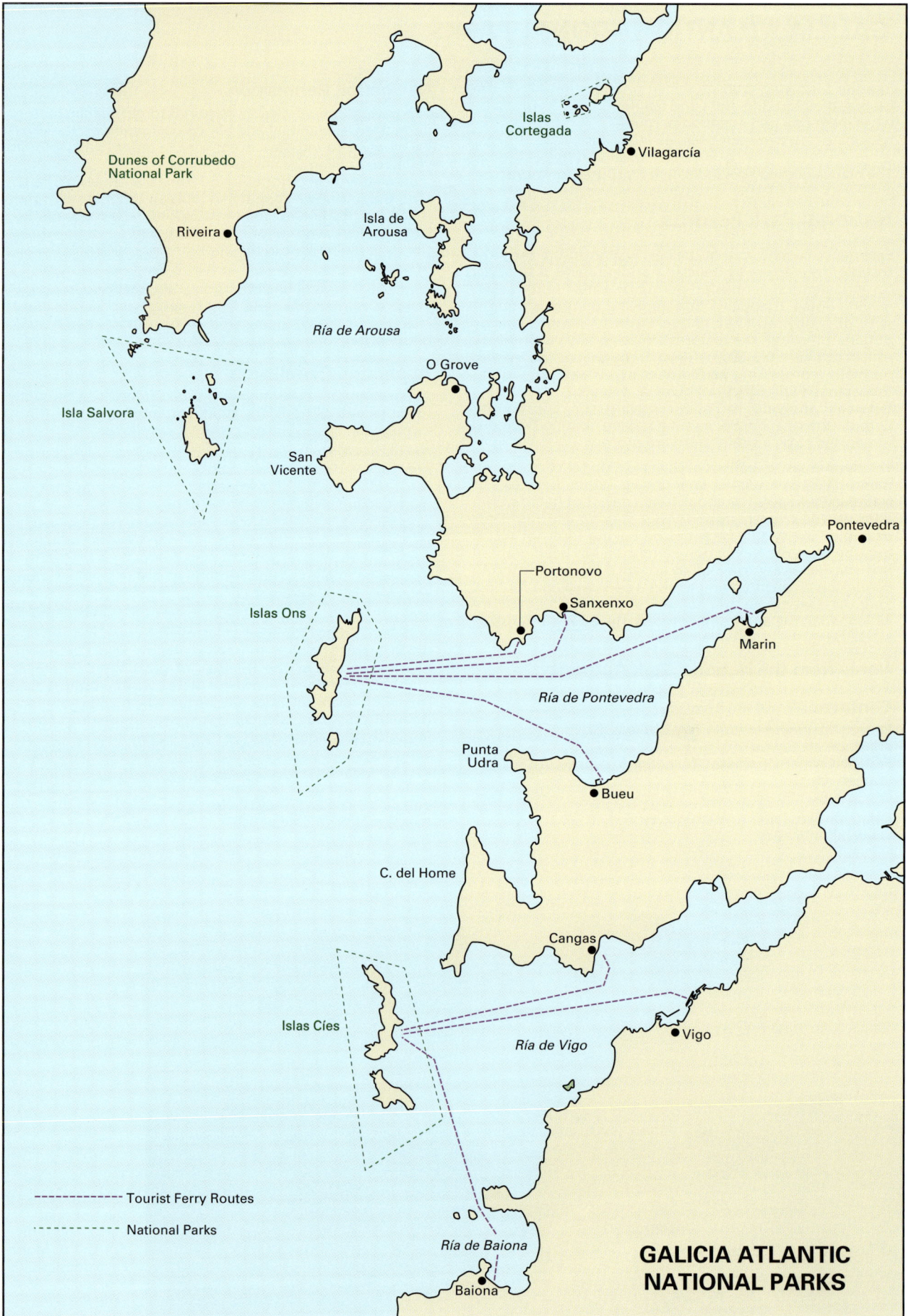

Dunes of Corrubedo
National Park

Riveira ●

Islas
Cortegada

● Vilagarcía

Isla de
Arousa

Ría de Arousa

O Grove
●

Isla Salvora

San
Vicente

Pontevedra ●

Portonovo

Islas Ons

● Sanxenxo

Marin ●

Ría de Pontevedra

Punta
Udra

● Bueu

C. del Home

Cangas ●

Islas Cíes

Ría de Vigo

● Vigo

- - - - - - - - Tourist Ferry Routes

- - - - - - - - National Parks

Ría de Baiona

**GALICIA ATLANTIC
NATIONAL PARKS**

Baiona ●

GALICIA

Islas Cíes *page 110*   Isla Ons *page 97*

Islas Cíes and Ons are well served by ferries and are popular
for walking – routes are shown on the two plans below.

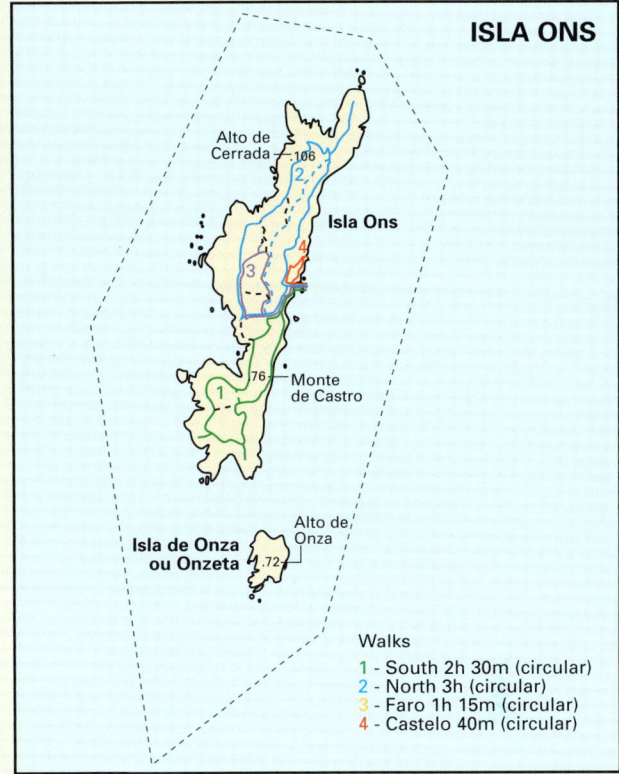

ISLAS CÍES

Alto das Cíes
.197
Monte Agudo .182
Isla del Norte
4
3
Alto do Principe .111
Isla del Faro
1 2
.175
Monte Faro

Monte Galeira .128
Isla del San Martino
.175 Monte Pereira

Isla Boeiro

Walks

1 - Monte Faro 2h 30m
2 - Faro da Porta 1h 45m
3 - Alto do Principe 1h 15m
4 - Monteagudo 1h 45m

ISLA ONS

Alto de Cerrada 106
2
Isla Ons
4
3
1 76 Monte de Castro

Alto de Onza
Isla de Onza ou Onzeta .72

Walks

1 - South 2h 30m (circular)
2 - North 3h (circular)
3 - Faro 1h 15m (circular)
4 - Castelo 40m (circular)

Islas Sálvora *page 73*   Islas Cortegada *page 85*

Islas Cortegada and Sálvora are not served by ferries and
visits by yachtsmen are not encouraged.

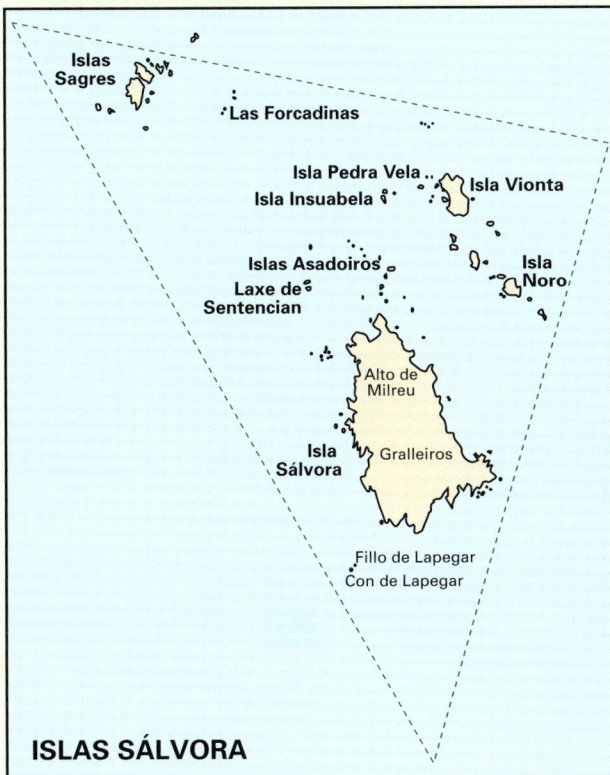

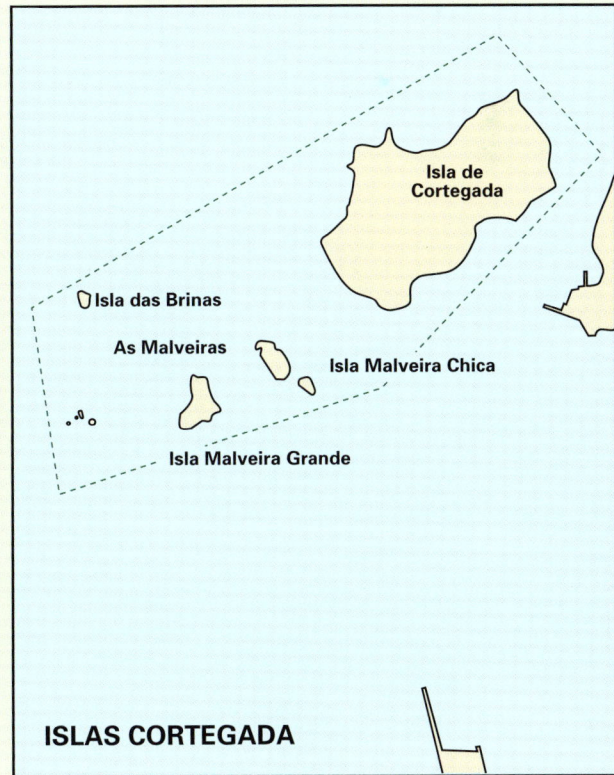

ISLAS SÁLVORA

Islas Sagres
Las Forcadinas
Isla Pedra Vela
Isla Insuabela **Isla Vionta**
Islas Asadoiros
Laxe de Sentencian **Isla Noro**
Alto de Milreu
Isla Sálvora Gralleiros
Fillo de Lapegar
Con de Lapegar

ISLAS CORTEGADA

Isla de Cortegada
Isla das Brinas
As Malveiras **Isla Malveira Chica**
Isla Malveira Grande

CABO ORTEGAL TO A CORUÑA

Depths in Metres

1686·3
Fl(2+1)15s
122m18M
AIS

34

48

Cabo Ortegal
45

Pta Candelaria
1687
Fl(3+1)24s87m21M
AIS

38

⊕2

43°40′
N

24

36

3

31

See plan p.19

Ría de
Cedeira

15

112

8

Punta de la Frouxeira
1690
Fl(5)15s73m20M

Cabo Prior
1692
Fl(1+2)15s105m22M

⊕3

9

1693
Fl(2)7s42m8M

Punta del Castro
EL FERROL

Cabo
Prioriño Chico
1694
Fl.5s34m23M

See plan p.23

30′

19

Ares

105

⊕4

Torre de Hércules
1704
Fl(4)20s104m23M
Racon
AIS

10

5

Fontan/
Sada

2

20′

A CORUÑA

30′   20′   10′   8°W   50′

Plan IA

⊕1	44°00′N	08°00′W	14M N Cabo Ortegal
⊕2	43°43′N	08°28′W	10M NW Cabo Prior
⊕3	43°31′N	08°25′·5W	4·2M W Cabo Prioriño
⊕4	43°24′·8N	08°28′·5W	Outer App West La Coruña

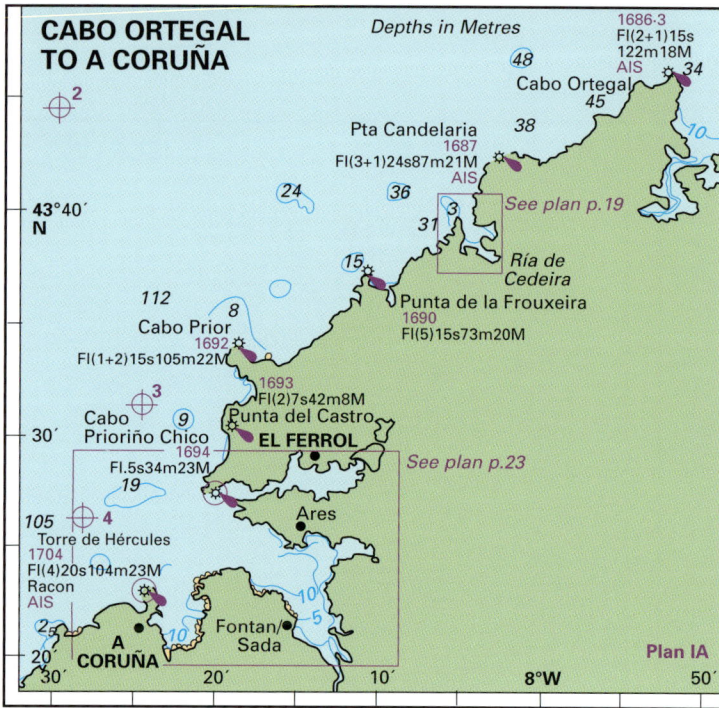

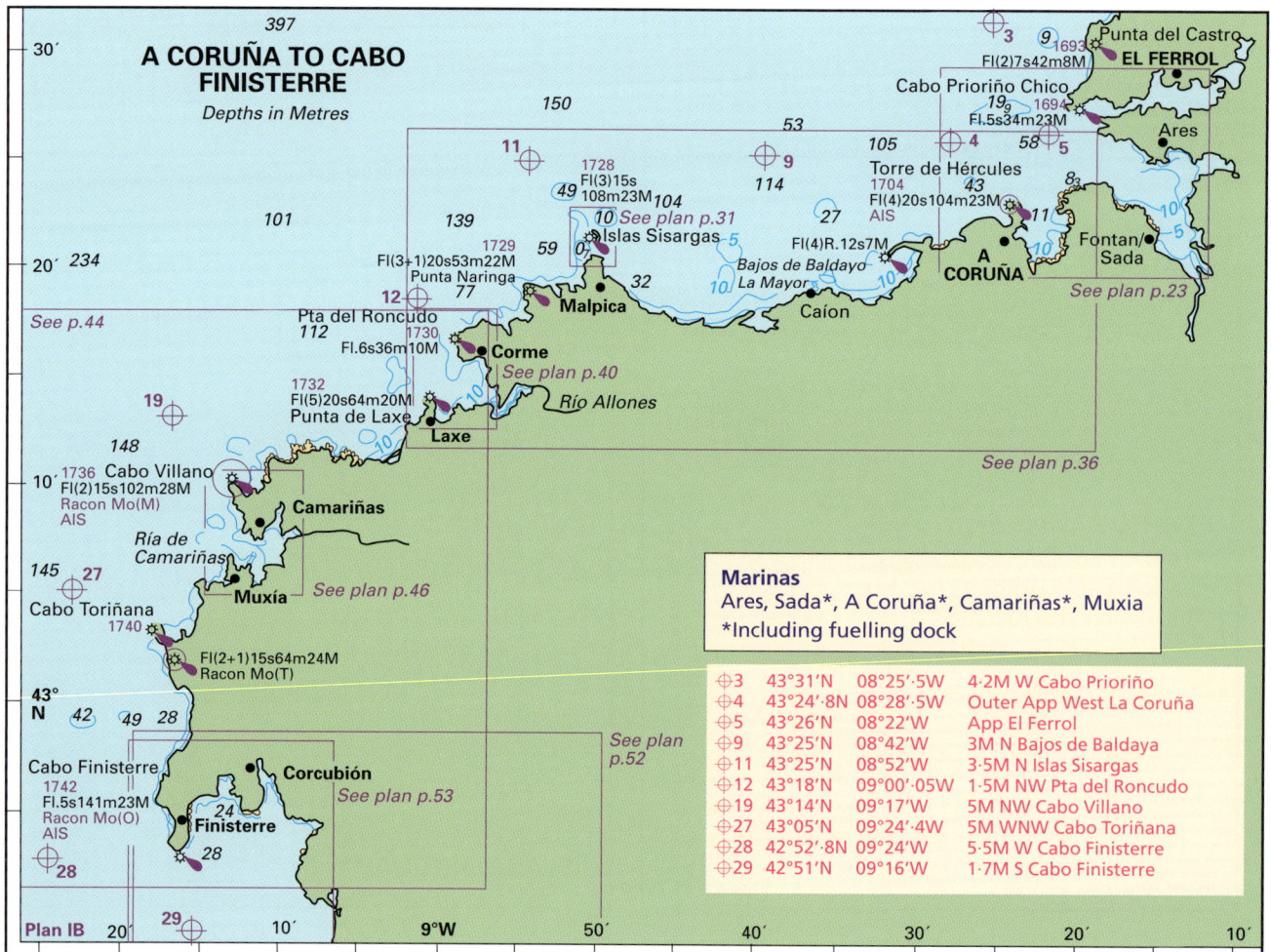

Coastguard
A Coruña
☎ +34 981 209 541/548
Sea Rescue Service
☎ +34 900 202 202

MRSC Coruña   Ch 10
MRCC Finisterre   Ch 11

Weather
Navtex (D)
Coruña Ch 26 at
   0840, 1240, 2010
Finisterre Ch 22 at
   0840, 1240, 2010

For details of the Rias Altas to the east of
Cabo Ortegal refer to RCCPF *South Biscay*

397

30′

A CORUÑA TO CABO FINISTERRE

Depths in Metres

150

⊕3

9
1693
Fl(2)7s42m8M

Punta del Castro
EL FERROL

53

Cabo Prioriño Chico
19
1694
Fl.5s34m23M

Ares

11

1728
Fl(3)15s
108m23M
AIS

⊕9

105

⊕4

58

⊕5

101

139

49

104

114

Torre de Hércules
1704
Fl(4)20s104m23M

43

8

10

See plan p.31

27

11

Fontan/
Sada

20′   234

1729
Fl(3+1)20s53m22M
Punta Naringa

59

0

Islas Sisargas

Fl(4)R.12s7M

A CORUÑA

10

5

See plan p.23

Bajos de Baldayo
La Mayor

10

⊕12

77

32

Malpica

Caíon

See p.44

Pta del Roncudo
112
1730
Fl.6s36m10M

Corme
See plan p.40

Río Allones

See plan p.36

1732
Fl(5)20s64m20M
Punta de Laxe

Laxe

⊕19

148

10′   1736 Cabo Villano
Fl(2)15s102m28M
Racon Mo(M)
AIS

Camariñas

Ría de
Camariñas

145   ⊕27

Cabo Toriñana
1740

Muxia
See plan p.46

Fl(2+1)15s64m24M
Racon Mo(T)

Marinas
Ares, Sada*, A Coruña*, Camariñas*, Muxia
*Including fuelling dock

43°
N

42

49

28

Cabo Finisterre
1742
Fl.5s141m23M
Racon Mo(O)
AIS

Corcubión
See plan p.53

Finisterre

24

28

⊕28

*See plan
p.52*

⊕3	43°31′N	08°25′·5W	4·2M W Cabo Prioriño
⊕4	43°24′·8N	08°28′·5W	Outer App West La Coruña
⊕5	43°26′N	08°22′W	App El Ferrol
⊕9	43°25′N	08°42′W	3M N Bajos de Baldaya
⊕11	43°25′N	08°52′W	3·5M N Islas Sisargas
⊕12	43°18′N	09°00′·05W	1·5M NW Pta del Roncudo
⊕19	43°14′N	09°17′W	5M NW Cabo Villano
⊕27	43°05′N	09°24′·4W	5M WNW Cabo Toriñana
⊕28	42°52′·8N	09°24′W	5·5M W Cabo Finisterre
⊕29	42°51′N	09°16′W	1·7M S Cabo Finisterre

Plan IB   20′   ⊕29   10′   9°W   50′   40′   30′   20′   10′

I.1.1 Ría de Cedeira to A Coruña

GALICIA

Cedeira

Location
43°40'·00N 08°04'·00W

Shelter
Not too good in NW gale

Warning
Offlying rocks off W entrance

Depth restrictions
Min 6m in approaches

Night entry
Well lit

Tidal information
HW A Coruña +0050
LW A Coruña +0050

Mean height of tide (m)

MHWS	MHWN	MLWN	MLWS
4.1	3·2	1·5	0·6

Berthing
Anchorage only

Facilities
All a dinghy ride away

Charts
BA 1290 (175), 1122 (25)
Spanish 930 (40) (20)
Imray C43, C48

Weather
A Coruña Ch 26 at 0840, 1240 and 2010
Navtex D

Radio and telephone
Try *Cedeira Practicos* on Ch 12

Beautiful ria behind an open bay conceals anchorage sheltered from Atlantic swell

The fishermen, although friendly, use all the facilities; watering, fuelling and provisioning entail some effort.

Approaches

By day or night

Give Punta Chirlateira a good 0·5M berth if coming from the west to avoid the offliers and approach the entrance from the north or northwest. The entrance to the Ría de Cedeira can be difficult to make out from seaward.

Entrance

Proceed down the bearing of 155° on Punta Promontorio (white hexagonal tower, Oc(4)10s) just open of Punta Sarridal (red round tower, Oc.WR.6s) in the white sector of the latter. Shortly after, the track passes into the west, red sector of Punta Sarridal which should be left at least 50m to port. Thence round the breakwater end (Fl(2)R.7s) and proceed to the anchorage.

Anchoring

In 2–4m to the southeast of the moorings, good holding in grey sand with weed patches and some detritus (mooring lines and fishing gear) on the seabed. A windy spot, the high hills funnel the wind giving the impression that it is much rougher outside. Generally well-protected from the Atlantic swell, which can be a problem on this coast, once you have turned in past the breakwater.

Moorings

None for visitors.

Berthing

The old quay can be used for embarking fuel and water, and landing; there is from 1·7–2·2m alongside the east half of the south side of it. There is one short pontoon with a gate at the top on the east end of the quay but it is for locals.

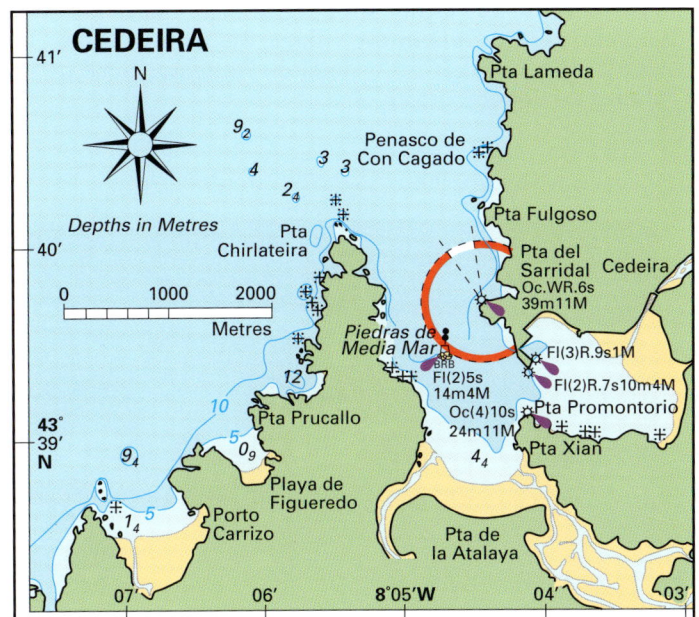

CEDEIRA

Cedeira looking East

Ashore

Cedeira has always welcomed visiting yachtsmen but not done much for them. There is a travel-lift and some hard standing used by fishermen possibly usable in extremis.

Facilities

Daily weather updates – including windguru – posted on Cruz Roja office near the dinghy landing on the old quay. Water from the old quay; garage (☎ +34 981 480 34 30) will deliver fuel here if more than 70 litres; 100-tonne travel-lift; shops are a good 0·5M walk but easier by dinghy near highwater; several restaurants in the village; ice from the new lonja; supermarket in Avienda de Castelao, close to Praza de Lopez Corton.

Leisure

Good beaches round the ria and the Río Loira is worth a dinghy trip provided it is not breaking at the mouth. Visits to La Concepcion castle, the church of Nuestra Señora Maria del Mar and chapel of San Antonio are worthwhile.

Travel

Occasional local buses to El Ferrol and A Coruña; nearest airport at the latter (60km).

Fiesta

14–30 August for Nuestra Señora Maria del Mar, when the port will be full.

Cedeira, old quay

The little chapel of San Antonio, high above the eastern side of the ria entrance, is a pleasant walk from the harbour *Jane Russell*

Cedeira anchorage looking SW *Jane Russell*

Cedeira fishing harbour looking S over breakwater end towards the anchoring area and the light on Punta Promontorio *Jane Russell*

The entrance to Ría de Cedeira looking W. Breaking seas can be seen over rocks off Punta Chirlateira *Jane Russell*

You can dinghy into the centre of Cedeira, but not at low tide! *Jane Russell*

Punta del Frouxeira

43°38'·54'N 08°10'·79W

An open anchorage
One of the few anchorages well-sheltered from the west behind the Punta in 2–10m, sand.

Punta del Frouseira looking southwest

Cabo Prior

43°33'·01'N 08°20'·08W

The only shelter from the east between Cedeira and El Ferrol
A small bay 2M south of Cabo Prior in 2–8m on sand has good protection. The only anchorage in less than 10m lies east of Isla Blanca in 4m but stay two cables clear because of the dangerous rocks that surround it.

Cabo Prior looking northeast

Approaches to Rías de Ferrol, de Ares, de Betanzos and A Coruña

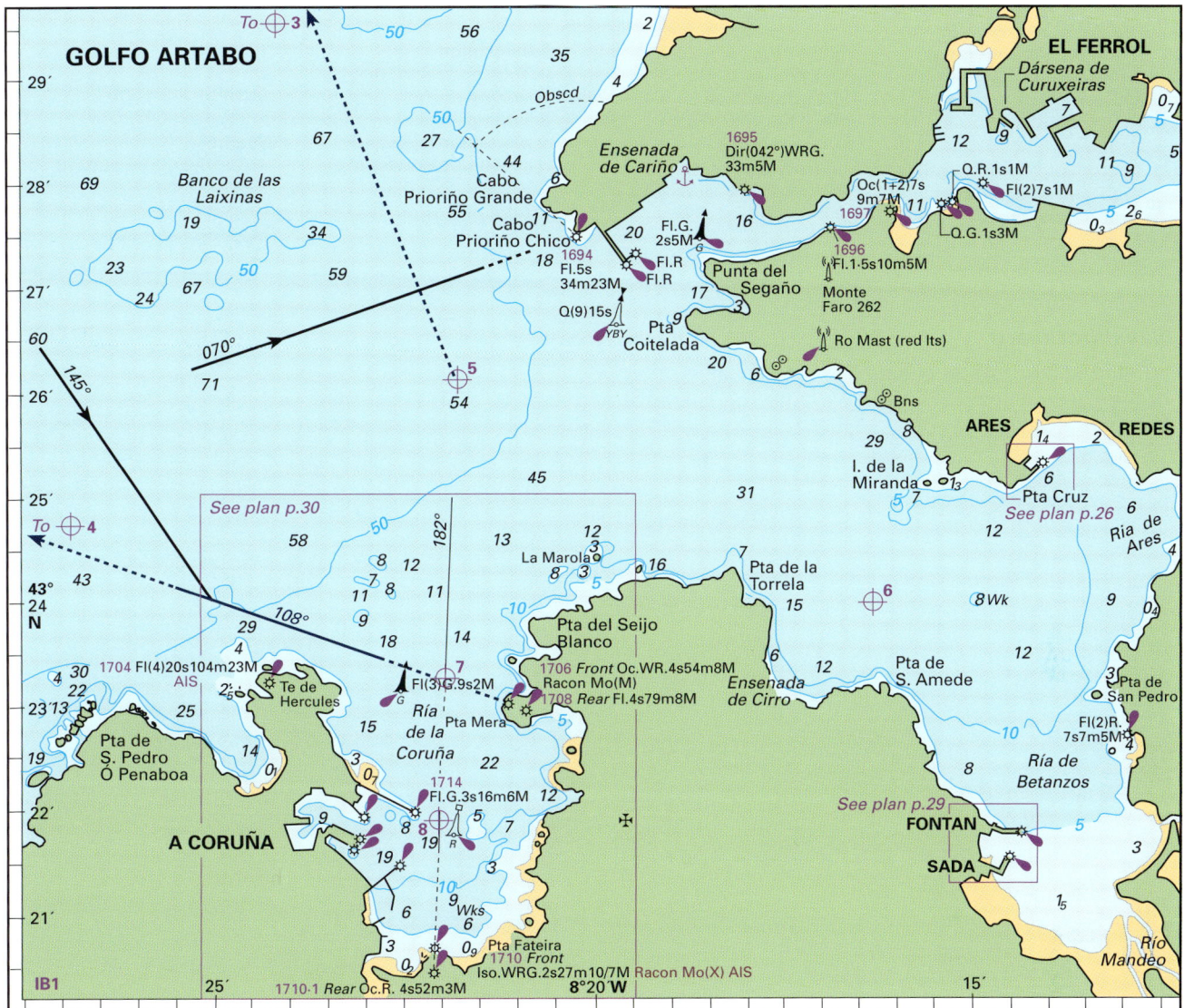

GALICIA

Chart labels (as read):

GOLFO ARTABO

To ⊕3 · 50 · 56 · 2
35
Obscd · 4
50
27 · 44
Cabo
Prioriño Grande 55
Cabo 11
Prioriño Chico
1694 FI.5s 34m23M
Q(9)15s
Ensenada de Cariño
1695 Dir(042°)WRG. 33m5M
20 FI.G. 2s5M
FI.R
FI.R
16
Punta del Segaño
1697
Oc(1+2)7s 9m7M 11
Q.R.1s1M
FI(2)7s1M
Q.G.1s3M
1696 FI.1.5s10m5M
Monte Faro 262
Ro Mast (red lts)
EL FERROL
Dársena de Curuxeiras
12
7
070°
145°
71
71
Banco de las Laixinas
69 19 34 50 59
23 24 67
60
54 ⊕5
17
Pta Coitelada
20
Bns
29
I. de la Miranda
ARES
REDES
14 2
Pta Cruz
See plan p.26
Ría de Ares
To ⊕4
See plan p.30
58 50 · 12 13
La Marola
8 12
8 11 11 9 18 14
108° 29 4
45
31
Pta de la Torrela
15
6
8 Wk
12
9
1704 FI(4)20s104m23M AIS
Te de Hercules
Ría de la Coruña
Pta Mera
FI(3)G.9s2M
7
1706 Front Oc.WR.4s54m8M Racon Mo(M)
1708 Rear FI.4s79m8M
Pta del Seijo Blanco
Ensenada de Cirro
Pta de S. Amede
12
Pta de San Pedro
FI(2)R. 7s7m5M
Ría de Betanzos
Pta de S. Pedro Ó Penaboa
1714 FI.G.3s16m6M 12
A CORUÑA
19 19
Wks 6
See plan p.29
FONTAN
SADA
Pta Fateira
1710 Front Iso.WRG.2s27m10/7M Racon Mo(X) AIS
1710·1 Rear Oc.R. 4s52m3M
Río Mandeo
IB1 · 25′ · 8°20′W · 15′

Waypoint list:

⊕3 43°31′N 08°25′·5W 4.2M W Cabo Prioriño
⊕4 43°24′·8N 08°28′·5W Outer App West A Coruña
⊕5 43°26′N 08°22′W App El Ferrol
⊕6 43°24′N 08°16′W App for Ares and Marina Sada
⊕7 43°23′·2N 08°22′·1W Ría de La Coruña
⊕8 43°21′·9N 08°22′·2W Off breakwater A Coruña

Charts	Approach	Rías
Admiralty	1111, 1094	1110, 1117, 1118
Spanish	928, 412A	4122, 4123, 4125, 4126
Imray	C18, C48	C18, C48

Tides

See A Coruña page 31

This group of rías in the Golfo Artabo include the major commercial and Naval port of El Ferrol, the small friendly marina at Ares, and the major marinas at Sada and A Coruña.

Hazards

In rough weather the sea breaks over two banks about 1M off the coast north of Cabo Prioriño – Bajos Tarracidos and Cabaleiro – and a third, Banco de las Laixinas some 2–4M west of that Cape. Under such conditions it is advisable to approach these rías from the west and remain well clear of Banco de las Laixinas. Clearing lines are shown on the plan.

Approach

From the north under settled conditions The route from ⊕3 to ⊕5 (5·5M) clears the dangers. From the area of ⊕5 set course as appropriate or look south for ⊕7 and ⊕8 to pick up the leading lights for A Coruña (1706 and 1708).

From the west (the all-weather route) The route from ⊕4 to ⊕5 (5M) will keep a yacht south of Banco de las Laixinas. If bound for A Coruña ⊕4 to ⊕7, lie on the leading line onto marks 1706 and 1708, then turn south at ⊕7 (see plan page 30).

El Ferrol

Location
43°28'·00N 08°18'·00W

Shelter
Perfect inside

Warning
Keep clear of works and
shipping in approaches

Depth restrictions
None

Night entry
Very well lit

Tidal information
HW A Coruña +0005
LW A Coruña +0010

Mean height of tide (m)

MHWS	MHWN	MLWN	MLWS
4·2	2·8	1·6	0·3

Tidal stream
Up to 3 knots in the
narrows

Berthing
La Graña marina and
Darsena de Curuxeiros

Facilities
Those of a large city

Charts
BA 1117, 1118 (10)
Spanish 412A (25)
Imray C42, C43, C48

Weather
A Coruña Ch 26 at 0840,
1240, 2010
Navtex D

Telephone and radio
None

Naval Dockyard

Stirring scenery starts behind the massive new outer
breakwater; a few facilities 4M from the entrance
for visiting yachts.

El Ferrol from the west with the forts of San Felipe to port and La Palma to starboard in the narrows

Approach and entrance

By day or night

A track of 065° from F5 will clear the outer end of the new breakwater seen in the photograph to line up 045° in the white sector of San Cristobal light (white truncated tower Dir.WRG.33m5M). Before reaching Punta Segaño align the next marks on 085° (both white truncated towers front Pta de San Martin Fl.1·5s, rear Oc.4s) taking care to leave the starboard hand buoy and shallows off Pta del Segaño to starboard. Then follow the buoyed channel inwards and identify the entrance to Darsena de Curuxeiros beyond the Ro-Ro berth (Fl(4)R.11s).

Berthing

The only yacht berths now are in Darsena de Curuxeiros (which is also busy with local ferries) and it will be a question of taking what is available, an alongside berth may be found here.

There are a number of small marinas:

The small marina at La Graña has been renovated and can accept the occasional visitor up to 12m in 4–6m but with only a few facilities. The moorings off it are often poorly anchored and the anchorage itself is subject to violent downdrafts in any W wind.

Marina Playa de Mugardos
43°27'·80N 08°15'·59W

Another marina with a good anchorage and some mooring buoys off it.

Anchoring

Temporary anchorages can be found in the following places:
Ensenada de Cariño, the new breakwater gives good shelter from the swell. (See plan p.23)
To the East of Castillo de San Felipe.
Ensenada de Baño.
Off La Graña.

Ashore in El Ferrol

There is an excellent walkway around the northern defences to El Ferrol.

GALICIA

The outer mole at El Ferrol and the approach to the narrows

Ares Marina

43°25'·35N 08°14'·33W

Shelter
Good except from northeast

Depth restrictions
2–2·5m in marina; deep approach

Night entry
Possible

Tidal information
As for A Coruña (Standard Port)

Mean height of tide (m)

MHWS	MHWN	MLWN	MLWS
4·2	2·8	1·6	0·3

Berthing
On fingers or pontoons

Facilities
Usual marina and small town

Charts
BA 1094 (25)
Spanish 412A (25)
Imray C42, C43, C48

Weather
A Coruña Ch 26 0840, 1240, 2010
Navtex D

Radio
Ch 09 (English spoken)

Telephone
☎ +34 610 73 73 44 or +34 981 46 87 87
Email
secretaria@nauticoares.com
www.nauticoares.com

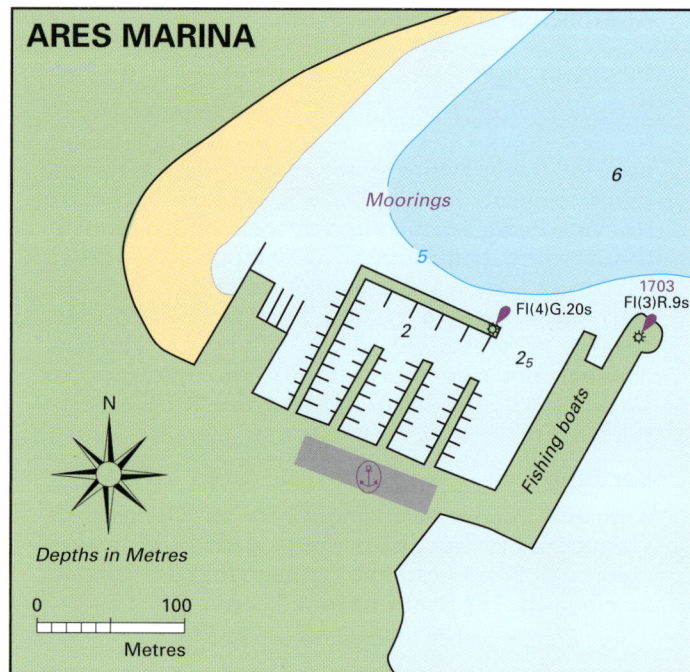

ARES MARINA

Moorings

6

5

2

2₅

1703
Fl(4)G.20s   Fl(3)R.9s

Fishing boats

N

Depths in Metres

0   100
Metres

Ares Marina looking north-northeast

Small marina with a great outlook onto sands, beach and town

Ares is a modern town and has the usual distractions of a seaside resort with good but crowded beaches.

Approach and entrance by day or night

From the west in any swell keep south of Bajo de Miranda with 3·7m over it to the southwest of Isla de Miranda lying 1M west of Ares breakwater(Fl(3)R.9s). The east end of the long pontoon is lit Fl(4)G20s. Berth here but if not directed otherwise call on Ch 09 for a berth (0900–2200; English spoken).

Berthing

Ares Marina has visitors' berths on finger pontoons with minimum depth 2-2·5m, and provides good protection, except in a NE wind. There are 26 visitors' berths (yachts up to 14m) either on fingers on the south side of the north pontoon or alongside the north of that pontoon.

Moorings

All private.

Anchoring

Moorings take up most of the space to the northeast of the marina but anchorage can be found in 2–3m to the east or northeast of the breakwater with shelter from the west. If anchored, there is a slip for dinghy use in the middle of the beach.

Facilities

Water and electricity on the pontoons; showers, laundry and heads in the marina building; craneage available and a 35-tonne travel-lift; fuel at the moment only by cans from garage who will deliver in quantity; repairs by arrangement; shops and provisioning a 10-minute walk into Ares, bread from just by the church; restaurant and café in marina building and many more in the town. Clubhouse and meteorological information in marina office. Cycle hire from here also.

Travel

Half-hourly bus service to El Ferrol (20 minutes) whence there are bus and rail connections to the rest of Spain. Nearest airports A Coruña (40 minutes) and Santiago de Compostela (one hour).

Ría de Ares

The ría extends eastward for three miles from Ares to Betanzos and the Río Eume. The north shore is now much obstructed by fish farms but the one at Ensenada de Redes has gone. Anchor outside moorings in 3–4m. Popular weekend spot for boats from Sada. Pretty houses in the village but not much else.

It may also be possible to anchor to the north of a farm between Isolete Mouron and Punta Modias with some shelter from the west but Spanish charts 4125 or 412A would be needed.

The ría shallows gradually up to the low railway bridge before Puentedueme town where there is 1m but no discernible channel.

Puentedueme is a historical town and worth a dinghy trip at most stages of the tide; the Castelo de Andrade perched over the town is worth a visit.

Ría de Betanzos

Río Mandeo may be entered to the south of Miño peninsula which lies 1M south-southeast of Sada. There is a small drying harbour on the south side of Miño. From here the río winds 4M to Betanzos, passing under a bridge with a clearance of approximately 20m. Spanish chart 412A is the only guide to the run of the channel and although excursion boats run up to the drying quay at Betanzos on the tide, it would be an adventurous stranger that tried it in a deep-draught yacht.

Betanzos is an ancient medieval city with many historical attractions including the 12th-century church of Santa Maria de Azogue, an excellent museum and many restaurants around the main square and waterfront.

GALICIA

Ares Marina building

Sada Marina (Fontán)

43°21'·00N 08°14'·00W

Shelter
Good in the marina

Depth restrictions
4m in entrance, 2·6–2m at berths

Night entry
Well lit, no leading lights

Tidal information
As for A Coruña (Standard Port)

Mean height of tide (m)

MHWS	MHWN	MLWN	MLWS
4·2	2·8	1·6	0·3

Berthing
At pontoons with fingers

Facilities
Those of a large modern marina

Charts
BA 1094 (25)
Spanish 412A (25)
Imray C42, C43, C48

Weather
A Coruña Ch 26 at 0840, 1240, 2010
Navtex D

Radio
Marina Sada Ch 09

Telephone
℡ +34 981 61 90 15
Email administracion@marina
sada.com
(Manager) teijido@marinasada.com
www.marinasada.com
www.marinasdegalicia.com

Large expanding marina with all facilities and security; a good place to lay up

The fishing harbour in Fontán and the marina at Sada have developed in parallel. Much progress has been made to the marina side in recent years and continues. The scope of the harbour was much enhanced by the removal of La Pulgeira rock and beacon in the middle of the harbour near the end of the pier for the local boats on the West side.

Sada Marina looking north

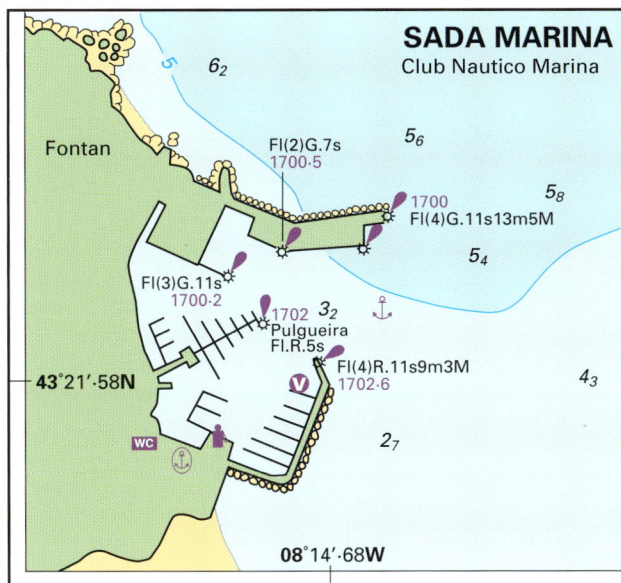

SADA MARINA
Club Nautico Marina

Fontan

Fl(2)G.7s
1700·5

Fl(3)G.11s
1700·2

1700
Fl(4)G.11s13m5M

1702 Pulgueira
Fl.R.5s

Fl(4)R.11s9m3M
1702·6

43°21'·58N

WC

08°14'·68W

Approaches

By day or night

From off the entrance to El Ferrol there are no offlying dangers provided 0·5M is kept offshore and a track of 120° on Punta de San Pedro (Fl(2)WR.7s7m5M) maintained until the Sada breakwater (Fl(4)G.11s) is sighted and the way is clear to the entrance.

Entrance

Wide and straightforward except for anchored and possibly unlit boats. Sada marina lies to port on entry to the main harbour.

Berthing

A prior call on Ch 09 may get a berth allocated. Otherwise select a vacant one on the outer pontoons of the eastern breakwater and check with the office. An additional marina – Club Nautico de Sada – with 313 berths up to 22m fills the centre of the harbour. It has its own travel lift.

Moorings

None for visitors.

Anchoring

Outside clear of the entrance in 1–3m.

Ashore

There are good laying up facilities and security and this is probably the best place to overwinter along the coast.

Facilities

Water and electricity on the pontoons to which access is by card; diesel and petrol at the fuel berth; 32-tonne travel-lift; craneage up to 10-tonnes; heads and showers; repair facilities under cover if needed; chandlery; free WiFi. There are adequate shops within easy walking distance, a market and a large supermarcado south of the marina.

Leisure

Sada is a popular seaside resort and there is the usual range of restaurants, shops, cafés and entertainments. Otherwise a dinghy trip up the Río Mondeo to the ancient town of Betanzos on the tide, or by one of the excursion boats that run up the river might amuse. See above for some details of Betanzos. There is a good beach at Playa de Sada.

Fiestas

16 July Feast of Our Lady of Mount Carmel; 15–18 Aug St Roch.

Travel

Sada is off the main rail and motorway routes (but not by much) and buses run to Betanzos to connect. If laying up here, A Coruña airport, with direct flights to London Heathrow or to other destinations via Madrid, is only 15km, with Santiago de Compostela international airport 45 minutes along the motorway.

Ensenada de Cirro

43°23'·31N 08°17'·92W

An alternative to the busy marinas hereabouts

Behind the extensive fish farm lies a small harbour with a West Country (UK) feel. Entirely given over to fishing, an anchorage may be found just off the beach (see plan page 23). An entry channel is marked by port and starboard markers but is encumbered by fishing rafts. Any route through the rafts can be used.

Ensenada de Cirro, harbour

Ensenada de Cirro © *Google earth*

GALICIA

Final approaches to Ría de la Coruña

Depths in Metres

27

33

56

12

8_8

8_5 7_5

Banco Yacentes
ó Basuril

26

13

18

9 La Marola

8

8

8

43°
24′
N

⊕ 4

19

11

8_2

11

9

Pta del Seijo Blanco

9

⊕ 5

182°

12

Islote Canabal

18

Pta del Canabal

1706
Front Oc.WR.4s54m8/3M
Racon Mo(M)
1708
Rear LFl.8s79m8M

47

108.5°

31

18

La Galera

Pta Herminio

35

35

Pta Pragueira

31

⊕ 1

24

29

4_6

☼ Torre de Hércules (49)
1704
Fl(4)20s104m23M
AIS

Fl(3)G.9s2M

Pta Mera

② ⚓

Ensenada
de Mera

23′

21

Moreira
3_6

Ría de la
Coruña

25

22

15 Islote
de Portelo

Ensenada
del Orzan

5

See
plan
p.33

Pta de la
Estrada

5 Pedrido Gde

Morro de Canido

Marina
Nautico

Marina
Coruña

White Tr

1714
Fl.G.3s
16m6M

18

18

22′

1716
Fl(2)G.7s

Castillo de
San Anton

Bajo Guisanda

10

5

1716·4
Fl(2)R.9s.3M
1716·6
Oc(2)G.9s.4M

18

18

9

5_1

Fl.R.5s4M

A CORUÑA

1723
Fl(2+1)R.
21s3M

⊕ 8

13

11

3_2

7

Pta Boy de Canto

⊕7 43°23′·2N 08°22′·1W
Ría de A Coruña
⊕8 43°21′·9N 08°22′·2W
Off breakwater A Coruña

Oil Tanks

10

8

0_8

2

21′

Dársena
de Oza

0_4

6

5

Marina
Seca

2_7

See plan 35

①

RÍA DE LA CORUÑA

Isla Sta
Cristina

Pta Fiateira
1710
Front Iso.WRG.2s27m10/7M
Racon Mo(X)
1710·1
☼ *Rear* Oc.R.4s52m3M

Playa del Burgo

2_3

24′

23′

22′

21′

8°20′W

Lights
Pta Mera Ldg Lts 108°30′
1706 *Front* Oc.WR.4s54m8/3M White 8-sided tower
1708 *Rear* LFl.8s79m8M White 8-sided tower
Pta Fiateira LdgLts 182°
1710 *Front* Iso.WRG.2s27m10/7M Red and white
   chequered square tower
1710.1 *Rear* Oc.R.4s52m3M Red and white chequered
   square tower
1714 **Breakwater head** 43°21′·9N 08°22′·47W
   Fl.G.5s16m6M Truncated conical tower

Torre de Hércules

Coruña breakwater tower

A Coruña (La Coruña)

43°21'·9N 08°22'·47W
(Outer breakwater light)

Warning
Banco Yacentes must be avoided and the leading lines followed in heavy weather or swell

Tides
Standard Port A Coruña
Heights in metres

MHWS	MHWN	MLWN	MLWS
3·8	2·8	1·5	0·5

Charts

	Approach	Harbour
Admiralty	1111, 1094	1110
Spanish	928, 412A	4126
Imray	C18, C48	C18, C48

Radio
Port Control Ch 12
Marinas Ch 09

Navtex
518kHz (D) at 0030, 0430, 0830*, 1230, 1630, 2030*
(*weather only)
490kHz (W) (Spanish) at 0340, 0740, 1140, 1540, 1940, 2340

Weather bulletins
MF 1698kHz at 0703, 1303, 1903
VHF Ch 26 at 0840, 1240, 2010
MRSC Ch 10 at 0005, 0405, 0805, 1205, 1605, 2005

Navigational warnings
MF 1698kHz at 0703, 1903
VHF Ch 26 at 0840, 2010
MRSC Ch 10 at 0205, 0605, 1005, 1405, 1805, 2205

Primary working freqs
c/s Coruña Radio
Manual Ch 26 Tx 1698 Rx 2123
Autolink Ch 28 Tx 2806 Rx 3283
DSC Ch 70 2187·5kHz

A major city port with modern marina facilities

A Coruña is the major city of northern Galicia, offering good communications by road and air. It has a busy commercial port with welcoming marinas. The old city is picturesque with narrow paved streets, houses with characteristic glassed-in balconies, and numerous small restaurants and cafés. North of the town is the Torre de Hércules, begun by the Romans, and the oldest functioning lighthouse in the world.

The people of A Coruña erected a monument to their hero Lieutenant-General Sir John Moore who was killed leading the defence of A Coruña in the Peninsular War. The monument can be found in the beautiful memorial garden of St. Carlos (Jardin de San Carlos) that was built in 1843 and overlooks the bay and Castillo de San Anton. This balance of history is reassuring. The city's more prominent hero is Maria Pita whose statue gazes over the main square, Plaza Maria Pita, and the Town Hall. Maria Pita is honoured for her heroic part in the defense of A Coruña against the English 'pirate' Francis Drake in 1589.

Santiago de Compostela is an easy day trip away by train.

Approach

Caution

The only safe approach in heavy swell or storm conditions is on the Punta Mera leading line south of Banco Yacentes. The latter should be avoided in any seaway. Note also that the lit yellow buoy to the north of this bank is reported as small and difficult to identify.

For the outer approach refer to page 22.

From the north: This is potentially dangerous in strong southwest or northwest winds. Pick up the Punta Fiateira leading line on the track of 182° and follow it through ⊕5, ⊕7 and ⊕8. The white tower on the mole will be conspicuous on this approach. After passing the outer mole turn onto 280° for Marina Coruña and Marina Nautico.

From the west: This is the big ship route and the safest in bad weather. Pick up the Pta Mera leading line on the track of 108°and follow it through ⊕4 to ⊕7. Conspicuous to starboard will be the Torre de Hércules followed by the white tower on the mole. Once clear of the green channel mark Fl(3)G.9s the course may be altered towards the mole end or the Pta Fiateira leading line.

Berthing and anchorage

A Coruña offers visitors two main marinas:

Marina Coruña, close south of the prominent tower on the breakwater, has a secondary marina for engineering services and lay-up facilities at Marina Seca. The latter has a waiting/service pontoon only.

Marina Nautico (RCN de A Coruña Marina) which lies tucked in further west beyond Castillo de San Anton.

There is now less space to anchor behind the breakwater and the authorities may restrict or forbid this. The bottom is mud with patchy holding and foul in places so it is advisable to use a tripping line.

In gales from southwest through to northwest, swell is likely to be reflected around the Ría de la Coruña making Anchorages 1 and 2 (Plan page 30) untenable and affecting visitor pontoons in the marinas. The resulting surge and snatch on mooring lines can be quite violent. Take precautions if leaving a boat unattended for some time. The locals use substantial steel springs as mooring points.

Maria Pita, heroine of the defense of A Coruña against Francis Drake *Jane Russell*

A Coruña from the northwest

Marina Coruña   Marina Nautico (RCN)   Marina Seca

A Coruña marinas from the northwest

Marina Nautico

43°22'N 8°23'·7W

☎ + 34 981 226 880

Email marina@rcncoruna.com www.rcncoruna.com

VHF Ch 09

There is a video introduction to A Coruña and Marina
Nautico at www.youtube.com/v/gcWpQuXFfts

The Marina Nautico is conveniently placed for the
city facilities; it is owned by the Real Club Náutico
(which is very formal) and includes 44 reserved
visitors' berths, including four for vessels up to 30m.
Call ahead on VHF Ch 09.

After rounding the breakwater, head towards
Castillo de St Anton (on approximately 280°) and
continue to the dock entrance about 300m beyond
the Castillo. The three pontoons for visitors are
immediately ahead on entering, and can be affected
by swell entering the harbour. Forty-four berths are
reserved for visitors including four for vessels to 30m.

Marina Nautico

Facilities

There is water and electricity on the pontoons; major
repairs to hull, engine, electrics and electronics are
possible; a 32 tonne travel-lift and craneage is
available.

A modern wooden building houses the marina
office at its east end and a bright taverna restaurant
at the other while domestic facilities lie in between.

The tourist office is at the northwest corner of the
marina, and there is an internet café off Plaza de
Maria Pita just west of the Plaza.

Entrance to the marina seen from the office *Martin Walker*

RCN building from the north *Martin Walker*

GALICIA

A CORUÑA MARINAS

Marina Coruña

43°22'N 8°23'W
☎ +34 881 92 04 82
Email marinacoruna@marinacoruna.es
www.northwestmarinas.com
www.marinasdegalicia.com
VHF Ch 09

This large marina has been built beneath the prominent tower on the harbour breakwater and is protected by two yellow striped wave breakers. Enter through the central gap marked by red and green lit posts. Substantial pontoons with finger berths run off a massive central pontoon. Call VHF Ch 09 on the approach.

Swell can make any of the berths here liable to quite severe snatching on the mooring lines. Use metal spring attachments to absorb the snatching if leaving the boat unattended for any length of time.

Facilities

There is water and electricity on the pontoons; Fuel and pump out are available close to the office building; laundry; fuel; small grocery shop and chandlery; cash machine and WiFi; restaurant on site.

Electric buggies are available to those berthed a long way from the shore and facilities. The nearest supermarket is some 10 minutes' walk away.

The associate marina at Marina Seca, in the south of the Ría de la Coruna, provides engineering services and lay-up facilities. It has a waiting/service pontoon only.

After passing through the wave-breakers turn to starboard for fuel *Martin Walker*

Marina Coruña

The port authority may order boats to leave the anchorage *Martin Walker*

Office, shop, restaurant, domestic facilities.
Fuel and pump out *Martin Walker*

Marina Seca
43° 20'·87 N 8° 22'·59 W
Darsena Deportiva Faro de Oza s/n, 15006 A Coruña.
① +34 881 913 651
Email marinaseca@marinaseca.com
www.northwestmarinas.com VHF 09

Marina Seca from the southeast *Northwest Marinas*

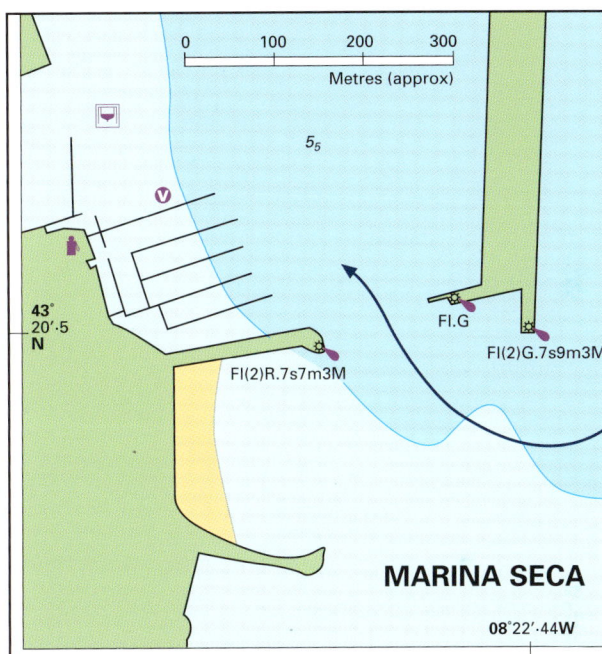

It should be noted that Marina Seca is a service marina only, with just one long pontoon at the northern side of the other four pontoons in the photograph. The latter are the property of a private fishing and ship repair enterprise that does not take visitors. The Marina Seca pontoon is a waiting/service pontoon only for use while repairs are being undertaken or a lift out arranged.

It is part of Marina Coruña in the Northwest Marinas group and is the main site for yacht work in A Coruña. There is a dry storage facility for small boats and most technical work can be undertaken. There is a small chandlery on site but domestic facilities are very limited and there are no shops nearby.

Arrivals berth, looking towards entrance from fuel dock
Martin Walker

MARINA SECA

Alternative anchorages *(see plan p.30)*

1. **Playa del Burgo** 43°20'·7N 08°22'·6W
   Off the east end of the Playa del Burgo, partly sheltered by the Isla de Santa Cristina, in 2–3m with good holding over sand and weed. Dinghies can be left on the sandy beach. There is a small restaurant ashore and a supermarket one road further back. The ferry to A Coruña departs from the tiny pier every hour, and must not be impeded.

2. **Ensenada de Mera** 43°22'·8N 08°20'·4W
   In the Ensenada de Mera, protected from northwest clockwise to south. Beware the unmarked rock some distance from the mole, which only shows near low water. Anchor as moorings and depth permit in 3–4m over sand and weed, surrounded by a crescent of sandy beach (a line of closely spaced yellow buoys may define the swimming area). The village is very much a holiday resort, with restaurants and limited shopping plus a ferry to/from A Coruña.

Early morning in Playa del Burgo anchorage looking NNW
Lilian Duckworth

A misty Ensenada de Mera at Low Water Springs.
The unmarked rock is just visible *Jane Russell*

I.1.2 A Coruña to Laxe (Lage)

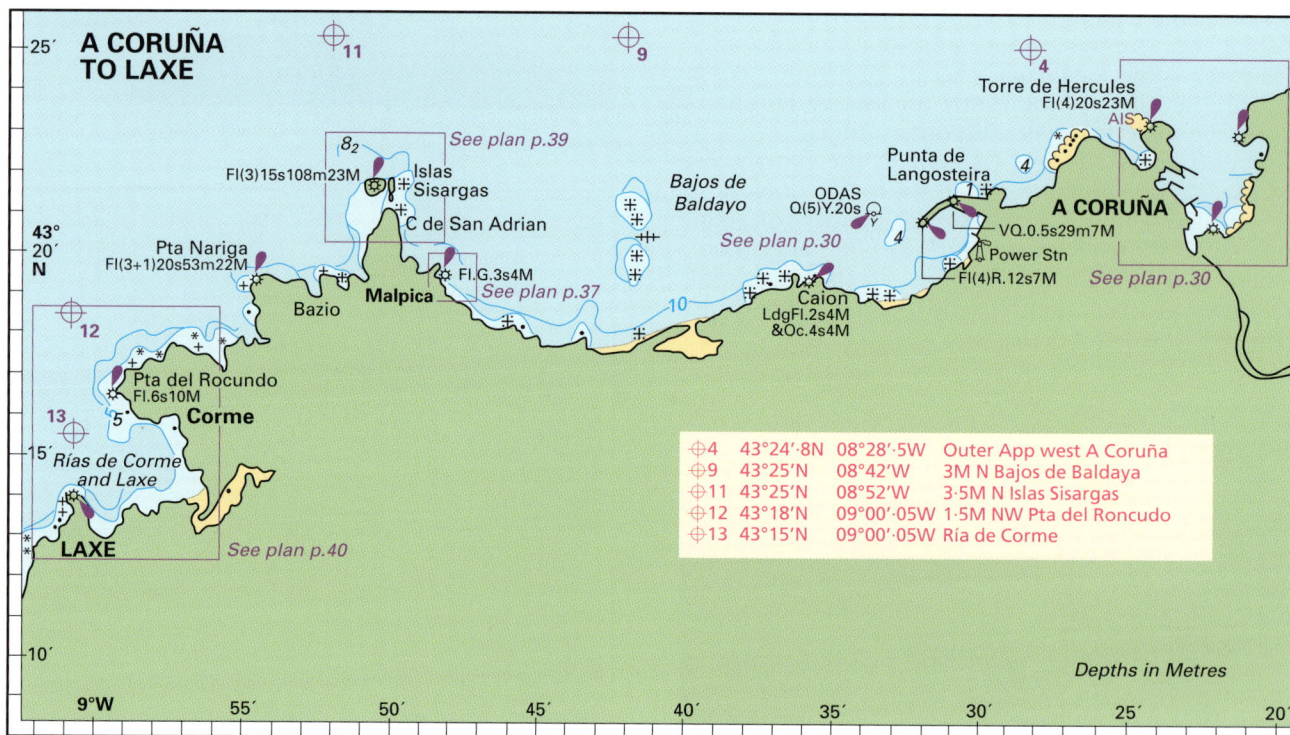

A CORUÑA TO LAXE

Torre de Hercules
Fl(4)20s23M
AIS

Fl(3)15s108m23M

8₂ See plan p.39

Islas Sisargas

C de San Adrian

Bajos de Baldayo

See plan p.30

Punta de Langosteira

A CORUÑA

ODAS Q(5)Y.20s

VQ.0.5s29m7M
Power Stn
Fl(4)R.12s7M

See plan p.30

Pta Nariga
Fl(3+1)20s53m22M

Bazio

Malpica

See plan p.37

Caion
LdgFl.2s4M
&Oc.4s4M

12

Pta del Rocundo
Fl.6s10M

13 5 Corme

Rías de Corme and Laxe

LAXE See plan p.40

⊕			
⊕4	43°24'·8N	08°28'·5W	Outer App west A Coruña
⊕9	43°25'N	08°42'W	3M N Bajos de Baldaya
⊕11	43°25'N	08°52'W	3·5M N Islas Sisargas
⊕12	43°18'N	09°00'·05W	1·5M NW Pta del Roncudo
⊕13	43°15'N	09°00'·05W	Ría de Corme

Depths in Metres

Industrial developments

A very large commercial harbour/gas terminal has been constructed approximately four miles west of A Coruña extending southwest from the coast at Punta Langosteira. This complex has at its northern extremity a quay 1·8M long with its end at approximately 43°20'·74N 08° 32'·00W. This point is also about 4M northeast of Caion. This area should be avoided by mariners.

Passage overview

This rugged coast continues to justify its name as Costa del Morte. Only in the most settled weather will yachtsmen wish to close the coast between A Coruña and Laxe. Most will choose to keep offshore. It would be unwise to go rock hopping without a large-scale chart. Heavy swell builds rapidly in a northerly wind. Malpica offers some protection but has extensive unmarked dangerous shallows to the east. There are shallows off Isla Sisargas with its massive lighthouse. Beyond that the wind farms start high above Pta Nariga and continue southwards. Malpica is a typical fishing

harbour: shallow at the head and subject to swell around the breakwater; a launching ramp, crane and inner harbour with travel lift, high walls, full of fishing boats and fuel not available to yachts. Such harbours cater for the fishing industry but are generally of only limited use to the leisure sailor who may have difficulty finding a place to secure.

Lights

1704 **Torre de Hércules** Fl(4)20s104m23M Square stone tower, 8-sided top
1728 **Sisargas** Fl(3)15s108m23M 8-sided tower with white house
1729 **Pta Nariga** Fl(3+1)20s53m22M Round tower on grey building
1730 **Pta del Roncondo** Fl.6s36m10M White round tower

Tides

See A Coruña standard port page 31

Charts

Admiralty 1111, 3633, 1094, 1113, 3764
Spanish   412, 928
Imray   C18, C48

Malpica

43°19'·31N 08°48'·12W

Charts
   Admiralty 3633
   Spanish   412
   Imray   C48

Light
   Breakwater Fl.G.3s18m4M. Green column

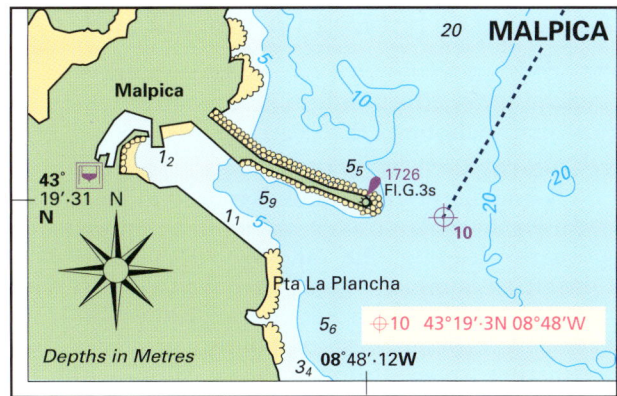

A harbour devoted to fishing

Malpica is a fishing port on a rugged coastline, and a minor tourist outlet for A Coruña. The harbour is colourful and there are good beaches nearby. The 420m mole is backed by a high wall over which heavy spray breaks in gales. There is good protection from south through west and north and northeast but a swell builds rapidly in a northerly wind and a northeasterly swell may come some way round the corner of the mole. The main harbour is full of fishing boat moorings. A small, shallow inner harbour (which now includes a 100-tonne travel lift and hardstanding) is not normally open to yachts, neither is the fuel station.

The town has everyday provisions and restaurants.

Approach

From the east The unmarked Bajos de Baldayo must be avoided. There is a fair-weather inside route about 0·7M offshore. Normally keep at least 5M off shore ($\oplus$9) before turning southwest (towards $\oplus$10) for the harbour.

Round the mole head well clear of the shore as there are reported to be unmarked rocks near the entrance.

From the west Other than Isla Sisargas there are no offshore hazards.

Anchorage

Anchor in the entrance clear of the fishing boats or negotiate the temporary use of a buoy or space against the very high harbour wall.

Facilities

Expect none, except in an emergency.

Malpica harbour looking southwest

Anchorages between A Coruña and Corme

Depending on the conditions there are five other potential anchorages in this area:

1. **Caion** 43°19'·2N 08°36'·1W

   The tiny harbour of Caion is tucked to the east of Punta Insua de Caion and should be approached on the leading line on 147°. Something of a Malpica in miniature, the harbour faces east with a high stone breakwater offering protection from north through west to south. Strictly a fair weather spot; although lit, it should not be approached in darkness. It may be possible to lie alongside for a short period if the fishing boats are out and there is no swell.

2. Off the beach immediately west of Malpica sheltered from the south.

3. **Playa de Seaya SE of Cabo de San Adrián**

   43°19'·8N 08°49'·6W

   Sheltered from the south and west.

4. **Islas Sisargas**

5. **Ensenada de Barizo**

   (entrance 43°19'·2N 08°52'·85W)

   The bay is 3M southwest of Isla Sisargas and is overlooked by cliffs and the Punta Nariga wind farm. A ledge runs out from the eastern headland leaving a usable width of about 250m in the entrance. The bay, which is open to the northwest and subject to swell from that quarter, opens out inside and provides shelter for small fishing

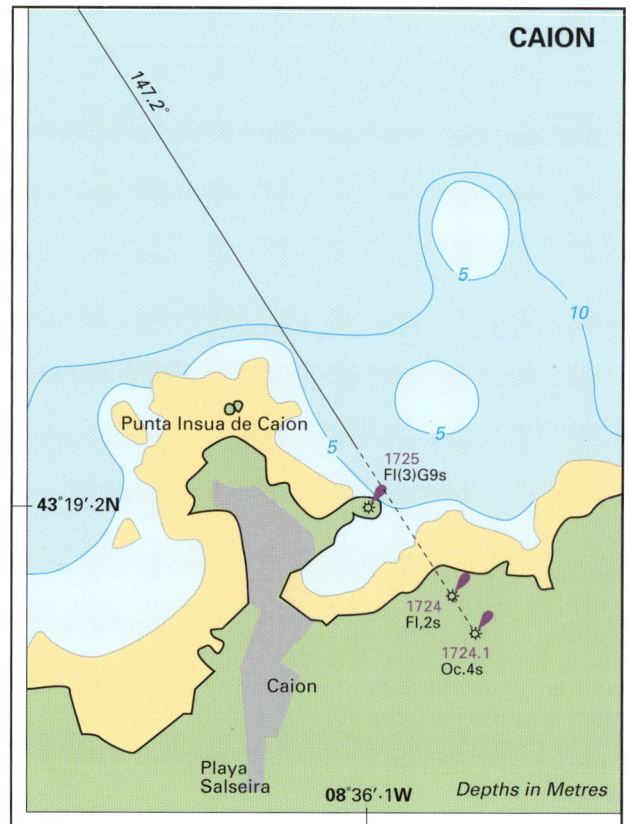

vessels to lie to summer moorings, with more craned ashore. A concrete mole, slipway and green light structure lie in the southwest corner.

There is a fine sandy beach at the head of the bay, but otherwise the bottom is rock and sand.

Over the leading line for Caion - two white marks just visible on hillside

Islas Sisargas

(landing 43°21'·47N 08°50'·30W)

The Islas Sisargas landing, in the cone between Sisarga Grande and Sisarga Chica (sometimes referred to as Sisarga Pequeña) is sheltered from the north. The gap between the two islands is very narrow, and virtually non-existent at low water. Anchor southeast of the stone quay in 3–4m: holding is variable over sand and rock. There are steps at the quay, and a track leading up to the lighthouse on the island's summit. The islands are a seabird reserve, and audible from a considerable distance. If walking ashore in June wear headgear as the herring gulls protect their young aggressively.

The Sisargas channel is hazardous. Both east and west winds can produce breakers and there are strong tidal streams. The approaches, which should not be attempted without large-scale charts (e.g. inset to Spanish 928), are as follows:

a. From the northwest, keep the left-hand edge of the Cabo de San Adrian in line with the left-hand edge of the prominent headland of Atalaya de Malpica on 133°.

b. From the southwest, keep to the south of La Carreira and Laxe de Barizo.

c. From the east, by following a leading bearing of 265° towards the rock Pedra do Lobo and changing towards Punta del Rostro when this

bears 314°. The channel is about 400m wide; keep closer to Punta Pedro d'Areas than Isla Sisarga Chica (which has a rock, La Chan, awash some 250m to the south).

GALICIA

Islas Sisargas - two yachts at anchor off the landing quay

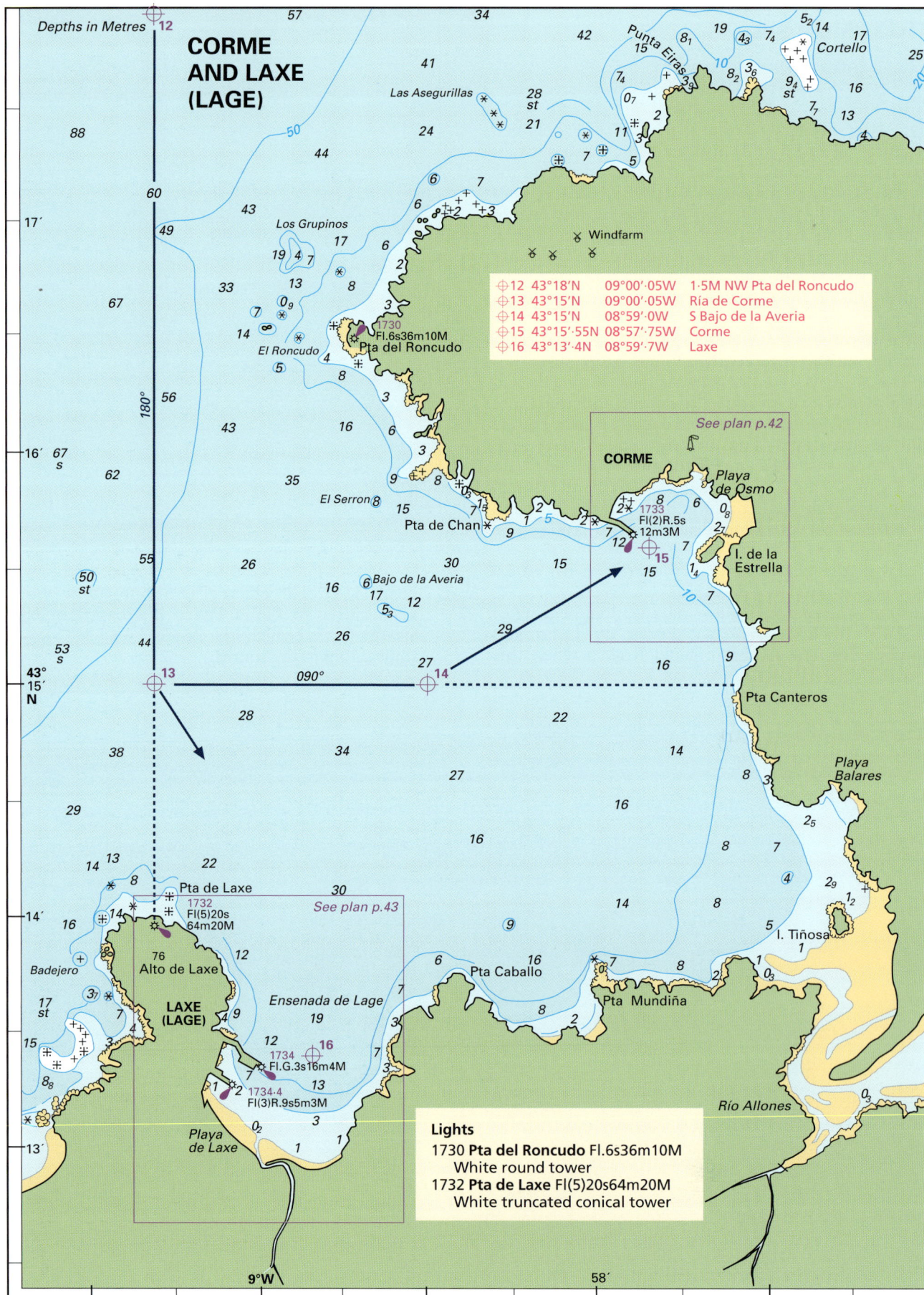

Depths in Metres

**CORME
AND LAXE
(LAGE)**

57 34 42 52 14 17
Punta Eiras 19 43 74 Cortello 25
41 81 74
Las Asegurillas 28 st 74 36 st 94 16
24 21 07 82 st
11 13
Los Grupinos 6 7 5 4
Windfarm

⊕12	43°18'N	09°00'·05W	1·5M NW Pta del Roncudo
⊕13	43°15'N	09°00'·05W	Ría de Corme
⊕14	43°15'N	08°59'·0W	S Bajo de la Averia
⊕15	43°15'·55N	08°57'·75W	Corme
⊕16	43°13'·4N	08°59'·7W	Laxe

El Roncudo
1730
Fl.6s36m10M
Pta del Roncudo

See plan p.42

CORME
Playa
de Osmo
1733
Fl(2)R.5s
12m3M
I. de la
Estrella

Pta de Chan
El Serron
15
Bajo de la Averia

Pta Canteros

Playa
Balares

090°
⊕13 ⊕14

I. Tiñosa

Pta de Laxe
1732
Fl(5)20s
64m20M
See plan p.43

Alto de Laxe
76
**LAXE
(LAGE)**
Badejero
Ensenada de Lage
Pta Caballo
Pta Mundiña

1734
Fl.G.3s16m4M ⊕16
1734·4
Fl(3)R.9s5m3M

Río Allones

Playa
de Laxe

Lights
1730 **Pta del Roncudo** Fl.6s36m10M
White round tower
1732 **Pta de Laxe** Fl(5)20s64m20M
White truncated conical tower

9°W 58'

Ría de Corme y Laxe

Entrance
22°43′·15N 09°00′·63W

Tides
Standard port A Coruña
Mean time differences
HW +0045; LW +0045
Heights in metres

MHWS	MHWN	MLWN	MLWS
3·7	2·8	1·5	0·5

Charts
Admiralty 3633, 1113
Spanish 928
Imray C48

Warning
Note offlyers off Pta del Roncudo and Pta de Laxe; also note Bajo de la Avería to the southwest of Pta de Chan

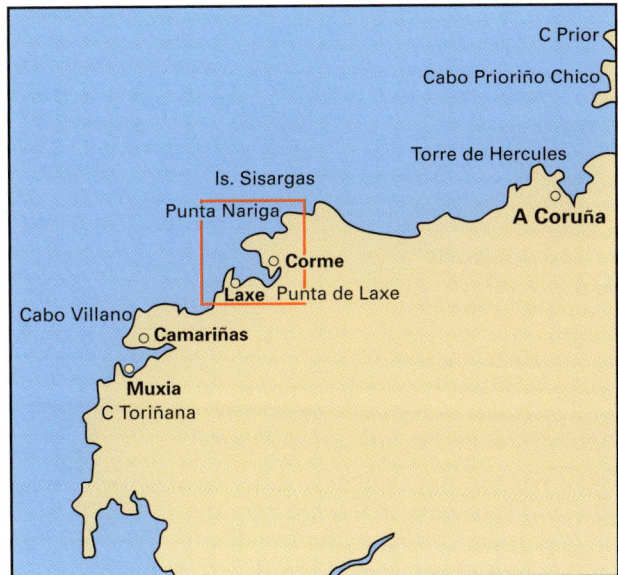

A pleasant ría

For many, the Ría de Corme y Laxe offers welcome anchorage following the 35M coastal passage from A Coruña. The two could hardly be more different with the busy city being exchanged for dramatic scenery, quiet beaches and the chance to explore, by dinghy, the beautiful Río Allones as it winds its way 5M up to the picturesque old bridge at Pontecesco.

If heading north, into prevailing north or northwest winds, then departure from here, rather than A Coruña, avoids giving away considerable ground to windward.

Approach

From the north Islas Sisargas, Pta Nariga and Pta del Roncudo are well marked (see plan on page 36). Round Pta del Roncudo with an offing of at least 1M and make track of 180° towards Pta de Laxe (⊕12 to ⊕13). In heavy weather the seas break on all the banks in the area and it is advisable to pass west and south of Bajo de la Averia (5m).

For Corme, head initially for Pta Canteros (and ⊕14) to clear the bank and then for ⊕15 or the outer mole.

For Laxe (Lage), head for ⊕16 or the outer mole, keeping 500m offshore to clear the outlying rocks of Pta de Laxe.

Corme. Anchorage between *viveros* and the harbour
Martin Walker

From the south Keep 1M off the coast northeast of Cabo Villano, with its attendant windfarm (plan page 46). Keep out 500m or more rounding Pta de Laxe, and follow the coast around at that distance to pick up Laxe breakwater, or head east until Corme breakwater bears 050°.

Laxe. Anchorage off the small boat pontoon   *Roddy Innes*

GALICIA

Corme

43°15'·64N 08°57'·78W

Charts
Admiralty 1113
Spanish   928
Imray   C48

Tides
See ría page 40

Final approaches ⊕
⊕15 from ⊕14

Light
Breakwater beacon Fl(2)R.5s12m3M Red Column

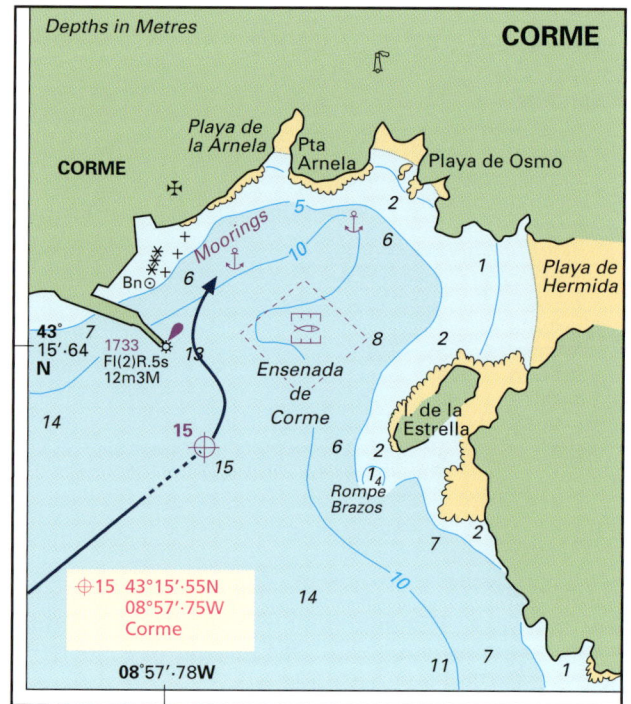

Attractive anchorage off a village

Despite the improvement in the road system, and some development, Corme remains a small and picturesque fishing village. There are limited facilities and none specifically for yachts. The anchorage is well sheltered other than from the south when Laxe (Lage) may be preferable.

Energetic crews will enjoy the walk amidst wild granite scenery out to the lighthouse on Punta del Roncudo.

Approach

See the approach to the Ría on page 40. Note the recommended route to the anchorage which passes between the breakwater and two small green buoys 'guarding' the *viveros*.

Anchorage

Fishing boats use the inside of the breakwater, while the small area to the northeast is filled with moorings. There are rocks inshore of the moorings, marked by an unlit green beacon.

Anchor to the west of the *viveros* in 10m or less, or further round the bay towards the beaches.

Facilities

Adequate shopping, restaurants, hotels and a bank.

Corme from the south – anchor west or north of viveros

Laxe (Lage)

43°13'·37N 08°59'·97W

Charts
Admiralty 1113
Spanish 928
Imray C48

Tides
See ría page 40

Final approaches ⊕
⊕16 from ⊕13

Light
Breakwater beacon Fl.G.3s15m4M Green column

Communications
Club Náutico de Laxe
Fax +34 981 728 255
Email náuticolaxe@hotmail.com
VHF Ch 09

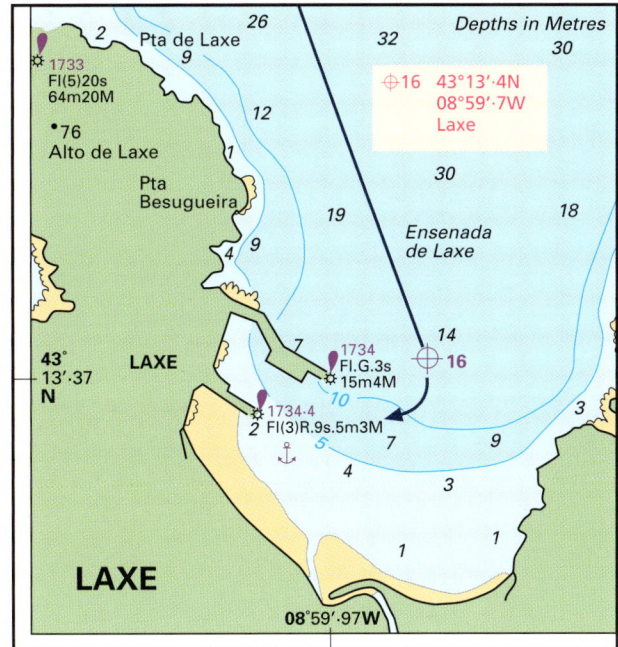

Limited facilities for yachts

Laxe (the common name) is a holiday resort around a fishing village with a small port. There is a long sandy beach to the south and the 14th-century church of Santiago de Lage overlooks the harbour. This is a popular area for sailing dinghies. There is a street market on Fridays. Good walks, impressive scenery.

Approach

See under Ría de Corme y Laxe approaches on page 40.

Anchorage

The 300m breakwater offers good shelter in most conditions, though swell may work in. In fair weather, and south or west winds, anchor off the beach near the south mole but clear of the harbour approach in 5m or less over sand. Small buoys may impede swinging room. This would become untenable in a north wind when Corme will provide better shelter. Fishing boats enter day and night, timber-loading ships berth along the north mole.

There are many small-craft moorings within the harbour, some trail floating lines.

Facilities

It may be possible to berth at the end of the small boat pontoon to take on water. Water on the quay, shops, hardware store, banks, restaurants and bars.

Laxe - note the anchoring options

GALICIA

I.1.3 Laxe (Lage) to Cabo Finisterre

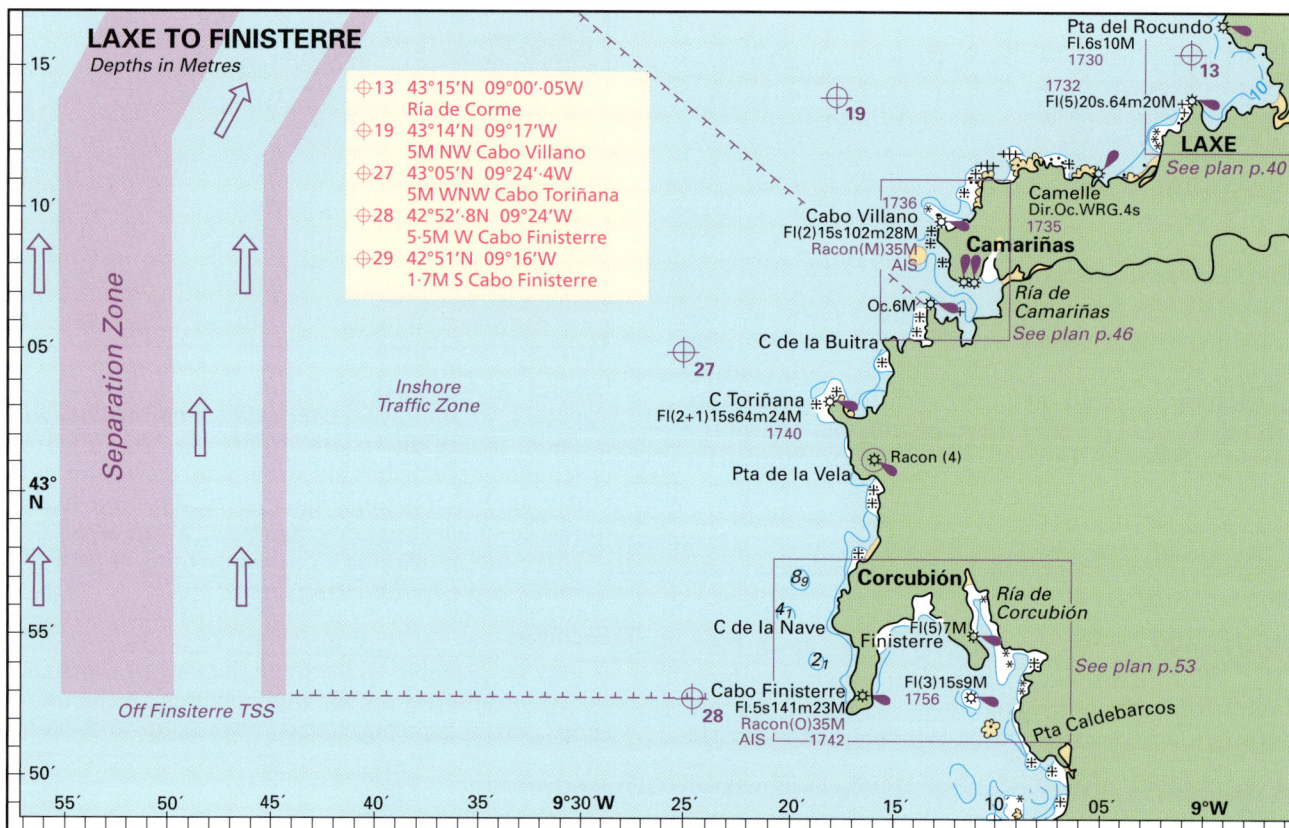

LAXE TO FINISTERRE
Depths in Metres

⊕13	43°15'N 09°00'·05W
	Ría de Corme
⊕19	43°14'N 09°17'W
	5M NW Cabo Villano
⊕27	43°05'N 09°24'·4W
	5M WNW Cabo Toriñana
⊕28	42°52'·8N 09°24'W
	5·5M W Cabo Finisterre
⊕29	42°51'N 09°16'W
	1·7M S Cabo Finisterre

Pta del Rocundo
Fl.6s10M
1730
1732
Fl(5)20s.64m20M
LAXE
See plan p.40
Camelle
Dir.Oc.WRG.4s
1735
1736
Cabo Villano
Fl(2)15s102m28M
Racon(M)35M
AIS
Camariñas
Ría de Camariñas
See plan p.46
Oc.6M
C de la Buitra
C Toriñana
Fl(2+1)15s64m24M
1740
Racon (4)
Pta de la Vela
8 9
Corcubión
Ría de Corcubión
4 7
C de la Nave
Fl(5)7M
Finisterre
2 7
See plan p.53
Fl(3)15s9M
1756
Cabo Finisterre
Fl.5s141m23M
Racon(O)35M
AIS — 1742
Pta Caldebarcos

Separation Zone
Inshore Traffic Zone
43° N
Off Finisterre TSS

Lights
1730 **Pta del Rocundo** Fl.6s36m10M White round tower
1732 **Punta Laxe** Fl(5)20s64m20M
White truncated conical tower
1736 **Cabo Villano** Fl(2)15s102m28M
8-sided tower, grey cupola
1737 **Pta de la Barca** Oc.4s11m10M
Grey truncated conical tower
1740 **Cabo Toriñana** Fl(2+1)15s63m24M
White round tower
1742 **Cabo Finisterre** Fl.5s142m23M
8-sided stone tower and white dwelling

Charts
Admiralty 1111, 3633, 3764
Spanish 927
Imray C48

Warning
A local magnetic anomaly has been reported within a radius of 13M of Cabo Toriñana

Laxe from the anchorage off the south mole, looking NW   *Jane Russell*

Overview

The rugged Costa da Morte continues on to Cabo Finisterre from Laxe. Unless wishing to enter the delightful ría de Camariñas, for Camariñas and Muxia, the mariner should make passage well out to sea. If sailing between Corme/Laxe and Camariñas, do not cut the corner, avoid Camelle and stand well out towards ⊕19. Stay away from Cabo Toriñana where, even on the calmest days, the Atlantic swell crashes on the outlying rocks off the lighthouse sitting on the edge of the barren peninsula.

Traffic Separation Zone

A very busy 19M wide Traffic Separation Zone (TSZ) lies off Cabo Finisterre. Yachts should use the Inshore Traffic Zone, also 19M wide, and only cross the TSZ at right angles in accordance with regulations.

Finisterre Vessel Traffic Services (Finisterre VTS)

The VTS monitors all traffic and will give advice to particular vessels and those nearby. It provides regular navigational and weather information - see page 51.

c/s Finisterre Traffic (Finisterre Trafico)

☎ +34 981 76 73 20 & 76 77 38 VHF Ch 11, 16 (74)

Camelle

43°11'·34N 09°05'·19W
(outer breakwater green column)

Charts

Admiralty	1111, 3633
Spanish	927
Imray	C48

No place for sailing yachts

Camelle is a small harbour lying between Laxe (Lage) and Camariñas. Any rock hopping, inquisitive yachtsman considering making this a lunchtime stop is strongly advised to remain well offshore. In winds from the north to west this is a dangerous lee shore.

Swell works into the outer harbour which is narrow and with isolated rocks inside the breakwater; the inner harbour is shallow, except by the quay but that lies beyond a criss-cross of mooring lines lying on and beneath the surface. The harbour is recorded here only as a place to avoid – unless coming by land to beachcomb in which case it has a charm of its own.

GALICIA

Camelle

Ría de Camariñas

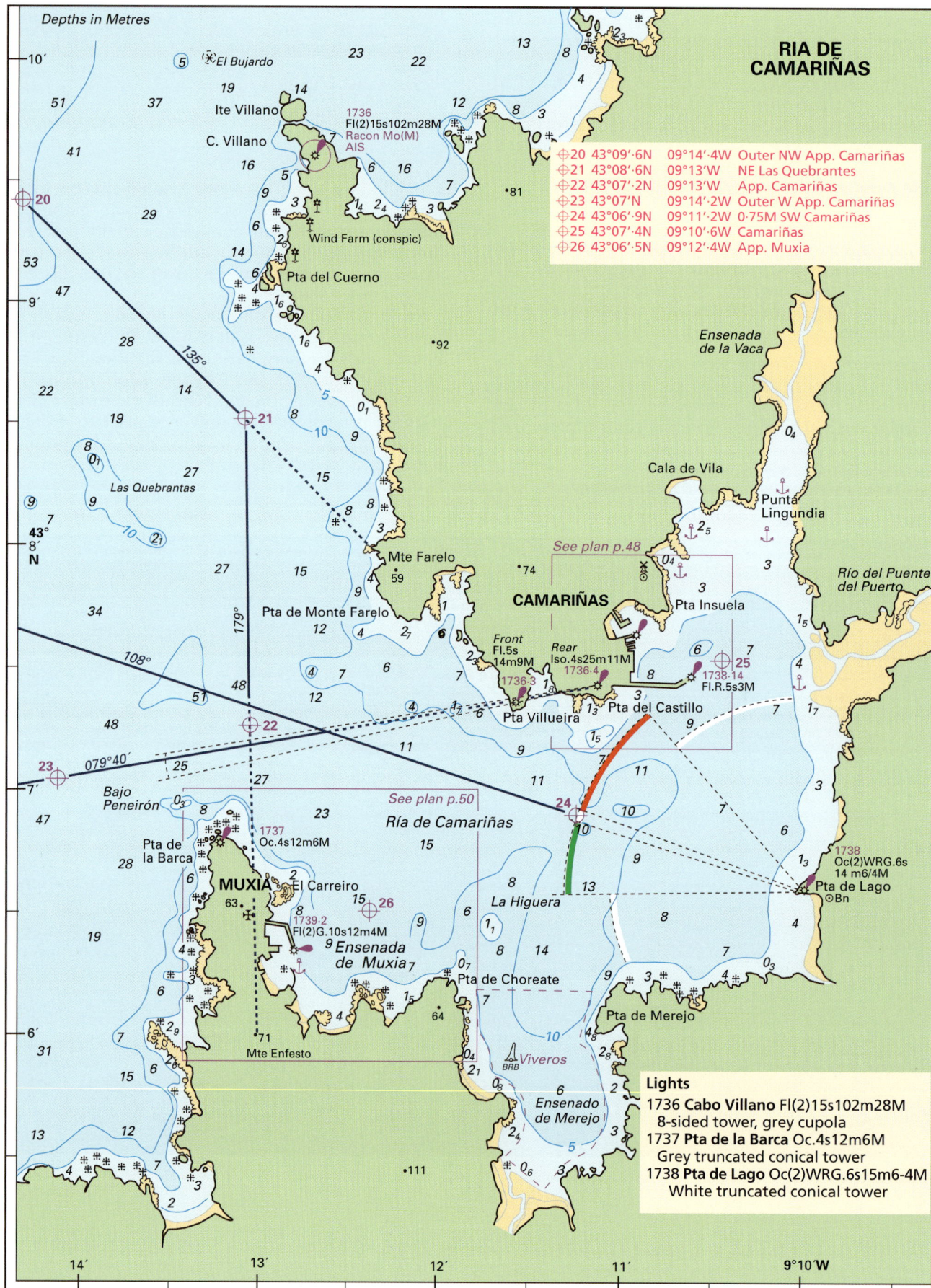

Depths in Metres

RIA DE CAMARIÑAS

⊕20 43°09'·6N 09°14'·4W Outer NW App. Camariñas
⊕21 43°08'·6N 09°13'W NE Las Quebrantes
⊕22 43°07'·2N 09°13'W App. Camariñas
⊕23 43°07'N 09°14'·2W Outer W App. Camariñas
⊕24 43°06'·9N 09°11'·2W 0·75M SW Camariñas
⊕25 43°07'·4N 09°10'·6W Camariñas
⊕26 43°06'·5N 09°12'·4W App. Muxia

El Bujardo

Ite Villano

C. Villano

1736
Fl(2)15s102m28M
Racon Mo(M)
AIS

Wind Farm (conspic)

Pta del Cuerno

Ensenada de la Vaca

Cala de Vila

Punta Lingundia

Río del Puente del Puerto

Las Quebrantas

Mte Farelo

See plan p.48

CAMARIÑAS

Pta Insuela

Pta de Monte Farelo

Front
Fl.5s
14m9M
1736·3

Rear
Iso.4s25m11M
1736·4

1738·14
Fl.R.5s3M

Pta Villueira

Pta del Castillo

Bajo Peneirón

See plan p.50

Ría de Camariñas

1737
Oc.4s12m6M

Pta de la Barca

MUXIA

El Carreiro

1739·2
Fl(2)G.10s12m4M

Ensenada de Muxia

La Higuera

1738
Oc(2)WRG.6s
14 m6/4M
Pta de Lago
Bn

Pta de Choreate

Mte Enfesto

Viveros
BRB

Pta de Merejo

Ensenado de Merejo

Lights
1736 **Cabo Villano** Fl(2)15s102m28M
8-sided tower, grey cupola
1737 **Pta de la Barca** Oc.4s12m6M
Grey truncated conical tower
1738 **Pta de Lago** Oc(2)WRG.6s15m6-4M
White truncated conical tower

Ría de Camariñas

43°07'·28N 09°13'·00W

Tides

Standard port A Coruña
Mean time differences
HW +0005; LW −0005
Heights in metres

MHWS	MHWN	MLWN	MLWS
3·8	2·8	1·5	0·5

Charts

Admiralty	1111, 3633, 1113
Spanish	927
Imray	C48

Warning

Note hazards of El Bujardo, Las Quebrantas, Bajo Peneiron and the shallows southwest of Monte Farelo, and further note the warning below regarding Leixon de Juanboy. The only sound signal in the area is on Cabo Villano.

West of the plan, and lying between the two leading lines shown, is the small but dangerous 5m shoal of Leixon de Juanboy – position 43°07'·48N 09°14'·97W.

Approach ⊕

⊕20 43°09'·6N 09°14'·4W or ⊕23 43°07'N 09°14'·2W

Entrance ⊕22 43°07'·2N 09°13'W

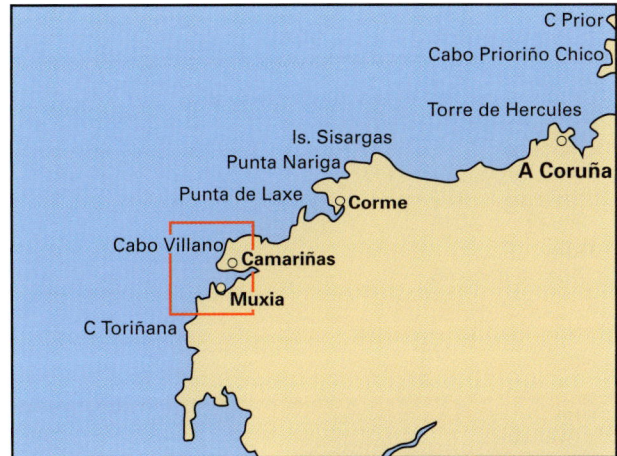

Camariñas rear leading light 1736.4 on Pta Villueira line *Martin Walker*

Well placed, scenic and useful ría

Many would consider the Ría de Camariñas amongst Galicia's loveliest, with the added advantage that it contains anchorages protected from almost every direction. However, the entrance to the Ría is fully exposed to winds and seas from the northwest and may be inaccessible in rough weather. The two towns of Camariñas and Muxia meet the daily needs of the cruising yachtsman. Camariñas is a pleasant town which thrives on tourists and a well-established welcoming marina. Muxia's new southern curving mole has improved protection within the harbour and shields a new marina. Crews can dig for their shell-fish lunch on the beaches or walk through the unspoilt countryside.

Approach

Full use should be made of the leading lines by both day and night; ⊕ are positioned to ease the recognition of the key lights and headlands, although a first entry by night is not recommended.

Camarinas looking N from anchorage off Cala de Vila *Jane Russell*

From the north Keep well off Cabo Villano, with its wind farm, to avoid El Bujardo, a pinnacle rock awash at low tide. Either stay well off shore, to avoid Las Quebrantas, until Pta de Lago bears 108° (white sector) or come inside that bank tracking via ⊕20, ⊕21, ⊕22 as indicated on the plan opposite.

From the southwest Keep well off Cape Toriñana and do not cut the corner around Pta de la Barca. ⊕23 lies on the leading line to Pta Villueira. Follow until Pta de Lago bears 108° (white sector) or route through ⊕22.

From ⊕22, or the crossing of the leading lines, maintain the line towards ⊕24 and Pta de Lago until shaping course for Camariñas or Muxia.

Anchorages

The plan shows anchorages north and east of Camariñas which may offer solitude, shelter from north or northeast winds or the chance to enjoy the fine beaches. Excellent shelter and good holding has been reported here.

A settled weather anchorage off the mouth of the Río del Puente del Puerto offers the chance to take the dinghy 2M up the river to the town (of the same name) with its shops, restaurants, banks etc.

Camariñas

On the north side of the Ría de Camariñas
43°07'·47N 09°10'·70W

Charts
 Admiralty 3633, 1113
 Spanish 927
 Imray C48

Tides
 See ría page 46

Final approaches ⊕
 ⊕25 (037°/0·7M from ⊕24)

Light
 Breakwater beacon Fl.R.5s3M Red concrete beacon

Fuel
 Available

Communications
 Club Náutico de Camariñas
 Peirao Novo s/n, 15123 – Camariñas
 ☎ +34 981 737 130
 cnc@cibergal.com www.cncamarinas.com
 VHF Ch 09

Welcoming and efficient marina

Camariñas has an attractive harbour enclosed by a long breakwater which gives excellent shelter from all directions other than east and northeast. There was talk of building a mole extending southeast from Pta Insuela to improve protection from that quarter. Shelter from these winds can be found across the ría. The Club Náutico Camariñas has an active dinghy club and a long well-deserved reputation for making visiting yachtsmen welcome.

Approach

See page 47 for Approach to the ría; make the final approach to the Camariñas breakwater from ⊕24. Note shallows extend south of the rear light on Pta del Castillo.

Berthing and anchorage

Visiting yachts are berthed on substantial finger pontoons with visitors generally towards the outer ends. Catamarans and larger yachts use the T-ends. There are 83 berths of which 60 are reserved for visitors up to 18m, in a depth of 3-5m. There is electricity and water available on the pontoons.

The berthing master's office is the small wooden hut at the top of the centre pontoon. The fuelling pontoon is immediately beneath that.

At the busiest time of the year it may be necessary to anchor off. Holding is reported to be excellent in 4–5m sand and mud though extensive weed has been reported later in a year.

Facilities

The club marina provides, or can arrange, most support facilities but it does not have a travel-lift. There are several walls in the old harbour where it might be possible to dry out. Fuel is available on site for normal top up; larger quantities will be readily arranged for delivery by tanker to the main

quay – yachts would find this position bumpy in an east wind. Otherwise the nearest alongside fuel pumps are in A Coruña or Muros.

Apart from providing showers, the club has an excellent small bar/restaurant and two computers for visiting yachtsmen and WiFi. A same-day laundry service is available close to the marina.

The town of Camariñas has a market and shops for reprovisioning. Tourism is increasing and cafés and restaurants are close to the harbour.

CAMARIÑAS chart — ⊕25 43°07'·4N 09°10'·6W

The best goose barnacles are harvested along the Costa da Morte *Martin Walker*

Camariñas

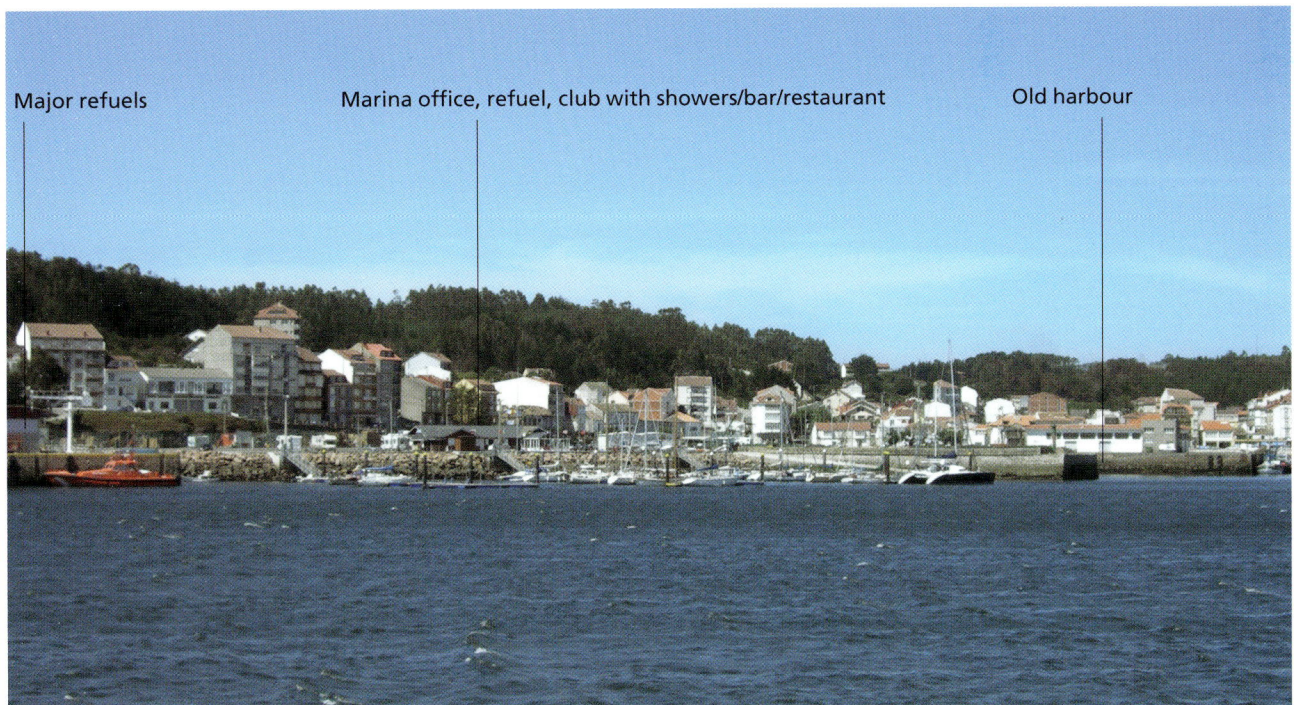

Major refuels | Marina office, refuel, club with showers/bar/restaurant | Old harbour

Camariñas. Club Náutico Camariñas from the outer mole looking northwest   *Martin Walker*

GALICIA

Muxia (Mugia)

43°06'·43N 09°12'·92W
On the south side of the Ría de Camariñas

Charts
Admiralty   3633, 1113
Spanish   927
Imray   C48

Tides
See ría page 46

Final approaches ⊕
⊕26 43°06'·5N 09°12'·4W (150°/0·9M from
⊕22 43°07'·2N 09°13'W)

Lights
Breakwater beacon Fl(4)G.11s14m5M Concrete beacon, green top

Communications
Marina Muxía Marina Cataventos
Puerto deportivo Muxia S/N, 15124 Muxia A Coruña
Marina Office: ☎ +34 673 168 199
Manager: +34 652 97 16 67
Admin: ☎ +34 666 36 93 24
Email info@cataventos.net or info@marinamuxia.com
www.cataventos.net www.marinamuxia.com
www.marinasdegalicia.com
VHF Ch 09

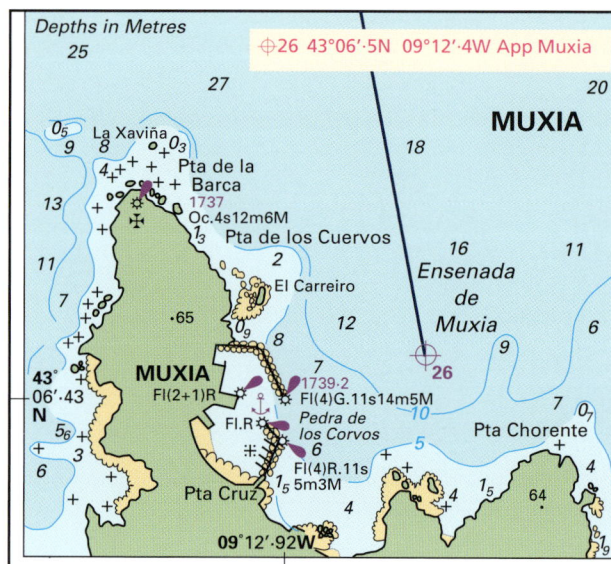

Fishing harbour with a marina in its south side

Muxía is a minor fishing harbour including a marina known as the Puerto Deportivo de Muxía. A few old buildings remain amidst the modern blocks as tourism is developed. The 17th-century church of La Virgen de la Barca on the northern point was destroyed by fire started by lightning on Christmas Day 2013. There is a clean sandy beach to the south of the harbour and fine views over the ría from Punta de la Barca.

Approach

See under Ría de Camariñas on page 47 and note warnings.

Berthing

A southern mole has been constructed and provides shelter to a marina boasting 232 berths, all on finger pontoons. There are plenty of transit berths, for yachts from 6m to 14m, in 2m to 3m of water.

Anchorage

Anchor in the harbour if space can be found or over sand southeast of the outer mole. Space outside is limited and the position likely to be untenable in northerly winds.

Facilities

Water and electricity on the pontoons; showers; laundry; fuel by tanker truck; free wi-fi; security; berthing assistance 0900-2400.
Several small supermarkets, restaurants, bars, banks, a hardware store and post office are in the town.

Muxia Marina *Muxia Marina*

Cabo Finisterre (Fisterra)

42°54'N 9°15'W

Tides
Standard port Lisbon
Mean time differences
HW +0105 ±0010; LW +0130 ±0010
(the above allows for the difference in time zones)
Heights in metres

MHWS	MHWN	MLWN	MLWS
3·3	2·6	1·2	0·5

Note
A considerable inshore set may be encountered south of Cabo Finisterre with a westerly wind and flood tide

Charts
BA   3764
Spanish   927, 9270
Imray   C48

Navtex
518kHz (D) at 0030, 0430, 0830*, 1230, 1630, 2030*
(*weather only)

Weather bulletins
MF 1764kHz at 0703, 1303, 1903
VHF Ch 22 at 0840, 1240, 2010
MRCC Ch 11 at 0233, 0633, 1033,1433, 1833, 2233

Navigational warnings
MF 1764kHz at 0703, 1903
VHF Ch 22 at 0840, 2010
MRCC Ch 11 at 0033, 0433, 0833, 1233, 1633, 2033
AIS

Primary working frequencies
Manual Ch 22 Tx 1764 Rx 2108
Autolink Ch 27 Tx 2596 Rx 3280
DSC Ch 70 2187·5kHz. MMSI 992242117

GALICIA

Cabo Toriñana, the most western point of mainland Europe, looking south towards Cabo Finisterre *Jane Russell*

Finisterre lighthouse from the south. Finisterre harbour and anchorage visible east and north

I.2.1 Cabo Finisterre to Ría de Muros

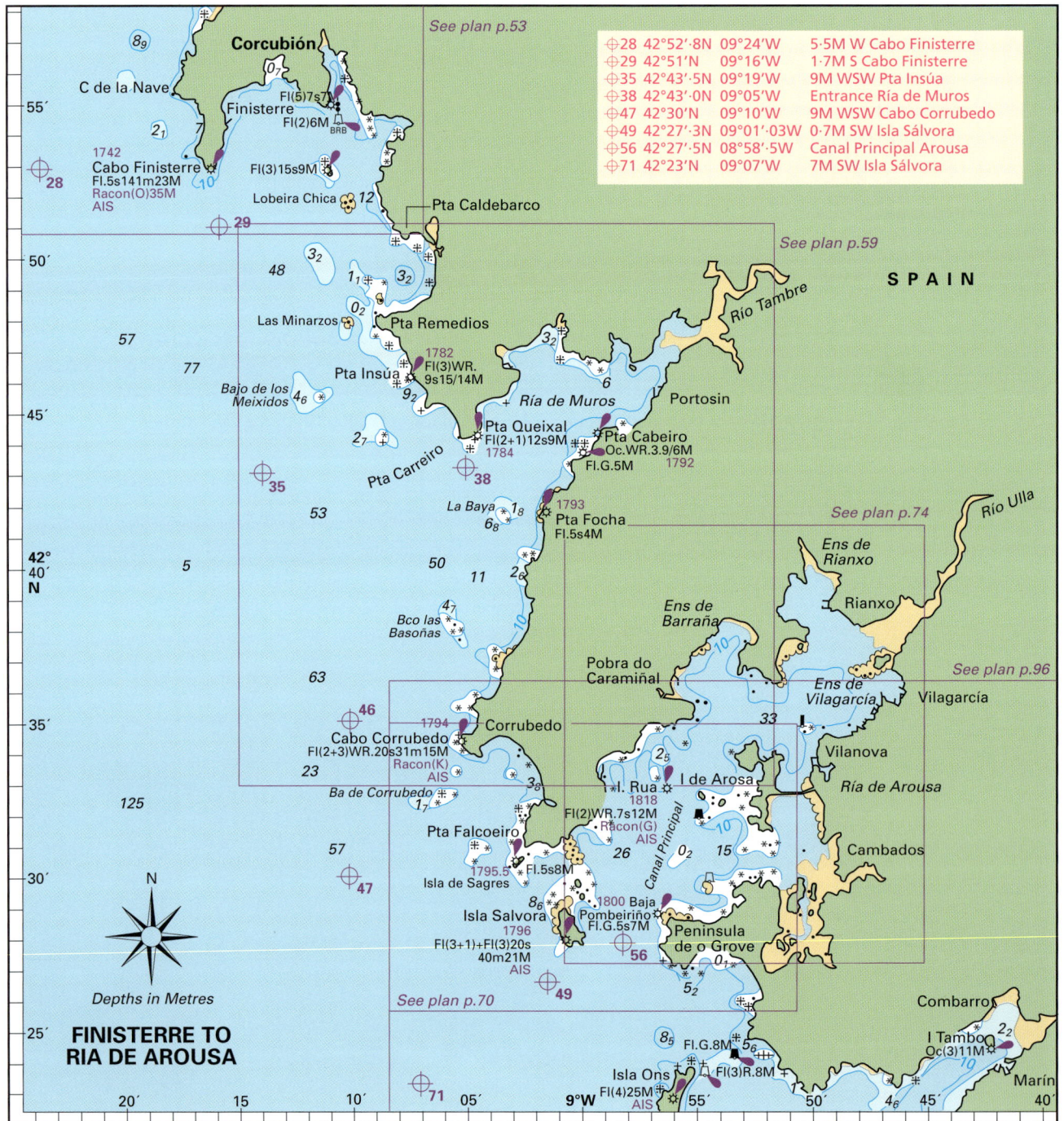

See plan p.53

⊕28 42°52'·8N 09°24'W	5·5M W Cabo Finisterre
⊕29 42°51'N 09°16'W	1·7M S Cabo Finisterre
⊕35 42°43'·5N 09°19'W	9M WSW Pta Insúa
⊕38 42°43'·0N 09°05'W	Entrance Ría de Muros
⊕47 42°30'N 09°10'W	9M WSW Cabo Corrubedo
⊕49 42°27'·3N 09°01'·03W	0·7M SW Isla Sálvora
⊕56 42°27'·5N 08°58'·5W	Canal Principal Arousa
⊕71 42°23'N 09°07'W	7M SW Isla Sálvora

Corcubión

C de la Nave

Finisterre

Fl(5)7s7M

Fl(2)6M BRB

1742
Cabo Finisterre
Fl.5s141m23M
Racon(O)35M
AIS

Fl(3)15s9M

Lobeira Chica 12

Pta Caldebarco

See plan p.59

SPAIN

Río Tambre

Las Minarzos

Pta Remedios

1782
Fl(3)WR.
9s15/14M

Pta Insúa

Bajo de los
Meixidos

Ría de Muros

Portosin

Pta Queixal
Fl(2+1)12s9M
1784

Pta Cabeiro
Oc.WR.3.9/6M
Fl.G.5M
1792

Pta Carreiro

La Baya

1793
Pta Focha
Fl.5s4M

See plan p.74

Río Ulla

Ens de
Rianxo

**42°
40'
N**

Rianxo

Ens de
Barraña

Bco las
Basoñas

Pobra do
Caramiñal

Ens de
Vilagarcía

Vilagarcía

1794

Corrubedo

46

Cabo Corrubedo
Fl(2+3)WR.20s31m15M
Racon(K)
AIS

Vilanova

33

Ba de Corrubedo

I. Rua

I de Arosa

Ría de Arousa

1818
Fl(2)WR.7s12M
Racon(G)
AIS

Pta Falcoeiro

1795.5

Fl.5s8M

Isla de Sagres

Cambados

26

Canal Principal

47

Isla Salvora

1800 Baja
Pombeiriño
Fl.G.5s7M

1796
Fl(3+1)+Fl(3)20s
40m21M
AIS

Peninsula
de o Grove

56

N

49

See plan p.70

Depths in Metres

Combarro

I Tambo
Oc(3)11M

**FINISTERRE TO
RIA DE AROUSA**

Isla Ons
Fl(4)25M
AIS

Fl.G.8M

Fl(3)R.8M

Marín

71

9°W

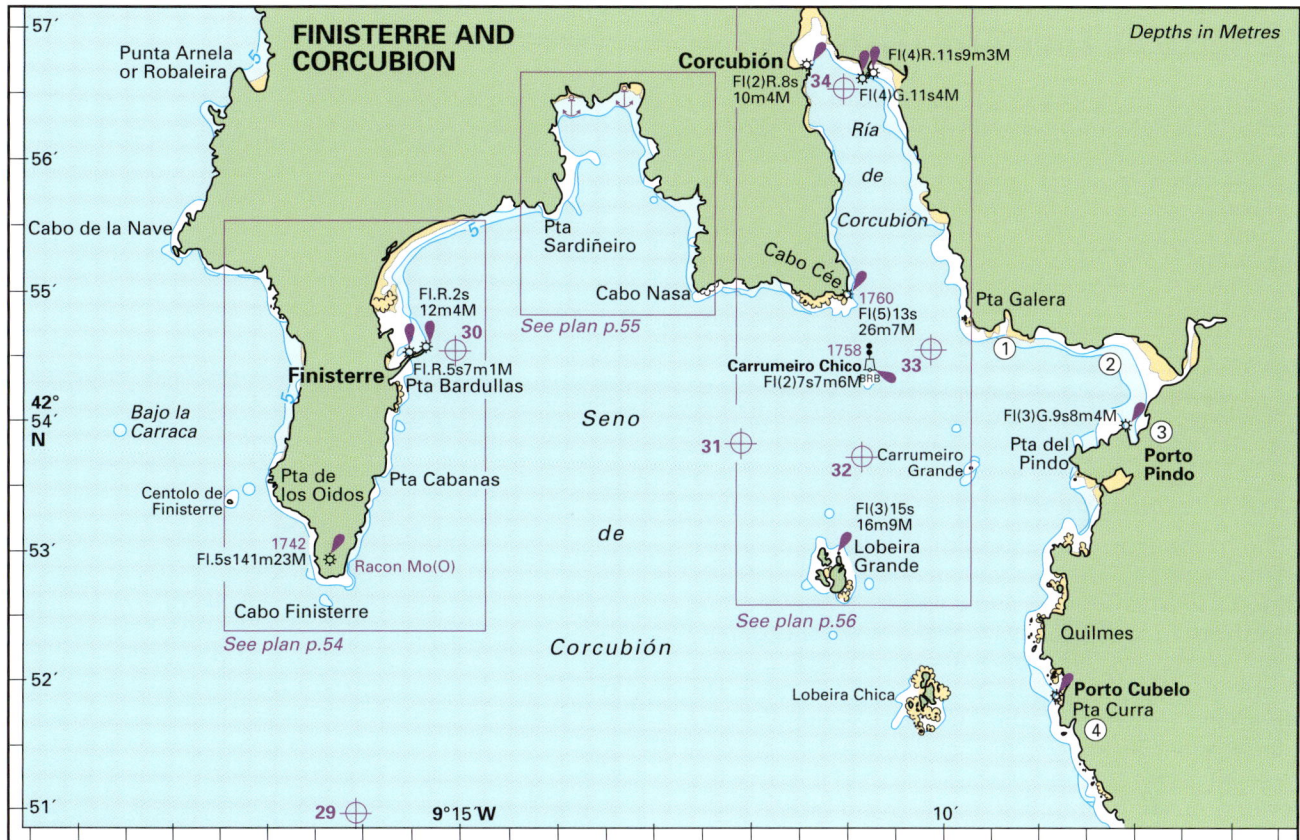

FINISTERRE AND CORCUBION

Depths in Metres

Punta Arnela or Robaleira

57′
56′
Cabo de la Nave
55′
42°
54′
N

Bajo la Carraca

Centolo de Finisterre

53′

52′

51′

29

9°15′W

Finisterre

Fl.R.2s 12m4M

30

Fl.R.5s7m1M
Pta Bardullas

Pta de los Oidos

Pta Cabanas

1742
Fl.5s141m23M   Racon Mo(O)

Cabo Finisterre

See plan p.54

Pta Sardiñeiro

Cabo Nasa

See plan p.55

Seno

de

Corcubión

Corcubión
Fl(2)R.8s
10m4M

Fl(4)R.11s9m3M

34
Fl(4)G.11s4M

Ría

de

Corcubíon

Cabo Cée

Pta Galera

1760
Fl(5)13s
26m7M

1758
Carrumeiro Chico PRB
Fl(2)7s7m6M

33

31

32

Carrumeiro Grande

Fl(3)15s
16m9M

Lobeira Grande

See plan p.56

Lobeira Chica

①

②

Fl(3)G.9s8m4M

Pta del Pindo

③

Porto Pindo

Quilmes

Porto Cubelo
Pta Curra

④

GALICIA

See plan p.54
See plan p.55
See plan p.56

⊕29	42°51′N	09°16′W	1·7M S Cabo Finisterre
⊕30	42°54′·5N	09°15′W	Finisterre
⊕31	42°53′·8N	09°12′·4W	Seno de Corcubión
⊕32	42°53′·7N	09°10′·9W	0·6M S Carrumeiro Chico
⊕33	42°54′·5N	09°10′·1W	0·5M E Carrumeiro Chico
⊕34	42°56′·5N	09°11′W	Corcubión

Coastguard
Fisterra ☎ +34 981 767 500

Sea Rescue Service
☎ +34 900 202 202 MRCC Finisterre Ch 11

Weather
Navtex (D)
Finisterre Ch 22 at 0840, 1240, 2919

Anchorage north of Puerto de Finisterre *Martin Walker*

Lights
1742 **Cabo Finisterre** Fl.5s142m23M 8-sided stone tower and white dwelling
1758 **Carrumeiro Chico** Fl(2)7s7m10M Black balls on black beacon, red bands
1760 **Cabo Cée** Fl(5)13s26m10M 8-sided tower on red roofed white dwelling
1782 **Punta Insua** Fl(3)WR.9s26m15/14M 6-sided tower, metal cupola and dwelling
1784 **Pta Queixal** Fl(2+1)12s26m10M 6-sided tower and white dwelling
1793 **Pta Focha** Fl.5s28m4M White tower and round building
1794 **Cabo Corrubedo** Fl(2+3)WR.20s31m15M Round masonry tower, white cupola
1796 **Isla Sálvora** Fl(3+1)20s39m21M White 8-sided tower, red band
1847.3 **Isla Ons** Fl(4)24s126m25M 8-sided white tower on corner of building

Finisterre lighthouse *Martin Walker*

Puerto de Finisterre (Fisterra)

Cabo Finisterre light 42°52'·94N 09°16'·32W
Puerto de Finisterre breakwater 42°54'·56N 09°15'·36W

Tides
See page 51
Charts
Admiralty 3764
Spanish 9270
Imray C48
Final approach ⊕
⊕30 42°54'·5N 09°15'W Finisterre
Light
Breakwater end beacon Fl.R.4s12m4M
Facilities
Little for yachts

A picturesque fishing harbour

The harbour is crowded with fishing boats and a densely populated small boat marina. It provides good shelter from west and south but is open to the northeast. The town has the usual small shops, bars and restaurants but it becomes crowded in summer with tourists and pilgrims on the Camino de Santiago for whom Cabo Finisterre is the ultimate destination. Most go to the lighthouse where there is a small restaurant and stunning views. Finisterre has two interesting churches, one 12th century and the other Baroque. There is a small museum within the Castello San Carlos.

Rounding Finisterre and final approach

From the north See Plans pages 52 and 53. The main options are either to keep 2M off and avoid the 2m patch Bajo La Carraca, 1M to the northwest of Centolo de Finisterre (an island some 20m high), or to come inside both – much will depend upon the weather. At the Cape there is a similar option: either pass more than 0·5M off or about 200m off in order to avoid El Turdeiro shoal – a large-scale chart is needed for the latter passage. Strong local winds are possible. Once round, keep at least 300m off until reaching Finisterre breakwater.

Puerto de Finisterre from the southeast

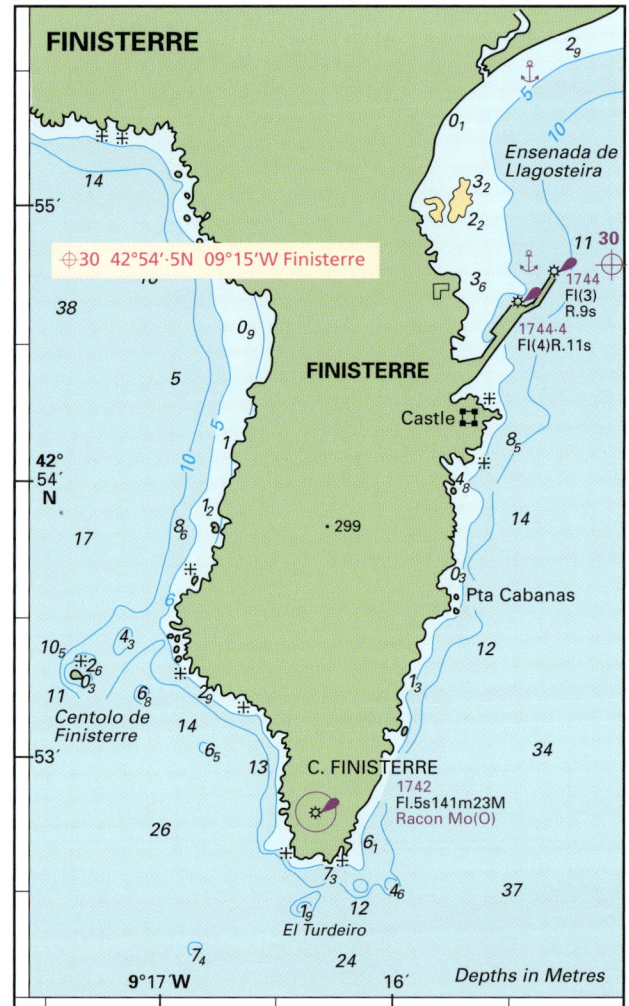

From the south Plan page 52. Give Punta Insúa a 5M offing to clear Bajo de los Meixidos and head straight for Finisterre mole. On a night approach, take the outside passages and keep at least 300m off the east coast of the Cape.

Anchorage

The harbour is full of moorings. Small yachts may find space to moor alongside the outer pontoons of the small boat marina or alongside the main breakwater. This may be uncomfortable, particularly in north or northeast winds. A popular anchorage, which provides protection from the summer northerly winds is off the sandy beach of Ensenada de Llagosteira. The southwest end is foul.

Seno de Corcubión

The area northeast and east of Cabo Finisterre offers a variety of anchorages depending on the direction of the wind and, to the east, interesting pilotage for rock-hopping sailors armed with chart BA 3764.

Passage planning

Keep well west of Cabo Finisterre through ⊕28 if making passage south to Muros or beyond. Otherwise refer to the section on Puerto de Finisterre for rounding the Cape above.

Ensenada del Sardiñeiro

Entrance
42°55·5N 09°13'·40W

Tides
See page 51

Charts
Admiralty 3764
Spanish   9270
Imray   C48

An unspoilt anchorage

Although open to the south, this unspoilt anchorage provides good protection from west through north to east. Both Playa Sardiñeiro and Playa Esordi are good bathing beaches.

Approach

Approach is straightforward but care is required to avoid the shallow patch of La Eyra.

Ensenada del Sardiñeiro anchorage *Roddy Innes*

Anchorage

Anchor in either bay to suit conditions. Both have been recommended and offer good holding in sand; Playa Sardiñeiro generally has the least swell.

Facilities

The village, with supermarkets, restaurants and camp site, straddles the road between Corcubión and Finisterre.

Pta Arnela (centre) divides the two anchorages of Ensenada del Sardiñeiro, seen from the south

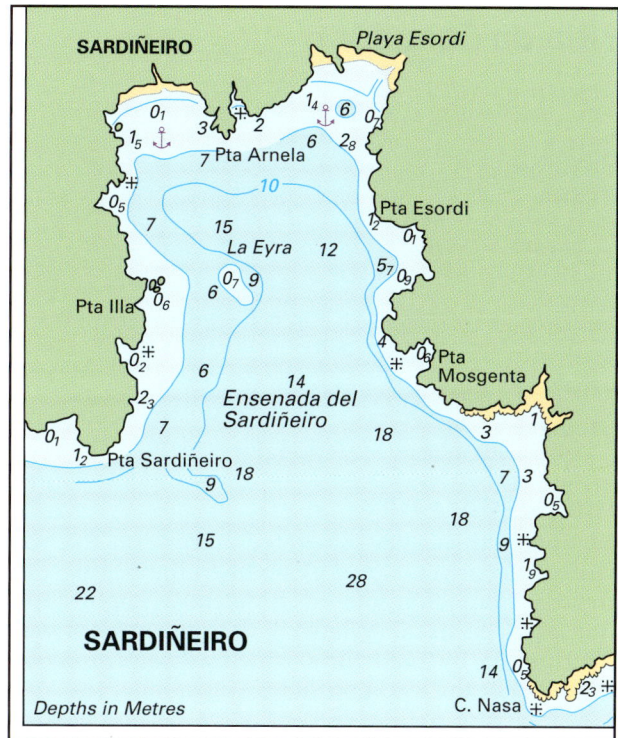

Ría de Corcubión

Mouth of ría (⊕33) 42°54'·5N 09°10'·1W
Corcubión fish quay 42°56'·6N 09°11'·35W

Tides
See page 51

Charts
Admiralty   3764
Spanish   9270
Imray   C48

Warning
There are considerable hazards on the approach to the ría and south and east of it

Port radio
Corcubión Practicos VHF Ch 14,16

Facilities
Usual village shops and restaurants

Little used by yachts

Most of the more sheltered spots in Ría de Corcubión are occupied by small craft moorings. In the past Corcubión enjoyed considerable importance, not least because its relatively narrow entrance was overlooked by twin forts which allowed it to be defended in a way not possible in most other rías.

The picturesque small town, which is on the west bank of the ría, is a summer holiday resort with banks, shops, restaurants and bars.

Waterborne processions mark the fiesta of the Virgen del Carmen on 16 July (also at Muros and in many other harbours).

Cee, a larger and beautifully developed town at the head of the estuary, can be reached by dinghy, on foot or by bus. It has a major supermarket along with a good general market and excellent shops. In contrast, the large industrial works and dock on the east side of the ría appears very run down with dangerous sea work extensions to the docks south of Pta Fornelos surrounded by just a low floating barrier.

Approach

From the west See page 54 regarding rounding Finisterre.

From the south See plan on page 52. Give Punta Insúa an offing of at least 5M to clear Bajo de los Meixidos, or if using the inner passage, hold the course towards Finisterre (and ⊕29) until the passage between Carrumeiro Chico and Islote Lobeira Grande can be approached from the southwest. ⊕31, ⊕32, ⊕33 and ⊕34 indicate the safe route.

Anchorages

(See photograph page 57). The Corcubión fishing quay becomes uncomfortable as soon as wind builds up. Be prepared to anchor. Anchorages in the ría, none of which offer shelter from southerly winds, are:

1. In the small bay of Playa de Quenje. Inshore is occupied by moorings, but some shelter will still be gained outside them – even so it would be uncomfortable in winds from south through east to north. There is a restaurant on the beach fringing the bay, and considerable recent development to the south.

2. Southeast of the main quay in 8–10m is probably the best bet, as it has yet to be filled with moorings.
3. North of the main quay in 3–4m, between the many small-craft moorings and the shoal water to the north. Holding is poor. If not busy it might be possible to lie alongside briefly.
4. In the northeast corner of the ría between the commercial quay and Punta Fornelos. Depths shoal rapidly once within the 5m line. This anchorage provides shelter in strong north winds.

The bottom in all these anchorages is a mixture of rock and sand and the holding is variable.

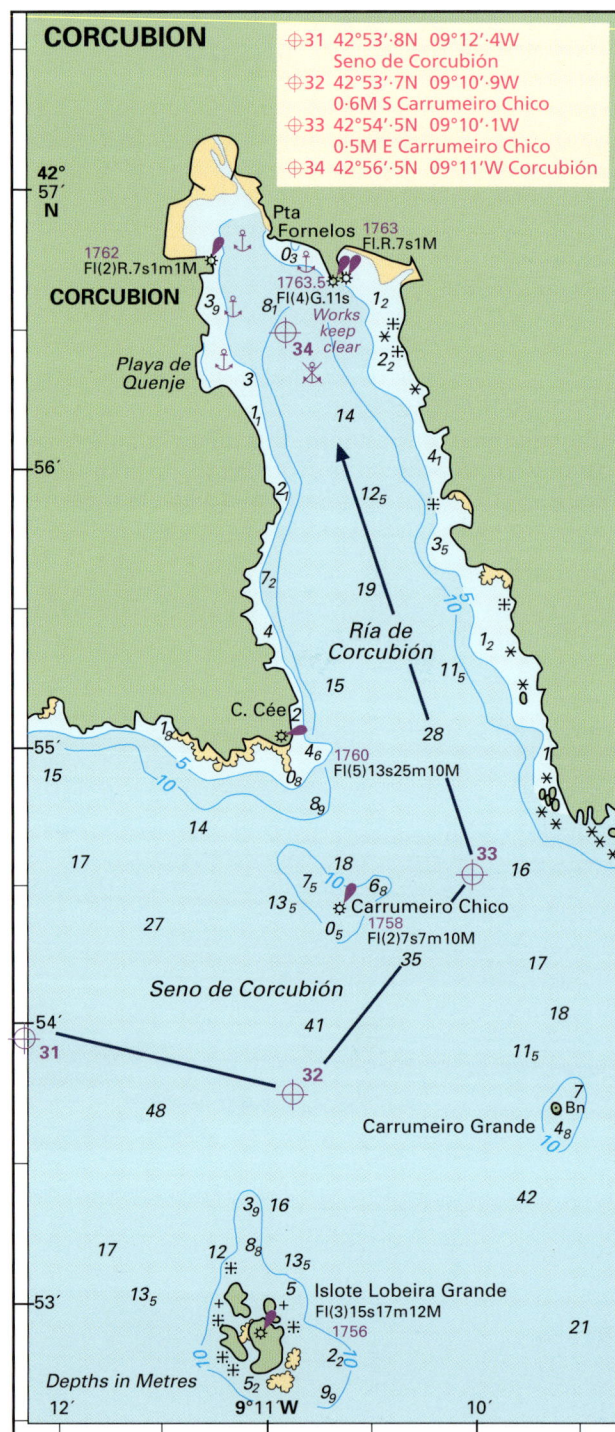

CORCUBION

⊕31 42°53'·8N 09°12'·4W
Seno de Corcubión
⊕32 42°53'·7N 09°10'·9W
0·6M S Carrumeiro Chico
⊕33 42°54'·5N 09°10'·1W
0·5M E Carrumeiro Chico
⊕34 42°56'·5N 09°11'W Corcubión

Corcubión   Fishing quay   Cée   Shipyard

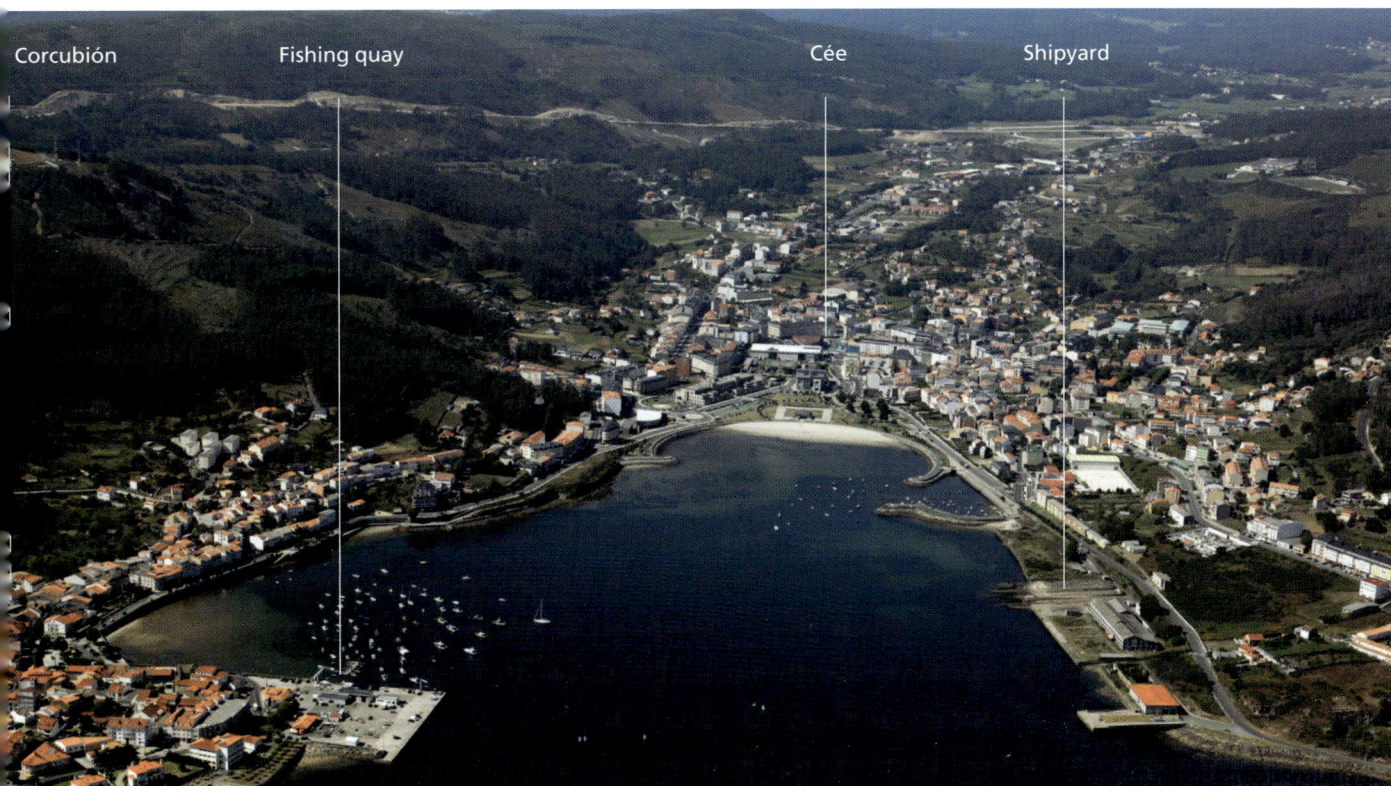

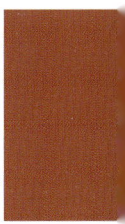

Corcubión and Cée

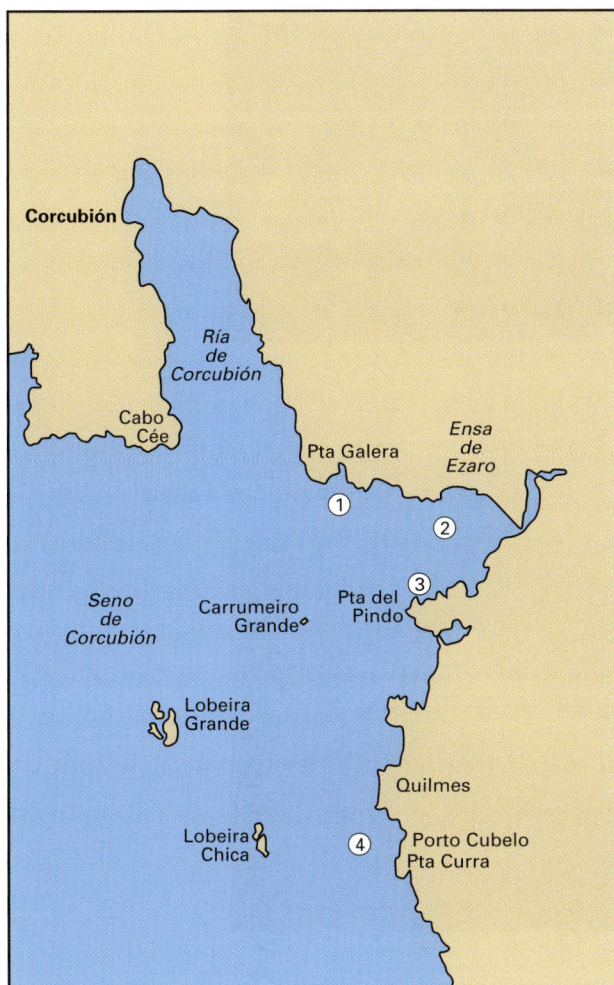

Anchorages between Ría Corcubión and Ría Muros

Yachts rarely visit the area surrounded by reefs and rocky outcrops off the coast heading south from Ría Corcubión. Given settled weather, chart 3764 and an escape plan, there are several anchorages worth visiting.

1. **Off Playa Gures** 42°54′·6N 09°08′·9W

Anchor in sand, avoiding the weed patches, with shelter from the north but with a possibility of squally winds.

2. **Ensenada de Ezaro** 42°54′N 09°08′W

This is a beautiful bay with fine beaches but totally exposed to the west. The rocky banks of Los Bois and El Asno might complicate a hasty departure.

3. **Porto del Pindo** Breakwater green column at 42°53′·81N 09°08′·04W

The harbour is open to the north but, with eyeball navigation on the approach, temporary space might be found near the head of the mole. The inner harbour is full of moorings. Pindo has restaurants and limited supplies.

4. **Porto Cubelo** Breakwater green column at 42°48′·45N 09°08′·13W

This harbour is best approached from the north/northeast to avoid the numerous rocks and reefs to the northwest and west. A short stop near the end of the breakwater, on a calm sunny day when eyeball navigation is possible, might be considered. Subject to fishing activities, short-term berthing may be found alongside the modern *lonja* (fish-handling building) but check depths. Limited facilities in the village about one mile away.

Anchorages between Ría Corcubión and Ría Muros *Above* Looking north over Pta del Pindo and the harbour (3) to Ensenada de Ezaro (2). Playa Gures (1) is just to the west   Below Porto Cubelo (4)

Left View from the hill above Pt Carreiro at the entrance to Ría de Muros, looking NW to Finisterre over the Canal de los Meixidos. Breaking seas are visible over the shoals
Jane Russell

I.2.2 Ría de Muros to Ría de Arousa

Approaches to Ría de Muros

Tides Standard port Lisbon
Mean time differences (at Muros)
HW +0100 ±0010; LW +0125 ±0010
(the above allows for the difference in time zones)
Heights in metres

MHWS	MHWN	MLWN	MLWS
3·5	2·7	1·3	0·5

Charts

	Approach	Ría
Admiralty	3633, 3764	1756
Spanish	415	415A
Imray	*C48*	

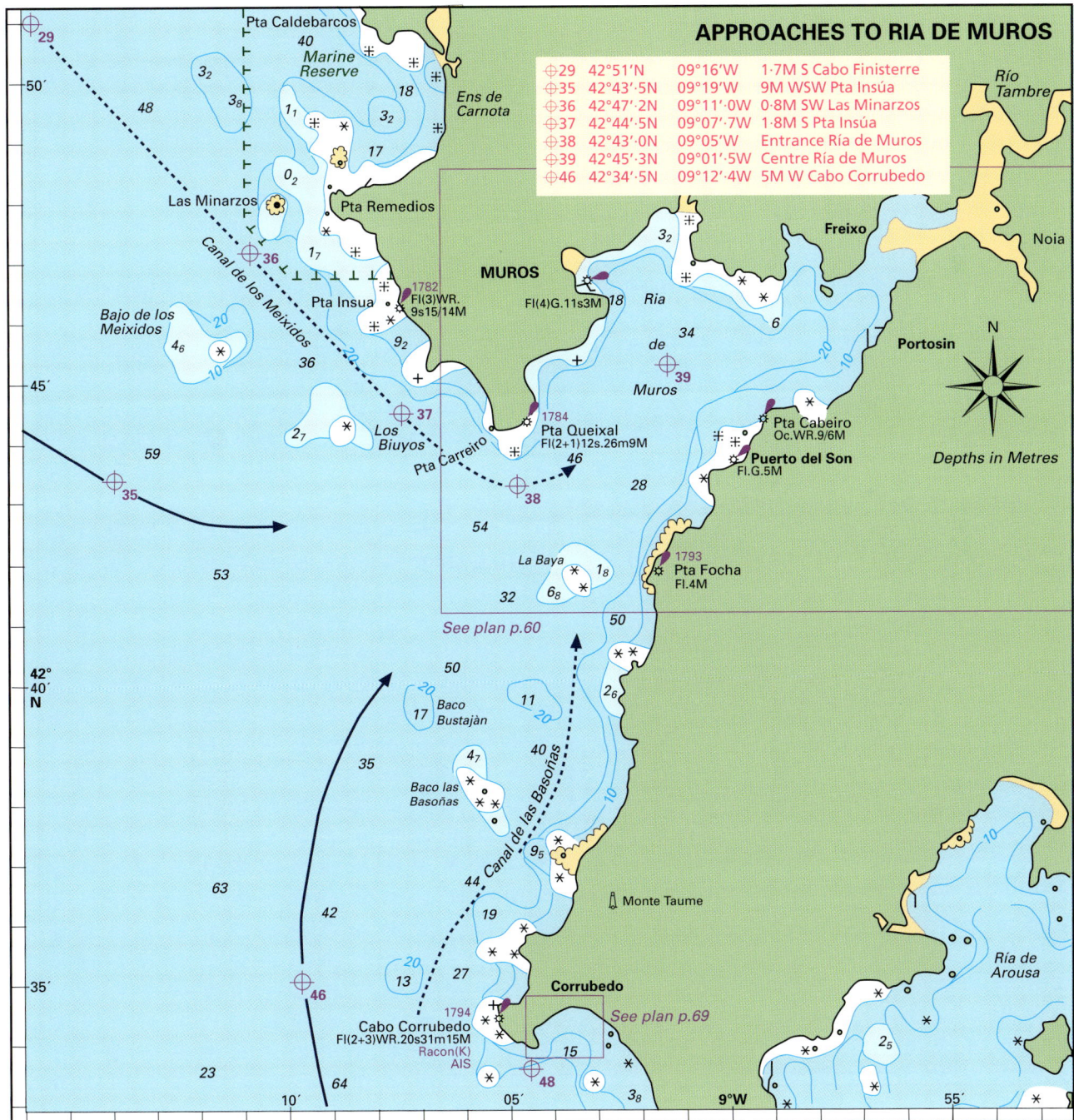

GALICIA

APPROACHES TO RIA DE MUROS

⊕29	42°51'N	09°16'W	1·7M S Cabo Finisterre
⊕35	42°43'·5N	09°19'W	9M WSW Pta Insúa
⊕36	42°47'·2N	09°11'·0W	0·8M SW Las Minarzos
⊕37	42°44'·5N	09°07'·7W	1·8M S Pta Insúa
⊕38	42°43'·0N	09°05'W	Entrance Ría de Muros
⊕39	42°45'·3N	09°01'·5W	Centre Ría de Muros
⊕46	42°34'·5N	09°12'·4W	5M W Cabo Corrubedo

(Chart labels:)

Pta Caldebarcos · Marine Reserve · Ens de Carnota · Las Minarzos · Pta Remedios · Bajo de los Meixidos · Pta Insua · Canal de los Meixidos · Los Biuyos · Pta Carreiro · Pta Queixal Fl(2+1)12s.26m9M · 1784 · 1782 Fl(3)WR. 9s15/14M · MUROS · Fl(4)G.11s3M · Ria · de · Muros · Río Tambre · Freixo · Noia · Portosin · Pta Cabeiro Oc.WR.9/6M · Puerto del Son Fl.G.5M · La Baya · Pta Focha Fl.4M · 1793 · Depths in Metres · See plan p.60 · Baco Bustajàn · Baco las Basoñas · Canal de las Basoñas · Monte Taume · Ría de Arousa · Corrubedo · See plan p.69 · 1794 Cabo Corrubedo Fl(2+3)WR.20s31m15M Racon(K) AIS

RIA DE MUROS

⊕38	42°43'·0N	09°05'·W	Entrance Ria de Muros
⊕39	42°45'·3N	09°01'·5W	Centre Ria de Muros
⊕40	42°46'·75N	09°03'·1W	Muros
⊕41	42°46'·7N	08°57'·W	0·25M SE Pta Cambrona
⊕42	42°47'·5N	08°56'·58W	App Freixo
⊕43	42°47'·6N	08°54'·6W	App Noia channel
⊕44	42°46'N	08°57'W	Portosin
⊕45	42°43'·9N	09°00'·2W	Puerto del Son

NOIA

Pta Barquiña
Pta de Carreira
Pta Testal
1791·3
1791
1791·2
43
Banco de la Misela
Pta Caballo de Ariba
Pta de Ornanda
Pta Mexilloeiro

See plan p.63

FREIXO
1790·3
Fl(2)R.5s7m4M
Pta del Corbeira
42
See plan p.64

PORTOSIN
Porto Refis del Con
1791·9
1791·95
1791·8
1791·84
44
15
Fl(2)7s5m8m
Fl(2)G.5s7m3M
1790·2
21
See plan p.66

Pta El Carballal
Pta Larga
Esteiro
Ensenada de Estero
I. Creba
3
4
Pta Borneira
Pta de S. Catalina
Pta Aguieira
Pta Cabeiro
1792
Fl.WRG.5s35m9/6M
Pta Corbeiro
1792·3
Fl.G.5s4m6M
PUERTO DEL SON
See plan p.68

Pta Insuela
Pedrais
El Xorexo
45
Pta Sagrada
Ría de Muros
39
Pta Avilleira
2
5
Ensenada de Bornalle
Ensenada de Muros
1786
Fl(2)R.7s18m7M
Cabo Rebordiño
Fl(4)G.11s3M
Fl(4)R.11s5M
40
MUROS
See plan p.61
Pta Magrio
Pta Sofocho
Punta Focha
1793
Fl.5s27m4M
Pta Castro
Pta Bouja
Ensenada de San Francisco
1
Pta Queixal
1784
Fl(2+1)12s26m9M
Leixoes
38
La Baya
Moyedor del W
Pta Carreiro
Laguna de Louro
Pedra do Cou
42°
44'
N
Depths in Metres

54'
56'
58'
9°W
9°W
48'
46'
42'
576'

A scenic ría

Ría Muros is the least developed of the rías. It has good anchorages, old towns and welcoming marinas at Portosin and Muros.

Approach

The safest approach, and in particular by night, is from the westsouthwest towards ⊕38. Keep 5M off Pta Insúa or 3M off Cabo Corrubedo. In fair weather:

From the north Canal de Los Meixidos may be used (⊕29, ⊕36, ⊕37, ⊕38) Do not cut inside the prominent rock off Pta Carreiro.

From the south Canal de Las Basoñas, the passage inside the banks, may be used.

⊕40 42°46'·75N 09°03'·1W

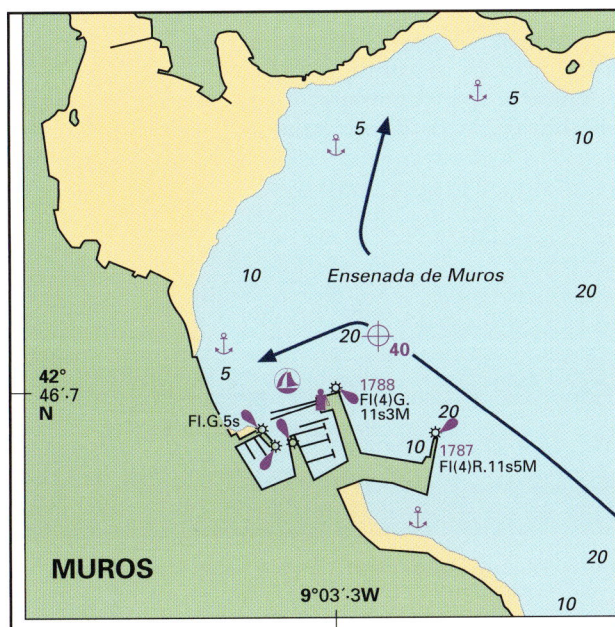

Muros marina looking north northwest *Henry Buchanan*

Muros

42°46'·30N 09°03'·16W

Tides
 See page 59

Charts
 Admiralty 1756
 Spanish   415A
 Imray   C48

Final approaches ⊕
 ⊕40 42°46'·75N 09°03'·1W

Lights
 Breakwater beacon Fl(4)R.13s8m4M
 White round tower

Fuel
 Available

Communications
 Address: Puerto de Muros.S/N 15250. Muros. A Coruna
 ☎ +34 981 82 76 60 *Mobile* +34 608 174 395
 Email muport@muport.es
 www.muport.es www.marinasdegalicia.com
 VHF: Ch 09

A picturesque fishing town with a new marina

The whole feeling of Galicia changes as the Lauro peninsula, past Pta Queixal, is rounded and the warmer, softer ría is entered with its immediate sense of increased shelter and temperature, tourism and prosperity. Inland, the fields of sweet-corn give way to massed vineyards. Muros is a picturesque old fishing town with colonnaded pavements, narrow streets, covered and open-air markets, a Romanesque church and a number of bars and restaurants. It has long been popular with cruising yachtsmen due to both its atmosphere and its facilities. Waterborne processions mark the fiesta of the Virgen del Carmen on 16 July, a practice which has spread throughout the area. The town is popular with tourists.

Approach

Head northeast from the mouth of the ría until Cabo Rebordiño lighthouse comes into view, then steer to clear it by 200m. Note recommended track. If approaching by night be aware that there are isolated unlit rafts inside 20m.

Security at Muros marina. The Repsol pump at left is for fishing boats only *Henry Buchanan*

Berthing

The new Marina in Muros is in full operation with friendly staff led by Pedro (2013). Approach around the west end of both the wavebreaker and the fishing boat pontoon just inside the wavebreaker, and turn east for the finger pontoons. The end of the wavebreaker is off the slip on the east shore of Muros town, marked with a red post and light at its west end (nearest the shore). There are berths for boats from length 6m to 20m and beam of 3m to 6·75m. There is one security gate with key access.

Anchorage

Anchorage is in the Ensenada de Muros as shown on the Plan. In several areas the ground is foul with lobster pots and other debris. A tripping line is advisable. Holding is variable.

Facilities

The Repsol fuel pump at the west side of the harbour is strictly for use by fishing boats only. The east side Repsol pumps on the quay with pontoon below are for use by leisure craft.

The marina office is in a converted house (blue building opposite security gate) with two lounge areas, and a small kitchen/laundry room including a fridge. An outside sitting area is shielded and fenced off from the public. There are two private outside showers in the garden, as well as a shower inside with a loo, all 24hr access.

WiFi is available in a special room in the office block, and to the pontoons but is weak at the outer edges. There is a Gadis supermarket 100m beyond the office.

Work and chandlery is geared generally to fishing boats but there is a good hardware store. There is a boat lift and 100-tonne travel lift and some space ashore to over-winter. There is a tidal scrubbing berth at a quay some 600m north of the harbour, on hard sand with about 2·5m at high water springs. It is well sheltered other than from southwesterly swell but inspect for debris before use – alternatively the sand in Ensenada de Muros is hard and clean.

The town is well provided with shops of all kinds, banks, hotels, restaurants and pavement cafés. There are excellent ones by the harbour. There is a good produce market, plus a fish market on the quay. Supermarkets and a good hardware store will be found near the north end of the town, some distance away from the harbour.

There is a free computer for use in the morning at the library. Also wi-fi at the Aclan Bar and at the Theatro Restaurant in the Plaza on the bend in the road around the corner of the marina.

Yacht entering Muros marina. Photo taken looking east
Henry Buchanan

Muros from the anchorage off the N shore *Jane Russell*

Anchorages in the Ría de Muros

1. **Ensenada de San Francisco** 42°45'·4N 09°04'·30W
In strong northerly winds, the Ensenada de San Francisco 1·5M southwest of Muros provides good shelter. Anchor in the northern part of the bay in 7m or less with excellent holding over sand. Land on the beach, where there are shops and cafés.

It has been reported that an anchor trapping pipe of some kind ran out into the bay from a point near the 'lollipop' lights on the road, terminating near the 10m line (see plan page 60). No more is known of its position or purpose.

2. **Ensenada de Bornalle** 42°47'·60N 09°01'·7W
In the northwest corner of the Ensenada de Bornalle, nearly 2M northeast of Muros, in 5m or less. There is a good bathing beach and a freshwater stream, but holding is variable due to large patches of very dense weed. The massed ranks of *viveros* in the entrance to the bay give some protection from southwesterly swell.

3. In the **Ensenada de Esteiro** 42°47'·20N 08°58'·50W about 4M east of Muros, well protected from west through north to east. The bay is effectively divided into two by a central rocky promontory (with shallow off-liers) and anchorage can be had on either side in 3–4m over sand and weed, avoiding the rock patches. There is a private quay on the west shore of the western arm and the entire surroundings are somewhat built up. Both arms of the bay shelter small but attractive beaches and there are normally some *viveros* moored in the entrance.

4. Close **northeast of Isla Crebra** 42°46'·60N 08°57'·6W, lit at its southerly extreme (Fl(2)7s5m8M Metal post 3m) and easily identified by the red-roofed building on its summit. Anchor north of the Vella rocks in 2–4m, sheltered from southwest to north. This is an isolated anchorage in the ría, with no facilities and notices forbidding landing.

See page 64 for Freixo and page 65 for Noia.
The latter can only be reached by dinghy having left the mother sip at anchor at
1. Freixo
2. Southeast of Pta Picouso
3. Off Pta Testal

Tides
West winds may increase tidal heights in the upper parts of the ría by up to 0·6m, but tidal flow in general is weak.

Training wall
Beacons are red and white and green and white. Pta Testal beacon is green and white. All are lit.

Ría de Muros, looking ENE up the ria from the peak above Pta Carreiro. Ensenada de San Francisco anchorage is off the long beach on the left *Jane Russell*

Muros *Jane Russell*

The anchorage at Ensenada de San Francisco looking SW towards the peak above Pta Carreiro and beyond towards Corrubedo *Jane Russell*

The anchorage at Pta Testal
Roddy Innes

GALICIA

Approaches to Freixo and Noia

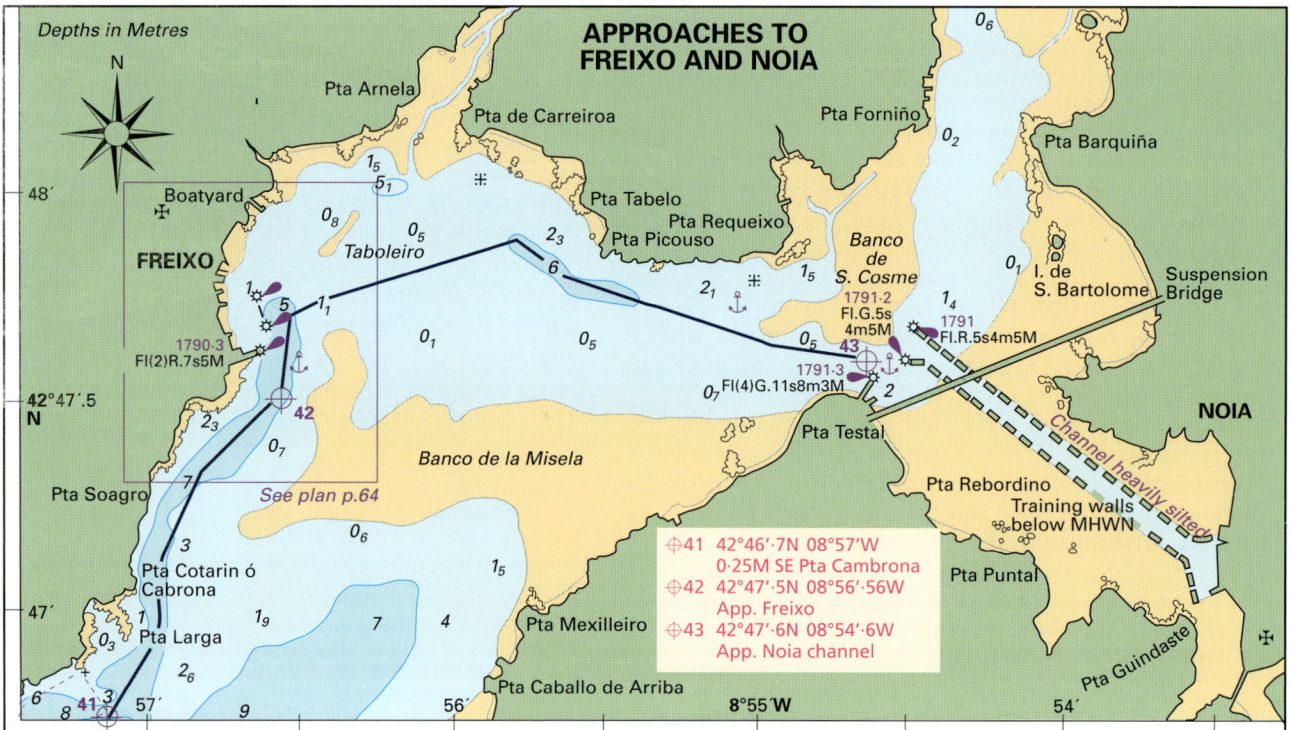

APPROACHES TO FREIXO AND NOIA

Depths in Metres

Pta Arnela
Pta de Carreiroa
Pta Forniño
Pta Barquiña
Pta Tabelo
Pta Requeixo
Pta Picouso
Banco de S. Cosme
I. de S. Bartolome
Suspension Bridge
Boatyard
Taboleiro
FREIXO
1790·3 Fl(2)R.7s5M
42°47'·5N
1791·2 Fl.G.5s 4m5M
1791 Fl.R.5s4m5M
1791·3 Fl(4)G.11s8m3M
NOIA
Channel heavily silted
42
Banco de la Misela
Pta Testal
Pta Soagro
See plan p.64
Pta Rebordino
Training walls below MHWN
Pta Puntal
Pta Cotarin ó Cabrona
Pta Larga
Pta Mexilleiro
Pta Guindaste
47'
Pta Caballo de Arriba
41
8°55'W
56'
54'

⊕41 42°46'·7N 08°57'W 0·25M SE Pta Cambrona
⊕42 42°47'·5N 08°56'·56W App. Freixo
⊕43 42°47'·6N 08°54'·6W App. Noia channel

Freixo (Freijo)

42°47'·62N 08°56'·62W

Tide
See page 59

Charts
Admiralty 1756
Spanish   415A
Imray   C48

Final approaches ⊕
⊕42 but not direct from ⊕41

Light
Breakwater beacon Fl(2)R.5s7m4M Red and white column
Wave breaker lights on thin posts (Green and BYB)

Muros
Freixo
Ria de Muros
Portosin
Pta Queixal
Pta Cabeiro

Straggling village with active boat yard

Freixo (Freijo) offers a sheltered anchorage, in 5m mud, and minor food shops and restaurants ashore. Yachts are also welcome on the outer pontoon but check depths carefully.

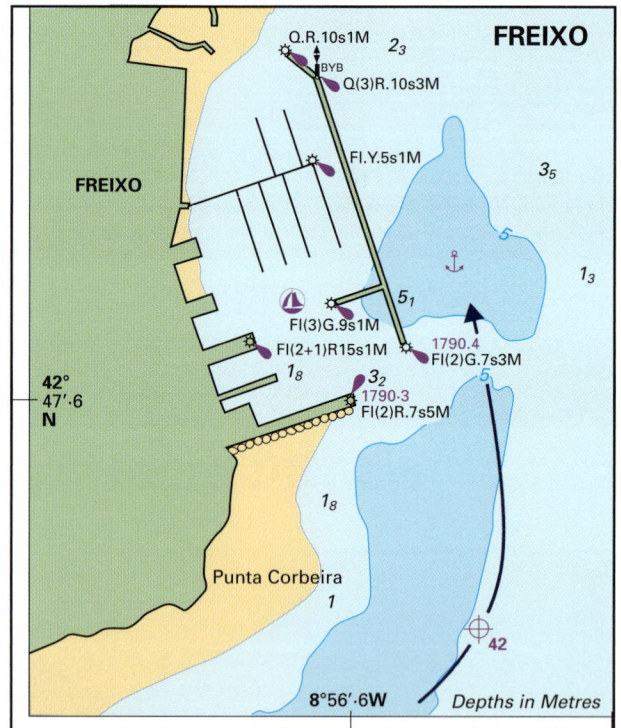

FREIXO

Q.R.10s1M
BYB
Q(3)R.10s3M
FREIXO
Fl.Y.5s1M
42° 47'·6 N
Fl(3)G.9s1M
Fl(2+1)R15s1M
1790·4 Fl(2)G.7s3M
1790·3 Fl(2)R.7s5M
Punta Corbeira
42
8°56'·6W
Depths in Metres

⊕41 42°46'·7N 08°57'W   0.25M SE Pta Cambrona
⊕42 42°47'·5N 08°56'·58W App Freixo

Approach (see plan and chart 1756)

The deep water becomes shallow as the *viveros* to the northwest of Isla Creba are passed. From ⊕41 pick up the channel as it follows the west bank past the reef extending from Pta Larga.

Freixo from the south

Caution

Watch the depth gauge at Punta Corbeira and north, before you reach the southern harbour wall. In 2013 the channel edge extended much further out than shown in the chartlet in the last Edition 6 of the pilot book. At low tide all local boats passed well to the south and east of the indicated route and local fishermen went out of their way to warn a yacht to pass much further out than indicated. ⊕42 has been adjusted in this 7th Edition to allow for this. There is also a lot of diving activity in the area to watch out for (diving for shellfish it is believed), but divers down flags are usually used.

Noia (Noya)

Noia lies 1M southeast from Pta Testal between training walls at F43 42°47′N 08°53′·5W

Silting and suspension bridge restrict access to old town and port

The harbour and approaches to Noia are now severely silted but at high water it is still possible for a yacht drawing less than 2m to get within 1M of the town off Punta Testal. Then continue by dinghy, or land at the quay at Punta Testal and walk into town, a distance of about 2·5km (taxis are available in the main square for the return journey). Punta Testal is fringed by clear sandy beach, where a yacht able to take the ground could dry out.

A very large suspension bridge across the estuary blocks access to Noia for yachts.

Approach

Leave Freixo after half flood, or as draught allows. From the 5m patch north of the Freixo mole head for Punta Tabelo until the 5–6m trench is reached. Follow the trench past Punta Picouso. When it starts to shoal, head just north of the tip of the Punta Testal sand, where red and green buoys mark the start of the channel within the training wall.

Anchorage (see plan page 63)

Anchor south of Pta Picouso or between the south training wall and Pta Testal molehead. The latter offers more shelter but is a holiday area, the water is shallower and there are many small boat moorings. There is little room for more than one visiting boat to anchor.

Facilities

All the domestic facilities of a bustling small town.

Looking towards the new suspension bridge from Noia Henning Dürr

Portosin

42°45'·94N 08°56'·91W

Tides
See page 59

Charts
Admiralty 1756
Spanish 415A
Imray C48

Final approaches
⊕44 42°46'N 08°57'W

Light
Breakwater beacon Fl(3)G.9s Green round tower

Communications
Club Náutico Portosin
☎ +34 981 766 583
Email info@cnportosin.com
www.cnportosin.com
VHF Ch 09

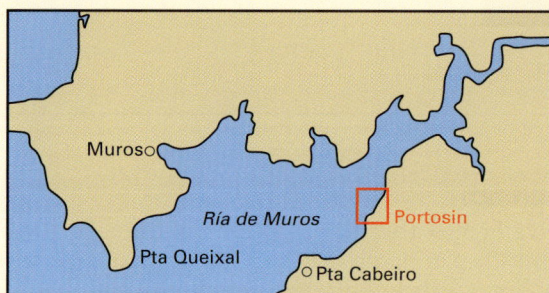

An efficient and pleasing marina

The large harbour houses an established marina, the Real Club Náutico, which was awarded its Royal status in 2013. This marina has long received unanimous praise from visitors and is the closest marina to Santiago de Compostela for a visit and to make use of its crew change airport, where a yacht can be left for extended periods in safety. The town is without any great charm, but the marina has an attractive setting backed by wooded hills and with a good beach nearby.

Approach

Head up the middle of the ría to the approach to the harbour at ⊕44 which is on the south shore opposite Isla Crebra. The marina is to port on entering harbour.

Berthing

Call ahead and, unless a berth has been pre-arranged, visitors should secure to the second hammerhead. Most berths are bows-on with finger pontoon or a mooring line provided astern; yachts up to 20m can be accommodated in depths of 2–5m. Shelter is good though some surge may be experienced in north easterlies.

Office hours are 1000–2000 weekdays, 1030–1330 Saturdays, closed Sundays. Charges are based on LOA x beam. The staff are very welcoming and helpful, and a range of European languages is spoken.

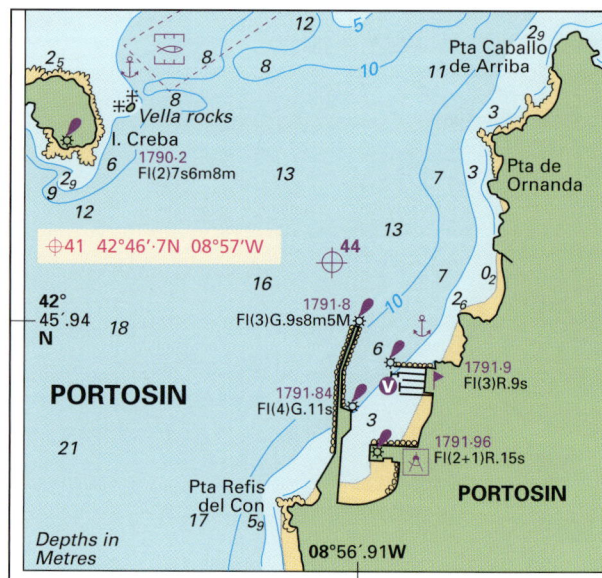

Anchorage

Yachts may anchor immediately north of the mole in 5–6m, sheltered from northeast through to south or southwest. Holding is reported to be good in sand.

Facilities

Facilities are very good within the marina, both for boat support and domestics. There is diesel on site, although depth may be limited at low tide. It has good showers and laundry facilities and the Club has WiFi, and a good bar and restaurant. Hire cars can be arranged from here and there is a bus service into Noia.

Ashore

Portosin has an excellent supermarket despite otherwise modest shops and there is a produce market on Saturdays.

At the head of the ría, the old town of Noia (declared an Area of Historical Importance) is a short bus-trip away. Noia offers supermarkets, an excellent covered market and a weekly general street market. Santiago de Compostela, its airport and the excellent 'Atlantic' motorway, are less than an hour away.

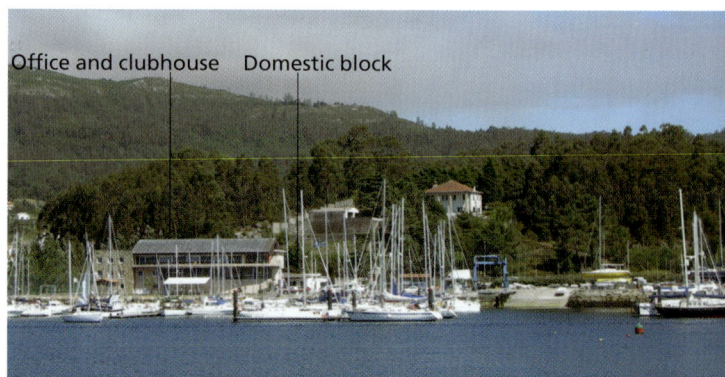

Portosin marina lies to port after entering harbour
Martin Walker

Portosin entrance

Anchorage between Portosin and Puerto del Son

42°46'·6N 08°58'·2W

The bay east of Punta Aguieira (1·5M southwest of Portosin) offers an attractive anchorage when the wind is in the southern quadrant. Depths are said to be greater than shown on Admiralty *1756* (shoaling to 2m some way off the beach), and it may be possible to tuck in behind the isthmus running out to the almost-islet of Punta Aguiera and thus avoid any swell running into the ría. Holding is good over sand off an inviting sandy beach.

Typical covered market with fruit, meat and fish, other foodstuffs and general goods *Roddy Innes*

Galicia has excellent fish stalls *Roddy Innes*

Puerto del Son

42°43'·74N 09°00'·05W

Tides
See page 59

Charts
Admiralty 1756
Spanish 415B
Imray C48

Final approaches ⊕
⊕45 42°43'·9N 09°00'·2W but from the west and only with great care

Lights
Breakwater beacon Fl.G.5s4m6M Green and white round concrete tower
Pta Cabeiro Oc.WR.3s36m9/6M Grey truncated pyramidal tower

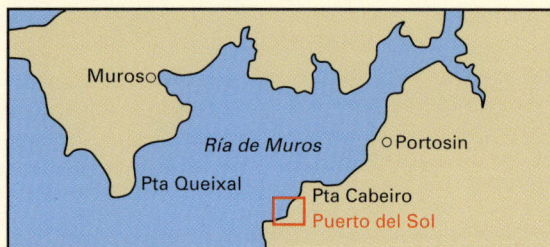

⊕45 42°43'·9N 09°00'·2W Puerto del Son

PUERTO DEL SON

09°00'·05W

Small fishing harbour

A yachtsman might find shelter here. The village has basic shops and there are good beaches nearby.

Approach

The bay between Puerto del Son and Punta Cabeiro is shallow and largely foul although under ideal conditions it is possible to approach the harbour breakwater on a heading of 180°. A safer route is from the southwest with Pta Cabeiro bearing 56·5° (the narrow-beam red sector of the light) until the end of Puerto del Son breakwater bears 170°.

Alternatively, approach ⊕45 from a westerly direction taking note of El Xorexo reef to the north and the shallows of Bajo Angostin.

Anchorage

Anchor in the outer harbour clear of the approach channel to the fishermen's quays. The likely spot will be abeam the distinctive orange lifeboat. In quiet periods it may be possible to lie alongside the quay for a short while.

Facilities

Water on the quay, shop, restaurants, post office but little else.

Looking S across the mouth of Ría de Muros from Pta Queixal, Puerto del Son on the far shore
Jane Russell

Puerto del Son

Corrubedo

42°34'·34N 09°04'20W

Tides
See page 59

Charts
Admiralty 1734 (essential)
Spanish 415B
Imray C48

Final approaches ⊕
⊕46 42°34'·5N 09°12'·4W 5M
W Cabo Corrubedo but only in good conditions and with great care

Lights
Breakwater beacon Iso.WRG.3s White truncated conical tower
Cabo Corrubedo Fl(2+3)WR.20s31m15M Round tower and daymark

Warning
Yachtsmen should avoid this area in poor weather conditions and at night

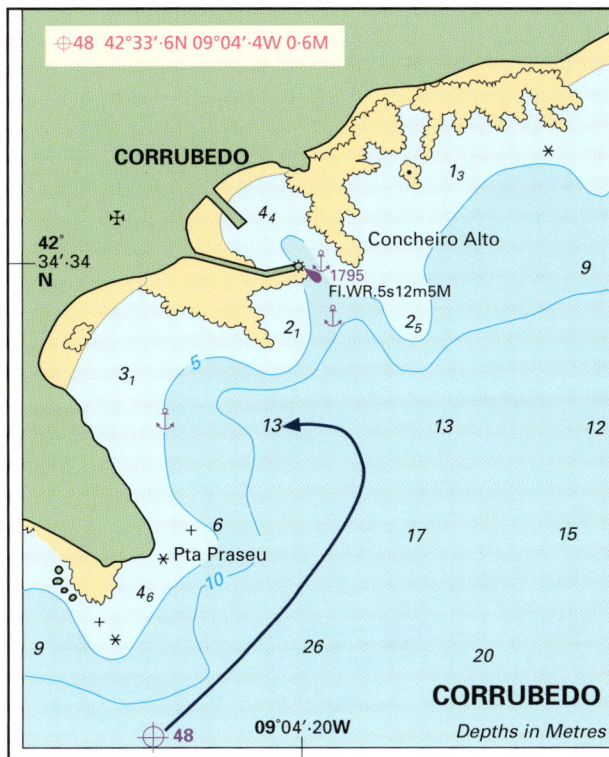

A small fishing harbour offering little space or protection

Corrubedo should be visited in fair weather only and using chart 1734. The approaches should only be attempted in calm weather and daylight. If a southerly develops it would be necessary to clear out. There are basic shops and restaurants ashore. To the east lies the Dunes National Park with vast sand dunes and nature trails.

Approach

See plan on page 70. (See chart 1734 for offshore dangers, not all are recorded here.)

From the north From ⊕46 a passage between the rocky ledges off Pta Posalgueiro and Bajo La Marosa to ⊕48 can be made.Continue on this line through ⊕48 until Corrubedo breakwater bears 350° and then turn in - but take care.

From the south The inshore passage from ⊕50 clears the dangers on a course of 356° towards Corrubedo breakwater Light (the narrow white sector of the light - not that the prudent mariner would want to do this at night!).

Anchorage

The bay to the southwest of the harbour may offer more room and greater comfort than the harbour itself but note the swell in the picture.

Corrubedo from the south

GALICIA

Approaches to Ría de Arousa

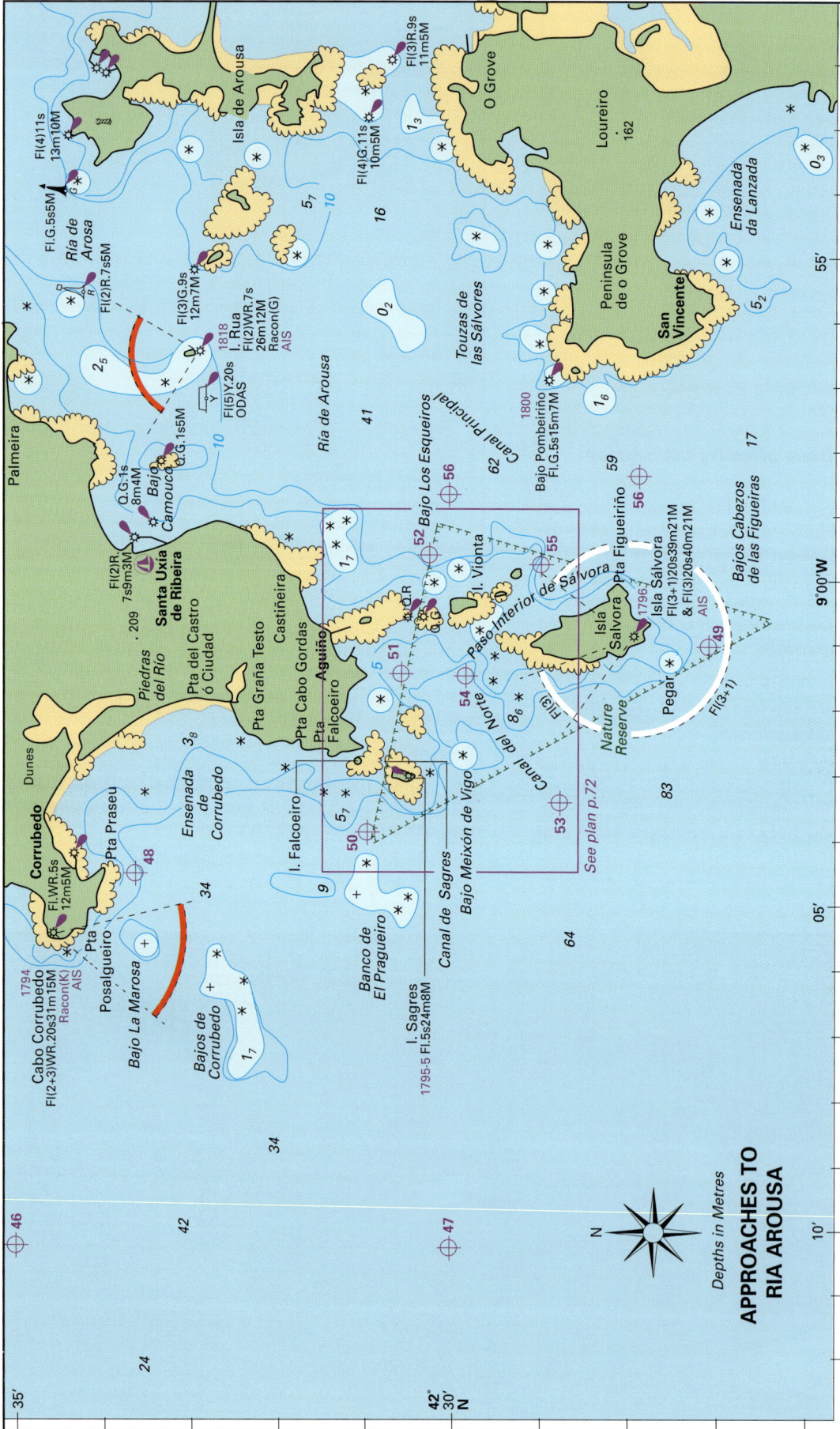

Fl(4)11s
13m10M

Fl(3)R.9s
11m5M

Isla de Arousa

O Grove

Loureiro
162

Fl.G.5s5M

Ría de
Arosa

Fl(4)G.11s
10m5M

1₃

Ensenada
da Lanzada

0₃

Fl(2)R.7s5M

Fl(3)G.9s
12m7M

5₇   10

16

Touzas de
las Sálvores

0₂

Peninsula
de o Grove

5₂

Palmeira

1818
I. Rua
Fl(2)WR.7s
26m12M
Racon(G)
AIS

2₅

Fl(5)Y.20s
ODAS

10

Q.G.1s5M

Ría de Arousa

41

62

1800
Bajo Pombeiriño
Fl.G.5s15m7M

1₆

San
Vincente

17

Q.G.1s
8m4M

Bajo
Camoucd

Santa Uxia
de Ribeira

Bajo Los Esqueiros

56

Canal Principal

59

56

Fl(2)R.
7s9m3M

Piedras
del Río

. 209

Pta del Castro
ó Ciudad

Pta Graña Testo

Castiñeira

52

I. Vionta

55

Paso Interior de Sálvora

Pta Figueiriño

Isla Sálvora
1796
Fl(3+1)20s39m21M
& Fl(3)20s40m21M
AIS

Bajos Cabezos
de las Figueiras

Corrubedo

Dunes

Pta Praseu

48

Ensenada
de
Corrubedo

3₈

Pta Cabo Gordas
Pta Falcoeiro

Aguiño

5   51

Q.R

54

8₆   Fl(3)

Canal del Norte

Isla
Sálvora

49

Pegar

Nature
Reserve

Fl(3+1)

83

See plan p.72

1794
Cabo Corrubedo
Racon(K)
AIS

Fl.WR.5s
12m5M

Pta
Posalgueiro

Pta

34

I. Falcoeiro

5₇

50

9

53

Fl(2+3)WR.20s31m15M

Bajo La Marosa

Bajos de
Corrubedo

1₇

Banco de
El Pragueiro

I. Sagres
1795·5 Fl.5s24m8M

Canal de Sagres

Bajo Meixón de Vigo

64

34

24

42

46

47

N

APPROACHES TO
RIA AROUSA

Depths in Metres

35'

55'

9°00'W

05'

10'

42°
30'
N

⊕46	42°34'·5N	09°12'·4W	5M W Cabo Corrubedo
⊕47	42°30'N	09°10'W	9M WSW Cabo Corrubedo
⊕48	42°33'·6N	09°04'·4W	0·6M S Corrubedo
⊕49	42°27'·3N	09°01'·03W	0·7M SW Isla Sálvora
⊕50	42°30'·95N	09°03'·85W	0·6M WNW Islas Sagres
⊕51	42°30'·55N	09°01'·40W	0·7M WSW Aguiño
⊕52	42°30'·4N	08°59'·5W	0·3M E Piedras del Sargo
⊕53	42°28'·9N	09°03'W	App Canal del Norte
⊕54	42°29'·9N	09°01'·4W	W App Passo Sálvora
⊕55	42°28'·85N	08°59'·5W	E App Passo Sálvora
⊕56	42°27'·5N	08°58'·5W	Canal Principal Arousa

I.2.3 Ría de Arousa to Isla Ons

GALICIA

Outer Approach (overview plan page 70)

The easiest and safest approach to the ría, particularly at night or in poor conditions, is from the southwest through the Canal Principal. This leads between Isla Sálvora and Pombeiriño, at the northwest point of the Península de o Grove. Isla Rúa light, that is some 7M into the ría, can be seen from well out to sea, and from offshore is safe to approach on a bearing of between 010° and 025°.

Coming from the north on passage, clear Cabo Corrubedo by 5M to avoid the dangers of Bajos de Corrubedo. When past them, steer to round Isla Sálvora giving the lighthouse a berth of 1M to avoid the Pegar rock group and enter by the Canal Principal. Alternatively ⊕46, ⊕47, ⊕49, ⊕56 apply.

Coming from the south on passage, ⊕56 marks the southern entrance to the Canal Principal.

Pombeiriño light with Aguiño in the distance looking NW from O Grove *Martin Walker*

Aguiño fisherman. Work continues beyond to enhance protection from the east

Shell-fish drags. The pole may be up to 25m long and trail behind the fishing boat; give a wide berth

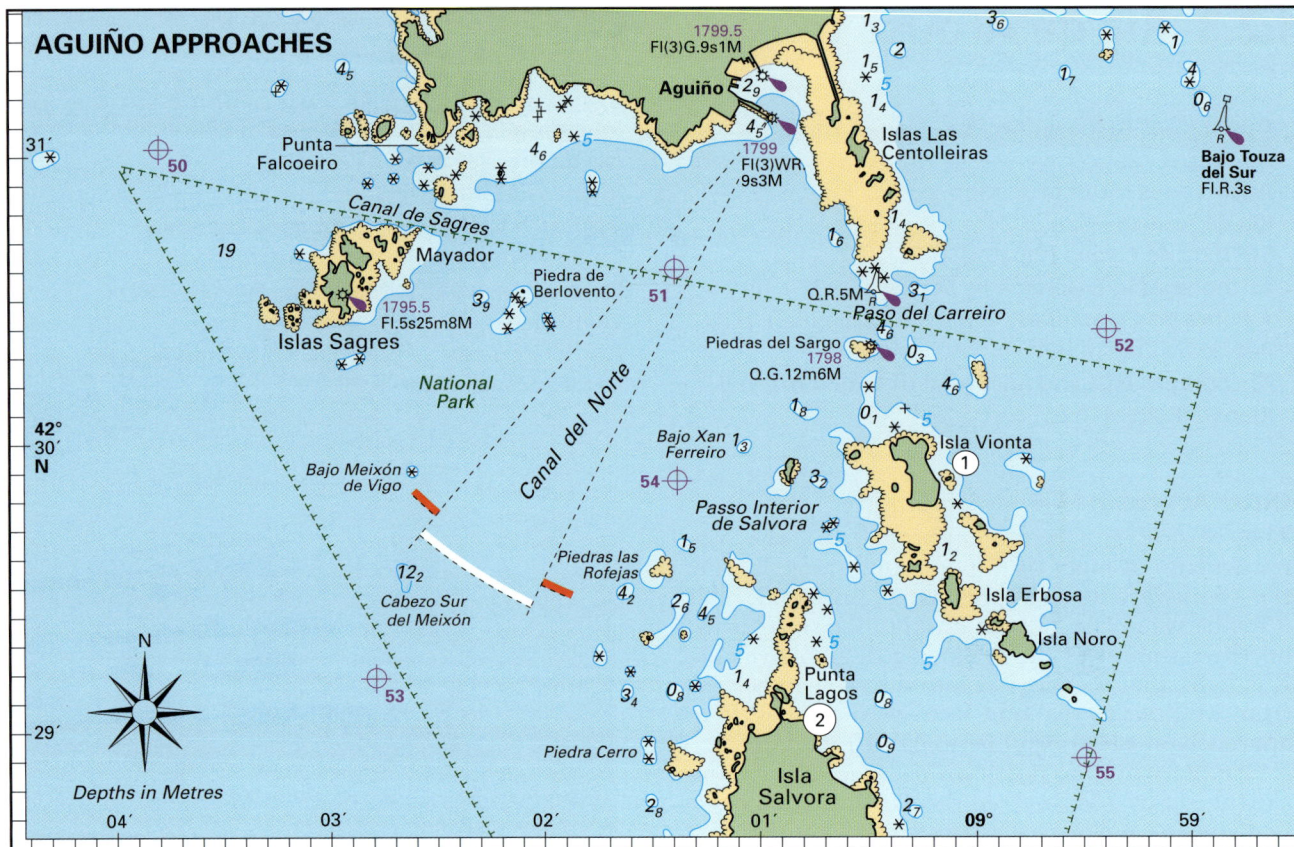

AGUIÑO APPROACHES

(nautical chart showing approaches to Aguiño)

Labels on chart:
- 1799.5 Fl(3)G.9s1M
- Aguiño
- Punta Falcoeiro
- Canal de Sagres
- 1799 Fl(3)WR.9s3M
- Islas Las Centolleiras
- Bajo Touza del Sur Fl.R.3s
- Mayador
- Piedra de Berlovento
- Q.R.5M
- Paso del Carreiro
- 1795.5 Fl.5s25m8M
- Islas Sagres
- National Park
- Piedras del Sargo 1798 Q.G.12m6M
- Canal del Norte
- Bajo Meixón de Vigo
- Bajo Xan Ferreiro
- Isla Vionta ①
- Passo Interior de Salvora
- Cabezo Sur del Meixón
- Piedras las Rofejas
- Isla Erbosa
- Isla Noro
- Punta Lagos ②
- Piedra Cerro
- Isla Salvora
- N — Depths in Metres

⊕50 42°30'·95N 09°03'·85W 0·6M WNW Islas Sagres
⊕51 42°30'·55N 09°01'·40W 0·7M WSW Aguiño
⊕52 42°30'·4N 08°59'·5W 0·3M E Piedras del Sargo
⊕53 42°28'·9N 09°03'W App Canal del Norte
⊕54 42°29'·9N 09°01'·4W W App Passo Sálvora

Aguiño

42°31'·12N 09°00'·95W

Tides
See page 75

Charts
Admiralty 1734 (essential)
Spanish 415B
Imray C48

Final approaches ⊕
⊕51 42°30'·65N 09°01'·40W
SW Aguiño then 030°/0·6M
to breakwater

Light
Breakwater beacon Fl(3)WR.9s3M Red post

Warning
Strong and unpredictable currents can run strongly through the channels which should not be attempted in less than perfect weather or at night

Facilities
Geared for the fishing fleet, usual town facilities

(inset locator map: Corrubedo, Aguiño, Isla Salvora Pta Besugueiros)

Fishing harbour

Aguiño is dedicated to fishing – primarily for shellfish. It lies at the head of numerous reefs and islands which form a National Park.

Approaches

There are four approaches or passages to or past Aguiño. (⊕ are used for reference; do not link for direct routing without plotting; visual pilotage is vital. The plan should not be used for navigation).

From the north and Canal de Sagres (⊕50 and ⊕51) Approach heading 170° from Corrubedo and continue south until turning for Canal Principal or turn for Canal de Sagres. This must be a visual passage; Piedras del Sargo should bear about 105°. The course passes about 80m north of the visible Mayador rocks and 150m south of the submerged rocks off Pta Falcoeiro. From ⊕51 head for Aguiño or other passages.

To/from the Ría – Paso del Carreiro (⊕51 and ⊕52) Piedras del Sargo light is prominent (white tower/green band). The passage is about 250m wide; keep 150m north of the tower to avoid its two offlying rocks. If heading up Ría de Arousa from this passage, beware Bajo Trouza del Sur to port; Isla Rúa, a distinctive clump of rocks with a prominent lighthouse, is 3M up the ría.

Canal del Norte (⊕53 and ⊕51) The centre line of the white sector is 032° to Aguiño breakwater light

Passo Interior de Sálvora (⊕54 and ⊕55) This route is suited to local fishermen or devoted rock-hoppers.

Anchorage

The Las Centolleiras reef continues to be filled in to form a causeway protecting the harbour from the east. As a result the harbour is reasonably sheltered,

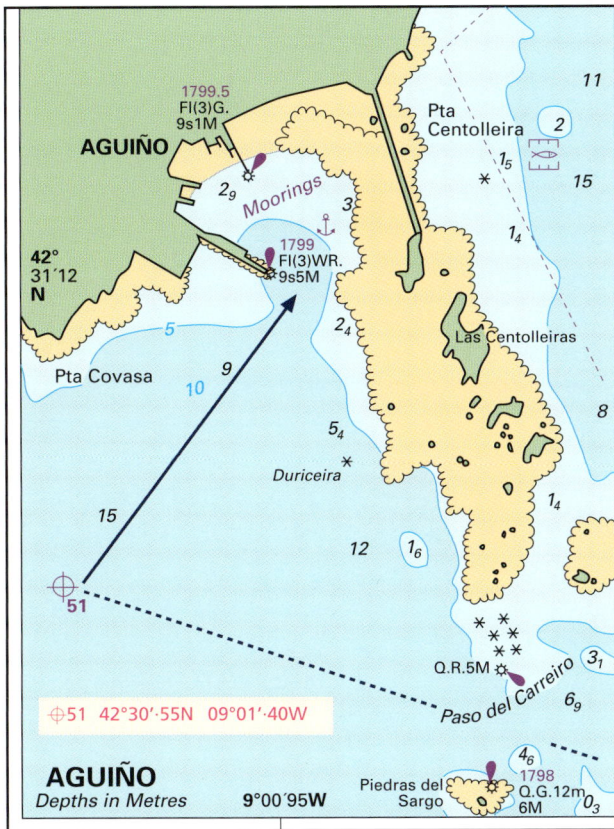

though the entrance is exposed to the southwest. The best anchorage is occupied by smallcraft moorings. Anchor about 150m north or northeast of the breakwater as space allows in 2–4m over sand, keeping clear of the approach to the fishermen's quay on the inside of the breakwater.

Anchorages south of Aguiño

(See plan page 72)

The following isolated anchorages offer interesting daytime exploring in settled weather, but have intricate approaches and in an easterly (not uncommon in the rías) would be difficult to leave. None are recommended for an overnight stop.

1. **Isla Vionta** (northeast coast 42°30'N 9°00'W). Off the small beach over sand, rock and weed.

2. **Isla Sálvora** (northeast coast 42°28'·9N 9°00'·5W). Off the beach over sand and weed. Take care to avoid isolated rocks. The island is a National Park patrolled by a vigilant warden; anchorage is only permitted with a permit (see page 15). The pontoon beside the quay is owned by the Vilagarcía Port Authority and may not be used without permission. From the beach the only access permitted on the island is the track to the lighthouse.

GALICIA

The map on the left shows:

AGUIÑO
Depths in Metres

1799.5
Fl(3)G.
9s1M

Pta Centolleira

1799
Fl(3)WR.
9s5M

Moorings

Pta Covasa

Duriceira

Las Centolleiras

Q.R.5M

Paso del Carreiro

Piedras del Sargo

1798
Q.G.12m
6M

⊕51 42°30'·55N 09°01'·40W

42°
31'12
N

9°00'·95W

Aguiño

RIA DE AROUSA

Warning

The numerous *viveros* moored near to and sometimes infringing on the channel north of Isla Rúa make it inadvisable to beat up the channel at night or in poor visibility. Their pattern shows up well on Google Earth, as do the shallows to the east of O Grove

Ría de Beluso

Pta Inobre

0_9

See plan p.82

Ensenada de Rianxo

2_6

2_3

Rianxo

Pta Fincheira

3 1843·1
Q(9)15s

Pta Bodión

See plan p.81

Pta Porta Mouro

3 **64**

Río Ulla

3

Escarabote

Fl(2)7s
BRB
9

3
8

9

14

Pta del Trove

See plan p.78

Fl.R.5s

1_4

9

12

Pta Ostral

I. Cortegada

2

Pta del Chazo

13

Aurora
Fl(4)R.11s

Carril

Vilagarcía
3 DirFl.WRG
1840·5

Pobra do Caramiñal

0_3

Fl(3)G.9s

2

Sinal de Ostreira

2

2

Fl.R.5s
7

Cabo Cruz

1831·5
F(2)G.7s

62

Q.G

22

1

2_7

Moscardiño (Findlay)

Fl.R.5s

Bn
La Barsa
BRB

21

2_7

63 Fl.Y.5s

El Seijo
Fl(3)G.10s
G

Vilaxuan

Fl.G.5s
G
Fl(2)
G.7s
Fl(3)R.9s
7
8

Palmeira
See plan p.77

0

35

Fl.Y.5s3M **61**

38

Fl.G.5s5M Pta Caballo
1826
Fl(4)11s12m10M

2_3 6

Pta Bornal

See plan p.84

See plan p.86

See plan p.70

Pta de Cabio

5

18

Sinal del Maño

0_9
Fl(2)R.7s

Bajo Ter
G
3 12

Fl.Y.5s3M

15

Vilanova de Arousa
1832
Fl(4)R.11s
Fl.R

8

12

See plan p.76

I. Perilla
2_1

I. Corosa

3_6

Lobeira Grande

63

Pta Barbafeita

27

S. Xulian
2_3

7

2

Pta Sartaxa

See plan p.90

Riviera

Fl(2)R.7s
9 12
Q.R
Camouco
Bn Q.G
0_3
de Terre
8
58

Llagareos

24

Piedra Seca

27
4

Jidoiro Arenoso

I. de Arousa
2 7 7

Pta del Vado
2_4

Bridge

I. Rúa
2_9
60
1824

Fl(3)G.9s
12m7M
I.Jidoiro Pedregoso

4

7

0_8

Pta Tragrove

Cambados

See plan p.93

Fl.Y.5s3M

1818
Fl(2)WR
7s26m12M
Racon(G)
AIS

34

Ría de Arousa

La Loba
1816
Fl(2)G.7s7M

I. Corbeiro
9

6

18 **66** 8

Praguero de Fuera
Fl(4)G.11s
3

6

5

0_2

2_9

Río Umia

Pta del Castro

Fl(2)WR.7s

Sinal del Castro

46

24

Los Mexos
0_2 G
Fl.G.5s

1_1

67
Golfeira
Lobeira de Cambados

1808
Fl(3)R.9s5M
Fl(3)R.9s

31

30

1798 Q.G.12m6M

Sargo

Canal del Norte

Los Esqueiros
Fl(2+1)G.14.5s
GRG
1_9
36
Fl.R.5s

19

1_1

Meloxo

0_8

Pta Borrelo

I. Vionta **52**

9

I. Noro

38

Piedras Salvores
8
2_7
1_3

7

20

S. Martin O Grove

I. Toxa Gde

57

Fl(3)G.10s5M
Laxes de S. Vicente
G
31

12

8

0_7

28

55
Isla Salvora

25

Bajo Pombeiriño
1800
Fl.G.5s14m7M
I. Pombeiro

15

Pta Pateiro ó Pedregal

Pta Antarde

See plan p.94

Ensenada del Grove

2

Depths in Metres

See plan p.72

1796
Fl(3+1)20s39m21M
Fl(3)20s

59

Canal Principal

Península O Grove

See plan p.95

San Vicente

27
Isla Salvora

46

12 Pta Miranda

6

12

0_3

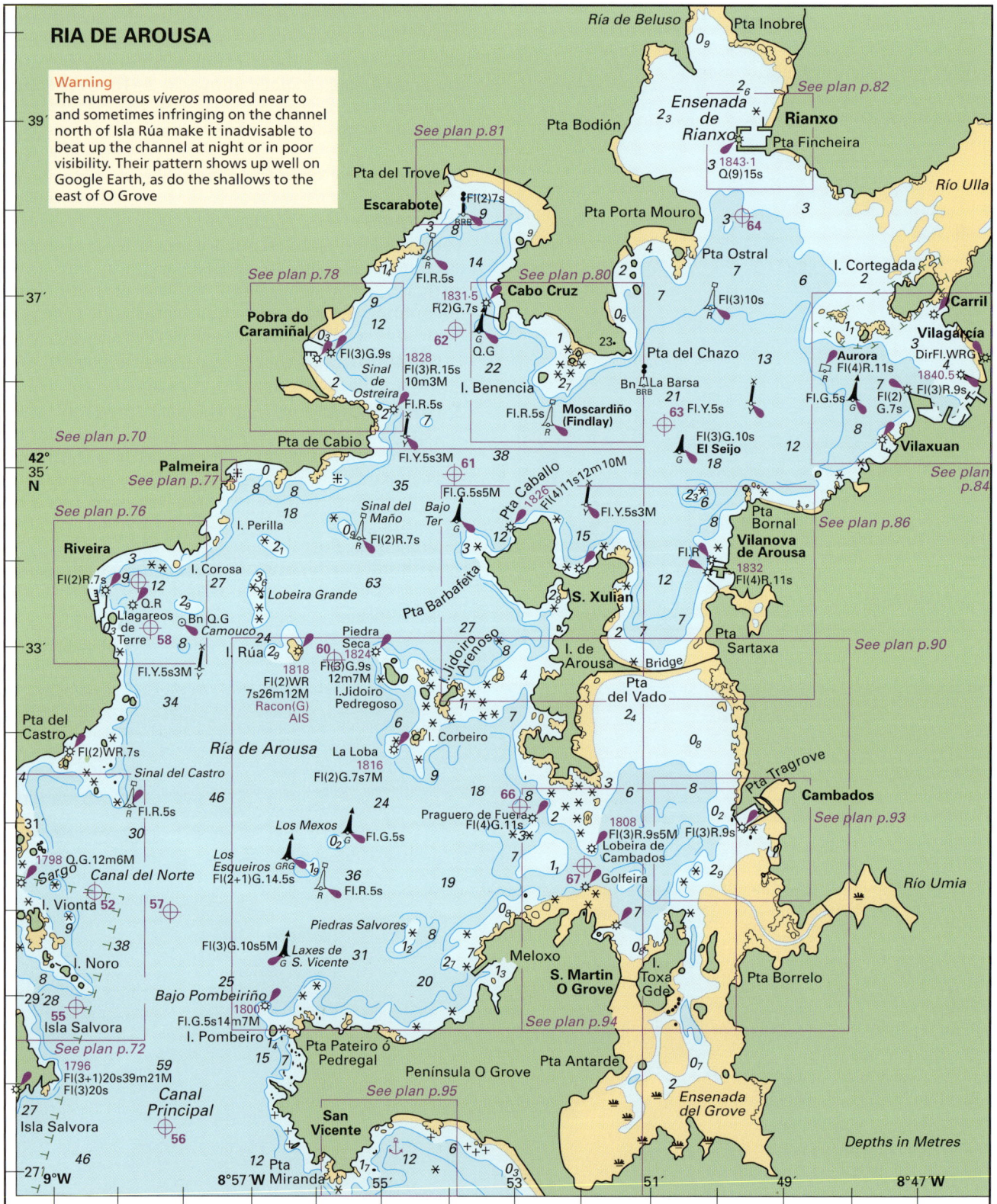

⊕52	42°30'·4N 08°59'·5W	0·3M E Piedras del Sargo
⊕56	42°27'·5N 08°58'·5W	Canal Principal Arousa
⊕57	42°30'N 08°58'W	1·5M NW Roca Pombeiriño
⊕60	42°32'·8N 08°55'·7W	0·5M ESE Isla Rúa
⊕61	42°35'N 08°54'W	1.0M WNW Pta Barbafeita
⊕62	42°36'·7N 08°54'W	0·5M W Puerto Cruz
⊕63	42°35'·5N 08°50'·9W	3M WSW Vilagarcía
⊕64	42°38'N 08°39'·5W	App Rianxo
⊕66	42°31'·2N 08°53'W	1·7M NW O Grove
⊕67	42°30'·5N 08°52'W	0·7M NNW O Grove
⊕70	42°27'N 08°54'·35W	App San Vicente

Lights
1796 **Isla Sálvora** Fl(3+1)20s39m21M White 8-sided tower, red band
1800 **Bajo Pombeiriño** FlG5s14m7M White truncated conical tower, green band
1798 **Piedras del Sargo** Q.G.12m6M White truncated conical tower, green band
1816 **Bajo La Loba** Fl(2)G 7s9m7M Green and White truncated conical tower.
1818 **Isla Rúa** Fl(2)WR7s12M. AIS Round masonry tower and dwelling
1824 **Bajo Piedra Seca** Fl(3)G.9s11m7M White truncated conical tower, green band
1826 **Punta del Caballo**, Isla Arosa Fl(4)11s12m10M 8-sided masonry tower, red and white dwelling
1828 **Bajo Sinal de Ostreira** FlR 5s9m5M Red and White truncated conical tower.

Ría de Arousa

Tides
Standard port Lisbon
Mean time differences (at Vilagarcía)
HW +0050 ±0015; LW +0115 ±0005
(the above allows for the difference in time zones)
Heights in metres

MHWS	MHWN	MLWN	MLWS
3·5	2·8	1·3	0·5

Charts

	Approach	Ría
Admiralty	3633, 1734	1768, 1764
Spanish	41B, 925, 926	415B, 415C, 9261, 9263
Imray	C48	C48

The largest Galician ría

The largest of the Galician rías and perhaps the most attractive for cruising, Ría de Arousa has many pleasant anchorages to explore and some interesting challenges in the way of pilotage. Not surprisingly it is also very popular with the Spanish, both afloat and on the many beaches. Food and other basics may be obtained in most of the small harbours on its shores, though the widest choice is undoubtedly to be had at Vilagarcía de Arousa, an otherwise unappealing town.

The variety of anchorages is such that shelter from any wind direction can be found relatively easily. The simplest harbours to enter in darkness are Santa Uxia de Riveira, Pobra do Caramiñal and Vilagarcía de Arousa – night approaches to other places would be easier with local knowledge, not least because of the dangers posed by unlit *viveros*, of which the Ría Arousa is particularly full.

In addition to the harbours detailed in the following pages, a number of nominal *puertos* exist, usually consisting of a short breakwater (sometimes lit) behind which small fishing vessels lie on moorings. Few can be approached by a keel yacht at all states of the tide. Similarly, not all the possible anchorages in this large ría can be described, though an attempt has been made to include those most popular.

All photos Martin Walker

Sta Uxia de Riveira (Ribeira)

42°33'·75N 08°59'·26W

Charts and tides
See ría page 75

Harbour chart
Admiralty 1755

Final approach ⊕
⊕59 42°33'·7N 08°59'W
App Sta Uxia de Riveira

Light
Marina breakwater beacon
Fl(2+1)G.15s3M GRG pillar
See plan for main harbour
lights

Communications
Club Náutico Deportivo de
Riveira
☎ +34 981 874 739 +34 648 187 170
Email secretaria@nauticoriveira.com
www.nauticoriveira.com
VHF Ch 09

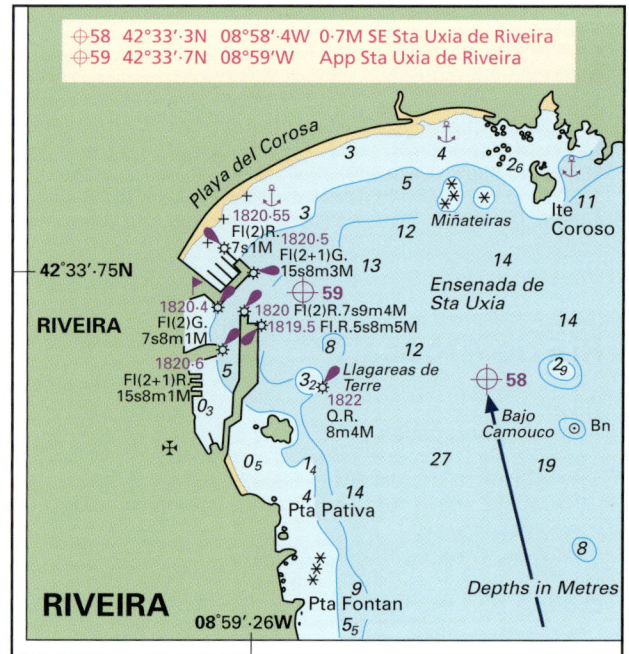

⊕58 42°33'·3N 08°58'·4W 0·7M SE Sta Uxia de Riveira
⊕59 42°33'·7N 08°59'W   App Sta Uxia de Riveira

Riveira with marina to the north of the main port

Small club marina next to large commercial harbour

The main harbour caters for coasters, fishing boats and small local boats. It is well marked and has a substantial breakwater. Yachts go to the marina immediately to the north which offers shelter.

Approach

Riveira lies in the bay to the west of the prominent Isla Rúa. Approach is straightforward via ⊕57, ⊕58, ⊕59. Head up the ría towards Isla Rúa until clear of Bajo Touza del Sur to the southeast of Castineira. As the bay opens, identify the harbour wall, and off-lying red topped tower of Llagareos de Terre Q.R, before closing the marina breakwater.

Berthing and anchorage

Visitors may be directed to lie bow to one of the inner pontoons in the northern part of the marina where depths are at least 5m. Boats of up to 16m can be accommodated. The outer pontoon is likely to be untenable in a northeaster.

Anchorage is possible off Playa del Corosa to the northeast of the marina in 3–5m over sand and mud.

Marina breakwater head with anchorage off beach beyond

Facilities

The on-site Club facilities are good. Fuel and technical support is available in the area, the Club is welcoming and has a pleasant restaurant. The marina is close to the large town with a wide choice of restaurants and all normal facilities. There is a good supermarket reasonably close by, plus a produce and fish market.

Anchorages to the northeast

1. **Northeast of Isolote Coroso**
   42°33′·95N 08°58′·05W
   In 3-4m over sand, surrounded by smooth, pinkish boulders. Approach only in good light. Use chart 1755.

2. **Ensenada de Palmeira** 42°34′·90N 08°57′·04W
   Use chart 1734 or 1764. There are isolated rocks shown in the east of part of the bay. Immediately west is the small village and harbour of Palmeira. It has little space and the shallow approach should be checked by dinghy before considering entering above half tide for minor provisions or a meal ashore. On the outer breakwater is one of a number of monuments seen on this coast to the many people who have emigrated from Galicia.

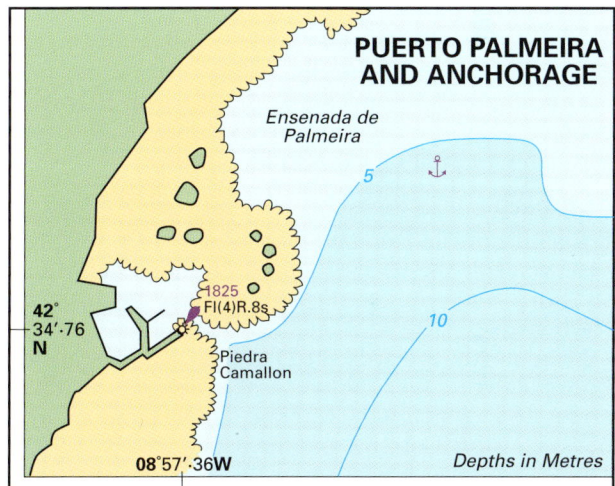

PUERTO PALMEIRA AND ANCHORAGE

Ensenada de Palmeira

5

10

42° 34′·76 N

1825
Fl(4)R.8s

Piedra Camallon

08°57′·36W

Depths in Metres

Palmeira outer harbour pontoon *Martin Walker*

Monument to emigrants pointing west, Palmeira
Martin Walker

A Pobra do Caramiñal

42°36'·25N 08°56'·00W

Charts and tides
See ría page 75
Harbour chart Admiralty 1755

Final approaches ⊕
⊕61 42°35'N 08°54'W
1·0M WNW Pta Barbafeita
⊕62 42°36'·7N 08°54'W
0·5M W Puerto Cruz

Lights
Harbour breakwater
Fl(3)G.9s9m5M White and green round tower
Marina mole head
Fl(2+1)R.12s3M White and red round tower (low red green red pillar at pontoon head)

Communications
Club Náutico do Caramiñal
☎ +34 981 832 504
Email info@cncaraminal.es
www.nauticocaraminal.es www.marinasdegalicia.com
VHF Ch 09

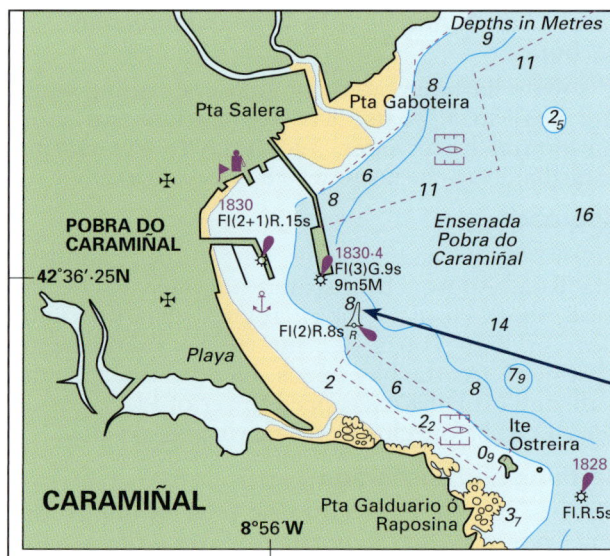

⊕61 42°35'N   08°54'W 1·0M WNW Pta Barbafeita
⊕62 42°36'·7N 08°54'W 0·5M W Puerto Cruz

Well-liked marina and a town with good restaurants

Yachtsmen welcome the substantial pontoons at Pobra (as it is known locally) which provides normal marina facilities alongside a useful town. It is well protected by the big ship breakwater from north through west, but exposed to the southeast.

Approach

From abeam Isla Rúa (⊕60) maintain 030° towards ⊕61 to clear the buoyed dangers of Sinal del Maño to port and the shallows off Isla Arousa to starboard.

Head north (towards ⊕62) until a clear passage to Pobra can be seen between the *viveros* heading about 285° which will clear the dangers and *viveros* between Islote Ostreira and the harbour.

Anchorage and berthing

Yachts may anchor off the beach clear of the marina entrance. If berthing has not been pre-arranged in the marina secure to a pontoon and check at the marina office at the top of the gangway.

Facilities

Marina facilities are good, and in August 2014 a fuel berth was about to be opened at the north of the harbour in the position shown on the Plan. The town offers all the normal facilities and there are now two excellent supermarkets (Gadis and Eroski) in the refurbished building overlooking the anchorage.

Alternative anchorage

Southeast of Pobra towards Islote Ostreira inside the *viveros* in 3–5m.

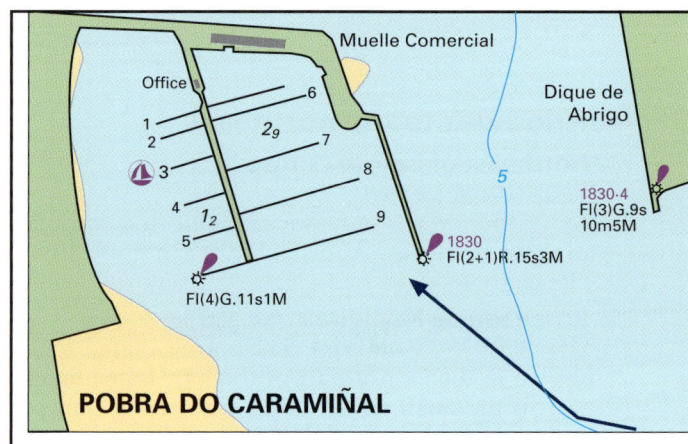

Yacht at anchor beyond marina entrance *Martin Walker*

Pobra do Caramiñal. Works yard, including travel-lift and chandlery, is on the northern quay

Marina from the outer breakwater across a mussel boat inbound from a day at the *viveros Martin Walker*

Puerto de Cruz

42°36'·89N 08°53'·43W

Charts and tides
See ría page 75

Final approach ⊕
⊕62 42°36'·7N 08°54'W
0·35M SW of the entrance

Light
Breakwater beacon
Fl(2)G.4s1M White and
green round tower

Communications
Club Nautico de Boiro -
Marina Cabo de Cruz
Ensenada de Corbiño S/N
Boiro - Cabo de Cruz 15939 A Coruña Spain
☎ +34 622 884 846
Email info@nauticoboiro.com
Web www.nauticoboiro.com
VHF Ch 09

A busy fishing harbour with a new (2013) marina

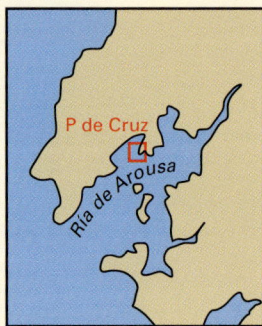

A fishing village in an attractive setting with new harbour moles enclosing a large harbour outside the existing one. A marina has been built in the northern part of this harbour. Entry to the harbour complex is from the west and note that Puerto de Cruz remains dedicated to the fishing industry.

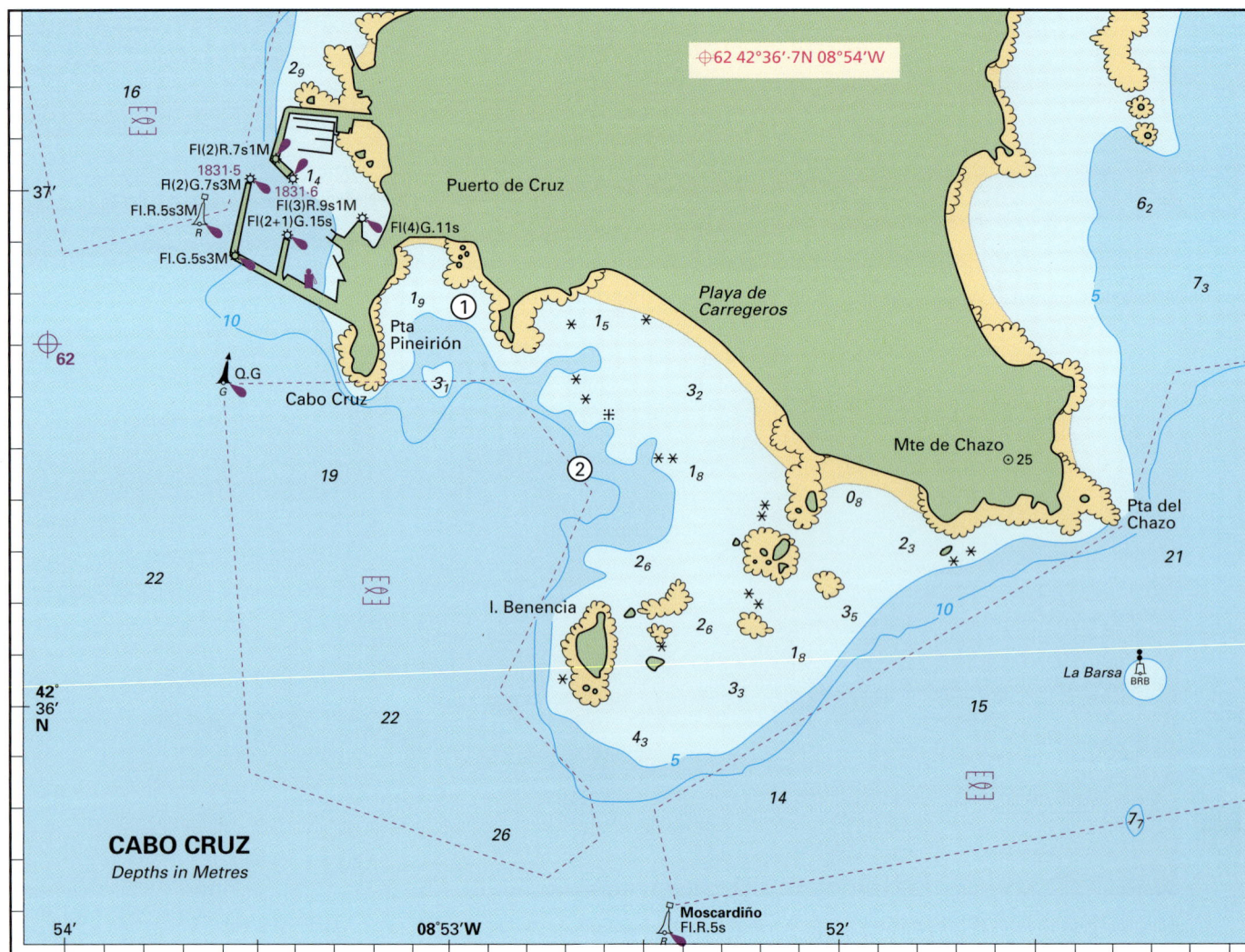

The harbour gives shelter from all winds while the open bays to the south provide shelter from west through north to east. The village depends on the cultivation and canning of mussels for its livelihood, and there are many *viveros* close offshore.

Approach

There is much foul ground to the southeast of Cabo Cruz, and the safe approach lies west of the distinctive humped Isla Benencia (about 0·7M southeast of Cabo Cruz), 16m high with a rocky ridge and a reef extending south-southwest from its southern tip.

Head north up the ría keeping west of Isla Benencia or make for the breakwater from ⊕62.

Caution

There is a wave breaker extending south from light 1831·6.

Berthing

200 berths, including 30 for visitors, from 6 to 22m. Depth in the marina 2m to 5m. Water and electricity on pontoons. Video surveillance service 24/7 and magnetic card access to the pontoons.

CABO CRUZ
Depths in Metres

Puerto de Cruz - the new marina is to port on entry

Facilities

Showers and WC, Laundry, Fuel, WiFi, Restaurant, Bicycle Rental

The village has a small supermarket, restaurants and a bank

Anchorages

Anchor north of the breakwater in mud as space allows but watch depths carefully.

Alternative anchorages

East of Cabo Cruz

1. **South Bay** 42°36'·74N 08°53'·05W

   Anchor in the centre of the bay clear of the fishing boat moorings in 5m over sand and weed, exposed to southeast round to southwest. There are rocks in the eastern part of the bay off Punta Pineirón.

2. **Playa de Carregeros** 42°36'·38N 08°52'·55

   Anchor in the angle between the southeast end of the beach and Isla Benencia with its associated reef, in 2–3m over sand. There is reasonable clearance between the island and an isolated half-tide rock to the northeast, but approach should only be made in flat conditions and good light. The reef (largely exposed at low tide) and the closely-packed *viveros* give some shelter from the south.

Northwest of Cabo Cruz

3. **Playa Barrana (Escarabote)** (see plan page 74 but use chart 1764)

   Holding is good in 3m over mud and sand. The bay is exposed from the southeast through to southwest. Escarabote offers a place to land; small yachts might anchor near the harbour mouth.

Escarabote   *Martin Walker*

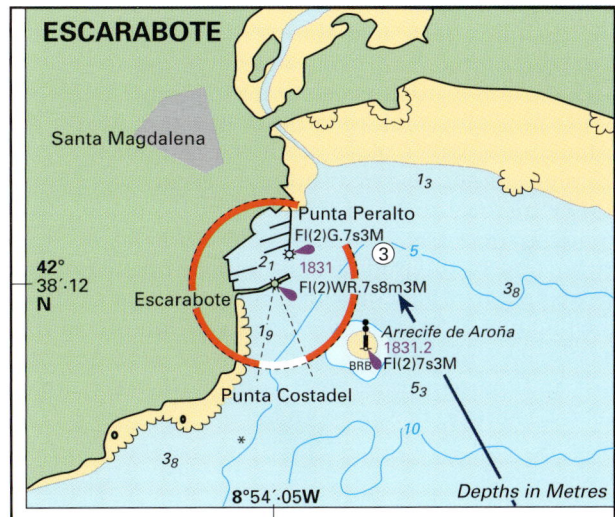

Rianxo (Rianjo)

42°39'·00N 08°49'·40W

Charts and tides
See ría page 75, and chart 1764

Final approaches ⊕
⊕64 42°38'N 08°49'·5W (0·7m south of harbour)

Lights
Breakwater elbow Q(9)15s3M ⌷ card bn
Entrance beacons Fl(3)G Green pillar
Fl(3)R.11s Metal post

Communications
Club Náutico de Rianxo
☏ +34 981 866 107
Mobile +34 609 833 433
Email info@nauticorianxo.com
www.nauticorianxo.com

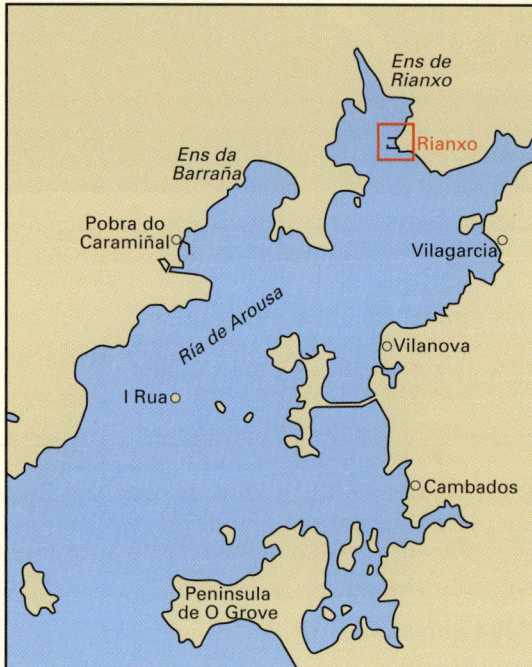

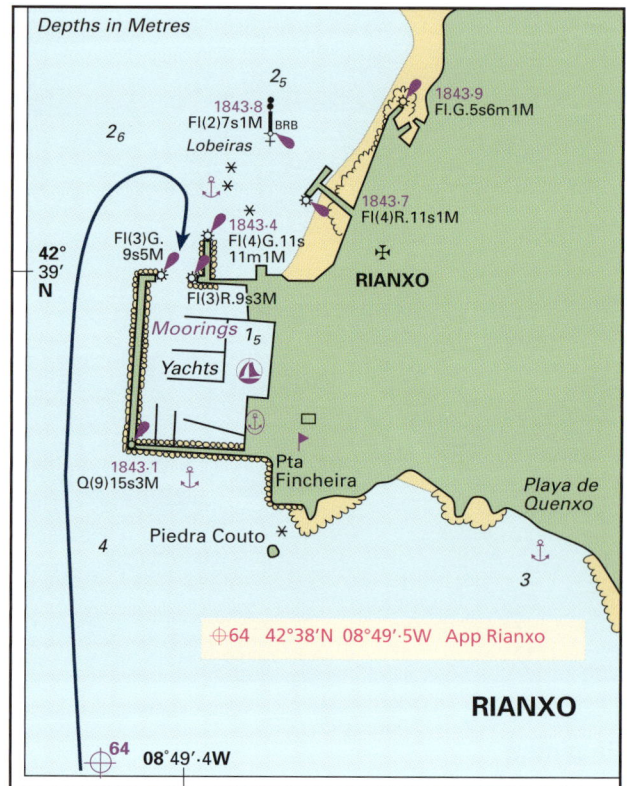

⊕64   42°38'N 08°49'·5W   App Rianxo

RIANXO

Approach

Come up the centre of the ría and continue past ⊕63 for 0·35M until ⊕64 (and Rianxo) bears 010° and a clear but watchful approach can be made through the mass of *viveros*. Head north 0·75M from ⊕64 and follow the mole around to the entrance on the north side. A west cardinal beacon is on the southwest corner of the harbour.

A protected fishing harbour with facilities for yachts

The majority of the harbour remains in active use by the fishing fleet but limited berthing may be available on the yacht pontoons.

A sardine festival is celebrated in June, while in September the week-long fiesta of Santa Maria de Guadaloupe takes place, with entertainment every evening culminating in an all-night event.

The historic town of Padrón lies 16km away by road. Called Iris Flavia by the Romans, it was important in the middle ages and still displays the stone post to which, legend claims, the boat bearing the remains of St James the Great was moored in the headwaters of the ría. The relics were subsequently lost and rediscovered before coming to rest at what is now Santiago de Compostela.

The pilgrims' symbol, the scallop shell of St James, is a ubiquitous image in Santiago and throughout the region
David Russell

Rianxo from the south

Berthing and anchorage

Proceed with care on entering harbour as many fishing boats lie to moorings and depths are reported to range from 4–2m. Secure to the marina pontoons and seek advice from the security box at the gangway to the pontoons.

Anchoring is not permitted in the harbour but is possible north of the entrance and west of the Lobeiras rocks.

Facilities

There is adequate technical and domestic support available within, or close to, the harbour and the small club is welcoming. The town offers all the normal facilities of a small town, including a good fish market.

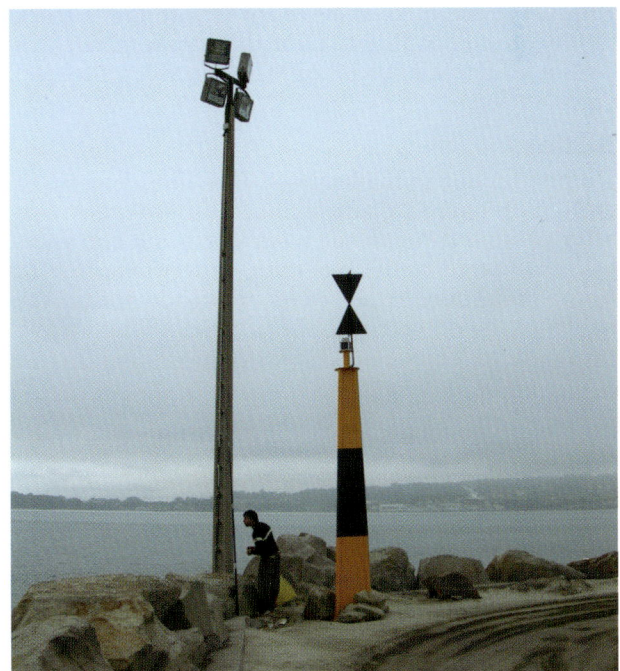

West cardinal beacon on breakwater southwest corner
Martin Walker

Vilagarcía
(Villagarcía de Arousa)

42°36'·04N 8°46'·20W

Tides
  See page 75
Charts
  Admiralty 1764, 1762
  Spanish   415C
  Imray   C48
Final approaches ⊕
  ⊕65 42°36'·2N 08°46'·6W
Lights
  1840.5 **Muelle head** Iso.2s2m10M Round masonry tower
  Marina entrance beacons 3-sided towers, red and green, flashing Q.R and Q.G
Communications
  Marina Vilagarcía
  ✆ +34 986 511 175
  Email marinavilagarcia@marinavilagarcia.com
  www.marinavilagarcia.com www.marinasdegalicia.com
  VHF Ch 09

An efficient and welcoming marina

Vilagarcía Marina is self-contained within the arms of the commercial port and is run pleasantly and efficiently by the port authority. The staff are particularly helpful and will arrange lift out, technical support and will also handle travel and hotel services. There is a pleasant Club de Mar on the outer mole. Yachts may safely be left here while visiting Santiago de Compostela or else laid up. Vilagarcía is a good place for crew change or re-provisioning.

Approach

Approach up the centre of the ría. From abeam Isla Rúa ⊕60, use ⊕61 and ⊕63 which follow a track of 030° from Isla Rúa to clear the northeast hazards of Isla de Arousa and then 075° between the vast *viveros* fields.

Berthing

Do not anchor in the harbour. Call ahead by radio and be prepared to turn immediately to starboard after passing through the narrow marina entrance. Unless ordered to the fuel jetty, expect to secure to finger pontoons (the outer pontoon near the entrance is reported to be untenable in strong northerly winds).

Facilities

Vilagarcía is a good marina with technical support facilities available, a 35-tonne travel lift and a fuel berth for diesel and petrol.
The modern office building includes a restaurant and showers. Weather forecasts are posted daily in the marina office.

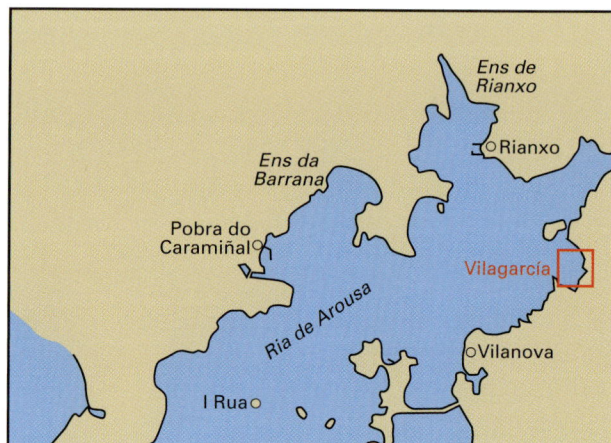

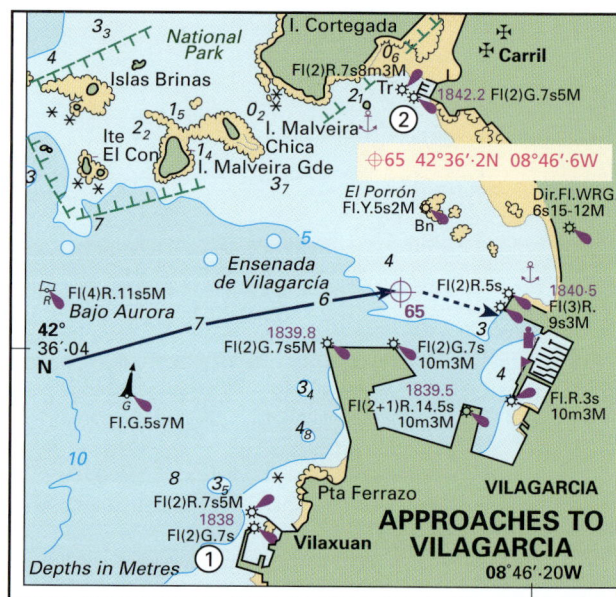

Vilagarcía marina *Martin Walker*

Entrance to Vilagarcía marina *Roddy Innes*

Approach to Vilagarcía Marina

Alternative anchorages

1. **Vilaxoan (Villajuan)** 42°35'·41N 08°47'·47W
   Small fishing harbour southwest of Vilagarcía. (See main air photo.) It may be possible to anchor in the shelter of the breakwater or moor alongside the inner quay.

2. **South of Carril** 42°36'·7N 08°46'·85W and the nearby Bahia de Tierra beacon (white tower red band) Approach from the southwest and keep clear of the El Porron beacon (yellow lattice metal tower). Keep well clear of the lines of stakes which mark the shell-fish beds. Most are covered at high tide. Their outer limits tend to be marked with a yellow beacon with an **x** topmark. Enter the harbour only by dinghy. Isla Cortegada, and the small islands to the southwest are a National Park (see page 15) and a permit is required before landing to walk around or across the island. There is an excellent, and expensive, fish restaurant close to the harbour.

Vilaxoan

Carril. Anchor and take the dinghy to harbour

Isla de Arousa

42°34'N 08°52'W

Tides
See page 75
Charts
Admiralty 1764, 1755
Final approaches ⊕
⊕61 42°35'N 08°54'W (1.0M WNW Pta Barbafeita)

Anchorages, good beaches, dense fishing activity

The Isla de Arousa comprises two islands connected by an isthmus on which the holiday and fishing village of San Xulian (San Julian) sits. It is connected to the mainland by the long El Vado bridge which is conspicuous from the north. The west coast has a number of islets and parts require very careful navigation. The northern approach is clear until closing the shore. The *viveros* are numerous, as are their support boats, but there are clear routes around and between them.

Isla de Arousa Anchorages

1. **Porto O Xufre (Ensenada Norte de San Xulian)** 42°34'·0N 08°52'·1W
   This is a friendly, bustling little harbour with a small boat marina and many moored fishing boats. Finding space to anchor (in sand / mud /

Port O Xufre and fuel jetty (Anchorage 1) *Martin Walker*

stones) will be difficult. Enquire for a fisherman's mooring; those without pickup lines are generally not in use. Fuel is available on the jetty where sports boats, fishing boats and cars squeeze in as best they can. Good supermarket south of the pier.

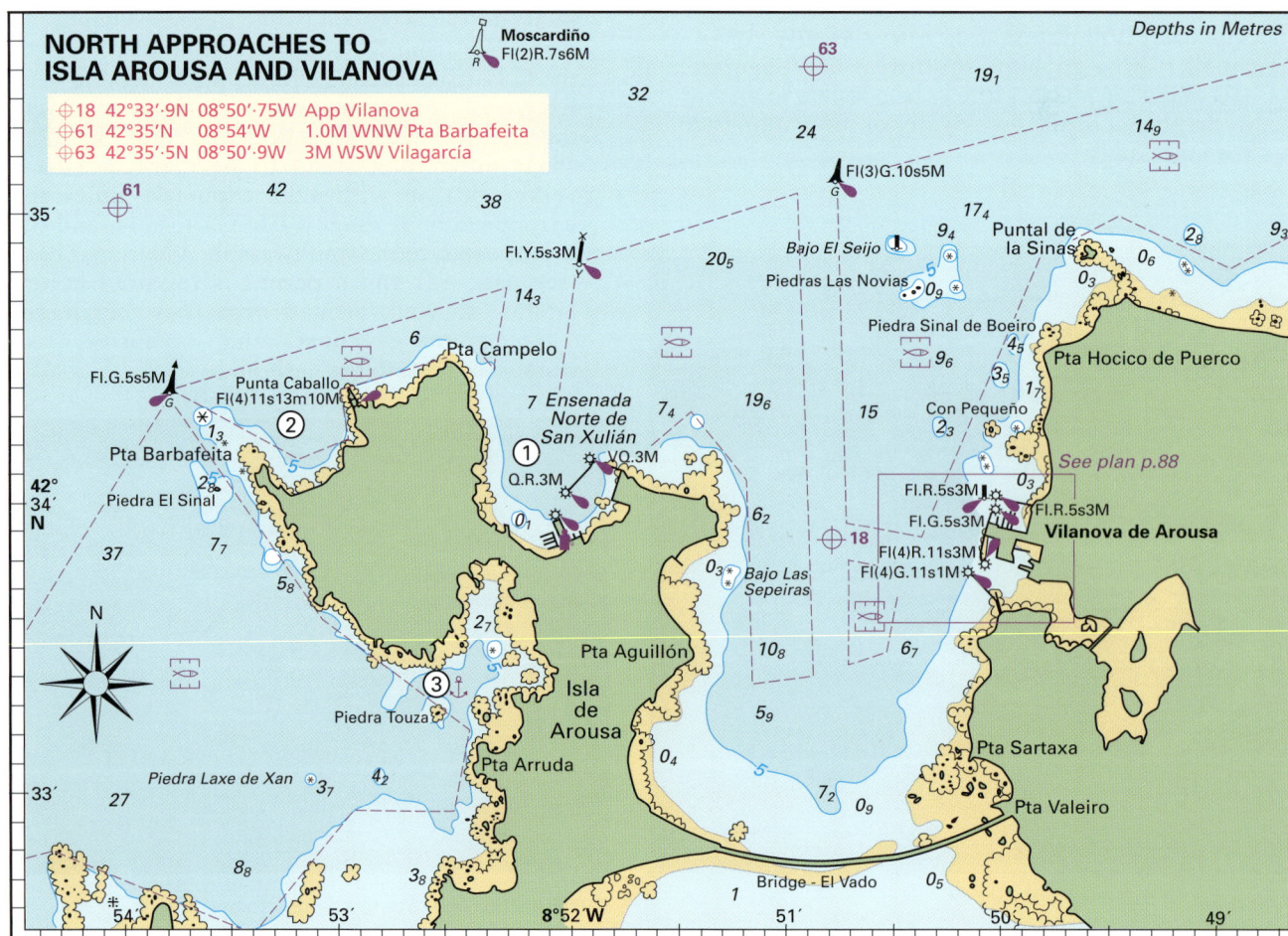

NORTH APPROACHES TO ISLA AROUSA AND VILANOVA

Depths in Metres

⊕18 42°33'·9N 08°50'·75W App Vilanova
⊕61 42°35'N 08°54'W 1.0M WNW Pta Barbafeita
⊕63 42°35'·5N 08°50'·9W 3M WSW Vilagarcía

Pta Caballo lighthouse is set back from giant granite rocks. Anchor in the bay beyond (Anchorage 2) *Martin Walker*

Seek space to anchor beyond moorings (Anchorage 3) *Martin Walker*

2. Southwest of Pta Caballo off the beach

42°34'·15N 08°53'·22W

A long sandy beach generally clear of the fishing fleet. Approach from the north to anchor in 5–10m clear of the shoreline rocks.

3. Ensenada Sur de San Xulian

42°33'·38N 08°52'·56W

A small harbour, guarded by rocks and filled with small boats. Under good light one might work in and find space before the moorings to anchor. This is a quiet harbour with shoreside restaurants and calm compared to the main port just the other-side of the isthmus to the north. There is good shelter except from the southwest. The church carillon of bells ring *Ave Maria* at midday.

Looking east from San Xulian with Anchorages 1 and 3 left and right of the isthmus. The route through the *viveros* to Vilanova – central on the far shore – can be seen. Vilagarcía is at top left

Vilanova Marina

42°33′·97N 08°50′·04W

Tides
See page 75

Charts
Admiralty 1764, 1755
Spanish 415C
Imray C48

Final approach ⊕
⊕18 42°33′·9N 08°50′·75W (0·5m west of entrance)

Harbour entrance
Mole heads carry green and white and red and white pillars and lights.

Communications
☎ +34 666 536 411
www.marinaarousa.es

Ens de Rianxo
Rianxo
Ría de Arousa
Ens de Vilagarcía
Vilanova

A pleasant modern marina

This is a welcoming marina and has received praise for its helpful attitude and facilities. Known as El Puerto Deportivo de Vilanova de Arousa it is the northern part of the Marina Arousa harbour.

Vilanova

Approaches to Vilanova

Follow the centre of the ría as if for Vilagarcía (⊕60, ⊕61, ⊕63) and at ⊕63, north of El Seijo green buoy, turn south and follow the passage 1·5M through the *viveros* until ⊕18, when Vilanova bears east.

Berthing

Visitors' berths for up to 16m yachts are on finger pontoons on the west outer end of the centre pontoon. Larger yachts up to 20m use the three hammerheads. There is water and electricity on the pontoons.

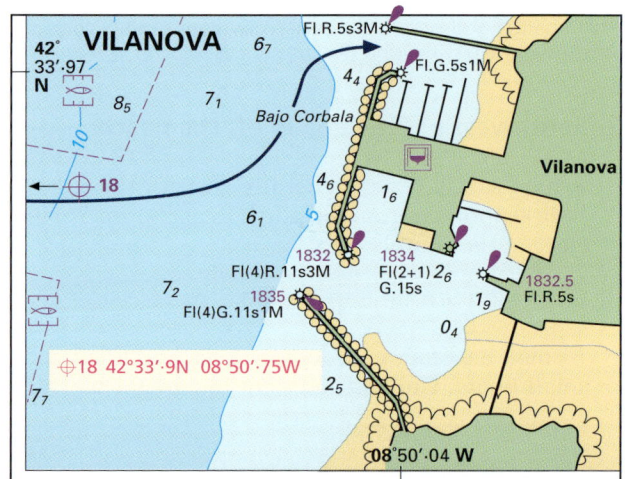

VILANOVA
Bajo Corbala
Fl.R.5s3M
Fl.G.5s1M
Vilanova
⊕18 42°33′·9N 08°50′·75W
1832 Fl(4)R.11s3M
1834 Fl(2+1) G.15s
1835 Fl(4)G.11s1M
1832.5 Fl.R.5s
08°50′·04 W

Facilities

A travel-lift (35 tonne) and large lay-up ashore area is available. A fuelling berth is not available.

The marina has a well-stocked chandlery, and engineering and electrical work can be undertaken.

There is a small restaurant on site and good shopping facilities in town, a Friday market and a bus service to Vilagarcia.

Santiago de Compostela

Since the discovery of the tomb of St James at the beginning of the 9th century, Santiago de Compostela has been the focus for thousands of pilgrims as one of the greatest shrines in Christianity. No lesser numbers come today, many on foot following the old medieval routes, and thousands by air. Web search 'Pilgrim routes Santiago de Compostela' for a wealth of information.

The cathedral is magnificent and the old city built of local granite glistens in the rain. It is compact and can be explored in a few hours. Those looking for accommodation can stay in style at the Hostal de los Reyes Catolics, now a Parador Hotel.

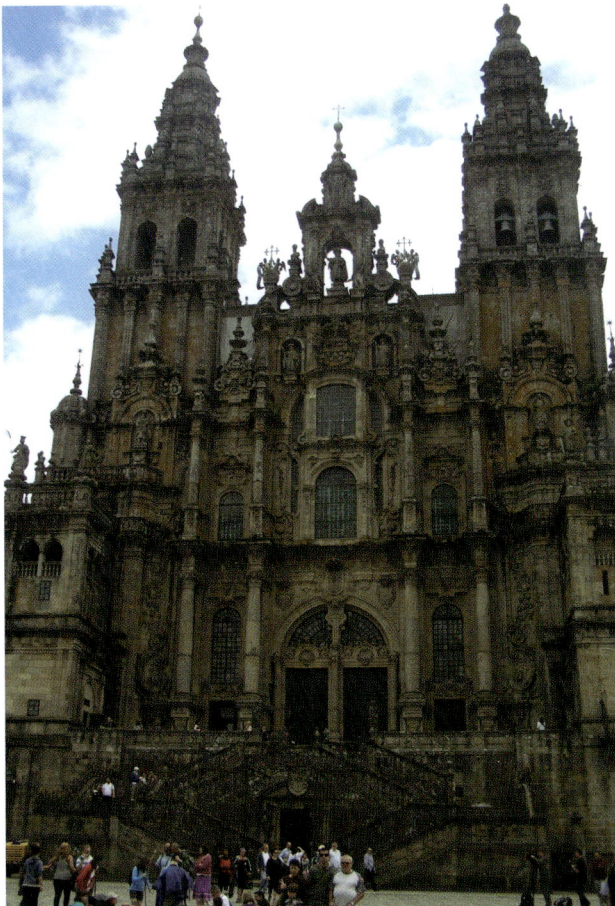

The fiesta of St James (celebrated throughout the province as Galicia Day) takes place on 25th July with associated cultural events for a week or so on either side. When this date falls on a Sunday the entire year is declared a 'Holy Year' and the fiesta celebrated with even greater enthusiasm. A visit to the basilica on holy days, when the huge incense burner is swung over the crowd by eight priests, is not to be missed.

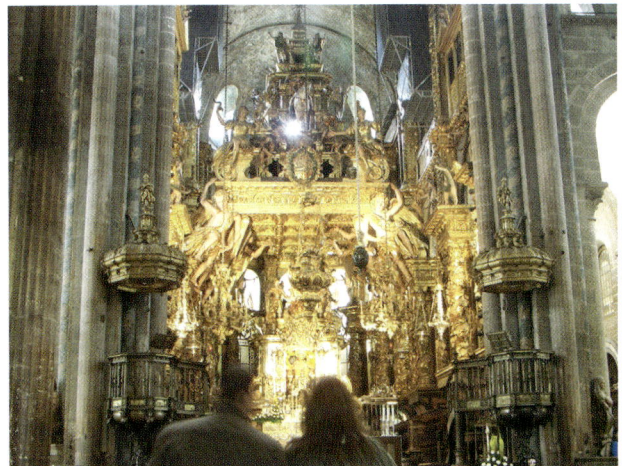

Pilgrims queue to pass through the ornate golden baldachin where they can kiss the mantle of St James *David Russell*

The enormous edifice of the cathedral of Santiago de Compostela *David Russell*

Martin Walker

GALICIA

The approach to O Grove, Cambados and Toxa anchorages

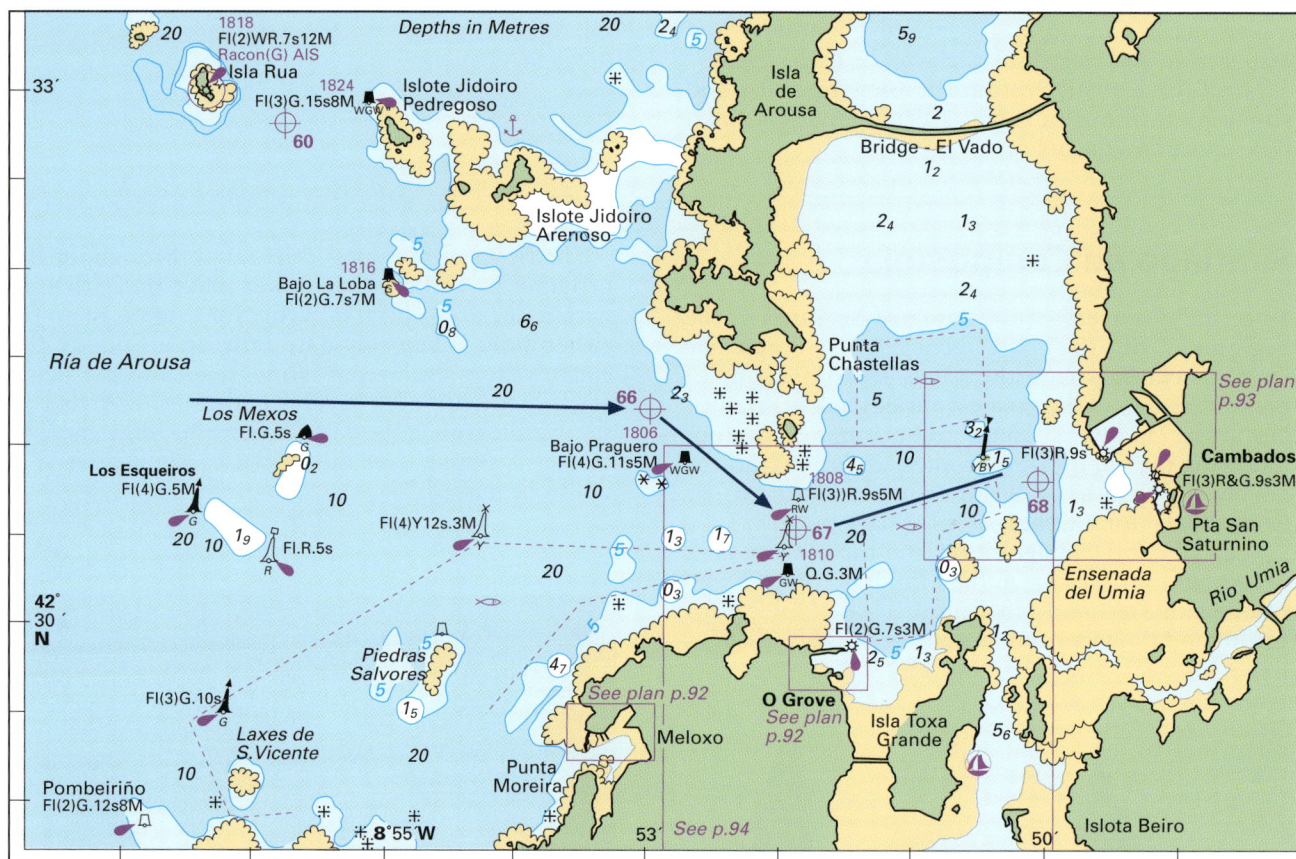

Depths in Metres

1818
Fl(2)WR.7s12M
Racon(G) AIS
Isla Rua
1824
Fl(3)G.15s8M
Islote Jidoiro Pedregoso
60

Islote Jidoiro Arenoso

1816
Bajo La Loba
Fl(2)G.7s7M

Ría de Arousa

Los Mexos
Fl.G.5s

Los Esqueiros
Fl(4)G.5M

Fl.R.5s

Fl(4)Y12s.3M

66

1806
Bajo Praguero
Fl(4)G.11s5M

WGW

1808
Fl(3)R.9s5M
RW
67

1810
Q.G.3M
GW

68

Isla de Arousa

Bridge - El Vado

Punta Chastellas

Cambados
Fl(3)R&G.9s3M

Pta San Saturnino

Ensenada del Umia

Rio Umia

See plan p.93

Fl(3)R.9s

42°
30′
N

Piedras Salvores

Fl(3)G.10s

Laxes de S.Vicente

Pombeiriño
Fl(2)G.12s8M

Punta Moreira

See plan p.92

Meloxo

O Grove
See plan p.92

Fl(2)G.7s3M

Isla Toxa Grande

Islota Beiro

See p.94

8°55′W

⊕60	42°32′·8N	08°55′·7W	0·5M ESE Isla Rúa
⊕66	42°31′·2N	08°53′W	1·7M NW O Grove
⊕67	42°30′·5N	08°52′W	0·7M NNW O Grove
⊕68	42°30′·9N	08°50′·0W	Ensenada de Cambados

Lights
1816 **Bajo La Loba** Fl(2)G.7s9m7M Grey truncated conical tower, green top

1806 **Bajo Praguero** Fl(4)G.11s9m5M White truncated conical tower, green band

1808 **Bajo Lobeira de Cambados**, Fl(3)R.9s10m5M White truncated conical tower, red top

1810 **Bajo Golfeira** Q.G.10m3M White truncated conical tower, green top

Location
Centred on 42°30′·5N 08°51′·2W

Tides
See page 75

Charts
Admiralty   1764, 1755
Spanish   4152
Imray   C48

Approach
⊕66 42°31′·2N 08°53′W 1·7M NW O Grove
⊕67 42°30′·5N 08°52′W 0·7M NNW O Grove
⊕68 42°30′·9N 08°50′·0W Ensenada de Cambados

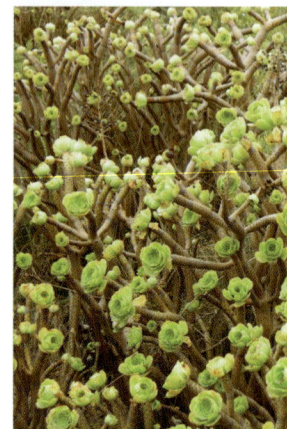

A chance to stray from the beaten track

O Grove is popular with tourists in season and numerous tripper boats operate from here.

Cambados is a sophisticated old town with limited mooring facilities for yachtsmen.

Toxa (Isla Toxa Grande) is for the smart set and offers pleasant anchorages.

Approach

The area north of the Peninsula de O Grove and approaching Cambados has numerous shallows, rocks and fields of *viveros*. Although it is well marked, the repetitive nature of the area means it is important for navigators to absorb the key features and maintain a plot. Newcomers may find waypoint navigation, whilst monitoring the physical marks, of benefit.

Leave the centre of the ría south of Isla Rúa, heading east for ⊕66 and passing around midway between La Loba in the north and Los Mexos in the south. Both are clearly marked dangers. Note plan on page 90 and use chart 1764. From ⊕66 (use chart 1755) track 132°/1M to ⊕67, leaving the beacons of Bajo Praguero to starboard and Lobeira de Cambos to port.

For O Grove Maintain a broad heading southeast, to leave Viveros yellow buoy to starboard, and then run down the line of *viveros* to O Grove harbour.

For Cambados Track between *viveros* on about 075°/1·5M to ⊕68.

For the Toxa anchorages head almost to Cambados before working south through the shallows.

Local boats use a route westwards through the *viveros* from north of Golfeira beacon (light 1810), passing north or south of Piedras Salvores.

Alternative anchorage

The large bay to the north between Isla de Arousa and the mainland shoals gradually towards the shores and the bridge. It has fine beaches. Anchor in 2–4m.

Looking east over O Grove with Isla Toxa Grande middle right (anchorages beyond) and Cambados at top

GALICIA

Puerto O Grove (San Martin del Grove)

(See photo page 91)
42°29'·88N 08°51'·52W

Tides
See page 75

Charts
Admiralty   1764, 1755
Spanish   415C
Imray   C48

Final approaches ⊕
⊕67 42°30'·5N 08°52'W

Light
Breakwater Fl(2)G.7s Green round tower

A shallow fishing and tripper boat harbour

O Grove is a major holiday resort and the shallow fishing harbour has been developed for fast tripper boats to visit the offlying islands.

Approach

Route around *viveros* fields from the north, from ⊕67 between the beacons of Lobeira de Cambados and Golfeira (see pages 94). Do not cut the corner, rocks protrude well beyond the line between Golfeira and the harbour.

Mooring and anchorage

There is a small pontoon within the harbour or berth alongside the north breakwater. There is little room for shallow-draught boats to anchor in the harbour itself, and very limited space outside as the water shoals rapidly immediately south of the harbour. Pick up a mooring buoy outside the harbour but do not leave the boat unattended for long.

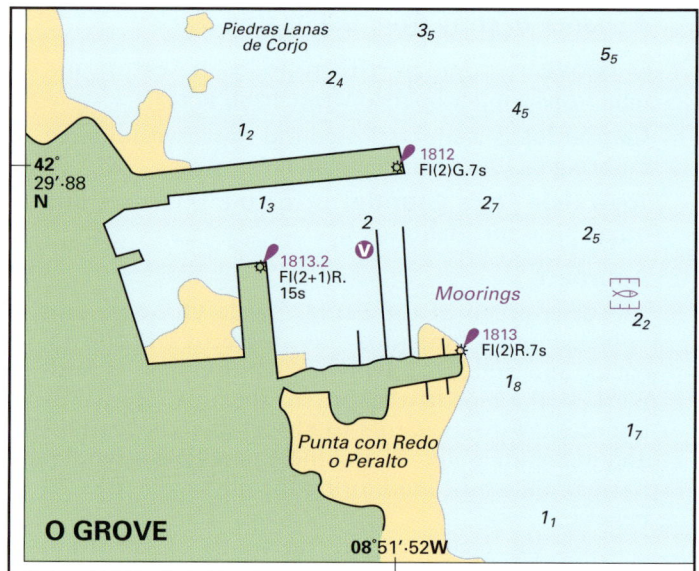

Facilities

Water on the quay, usual shops and many restaurants. A seafood festival takes place at O Grove on 14 September.

Alternative anchorage

Porto de Meloxo (Melojo) 42°29'·32N 08°53'·51W (Breakwater end with red light) is a fishing harbour on the northwest of the peninsula and exposed to the west. The harbour is full of fishing boats on moorings. One might negotiate to borrow a mooring or anchor outside, although the harbour and the small village appears to have little to offer the yachtsman.

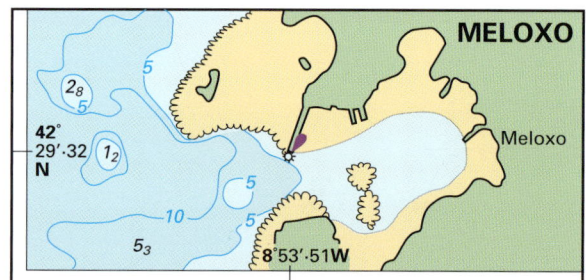

Meloxo is devoted to the fishing fleet *Martin Walker*

Cambados (Puerto de Tragove and Cambados old harbour)

(See also plan page 82)
42°30'·91N 08°49'·58W

Tides
See page 75

Charts
Admiralty 1764, 1755
Spanish   415C
Imray   C48

Final approaches ⊕
⊕68 42°30'·9N 08°50'·0W Ensenada de Cambados

Light
Breakwater Fl(3)G.9s Green round tower

Fuel
Old harbour

Attractive old town, shallow harbours

The modern harbour (Puerto de Tragove) is large but shallow and supports the major mussel industry. The old harbour (Cambados-San Tome) is small and shallow but has fuel.

Cambados is a small town with an attractive and historic central square and imposing buildings. It is the home of *O Albariño*, considered by many to be Galicia's best wine. A *sardiñada* (sardine festival) is held on 25 July (Galicia Day) and a wine festival on the first Sunday in August.

Approach

See page 90.

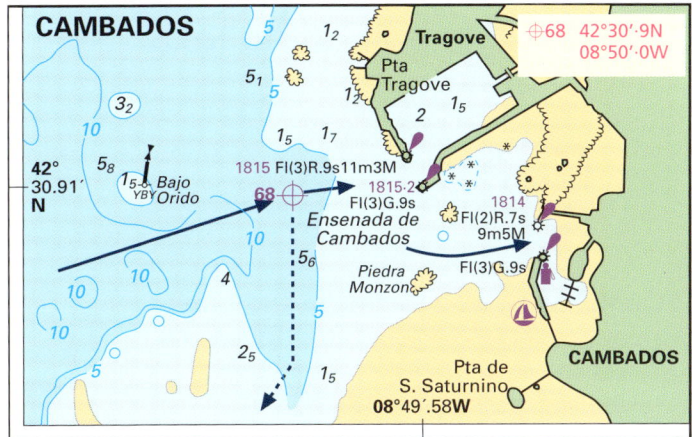

Anchorage and berthing

Main Harbour (Tragove Marina) The harbour shallows rapidly from the major fishing boat pontoon. Only the outer sides of the yacht pontoon should be considered; inside is very rocky. Lying to anchor, facing the harbour mouth, with stern to the pontoon offers greatest depth. Anchoring may be possible behind the fishing boats depending on the random moorings and the busy boat traffic.

Old Harbour (Cambados Marina) This is small, attractive, well placed for the town and claims depths of 2·3m – significantly more than charted. Approach and enter with caution, and check at the fuel dock for mooring opportunities on wall or pontoon. Boats which take the ground may find space beyond the pontoons.

GALICIA

Cambados harbours from the west

Anchorages east of Isla Toxa (Toja) Grande

(Use chart 1755)

Warning
Silting has been reported in the approaches to the anchorages

Careful navigation leading to anchorages

Toxa is a smart, well groomed island. The bridge access to the west crosses over drying sands; the anchorages all lie to the east.

Approach

The routes cross sandbanks and should only be made on a rising tide.

From the main channel north of O Grove (shallow-draught vessels) From ⊕67 head on a bearing of about 108° to cross the bank north of Toxa at least 100m offshore; turn to 175° when deep water is reached. On no account attempt to pass inside the rock off Pta Cabreiron.

From off Cambados From Orido buoy head for the middle of the gap between Toxa Grande and Toxa Pequeña on 175°.

From ⊕68 (the 'normal, deeper route'). Head south from ⊕68 on westing 08°50' until on a line of 210° Cambados main harbour entrance and Punta Cabreiron, and then onto 175° shortly before reaching Punta Cabreiron.

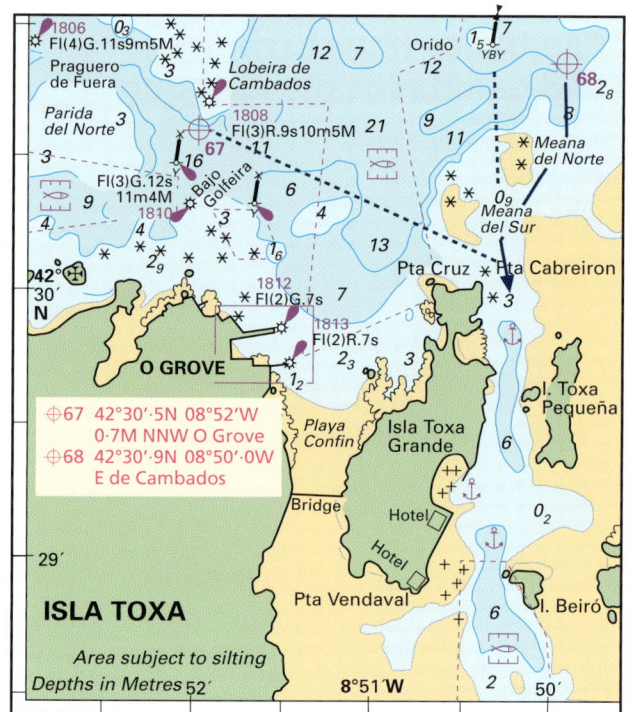

Anchorages (and berthing)

See plan, eyeball to avoid shallows and kelp; anchor in 3–5m over sand.

Occasionally space may be available on Marina Isla da Toja jetty ☎ +34 616 954 252.

Anchorages of Isla Grande Toxa – O Grove at top left

San Vicente del Mar
(Porto Pedras Negras)

42°27'·47N 08°55'·06W

Charts and tides
See ría page 75

Final approaches ⊕
⊕70 42°27'N
08°54·35'W
(0·7M southwest of
harbour)

Lights
Breakwater beacon
Fl(4)WR.11s5m4/3M
Red post
Approach buoys
Fl(2)G.9s Green buoy
Fl(3)R.9s Red buoy

Communications
☎ Office
+34 986 738 325
Marineros +34 986 738 430
Email administracion@cnsvicente.org
www.cnsvicente.org
VHF Ch 09

Facilities
Good on-site, including club restaurant

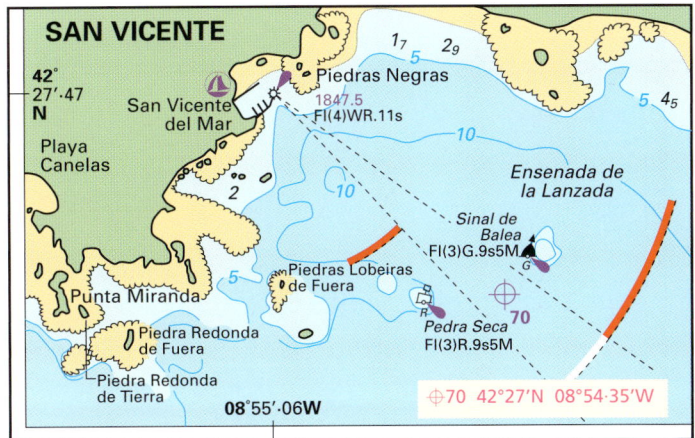

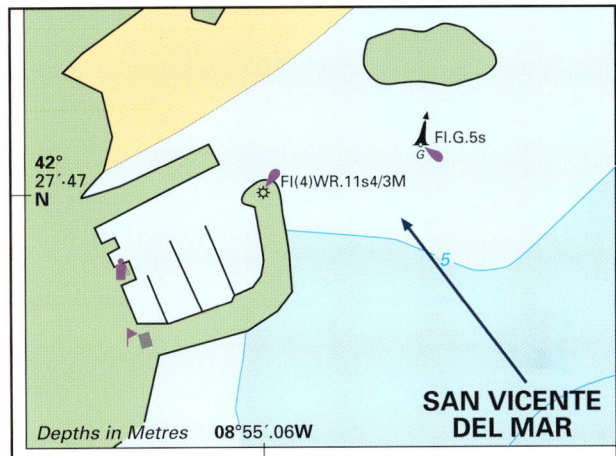

A small, smart marina with good facilities

There is little outside the marina except houses, hotels and a small supermarket. This is a place to relax, enjoy the stunning walk to Pta Miranda or visit the beach.

Approach

If coming from Ría de Arousa keep clear outside the *viveros* of the northwest shores of Peninsula de O Grove and the Roca Pombeirino beacon. Keep at least 800m offshore rounding the complete headland before heading towards the long sandy beach La Lanzada and ⊕70. This is in the white sector of the breakwater light and between the red and green buoys. Then head direct to harbour.

San Vicente from the south

Berthing and anchoring

There are 134 berths, 10 reserved for visitors for boats 6-12m in 4m depth.
The pontoons are very small for a 12m yacht, otherwise anchor off the beach as close to the rocks as you dare.

Facilities

Electricity and Water on the pontoons. Fuel available, good showers, a small bread shop and supermarket. WiFi - ask at the Yacht Club.
The Board Walk going north is a must with many cafes and restaurants plus the benefit of coves and sandy beaches.

GALICIA

Lights
1796 **Isla Sálvora**
Fl(3+1)20s39m21M
White 8-sided
tower, red band
1847.3 **Isla Ons**
Fl(4)24s126m25M
8-sided white
tower on corner of
building
1884 **Monte del Faro**
Fl(2)8s185m22M
Tower and dwelling
1916 **Cabo Silleiro**
Fl(2+1)15s83m24M
White 8-sided
tower, red bands
on white dwelling

Pobra do
Caramiñal

45
52
2.8
10
35' 13
52
Corrubedo
Cabo Corrubedo
1794
Fl(2+3)WR.20s
31m15M
Racon AIS
Playa Ferreira
32
Vilanova
31
Sta
Uxia
de
Riveira
29
36
Ba de
Corrubedo
1₇
C de Sagres
30
Aguiño
Isla Rúa
I. de Arousa
8
2
Ría
de
62
Arousa
Cambados
Pta
Falcoeiro
76
Banco de
Praqueiro
1795·5
Fl.5s
24m8M
9
25
29
8
Canal del Norte
12
5
58
26
7
50
15
O₂
1₈
O
Grove
Bajo
Pombeiriño
1800
Fl.G.5s
14m7M
29
10
National
Park
Isla Sálvora
1796
Fl(3+1)+Fl(3)20s
40m21M
AIS
49
40
8
Península de
O Grove
San
Vicente
8
15
15

47

99
43
16
8
See p.70
69
O₃
Canal Principal
See p.74

Combarro
25'
72
12
Pta Fagilda
I. Tambo
10
71
64
3
3₉
14
1847.3
Fl(4)24s126m25M
AIS
Porto
Novo
Sanxenxo
Marin
See p.104
100
See p.52
35
4
Isla Ons
13
9
41
Pta
Cabicastro
17
Aguete
National
Park
6
44
17
Ría de Pontevedra
98
4
42°
20'
N
Pan de
Centena
See p.97
3
8
11
3
8
50
42
15
Beluso
9
74
15
Bueu
Boca del Sudoeste
1873
Fl(3)WG.10·5s
18m10/8M
Pta Couso
8
Ría
de
Aldan
Península
de
Morrazo
See p.98
See p.112
70
27
See plan
p.109
28
2₇
80
Cangas
8
10
73
125
C. del Home
1876
Fl.3s
36m9M
81
35
Ría de Vigo
28
15'
National
Park
12
24
9
16
26
3
VIGO
8
Islas Cíes
15
RIA DE AROUSA
TO BAIONA
N
Monte del Faro
1884
Fl(2)8s186m22M
AIS
43
I. de S. Martín
C. Vicos
1888 Fl(3)R.9s93m10M
38
Cabo Estay
1890·1
Rear Oc.4s48m18M
2₈
1₁
140
1889
Fl(2)R.8s22m5M
I. Boeiro Sur
1890
Front Iso.2s16m18M
Horn Mo(V)60s
Racon Mo(B)
93
Castrol de
Agoeiro
4
Canal del Norte
Canal   del   Sur
50
88
6₃
20
5
10'
89
069°
12
1907
Fl.G.4s
9m5M
Mte Ferro
10
61
91
Las
Seralleiras
40
94
1916
Fl(2+1)15s83m24M
Siren Mo(S)30s
BAIONA
Depths in Metres
5'
120
9°W
95
C. Silleiro
55'
50'
See plan
p.122
45'

⊕47 42°30′N 09°10′W 9M WSW Cabo Corrubedo
⊕71 42°23′N 09°07′W 7M SW Isla Sálvora
⊕73 42°17′N 09°00′W Outer App Ría de Pontevedra
⊕87 42°17′·3N 08°39′·7W Vigo high bridge (de rande)

I.3.1 Isla Ons, Ría de Pontevedra to Islas Cies

Isla Ons

See pages 15–17
42°22'·62N 08°55'·77W

Charts
Admiralty 1732, 1734
Spanish   416A
Imray   C48

Communications
See Notes on National Parks' Permits p.15

National Park, limited anchorages

Visiting yachts require a permit to visit, anchor or dive around Isla Ons – see page 15 – National Parks' Permits.

Isla Ons helps protect the Ría de Pontevedra from westerly seas and winds. It is a rugged and attractive island with few permanent inhabitants. It is much visited by campers in the summer, tripper boats from Ría de Arousa and Ría de Pontevedra, and regular ferries from Porto Novo, Sanxenxo and Marin. All land at Almacén. Shelter is limited on the east coast which offers the only normal anchorages. Landing is forbidden on the small southern island of Onza (Onceta) which is a bird sanctuary.

Approach

See Ría de Pontevedra page 96 and close the island from the east.

Anchorages

Anchorages should be vacated if the wind gains an easterly component

1. **Almacén** 42°22'·62N 08°55'·77W
   The mole at Almacén is not a good place to lie. There is little room and frequent ferries. Visitors' buoys may be positioned either side of the mole head. If picking up a blue buoy and requiring a lift ashore ☎ Hostal Casa Checho +34 629 71 81 04 or +34 639 56 35 72. This is the first restaurant on the left when stepping ashore. At the head of the slip is a tourist office and 500m beyond a first aid station. There is a campsite at Almacén.
   Reefs extend north and south of the entrance but it is possible to anchor east-northeast of the mole head in 12m or more over rock and weed.

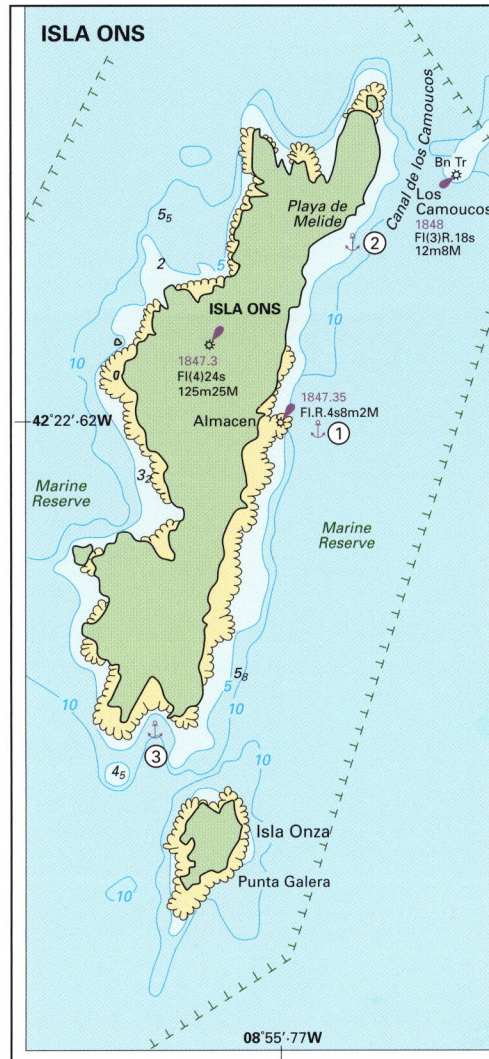

ISLA ONS

2. **Playa de Melide** 42°23'·33N 08°55'·43W
   The beach is about 1M north of Almacén mole. Anchor in 4m over sand, rock and weed. The anchorage is sheltered from north through west to southwest. The beach is favoured by nudists.
3. **Southern Bay** 42°21'·23N 08°56'·47W
   A short stay possibility in a light northerly is the small bay between Punta Fedoranto and Punta Rab d'Egua on the south coast.

Anchored off Southern Bay (anchorage 3)

GALICIA

RIA DE PONTEVEDRA

COMBARRO

MARIN

See p.104

Cabezo de la Mourisca

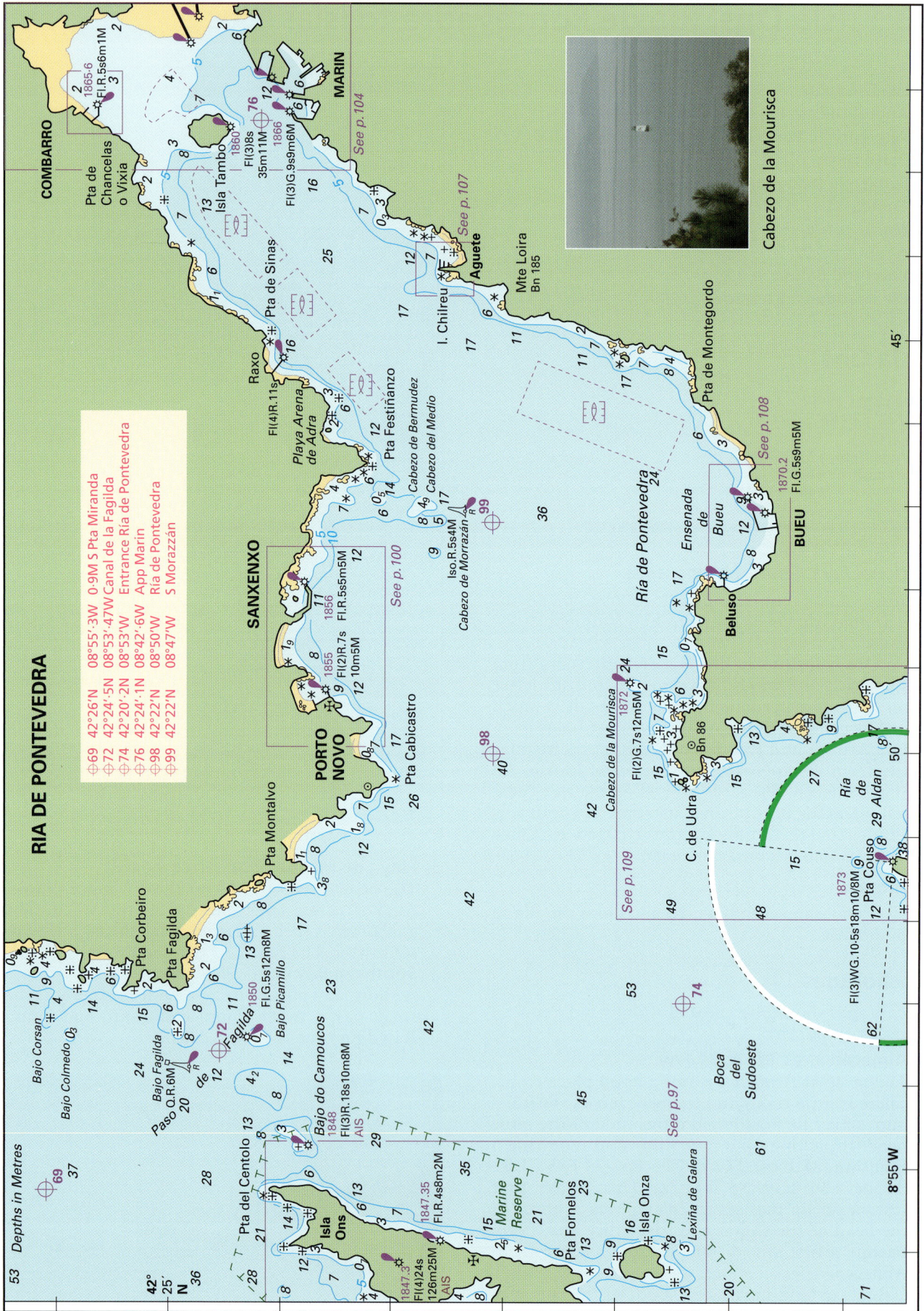

Pta de
Chancelas
o Vixia

1865.6
Fl.R.5s6m1M
3
2

Isla Tambo
1860
Fl(3)8s
35m11M
1866
Fl(3)G.9s9m6M

76

See p.107

Aguete

Mte Loira
Bn 185

I. Chilreu

Pta de Montegordo

Pta de Sinas

Raxo

Playa Arena
de Adra

Fl(4)R.11s

Pta Festiñanzo

Cabezo de Bermudez
Cabezo del Medio

See p.100

Cabezo de Morrazán

Iso.R.5s4M

99

See p.108

1870.2
Fl.G.5s9m5M

BUEU

Ensenada
de
Bueu

Ría de Pontevedra

Beluso

SANXENXO

1856
Fl.R.5s5m5M

1855
Fl(2)R.7s
10m5M

PORTO
NOVO

Pta Cabicastro

98

Cabezo de la Mourisca
1872
Fl(2)G.7s12m5M
Bn 86

See p.109

C. de Udra

1873
Fl(3)WG.10-5s18m10/8M
Pta Couso

Ría
de
Aldan

Pta Montalvo

Pta Corbeiro

Pta Fagilda

Pta Picamillo
1850
Fl.G.5s12m8M

Bajo Corsan

Bajo Colmedo

Bajo Fagilda
Paso Q.R.6M
Fagilda

74

Bajo do Camoucos
1848
Fl(3)R.18s10m8M
AIS

Boca
del
Sudoeste

See p.97

Depths in Metres

69

Pta del Centolo

Isla
Ons

1847.35
Fl.R.4s8m2M

Marine
Reserve

Pta Fornelos

Isla Onza

Lexiña de Galera

1847.3
Fl(4)24s
126m25M
AIS

**42°
25'
N**

8°55'W

20'

ATLANTIC SPAIN AND PORTUGAL

⊕69	42°26'N	08°55'.3W	0.9M S Pta Miranda
⊕72	42°24'.5N	08°53'.47W	Canal de la Fagilda
⊕74	42°20'.2N	08°53'W	Entrance Ria de Pontevedra
⊕76	42°24'.1N	08°42'.6W	App Marin
⊕98	42°22'N	08°50'W	Ria de Pontevedra
⊕99	42°22'N	08°47'W	S Morazzán

Approaches to Ría de Pontevedra

42°22'N 08°53'W

Tides
Standard port Lisbon
Mean time differences (at Marín)
HW +0100 ±0010; LW +0125 ±0005
(the above allows for the difference in time zones)
Heights in metres

MHWS	MHWN	MLWN	MLWS
3·3	2·6	1·2	0·5

Charts

	Approach	Ria
Admiralty	3633	1732, 1733, 1734
Spanish	416,	416A
Imray	C48	C48

Coastguard
Vigo ☽ +34 981 297 403
Sea Rescue Service ☽ +34 900 202 202
MRCC Finisterre Ch 11
MRSC Vigo Ch 10

Navtex
518kHz (D) at 0030, 0730, 0830*1230, 1630, 2030*
(*weather only)

Weather bulletins VHF
Vigo Ch 65 at 0840, 1240, 2010
MRSC Vigo Ch 10 at 0015, 0415, 0815, 1215, 1615, 2015

Navigational warnings VHF
Vigo Ch 65 at 0840, 2010
MRSC Ch 10 at 0215, 0615, 1015, 1415, 1815, 2215

Primary working freqs
c/s Coruña Radio
Vigo Manual Ch 65
Autolink Ch 62 Tx 2596 Rx 3280
DSC Ch 70 2187·5kHz

Lights (opposite page)
1847.3 **Isla Ons** Fl(4)24s126m25M 8-sided white tower on
   corner of building 1848 Los Camoucos
   Fl(3)R.18s11m8M Red and White Tower
1850 **Bajo Picamillo** Fl.G.5s10m8M Green and White
   Tower
1860 **Isla Tambo** Fl(3)8s34m11M Round tower, on
   truncated conical base
1872 **Bajo Cabezo de la Mourisca** Fl(2)G.7s11m5M Green
   and White Tower
1873 **Punta Couso** Fl(3)WG.10·5s19m10/8M White
   truncated conical tower, green top

A ría much developed in recent years

The fast road to Sanxenxo continues to bring development in its wake, both with tourism and the upgrading of harbour facilities. These include Porto Novo, Sanxenxo which is a major marina and Combarro, on the northern shore towards the head of the ría. This attractive old village is worth visiting by sea or land, preferably for a leisurely lunch in one of its numerous restaurants. Pontevedra itself lies upriver and is reachable only by small yacht. The Spanish Naval College has its home and marina at Marin but this is not open to visiting yachts.

Approach

From the north or Ría de Arousa ⊕69, ⊕72, ⊕98 through Paso de Fagilda marked by a red buoy Bajo Fagilda in the north and a beacon on Bajo Picamillo in the south. This tower may be passed up to 0·5M either side or else the route west of Los Camoucos tower may be used (Canal de los Camoucos). Refer to large scale chart.

From the southwest The main channel ⊕73, ⊕74, through Boca del Sudoeste between Isla Ons and the mainland.

From the south and Ría de Vigo ⊕81, ⊕80, ⊕74, through Canal del Norte between Islas Cíes and the mainland.

Note The entrance to the ría proper lies between the unmarked Punta Cabicastro, which has a rock off it, and Cabo de Udra which is surrounded by foul ground (see plan opposite).

⊕47	42°30'N	09°10'W	9M WSW Cabo Corrubedo
⊕56	42°27'·5N	08°58'·5W	Canal Principal Arousa
⊕69	42°26'N	08°55'·3W	0·9M S Pta Miranda
⊕71	42°23'N	09°07'W	7M SW Isla Sálvora
⊕72	42°24'·5N	08°53'·47W	Canal de la Fagilda
⊕73	42°17'N	09°00'W	Outer App Ría de Pontevedra
⊕74	42°20'·2N	08°53'W	Entrance Ría de Pontevedra
⊕76	42°24'·1N	08°42'·6W	App Marin
⊕80	42°15'·65N	08°53'·3W	N Canal del Norte
⊕81	42°14'·45N	08°52'·65W	S Canal del Norte
⊕88	42°10'N	08°52'·7W	Canal del Sur
⊕89	42°08'·5N	08°58'W	Outer App Canal del Sur
⊕91	42°07'·95N	08°53'W	0·8M SSW Islotes Las Serralleiras
⊕95	42°06'·5N	08°56'·6W	2M W Cabo Silleiro

Approach to Ría de Pontevedra from the north with Isla Ons right and Punta Fagilda left

GALICIA

Approach to Porto Novo and Sanxenxo

42°23'·5N 08°48'·7W (between ports)

Charts and tides
See page 99

Approach ⊕
⊕75 42°23'·4N 08°48'·6W

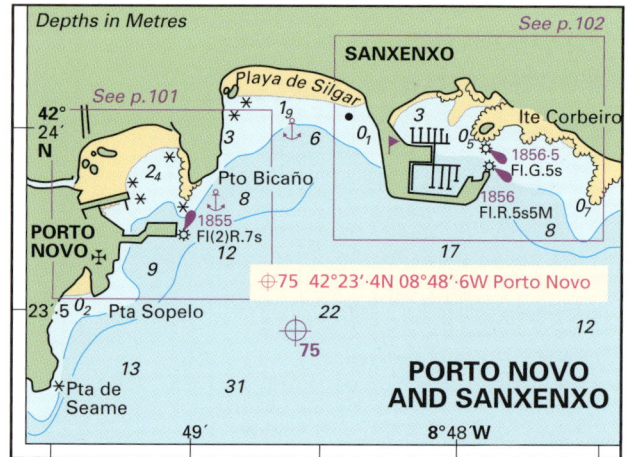

Marinas in a major holiday area

The VRG (Via Rapida Galicia) connects the Sanxenxo area to the main Motorway Atlantic and the cities of Santiago de Compostela and the rest of Galicia. Holidaymakers and business firms pour down this road making this part of Galicia both thriving and developing. The yachtsman can now choose between seeking space at the club marina of Port Novo, making use of the vast Sanxenxo marina or anchoring in between them off Playa de Silgar.

Approach

Approach is straightforward (although headlands should be given an offing of at least 200m) except from the east where shallows extend up to 600m southwest off Pta Festiñanzo. In normal weather a yacht may safely pass about midway between the warning Cabezo de Morrazan port hand buoy and the shore.

Berthing and anchorage

From ⊕75 head to port for the small club marina of Porto Novo, ahead to anchor, or to starboard to the major full service marina of Sanxenxo.

Playa Silgar anchorage *Martin Walker*

Playa Silgar anchorage between Sanxenxo and Porto Novo

Porto Novo

42°23'·64N 08°49'·12W

Charts and tides
See ría page 99

Chart
Admiralty 1732

Final approach ⊕
  ⊕75 42°23'·4N 08°48'·6W (0·45M SE of harbour)

Light
Marina breakwater beacon Fl(3)R.6s3M Red tower

Communications
Club Nautico Portonovo ☏ +34 986 723 266
www.nauticoportonovo.com
Email administracion@nauticoportonovo.com
VHF Ch 09

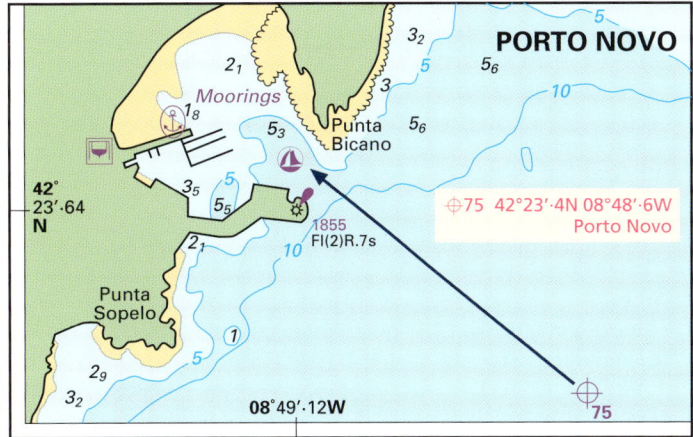

PORTO NOVO

⊕75 42°23'·4N 08°48'·6W
Porto Novo

GALICIA

Attractive fishing harbour with club marina

Porto Novo is a fishing village and holiday resort with an easy approach.

The Club Náutico de Portonovo has a small club house housing a restaurant and bar, with facilities at the end of the inner quay from which sprout the boat pontoons.

Approach

See pages 98 and 100.

Porto Novo

Berthing and anchorage

There are 106 berths at CN Portonovo on finger pontoons for vessels of 6 to 20m with maximum draught 4m. On arrival, secure to an outer pontoon and seek a berth. There is no anchoring in the harbour.

Facilities

Electricity and water on the pontoons, 110 tonne travel-lift. Showers and laundry, WiFi, bar and restaurants.

Nearby are further bars and restaurants, shops and a supermarket and a fine beach.

Sanxenxo (Sangenjo)

42°23'·80N 08°48'·06W

Tides
See page 99

Chart
Admiralty 1758
SHOM 7596

Final approaches ⊕
⊕75 42°23'·4N 08°48'·6W (0·6M SW of harbour)

Light
Breakwater beacon Q.R Red and white round tower

Communications
Nauta Sanxenxo
Avda. Augusto Gonzalez Besada, s/n 36960 Sanxenxo
(Pontevedra)
☎ +34 986 720 517
Email nauta@sanxenxo.org www.sanxenxo.org
www.marinasdegalicia.com
VHF Ch 09

SANXENXO
⊕75 42°23'·4N 08°48'·6W Sanxenxo

1856·5
Fl.G.5s4m3M

1856
Fl.R.5s6m5M

42°
23'.8
N

Depths in Metres
08°48'.06W

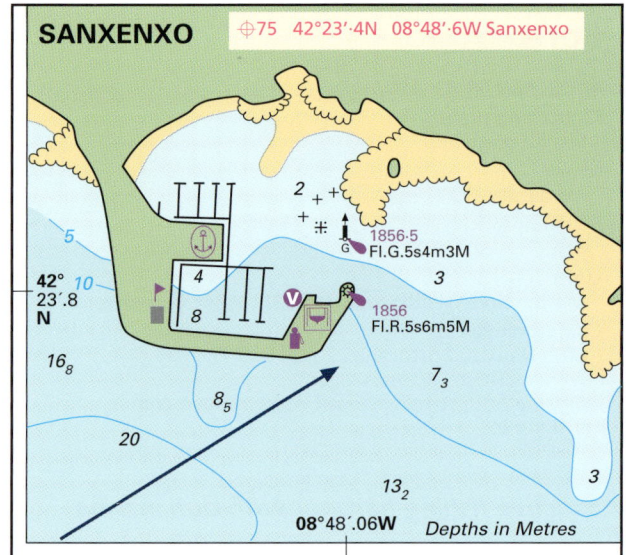

An easily accessible major marina (pronounced Sanshensho)

Sanxenxo Marina has three main areas: The mole head - with fuel dock, lift, workshops and ferry pontoon. The central quay - orange roofs with the harbour office, domestic facilities, shops and restaurants. The western end - the prominent RCN Club house and a large covered carpark.

Approach

Straightforward – see pages 98–100. Be aware of the ferries, to the ría and the outlying islands, which operate from a small pontoon on the very end of the main breakwater.

Berthing and anchoring

The marina has 379 berths to take boats of 8m-44m in length. Water depths vary from 3·5m to 7·5m. Call ahead for a berth, or alternatively proceed between the two parts of the marina towards the central mole and the arrivals pontoon. At crowded times it may be necessary to moor initially along the extended fuel pontoon but it is a very long walk from here to the office marina facilities.

Office hours are 09:30 to 13:30 and 16:00 to 20:00. The marina staff are friendly, helpful and speak good English.

Anchoring is not allowed in the harbour.

Facilities

Electricity and water at the berths; Fuel berth; 64 tonne travel lift; Camping gas; Showers; WiFi; Shops and numerous restaurants close to the marina. There is a major Froiz supermarket about a mile away at the roundabout leading to the highway out of town.

Sanxenxo fuel dock and technical area *Martin Walker*

Sanxenxo looking north

Anchorage

Raxo anchorage looking towards Isla Tambo and Marin. Anchorage is possible off the north shore beyond Cabo de Morrazán, particularly outside the line of local boat mooring buoys off Raxo quay (red beacon) (42°24'·1N 08°45'·28W)   *Martin Walker*

Combarro

42°25'·62N 08°42'·22W

Charts and Tides
See ría page 99

Charts
Admiralty   1733
Spanish   416A
Imray   C48

Final approaches ⊕
⊕77 42°25'·5N 08°42'W

Lights
Marina breakwater beacon Fl(2)R.6s3M Red round tower

Communications
Edificio de Capitania 36993 Combarro – Poio (Pontevedra)
☎ +34 986 778 415 or +34 607 427 726 (24h)
Mobile +34 695 955 750
Email comercial@combarromar.com
www.combarromar.com
VHF Ch 09, 10

Modern marina, anchorage, gem of a village

It would be a shame to visit this part of Galicia and miss seeing Combarro. This restored old fishing village, of massive granite and surrounded by vineyards, is very picturesque; numerous restaurants serve excellent seafood. In addition to the attractions of the old village, all routine shops are available plus a morning fruit market in the square.

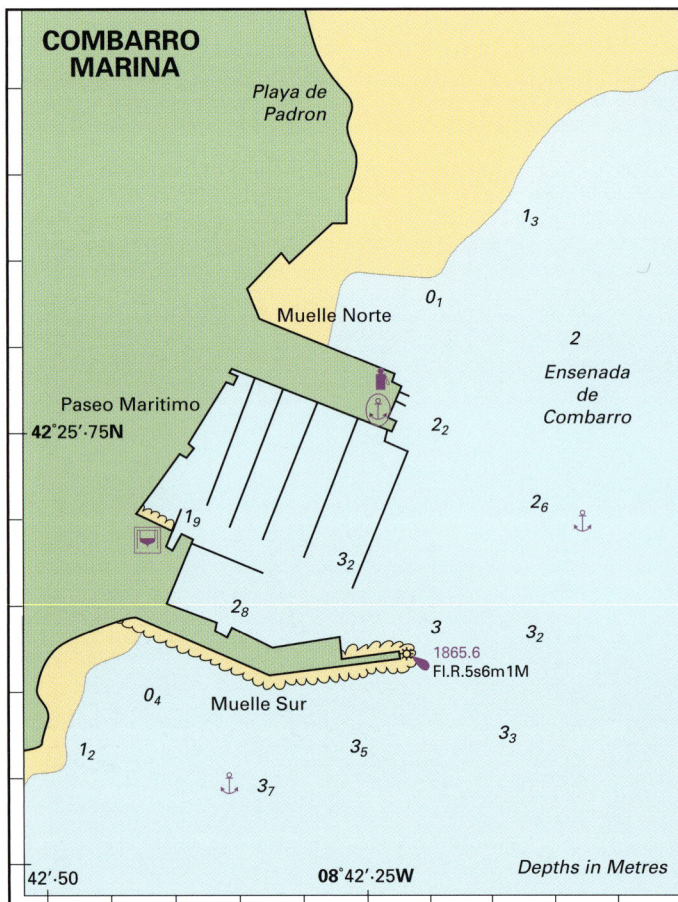

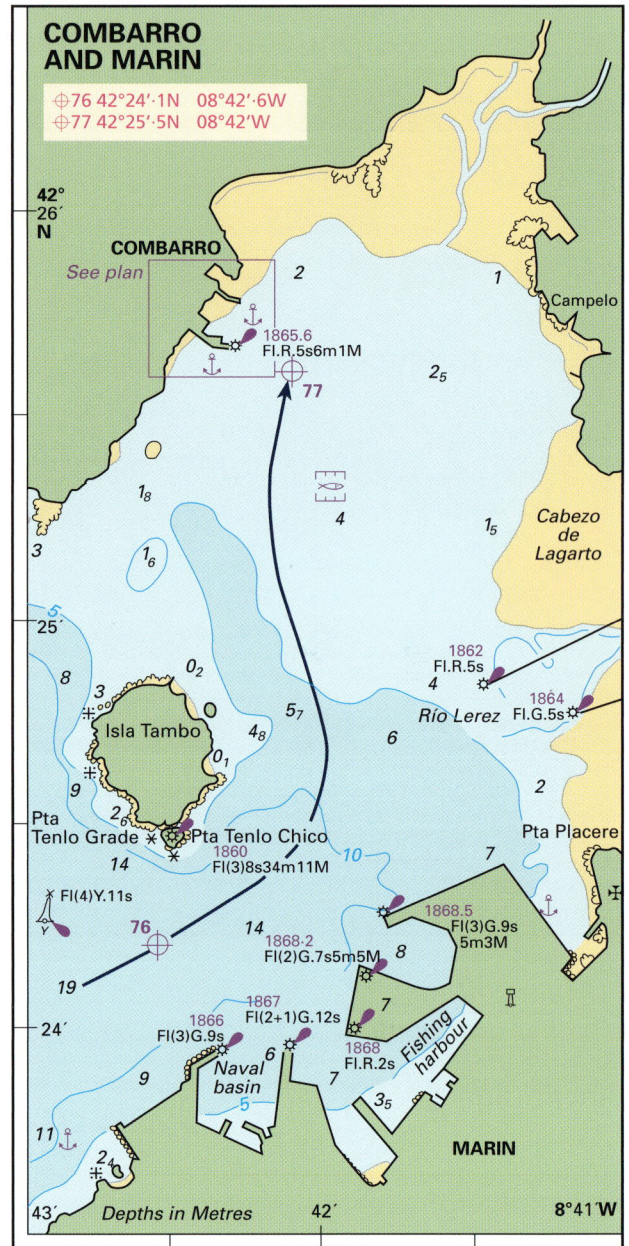

Approach and berthing

The best approach is from east of Isla Tambo. Call VHF Ch 09 for a berth. The marina has 335 berths for boat lengths from 6m to 16m. The maximum water depth of 3m is at the inside of the outer pontoon.

Facilities

Full service marina: Water and electricity at the berths; 50-tonne travel-lift; Fuel and pump out pontoons are outside the marina alongside the red office building; 24hr security; WiFi.

Small town shopping and numerous restaurants nearby.

Anchorage

Anchor off the marina, clear of viveiro rafts and away from the entrance. Good holding in sand and mud.

Left Combarro looking north; haul out, repair and chandlery around top left hard-standing. Red office block has domestic facilities and snack bar. Numerous restaurants from the root of the north quay, around the square and in the old village to the right

Below Approaching Combarro marina looking NW *Jane Russell*

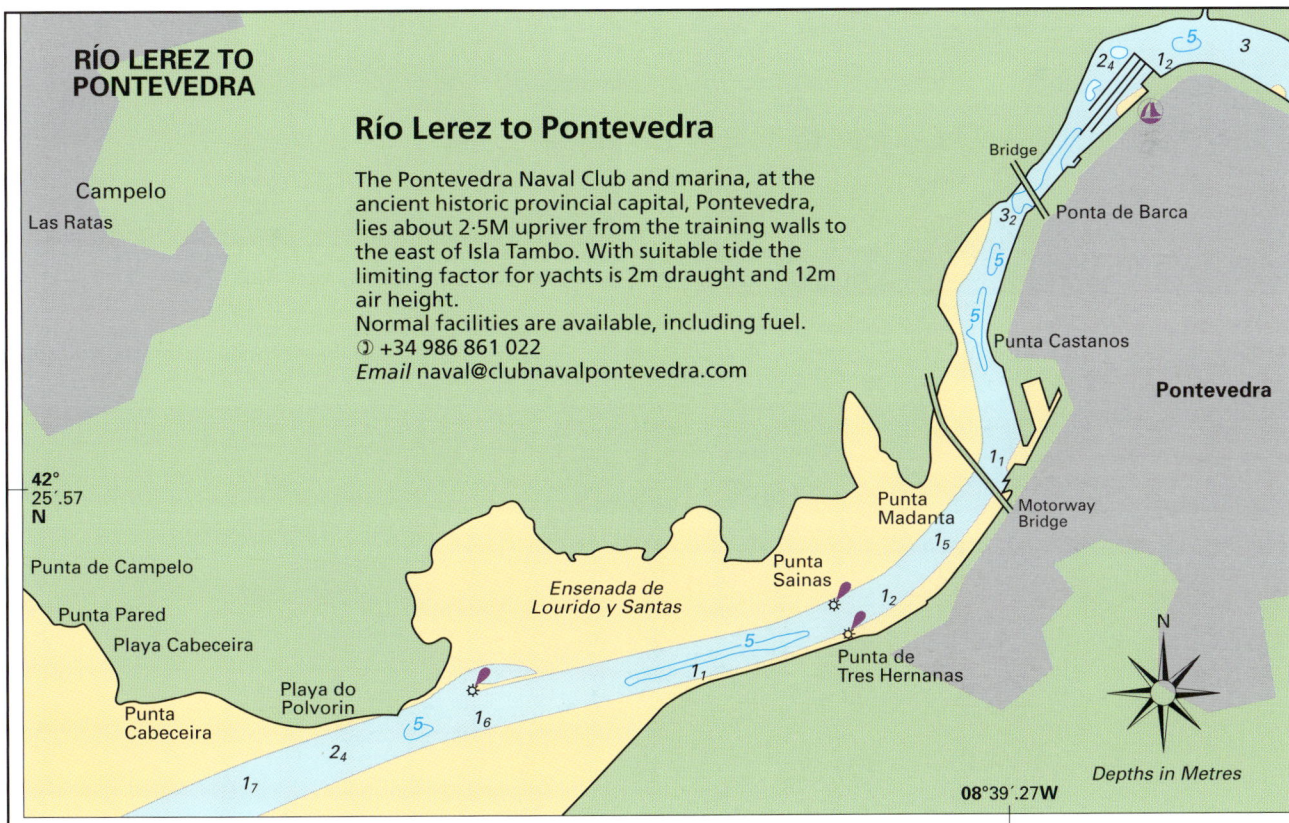

RÍO LEREZ TO PONTEVEDRA

Campelo

Las Ratas

Río Lerez to Pontevedra

The Pontevedra Naval Club and marina, at the ancient historic provincial capital, Pontevedra, lies about 2·5M upriver from the training walls to the east of Isla Tambo. With suitable tide the limiting factor for yachts is 2m draught and 12m air height.
Normal facilities are available, including fuel.
☎ +34 986 861 022
Email naval@clubnavalpontevedra.com

Bridge

Ponta de Barca

Punta Castanos

Pontevedra

42°
25′.57
N

Punta de Campelo

Punta Pared

Playa Cabeceira

Punta
Cabeceira

Playa do
Polvorin

*Ensenada de
Lourido y Santas*

Punta
Sainas

Punta
Madanta

Motorway
Bridge

Punta de
Tres Hernanas

Depths in Metres

08°39′.27W

N

Marin

(See plan page 104)
42°24'N 08°42'W

Charts
Admiralty 1733
Spanish 416A
Imray C48

Approaches ⊕
⊕76 42°24'·1N
08°42'·6W

Consider only as a port of refuge

Marin is a commercial fishing and naval port and the home of the Spanish Naval College. The west basin (with its marina) and offlying Isla Tomba are restricted military areas. Two other pontoon areas are for small local boats only.

Anchorages

Shelter from strong southerlies might be sought off Playa Placere (42°24'·5N 08°41'·4W) before the shallows which protrude immediately north of that area. In other winds, anchoring in the lee of Isla Tomba might be more satisfactory. Note from charts 1732 and 1733, that a cable runs from the yellow lightbuoy to the southwest of Isla Tomba to Pta Placere.

Traditional craft passing Isla Tampo, Marin behind in the distance *David Russell*

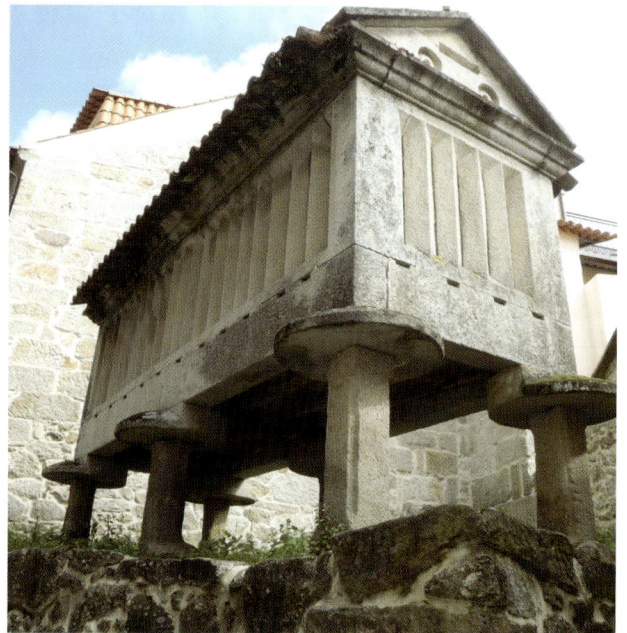

Traditional Combarro grain store *Jane Russell*

Marin, looking northeast with the Naval College in the foreground

Combarro cockle pickers *Jane Russell*

Aguete

42°22'·56N 08°44'·20W

Charts and tides
See ría page 99

Charts
Admiralty 1732
Spanish   416A
Imray   C48

Final approach ⊕
⊕78 42°22'·8N 08°44'.W

Lights
Pontoon wave breaker
Green/white post
Lit green buoy 0·1M off
marina promontory

Communications
☎ +34 986 702 373
Email rcma@ctv.es www.rcmaguete.com

Small club marina

Aguete has been an active recreational marina for Marin since 1974 and is situated in an attractive bay with steep hill behind. The Real Club de Mar de Aguete welcomes visitors and has an attractive clubhouse, with restaurant, overlooking the harbour.

Aguete is one of the many harbours in Galicia to celebrate the fiesta of the Virgen del Carmen on 16 July with a waterborne procession. A lifesize statue of the Virgin is taken on a tour of the harbour in the club launch accompanied by local craft of all sizes decked out with flags and bunting.

Approach

The approach (to ⊕78) is straightforward from west to northeast. There are rocks off Punta de Aguete and buoys marking the Bajo Los Pelados. A

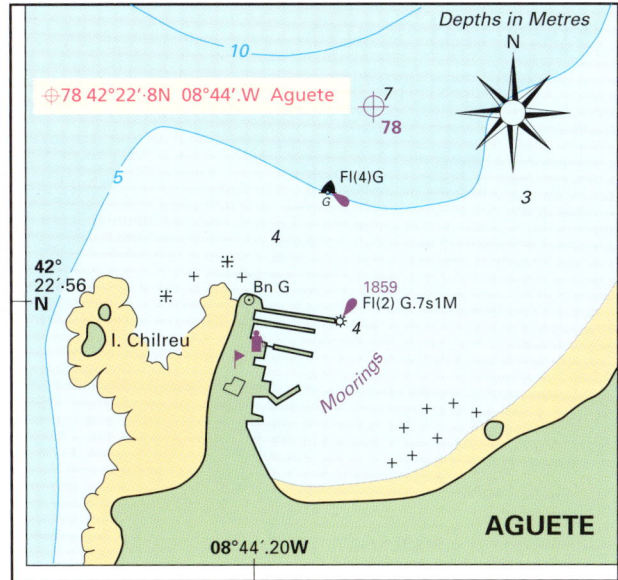

north cardinal buoy marks the rocky shoal and a preferred channel-to-port lateral mark (GRG) at 42°23'·03N 8°44'·44W (Fl(2+1)G 12s) marks the outer edge of the bank.

Berthing and anchoring

The outer separated pontoons act as a wave breaker. Berth on the first pontoon behind the wave breaker or anchor off the beach clear of the moorings. Even in calm weather, some swell from passing boats works in as the harbour and moorings are fully exposed to the north.

Facilities

Fuel available.

Aguete from the north – green buoy is bottom right

GALICIA

Bueu and Beluso

Bueu 42°19'·79N 08°47'·01W
Beluso 42°20'·01N
08°47'·90W

Charts and tides
See ría page 99

Charts
Admiralty   1732
Spanish   416A
Imray   C48

Final approaches ⊕
⊕79 43°20'·2N
08°47'·2W

Lights
Breakwater Bueu
Fl.G.3s4M Green column
Breakwater Beluso
Fl(3)G.9s3M Green
column

Communications (Beluso)
☏ +34 981 545 794
Email portosdeportivos@portosdegalicia.com
www.portosdegalicia.com

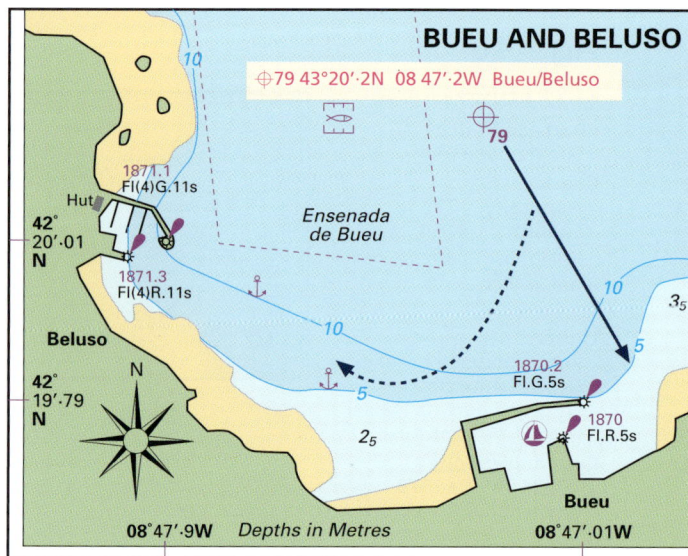

BUEU AND BELUSO
⊕79 43°20'·2N 08 47'·2W Bueu/Beluso

Busy fishing harbour/small marina

Bueu is a small fishing and market town with shops, restaurants, market and good beaches. 0.6M west is the small marina of Beluso with one nearby restaurant.

Approach

Straightforward from the north down a wide fairway between *viveros* to ⊕79; offlying rocks of Isolote El Caballo de Bueu to the west. There is a clear route inside the viveros between harbours.

Berthing and anchorage

No space is reserved for yachts in Bueu (though inquire at the harbour office if requiring lifting with the 100-tonne travel lift there). There may be room to anchor outside the harbour mouth and small

Bueu harbour with travel lift in southwest corner

moorings in 4–6m over mud. Try the first pontoon in Beluso, borrow a mooring there, or anchor midway between harbours in 3–5m over sand and mud. There are reported to be 62 berths for boats up to 12m in a maximum depth of 3m.

Beluso – best to anchor off

Ría de Aldan Anchorages

42°19'·6N 08°51'·2W

Charts and tides
See ría page 99

Chart
Admiralty 1732

Overview

The Ría de Aldan, between Punta Couso and Cabo de Udra is worth a visit in suitable conditions for its rocky shores and small secluded beaches. There are good walks through the woods on the peninsula up ancient, steep, stone-paved tracks.

There are numerous *viveros* lining the west side of the ría but space should be found inside them. The eastern side of the bay is deeper and somewhat prone to swell.

Ría de Aldan should be avoided if winds build from the north or northwest. Under other conditions it offers anchorage in several of the small bays on the west side of the ría (but note the offlying rocks) or in the southeast corner towards the head of the bay. There are moorings here and a large rock which tends to merge into the background. Anchorage may be found off the ramp in 10m mud.

Approach

From the north Cabo de Udra is foul and passage south of Cabezo de la Mourisca beacon inadvisable. (See photo on page 98).

From the south Pta Couso should be given a good berth.

Aldan

The short mole at Aldan (42°16'·95N 08°49'·37W red beacon) offers little protection for yachts but one can anchor off, or on the opposite shore, to seek provisions from the developing village.

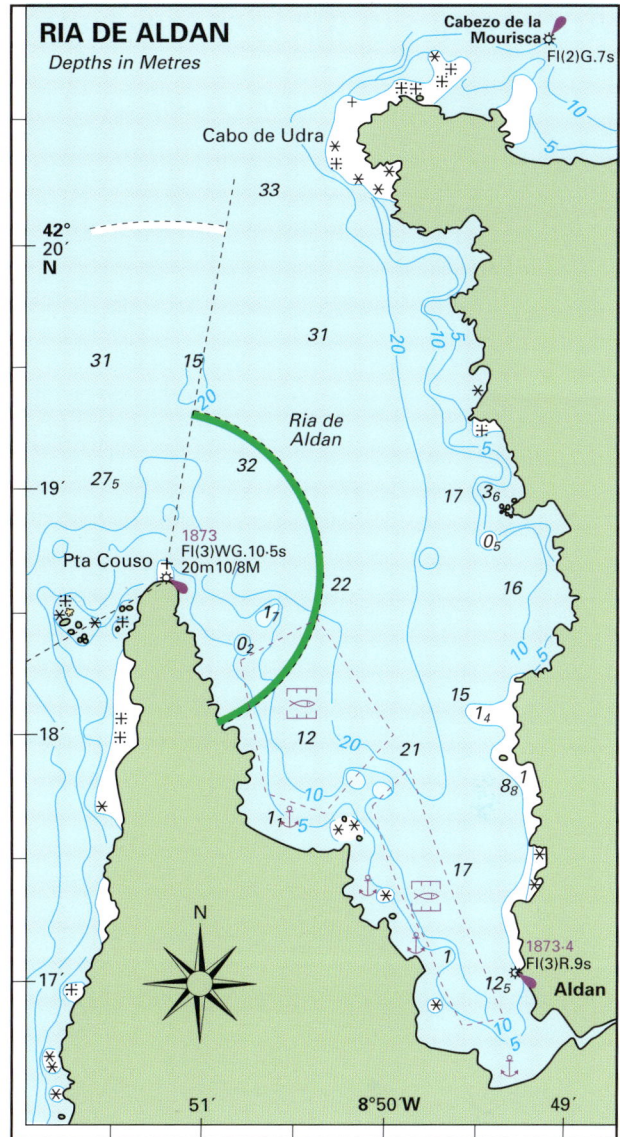

RIA DE ALDAN
Depths in Metres

The head of Ría de Aldan

Anchorages in the Islas Cies National Park

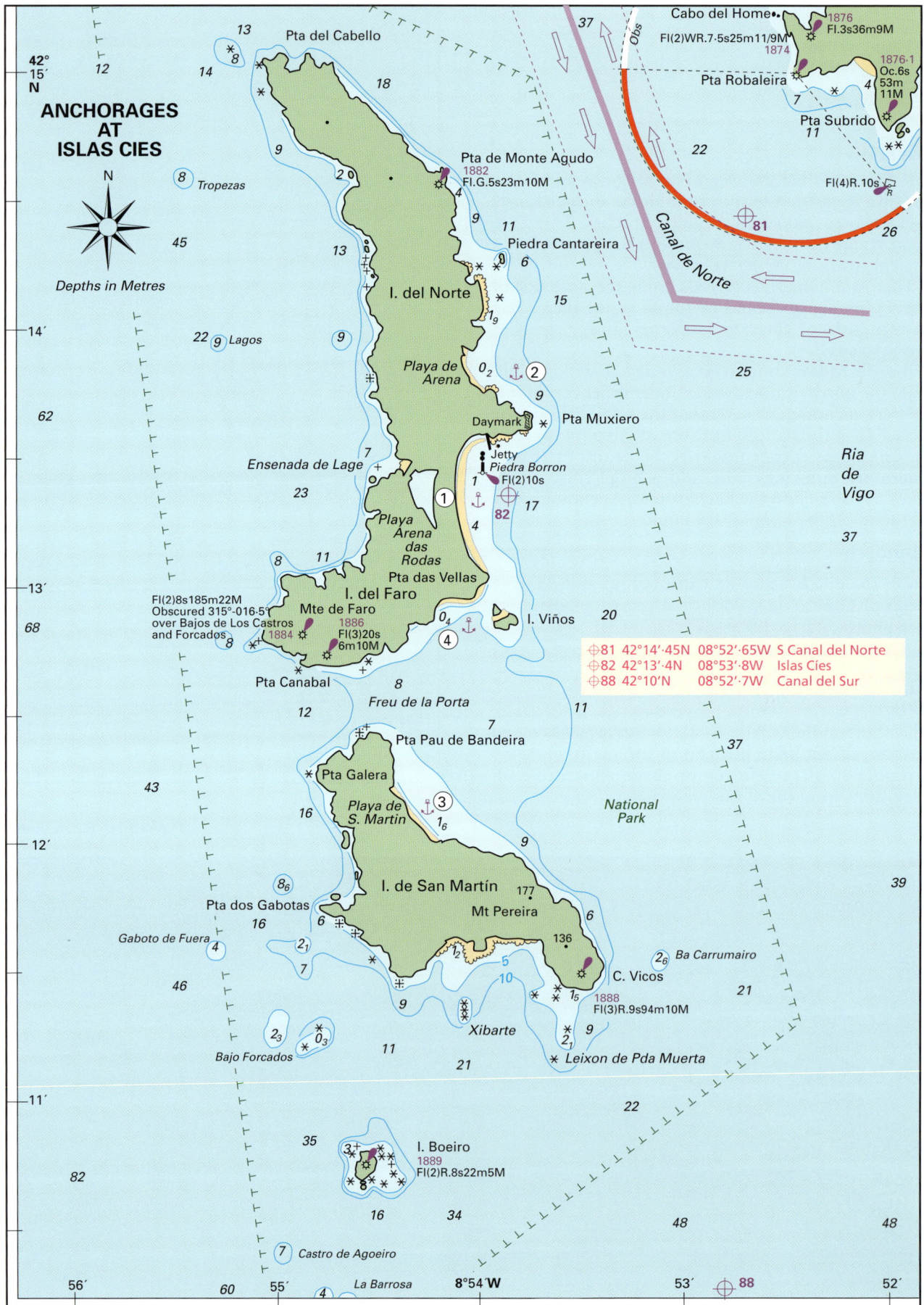

ANCHORAGES
AT
ISLAS CIES

N

Depths in Metres

42°
15'
N

12

13 · Pta del Cabello

14

18

8 · Tropezas

45

9 · Lagos

22 · 9

9

62

I. del Norte

13

9

Pta de Monte Agudo
1882
Fl.G.5s23m10M

9

11

Piedra Cantareira

6

15

Playa de Arena

0·2 ⚓2

9

14'

Ensenada de Lage

7

Daymark

Pta Muxiero

Jetty
Piedra Borron
Fl(2)10s

1

⚓1

Playa
Arena
das
Rodas

23

17

82

4

8

11

Pta das Vellas

Fl(2)8s185m22M
Obscured 315°-016·5°
over Bajos de Los Castros
and Forcados

I. del Faro

Mte de Faro
1886
Fl(3)20s
6m10M
1884

0·4

I. Viños

20

⚓4

13'

68

8

Pta Canabal

8

Freu de la Porta

11

12

7

Pta Pau de Bandeira

37

Pta Galera

Playa de
S. Martin

16

⚓3

1·6

National
Park

9

12'

8·6

I. de San Martín

177

39

Pta dos Gabotas

16

6

Mt Pereira

6

Gaboto de Fuera

4

2·1

136

2·6 · Ba Carrumairo

7

1·2

5
10

C. Vicos
1888
Fl(3)R.9s94m10M

21

46

2·3

0·3

11

Xibarte

1·5

2·1

9

Bajo Forcados

21

Leixon de Pda Muerta

11'

22

35

3·+

I. Boeiro
1889
Fl(2)R.8s22m5M

82

8

16

34

48

48

7 · Castro de Agoeiro

56'

60

55'

4

La Barrosa

8°54'W

53'

88

52'

Cabo del Home
Fl(2)WR.7·5s25m11/9M
1874

1876
Fl.3s36m9M

Pta Robaleira

1876·1
Oc.6s
53m
11M

7

4

37

Obs

11

Pta Subrido

22

Fl(4)R.10s

26

81

Canal de Norte

25

Ria
de
Vigo

37

⊕81	42°14'·45N	08°52'·65W	S Canal del Norte
⊕82	42°13'·4N	08°53'·8W	Islas Cíes
⊕88	42°10'N	08°52'·7W	Canal del Sur

I.3.2 Islas Cies and Ría de Vigo to Baiona

Islas Cíes

See National Parks pages 15–17
42°13'·00N 08°54'·00W
Tides
  See page 113
Charts
  Admiralty 1730
  Spanish   416B
  Imray   C48
Daymark
  42°13'·65N 08°53'·78W
Communications
  See Notes on National Parks' Permits page 15

National Park; a nature reserve with good anchorages

Visiting yachts require a permit to visit, anchor or dive around Isla Cíes – see page 15. It is strongly advised that these permits are arranged well before visiting, even before leaving home. The Islas Cíes are mountainous, wooded and very attractive. The whole area is a Nature Park, and in addition a large part of Isla del Norte, Isla del Faro and all of Isla de San Martín are bird sanctuaries (mostly herring gulls, lesser black-backed gulls and shags, plus a few guillemots) where access is forbidden. However, there are good tracks on Isla del Norte and Isla del Faro, which are linked by a narrow sandy isthmus, and it is worth studying the map displayed at the northern end of Playa Arena das Rodas. There are stunning views from the lighthouse with the evening sun.

Islas Cies anchorages from the north. *See also photo on p.15*

There are no cars on the islands and few permanent inhabitants, but in summer many campers and day visitors come by ferry from Vigo, Baiona and Cangas to enjoy the clean sandy beaches so time a visit for midweek if possible. In terms of their surroundings the anchorages, which are on the east side of the islands, are amongst the best in the rías, but all are open to the east.

Approach
Initially to ⊕82 or Daymark. Monte del Faro is easily identified, standing on the highest point of the central island, Isla del Faro, as is the long beach lining the isthmus between Isla del Faro and Isla del Norte.Be aware that when approaching the north end and also down the east side of the islands there may be marked acceleration in winds.

Anchorages

1. **Off Playa Arena das Rodas** 42°13'·36N 08°53'·89W Anchor over sand, rock and weed towards the middle of the beach as depth allows. Borron de Cíes, a submerged rock some 20m across, lies about 200m south of the stone mole. It shows at low water and is marked by a beacon (tall black pole, two balls, light). Avoid anchoring too close to the mole, which is in constant use by tourist ferries. It is possible for a shallow-draught boat to anchor inshore of the rocks, though in summer the beach itself is buoyed-off for swimming.Good anchorage, clear of both rocks and ferries, is to be found with the western white tower on Cabo del Home framed in the centre of a cleft in the rocks at the end of Punta Muxiero. Holding is good in sand.

2. In southerlies, anchor in the bay (42°13'·93N 08°53'·89W) north of Punta Muxiero and its daymark.

3. In south to northwest conditions, better anchorage is to be had on the north coast of Isla de San Martín off the Playa de San Martín (42°12'·23N 08°54'·18W), in 3–5m over rock and sand. This is a particularly quiet and attractive spot although without access to facilities of any kind. The island is a bird sanctuary where landing is forbidden.

4. In east winds some shelter may be found in a small bay on the south coast of the Isla del Faro immediately west, and in the lee, of Isla Viños (42°12'·88N 08°54'·09W). It is occasionally used by fishing boats and there is not much room. The Monte Faro jetty some 600m to the west is used by fishing boats and the occasional ferry, and yachts are not welcome.

Facilities
A few restaurants and a small supermarket at Playa Arena das Rodos and a good visitors' centre above the campsite.

GALICIA

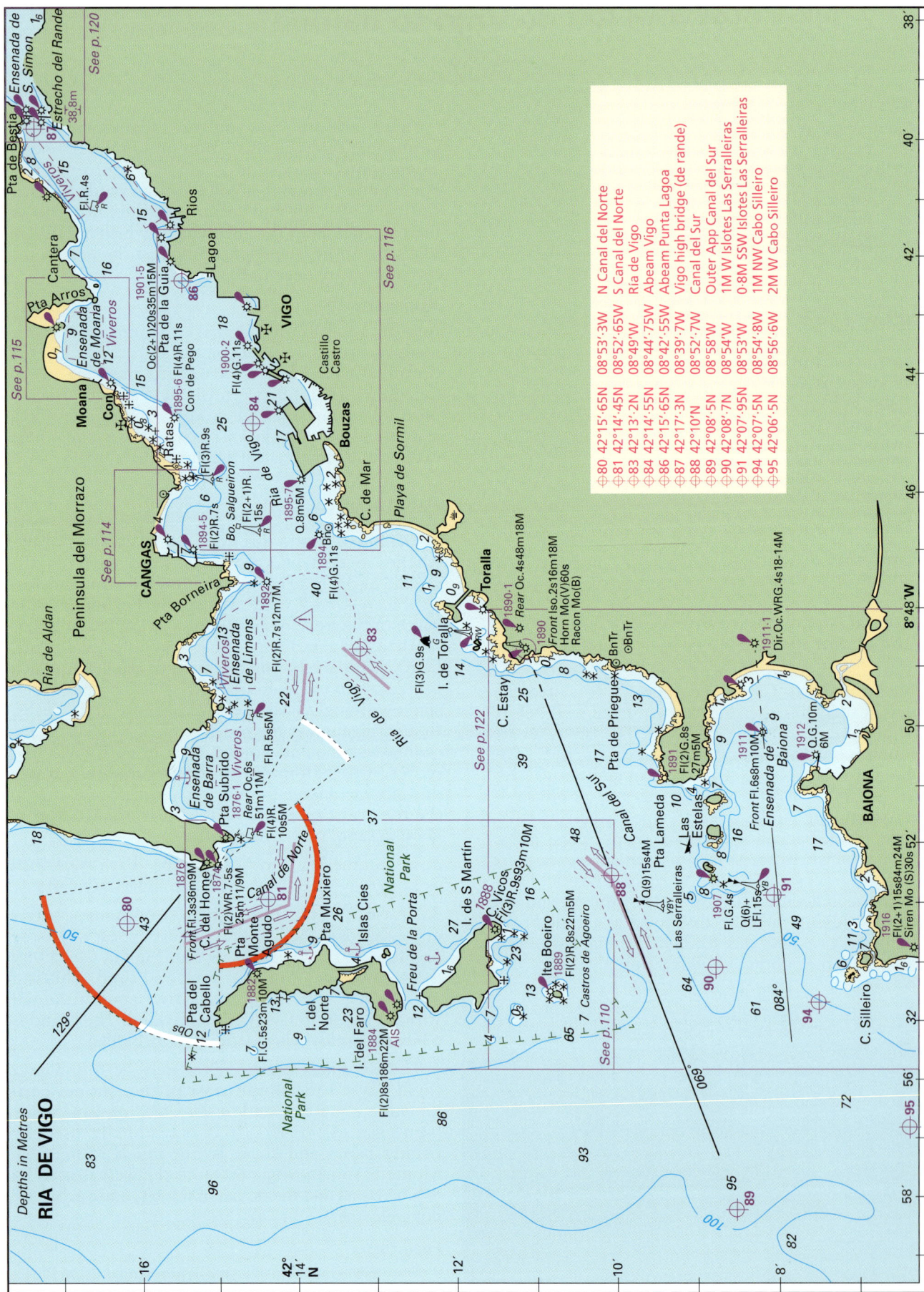

Depths in Metres
RIA DE VIGO

⊕ 80	42°15'·65N	08°53'·3W	N Canal del Norte
⊕ 81	42°14'·45N	08°52'·65W	S Canal del Norte
⊕ 83	42°13'·2N	08°49'W	Ria de Vigo
⊕ 84	42°14'·55N	08°44'·75W	Abeam Vigo
⊕ 86	42°15'·65N	08°42'·55W	Abeam Punta Lagoa
⊕ 87	42°17'·3N	08°39'·7W	Vigo high bridge (de rande)
⊕ 88	42°10'N	08°52'·7W	Canal del Sur
⊕ 89	42°08'·5N	08°58'W	Outer App Canal del Sur
⊕ 90	42°08'·7N	08°54'W	1M W Islotes Las Serralleiras
⊕ 91	42°07'·95N	08°53'W	0·8M SSW Islotes Las Serralleiras
⊕ 94	42°07'·5N	08°54'·8W	1M NW Cabo Silleiro
⊕ 95	42°06'·5N	08°56'·6W	2M W Cabo Silleiro

See p.120
See p.115
See p.114
See p.116
See p.122
See p.110

Ensenada de S. Simon
Estrecho del Rande 38.8m
Pta de Bestia
Viveiros
F.I.R.4s
Rios
Lagoa
Cantera
Pta Arros
Moana
Ensenada de Moana
Con
Viveros
Pta de la Guia
Con de Pego
Oc(2+1)20s35m15M 1901·5
1895·6 Fl(4)R.11s
Ratas
Fl(3)R.9s
VIGO
Castillo
Castro
1900·2 Fl(4)G.11s
Vigo
Fl(2+1)R. 15s
Bo, Salgueiron
Bouzas
C. de Mar
Playa de Sormil
Fl(2)R.7s
Fl(4)R. 1894·5
1895·7
Q.8m5M
CANGAS
Fl(4)G.11s 1894
Pta Borneira
Viveros
Ensenada de Limens
Fl(2)R.7s12m7M 1892
Peninsula del Morrazo
Ria de Aldan
Fl(3)G.9s
I. de Toralja
Toralla
Rear Oc.4s48m18M
Front Iso.2s16m18M
Horn Mo(V)60s
Racon Mo(B)
C. Estay
Ria de Vigo
83
Ensenada de Barra
Pta Subrido
Viveros
Rear Oc.6s 1876·1
51m11M
Fl.R.5s5M
Fl(3)R.9s93m10M
National Park
Canal del Norte
Front Fl.3s36m9M 1876
C. del Home 1874
Fl(2)WR.7·5s 25m11/9M
Monte Agudo
Pta Muxiero
Islas Cies
I. de S Martin
C. Vicos
Fl(3)R.9s
Ite Boeiro 1889
Fl(2)R.8s22m5M 1888
Castros de Agoeiro
National Park
Pta del Cabello
Monte
Fl(4)R. 10s5M
1882 Fl.R.8s23m10M
I. del Norte
I. del Faro
Fl.G.5s23m9M
I. del Faro 1884
Fl(2)8s186m22M
AIS
Fl(2)8s186m22M
National Park
Pta de Priegue
Pta Lameda
Las Estelas
Las Serralleiras
Canal del Sur
Q(9)15s4M
Fl.G.4s 1907
Q(6)+ LFl.15s
Ensenada de Baiona
Front Fl.6s8m10M 1911
Q.G.10m 1912
6M
BAIONA
Dir.Oc.WRG.4s18·14M 1911·1
C. Silleiro
Siren Mo (S)30s 52
Fl(2+1)15s84m24M 1916

Approach lights (opposite page)

Canal de Norte
1874 **Cabo del Home** Fl(2)WR.7·5s25m11/9M Red round tower
1876 **Ldg Lts 129°** *Front* Fl.3s36m9M White round tower
1876.1 **Punta Subrido** *Rear* Oc.6s51m11M White round tower
1882 **Monte Agudo** Fl.G.5s23m10M White round tower with white wall

Canal del Sur
1890 **Cabo Estay Ldg Lts 069°20'** *Front* Iso.2s16m18M White 4-sided tower, red bands
1890.1 **Cabo Estay** *Rear* Oc.4s48m18M Red truncated pyramidal tower, white bands

Vigo Narrows
1892 **Bajo Borneira No.6** Fl(2)R.7s11m7M Red and white tower
1894 **Bajo Tofiño No.3** Fl(4)G.11s9m7M Red and white tower

Baiona approaches
1911 **Cabezo de San Juan Ldg Lts 084°** Fl.6s7m10M White truncated cónical tower
1911.1 **Playa de Panjon** *Rear* Dir.Oc.WRG.4s18m9m White truncated tower on 8-sided base

Islas Cíes
1884 **Monte Faro** Fl(2)8s185m22M Tower and dwelling

Ría de Vigo

Tides
Standard port Lisbon
Mean time differences (at Vigo)
HW +0050 ±0010; LW +0115 ±0010
(the above allows for the difference in time zones)
Heights in metres

MHWS	MHWN	MLWN	MLWS
3·4	2·7	1·3	0·5

Charts	Approach	Ria
Admiralty	3633	1730, 1731
Spanish	417	416B
Imray	C18, C48	C18, C48

Note A traffic separation scheme operates through Canal de Norte and Canal del Sur. There are sound signals on Cabo Silleiro and Cabo Estay.

Warning
Ría de Vigo and Ensenada de Baiona are separated by the Islas Las Estelas and Isolas Serrolleiras with their offlying, extensive and dangerous reefs and individual rocks. North/south passage between islands is not recommended without local knowledge, or in fair weather and using Spanish chart 4167

A partly industrial ría but with good marinas and attractive anchorages

The Islas Cíes shelter Ría de Vigo from the worst of the Atlantic swell. Industrial dockland Vigo dominates the upper part of the ría on the south side and its suburbs and dormitory towns spread down both sides. With them come harbours, ferries and marinas. There is peace as well, both in Ensenada de San Simón beyond the giant Rande Suspension bridge, or off the lovely beach at Ensenada de Barra; note that this is a popular nudist beach on weekends and holidays. Buoys or beacons mark the shallows off most headlands on both sides of the ría.

Approach

From the north or the northern rías Canal de Norte is well marked and free from dangers. (If coming from seaward note the dangers extending well north of Isla del Norte (Islas Cíes), if approaching from Ría de Pontevedra do not cut the corner off Pta Couso). ⊕80 and ⊕81 are positioned on the mainland side of the TSS at 160°. Pick up the line of red buoys after clearing Cabo del Home and Pta Subrido or head up ría on 095° from ⊕81.

From the west or south ⊕89 and ⊕88 lie on the Canal del Sur Cabo Estay 069° leading lights switching, to ⊕88, ⊕83 on 041°. These ⊕ are on the TSS centre line, track to starboard.

From Baiona (See plan on page 122). In fair weather and towards high tide, Canal de la Porta, between Monte Ferro and the easternmost of the three Estelas Islands, may be used. There is a 0·9m patch in the middle of this channel and a separate 1·6m patch about 0·1M further northwest. Favour the west side, use Spanish chart 4167 and then keep 1M clear of the headland, and Cabo Estay, before heading up Ría de Vigo.

Marinas

The ría is well served by marinas.

Ría de Vigo Ensenada de Barra looking SSW *Jane Russell*

Ensenada de Barra anchorage looking E up Ría de Vigo *Jane Russell*

Cangas

42°15'·63N 08°46'·95W

Charts and tides
See ría page 113

Charts
Admiralty 1730, 1731
Spanish 416B
Imray C48

Final approach ⊕
⊕85 42°15'·5N
08°46'·7W Cangas

Light
Outer breakwater
beacon Fl(2)R.7s3M
Red round tower

Communications
Club Náutico de Rodeira
☎ +34 986 304 246 or +34 671 660 105
Email club@nauticorodeira.com
www.nauticorodeira.com
VHF Ch 06

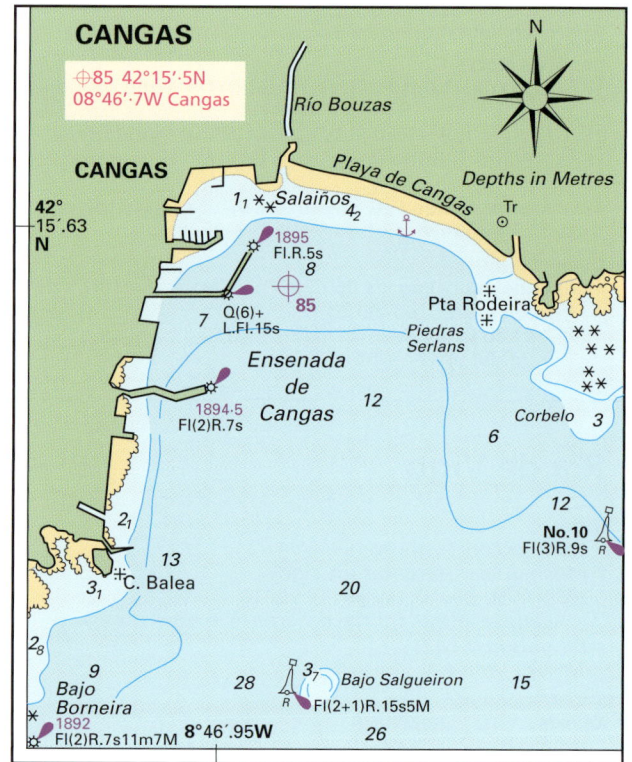

Cheerful welcome from a modern marina

Cangas has a small, friendly marina alongside an attractive town with fishing and some industry. There are regular ferries to Vigo.

Approach

Buoys mark the extent of the rocks off the headlands to east and west. If coming up the ría, Ensenada de Barra offers a good anchorage in 6m over sand and weed, open southwest to east. Approach Cangas between Piedra Barneira and Bajo Salgueiron – line of 010° to ⊕85. Alternatively head northwest from the centre of Vigo passing midway between the buoys off headland. Do not close the buoy.

Anchorage and berthing

On rounding the breakwater there are three sections to the harbour, fishing boats to main harbour left, ferries to the right hand pier and yachts to the marina in the middle harbour. There are 269 berths for boats up to 20m length. The minimum depth is 2m. An anchorage is available off Playa de Cangas in 5–6m over sand.

Facilities

Electricity and water; Fuel; 64 tonne travel lift; wi-fi; security.

The domestic facilities (including washing machine) and restaurant are in the end of the main blue roofed building on the centre mole. The main club house is next to the Shell fuel station immediately outside the harbour road entrance. There is a seafront market on Friday.

Cangas from the south

Moana

42°16'·68N 08°43'·99W

Final approach
⊕17 42°16'·5N 08°44'W

Communications
☎ +34 986 31 11 40
Email info@moanamar.es   www.moanamar.es
VHF Ch 09

A small marina with easy access to Vigo via the adjacent ferry jetty

Approach

Approach the northeast entrance through the *viveros*. The arrivals pontoon is to starboard beyond the outer pontoon with visitors' berths close to the entrance.

Berthing

In June 2014 new berths where being put in place to take boats of lengths from 8m to 16m.

Moana marina and anchorage from the south

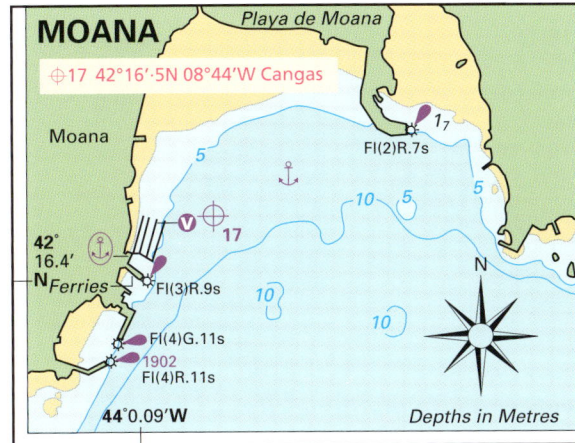

MOANA
⊕17 42°16'·5N 08°44'W Cangas
Playa de Moana
Moana
Fl(2)R.7s
5
10 5 5
42°
16.4'
N *Ferries*
Fl(3)R.9s
10
10
Fl(4)G.11s
1902
Fl(4)R.11s
44°0.09'W
Depths in Metres

Facilities

The marina office has bikes for hire. Domestic facilities are temporary but adequate.

Anchorage

Alternatively anchor outside the marina in mud and sand.

GALICIA

Anchorage / berthing further up the ría

Domaio Marina 42°17'·3N 08°40'·5W

Two miles beyond Moana, anchorage is just possible inside the viveros between the tiny Puerto de Domaio and a large factory. There is also a private marina with good pontoons and protection from the swell. Visitors are not catered for, there are no shore-side facilities, and security gates prevent access to/from the pontoons.

Domaio – tight anchorage and private marina

Vigo

Centred 42°14'N 08°45'W

Tides
  See page 113

Charts
  Admiralty 1730, 1731
  Spanish   416B
  Imray   C48

Final approach ⊕
  ⊕84 42°14'·55N
  08°44'·75W abeam Vigo

Ría de Vigo
Vigo
BAIONA

Facilities

Any repair work is possible in Vigo. In addition to the facilities at the marinas, the long established Astilleros Lagos boatyard in Darsena de Bouzas continues to offer major technical support and repair.

Astilleros Lagos Avda. Eduardo Cabello 2, 36208 Vigo, Spain
☎ +34 986 232 626
www.astilleroslagos.es
Email astillero@astilleroslagos.com

A lively, modern maritime city

Vigo has an ancient history and strong maritime connections. Its wharfs stretch for two miles handling cargo, deep-sea fishing and cruise ships as well as building coasters and fishing vessels.

Marinas

There are four marinas in the Vigo area that will accept visiting yachts. Three are in the main waterfront dock area and the fourth, Punta Lagoa, is to the northeast of the docks (entrance ⊕86) under the wooded Monte de la Guia. Other marinas can be seen, particularly by Bouzas bridge, but they are generally private or rather shallow.

Festa dos Maios, Vigo David Russell

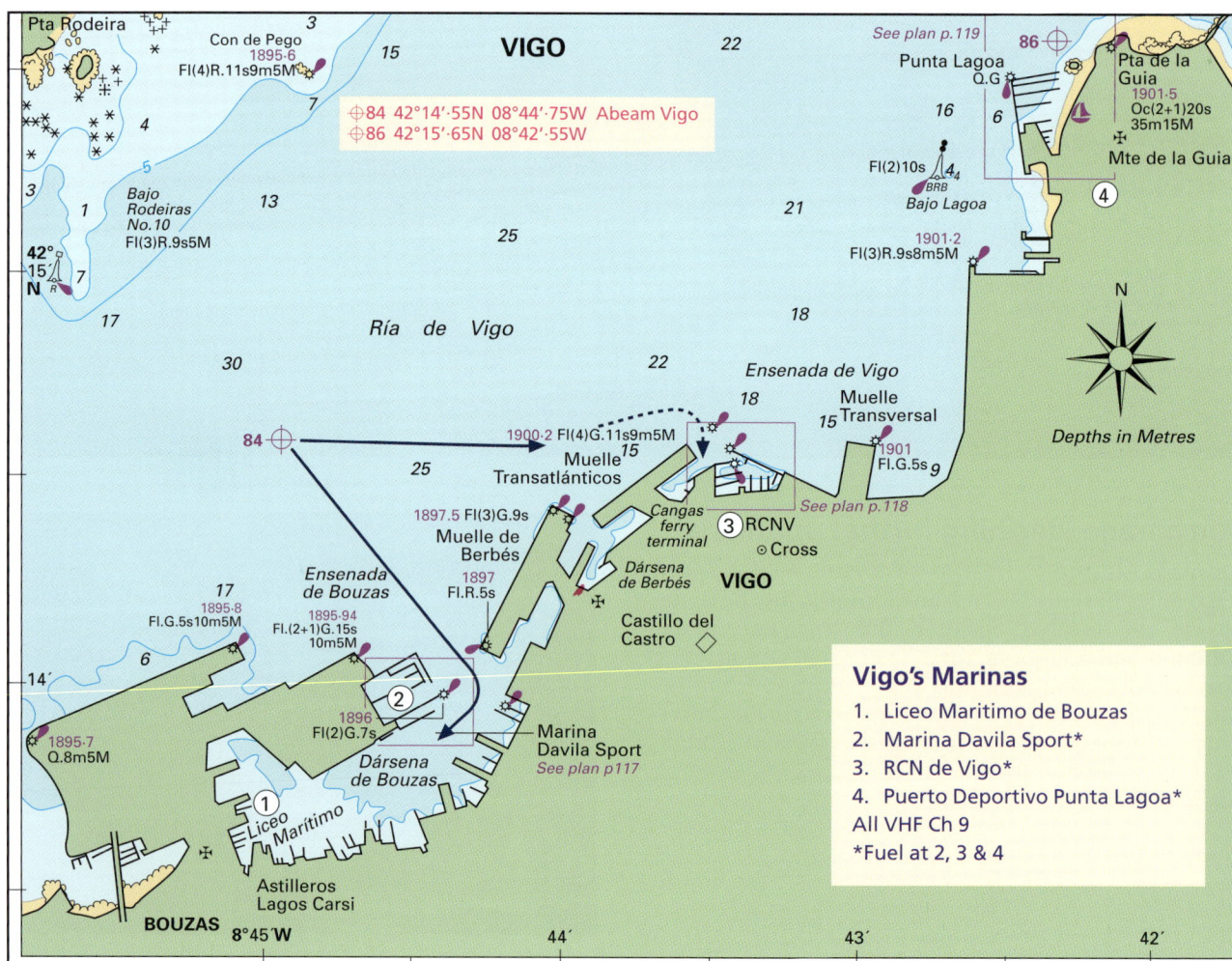

⊕84 42°14'·55N 08°44'·75W Abeam Vigo
⊕86 42°15'·65N 08°42'·55W

Vigo's Marinas

1. Liceo Maritimo de Bouzas
2. Marina Davila Sport*
3. RCN de Vigo*
4. Puerto Deportivo Punta Lagoa*

All VHF Ch 9

*Fuel at 2, 3 & 4

Depths in Metres

Darsena de Bourgas

1. Liceo Maritimo 42°13'·70N 08°44'·95W

A long established marina, close to the noise and dust of shipyards and some way from town. There are 277 finger berths from 6m to 12m. WiFi available.

☎+34 986 232 442
Email info@liceobouzas.com.
www.liceobouzas.com

2. Marina Davila Sport 42°13'·9N 08°44'·5W

This marina was built for megayachts with all the facilities that entails. It is north of the main southwest/northeast mole in the Dársena de Bouzas and protected by a wavebreaker pontoon. The marina offers good shelter as well as modern technical and shore-side layup facilities, but is a very long way from town.

☎ +34 986 244 612
Email marina@davilasport.es
www.davilasport.com www.marinasdegalicia.com
VHF Ch 09

Facilities at Marina Davila Sport

Electricity and water Available on the finger pontoons
Fuel The easily accessible fuel dock and travel lift (inside a long pontoon) are south of the southern mole in the shelter of Dársena de Bouzas.
Ship lift There is a 70 tonne travel lift.
Chandlery Jose Betanoz in the village for a well-stocked chandlery.
Travel The Marina is a walk of 20 minutes from the shops and supermarkets, but bicycles are provided free of charge making it a 5 minute trip. For major provisioning the El Campo mega supermarket is 10 minutes on a bicycle.
  The marineros will order taxis for anywhere and car hire is available in central Vigo.
Internet Access WiFi is provided free of charge.
Laundry Washing machines available.
National Park Permits The marina office will arrange these permits.
Restaurants An excellent restaurant is above the office and offers superb views up and down the ría.

Liceo Marina

Convenient refuelling at Davila Sport

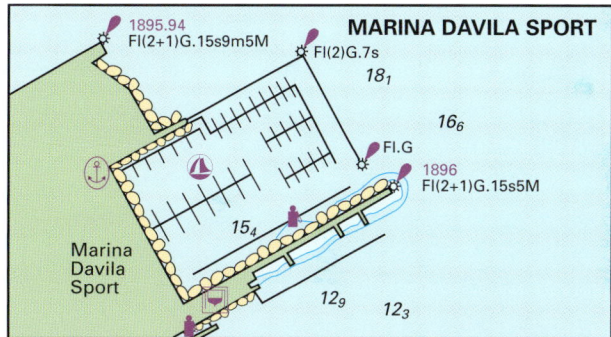
MARINA DAVILA SPORT

Marina Davila Sport looking east

East of Muelle Transatlanticos

3. **Real Club Náutico de Vigo** 42°14'·57N 08°43'·43W
   ☎ +34 986 44 96 94
   Berthing reservations: +34 902 104 762
   www.rcnauticovigo.com info@rcnauticovigo.com
   VHF Ch 09

Approach

Approach square on heading south but beware ferries emerging from starboard. Secure to the reception/fuel pontoon immediately in the entrance (see photo) and seek instructions.

Berthing

The entrance to the original berthing area, bow/stern-to mooring, is immediately to port on entry, but a marina extension has been built to the southwest entrance (see photo). The RCNV is a very congested marina with little space to manoeuvre. The main basin to the east has 320 berths for 8m (53) to 22m (5) boats. The smaller basin to the west past the ferry terminal can only take boats up to 10m on finger pontoons. Minimum depth 2m, 12m in the entrance.

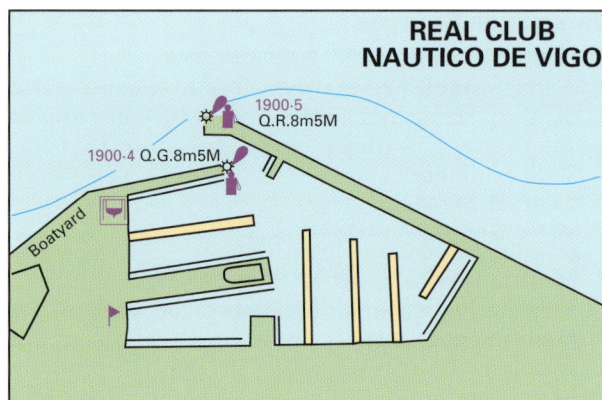

REAL CLUB
NAUTICO DE VIGO

1900·5 Q.R.8m5M
1900·4 Q.G.8m5M
Boatyard

Facilities

Water and electricity on pontoons.
Travel-lift 32 tonne; fuel; WiFi
   There are good facilities on site and easy access to the city.

RCN de Vigo Marina (note that the marina extension to the right of the picture (west) is not shown)

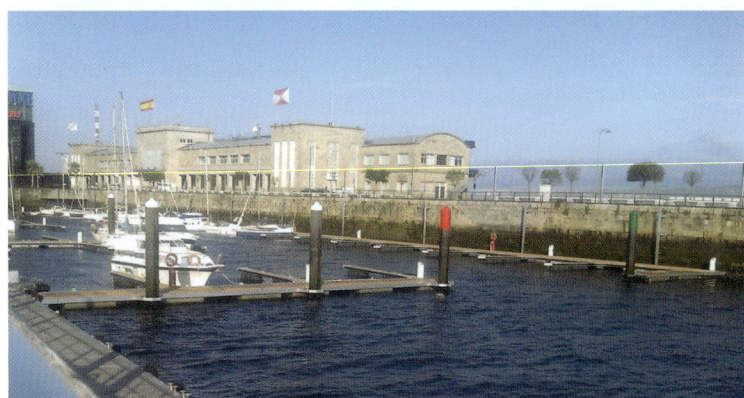

Looking southwest to the RCNV marina extension from the reception pontoon *Henry Buchanan*

Looking east into the main berthing area entrance from the reception pontoon *Henry Buchanan*

Puerto Deportivo Punta Lagoa

42°15'·55N 08°42'·30W Close west of Islote Cabron

Tides
See page 113

Charts
Admiralty 1730, 1731
Spanish   416B
Imray   C48

Final approach ⊕
⊕86 42°15'·65N 08°45'·55W Abeam Punta Lagoa

Lights
Pta de la Guia Oc(2+1)20s36m15M White round masonry tower
Breakwater 42°15'·52N 08°42'·45W Q.G.3M Green post
Entrance Green post

Communications
☎ +34 986 374 305
www.marinapuntalagoa.com
Email info@marinapuntalagoa.com
VHF Ch 09

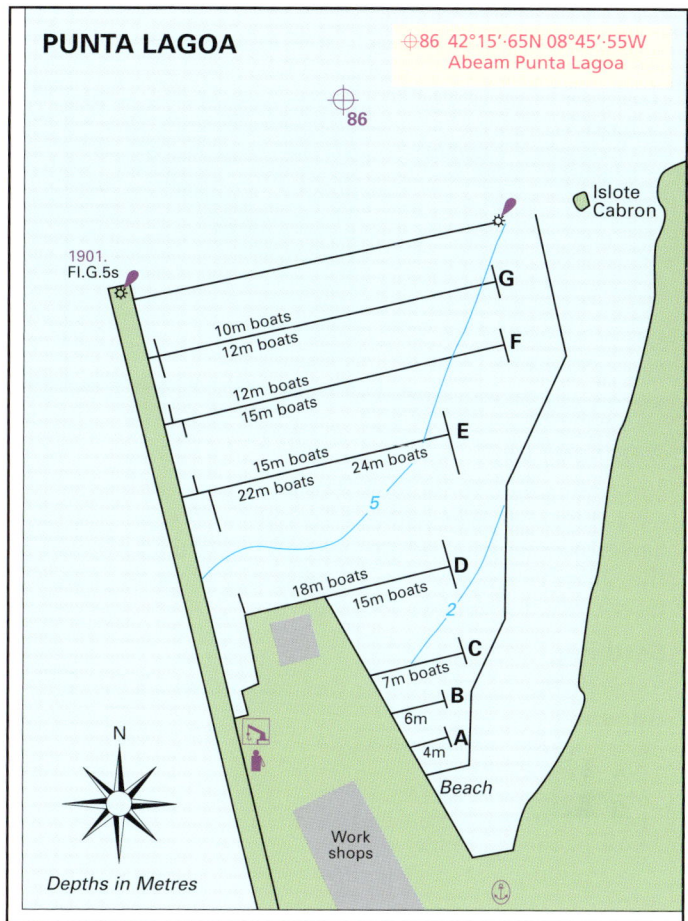

PUNTA LAGOA

⊕86 42°15'·65N 08°45'·55W
Abeam Punta Lagoa

A snug and friendly marina

Punta Lagoa marina is just north of Vigo and nestles between the wooded slopes of the prominent Monte de la Guia and a long breakwater stretching out north from the old Punta Lagoa commercial area. It offers good protection from swell and is a comfortable place to berth a boat with good security. There are magnificent views down the ría from here across the full frontage of Vigo and out to the Islas Cíes.

Approach

Head up the ría towards ⊕86 on about 070°. Punta de la Guia is high, tree-clad and prominent as it juts out into the ría beyond all the docks and industry of the city of Vigo. Turn south into the marina leaving the Islote Cabron and a line of posts to port against the shoreline.

Berthing

There are a total of 300 moorings on finger pontoons for boats of between 6m(27) and 39m(1). Depths reduce from some 4m in the entrance to 3 meters in the inner harbour at low water, but 2m beyond pontoon D.

Facilities

Electricity and water On the pontoons.
Fuel Diesel and petrol pumps.
Travel-lift 2 Travel-lifts of 110 and 50 tonnes and a fixed crane.
Security 24 hours a day security with a hut on the breakwater and at the marina road entrance gate.
Pump out Greywater and sewage.
Showers and WC These left a little to be desired in 2013 unless access was achieved to the cafe/bar/restaurant that had been shut down over a local planning dispute. Hopefully this will have been resolved.
Travel Being a little out of Vigo it is a twenty minutes' walk up a steep hill to shops and public transport in Guia, but good for fitness. There are numerous buses into Vigo from Guia, the No 17 has a stop nearest to the marina. The office or guard (24 hrs) at the main gate can order taxis.

The airport at Vigo is 15 minutes away by bus or taxi.
Engineering services There are engineering services on site managed by Yatesport (www.yatesport.com.es) or contracted in from Vigo yards. Yatesport have mechanical, rigging, electronics, carpentry, GRP expertise, but no longer build boats.
Internet WiFi in the marina.

Puerto Deportivo Punta Lagoa looking southwest towards the Islas Cies *Henry Buchanan*

GALICIA

Ensenada de San Simón

Entry 42°17'·3N 08°39'·6W

Charts

Admiralty	1730, 1731
Spanish	416B
Imray	C48

A tranquil bay

Sail under the 38·8m high Rande suspension bridge (⊕87) leaving Vigo astern to enter the Ensenada de San Simón which tends to be shallow particularly in the northern part. It is peaceful despite the motorway that crosses the bridge.

Berthing

A berth may be found in the club marina of San Adrián:

42°18'·05N 08°39'·14W Entrance
☎ + 34 986 67 38 07
Mobile +34 618 82 63 30
Email info@puertodesanadrian.com
www.puertodesanadrian.com

There are 204 berths from 6m(78) to 18m(2), beam 2·5m to 3m. Berthing is free whilst dining at the superb and well-priced restaurant.

From the west Isla de San Simón is above the left-hand bridge tower.
Anchorage 1 is beyond the cranes to the right; Anchorage 2 is south of the islands

Facilities

Electricity and water; 24hr security; Good showers/toilets; WiFi.

There is a small shop about 1km towards Pontevedra.

Anchorages

The following are suggested anchorages:

1. On the south shore beyond the cranes off Punta Soutelo, before the shallows, in 3–4m mud. Beware the shallows extending off the mouth of the Ría de Redondela and the training walls which cover at half tide.

2. The tip of the island off two stone crosses or southwest of the reef which extends south from the Islas de San Simón (two islands linked by a distinctive bridge). Anchor clear of the beacon in 3m mud or work in between moorings towards the sand shore. There is a restaurant on the spit of beach, and a bakery and shop 400m inland, or take the dinghy to the small harbour of Cesantes (there are food shops but up a steep hill).

3. South of Pta Pereiro with its pontoons shielded in shallow water behind Islote Pedro.

4. Muelle de San Adrián de Cobres 42°18′·14N 08°39′·27W village mole, red beacon. Anchor off the pier in 4m, small restaurant by the dock.

Marina and clubhouse at San Adrián looking south
Martin Walker

GALICIA

Punta Lagoa   Vigo

From the northeast San Adrián Anchorage 4 off quay, and San Adrián Marina. Punta Lagoa marina is beyond the prominent tree-clad hill on the left down the ría

I.3.3 Baiona to the Portuguese border

Approaches to Baiona *p122*
Baiona *p123*
La Guardia *p126*

⊕88	42°10'N	08°52'·7W	Canal del Sur
⊕90	42°08'·7N	08°54'W	1M W Islotes Las Serralleiras
⊕91	42°07'·95N	08°53'W	0·8M SSW Islotes Las Serralleiras
⊕92	42°08'N	08°51'W	0·3M WNW Punta del Buey
⊕93	42°07'·6N	08°50'·3W	App Baiona
⊕94	42°07'·5N	08°54'·8W	1M NW Cabo Silleiro

Lights
Canal del Sur Ldg Lts 069°20'
1890 **Cabo Estay** *Front* Iso.2s17m18M Red truncated pyramid tower red bands
1890.1 **Cabo Estay** *Rear* Oc.4s49m18M as above
Baiona approach Ldg Lts 084°
1911 **Cabezo de san Juan** *Front* Fl.6s8m10M White truncated conical tower
1911.1 **Playa de Panjón** *Rear* Dir.Oc.WRG.4s18m9M White truncated tower on 8-sided base
1916 **Cabo Silleiro** Fl(2+1)15s84m24M White 8-sided tower, red bands, on dwelling

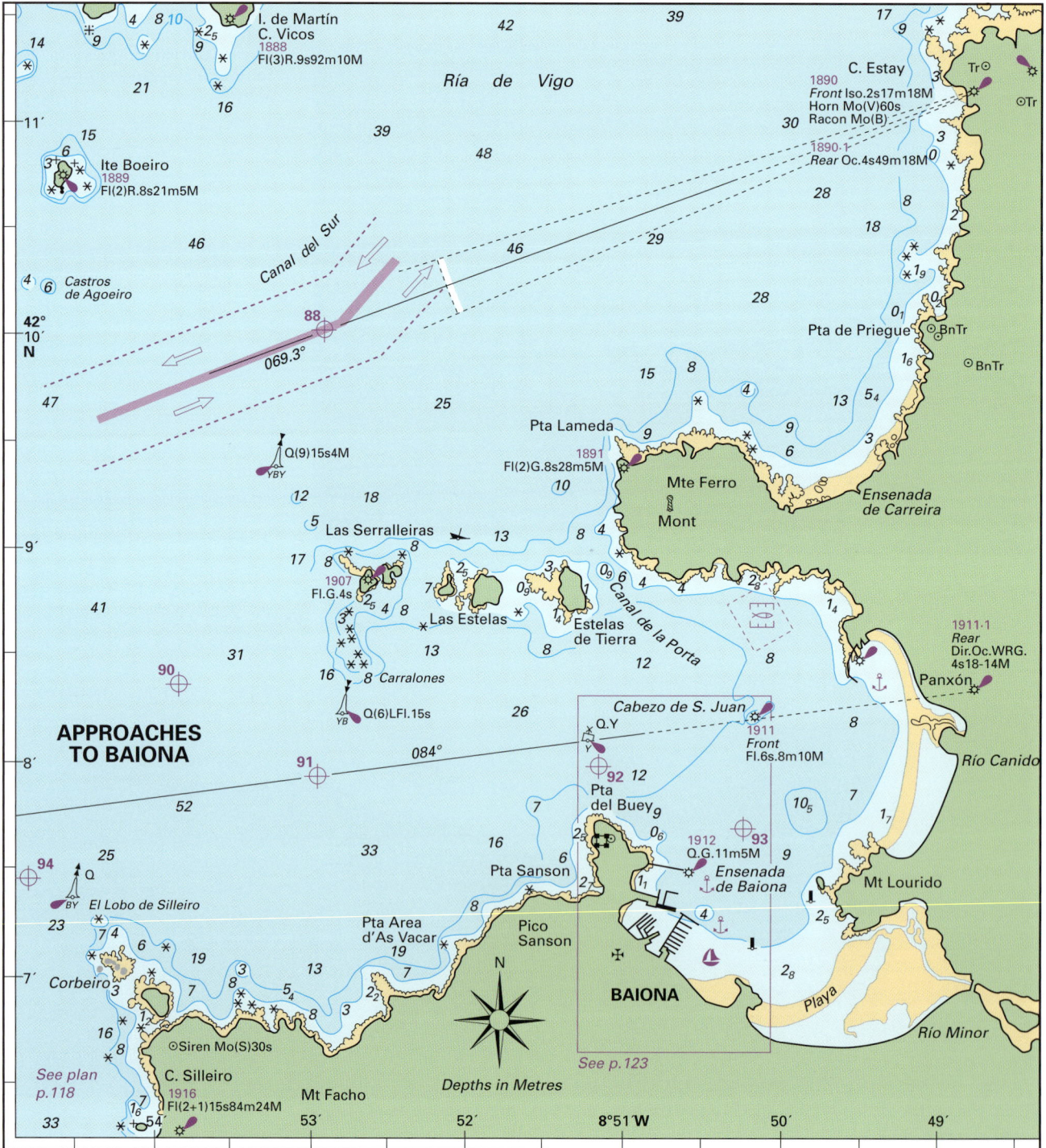

Baiona (Bayona)

42°07'·47N 08°50'·55W

Tides
Standard port Lisbon
Mean time differences
HW +0045 ±0010; LW +0110 ±0010
(the above allows for the difference in time zones)
Heights in metres

MHWS	MHWN	MLWN	MLWS
3·5	2·7	1·3	0·5

Charts
Admiralty 3633
Spanish 4167
Imray C48

Final approaches ⊕
⊕93 (northeast of breakwater)

Light
Breakwater beacon Q.G.5M Green and white tower

Communications
Monte Real Club de Yates
☎ +34 986 385 000
Email secretaria@mrcyb.com www.mrcyb.es
VHF Ch 06 or 71 Monte Real Club de Yates
Porto Deportivo Baiona
☎ +34 986 38 51 07
Email puertobaiona@puertobaiona.com
www.puertobaiona.com
VHF Ch 09 Baiona Sport Harbour

First European harbour to hear that Columbus had discovered America

Baiona is easily approached by day or night and is an excellent port of call whether arriving from transatlantic passage, working north or heading south. It offers the chance to relax, to wait out inclement weather and to re-provision. It is generally well protected except from strong winds with an easterly component, although prevailing northerlies also bring a swell into the harbour, the more marked beyond the protection of the main breakwater running out from Monte Real. Anchorage can be found in the southeast of the bay beyond the two marinas.

The town is attractive and thriving as a tourist resort, with well protected beaches and a secure place in history as Columbus' first mainland landfall

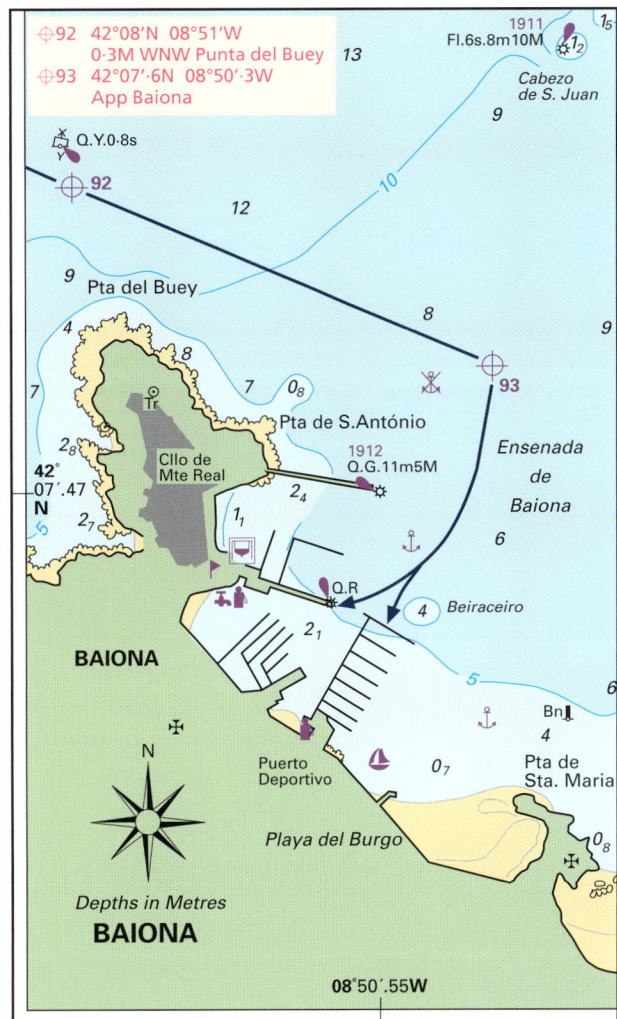

in 1493 after returning from the New World. This is commemorated by a replica of the Pinta permanently berthed in the harbour. The old part of the town is surprisingly un-commercialised compared to the tourist shops along the front, and a cool place to take a leisurely stroll on a hot day. Medieval walls surround the Parador Conde do Gondomar on the northern headland, commanding the harbour and its approaches, and there are

Looking NNW from Pta del Buey across Las Estelas in the approaches to Baiona. Islas Cies beyond *Jane Russell*

Baiona – Puerto Deportivo and MRCY from the north

pleasant walks among the pine forests beyond, where stands the enormous statue of the Virgen de la Roca. WiFi in Bayona is difficult to find and signals are weak. Cafe Erizana on the waterfront, half way between the two main marinas provides the best service.

Approach

⊕91 lies on the leading line of 084° through Cabezo de San Juan and Panjón.

From the north In fair weather keep west of 08°57'W to clear the hazards northwest of Islas Cíes, before setting heading for Cabo Silleiro ⊕94 and then Ensenada de Baiona. With an Atlantic swell running it can be quite a boisterous ride in to Pta del Buey, but everything starts to calm down as you close the end of the breakwater.

From Ría de Vigo With settled weather and with good visibility Canal de la Porta may be used (but see warning on page 113). Otherwise ⊕88, ⊕90,

Go aboard the Pinta and discover how Columbus' men lived
David Russell

⊕91, ⊕92, ⊕93 indicate a route around the dangers of Las Serralleiras and the Las Estelas group of islands and rocks.

From the south Stay off shore, coming no closer than 2M off Cabo Silleiro (⊕95 then ⊕94) before turning onto the approach. ⊕94, ⊕91, ⊕92, ⊕93 apply.

Caution

For about 10M south of Cape Silleiro there is a multitude of unmarked fishing pot floats inshore without flags, plastic and mostly coloured grey or black.

Berthing and Anchoring

1. Monte Real Club de Yates 42°07'·20N 08°50'·40W

The MRCY is a long established club in a superb situation on the harbour ramparts of the headland. The old defensive walls tower above it and house the Parador hotel.

There are 222 berths for boats up to 40m and maximum draught 6m on two long pontoons, one with fingers, one without (pick a rope up from the pontoon, walk it out to the bow, or stern, to tie it off). (It was (2014) €20 more expensive for a 13m boat in a finger berth. Office and domestic facilities are on the lower level beneath the restaurant.

Facilities

Services Water and electricity
Fuel Diesel and petrol
Engineering Repair shop
Travelift 17 tonne
Internet WiFi
Restaurant The club restaurant provides good food and an excellent view over the harbour. Visitors are welcome and are expected to match the dress code of members. restaurante@mrcyb.com ☎ +34 986 356 226

Baiona marinas and anchorage from Mte Real, looking SE   *Jane Russell*

Mte Real from Baiona anchorage, looking NW   *Jane Russell*

2. Puerto Deportivo de Baiona, Baiona Sports Harbour

This marina is popular and a little closer to town than the MRCY, but the planned shoreside development has stalled and the facilities are provided in portacabins (see photo below). A concrete wave breaker connects to the long feeder pontoon that has finger pontoons branching off it. There are 370 berths for vessels of up to 40m in length.

PD de Baiona facilities' buildings – office to the left
Henry Buchanan

Facilities

Services Water and electricity
Fuel Diesel and petrol
Travelift 50 tonne
Technical Services Ronautica, Avenida Monte Real s/n
   36300 Baiona (Pontevedra)Spain.
   ☎ +34 986 385 104
   Email patricia@ronautica.com   www.ronautica.com

Anchoring

The best anchorage close to Baiona is between the Puerto Deportivo and the Bajo Baiño.

Anchorage to the northeast of the Bay

(See plan page 122)

42°08′·5N 08°49′·4W

In settled or easterly conditions it is possible to anchor off the small town of Panjón (Panxón) on the eastern side of the Ensenada de Baiona, with some protection from northwest round to south. The short stone mole (Fl(3)R.9s12m5M Red column 7m) shelters a small harbour packed with moorings, but it provides convenient steps ashore while the Club Náutico de Panjón at its root has showers, a restaurant and bar. South of the harbour is a long sandy beach, the Playa de América. Basic shopping is available in the town, which is dominated by a spectacular church.

La Guardia

41°54'·04N 08°52'·90W

Tides
Standard port Lisbon
Mean time differences
HW +0050 ±0010; LW +0115 ±0010
(the above allows for the difference in time zones)
Heights in metres

MHWS	MHWN	MLWN	MLWS
3·3	2·6	1·2	0·4

Charts
Admiralty 3633
Spanish 417
Imray C48

Final approach ⊕
⊕96, ⊕97

Lights
North breakwater Fl(2)R.7s5M Red truncated conical tower
Cabo Silleiro Fl(2+1)15s84m24M

Navtex
518kHz (D) at 0030, 0630, 0830*, 1230, 1630, 2030*
(*weather only)

Weather bulletins VHF
Vigo Ch 65
La Guardia Ch 21 at 0840, 1240, 2010
Vigo MRSC Ch 10 at 0015, 0415, 0815, 1215, 1615, 2015

Navigational warnings VHF
Vigo Ch 65
La Guardia Ch 21 at 0840, 2010
MRSC Vigo Ch 10 at 0215, 0615, 1015, 1415, 1815, 2215

Primary working frequencies
c/s Coruña Radio
Manual: Vigo Ch 65; La Guardia Ch 21
Autolink: Vigo Ch 62 Tx 2596 Rx 3280
DSC Ch 70 2187·5kHz

A harbour of limited use to yachtsmen

A border town and centre of seafood gastronomy in an attractive setting, La Guardia has more shops, restaurants, hotels and banks than might be expected. It is a busy fishing port with few opportunities to anchor in the harbour, and despite a mole partially closing the entrance from the north heavy swells from the west can set in. A visit in settled conditions can be rewarding, but be prepared to leave at once if conditions deteriorate.

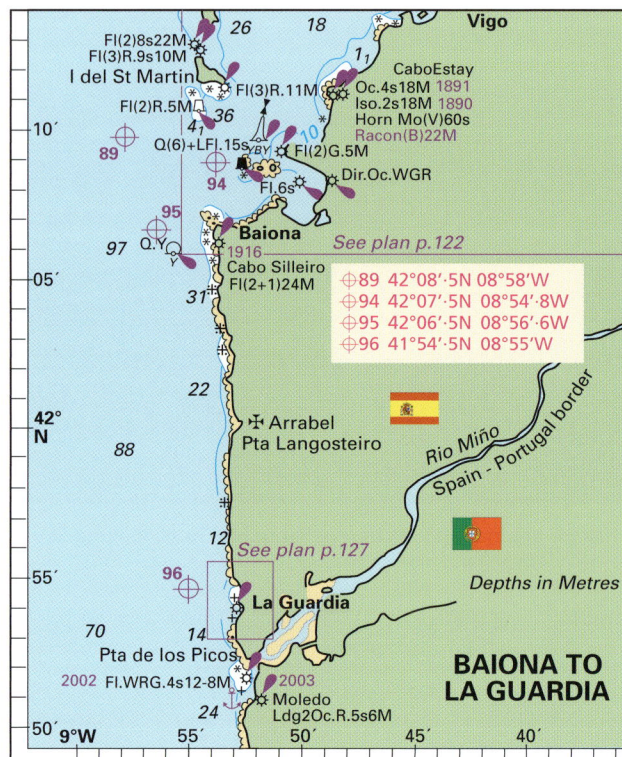

Monte de Santa Tecla, which rises steeply behind the town, repays the effort of the 350m climb. Near the summit is a remarkable Roman-Celtic hut settlement, though somewhat over-restored, and beyond this a series of large stone crosses leads to a tiny church, a restaurant and a hotel. In clear weather there are magnificent views south to the Río Miño, and Portugal, and as far north as the Islas Cíes.

Several fiestas take place in La Guardia during the course of the year, including that of the Virgen del Carmen on 16 July, and those of Monte de Santa Tecla during the second week of August.

⊕89 42°08'·5N 08°58'W
⊕94 42°07'·5N 08°54'·8W
⊕95 42°06'·5N 08°56'·6W
⊕96 41°54'·5N 08°55'W

BAIONA TO LA GUARDIA

The hazards off Cabo Silleiro

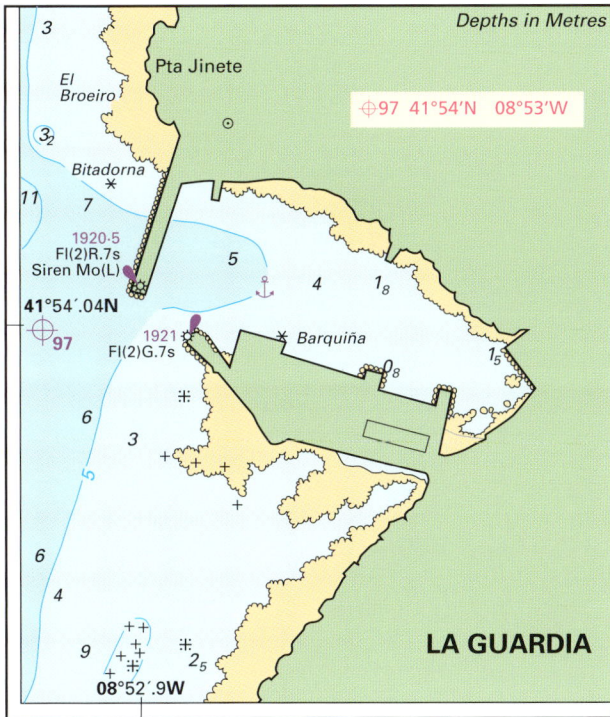

Depths in Metres

Pta Jinete

El Broeiro

Bitadorna

1920·5
Fl(2)R.7s
Siren Mo(L)

41°54'.04N

97

1921
Fl(2)G.7s

Barquiña

⊕97 41°54'N 08°53'W

08°52'.9W

LA GUARDIA

Approach

From the north The coast south from Baiona or Cabo Silleiro holds nothing for the yachtsman but potential hazards. Rocks awash extend up to 0·7M to the northwest of Cabo Silleiro. Swell builds up to crash on what is generally a lee shore and fog can obscure the shoreline although the tops of the hills behind may be in the clear. Straggling buildings run along the coast road as far as the village of Arrabel with its ancient church.

Stay at least a mile offshore until La Guardia has been identified close north of Monte de Santa Tecla. There are two chimneys on the coast just north of La Guardia. From the north, note ⊕89, ⊕96. From Baiona or Ría de Vigo ⊕94, ⊕95 and ⊕96 apply.

Caution

For about 10M south of Cape Silleiro there is a multitude of unmarked fishing pot floats inshore without flags, plastic and mostly coloured grey or black.

From the south. Keep at least 1M off. Conical Monte de Santa Tecla stands out prominently with a clutch of stone buildings and radio aerials on the summit – and the two chimneys near the shore.

Do not approach La Guardia at night, in thick foggy weather, or if there is any noticeable swell.

Entrance

Make final approach to ⊕97 from ⊕96 or the west. The gap between the two moleheads is no more than 70m wide: enter on approximately 105°, staying near the centre as neither wall goes down sheer. Favour the north side of the harbour once inside, and keep well outside a line drawn from the molehead to the corner of the inner wharf in order to clear Barquiña, a rocky shoal some 20m outside this line.

Depths shoal from 8m at the entrance to 0·5m off the quay at the head of the harbour, and on either side it shoals rapidly.

Anchorage and mooring

Very little space remains in which to anchor, as the centre of the harbour is taken up by closely packed fishing boat moorings, while to the south the fairway to the quay must not be obstructed. North of the moorings the water is shallow with an uneven, rocky floor likely to foul an anchor – should it hold at all.

Enlist the help of local fishermen, who may be able to advise if a mooring is free. It is essential to ask (preferably attempting some Spanish) rather than to help oneself.

La Guardia

Left panel:

Pontevedra

SPAIN

Islas Cies
Fl(2)8s186m22M

VIGO

II.1
See plan p.132

Fl(2+1)15s
83m24M

Cabo Silleiro

Tuy

Rio Minho

La Guardia
See plan
p.134

Montedor
Fl(2)9·5s102m22M

Viana do Castelo
See plan
p.138

Esposende
Fl.5s20m20M

See plan
p.141

Póvoa de Varzim

Leixões

II.2
See plan p.150

See plan p.146

Leça
Fl(3)14s57m28M

PORTO
See plan p.152

Fl(4)13s65m23M

Aveiro

See plans
pp.156 & 160

II.3
See plan
p.166

Fl.5s96m28M

Cabo Mondego

See plan
p.162

Figueira da Foz

Penedo da Saudade
Fl(2)15s54m30M

Nazaré
Oc.3s49m14M

See plan p.168

Os Farilhões
Fl(3)5s99m13M

São Martinho
See plan p.171

Berlenga

Peniche   See plan p.174

Cabo Carvoeiro
Fl(3)R.15s56m15M

Assenta
LFl.5s74m13M

Rio Tejo

II.4   See plan p.180

Cabo de Roca
Fl(4)18s
164m26M

LISBON

Cabo Raso
Fl(3)9s
22m20M

Cascais
See plan p.186

Fort Bugio
Fl.G.5s27m9M

Setúbal

Cabo Espichel
Fl.4s167m26M

30′   9°   30′

42°N
30′
41°
30′
40°N
30′
39°

Right panel:

Nazaré
Oc.3s49m14M
See plan p.168

São Martinho
See plan p.171

Fl.5s99m13M

Os Farilhões
Fl(3)20s120m27M

Berlenga

Peniche   See plan p.174

Cabo Carvoeiro
Fl(3)R.15s56m15M

Assenta
LFl.5s74m13M

See plan p.180

II.4

Cabo da Roca
Fl(4)18s164m26M

Cabo
Raso
Fl(3)15s22m20M

Cascais

LISBON

See plan
p.186

Fort Bugio
Fl.G.5s27m9M

Seixal   See plan p.198

Setúbal

II.5
See plan
p.202

Sesimbra

Cabo Espichel
Fl.4s167m26M

Cabo de Sines
Fl(2)15s
55m26M

Sines

Vila
Nova de
Milfontes

Cabo Sardão
Fl(3)15s67m23M

Arrifana

See
plan
p.222

Lagos

Cabo de São Vicente
Fl.5s85m32M

Pta Sagres
Iso.R.2s52m11M

III.1
See plan p.220

Depths in Metres

N

30′   9°W   30′

30′
39°
30′
38°N
30′
37°

II. Portugal – The West Coast

Foz do Minho to Cabo de São Vicente

PORTUGAL – THE WEST COAST

Statue of the great Portuguese explorer Dom Vasco da Gama at Sines *Henry Buchanan*

On passage down the Portuguese Coast *Sebastian Koziura*

Cabo de São Vicente – the springboard for the great Portuguese Discoveries

Foz do Minho to Cabo de São Vicente

In the past many yachtsmen viewed the west coast of Portugal as best avoided, or to be skirted at some distance offshore en route to the Algarve or beyond. This was their loss, as it has much to offer including pockets of stunning scenery, busy wildlife habitats and a mass of history. The increased accuracy of weather forecasts and almost universal use of GPS have played their part, since west-facing entrances can become dangerous in onshore swell, while long stretches of the coast are low and featureless and in summer may be lost in the haze.

Facilities for yachts are hugely improved with some provision for visiting yachts in almost every harbour. However, local yacht ownership is increasing in tandem, and in most places it is wise to telephone ahead to check that a berth will be available. Neither is berthing the relatively cheap option it once was, a situation compounded by there being relatively few all-weather anchorages.

A 'long stay' yacht tax is applied to all foreign-registered yachts kept anywhere in Portugal, either ashore or afloat, for a continuous period of more than 183 days in any tax year. There is then a 30-day period, within which the tax must be paid.

In Portugal, the calendar year is the tax year. This means that if a yacht arrives in Portugal after 2nd July, it cannot become liable in that tax year. If it is in Portugal on 1st January, it would only become liable for the tax on 4th July (and the tax must then be paid by 3rd August). Therefore, the standard 9-month winter contract avoids this tax.

Boats with an engine of less than 20Kw (26·82 HP) or registered before 1986, are exempt from the tax. There is no requirement to register or to claim this exemption. From 2008, 'Boat Tax' became based on engine power only. It uses Kilowatts as the measure. Collection is in the hands of the local *GNR–Brigada Fiscal*, and though non-payment can in theory lead to a fine of around €150 it is often poorly publicised. A certificate and receipt are issued on payment, valid for one year from the date of arrival in Portuguese waters (including the Azores and Madeira).

A few harbours have hazards of one sort or another on their approach, most commonly a bar which alters with the winter storms and can be dangerous if there is a swell running, particularly if it meets an ebbing tidal stream. Even though most river mouths are now dredged and no longer pose a threat in terms of depth – those of the Rio Minho in the north and Vila Nova de Milfontes in the south being notable exceptions – nearly all can be dangerous in heavy weather, and on average at least one yacht is lost (or at least capsized) each year while attempting to enter a harbour on the Portuguese Atlantic coast in the wrong conditions.

Caution

Check the datum of charts being used onboard but note that the plans and waypoints in this publication are all to WGS84.

Great care has been taken over the creation of waypoints, together with their associated courses and distances. However it remains the responsibility of the individual navigator to satisfy him or herself of each one's validity before placing any reliance on it.

Hazards – lobster and fish pots

Clusters of fish pots may be met with at intervals all along the Portuguese coast and particularly around the approaches to harbours. Others are laid well out to sea in surprising depths, and although most are reasonable well marked with flags, a minority rely on dark coloured plastic containers or even branches.

Winds

In April the prevailing northerly Portuguese trades – the *nortada* – begin to set in, generally blowing at around 15–25kn (Force 4–6), and becoming more firmly established from north to south as the season advances. In winter, fronts and occasionally secondary depressions may cross the area. Summer gales are unusual – in winter, onshore gales can close some harbours for days.

Particular mention should be made of the strength of the afternoon sea breezes. From early summer onwards these start to blow at around 1200 each day, regularly reaching 25kn (Force 6) and occasionally 30kn (Force 7) and continuing to blow until sundown. Typically they pick up from the east, swinging north and increasing during the afternoon. For this reason passages north, particularly in smaller yachts or if lightly crewed, are most easily made in short daily hops between dawn and midday with afternoons spent in harbour.

However it should be stressed that while these are the typical conditions, others can and do override them from time to time. In particular, September will occasionally see southwesterly winds gusting to 35kn (Force 8) blow without respite for a week or more, in which case the only prudent course is to stay put.

Winds are frequently stronger in river mouths and in the lee of headlands (due to the katabatic effects) and allowance should be made for this if entering under sail.

SWELL

Swell along this coast originates well offshore and as a result is seldom absent. In many ways it poses a greater danger than the wind, not least because it is extremely easy to underestimate its extent while still in deep water and be taken by surprise by its height and power on closing the coast. In winter it can come from anywhere between southwest and northwest; in summer it is more likely to come from northwest, with heavy swell occurring about 10% of the time. Monitor swell forecasts (see page 2)

Visibility

Poor visibility (less than 2M) can occur any time of year but there is a steep increase in its incidence (from 3% to 10%) 60M either side of Lisbon in July and an increase of approximately the same order further north in August and September. By October, all areas have returned to the 2–4% level. Coastal fog can occur at any time but generally comes with light onshore winds.

Shelter

Many Portuguese harbours provide excellent shelter once inside, but in strong onshore winds only Leixões, Nazaré, Peniche, Cascais, Lisbon and Sines are likely to be safe to enter. In really strong winds even the entrance to the Rio Tejo (Lisbon) can become dangerous.

Currents

The set of the current depends upon the recent dominant wind, but the basic trend is from north to south. Its speed averages about 0·5 knot, though this can double in summer when the *nortada* has been blowing for some time.

Tactics making a passage north

The choice of whether to head offshore or head up the coast is largely down to timing. With time available it is possible to day sail nearly the whole way and have a great cruise.

Favourable windows are more likely to be found in the Spring (May – June). Later in the summer the Portuguese Trades usually fill in and dominate wind and swell. But there are still periods of calm when excellent progress can be made under motor. Sometimes SW winds can occur but usually only for short periods.

Close inshore between Cabo de São Vicente and Lisbon, and Peniche and Baiona, a reduction in the current has been experienced. The problem with this tactic is that, even to some distance offshore, the Portuguese lay thousands of fishing pots, most of which are inadequately marked and unlit. In daylight a very good look out should be kept, and motoring close-in at night is definitely risky.

Tides

Tidal predictions throughout Portugal use Lisbon as the Standard Port, Volume 2 of the Admiralty *Tide Tables: The Atlantic and Indian Oceans including tidal stream predictions (NP 202)*, published annually, covering the entire coastline. Alternatively, consult the UK Hydrographic Office's *EasyTide* programme at www.ukho.gov.uk/easytide. Predictions for the current day and the next consecutive six days are available free of charge. Predictions and additional information for past or future dates can be obtained at a small charge.

The mean tidal range at Lisbon is 3·3m at springs and 1·6m at neaps, but both height and time of tide along the coast can be affected by wind. Offshore tidal streams are very weak and surprisingly little is known about them – at Cabo Carvoeiro it is said to flood to the southeast, roughly the opposite to the stream off Galicia, but it is not known where the change takes place.

Climate

Rain occurs mainly between November and March, with cloud following the same pattern. Cool in winter, warm in summer, cooler in the north, warmer in the south. July averages for Lisbon are 14–36°C with 57% humidity; in January 3–16°C with 75% humidity.

Maritime radio stations and weather/navigational services

Many Portuguese Maritime radio stations and those broadcasting weather and navigational information are situated between, rather than at, ports or harbours. Details will be found under the nearest harbour to the station. All Maritime radio stations are remotely controlled from Lisbon. Broadcast times are quoted in UT, but all other times (office hours etc) are given in LT.

Villa do Conde *James Peto*

PORTUGAL – THE WEST COAST

II.1 Foz do Minho to Leixões

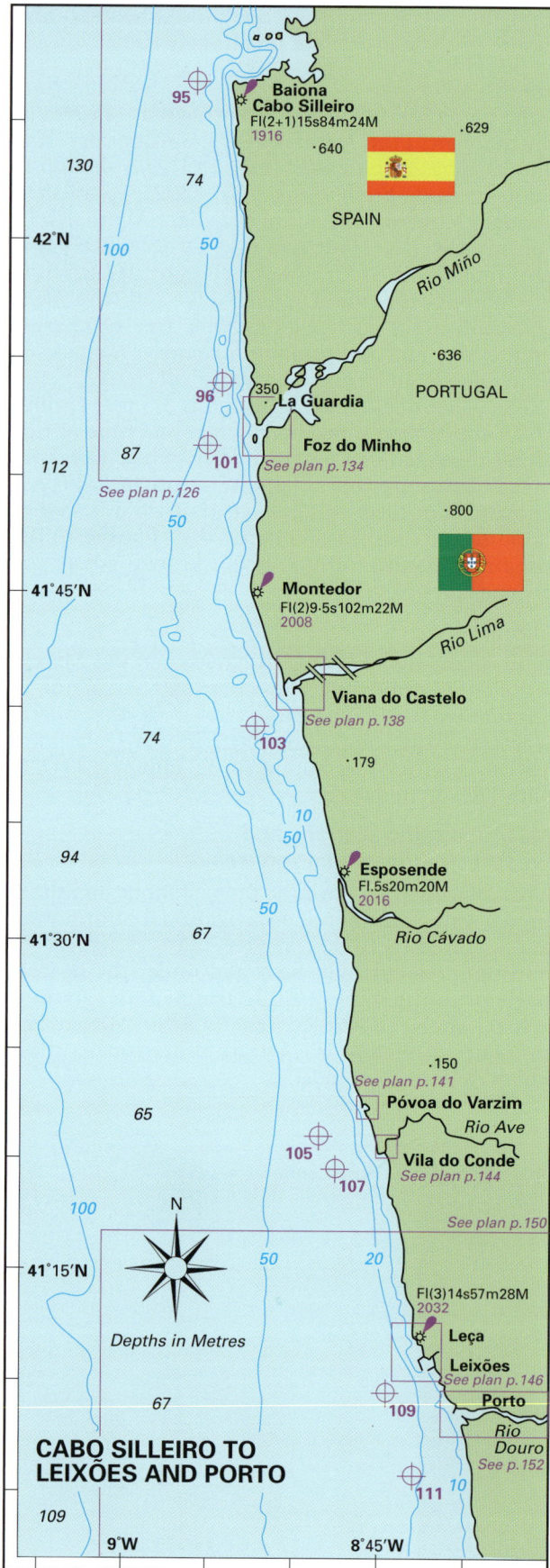

The map shows the coastline from Cabo Silleiro (Spain) to Porto/Rio Douro (Portugal), with labelled positions and lighthouses.

Map labels (north to south):

- Baiona
- Cabo Silleiro 95 Fl(2+1)15s84m24M 1916
- ·629
- ·640
- SPAIN
- 130
- 74
- 42°N
- 100   50
- Rio Miño
- ·636
- La Guardia 96 350
- PORTUGAL
- Foz do Minho 101
- See plan p.134
- See plan p.126
- 112   87
- 50
- ·800
- PORTUGAL
- 41°45'N
- Montedor Fl(2)9·5s102m22M 2008
- Rio Lima
- Viana do Castelo 103 See plan p.138
- 74
- ·179
- 10   50
- 94
- Esposende Fl.5s20m20M 2016
- 50
- 41°30'N   67
- Rio Cávado
- ·150
- See plan p.141
- Póvoa do Varzim
- Rio Ave
- 65
- 105   Vila do Conde 107 See plan p.144
- 100   See plan p.150
- N
- 41°15'N   50   20
- Depths in Metres
- Fl(3)14s57m28M 2032
- Leça
- Leixões See plan p.146
- 67   109   Porto
- Rio Douro See p.152
- 111   10
- CABO SILLEIRO TO LEIXÕES AND PORTO
- 109
- 9°W   8°45'W

95	42°06'·5N	8°56'·6W	2M W of Cabo Silleiro
96	41°45'·5N	8°55'·1W	1·6M WNW La Guardia
101	41°51'·3N	8°54'·9W	Foz do Minho approach
103	41°39'·2N	8°52'·5W	Viana do Castelo approach
105	41°21'·2N	8°48'·7W	Póvoa de Varzim approach
107	41°19'·7N	8°47'·5W	Vila do Conde approach
109	41°09'·2N	8°44'·7W	Leixões approach
111	41°08'·4N	8°43'W	Porto & the Rio Douro approach

PRINCIPAL LIGHTS

1916 **Cabo Silleiro** Fl(2+1)15s84m24M
White 8-sided tower, red bands on dwelling

2008 **Montedor** Fl(2)9·5s102m22M
Horn Mo 'S' (···)25s 800m WSW
Square masonry tower and building 28m

2016 **Esposende** Fl.5s20m20M Horn 20s 100m S
Red tower on white base and building 15m

2032 **Leça** Fl(3)14s57m28M
White tower, narrow grey bands, red lantern 46m

Ports

Foz do Minho
Viana do Castelo
Póvoa de Varzim*
Vila do Conde
Leixões*

* Fuel available alongside

The elegant front leading light on the corner of the Castelo de Santiago at Viana do Castelo
Anne Hammick

Foz do Minho

Courses and distances
⊕95 (Cabo Silleiro) – F101 = 15.3M, 175° or 355°
⊕101 – ⊕102 = 1·8M, 098° or 278°
⊕101 – ⊕103 (Viana do Castelo) = 14M, 173° or 353°

Tides
Standard port Lisbon
Mean time differences (at La Guardia)
HW –0010 ±0010; LW +0015 ±0010
Heights in metres

MHWS	MHWN	MLWN	MLWS
3·3	2·6	1·2	0·4

Charts	Approach	Entrance/river
Admiralty	3633	
Imray	C19, C48	
Portuguese	23202, (23201), 24201	51, (26301)

Principal lights
2002 Insua Nova Fl.WRG.4s16m12/8/9M
357°-W-204°-G-270°-R-357°
White conical tower on square base 7m
2003 Ldg Lts 100°
Front Moledo Oc.R.5s12m6M
White, red and yellow column on beach 3m
2003.1 *Rear* 25m from front Oc.R.5s16m6M
White, red and yellow column behind beach 7·5m
1926 Piedra Cabrón (Bajo de las Oliveiras)
Fl(2)5s3M Black beacon, red band, ⁑ topmark

Night entry
Not feasible, though in calm conditions it might be
possible to anchor in the entrance

Maritime radio station
Arga (41°48'·4N 8°41'·6W)
Remotely controlled from Lisbon)
Manual – VHF Ch 16, 24, 25, 28. *Autolink* – VHF Ch 83.

Attractive river with several anchorages but a difficult entrance

The Rio Minho (or Río Miño to those further north) forms part of the boundary between Spain and Portugal. It gives its name to Portugal's northern province, where the hilly landscape with its numerous villages and their vines, eucalyptus and fruit trees is as pretty as its produce is good.

The Minho valley itself is particularly attractive – though increasingly built-up near its mouth – and, with local knowledge and a current large-scale chart or plan, a yacht of modest draught can navigate a considerable distance up the river. Dinghies, multihulls and monohulls able to take the ground can penetrate as far as Valença on the Portuguese shore – Túy (Tui) on the Spanish side – where there are bridges with an estimated clearance 15m.

The shallow river mouth (*foz*) is continually changing in shape, particularly regarding the position of the deep channel, and local knowledge should be enlisted if at all possible.

Approach

If coastal sailing, the Rio Minho's northern approach is dominated by the 350m Monte de Santa Tecla, topped by grey stone buildings and an aerial. On the mountain's western flank lies a conspicuous factory with two tall chimneys. South of the entrance a narrow strip of land fronted by a wide sandy beach separates the sea from hills which rise to some 700m about 8km inland, while the entrance itself is guarded by the low-lying Insua Nova with its stone fortress.

From offshore, ⊕101 lies some 2M off the coast. A course of 097° for 1·8M leads to ⊕102, after which refer to the plan on page 134.

The approach to the mouth of the Rio Minho

PORTUGAL – THE WEST COAST

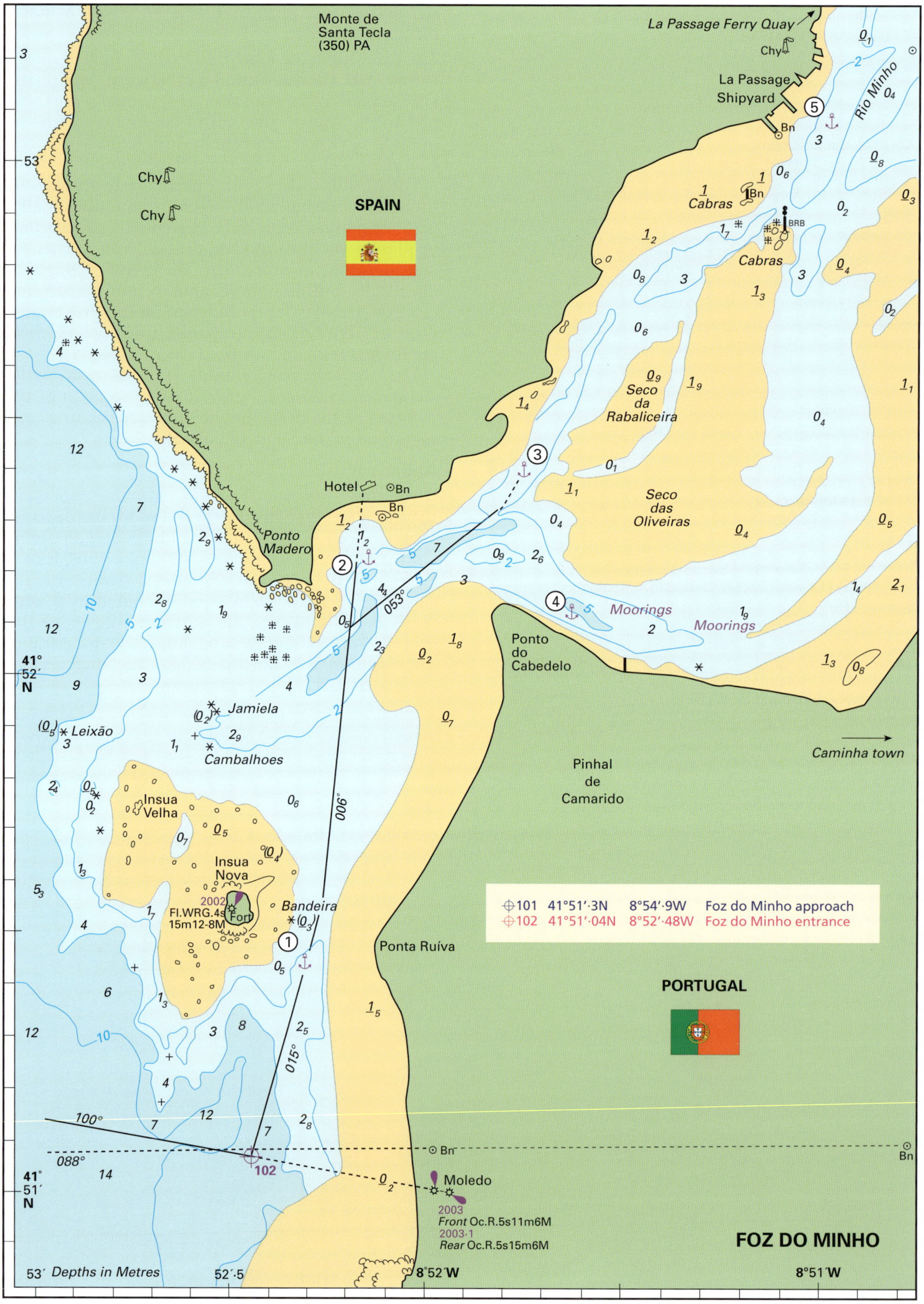

Monte de
Santa Tecla
(350) PA

La Passage Ferry Quay

Chy

La Passage
Shipyard

Chy

3

53

Chy

Chy

SPAIN

Rio Minho

Bn

Cabras

Bn

BRB

Cabras

Seco
da
Rabaliceira

Seco
das
Oliveiras

Hotel   Bn
Bn

053°

Ponto
Madero

Ponto
do
Cabedelo

Moorings
Moorings

Caminha town

*41°
52'
N*

Jamiela

Leixão

Cambalhoes

Pinhal
de
Camarido

Insua
Velha

Insua
Nova

900°

Bandeira

2002
Fl.WRG.4s
15m12-8M   Fort

101	41°51'·3N	8°54'·9W	Foz do Minho approach
102	41°51'·04N	8°52'·48W	Foz do Minho entrance

Ponta Ruíva

PORTUGAL

015°

100°

088°

102

*41°
51'
N*

Bn

Bn

Moledo

2003
Front Oc.R.5s11m6M
2003·1
Rear Oc.R.5s15m6M

FOZ DO MINHO

53' Depths in Metres   52'·5   8°52'W   8°51'W

A fish farm which incorporates a floating platform, marked by a south cardinal post, ⚏ topmark, Q(6)+LFl.6M, lies at 41°49'·3N 8°55'·6W (2M south-southwest of ⊕101).

Entrance

The entrance is difficult and can be dangerous, and has claimed more than one yacht as well as innumerable local craft. It is an option only in calm weather with little or no swell. Once inside, should westerly winds or swell get up a yacht can remain trapped inside for days, though well protected. There are many rocks, shoals and banks in the approaches and the river itself, the sands shift, and the currents run hard in the narrow entrance particularly after rain. Once in the channel there are no buoys or other channel markers.

If possible enter before half flood, when Bandeira rock, 150m east of Insua Nova, should be visible. At the same time some protection will be offered by the rocky shoals which largely block the north entrance (itself not a viable proposition without informed local knowledge).

If coming from the north keep at least 0·5M off Insua Nova and continue south until, by turning onto the Moledo leading line on 100°, one passes south of its fort by some 0·5M. If in doubt there is good water to the south. If coming from the south keep a good 0·5M offshore until able to turn onto 100°, as above. Although the Moledo leading marks are lit, night approach is out of the question. The nearby pair of beacons on 088° – see plan – may also be useful but the rear beacon, nearly a mile inland, is difficult to identify.

When the east side of Insua Nova bears 000°, turn onto approximately 015° to pass as close to the island as Bandeira rock allows. The sandbank off Ponta Ruíva opposite is growing westwards by the year, yet remains very steep-to and in the least swell is likely to be indicated by breaking water. If feasible, anchor about 250m southeast of the fort and reconnoitre by dinghy before pushing on. After leaving Bandeira rock close to port head straight for the conspicuous hotel on the Spanish shore on a bearing of approximately 006°, ignoring the leading marks to the east of the hotel. At approximately 41°52'·08N – or as depths begin to shoal off the rocky patch south of Ponto Madero – alter course to 053°, roughly parallel to the Spanish shore. South of the point depths shoal quickly inside the 5m contour.

If heading towards Caminha town, the channel lies approximately 200m off the southern shore. It shoals after the shore turns northeast.

If continuing north-northeast favour the north shore, keeping to the middle of the gap between the two Cabras (goat) rocks, awash at high tide but the southern group marked by a lit red and black beacon, ⦂ topmark. Note that a group of smaller rocks lie close north of the marked pair. More substantial beacons some 0·5M upstream indicate the ferry channel between the small towns of Composantos and Caminha.

Anchorages near the Foz

1. As already mentioned, temporary anchorage is possible 250m southeast of the fort on Insua Nova. Holding is good over clean sand, protected from west through north to southeast, but it is too exposed for an overnight stay in all but the very calmest conditions
2. South of the hotel on the Spanish side of the entrance, protected from the west by Ponto Madero, in 2–3m.
3. Between the Seco das Oliveiras sandbank and the Spanish shore in 2–3m, but very uncomfortable in wind against flood tide when strong NE winds blow.
4. Off the southern shore, east of Ponta do Cabedelo. This is a delightful anchorage with good holding and plenty of depth to moor inside, near the designated moorings full of small fishing boats.
5. Abeam of the La Passage shipyard, but keeping clear of the dredged ferry channel, indicated by beacons.

The Rio Minho seen from the heights of Monte de Santa Tecla to the north. The two sets of Cabras rocks are clearly visible at half left   *Anne Hammick*

The long white sand beach south of the Rio Minho
Anne Hammick

Formalities

Little notice is likely to be taken of a visiting yacht, though officials from the *Polícia Marítima* and/or the *GNR–Brigada Fiscal* may arrive alongside if in the area. There is a *Capitania* near the Caminha ferry berth which should be visited if anchored in the vicinity, but the nearby *Alfândega* (customs) office has long been closed.

Facilities and communications

On the Portuguese shore a restaurant and a campsite with a small general store will be found near anchorage No.4 above. Caminha itself (within walking distance) has a post office, shops, a market, banks, restaurants and several public telephones. Taxis are available, with bus and train services to Valença, Vigo and Porto.

On the Spanish side there is a small shipyard building trawlers at La Passage and a few buildings near the ferry landing at Goyan, but otherwise little between La Guardia and Túy.

Adjacent anchorage

41°49′N 08°52′·2W (approach)

Ancora, with its small stone fort and miniature harbour, lies just over 2M south of Foz de Minho entrance. There is no room to seek protection inside the tiny harbour – even local craft are hauled high up a wide concrete apron – but in the right conditions anchoring is possible in 2–3m just off the breakwater. However, even if the morning breeze is offshore, by lunchtime the nortada may well make the anchorage untenable and the yacht should never be left unattended.

If intent on exploration, remain at least 0·5M offshore until the harbour has been identified, then pick up the leading marks on 071° (two red and white posts on white pyramid bases). The cross on the hill above is almost in line. Although lit, Fl(2)R.5s11m9M and Fl(2)G.5s10m6M, on no account should the coast be closed in darkness.

The town has shops and restaurants.

The mouth of the Rio Minho from the southwest. On the right is the small harbour at Ancora, about 3M south of the Foz do Minho

Viana do Castelo

Waypoints
⊕103 – 41°39'·2N 8°52'·5W (approach)
⊕104 – 41°40'·34N 8°50'·43W (entrance)

Courses and distances
⊕95 (Cabo Silleiro) – ⊕103 = 27·5M, 174° or 354°
⊕101 (Foz do Minho) – ⊕103 = 14M, 173° or 353°
⊕103 – ⊕104 = 1·9M, 054° or 234°
⊕103 – ⊕105 (Póvoa de Varzim) = 18M, 171° or 351°
⊕103 – ⊕109 (Leixões) = 30·6M, 169° or 349°

Tides
Standard port Lisbon
Mean time differences (at La Guardia)
HW –0010 ±0010; LW +0015 ±0005
Heights in metres

MHWS	MHWN	MLWN	MLWS
3·5	2·7	1·4	0·5

Or refer to EasyTide at www.ukho.gov.uk/easytide

Charts

	Approach	Harbour
Admiralty	3633, 3634, 3257	3257
Imray	C19, C48	C48
Portuguese	23202, (23201), 24201	26401

Principal lights
2012.8 **Outer breakwater** Fl.R.3s9M Horn 30s White tower, red bands 10m
2012 **Fishing harbour Ldg Lts** 012° *Front* Castelo de Santiago Iso.R.4s14m5M 241°-vis-151° Red tower in corner of castle, white lantern 6m
2012.1 *Rear* **Senhora da Agonia** 400m from front Oc.R.6s33m5M 005°-vis-020° Red tower beside prominent church, white lantern 9m
Note The above lights lead from the main channel into the fishing harbour and should NOT be followed through the entrance itself
2012.6 **East (inner) breakwater** Fl.G.3s9M White tower, green bands 6m
2012.4 **Sectored entrance light** Oc.WRG.4s15m8–6M 035°-G-005°-W-010°-R-025°-obscd-350°
2013 **Fishing harbour, port side** Iso.R.1s5m3M White column, red bands 2m
2013.5 **Fishing harbour, starboard side** Iso.G.1s5m3M White column, green bands 2m

Night entry
Well lit (though buoys may occasionally be missing), and straightforward in all normal conditions

Harbour communications
Port Authority ☎ +351 258 359500 *Fax* +351 258 359535 *Email* ipn@ipnorte.pt
www.ipnorte.pt
VHF Ch 11, 16 (call *Capimarviana*) (0900–1200, 1400–1700 weekdays only)
Viana Marina ☎ +351 258 359 546 Fax +351 258 359 535 *Email* marina@apvc.pt
www.apvc.pt
VHF Ch 12.

An old and attractive town with commercial harbour and a small marina on the north bank of the river

Known to the Romans and situated on the banks of the Lethe – the river of forgetfulness – in the 15th century it gained importance as the one of the main ports from which Portuguese explorers set sail. As a result, in the 16th century, the town grew rich from trade with Brazil and from cod fishing on the Newfoundland Banks. The Portuguese swapped local wines for nets brought out by fishermen from England's West Country. This returned to England as 'Portuguese wine' later abbreviated to 'Port wine'. English merchants came to Viana do Castelo in the later 16th century to develop the trade, and links with England once warranted an English consul being based here. The trade moved to Vila Nova de Gaia on the Rio Douro, opposite Porto, when the harbour at Viana silted up. In the meantime the town's citizens had built the beautiful grey granite and white stucco houses that make the old town so attractive today.

A Rio style carnival takes place here every February, but one of the major festivals of the Minho area is the *romaria* dedicated to Nossa Senhora da Agonía which takes place in Viana do Castelo over the weekend nearest to 20 August. It includes impressive floats, displays of local crafts, carnival giants (*gigantones*), local music and a magnificent fireworks display.

This magnificent spectacle of song and dance with parades and fireworks display should not be missed *Henry Buchanan*

A float in the Romaria Festa parade – Viana do Castelo *Henry Buchanan*

Entrance to Viana Marina showing the swinging footbridge (open) and waiting pontoon just downstream to port *Henry Buchanan*

PORTUGAL – THE WEST COAST

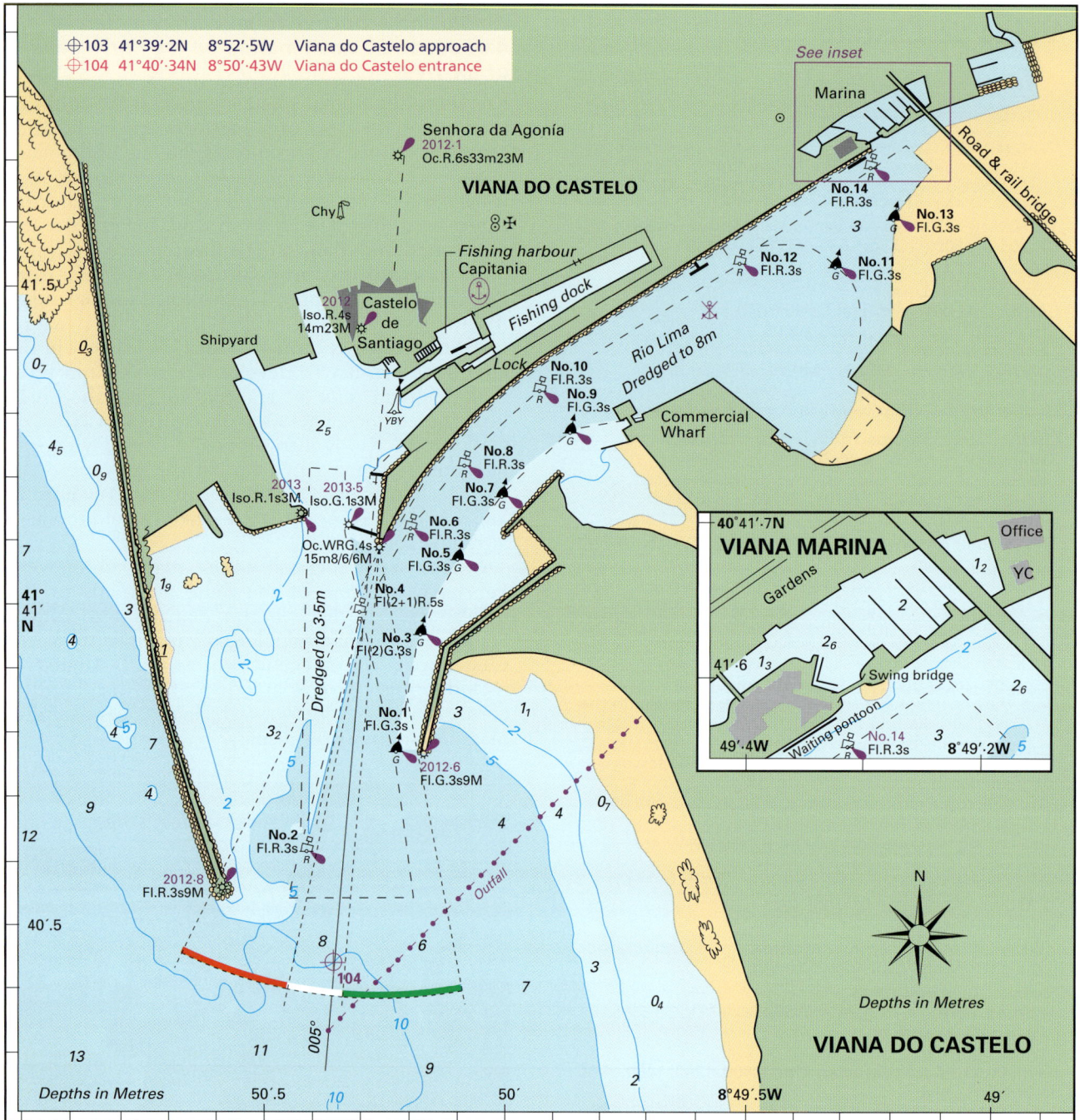

⊕103 41°39′·2N   8°52′·5W   Viana do Castelo approach
⊕104 41°40′·34N 8°50′·43W Viana do Castelo entrance

Senhora da Agonía
2012·1
Oc.R.6s33m23M

VIANA DO CASTELO

Chy

Fishing harbour
Capitania

2012
Iso.R.4s
14m23M

Castelo
de
Santiago

Shipyard

Fishing dock

Lock

No.10
Fl.R.3s

No.9
Fl.G.3s

Rio Lima
Dredged to 8m

Commercial
Wharf

YBY

2013   2013·5
Iso.R.1s3M Iso.G.1s3M

Oc.WRG.4s
15m8/6/6M

No.8
Fl.R.3s

No.7
Fl.G.3s

No.6
Fl.R.3s

No.5
Fl.G.3s

No.4
Fl(2+1)R.5s

No.3
Fl(2)G.3s

No.1
Fl.G.3s

2012·6
Fl.G.3s9M

Dredged to 3·5m

No.2
Fl.R.3s

2012·8
Fl.R.3s9M

Outfall

005°

104

No.14
Fl.R.3s

No.13
Fl.G.3s

No.12
Fl.R.3s

No.11
Fl.G.3s

Marina

See inset

Road & rail bridge

Viana Marina inset:
40°41′·7N
VIANA MARINA
Office
YC
Gardens
Swing bridge
Waiting pontoon
No.14
Fl.R.3s
41′·6
49′·4W
8°49′·2W

N

Depths in Metres

VIANA DO CASTELO

Depths in Metres

8°49′.5W

Approach

If coastal sailing, note that hazards lie close offshore both north and south of Viana do Castelo – for peace of mind keep outside the 20m line.

From offshore, ⊕103 lies 1·9M southwest of the entrance, a course of 054° leading to ⊕104, close outside the harbour mouth.

The major lights are Montedor to the north, Senhora da Agonia at Viana itself, and Esposende. There are a pair of leading lights at Neiva, 3·5M to the south, which are not relevant to Viana.

Entrance

From the north, take a wide swing eastwards at least 500m south of the outer breakwater. At night, do not turn into the harbour until within the white sector of the entrance light (see plan), to pass up the centre of the buoyed channel to pass up the centre of the buoyed channel.

From the south, head in from the 20m line with the radio aerial on Faro de Anha bearing around 080° until within the white sector, then proceed as above. The entrance is kept dredged to 8m, making it safe in all but the severest weather or swell.

The south-facing entrance to Viana do Castelo

Leaving the entrance to the shipyard and fishing harbour to port, follow the buoyed channel northeast past the commercial wharf on the starboard hand to the marina on the north bank. This is just short of the road and rail bridge and marked by the swinging 'gate' of a cantilevered footbridge across the entrance. The footbridge has no visible lights when viewed from the west and it is hard to detect, both during the day and at night, against the background of the old road/train bridge of Rio Lima. Ten buoys are shown as marking the channel between the fishing dock and marina entrance, though it appears rare for all to be in place and working at any given time. Thus while night entry is perfectly feasible it should be undertaken with some caution.

Beyond the commercial wharf depths decrease from 8m to 3m, shoaling to less than 2·5m in the marina approach. Beware strong cross-currents at the marina entrance on both the flood and the ebb.

Anchoring in the river is prohibited, but towage is available if required.

Caution

On the ebb at night, fishermen deploy drift nets across the entire width of the river marked by faint white lights and a brighter white light at each end.

Berthing

Viana Marina lies about 1·5M upriver from the entrance, with its eastern end beneath the two-tier road and rail bridge (designed by Gustaf Eiffel of Tower fame). The old town is a short walk away through public gardens which contain a children's playground.

Just downstream of the marina there is a reception pontoon beyond which is a swinging 'gate', of a cantilevered footbridge guarding the entrance. This

Viana Marina looking northeast

is controlled by the marina staff, who can be contacted on VHF Ch 9 or 16.

The marina contains some 160 berths, of which around 20 are nominally reserved for visiting yachts of up to 14m. In addition there is a single berth capable of taking a 20m vessel. The reception pontoon is just outside and downstream of the entrance, and electricity/water is available here. Visitors are berthed inside on either the westernmost of the four pontoons on the starboard hand or on the right-angled pontoon to be found on the port side, just inside the entrance. The westernmost pontoon has fingers whilst the right-angled pontoon to port has a combination of alongside berths and picking-up lines.

Formalities

The marina office will be found in the large new building at the east end of the basin. Although for many yachts this will be their first (or last) Portuguese harbour, formalities are kept to a minimum with computer-generated forms distributed automatically to the various officials. The usual passports, ship's papers and insurance documents will be required. Normally no other offices need be visited, though skippers of non-EU registered yachts, or with non–EU nationals amongst their crew, should check current requirements. Yachts which arrive outside office hours may be visited by a member of the *GNR–Brigada Fiscal*.

Facilities

Boatyard No boatyard at the marina, but extensive shipyards west of the fishing dock where commercial vessels, as well as GRP and timber fishing boats, are built. In an emergency there is little doubt that yacht repairs in most materials could be undertaken. Enquire at the marina office.

Travel-lift Not as such, but the marina has a mobile crane capable of lifting at least 20 tonnes, with larger ones available in the new commercial harbour on the south bank of the river. Yachts of suitable underwater shape may also use the tidal grid.

Engineers Costa & Rego Lda, ℡ 258 806140, situated between the river and the old commercial basin, are precision engineers and machinists. They can arrange engine repairs and will copy any unobtainable metal parts.

    Next to them will be found Mechanica Magalhães (run by two brothers, it is sometimes referred to as Magalhães & Magalhães Lda), ℡ 258 823950, mobile 93 8344 797. Neither speak much English but the marina staff are happy to translate if necessary.

    Finally Manuel Carvalhosa & Ca Lda, ℡/Fax 258 832133, mobile 96 9024 743, has been recommended as 'fast, efficient and reliable' for work on diesel engines/electrics/fabrication/ welding etc.

Electronic and radio repairs Arrange through the marina office, who may well suggest Engineering Pires, mobile 91 7540 233.

Sail repairs Minor repairs may also be done locally (enquire at the marina office). For anything major try Pires de Lima in Porto (see page 149).

Chandlery A good range will be found at Angelo Silva Lda, ℡ 258 801465 Fax 258 801469 www.marinehardware.en.ecplaza.net *Email* geral@nautigas.pt, overlooking the old commercial basin. Items not in stock can be ordered from a wide variety of suppliers. Ferraz & Ferraz Lda just beyond sells some chandlery in addition to all kinds of fishing tackle.

    A chandlery is planned for the large building where the marina office is situated.

Water On the pontoons.

Showers Immaculate showers and toilets at the back of the block housing the marina office. The latter are open to all, the former accessed by key obtained from the marina office.

Launderette A washer and a dryer are provided in both the men's and the ladies' ablutions areas. There are several commercial launderettes in the town.

Electricity On the pontoons.

Fuel There is no longer fuel available at the marina entrance. Diesel and petrol from a filling station just beyond the road/rail bridge.

Bottled gas Camping Gaz is readily available. Angelo Silva Lda (see Chandlery above) can arrange for other bottles to be refilled, but allow a minimum of 24 hours.

Clube náutico Small but friendly *clube náutico* at the east end of the marina basin, which welcomes visiting yachtsmen.

Weather forecast At the marina office.

Banks Several in the town, nearly all with cash dispensers.

Shops/provisioning Good shopping of all kinds in the town, including several supermarkets, with a hypermarket about 1·5km inland.

Produce market Fish and produce market daily, plus open-air general market on Friday near the Castelo de Santiago at the seaward end of the town.

Cafés, restaurants and hotels A wide choice in and around the town. The *clube náutico* has a bar overlooking the marina which also serves light meals.

Medical services Hospital etc in the town.

Communications

Post office In the town.

Mailing address The marina office will hold mail for visiting yachts – c/o Instituto Portuário do Norte, Marina de Viana do Castelo, Rua da Lima, 4900-405 Viana do Castelo, Portugal. It is important that the envelope carries the name of the yacht in addition to that of the addressee.

Internet access There is no WiFi at the marina, but several terminals in the nearby youth hostel (the rather boxy building just upstream of the two-tier bridge) and a facility on the Rua General Luis do Rêgo (open 0900–1900 weekdays, 0900–1800 Saturday, closed Sunday), the latter also has printers.

Public telephones In the entrance to the *clube náutico* and elsewhere.

Fax service At the marina office, Fax 258 359546.

Car hire/taxis In the town. Taxis can be ordered from the marina office.

Buses and trains To Porto, Vigo and beyond.

Air services International airport at Porto some 50km away.

Not feasible – Esposende

Esposende (41°32'·5N 8°47'·5W), just under 10M south of Viana do Castelo, should be mentioned in passing – literally. A long sandbank blocks the mouth of the Rio Cávado, leaving a very shallow entrance some 50m wide which gives onto an equally shallow lagoon where a few small boats are moored. Shoals and isolated rocks (the Cavalos de Fão and Baixo da Foz) extend up to 1·5M offshore opposite the lighthouse. Give it a wide berth.

Póvoa de Varzim

Waypoints
⊕105 – 41°21'·2N 8°48'·7W (approach)
⊕106 – 41°22'·15N 8°46'·14W (entrance)

Courses and distances
⊕95 (Cabo Silleiro) – ⊕105 = 45·7m, 173° or 353°
⊕103 (Viana do Castelo) – ⊕105 = 18M, 171° or 351°
⊕105 – ⊕106 = 2·1M, 064° or 244°
⊕105 – ⊕107 (Vila do Conde) = 1·8M, 149° or 329°
⊕105 – ⊕109 (Leixões) = 12·4M, 166° or 346°

Tides
Standard port Lisbon
Mean time differences
HW –0010 ±0010; LW +0015 ±0005
Heights in metres

MHWS	MHWN	MLWN	MLWS
3·5	2·7	1·4	0·5

Or refer to EasyTide at www.ukho.gov.uk/easytide

Charts

Charts	Approach	Harbour
Admiralty	3634	
Imray	C19, C48	C48
Portuguese	23202, (23201), 24201	(27501)

Principal harbour lights
2020.4 **North breakwater** Fl.R.3s14m12M
   White tower, red bands 5m Siren 40s
Note The breakwater projects some distance beyond the
light structure
2020.6 **South breakwater** LFl.G.6s13m4M
   White post, green bands 4m

Night entry
Straightforward, though care must be taken to observe
the small, unlit, starboard hand buoys

Maritime radio station
Apúlia – *Digital Selective Calling* (MF)
MMSI 002630200 (planned)

Harbour communications
Marina da Póvoa ☎ +351 252 688121 *Fax* +351 252
622791 *Email* clubenavalpovoense@mail.telepac.pt
www.clubenavalpovoense.com
VHF Ch 09, 12,16 (0900–1200, 1400–1700).

| ⊕105 | 41°21'·2N | 8°48'·7W | Póvoa de Varzim approach |
| ⊕106 | 41°22'·15N | 8°46'·14W | Póvoa de Varzim entrance |

The semi-circular harbour at Póvoa de Varzim, seen from a
little west of south. The Marina da Póvoa can been seen in
the foreground, with the fishing boat berths beyond

Small, friendly marina in busy fishing harbour

Coming in from the sea, the view of Póvoa de
Varzim's newer high-rise buildings belies the largely
18th-century town which lies to the east and south.
Hotels and a casino front the beach, but the harbour
still boasts an active fishing fleet and the Marina da
Póvoa has gained a well-deserved reputation for
friendly and efficient service since its opening in
1999.

A colourful *romaria* is held on 15 August each
year to commemorate those lost at sea, while the
Museu Municipal de Etnografica e História on Rua
do Visconde de Azevedo often has interesting
displays relating to local fishing and other maritime
pursuits in its handsome 18th-century headquarters.

South of Povoa, at Rio Mau, lies the church of Sao
Christovao completed in 1151, with some excellent

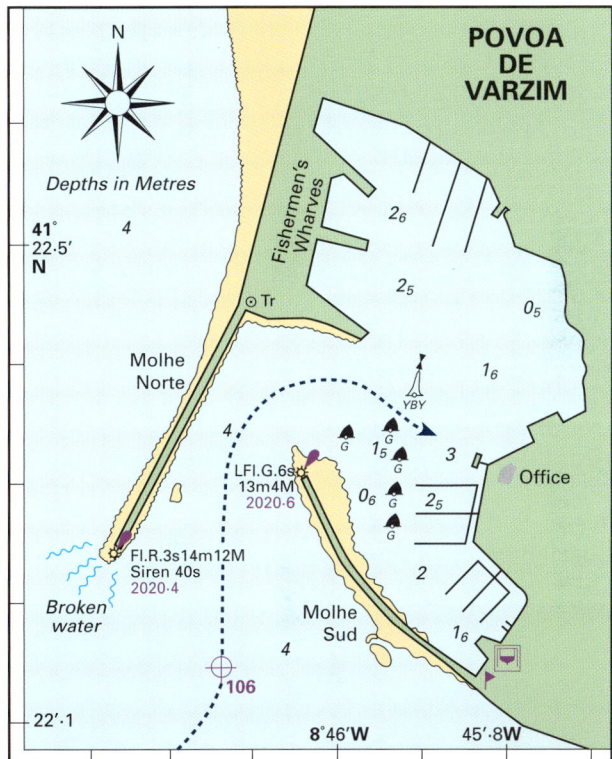

PORTUGAL – THE WEST COAST

carvings from this period. Two kilometres further on the same road, a left hand turn leads to Rates, where the 13th-century church of São Pedro de Rates is one of the best examples of Romanesque architecture in Portugal, boasting a magnificent rose window and some gracefully sculpted statues of saints.

Approach

If coastal sailing, the coast between Viana do Castelo and Esposende has offlying dangers and should be given 2M clearance. From Esposende southwards there are sandy beaches and rocks with further isolated hazards all the way to Leixões. For relaxed sailing, keep outside the 20m contour, but beware of fishing floats and an offshore alternative energy generation site just inside the 50m contour, about 6·8nm NNW of Povoa de Varzim. The area is marked by four cardinal buoys as follows:

1. Northwest NCB 41°28'·29N 008°50'·82W VQ 0·6s
2. Northeast ECB 41°28'·20N 008°50'·12W VQ(3)5s
3. Southwest WCB 41°27'.52N 008°50'·99W VQ(9) 10s
4. Southeast SCB 41°27'.43N 008°50'·28W VQ(6)+LFl 10s

The massive structure of a single wind generator has been erected at this site, where it is likely that an earlier experimental wave generator has been removed. The structure has a white strobe light flashing 1 every 3 seconds at its top and is painted white, so difficult to see in a mist. The prudent mariner will give the area a wide berth (see photo).

From offshore, ⊕105 lies 2·1M west-southwest of the entrance, a course of 064° leading to ⊕106, close outside the harbour mouth.

A distinctive white apartment block stands a short distance north of the harbour. The latter may be identified by its tower – reminiscent of an airport

Wind Turbine in 50m, 3nm from the coast, NW of Póvoa de Varzim *Henry Buchanan*

control tower – which also serves as an excellent landmark. A range of fish-handling buildings stand behind it.

Entrance

If approaching from the north, swing wide of the breakwater end and its associated breaking water, and note that it is also foul up to 30m off on the south side. Approach heading north-northeast towards the spur which projects at right angles from the north breakwater, giving the latter a 50m offing. When the southern breakwater head has been cleared, turn to starboard for the marina or anchorage, leaving the line of small, unlit, green buoys (which mark shoals on the inside of the breakwater) well to starboard and the (unlit) west cardinal buoy (believed to mark a rock) to port. Depth unknown.

The friendly and well-run Marina da Póvoa

The harbour is well protected from the northwest, but the entrance may be rough if the swell is heavy and, even in moderate conditions, breaking water can be expected off the breakwater end.

In bad weather the harbour can be closed in which case the following marks/signals are displayed from the radar tower at the root of the west breakwater:

By day: A black cylinder

By night: Red, green, red vertical lights.

Berthing

The Marina da Póvoa offers 241 berths on its six pontoons. There are about 50 berths for yachts of 10m or more with depth of at least 2.4m, and four berths for yachts of up to 18m with depth of at least 3m.

The marina lies in the shelter of the south breakwater, and even in gale force west-northwesterlies experiences remarkably little movement inside, although a vigorous chop comes across the harbour in fresh northerlies. All berths are provided with finger pontoons of appropriate length.

On arrival yachts should berth on the short hammerhead by the marina office. Office hours are 0900–2000 daily in summer, 0900–1230 and 1400–1730 in winter, with a night watchman providing 24 hour security.

Anchorage

Anchoring in the harbour is permitted, provided neither the marina approach nor the many fishing boat movements to and from the north breakwater are impeded. The most obvious spot is in the northeast of the harbour, clear of the yacht and small craft moorings, in about 3m over mud and sand, but space is limited. Depths shoal gradually at some distance from the shore.

Formalities

If berthed in the marina (or anchored), visit the marina office taking passports, ship's papers and insurance documents. There are no forms to complete but copies of passports and boat's papers are needed. It is also not necessary to clear out from each port in Portugal as details are kept in computer systems which most ports have access to. If a change of crew is made, however, the authorities need to be informed for safety reasons.

Facilities

Boatyard Several businesses operate within the marina's secure area – ask at the office. There is a large area of open space fronting the marina, part of which is designated for use as hardstanding. A small covered workshop has been provided in the central marina building, next to the main gate.

Travel-lift A 32-tonne capacity hoist operates in the southern part of the secure area.

Engineers, electronic and radio repairs All skills available amongst those who service the fishing fleet – enquire at the marina office. A professional diver is also available.

Sail repairs Nothing nearby – try Pires de Lima in Porto (see page 155).

Chandlery Náutica Vaga, tucked away behind the old fort opposite the fishing harbour, has only limited stock. For anything major contact Angelo Silva Lda in Viana do Castelo or Nautileça in Leixões (see pages 140 and 149 respectively).

Water On the pontoons.

Showers In the central marina building.

Launderette In the central marina building.

Electricity At every berth.

Fuel No fuel at the marina, the original plan to install pumps on the reception pontoon having been shelved indefinitely. However diesel can be obtained in the fishing harbour (no minimum quantity) and small quantities of petrol, for outboards or generators, from the marina office.

Bottled gas Camping Gaz exchanges are readily available in the town, and Calor Gas bottles can be refilled. Ask at the office for directions.

Clube naval The Clube Naval Povoense, which in 2004 celebrated its centenary, has large premises overlooking the south breakwater, where members' dinghies and jet-skis are stored on the ground floor with a bar and restaurant above. Visiting yachtsmen are made particularly welcome. WiFi available.

Weather forecast 48-hour forecast posted daily outside the marina office.

Banks In the town, about ten minutes' walk.

Shops/provisioning Good range in the town, with a large supermarket about 2km distant.

Produce market In the town.

Cafés, restaurants and hotels Wide variety in the town, as well as a restaurant at the *clube naval*.

Medical services Well equipped first aid post in the marina's central building, with doctors and a hospital in the town.

Communications

Post offices In the town.

Mailing address By courier: Marina da Povoa, Porto de Abrigo da Povoa de Varzim, Mollhe Sul, 4490 Povoa de Varzim, Portugal.

By Post: Club Naval Povoense, Rua da Ponte No 2,4490 523 Povoa de Varzim, Portugal.

The *Clube Naval* will hold mail for visiting yachts – c/o Marina da Póvoa, Rua da Ponte No.2, Apartado 24, 4491 Póvoa de Varzim, Portugal. It is important that the envelope carries the name of the yacht in addition to that of the addressee.

Internet access There is good WiFi on the marina pontoons and further access points in the town.

Public telephones At the marina's central building, with cards available from the office.

Fax service At the marina office, *Fax* 252 688123.

Car hire/taxis In the town. A taxi can be ordered via the marina office. Bicycles (some with small trailers) can be hired from an office at the root of the main breakwater.

Buses and trains To Porto, Viana do Castelo etc. The metro is fully open and there is an hourly express service into Porto and to near the airport (1hr). Several yachtsmen have also recommended the 'direct' bus as a convenient way to visit the city.

Air services International airport at Porto some 20km away. The metro provides easy access for crew changes.

PORTUGAL – THE WEST COAST

Vila do Conde

Waypoints
⊕107 – 41°19'·7N 8°47'·5W (approach)
⊕108 – 41°20'·1N 8°44'·88W (entrance)

Courses and distances
⊕105 (Póvoa de Varzim) – ⊕107 = 1·8M, 149° or 329°
⊕107 – ⊕108 = 2M, 079° or 259°
⊕107 – ⊕109 (Leixões) = 10·7M, 169° or 349°

Tides
See Póvoa de Varzim, page 141

Charts

	Approach	Harbour
Admiralty	3634	
Imray	C19, C48	
Portuguese	23202, (23201), 24201	(27501)

Principal lights
2023.7 **Breakwater** Fl.R.4s8m9M Siren 30s
  Red column, white bands 8m
2023 **Outer Ldg Lts 079°**
  Front **Azurara** Iso.G.4s9m6M
  White post, red bands 7m, at rear of beach
2023.1 *Rear* 370m from front Iso.G.4s26m6M
  Square white tower, red bands and ▲ 6m
2024 **Inner Ldg Lts 357°** *Front* Barra Oc.R.3s6m6M
  White column, red bands 3m
2024.1 *Rear* 86m from front Oc.R.3s7m6M
  White column, red bands 5m

Night entry
  Not feasible without local knowledge

Harbour communications
  Capimarviconde VHF Ch 11, 16 (0900–1200, 1400–1700
  Monday–Friday).

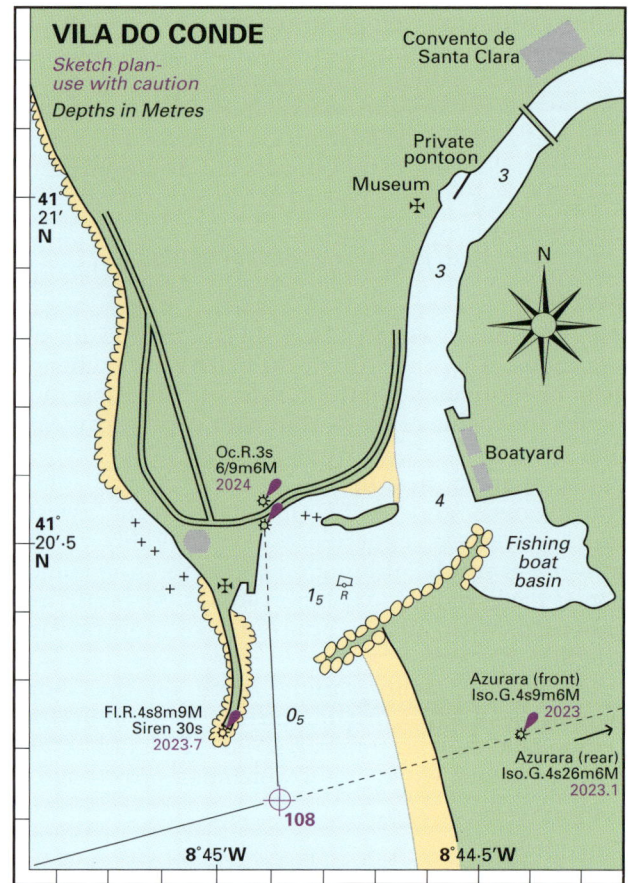

Looking into Vila do Conde from the south, with the white
bulk of the Convento de Santa Clara clearly visible just left of
centre

⊕107	41°19'·7N	8°47'·5W	Vila do Conde approach
⊕108	41°20'·1N	8°44'·88W	Vila do Conde entrance

Pontoon, Convento de Santa Clara and road bridge looking upstream *James Peto*

Narrow river offering possible berth and anchorage

A small harbour only suitable for entry in calm weather, in daylight, and towards high tide. The town enjoyed its boom years as a shipbuilding centre during Portugal's Age of Discovery in the 15th and 16th centuries. The old fishing village, renowned for its lace, is dominated by the imposing Convento de Santa Clara. Traces of the old shipyard can still be made out, though now supplanted by the impressive building and repair yard overlooking the fishing basin. Lace-making is kept alive today at the Escola de Rendas (Lace-making School) installed on the premises of the town's Lace Museum on Rua de São Bento.

Five kilometres inland at the confluence of the rivers Ave and Este there is the pre-Roman site of Bagunte.

Approach and entrance

The entrance lies at the southern end of the line of high-rise blocks strung out along the beach between Póvoa and Vila do Conde. The low breakwater is some 350m long and has a small chapel dedicated to Senhora da Gaia at its root.

From offshore the outer leading marks, on 079°, clear the mole but are difficult to identify from offshore. ⊕107 lies on this line and 2M offshore. The inner pair, on 357°, lead over the bar – which may shoal to 0·5m at low water springs – but as the bar shifts these do not always indicate best water. ⊕108 lies at the intersection of the two leading lines.

Once round the eastern (inner) mole the channel swings to pass south of a small, L-shaped sandbank, marked by a single red buoy. A sizeable fishing boat basin, not available to yachts, lies to the east of the bend.

Tidal streams in the relatively narrow entrance can run strongly on both ebb and flood. It is advisable to enter the river at the end of the flood.

Berthing

There is a pontoon in the river just downstream of the road bridge (see photograph). It is private but it is reported to be possible to berth for a night against a vessel of suitable size, or in a gap on the basis that the owner may return. There is a gate at the end of the pontoon.

Anchorage

Anchor just short of the road bridge in 3–4m, taking care to buoy the anchor as the bottom is mainly foul. On the north bank there is an unusual fortified church with an almost Moorish white dome, while the entire area is overshadowed by the vast bulk of the Convento de Santa Clara.

Facilities and communications

Food shops, banks, and restaurants are all available as well as a lively produce market on Fridays. There is a post office and public telephones sited throughout the town. The metro and regular bus service provide transport north to Póvoa de Varzim and south to Porto.

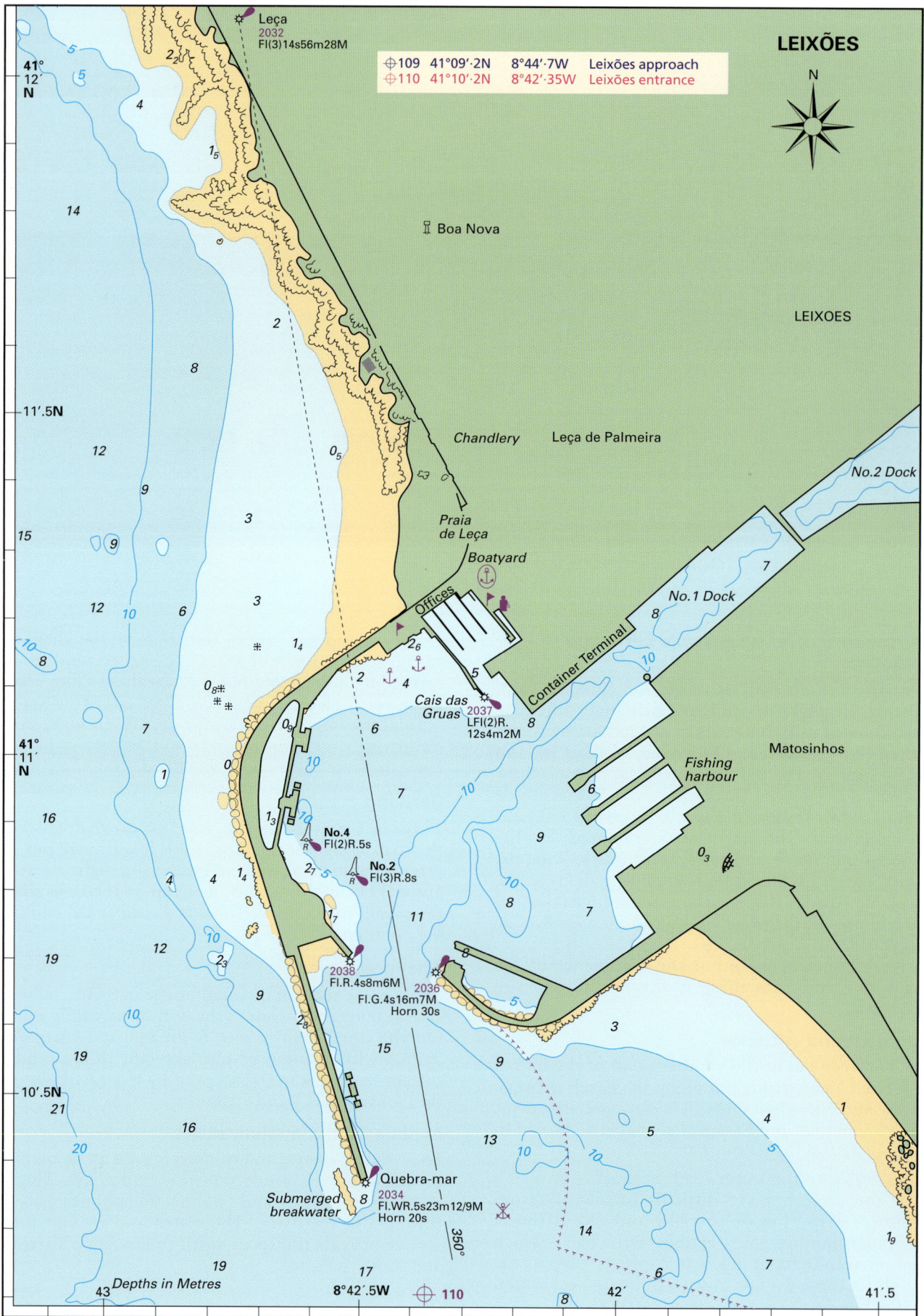

LEIXÕES

N

Leça
2032
Fl(3)14s56m28M

⊕109	41°09'·2N	8°44'·7W	Leixões approach
⊕110	41°10'·2N	8°42'·35W	Leixões entrance

Boa Nova

LEIXOES

Chandlery   Leça de Palmeira

No.2 Dock

Praia
de Leça

Boatyard

Offices

No.1 Dock

Container Terminal

Matosinhos

Cais das
Gruas
2037
LFl(2)R.
12s4m2M

Fishing
harbour

No.4
Fl(2)R.5s

No.2
Fl(3)R.8s

2038
Fl.R.4s8m6M

2036
Fl.G.4s16m7M
Horn 30s

Quebra-mar
2034
Fl.WR.5s23m12/9M
Horn 20s

Submerged
breakwater

350°

41°
12'
N

11'.5N

41°
11'
N

10'.5N

Depths in Metres

8°42'·5W

⊕ 110

8'

42'

41'.5

Leixões

⊕109 – 41°09'·2N 8°44'·7W (approach)
⊕110 – 41°10'·2N 8°42'·35W (entrance)

Courses and distances
⊕103 (Viana do Castelo) – ⊕109 = 30·6M, 169° or 349°
⊕105 (Póvoa de Varzim) – ⊕109 = 12.4M, 166° or 346°
⊕107 (Vila do Conde) – ⊕109 = 10·7M, 169° or 349°
⊕109 – ⊕110 = 2M, 061° or 241°
⊕109 – ⊕111 (Porto and the Rio Douro) = 1·5M, 122° or 302°
⊕109 – ⊕113 (Ria de Aveiro) = 31·7M, 185° or 005°
⊕109 – ⊕116 (Figueira da Foz, via F115) = 61·7M, 189° & 162° or 342°&009°
⊕109 – ⊕118 (Nazaré) = 95.1M, 190° or 010°

Tides
Standard port Lisbon
Mean time differences
HW −0015 ±0010; LW +0005 ±0005
Heights in metres

MHWS	MHWN	MLWN	MLWS
3·5	2·7	1·3	0·5

Or refer to EasyTide at www.ukho.gov.uk/easytide

Charts

	Approach	*Harbour*
Admiralty	3634	3258
Imray	C19, C48	C19, C48
Portuguese	23202, (23201), 24201	26402

Principal lights
2032 Leça
Fl(3)14s28M White tower, narrow grey bands 46m
2034 West breakwater head (Quebramar)
Fl.WR.5s23m12/9M 001°-R-180°-W-001°
Horn 20s Grey tower 10m
2038 West breakwater spur
Fl.R.4s8m6M Red lantern 4m
2036 South breakwater
Fl.G.4s16m7M 328°-vis-285° Horn 30s
Hexagonal tower, green lantern 10m
2037 Marina mole (Cais das Gruas)
LFl(2)R.12s4m2M White post, red bands 3m

Night entry
Straightforward – the entrance is wide and the harbour well-lit. However it might be wise to anchor until daylight rather than enter the crowded marina

Weather bulletins and navigational warnings
Weather bulletins in Portuguese only, from the Rio Minho to Cabo de São Vicente to 20 miles offshore, are broadcast on VHF Ch 11 at 0705 and 1905 UT.
Navigational warnings in Portuguese and English within 200 miles offshore: VHF Ch 11 at 0705, 1905 UT

Harbour communications
Marina Porto Atlântico ☎ +351 229 964895 *Fax* +351 229 966636 *Email* info@marinaportoatlantico.net www.marinaportoatlantico.net (with English translation) VHF Ch 09, 16 (0900–1230 & 1400–2000 daily 16 June–15 September, otherwise 0900–1230 & 1400–1830 Monday–Saturday).

The large harbour at Leixões with the marina tucked in the north corner by the beach

PORTUGAL – THE WEST COAST

A secure marina and adjacent anchorage which can be entered in all weather conditions

Leixões (pronounced '*layshoinsh*'), with its wide entrance, is by far the best port of refuge on this stretch of the coast and can be entered in almost any weather. The busy commercial port is centred on oil, fishing and general trade, while the Marina Porto Atlântico in its north corner was one of the first yacht harbours to be established on the Portuguese Atlantic coast. The marina provides good shelter and is an excellent base from which to explore the fascinating city of Porto, easily accessible by bus, taxi or *metro*. Those cruising with small children may be interested to know that the infant school on the road which runs north past the marina allows visiting youngsters to use the play area in its grounds.

Perhaps inevitably, bearing in mind its position in the corner of a commercial harbour, with a refinery nearby, the marina sometimes suffers from poor water quality, but effective measures have been made to overcome this.

Approach

Compared to the coastline further north, the area around Leixões is somewhat featureless. The oil refinery 1·5M north is a good mark by day or night, with the powerful Leça light lying between it and the harbour.

A spherical yellow outfall buoy (Fl.Y.4s6M Horn 30s) and a yellow tanker discharge 'superbuoy' (Fl(3)15s6M Horn (3)30s) lie 2·2M northwest of the west breakwater at 41°12′·5N 8°44′·7W and 41°12′·2N 8°45′W respectively. If in the vicinity after dark, note that both have occasionally been reported as unlit, and that other unlit yellow buoys have been reported nearby. A prohibited zone extends 1000m in all directions from the superbuoy, which is located about 1·6M offshore and well outside the 20m depth contour.

Harbour regulations state that vessels must give the outside of the west breakwater a berth of at least 1M, but few fishing boats appear to observe this. There are, however, shoals up to 200m off the seaward side of this breakwater as well as obstructions off its end. There are fewer hazards if approaching from the south, though several lit yellow buoys may be encountered within 1M of the shore. The buildings of Porto can be seen from a good distance, with the entrance to Leixões 2M northwest.

From offshore, ⊕109 lies 2M west-southwest of the entrance, a course of 061° leading to ⊕110, close outside the harbour mouth.

Entrance

The breakwater light may be difficult to identify against shore lights, but from south of the harbour – or ⊕110 – Leça light on 350° leads between the breakwater spur and the south breakwater, after which the marina will become visible. During westerly gales the swell at the entrance may be heavy, but it decreases rapidly once inside. Floating debris can be a hazard when crossing the harbour, and it is also best to avoid entry in the early evening when the many fishing trawlers are heading out to sea.

A parallel mole to the east mole at Leixoes, being built in the photograph on page 147, has been completed. Between these two moles, a number of piles have been put in place with pontoons. These have water and electricity points but are probably intended for use by local craft. The large building nearby is a cruise ship terminal for ships that will berth on the harbour side of the new mole.

Berthing

The three yacht clubs and the Marina Porto Atlântico are all located around the old fishing harbour at the north corner of the main harbour, behind a short mole (the Cais das Gruas). The narrow entrance (less than 50m wide) faces southeast, but even so considerable swell may work in during strong southwesterlies. Boats berthed near the entrance will obviously bear the brunt.

The marina, which has been dredged to 5m, can berth about 240 boats alongside narrow finger pontoons. It is crowded with local craft, but it is claimed that space can always be found for a visitor, even if this means rafting up at the reception berth.

The waiting/welcome pontoon is on the port side just after the turn into the marina, hard against the mole. The marina office and showers are at the root of the mole, through the self-closing and card accessed gate. Office hours are 0900–1230 and 1400–1830 daily from 16/6 until 15/9, closing all day Sunday outside the high season. The marina personnel have been consistently praised for their helpfulness and efficiency, and all office staff (though not all the *marineros*) speak good English.

Anchorage

A designated public anchorage exists just outside the marina, in the angle formed by the marina mole and the breakwater, in 5m or more. Holding, particularly near the mole, is reported to be good over mud. There is a single ladder on the outside of the marina mole at which a dinghy might be left (though note the 3m spring range), while the short pontoon belonging to the Yate Clube de Porto is closed off by security gates from early evening. It is normally possible to leave a dinghy in the marina, in which case a small charge is made.

Leixões fuel berth looking southeast *James Peto*

Formalities

Visit the marina office equipped with passports, ship's papers, and insurance documents whether berthed in the marina or anchored off. There are no forms to complete but copies of passports and boat's papers are taken. There is also no need to clear out from each port in Portugal as details are kept in computer systems which most ports have access to. If a change of crew is made, however, the authorities need to be informed, for safety reasons.

Facilities

Boatyard The boatyard next to the marina is able to handle repairs in GRP, wood, steel and aluminium.

Travel-lift No travel-lift, but 6.3-tonne capacity crane at the boatyard. The nearest large (ie 32-tonne capacity) travel-lift is at Póvoa de Varzim, 12M north.

Engineers, electronic and radio repairs Inboard and outboard engine specialists, and electrical and electronic workshops, are all available, though geared more to commercial vessels than yachts. Ask at the marina office. Lisbon-based NautiRadar Lda (see page 195) has a local agent, Antonio Rocha ② 229 381391.

Sailmaker The Pires de Lima loft, Rua Joaquim Vieira Moutinho 35, 4460 Santa Cruz de Bispo, ② 229 952218 *Fax* 229952 209 *Email* ukportugal@mail.telepac.pt, is situated a taxi-ride away near the airport. Sails are both made and repaired.

Chandlery Nautileça, ②/*Fax* 229 951463, that used to be found about 50m north of the main harbour gates is reported to be closed.

Charts Portuguese charts and other publications may be available from 'Sailing', at Traversa des Laranjeiras 34, Foz do Douro, 4100 Porto, ② 226 179936 *Fax* 226 103716.

Liferaft servicing Can be arranged via the Nautileça chandlery, see above.

Water On the pontoons.

Showers At the marina – free if occupying a berth, but charged for if anchored off. The Yate Clube de Porto also has showers, which it may be possible to use by arrangement.

Laundry In the town. Washing left at the marina office will normally be returned within 24 hours, clean, dry and ironed.

Electricity On the pontoons.

Fuel The fuel berth has been moved in recent years to the NE side of the marina. A rock is apparently just off the NE end of the fuel pontoon. The pontoons have been doubled up from the SE end to the fuel area so that there is a step in the end which is best avoided. Going in forward, it is quite difficult to reverse out and there is very little room to do a U-turn, especially as water depths are limited. It is suggested that the fuel berth is best approached going astern and after half tide, feeling the way in. It would be prudent to walk round from the waiting pontoon to check first. The fuel berth is open from 1000 to 1830 subject to there being enough water.

Bottled gas Cylinders taken to the Petrogal refinery about 2km north of the marina will be exchanged or refilled as necessary.

Clube náuticos The Yate Clube de Porto, the Clube Vela Atlântico and the Clube Náutico de Leça all overlook the harbour and marina.

Weather forecast Posted daily at the marina office.

Banks In Leça da Palmeira (about 1km away), Matosinhos and Porto.

Shops/provisioning Good shopping locally, and a very wide choice in Porto.

Produce market In Matosinhos, a taxi-ride away – or at least for the return, if heavy laden.

Cafés, restaurants and hotels Numerous in Leça da Palmeira and Porto, but nearly all at some distance from the harbour. However the Yate Clube de Porto has a formal restaurant as well as a very pleasant terrace bar.

Medical services In Leça da Palmeira, with a large modern hospital in Porto.

Communications

Post offices In Leça da Palmeira, Matosinhos and Porto.

Mailing address The marina office will hold mail for visiting yachts – c/o Marina Porto Atlântico, Molhe Norte de Leixões, 4450-718 Leça da Palmeira, Portugal. It is important that the envelope carries the name of the yacht in addition to that of the addressee.

Internet access A public computer terminal is installed in the marina office. Good WiFi is available.

Public telephones In the marina and elsewhere, with cards on sale at the office.

Fax service At the marina office, *Fax* 229 964899.

Car hire/taxis Both can be arranged via the marina office, though there is a good chance of flagging down a taxi on the main road outside the harbour gates.

Buses Number 507 runs into Porto (a city not to be missed) every 15/20 minutes. A convenient bus stop will be found on the main road just outside the harbour gates.

Trains Stations at Leça da Palmeira and Porto, both of which can be reached by bus. The *metro* line links Matosinhos to the city centre. Unlike most of its fellows, much of the line is above ground and a good part of that runs, tram-like, along city streets, making it scenic as well as practical.

Air services Porto International Airport lies about 6km northeast of the harbour and is (or soon will be) reachable by *metro*.

The Marina Porto Atlântico at Leixões looking east. The anchorage is in the clear area

II.2 Porto to Figueira da Foz

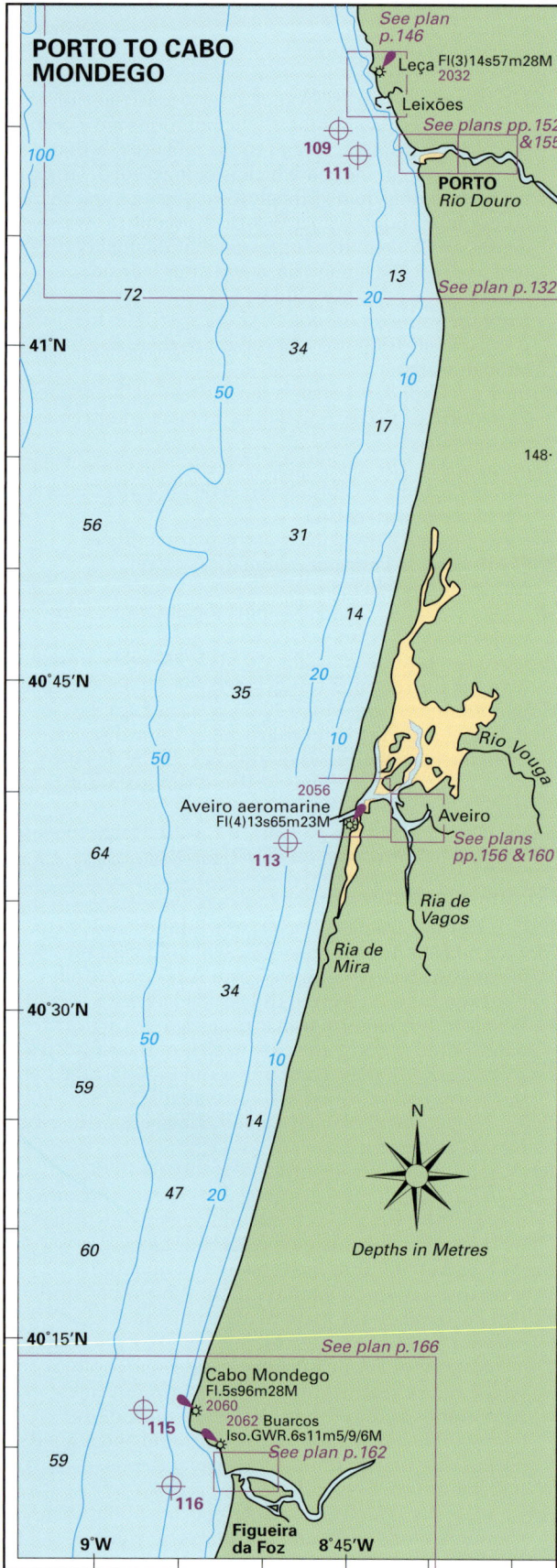

PORTO TO CABO MONDEGO

See plan p.146

Leça Fl(3)14s57m28M
2032

Leixões

See plans pp.152 &155

109
111

PORTO
Rio Douro

See plan p.132

100

72

41°N

13
20

34

50

10

17

148·

56

31

14

20

40°45′N

35

10

50

2056
Aveiro aeromarine
Fl(4)13s65m23M

Rio Vouga

Aveiro

See plans pp.156 &160

64

113

Ria de Vagos

Ria de Mira

34

40°30′N

50

10

59

14

47 20

N

60

Depths in Metres

40°15′N

See plan p.166

Cabo Mondego
Fl.5s96m28M
2060
2062 Buarcos
Iso.GWR.6s11m5/9/6M
See plan p.162

115

59

116

Figueira da Foz

9°W

8°45′W

⊕109	41°09′·2N	8°44′·7W	Leixões approach
⊕111	41°08′·4N	8°43′W	Porto & the Rio Douro approach
⊕113	40°37′·6N	8°48′·5W	Ria de Aveiro approach
⊕115	40°11′·4N	8°56′·5W	1·7M W of Cabo Mondego
⊕116	40°08′·4N	8°55′·2W	Figueira da Foz approach

PRINCIPAL LIGHTS

2032 **Leça** Fl(3)14s57m28M
  White tower, narrow grey bands 46m
2056 **Aveiro** Fl(4)13s65m23M
  Red tower, white bands and building 62m
2060 **Cabo Mondego** Fl.5s96m28M Horn 30s
  Square white tower and building, red cupola 15m
2062 **Buarcos** Iso.GWR.6s11m5/9/6M
  004°-G-028°-W-048°-R-086°
  White tower, red bands 7m

Ports

Porto and the Rio Douro
Aveiro anchorages
Figueira da Foz*

* Fuel available alongside

Rio Douro Tide Gauge at Cantareira mole *Jane Russell*

Traditional port barges off Vila Nova de Gaia *Jane Russell*

Porto and the Rio Douro

A fascinating old city on the Rio Douro which has improved entrance breakwaters and navigation marks/lights, and the Douro Marina on the south bank

The second city of Portugal, Porto rises magnificently above the gorge at the mouth of the Douro. Its historic involvement with the rest of Europe, the Americas and the East makes a fascinating tale. The reverberations remain in its architecture, its customs and its behaviour, as well as in its present commercial life.

Although there are few buildings of great historical significance, as a working city with a long and fascinating history (the bishopric is of very

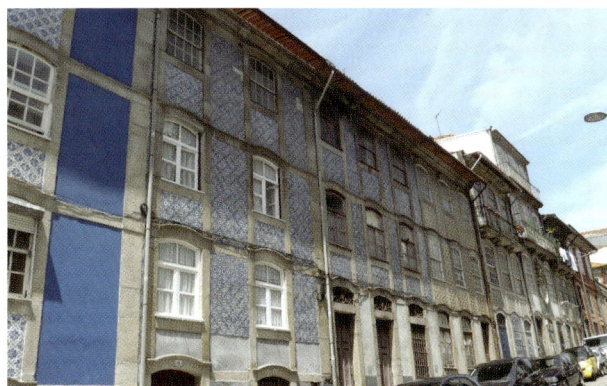

Tiled house fronts are typical in Porto *Jane Russell*

The Rio Douro looking East into Porto *Douro Marina*

RIVER DOURO

N

Depths in Metres

Porto and the Rio Douro approach
Porto and the Rio Douro entrance

⊕111	41°08'·4N	8°43'W	Porto and the Rio Douro approach
⊕112	41°08'·54N	8°41'W	Porto and the Rio Douro entrance

Porto

River Douro

5_5

No.5 3
G 2_3

5_6

6_2 5

5_7 5

No.4 3
R Fl(2)R.5s

5_2

3_5 1_5

2 2_9

Reception
Douro
Marina

F C D
A B E

WC

See plan p.155

No.3
G Fl(2)G.5s

0_7

2_2

Pedras do
Lima

No.2
Fl.R.3s 5_3
5

3

Ponta do
Cabadelo

3_1

5_4
5

1_1

2_6

São João da Foz
Oc.Y.5s38m6M

Cantareira
Lt structure

No.1
G Fl.G.3s

1_7 5
2_4

Molhe S
Fl.G.5s15m6M

8

Castelo da Foz
Oc.Y.5s12m5M

6_8 5

5

3_7

3_7 5

9

10

11

Felgueiras
Lt structure

7
5

Molhe N
Fl.R.5s17m9M

10

4_8

112 ⊕

10

12

059°

13

14

5

6

8

10

11

10

10

13

41°09'·N

41°08'·5N

39'W

8°40'W

41'W

Entrance to the Rio Douro from seaward – Leading Line just open to starboard *Henry Buchanan*

ancient origin), it is a delightful town through which to wander, although a certain fitness is needed to cope with the city's hills. The cathedral area deserves to be explored, and the densely populated quarter of Barredo, which appears not to have changed since medieval times. The riverside quarter of Ribeira is also delightful, with narrow streets, typical houses and attractive life-style. It has been restored and now includes fashionable restaurants and bars. Equally lively and colourful is the market of Bolhão. More elegant shops can be seen nearby in the Baixa (down-town). There are continuous reminders of the town's long-standing and prosperous connection with the wine trade which flourished in the 18th century, after the English merchants began to lace the best Douro wines with brandy. A highlight of any visit to the city must be a trip to one or more of the port warehouses at Vila Nova de Gaia, on the south bank opposite the Cais da Estiva, for a guided tour and tasting.

Approach

If coastal sailing, the low hills along the coast between Leixões and Porto extend south beyond the mouth (*foz*) of the Rio Douro. Further south the foreshore is flat, with sandy beaches and marshes behind, and from that direction the buildings on the hill immediately north of the Rio Douro are conspicuous.

From offshore, ⊕111 lies 1·7M southwest of the river mouth. ⊕112 lies near the leading line into the harbour. Extensive works involving the building of new breakwaters and the erection of new lights and marks have improved the approach to the Rio Douro.

Entrance

The bar is dangerous in strong winds or when there is heavy swell, with a 6–7 knot current on the spring ebb which may be even stronger after rain. In winter, storms may close the entrance for weeks. To add to the challenge both the narrows and the 'bag' inside are frequently crowded with dozens of small, open boats lying at anchor whilst their owners fish. It hardly needs saying that entry should only be attempted in daylight and settled weather.

The leading line through the new breakwaters into the Rio Douro has been established on a transit of 059° between two Barra Foz red/white horizontally striped beacons. The characteristics of both are Oc(1)Y.5s. The forward light is 12m high and the rear light 37m high. The rear mark/light is just by the tower of the little church (S.Joao da Foz). (see photograph of the entrance above and plan opposite). Once inside favour the northern shore towards Cantareira point rounding SHB No.1. The bar is claimed to carry at least 3m at MLWS, but this figure fluctuates from year to year. Cantareira mole has a rocky shoal off its southeast tip and should be given a wide berth before rounding PHB No.2 a little further in. Skirt No.2 buoy closely to keep well clear of the opposing Ponta do Cabadelo, a long sandspit which has been extending north and east.

Once in the Rio Douro, the channel as far as the Ponte de Arrábida (60·5m clearance) is well-buoyed and should present no problems. Beyond the bridge there are only two more buoys, but at least 6m should be found in mid-channel up to the Ponte Dom Luís I (8·8m).

Douro Marina looking westward *Douro Marina*

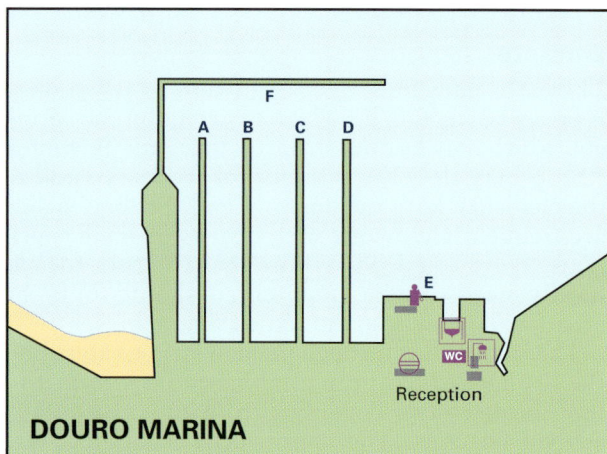

DOURO MARINA

Berthing

Navigate the channel into the Rio Douro and, when port-hand buoy No.4 bears north, steer 161° towards the marina entrance, a distance of about 0·3M. The depth in this access channel is 3·5m, but there is a small area (2014) outside and upstream of the channel that is shallow. Douro Marina is working with the port authority to have this area dredged, so it can be eliminated.

It should be noted that the marina normally meets visitors' boats with a rib as a courtesy service and this service is always available if a skipper has any concerns about the depth of the channel.

Douro Marina from north shore. No 4 port hand buoy in foreground *Jane Russell*

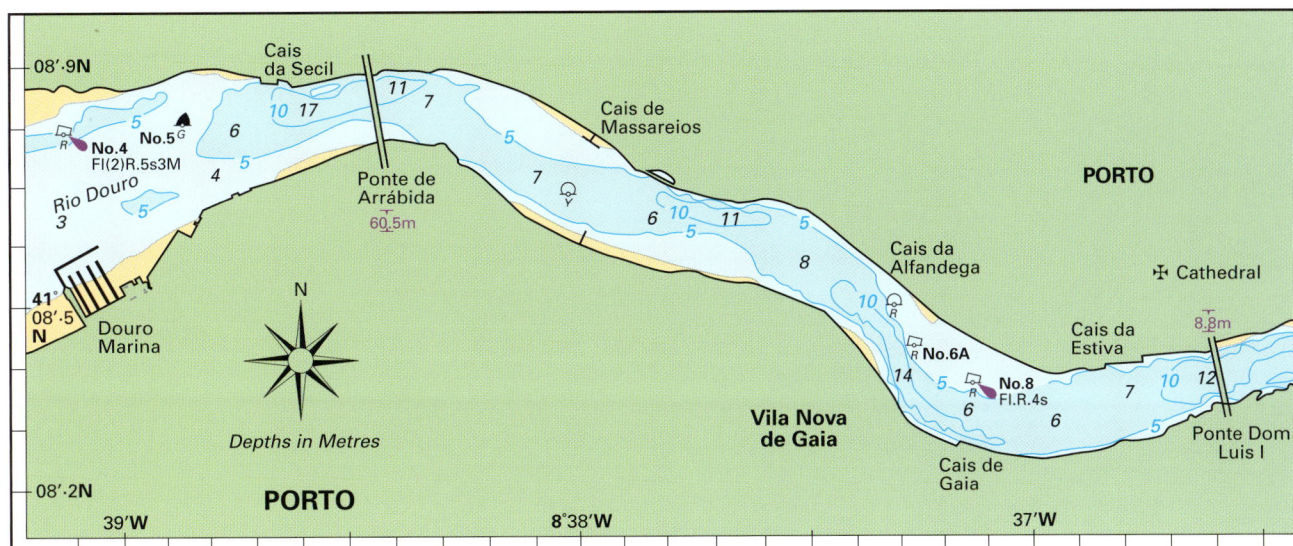

The depth in the marina is reported to be 3·5m. There are 300 berths, 60 of them for visitors and boats up to 30m can be accommodated.

Douro Marina has a pontoon reserved for catamarans and applies the same prices as a monohull meaning that rates are calculated by the length and not by the beam.

Formalities

Visit the marina office equipped with passports, ship's papers and insurance documents. There are no forms to complete but copies of passports and boat's papers are taken. There is also no need to clear out from each port in Portugal as details are kept in computer systems which most ports have access to. If a change of crew is made, however, the authorities need to be informed, for safety reasons.

Facilities

Security 24hr security.

Boatyard A workshop for maintenance and repair of boats with brand expertise available such as Volvo, Yanmar, Dupon Marina Paint and International Paint.

Travel-lift 75 ton, Crane 3·2 ton, and a ramp.

Engineers, electronic and radio repairs Enquire at the marina office.

Diving Diver available at the marina.

Sailmaker/sail repairs Sails in need of repair are normally sent to Lisbon for attention – ask at the marina office.

Chandlery There is a small, helpful chandlery at the marina.

Water On the pontoons.

Showers In containers while permanent facilities are completed.

Launderette In containers while permanent facilities are completed.

Electricity On the pontoons.

Fuel Diesel and Petrol at the reception/fuel pontoon.

Bottled gas Enquire at the marina office.

Weather forecast Posted daily outside the marina office.

Banks ATM at the marina.

Shops/provisioning Good shopping of all types in Porto.

Cafés, restaurants Additional facilities planned for the marina are buildings comprising restaurants, bars, stores, fitness and wellness spa, etc.

Medical services In Porto.

Communications

Post office In Porto.

Mailing address Marina Douro Rua da Praia, 430, 4400-554 Vila Nova de Gaia, Portugal

It is important that the envelope carries the name of the yacht in addition to that of the addressee.

Internet access WiFi in the marina.

Fax service +351 220 907 309

Car/Bicycle hire Rent-a-car and Rent-a-bike at the marina.

Transport Buses into Porto. Tourist ferry pier. Taxi Boat. Cycle path along the bank of the Rio Douro.

Airport Douro Marina is 15km far from the international airport of Porto.

Upriver

Motorboats, or yachts with masts which can be lowered, can explore as far as Barca de Alva, 200km upstream, following cruise boats into the large locks. The approaches require care and 6kn of boat speed in some conditions.

The upper reaches of the Rio Douro are particularly attractive, and if unable to venture by yacht it could be worth jumping ship to spend a few days aboard one of the many hotel-boats which ply the river.

Not feasible – Lagoa de Esmoriz

The Lagoa de Esmoriz (40°57'·6N 8°39'·5W), close south of Espinho and some 11M south of Porto, bears more than a passing resemblance to Esposende – but on an even smaller scale. Sail on by.

AVEIRO

N

Depths in Metres

⊕113	40°37'·6N	8°48'·5W	Ria de Aveiro approach
⊕114	40°38'·41N	8°46'·11W	Ria de Aveiro entrance

Shipyard

Ilho do Monte Farinho

2Fl.Y
2Fl.Y
2Fl.Y

Fl.G.1.5s2M

Canal Principal de Navagação

5

Continued on plan p.152

4₁

10 5

Works in progress

Ilha da Mó dó Meio

12

2059.6
Fl(2+1)R.
6s7m4M

2059.36
Fl.G.4s7m3M

2059.5
Fl.R.5s6m4M

11

Commercial Harbour

São Jacinto

13 Ferries

2059.55
Fl.G.6s8m3M

2059.1
Fl.G.3s21m6M

12

Baia de São Jacinto

2059.37
Fl.R.3s7m4M

12

5₄

5₂

G
R

2059.35
Fl(2+1)G.6s6m

Fl.R.4s5m8M

Commercial sector

Military Area

YB

Airport Control Tower

RW

Military Airport

0₉

14

2059.2
Fl.G.3s4m

5

2058.55
Fl.R.2s7m3M

Triângulo

Power Cables

BARRA

3M
Fl(2)G.
6s3M

1M
Fl.G.3s3M

5M
Fl(3)G.
9s3M

7M
Fl.G.
3s3M

6₁

Canal de Mira

9M
Fl(2)G.
6s3M

11M
Fl(3)G.9s3M

1₄

0₁

Nature Reserve

2056.21
Oc.R.6s16m9M

2059
Fl(2+1)G.6s8m6M

16

089°

Canal da Embocadura

19

Molhe Central
LFl.G.5s9m3M

2056 & 2058.1
Aveiro
Fl(4)13s66m23M

0₄

Praia de São Jacinto

Marine Nature Reserve

1₉

7₃

2₆

5

2₃

8₁

10

11

2056.2
Oc.R.3s8m9M

3₉

7₇

5

1₆

3₆

7₄

7₆

8°44'W

8°45'W

2058
Fl.G.3s17m9M

2057
Fl.R.3s12m8M

Works in progress to extend breakwater

114

059°·9

9₁

12

10

8₁

12

11

8°46'W

39'·5

40'39'N

38'·5

38'

43'

Ria de Aveiro

Waypoints
- ⊕113 – 40°37'·6N 8°48'·5W (approach)
- ⊕114 – 40°38'·41N 8°46'·11W (entrance)

Courses and distances
- ⊕109 (Leixões) – ⊕113 = 31·7M, 185° or 005°
- ⊕111 (Porto and the Rio Douro) – ⊕113 = 31·1M, 188° or 008°
- ⊕113 – ⊕114 = 2M, 066° or 246°
- ⊕113 – ⊕116 (Figueira da Foz, via ⊕115) = 30·1M, 193°&162° or 342°&013°

Tides
Standard port Lisbon
Mean time differences (at entrance)
HW +0005 ±0005; LW +0010 ±005
Heights in metres

MHWS	MHWN	MLWN	MLWS
3·2	2·6	1·4	0·7

Or refer to EasyTide at www.ukho.gov.uk/easytide

Charts

	Approach	River
Admiralty	3634	3227
Imray	C19, C49	
Portuguese	23202, 24201, 24202	26403

Principal lights
2056 **Aveiro** Fl(4)13s66m23M Red tower, white bands and building 62m
2057 **North breakwater** Fl.R.3s12m8M Horn 15s White tower, red bands 6m
2058 **South breakwater** Fl.G.3s17m9M White tower, green bands 12m (20m from outer end)
2058 **Outer Ldg Lts 085°** *Front* South breakwater
2058.1 *Rear* 850m from front Fl.G.4s54m9M 065·4°-vis°-105·4° Shares tower with Aveiro (above), at 50m
2058.55 **Entrance channel north side** Fl.R.2s7m3M Red tower 4m
2056.2 **Entrance Ldg Lts 066°** *Front* Oc.R.3s8m9M 060·6°-vis-070·6° Red column 4m
2056.21 *Rear* 440m from front Oc.R.6s16m9M 060.6°-vis-070.6° Red column 13m
2058.5 **South inner mole** LFl.G.5s9m3M White tower, green bands 4m
2059 **Triangle – west corner** Fl(2+1)G.6s8m6M Green tower, red band 4m
2059 **Inner Ldg Lts 089°** *Front* **Triangle – west corner** (above)
2059.1 *Rear* **Fuerte de Barra** 870m from front Fl.G.3s21m6M 084·5°-vis°-094·5° White tower 19m
2059.6 **Monte Farinha** Red tower, green band Fl(2+1)R.6s4M
Plus numerous lit and unlit beacons and buoys on the Canal Principal de Navegação, leading to the Canal das Pirâmides lock – see plan on page 160.

Night entry
Not recommended, even in light conditions. Although the entrance is well lit this does not extend to any of the yacht berths or anchorages

Maritime radio station
Arestal (40°46'·8N 8°21'4W)
Remotely controlled from Lisbon)
Manual – VHF Ch 16, 24, 25, 26. *Autolink* – VHF Ch 85.

Harbour communications
Capimaraveiro VHF Ch 11, 16 (0900–1200, 1400–1700 Monday–Friday)
Associação Aveirense de Vela de Cruzeiro (AVELA)
☎ +351 234 422142, *Email* avela@avela.pt
www.avela.pt (in Portuguese only).

Windswept channels and lagoons, inside a potentially dangerous entrance

The Aveiro estuary is made up of salt marshes and sand spits, low-lying and often deceptive. The ría has been developed as an oil, timber and general port but it is possible to escape into unspoilt, almost desolate, surroundings. The fishing port of Aveiro, some 12km from the entrance, was an ancient bishopric and the town prospered from fishing off Newfoundland and salt, until a storm in the 16th century effectively closed the entrance. It was re-opened early in the 19th century and Aveiro recovered its prosperity. With its humpbacked bridges the slightly Dutch air to the town is reinforced by the range and quantities of food originating here. Today it combines modern business and industry with reminders of the past, and is one of the more attractive towns along the coast. The historic Feira de Março takes place from late March to late April featuring many folk and rock concerts, but the Festa da Ría in mid-Summer with its historic heritage of painted boats – moliceiros – is probably more appropriate for the nautically minded. The town is known for its general merrymaking during the festival. The Festas do Sao Paio in early September features a traditional boat race on the northern lagoon.

Approach

If coastal sailing from the north, from the Rio Douro to Espinho the coast is backed by low hills some 7km inland and has isolated rocks inshore. South from Espinho one continuous beach backed by sand dunes and lagoons – known locally as the *Costa de Prata* or 'silver coast' – stretches for over 50M to Cabo Mondego, with the Barra de Aveiro rather less than halfway down its length. A dangerous wreck lies just over 2M southwest of the entrance at approximately 40°36'·7N 8°47'W.

From offshore, ⊕113 lies 2M west-southwest of the entrance, from which a course of 066° leads to ⊕114, on the leading line and about 500m from the north breakwater head.

Entrance

The potential dangers of the entrance should not be underestimated. Winds from between northwest and southwest can quickly produce a vicious sea, at its worst on the ebb tide – which may reach 8kn in the entrance at springs following heavy rain. The ebb runs for about seven hours and the flood for five, the best time to enter or leave being shortly before high water.

The northern breakwater to Aviero was being extended in 2013, and provided useful shelter in its lee to a yacht arriving in a 35kn northwester about 1·5 hours before high water, encountering overfalls before being swept up the channel at over 9kn. If coming from the north, give the end of the north

PORTUGAL – THE WEST COAST

The potentially dangerous entrance to the Ria de Aveiro looking east-northeast.
Note that the north breakwater was extended in 2013 after this photograph was taken.
Yachts can just be seen anchored in Baía de São Jacinto, top left

breakwater a wide berth, as shoals often build around its tip, while least depths, and hence the worst seas, are also to be found in this area.

There are two leading lines for the outer entrance. The northern line, on 085·4°, consists of the south breakwater light structure in line with Aveiro lighthouse and should be visible from some distance offshore. The southern line, on 059·9° and consisting of two red columns, is much harder to pick out but flatter water is likely to be found to the south. A third leading line, on 089°, has been established inside the entrance, but is intended mainly for commercial traffic heading for the Canal de Mira.

Once the protection of the river mouth is gained, while the tide may still run strongly, there should never be less than 7m depths and frequently much more. Leave the Triângulo (islet) to starboard and continue up the Canal de Embocadura. In contrast to some Portuguese harbours the channels buoys appear to be well maintained.

Anchorages and berthing
(see plans on pages 156 and 160)

There are very limited facilities for yachts, and the two small marinas in the Canal de Mira to the south (see plan) are not only shallow, but inaccessible to most cruising yachts due to the 8–10m power cables which cross the Canal at its northern end.

1. Good anchorage will be found in the Baía de São Jacinto, about 1·5M northeast of the river mouth. The entrance is shallow although there are good depths once inside, and it is essential to observe the buoyage – currently red and green buoys to port and starboard on entering, with a further

green buoy marking the western edge of the north shoal. The outer moles are both lit (F.R and F.G), but movement after dark is not recommended. Strong currents, with unpredictable eddies, run across and into the entrance on both the flood and the ebb.

If the inner buoy is not in place and no local craft are on hand to offer a lead in, after passing between the entrance buoys, head for a conspicuous yellow and black water tower on approximately 330°. Remain on this bearing until past the shallowest part of the bar (0·5–1m at datum). When the Military Base pier (often with small military craft alongside) bears 015°, head in towards it, following the shore in 5–6m towards the ferry pier.

Local moorings now occupy the north end of the bay, behind which are steps and a broad slipway. The ferry pier carries prominent 'no mooring' notices, and though it might be possible to land by dinghy at the small craft pontoon beyond, there is no possibility of lying alongside, even for a few minutes.

Anchor south of the moorings in 7–10m. The bottom is somewhat uneven, with holding poor in places and excellent in others. One yacht has reported holding absolutely firm while laid over by gusts exceeding 50kn, while another tried five times to hold, only to be told later that a minimum of 50m of chain should have been veered. In the latter case the yacht was waved over to the ferry pontoon and secured against an old ferry in 'perfect peace'.

An alternative used by another Yacht that could not get its anchor to hold was to go to the

Work underway extending the north breakwater 2013 *James Peto*

southwest corner of the harbour although care is needed as the channel to that part is quite narrow, but there is over 3m depth.

São Jacinto is very much a holiday town, with numerous cafés and restaurants, small shops, a post office and several public telephones. There is WiFi and English spoken in the bar nearby.

This is a good place to stay, weather permitting, to visit both Aveiro, which is a must to visit, and to catch the train to Coimbra. The ferry is co-ordinated with the bus in both directions which goes to the rail station, all within an hour.

There is nothing specifically for yachts, though a small shipyard lies just to the north. There is a nature reserve along the beach to the west but the large military area, including the airfield, is off limits.

2. It is also possible to anchor further north in the Canal de Ovar, a lagoon separated from the sea by a sandbank carrying the access road to São Jacinto. Tidal currents weaken beyond São Jacinto, and though relatively shallow (2·5–3m) where the Canal is wide, the narrow stretches contain pools with 5–7m. If very shoal draught or able to take the ground it is possible to work a good distance up the channel.

3. Space may be found for a small visiting yacht at the Marina da Costa Nova on the Canal Mira, but air height is restricted to an estimated 8–10m by the power cables already mentioned. The channel is indicated by buoys and posts.

4. Yachts have in the past anchored in the Canal Principal de Navagação, a buoyed channel carrying 3–4m and leading to the town of Aveiro (see plan overleaf). However tidal currents are strong and it would be difficult to find swinging room without impeding local traffic. The Clube Naval de Aveiro and neighbouring Sporting Clube de Aveiro have no more than 1m at their quays – local smallcraft are craned ashore when not in use – but for short periods it may be possible to lie alongside the jetty at either the Ría-Marine or Fracon yards – see under Facilities, below. Berthing at any of the fishermen's or commercial quays is strongly discouraged.

5. Space may be found alongside the 200m pontoon installed by AVELA (the Associação Aveirense de Vela de Cruzeiro) in the Canal de Veia, close to the Canal das Pirâmides lock. Though privately

The entrance to São Jacinto *James Peto*

PORTUGAL – THE WEST COAST

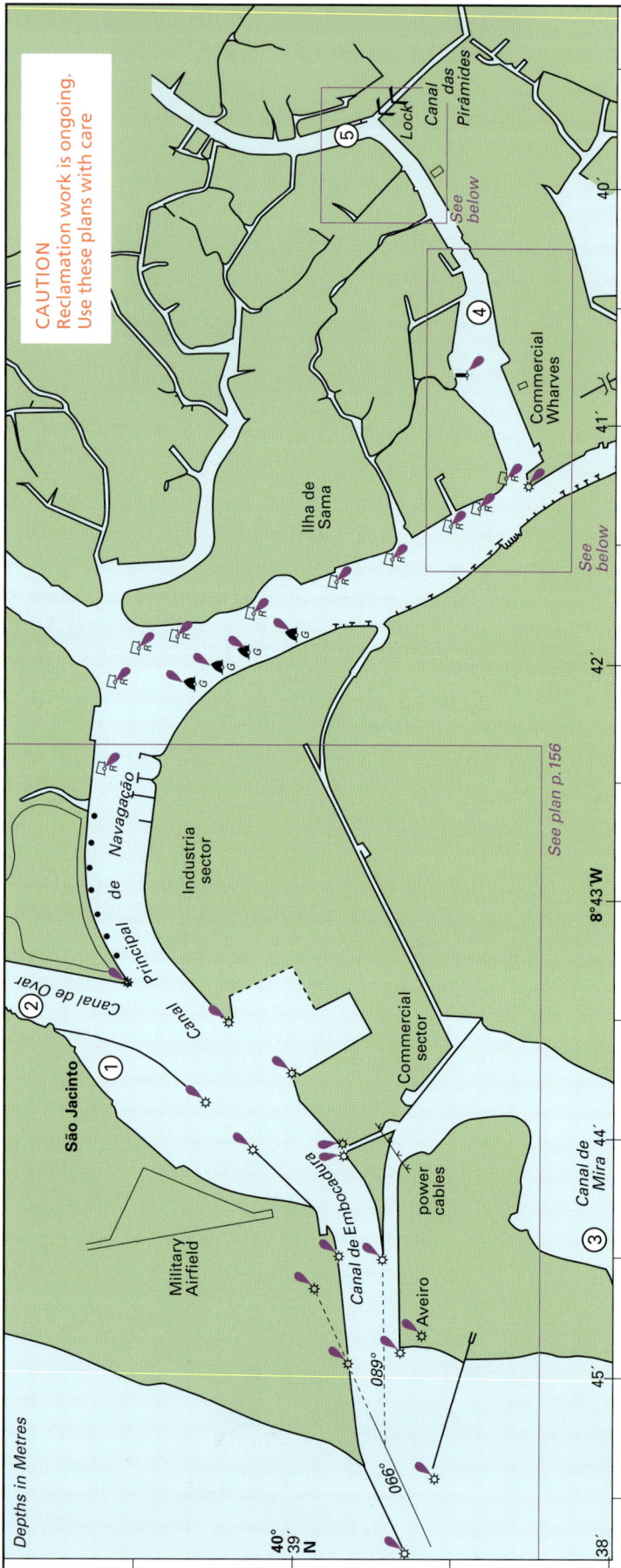

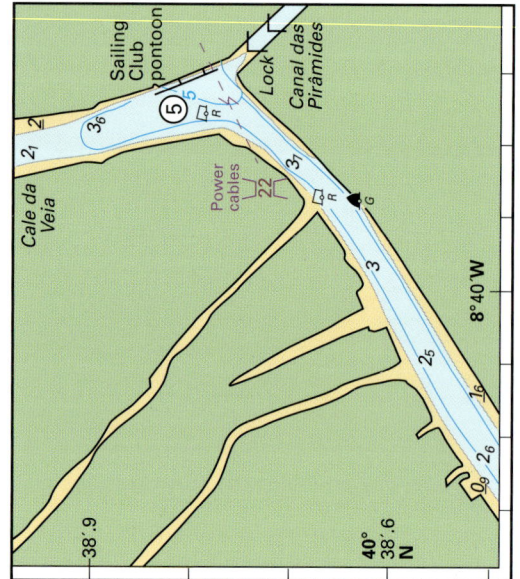

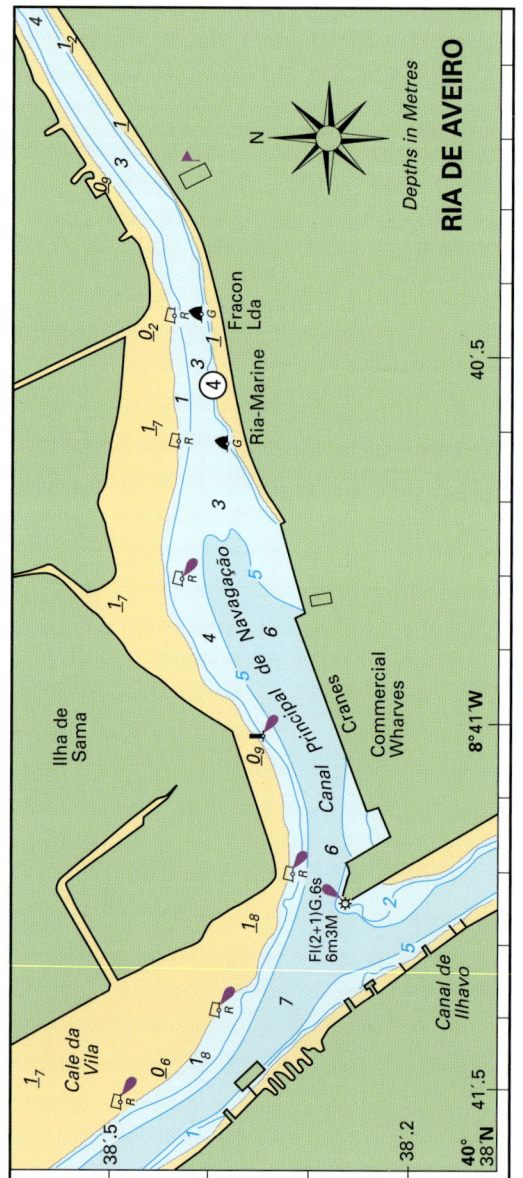

RIA DE AVEIRO

Depths in Metres

The AVELA pontoon, close north of the Canal das Pirâmides Lock *James Peto*

owned, visiting yachts are most welcome. Water and electricity are installed. Club rooms are at the end of a long building, just opposite the ramp from the pontoon.

Shower available. AVELA provide a key for the security gate on the ramp.

Power cables with a reported air height of 22m crossing the Canal just downstream of the pontoon will restrict larger yachts.

Visiting yachts are no longer permitted to enter the Canal das Pirâmides, which runs through the centre of the old town of Aveiro, but it would make an interesting dinghy excursion. The Canal is administered by the Associação Turistica Vigilância, with the lock reported to open for one hour either side of high water and on demand at other times – most often for small tourist vessels with which a dinghy could double up (the lock measures 18m by 5m). Strong tidal eddies may be encountered at the entrance.

Formalities

The *GNR–Brigada Fiscal* and possibly the *Polícia Marítima* may visit if anchored in the Baía de São Jacinto or moored at the AVELA pontoon.

Facilities

Boatyard Fracon Lda ① 234 422297 *Fax* 234 420561 *Email* fracon@fracon.pt www.fracon.pt on the Canal Principal de Navegação can handle repairs in all materials including GRP in large covered workshops. Staff are helpful with some English and German spoken, and security appears to be good. There is plenty of outdoor hardstanding for potential winter lay-up.

Ria-Marine Lda, ① +351 234 384049/426686, just downstream of Fracon, can handle work on yachts of all sizes in GRP, wood and steel. Little or no English is spoken. In the mid 1990s the yard was given responsibility for rebuilding Portugal's last surviving East Indiaman, the *D Fernando II e Glória*, for the Lisbon Maritime Museum, a commission which they carried out to a high standard.

Travel-lift Not as such, but Fracon has a 10-tonne capacity crane and can arrange for a 30 tonner to visit, and also has a marine railway (unsuitable for deep keels). Ría-Marine can haul yachts of all sizes by crane or on one of their two marine railways.

Engineers, mechanics, electricians At both Fracon and Ría-Marine as well as Quatro-Ventos (see *Chandlery*, below).

Sail repairs Can be organised via Quatro-Ventos, below.

Chandlery Good range at Quatro-Ventos, 230 Avenida Fernandes Lavrador, Praia da Barra (accessible by ferry from the São Jacinto anchorage), ① +351 243 394654, *Fax* +351 234 394 655, *email* quatro-ventos@quatro-ventos.com, website www.quatro-ventos.com. Owner Augusto Pereir (who also runs a sailing school and is an agent for Bénéteau) is reported to be helpful and efficient, and to speak fluent English and French. He can arrange for maintenance and repairs to anything from engines to sails etc.

Charts Portuguese charts and other publications may be available from Bolivar, on Rua da Aviação Naval 51, 3810 Aveiro.

Water On the AVELA pontoon, or by can from the Clube Naval de Aveiro or one of the boatyards.

Showers May be available at the Clube Naval de Aveiro or at one of the yards.

Electricity On the AVELA pontoon, though see above.

Fuel By can from a filling station in Aveiro. In an emergency it might be possible to buy a few litres from Fracon's own supply, but they are not officially licensed to sell retail.

Clube naval The Clube Naval de Aveiro and the Sporting Clube de Aveiro both have premises on the Canal Principal de Navegação, but only the former appears to be open regularly.

Banks In Aveiro.

Shops/provisioning Good shopping in Aveiro, but a much more restricted choice in São Jacinto.

Cafés, restaurants and hotels Wide choice in Aveiro, with plenty of cafés and restaurants (but apparently no hotels) in São Jacinto.

Medical services In Aveiro.

Communications

Post offices In both Aveiro and São Jacinto

Telephones Public telephones in both towns.

Car hire/taxis In Aveiro.

Ferries Regular ferries from the pier at São Jacinto across the Canal de Embocadura to Barra, on the south side of the estuary, and tourist excursions downstream from Aveiro via the Canal das Pirâmides.

Trains Direct rail link to Porto, amongst other destinations.

Air services Porto International Airport lies about 70km to the north.

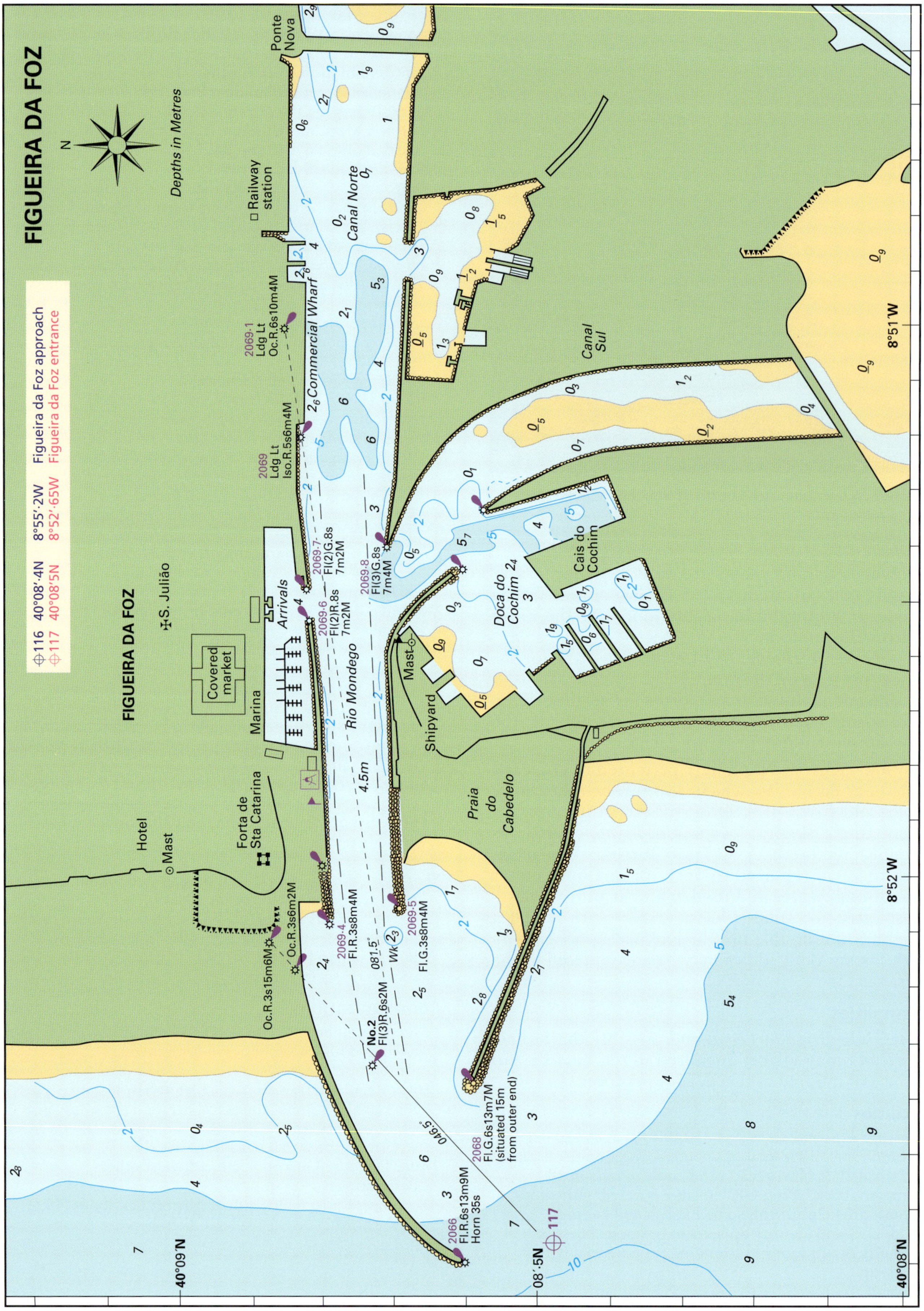

FIGUEIRA DA FOZ

N

Depths in Metres

FIGUEIRA DA FOZ

⬧116 40°08'·4N 8°55'·2W Figueira da Foz approach
⬧117 40°08'5N 8°52'·65W Figueira da Foz entrance

Ponte Nova

Railway station

Canal Norte

Canal Sul

2069·1 Ldg Lt Oc.R.6s10m4M

Commercial Wharf

2069 Ldg Lt Iso.R.5s6m4M

Cais do Cochim

2069·7 Fl(2)G.8s 7m2M

2069·8 Fl(3)G.8s 7m4M

2069·6 Fl(2)R.8s 7m2M

Doca do Cochim

Arrivals

Rio Mondego

Mast

Shipyard

⚓ S. Julião

Covered market

Marina

Praia do Cabedelo

Hotel
◉ Mast

Forte de Sta Catarina

4·5m

Oc.R.3s15m6M

Oc.R.3s6m2M

2069·4 Fl.R.3s8m4M

No.2 Fl(3)R.6s2M

Wk 2₃

2069·5 Fl.G.3s8m4M

081·5°

046°·5

2068 Fl.G.6s13m7M (situated 15m from outer end)

2066 Fl.R.6s13m9M Horn 35s

08'·5N

⬧117

40°09'N

40°08'N

8°52'W

8°51'W

Figueira da Foz

Waypoints
- ⊕15 – 40°11'·4N 8°56'·5W (1·7M W of Cabo Mondego)
- ⊕116 – 40°07'·66N 8°53'·82W (approach)
- ⊕117 – 40°08'·50N 8°52'·65W (entrance)

Courses and distances
- ⊕109 (Leixões) – ⊕116 (via ⊕115) = 61·7M, 189°&162° or 342°&009°
- ⊕111 (Porto and the Rio Douro) – ⊕116 (via ⊕115) = 61·1M, 190°&162° or 342°&010°
- ⊕113 (Ria de Aveiro) – ⊕116 (via ⊕115) = 30·1M, 193°&162° or 342°&013°
- ⊕116 – ⊕117 = 2M, 082° or 262°
- ⊕116 – ⊕118 (Nazaré) = 34M, 196° or 016°

Tides
Standard port Lisbon
Mean time differences
HW –0010 minutes ±0010; LW +0015 minutes ±0005
Heights in metres

MHWS	MHWN	MLWN	MLWS
3·5	2·6	1·3	0·6

Or refer to EasyTide at www.ukho.gov.uk/easytide

Charts

	Approach	Harbour
Admiralty	3634, 3635	3228
Imray	C19, C49	C19, C49
Portuguese	34, 23202, 24202	64, 26404

Principal lights
- 2066 **North breakwater** Fl.R.6s14m9M Horn 35s
  White tower, red bands 9m
- 2068 **South breakwater** Fl.G.6s14m7M
  White tower, green bands 7m (15m from outer end)
- 2069 **Ldg Lts** *Front* Occ(1)R3s6m. Red-White horizontal striped stone pylon.
- 2069.1 *Rear* Occ(1)R3s15m. Red-White horizontal striped stone pylon.
- 2069.4 **North inner mole** Fl.R.3s9m4M
  Red tower, white bands 4m
- 2069.5 **South inner mole** Fl.G.3s9m4M
  Green tower, white bands 5m
- 2069.6 **Marina, west mole** Fl(2).R.8s7m2M Red column 3m
- 2069.7 **Marina, east mole** Fl(2).G.8s7m2M Green column 3m
- 2069.8 **Confluência** Fl(3)G.8s8m4M
  Green tower, red band 4m

Night entry
Straightforward other than in heavy onshore swell. The marina entrance is well lit with the reception/fuel berth opposite. However anchored smallcraft may be encountered in the entrance – see below

Harbour communications
Instituto Portuário e dos Transportes Marítimos (IPTM)
☎ +351 233 402910 *Fax* +351 233 402920
Email geral.ffoz@imarpor.pt Ch 11, 16
Marina da Figueira da Foz ☎ +351 233 402918
VHF Ch 11, 16.

Attractive old town with small marina opposite a large commercial port

Figueira da Foz is on the north bank of the Mondego, the longest river to rise in Portugal. Although a modern town, depending largely on ship-building and tourism for its income, a large part of the attractive old town remains. Figueira da Foz saw action during the Peninsula War, with Wellington landing here in August 1808. The Casa do Paco has an interesting wall covered in Dutch tiles, and nearby is the Gulbenkian Museu do Dr Santo Rocha, an interesting archaeological museum with a marine section.

The city of Coimbra, some 48km upstream, is worth visiting by bus or train. Coimbra is the successor to the city of Conimbriga, the heart of Roman Portugal and was briefly the capital of Portugal in the 12th century. The university, in the upper part of the town, transferred there from Lisbon in 1320 and has played a major role in Portuguese life ever since. The university library (built as a direct legacy of Portugal's great age of exploration) is magnificent and the old city, including the crenellated 12th-century cathedral, is memorable. In the lower part of the town the church of Santa Cruz (containing medieval royal tombs) is not only significant historically, but was a British Army HQ during the Peninsula War.

Also in the upper part of the town, the fortress-like old Cathedral is a one of the finest Romanesque buildings in Portugal. Behind the cathedral is the old Bishop's Palace now the Museum of Machado de Castro containing some fine late medieval paintings and sculpture and subterranean passages dating back to Roman times. Although these are the highlights of Coimbra, the city is full of surprises and justifies time spent wandering its narrow streets.

Approach

Figueira da Foz lies 2·5M south of Cabo which at a distance, from both north and south, can be mistaken for an island. The shore to the south of the town forms a continuous low, sandy, beach backed by one of the largest coniferous forests in Europe. The major mark to the south is Penedo da Saudade, 25M distant.

Note that there is a concentration of fishing floats between Cabo Mondego and the harbour.

From offshore, ⊕116 lies 1·3M southwest of the entrance on the leading line of 046·5° into the harbour. ⊕117 is 200m south of the end of the north breakwater, also on the leading line. The pale grey suspension bridge 1·5M upriver from the entrance is conspicuous.

Entrance

Regular dredging of the previously shallow bar has greatly improved the entrance and a minimum of 5m should be found at all times. However, in strong onshore winds it can be dangerous as waves frequently break all the way across the gap. At springs the ebb can run at up to 7kns, particularly if there has been heavy rain inland, though this rate is unlikely to be reached during the summer.

Danger signals are displayed if necessary from Forte de Santa Catarina (on the north side of the entrance) as follows:

Black ball or vertical green, red, green lights – entrance closed; black ball at half-mast or vertical green, flashing red, green lights – entrance dangerous. These signals, which are near some strong sodium lights and difficult to see from offshore, are mandatory and instructions may also be given by radio. If no signals are displayed the entrance is considered to be safe, at least for large commercial vessels.

Care must be taken to avoid the many local fishermen who anchor in the main channel apparently at random, peacefully line-fishing from small rowing boats and motor vessels. Although most either depart before dusk or show lights, this should not be relied upon. It is reported that nets are sometimes strung across the river, in which case a yacht will be guided through the gaps by hand signals.

Berthing

The entrance to the Marina da Figueira da Foz lies on the port hand about 0·7M inside the river mouth. Beware of cross-currents, particularly on the ebb. Opposite the entrance, secure to the reception pontoon which has the marina office behind it open 0830–1230 and 1400–2200 daily.

The marina consists of a single long pontoon from which seven spurs run southward. All are fitted with individual finger pontoons and the two easternmost, some 36 berths, are reserved for visitors, though more will be fitted in elsewhere if necessary. Though easy to access, both eastern spurs are reported to suffer from strong cross-currents that can be the opposite to that experienced at the reception berth! There is a swell on the ebb.

This area is nominally dredged to 4·5m and able to take yachts of up to 25m LOA, though some would consider this optimistic.

A problem is that until a footbridge is built between the visitor pontoons and the marina office, it is a long walk between the two.

Reception, fuel pontoons and marina offices
Henry Buchanan

Formalities

Visit the marina office equipped with passports, ship's papers and insurance documents. There are no forms to complete but copies of passports and boat's papers are taken. There is also no need to clear out from each port as details are kept in computer systems which most ports have access to. If a change of crew is made, however, the authorities need to be informed, for safety reasons.

Facilities

Boatyard Not as such, though there are several concerns which could handle minor work. Papiro, ☎ +351 233 411849, at the west end of the basin advertises GRP work, including osmosis treatment, but appears fairly small.

There is a wide concrete slipway in the southwest corner of the basin where yachts of medium draught can dry out for scrubbing. A pressure washer (with operator) can be hired – enquire at the marine office. As with all such facilities it would plainly be wise to inspect thoroughly at low water before committing oneself.

Looking east-northeast past the outer breakwaters at Figueira da Foz, with the marina at centre and the impressive Ponte Nova on the right

The Marina da Figueira da Foz, with the town's park and the double-gabled covered market behind

Travel-lift None at present, though it is possible that a 50-tonne lift may be installed in the commercial area on the south side of the river. Enquire at the marina office.

Engineers, electronic and radio repairs Available in the commercial harbour – enquire at the marina office.

Sailmaker/sail repairs Sails in need of repair are normally sent to Lisbon for attention – ask at the marina office.

Chandlery Limited stocks at Figueira Iates at the west end of the basin. Papiro (see above) stocks a full range of International Paints including antifouling, thinners etc.

Water On the pontoons, with a generous number of long hoses.

Showers In the marina office building.

Launderette Next to the showers in the marina office building.

Electricity On the pontoons.

Fuel Diesel and petrol on the fuel pontoon open during office hours.

Bottled gas Camping Gaz from Alavanca (which also stocks an enormous range of tools), on the road leading east from the marina basin.

Clube náutico The Clube Náutico de Figueira da Foz has a small clubhouse at the west end of the marina. The children's play area behind the building is a particularly nice touch.

Weather forecast Posted daily outside the marina office.

Banks In the town.

Harbour entrance Figueira da Foz. Leading marks almost in line with the right hand edge of rectangular building to the right of the blue skyscraper *Henry Buchanan*

Shops/provisioning Good shopping of all types in the town. The nearest supermarket (open 0730) will be found across the road and slightly west from the marina gate, up a small side street.

Produce market The impressive covered market opposite the marina is amongst the best of its genre, and sells consumables of all types, clothing, souvenirs etc.

Cafés, restaurants and hotels A small café is planned for the new (2013) marina office building. The *clube náutico* has a pleasant bar/restaurant with indoor and outdoor tables, with others across the road from the marina entrance and dozens in the town proper.

Communications

Post office Just off the square of public gardens which face the yacht basin.

Mailing address The marina office will hold mail for visiting yachts – c/o Instituto Portuário do Centro, AP 2008–3080, Figueira da Foz, Portugal. It is important that the envelope carries the name of the yacht in addition to that of the addressee.

Internet access Several possibilities, including WebSymbol on Rua dos Bombeiros, which also sells computer equipment and expendables.

Public telephones At the post office.

Fax service The marina office will receive faxes for yachts, Fax 233 402920, but they must be sent from the post office.

Car hire/taxis In the town.

Buses and trains In the town. The station is less than 0·5km east of the marina.

PORTUGAL – THE WEST COAST

II.3 Figueira da Foz to Cabo da Roca

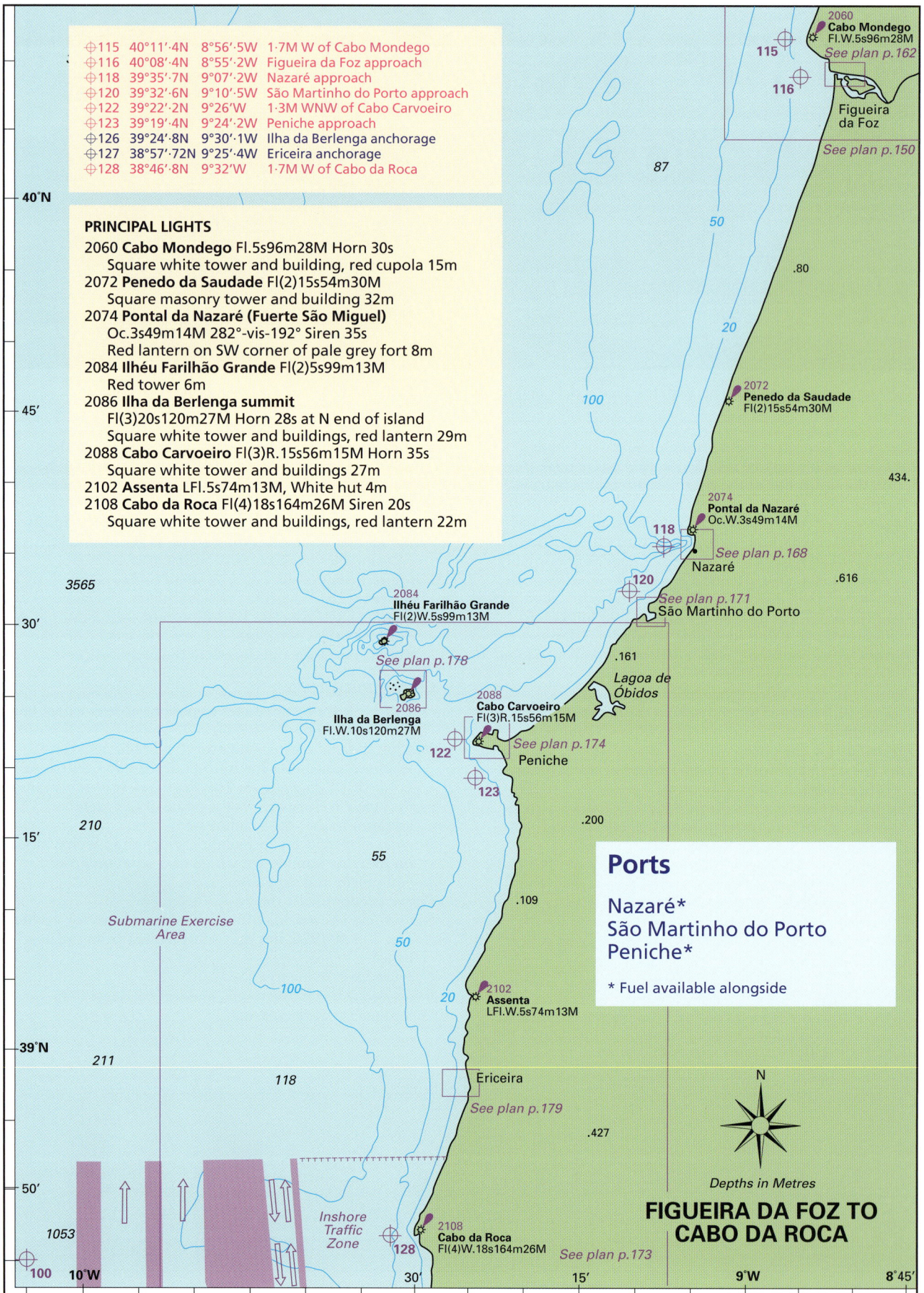

⊕115 40°11'·4N 8°56'·5W 1·7M W of Cabo Mondego
⊕116 40°08'·4N 8°55'·2W Figueira da Foz approach
⊕118 39°35'·7N 9°07'·2W Nazaré approach
⊕120 39°32'·6N 9°10'·5W São Martinho do Porto approach
⊕122 39°22'·2N 9°26'W 1·3M WNW of Cabo Carvoeiro
⊕123 39°19'·4N 9°24'·2W Peniche approach
⊕126 39°24'·8N 9°30'·1W Ilha da Berlenga anchorage
⊕127 38°57'·72N 9°25'·4W Ericeira anchorage
⊕128 38°46'·8N 9°32'W 1·7M W of Cabo da Roca

PRINCIPAL LIGHTS

2060 **Cabo Mondego** Fl.5s96m28M Horn 30s
  Square white tower and building, red cupola 15m
2072 **Penedo da Saudade** Fl(2)15s54m30M
  Square masonry tower and building 32m
2074 **Pontal da Nazaré (Fuerte São Miguel)**
  Oc.3s49m14M 282°-vis-192° Siren 35s
  Red lantern on SW corner of pale grey fort 8m
2084 **Ilhéu Farilhão Grande** Fl(2)5s99m13M
  Red tower 6m
2086 **Ilha da Berlenga summit**
  Fl(3)20s120m27M Horn 28s at N end of island
  Square white tower and buildings, red lantern 29m
2088 **Cabo Carvoeiro** Fl(3)R.15s56m15M Horn 35s
  Square white tower and buildings 27m
2102 **Assenta** LFl.5s74m13M, White hut 4m
2108 **Cabo da Roca** Fl(4)18s164m26M Siren 20s
  Square white tower and buildings, red lantern 22m

2060 **Cabo Mondego** Fl.W.5s96m28M
See plan p.162

115

116

Figueira da Foz

See plan p.150

87

50

.80

20

2072 **Penedo da Saudade** Fl(2)15s54m30M

100

434.

2074 **Pontal da Nazaré** Oc.W.3s49m14M

118
See plan p.168
Nazaré

120
See plan p.171
São Martinho do Porto

.616

3565

2084 **Ilhéu Farilhão Grande** Fl(2)W.5s99m13M

.161

Lagoa de Óbidos

See plan p.178

2086 **Ilha da Berlenga** Fl.W.10s120m27M

2088 **Cabo Carvoeiro** Fl(3)R.15s56m15M

122
See plan p.174
Peniche

123

.200

210

55

.109

Submarine Exercise Area

50

100

20

2102 **Assenta** LFl.W.5s74m13M

Ports

Nazaré*
São Martinho do Porto
Peniche*

* Fuel available alongside

211

118

Ericeira
See plan p.179

.427

Depths in Metres

N

Inshore Traffic Zone

2108 **Cabo da Roca** Fl(4)W.18s164m26M

See plan p.173

128

1053

100

FIGUEIRA DA FOZ TO CABO DA ROCA

40°N
45'
30'
15'
39°N
50'

10°W 30' 15' 9°W 8°45'

Nazaré

Waypoints
⊕118 – 39°35'·7N 9°07'·2W (approach)
⊕119 – 39°35'·48N 9°04'·74W (entrance)

Courses and distances
⊕109 (Leixões) – ⊕118 = 95.1M, 190° or 010°
⊕116 (Figueira da Foz) – ⊕118 = 34M, 196° or 016°
⊕118 – ⊕119 = 1·9M, 097° or 277°
⊕118 – ⊕120 (São Martinho do Porto) = 4M,
   219° or 039°
⊕118 – ⊕123 (Peniche, via ⊕122 Cabo Carvoeiro) =
   22·9M, 227° & 153° or 333° & 047°

Tides
Standard port Lisbon
Mean time differences
HW –0020 ±0010 LW 0000 ±0005
Heights in metres

MHWS	MHWN	MLWN	MLWS
3·3	2·6	1·3	0·6

Or refer to EasyTide at www.ukho.gov.uk/easytide

Charts

Charts	Approach	Harbour
Admiralty	3635	
Imray	C19, C49	C49
Portuguese	34, 23202, 24202, 24203	34, (26302)

Principal lights
2074.3 **North breakwater** LFl.R.5s14m9M
   White tower, red bands 7m
2074.5 **South breakwater** LFl.G.5s14m8M
   White tower, green bands 7m

Night entry
Straightforward, though the small marina is crowded and it may be necessary to raft up to a fishing boat until daylight.

Harbour communications
Porto de Recreio da Nazaré ☾ +351 262 561401
Mobile 96 8074 254 (Celtic Marine Services)
Fax +351 262 553191 *Email* celticmarin@clix.pt
www.portaldomar.pt
VHF Ch 09 (0830–1800 weekdays only)

A base for visiting famous cultural and devotional sites with a small marina in a busy fishing harbour with safe, all-weather entry

The harbour is a purpose-built, well-sheltered fishing port with no hazards on the approach. Indeed it is claimed that Nazaré's harbour is never closed, even in conditions in which it would be foolhardy to attempt any of those further north other than Leixões. This is due to the Canhão da Nazaré, a deep trench which runs close offshore and markedly reduces swell. However, from the perspective of a sailing yacht this promised calming effect may not be very apparent.

The Portuguese Hydrographic Institute is working to understand how the waves become so huge close-inshore at the Praia do Norte just north of Nazaré. The area is home to one of the only deep-water canyons in Europe that runs all the way to shore, funneling large swells from the Atlantic Ocean. This is where a new world record for the tallest wave ever surfed, at about 30m (100ft), was claimed in 2012. But the corollary of this phenomenon is that the canyon, Canhão da Nazaré, markedly reduces swell on its south side, as described above, although the prudent mariner would wish to avoid the conditions that generate such extremes.

Though useful as a port of refuge and sheltering a small but friendly marina, many would claim that the harbour itself is somewhat bleak. It is also more than 1·5km from the town, though there is a bus service. (The harbour surroundings are very flat, however, and Nazaré is one of those places where bicycles come into their own). Old Nazaré (O Sítio), whose citizens claim Phoenician origin, occupies a fine position on the rocky promontory above the main part of the town and provides wonderful views over the bay and beach of Nazaré. It is accessible by funicular railway. One of the most famous fishing villages in Portugal, Nazaré does not contain the architectural jewels of other towns, but relies more on its traditions for its atmosphere. The Caldeirada à Nazarena is a rich fish-based stew typical of the area. The festival of Nossa Senhora da Nazre Romaria (September 8) is a major festival with a religious procession, bullfights and folk dancing.

Possibly the most compelling reason to visit Nazaré is as a base from which to visit a number of Portugal's most famous cultural and devotional sites, including Fatima, Obidos, Alcobaça and Caldas da Rainha, all of which can be reached by public transport. However the top 'must see' is undoubtedly the early 15th-century abbey of Batalha – literally Battle Abbey – one of Europe's greatest Gothic masterpieces and a World Heritage Site. The slightly tortuous 60-minute bus journey via Leiria will be amply rewarded.

Approach

The low-lying beach which reaches from Figueira da Foz to the light at Penedo da Saudade gives way to a more broken coastline backed by low hills leading south to the Pontal da Nazaré, with a light on the

The result of winter storms 2013. The sorry north breakwater light   *Henry Buchanan*

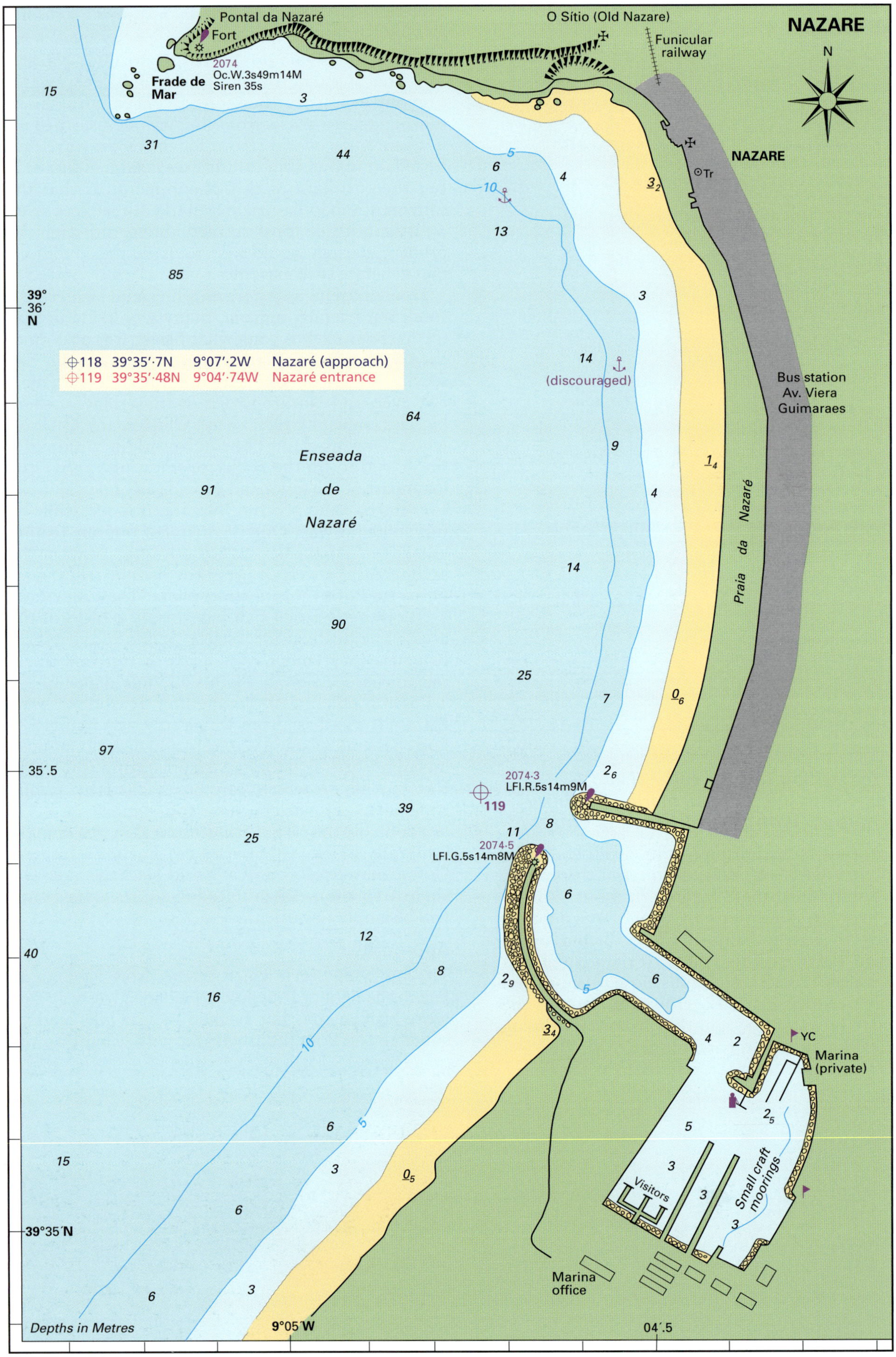

NAZARE

Pontal da Nazaré
Fort
2074
Oc.W.3s49m14M
Siren 35s

O Sítio (Old Nazare)

Funicular railway

Frade de Mar

N

NAZARE

Tr

15

3

31

44

5

6

4

3 2

10

13

3

85

39° 36′ N

| ⊕ | 118 | 39°35′·7N | 9°07′·2W | Nazaré (approach) |
| ⊕ | 119 | 39°35′·48N | 9°04′·74W | Nazaré entrance |

14
(discouraged)

Bus station
Av. Viera Guimaraes

64

9

1 4

Enseada

de

Nazaré

91

4

90

14

25

7

0 6

97

35′.5

39

25

2 6

2074·3
LFl.R.5s14m9M

119

11

8

2074·5
LFl.G.5s14m8M

6

12

40

8

2 9

6

16

3 4

5

4 2

YC

Marina (private)

2 5

6

5

3

10

Visitors

3

Small craft moorings

3

6

5

15

3

0 5

3

39°35′N

6

3

Marina office

Depths in Metres

9°05′W

04′.5

Praia da Nazaré

The Porto de Recreio da Nazaré and harbour looking north-northeast

wall of its fort, São Miguel. The point has rocks 200m offshore to the southwest, but within a further 60m the bottom drops to 50m or more. If approaching from this direction it is worth standing on until the harbour entrance bears 120° before turning, to avoid concentrations of pot buoys in the northeast part of the bay.

The coast 4M south of Nazaré loses its sand dunes and becomes rocky. South of São Martinho, towards the Lagoa de Obidos, there is a rugged stretch of higher coast. South of this the coast is again a sandy beach, here backed by cliffs, as far as Cabo Carvoeiro. Fishing nets may be laid on a line parallel to and up to 4M off this stretch of shore. On final approach from the south, particularly in thick weather, note that the Canhão da Nazaré underwater canyon trends north of east into the Enseada da Nazaré, and that its 100m line comes within 600m of the shore.

From offshore, ⊕118 lies 2M from the coast. A course of 097° leads to ⊕119, directly outside the harbour mouth.

Entrance

Straightforward, between the moles – though watch for fishing boats travelling at speed. The port hand entrance light, and the breakwater it was mounted on, was undermined by a storm in the winter of

Looking southwards from O Sítio towards Nazare harbour entrance *Jane Russell*

2012 and the original light fell over 90° to sea level. A replacement light was erected about 50m back but there is, as a result, rock, stone and broken sea wall extending at least 50m into the sea. So on entrance favour the starboard side of the channel.

Berthing

There are two marinas in the harbour, both small. Visiting yachts should head for the three pontoons in the southwest corner, known as the Porto de Recreio da Nazaré. Although officially administered by the Instituto Portuário e dos Transportes Marítimos, in practice the marina's reception and information office is run by Captain Michael Hadley and his wife Sally.

Yachts are generally met on arrival and directed to a berth but failing this, or outside office hours (officially 0830–1800, but often much later in summer), any suitable spot may be used. Depths are said to be a minimum of 3m throughout the marina. Fourteen of the 52 berths are nominally reserved for visitors, all alongside either main or finger pontoons, but by dint of rafting up, both at the marina and on the adjacent fishing boat jetties, nearly 50 visitors have been squeezed in on occasion. It should be noted, however, that in strong northwest winds, help from shore is required to secure to the central fishing dock. It is very high, not well laddered, covered in fish nets etc and not an ideal place to be moored, especially with small children on board.

Out of office hours, go to the security kiosk at the main road entrance to book in and obtain the keys to pontoons and showers.

Security throughout the entire port area is excellent though relaxed, with a watchman permanently on duty at the main gate and access to the pontoons via a key. There is CCTV surveillance for the whole port area.

In challenging conditions, the berthing master at the private *Clube Navale da Nazaré*, with premises in the east of the harbour, has been known to help when the Porto de Recreio da Nazaré is full, waving boats over to a pontoon berth adjacent to the fuel dock in the northeast corner of the harbour. However, there is seemingly an unpleasant local

Nazaré – northeast corner of the bay from the anchorage
Henry Buchanan

political dispute over rights to provide transient moorings. The *Clube Navale* want to be allowed to welcome visitors, so give it a try.

Anchorage

Anchoring is not permitted in the harbour or its approaches. However, in settled weather it is possible to anchor, best protected from the northerly swell, under the cliffs at Sitio on a plateau with good holding at 39°36'·121N 009°04'·704W. But beware the orange buoys with floating lines ashore just to the southeast and note this is also a popular spot for the friendly local fishermen. If anchored off the beach you may be asked to move by the *Policía Marítima*.

Formalities

Nazaré does not yet have the 'single form' system, but there is a *GNR–Brigada Fiscal* office in the same building as the marina office and, normally, no other officials need be seen. An Immigration Officer may visit your vessel to see passports etc.

Facilities

The first place to enquire about almost any need is at the marina reception and information office. Michael and Sally can advise on anything from major repair work by local contractors to the local bus timetable, and Sally will translate into Portuguese if necessary. They produce a very useful information sheet in a dozen or more languages, and find space for a multi-lingual book-swap.

Boatyard Near the main gate to the port area, and able to handle repairs in GRP and steel, painting etc. However visitors (particularly those who do not speak Portuguese) would be well advised to approach them through the marina office.

Travel-lift 50-tonne capacity hoist, backed by a large area of concrete hard-standing which serves both fishing boats and yachts (most of the latter in cradles with additional props). Electricity is laid on, and owners are free both to work on their own boats and to live aboard whilst ashore.

Engineers, electronic and radio repairs Again, all services are available but contact is best made via the marina office.

Sailmaker/sail repairs The nearest sailmakers are in Lisbon – again, enquire at the marina office.

Chandlery Some basic chandlery is held by Naval-Ship and a new company, Varga Laga. Otherwise the marina staff can arrange ordering and delivery from Lisbon.

Water On the pontoons.

Showers There are two male and two female showers and provision is soon to be made for the handicapped.

Launderette Washing machine next to the showers, but no dryer. There is a full-service launderette in the town.

Electricity On the pontoons.

Fuel Diesel and petrol pumps on the short hammerhead pontoon next to the *clube naval* marina, run by the nearby BP garage. Use the intercom at the gate off the pontoon to ask the fuel station staff to open it, and then go to the fuel station to get the pumps turned on. It is self-service with a return to the fuel station on completion.

Bottled gas Available at the mini-market next to the marina office.

Clube Naval da Nazaré Premises on the east side of the harbour. Clube Naval da Nazaré, Pavilhão Náutico do Clube Naval da Nazaré, Porto de abrigo da Nazaré, 2450 - 075 Nazaré. ☎/Fax +351 262 560 422 *Mobile* +351 917 50 0851. Weather forecast Posted daily outside the marina office.

Banks In the town.

Shops/provisioning Well-stocked mini-market facing the marina (where fresh bread is available twice a day), with good general shopping in Nazaré itself.

Produce market Good market in the town, open 0700–1300 daily in summer, closed Mondays in the winter. A large open market is held every Friday just behind the produce hall.

Cafés, restaurants and hotels Café/bar at the mini-market and another beside the *Clube Naval* pontoons, with a wide choice in the thriving holiday resort. Not surprisingly, all menus feature fish prominently.

Medical services In Nazaré, but visit the marina office for advice and assistance.

Communications

Post offices In the town, though stamped mail can be left at the marina office for posting.

Mailing address Mail is best sent via Michael and Sally Hadley – c/o Celtic Marine, Caixa Postal 1, Porto da Nazaré, 2450-075 Nazaré, Portugal. It is important that the envelope carries the name of the yacht in addition to that of the addressee.

Internet access There is free WiFi coverage across the marina. No password needed.

Public telephone Kiosks near the marina security gate and at the mini-market, which also sells the necessary card.

Fax service At the marina office *Fax* +351 262 561 402.

Car hire/taxis Best arranged via the marina office.

Buses Regular buses into Nazaré (though the walk is less than a mile over flat ground). A timetable is displayed outside the marina office. Express buses connect Nazaré with Lisbon airport (about 90 minutes), Porto etc.

Batalha, a top 'must-see' in Portugal *Jane Russell*

São Martinho do Porto

Waypoints
⊕120 – 39°32'·6N 9°10'·5W (approach)
⊕121 – 39°30'·76N 9°08'·9W (entrance)

Courses and distances
⊕118 (Nazaré) – ⊕120 = 4M, 219° or 039°
⊕120 – ⊕121 = 2·2M, 146° or 326°
⊕120 – ⊕123 (Peniche, via ⊕122 Cabo Carvoeiro) =
   19M, 229° & 153° or 333° & 049°

Peniche

Tides
See Nazaré, page 167

Charts

	Approach	Harbour
Admiralty	3635	
Imray	C19, C49	
Portuguese	34, 23202, 24202, 24203	34, (27501)

Principal lights
2076 **Ponta do Santo Antonío** LFl.R.6s33m9M Siren 60s
   White tower, red, bands
   Obscured on a bearing of more than 165°
2078 **Ldg Lts 145°** *Front* Carreira do Sul Iso.R.1.5s10m9M
   White column, red bands 6m
2078.1 *Rear* 129m from front Oc.R.6s12m9·5M
   White column, red bands, on square white base 8m

Night entry
Not feasible without local knowledge

Shallow but attractive fair-weather anchorage

Once a small fishing port but now a growing tourist town, São Martinho do Porto has a most attractive setting. The sea has widened a breach in the hard cliffs and excavated a crescent-shaped bay out of the softer rock behind. A foot tunnel runs through the cliff just short of the Ponta de Santo António, debouching onto a rocky shore where the unwary can get soaked.

Even though many of the buildings are new and most along the seafront are of four or five storeys, the town is surprisingly attractive with an almost Mediterranean feel to its architecture, pavement cafés, and tourist shops. The shallow, sheltered waters of the bay ensure warmer than average swimming temperatures.

Approach and entrance

The bay is shallow and should ideally only be entered in calm, settled weather. However, on advice from English speaking local fishermen it would appear that whilst in strong winds the entrance has to be treated with caution, if entering or leaving near the top of the tide then no problems should be experienced.

Once inside there is little movement even when breaking crests fill the entrance, but leaving in such weather would be impossible.

If coastal sailing, much of that written about Nazaré, page 167, also applies. On closing São Martinho, keep outside the enclosing headlands until the entrance is clearly seen. In particular, beware the rocks 300m off the unlit Ponta do Facho. This promontory, if one is close inshore to the northeast, masks Ponta do Santo António and its light, 0·5M to the south.

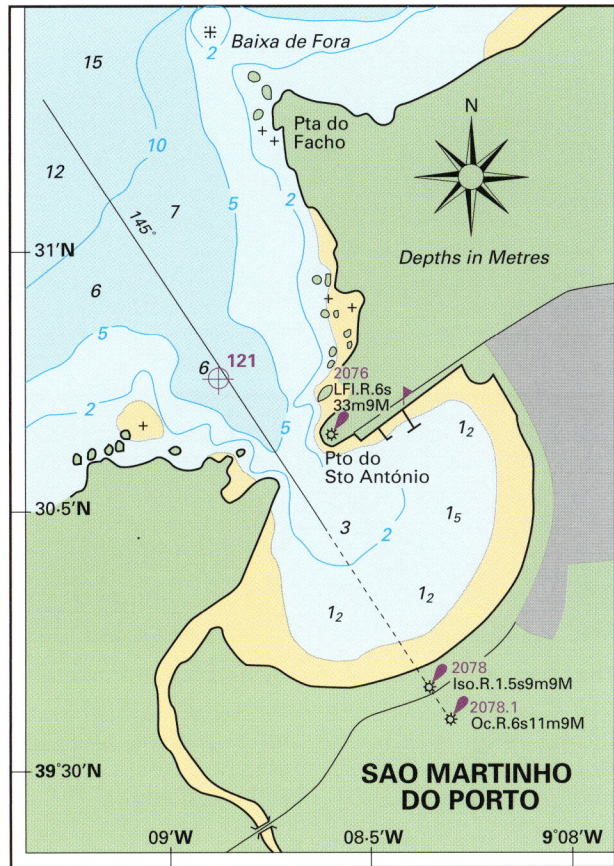

⊕120	39°32'·6N	9°10'·5W	São Martinho do Porto approach
⊕121	39°30'·76N	9°08'·9W	São Martinho do Porto entrance

From offshore ⊕120 lies 2·2M northwest of the entrance, a course of 146° leading to ⊕121 in the final approach.

The leading marks, on 145°, consist of two red and white banded columns 9m and 11m in height, which may be difficult to pick out against the sand and scrub background. Use them for the approach, but enter midway between Ponta do Santo António and Ponta Santana. Several dozen small white buoys are scattered across and just inside the entrance, presumably marking fish pots but posing an obvious hazard to propellers.

In even moderate weather, though the anchorage may be tenable a boat can be trapped by the swell at the exit. If the fishermen leave *en masse* it may be wise to follow.

Anchorage

Anchor outside the moorings in the northeast part of the harbour in about 2m over sand. The quay leading round from Ponta de Santo António has no more than this at its head, shoaling towards the town, and has underwater projections in places. There are two short jetties where one could land by dinghy, but there seems little point when the alternative is a clean, sandy beach.

Formalities

Call at the Policía Marítima office at the northeast corner of the beach (easily identified by its mast and

The narrow entrance to São Martinho do Porto's semicircular bay

lights) with passports, ship's papers and the documentation for the last port of call. An anchoring tax of €2 (2013) will be asked for.

Facilities and communications

The Clube Náutico de São Martinho do Porto has newly enlarged premises on the north quay. Water could doubtless be had for the asking, but there is no fuel available.

The town has reasonable shopping, banks, restaurants, bars etc., together with a post office and telephones. There is an excellent 'Union Jack Shop' behind the *Police Maritima* which sells English items not normally found, such as bacon, marmalade etc, but, more to the point, has an extensive book exchange and can provide good local advice.

Just beyond is the new Tourist Office which is very good and helpful for bus travel to Batalha etc., and has a lift at the back of the building to the higher levels. Frequent bus services are available but the tourist office does not recommend the railway.

The new *Intermarche* supermarket is adjacent to the bus-stops, and 15 minutes' walk from the pontoon where a dinghy can be left.

There are a number of good and relatively inexpensive restaurants there. WiFi in *Martinho* is excellent and the *Turismo* has a free to use computer.

In summary, this is a good place to stay, especially for those with children or who like warm seas and excellent beaches with showers etc.

Not feasible – Lagõa de Obidos

The Lagõa de Obidos (39°26′N 9°14′W), just south of Foz de Arelho and about halfway between São Martinho do Porto and Cabo Carvoeiro, may appear a possibility. However the mouth is almost totally blocked by sandbars and the tide runs swiftly through the gaps. Unlike the rather similar Esposende, there are no offlying hazards.

Looking southeast across the shallow bay at São Martinho do Porto from Ponta do Santo António   *Anne Hammick*

Peniche to Cascais, including Ilha da Berlenga

30′

Os Farilhões
2084
Fl(2)W.5s99m13M

Nature Reserve

See plan p.178

100

50

20

10

20

2086
Fl.W.10s120m16M
I.da Berlenga

122

See plan p.174

⊕ 2088
Cabo Carvoeiro
Fl(3).R.15s56m15M

Peniche
2094
Fl.R.3s13m9M

Lagoa de Óbidos

20′

123

50

100

⊕122	39°22′·2N	9°26′W	1·3M WNW of Cabo Carvoeiro
⊕123	39°19′·4N	9°24′·2W	Peniche approach
⊕127	38°57′·72N	9°25′·4W	Ericeira anchorage
⊕128	38°46′·8N	9°32′W	1·7M W of Cabo da Roca
⊕129	38°42′·3N	9°30′·3W	1M WSW of Cabo Raso
⊕130	38°37′·2N	9°23′·5W	Rio Tejo Fairway Buoy No.2
⊕131	38°40′N	9°25′·3W	Cascais approach

Porto das Barcas

Porto Dinheiro

10′

2102
Assenta
LFl.W.5s74m13M

39°00′N

See plan p.179

2106
Oc.R.3s36m6M

127 ⊕

Ericeira

100

50

20

10

*Traffic Separarion Scheme
Cabo da Roca*

100

100

50′

*Inshore
Traffic Zone*

See plan p.180

128 ⊕

See plan p.166

2108
Cabo da Roca
Fl(4)W.20s164m26M

2127·15
Mama Sul
Iso.6s153m21M

129 ⊕

See plan p.183

2127
Gibalta
Oc.R.3s21M

2127·1
Esteiro
Oc.R.6s21M

LISBON

2110
Cabo Raso
Fl(3)W.9s22m15M

Cascais

Oeiras

Rio Tejo

2118
131 ⊕ **Santa Marta**
Oc.WR.6s
24m18/14M

See plan p.186

See plan p.191

10

130 ⊕ **No 2**
Fl.R.10s
R

50′ 40′ 9°30′W 20′ 10′

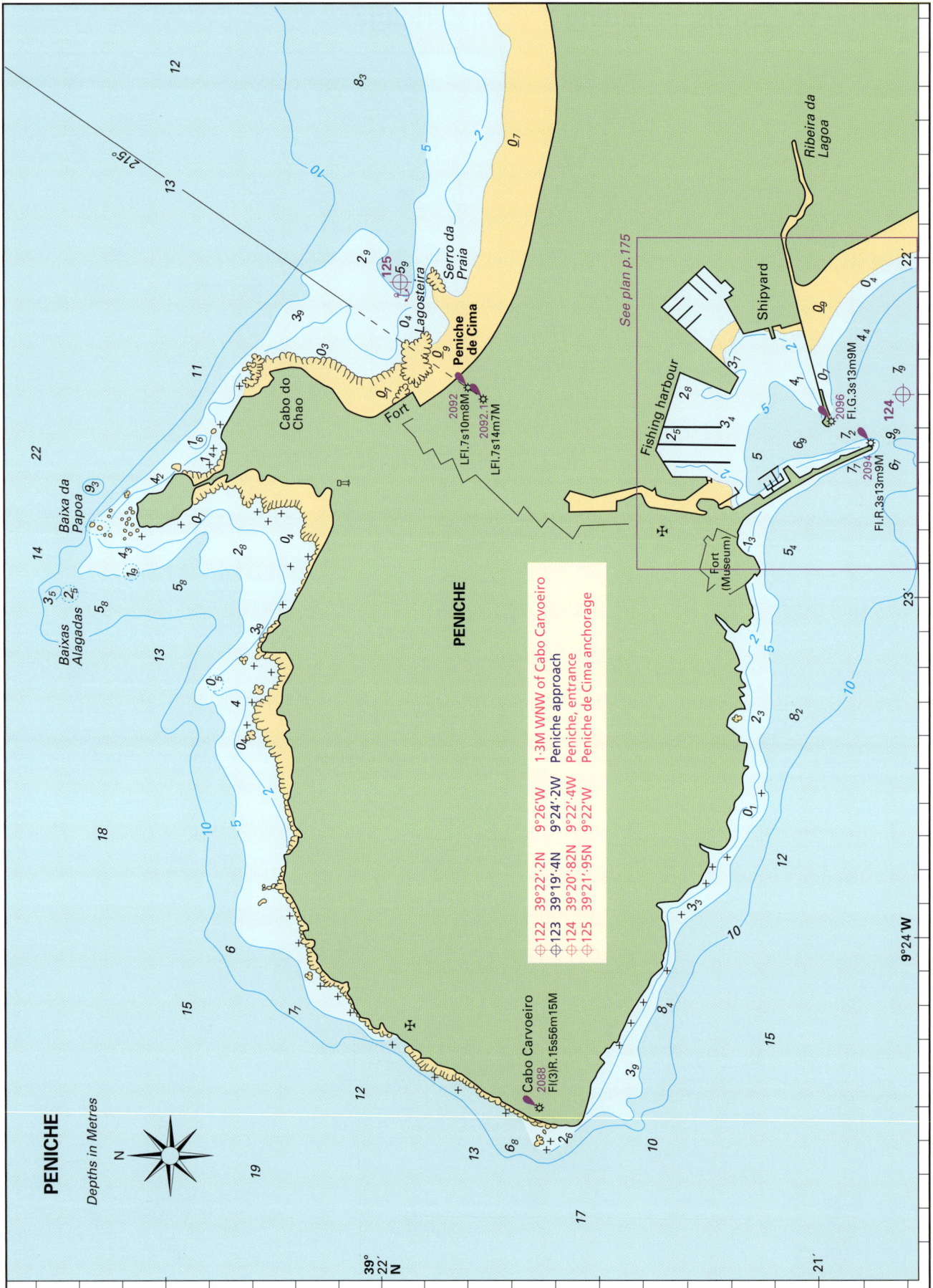

PENICHE

Depths in Metres

N

215°

Ribeira da Lagoa

Shipyard

Fishing harbour

See plan p.175

2096
Fl.G.3s13m9M
2094
Fl.R.3s13m9M

124

Fort (Museum)

PENICHE

Serro da Praia

Peniche de Cima

Fort

Cabo do Chao

2092
LFl.7s10m8M
2092.1
LFl.7s14m7M

Lagosteira

125

Baixa da Papoa

Baixas Alagadas

Cabo Carvoeiro
2088
Fl(3)R.15s56m15M

⊕			
⊕122	39°22'·2N	9°26'W	1·3M WNW of Cabo Carvoeiro
⊕123	39°19'·4N	9°24'·2W	Peniche approach
⊕124	39°20'·82N	9°22'·4W	Peniche, entrance
⊕125	39°21'·95N	9°22'W	Peniche de Cima anchorage

39° 22' N

9°24'W

Peniche, Ilha da Berlenga and Ericeira

Waypoints
⊕122 – 39°22'·2N 9°26'W (1·3M WNW of Cabo Carvoeiro)
⊕123 – 39°19'·4N 9°24'·2W (approach)
⊕124 – 39°20'·82N 9°22'·4W (entrance)
⊕125 – 39°21'·95N 9°22'W (Peniche de Cima anchorage)
⊕126 – 39°24'·63N 9°30'·25W (Ilha Berlenga anchorage waypoint)
⊕127 – 38°57'·72N 9°25'·4W (Ericeira anchorage)

Courses and distances
⊕118 (Nazaré) – ⊕123 (via ⊕122) = 22·9M, 227° & 153° or 333° & 047°
⊕123 – ⊕124 = 2M, 045° or 225°
⊕123 – ⊕126 = 7·1M, 320° or 140°
⊕124 – ⊕126 = 7·2M, 304° or 124°
⊕123 – ⊕127 = 21·7M, 182° or 002°
⊕123 – ⊕130 (Rio Tejo Fairway Buoy No.2, via ⊕128 & ⊕129) = 45·2M, 191° & 164°&134° or 314° & 344°&011°
⊕123 – ⊕131 (Cascais, via ⊕128 & ⊕129) = 42·4M, 191° & 164° & 120° or 300° & 344° & 011°
⊕127 – ⊕130 (Rio Tejo Fairway Buoy No.2, via ⊕128 & ⊕129) = 24·2M, 205° & 164°&134° or 314° & 344° & 025°

Tides
Standard port Lisbon
Mean time differences
HW –0025 ±0010; LW 0000 ±0005
Heights in metres

MHWS	MHWN	MLWN	MLWS
3·5	2·7	1·3	0·6

Or refer to EasyTide at www.ukho.gov.uk/easytide

Charts

	Approach	Harbour
Admiralty	3635	
Imray	C19, C49	C49
Portuguese	36, 23202, 24202, 24203, 26405	26405
Ilhas das Berlengas	26405	
Ilhéus dos Farilhões	26405	
Ericeira	(27501)	

Principal lights
2094 **West breakwater** Fl.R.3s13m9M Siren 120s White tower, red bands 8m
2096 **East breakwater** Fl.G.3s13m9M White tower, green bands 8m

Night entry
Well lit, and without problems other than in strong southerlies. However space at the marina is often limited.

Maritime radio station
Montejunto (39°10'·5N 9°03'·5W)
Remotely controlled from Lisbon
Manual – VHF Ch 16, 24, 25, 27. *Autolink* – VHF Ch 86.

Harbour communications
Port Authority ✆ +351 262 784109 *Fax* +351 262 784225 *Email* japcpen@mail.telepac.pt
VHF Ch 11, 16 (call *Capimarpeniche*) (0900–1200, 1400–1700 weekdays only)
Marina da Ribeira ✆ +351 262 781153, VHF Ch 11, 16
Fax +351 262 784 225

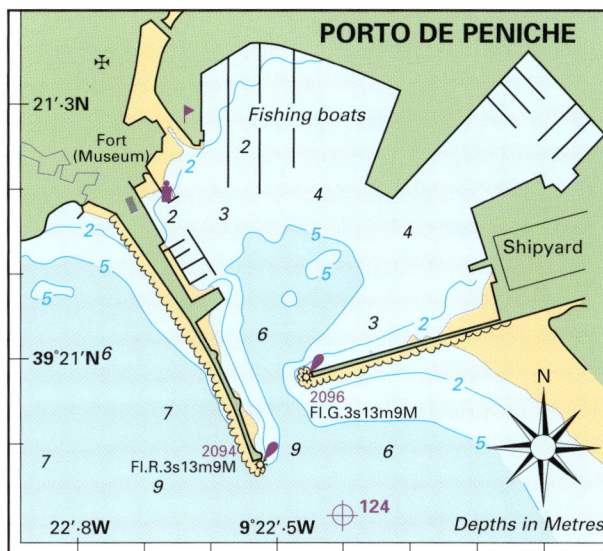

PORTO DE PENICHE

Depths in Metres

⊕123	39°19'·4N	9°24'·2W	Peniche approach
⊕124	39°20'·82N	9°22'·4W	Peniche, entrance

Busy fishing harbour with small yacht marina

Possibly settled by Phoenicians, and the scene of a landing in 1589 by an English force, Peniche today is an important fishing port with a large harbour. The town is of greater interest than many along this coast and the museum in the 16th-century Fortaleza, later converted into a political prison, is particularly recommended. Until the 15th century Peniche was effectively an island, and the defensive walls which protected its shoreward side still run unbroken from north to south.

The port is large and well sheltered from the prevailing northerlies with an easy entrance, but it is not picturesque, though the comings and goings of the fishing fleet certainly add interest (and wash), as do the Ilha da Berlenga tourist ferries. The festival of Nossa Senhora da Boa Viagem takes place over the first weekend in August and includes harbour processions and blessing of the fishing fleet.

Peniche looking north, with the small Marina da Ribeira tucked behind the breakwater on the left

PORTUGAL – THE WEST COAST

Peniche's Marina da Ribeira with visiting yachts rafted on both sides of the outer pontoon. Fishing boats line the concrete moles in the background

Approach

If coastal sailing from the north, most navigators will opt for the 5·5M wide channel between Ilha da Berlenga and Cabo Carvoeiro (⊕122), though tidal streams between the islands and the mainland may make for a rough passage. When seen from some distance to the north, Peniche can be mistaken for the island it once was. Also viable is the narrower, 3M gap between Ilha da Berlenga and Os Farilhões, though there are offlying rocks on both side and care is needed as the current sets south onto the larger island.

From Cabo Carvoeiro to Cabo da Roca, 33M to the south, the coast has steep cliffs with the occasional beach. A Traffic Separation Zone is situated off Cabo da Roca, 7M wide and approximately 10M from the headland. The major light en route is Assenta, 1M south of Ponta da Lamparoeira.

On closing Peniche, ⊕123 lies 2M due southwest of the entrance, a course of 045° leading to ⊕124, close outside the harbour mouth.

Entrance

On final approach from the west around Cabo Carvoeiro, the east breakwater light appears to the north of the west breakwater light. Approach the west breakwater within 50–100m and round in – the entrance is a little over 100m wide.

Peniche is a busy fishing port for vessels both large and small, and a greater than usual concentration of fish pots should be anticipated within 10–15M of the entrance. Some are well marked but the majority are not – be warned!

Berthing and formalities

Visiting yachts should secure to the long outer pontoon which shelters the marina proper, choosing a berth as space allows. Five or six yachts can moor in line ahead on the outside, rafting up from then on, while a few lucky ones may find places on the inside, though note that the northernmost inside berth is

Fish drying outside a house in Peniche *Anne Hammick*

reserved for the *GNR–Brigada Fiscal* vessel. All berths alongside finger pontoons are private. At least 5m should be found throughout.

The marina is reasonably well protected, particularly at its northern end, though may suffer from swell in winds out of the south. More of a problem is the constant wash from fishing boats approaching and leaving their three long jetties to the northeast, at all hours of the day and night and almost invariably at speed – despite the 3kn limit prominently displayed on the eastern breakwater end. Generous fendering is therefore essential, and particular care should be taken that masts are staggered to avoid rigging becoming entangled should two boats roll together.

The marina office shares premises at the root of the breakwater with the Ilha da Berlenga ferry booking offices, and is normally open 0700–0745, 0930–1200 and 1600–1830 weekdays, 0700–1200 and 1600–1800 weekends and holidays. If arriving outside these hours the skipper should in theory either walk round to the Instituto Portuário do Centro office at the main port gate, or call them on ℡ 262 781153, but it is unlikely that any English will be spoken. It may be simpler to await the arrival of a marina official or security guard, who amongst other things will issue a card to work the electronic gate. *GNR–Brigada Fiscal* and *Polícia Marítima* officials may also visit.

If going ashore before a card is issued it is essential for someone to remain inside the gate to let others back in. Even the most agile would have a tough time getting around the guard wires.

Anchorage

It used to be that anchoring was not permitted in the harbour, but having spent an unpleasant night at anchor outside the east breakwater, a yacht was subsequently told by marina staff that the boat could have anchored in the harbour on the starboard side of the entrance inside the east breakwater.

In winds from the northern quadrant good holding over sand in reasonably comfortable conditions can be found south of the east breakwater.

Facilities

Boatyard Several boatyards with marine railways operate near the root of the east breakwater, backed by mechanical, electrical and electronic engineering workshops. Though more accustomed to fishing boats, in an emergency yachts can also be hauled – at a price.

Electronic and radio repairs Estêvão Alexandre Henriques Lda, ℡ 262 085536 *Email* estevaoah@netvisao.pt www.estevaoah.com two streets back from the harbour on Rua José Estêvão, sell and repair marine electronics of all kinds. Most of their trade comes from the fishing fleet but the engineers (some of whom speak English) are happy to visit yachts.

Chandlery Estêvão Alexandre Henriques Lda (see above) stock a limited amount of general chandlery and are willing to order.

Water On the pontoons.

Showers Two toilet/shower cubicles behind the marina office.

Launderette Next to the above – one washer but no dryer.

Electricity On the pontoons.

Fuel Diesel and petrol pumps at the head of the jetty opposite the marina office, administered by the Clube Naval de Peniche (see below). Long hoses run down to the berth, which has black fendering and is frequently occupied by small fishing boats. Fuel is available during office hours only (which vary) so check well in advance. Payment must be made in cash.

Bottled gas Camping Gaz available in the town, but no refills.

Clube naval The Clube Naval de Peniche has its headquarters in the small fort near the root of the west breakwater, beyond the red-doored lifeboat house.

Weather forecast Posted daily on the back of the large display board near the Ilha da Berlenga ferry offices, but generally in Portuguese text only (ie no synoptic chart). An English translation may be available from the marina office.

Banks In the town, nearly all with cash dispensers.

Shops/provisioning Good provisioning and general shopping, including a large supermarket in a new housing development northeast of the harbour.

Produce market In the town.

Cafés, restaurants and hotels Many, though sadly the tradition of grilling sardines on charcoal braziers by the roadside appears to have succumbed to modern hygiene regulations.

Medical services Hospital etc in the town.

Communications

Post office In the town.

Mailing address The marina office will hold mail for visiting yachts – c/o Instituto Portuário e dos Transportes Marítimos, Porto de Pesca de Peniche, 2520 Peniche, Portugal. It is important that the envelope carries the name of the yacht in addition to that of the addressee.

Internet access There is no WiFi at the marina but it is available in many bars and at the *On Line* Cybercafé on Rua Antonio Cervantes (very close to the harbour).

Public telephones Kiosks on the root of the breakwater and elsewhere.

Fax service At the marina office, *Fax* 261 784225.

Car hire/taxis In the town. Taxis can be ordered via the marina office.

Buses Regular bus service to Lisbon (about 1hour 45 minutes) and elsewhere – a visit to the mediaeval walled town of Obidos is particularly recommended.

Ferries Tourist ferries to Ilha da Berlenga – and not a bad way to visit if one wishes to explore without the responsibility of a yacht at anchor (see below).

Air services International airport at Lisbon.

PORTUGAL – THE WEST COAST

Looking northwest over the anchorage at Peniche de Cima

Adjacent anchorages

1. **Peniche do Cima** (⊕125 – 39°21'·95N 9°22'W) on the north side of the peninsula southeast of Cabo do Chao. There are leading marks on 215° but they appear to lead straight onto a rocky shoal. Keep well east, sounding in to anchor close to the above position in 5–6m over sand. The entire bay is open to the north, and any northwesterly swell will also work around the corner.

2. **Ilha da Berlenga** (⊕126 – 39°24'·63N 9°30'·25W) remains desolate and largely unspoilt, despite the numerous tourist boats which ply from Peniche.

The entire island, together with its offlying rocks and the seabed out to the 3m contour, is a nature reserve frequented by seabirds including gulls, puffins and cormorants. For this reason parts of the island are off-limits to visitors – many of whom in any case appear unwilling to venture far from the landing quay at Carreiro do Mosteiro. (For those who enjoy their wildlife small but inquisitive, a small investment of damp bread will swiftly entice the resident lizards out of their crevasses, while walkers should watch out for their kamikaze brethren who dash across paths almost underfoot.)

Approach from the southeast or south in order to avoid off-lying rocks which fringe the island in all other directions, making for either Carreiro do Mosteiro or Carreiro da Fortaleza – in which stands the distinctive Forte de São João Batista – on the southeast coast or Cova do Sono to the southwest (taking care to avoid the offlying Baixo do Sota Cataláo). All three anchorages call for careful 'eyeball' pilotage in good light, made easier by the crystal clear water.

Both Carreiro do Mosteiro and Carreiro da Fortaleza have beaches at their heads, and in the former landing can also be made by dinghy at the stone quay used by the tourist ferries. It would be unwise to leave the yacht unattended for long in any but the calmest conditions, but a short tour by dinghy will be amply rewarded, viewing the impressive Forte de São João Baptista – built in 1502 by monks, tired of their undefended monastery being ransacked by pirates – and exploring the natural tunnels and caves. Once ashore, the small settlement of Bairro dos Pescadores overlooking the quay offers a café/restaurant and a small shop, the latter apparently selling little beyond ice cream.

The second possible anchorage, in the entrance to Cova do Sono in 8–10m over sand and rock, is somewhat better protected and has been used overnight in settled weather. However, although it

Ilha da Berlenga from the southeast, with the Ilhas Medas and Ilhas Estelas clearly visible behind

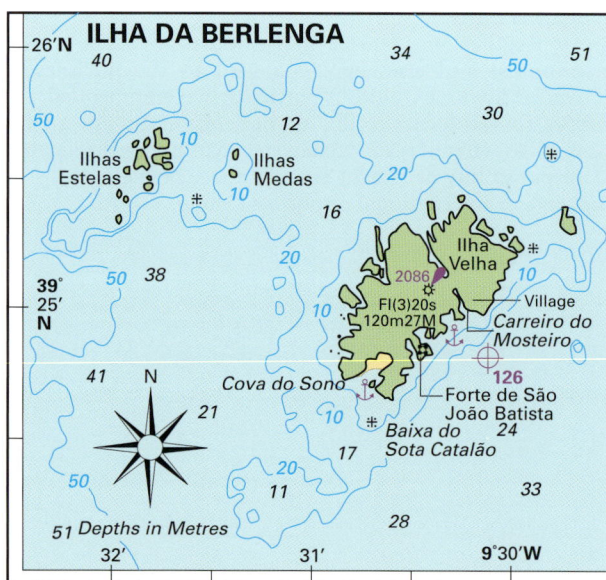

⊕126 39°24'·63N 9°30'·25W Ilha da Berlenga anchorage

The centre part of the Ilha da Berlenga with, from left to right, Forte de São João Batista, the island's 29m lighthouse, and the inlet and village of Carreiro do Mosteiro

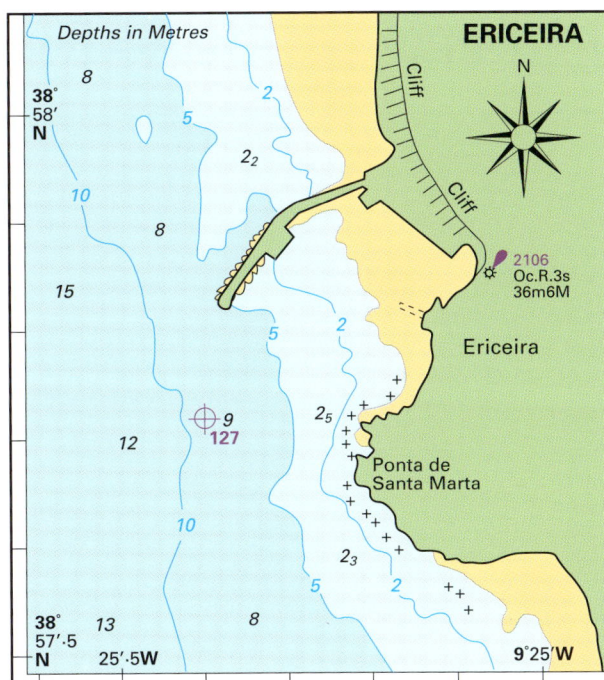

⊕127   38°57'·72N   9°25'·4W   Ericeira anchorage

is possible to land on the surrounding boulders, only a mountaineer – and one willing to ignore the bylaws which forbid roaming off the marked paths – could attain the island's virtually flat summit.

All official paths start and end at the quay in Carreiro do Mosteiro, but if intent on seeing the island in detail – and unless the crew is large enough to leave a person aboard at all times – it might be better to visit by ferry from Peniche, where several companies compete for business at the root of the main quay. A single day will be long enough to cover all the approved paths, but it is also possible to stay overnight, either in chalets or on the approved campsite – enquire at the tourist office in Peniche.

The Ilhéus dos Farilhões, some 4M north-northwest of Ilha da Berlenga, offer no feasible anchorages.

3. **Ericeira** (⊕127 – 38°57'·72N 9°25'·4W), 6M south of Assenta light and 11·5M north of Cabo da Roca, Ericeira offers a possible daytime anchorage in calm, settled weather. However the single breakwater provides absolutely no shelter from onshore winds or swell, and local craft are kept ashore on the wide slipway – not for nothing is the area popular with surfers from all over Europe. No large scale chart is currently available for the area, which is admitted to be poorly surveyed. Though lit, approach after dark would be most unwise.

Close the land keeping well clear of the breakwater head, which lost its outer section to a winter storm and has yet to be rebuilt. Although the outer block shows at all states of the tide, underwater rubble lies scattered in all directions. Best anchorage is to be found in the entrance to the bay, south of the breakwater head, in 5–6m over rock and sand. There is little depth off the small quay, though it has steps convenient for landing by dinghy.

Once a clifftop village – though now dwarfed by the inevitable high-rise buildings – the old town centre has nevertheless retained much of its character and is renowned for its shellfish restaurants. The Clube Naval de Ericeira has a small clubhouse below the cliffs and there are several beach cafés, while the town itself offers the usual banks, shops, post office etc.

In 1910 Portugal's last king, Dom Manuel II, chose Ericeira as his port of departure after a military revolt and following the assassination of his father and elder brother. One can only wonder whether it was the little harbour's apparent unsuitability which prompted his choice.

The small, exposed harbour at Ericeira looking east

II.4 Approaches to the Rio Tejo and Lisbon

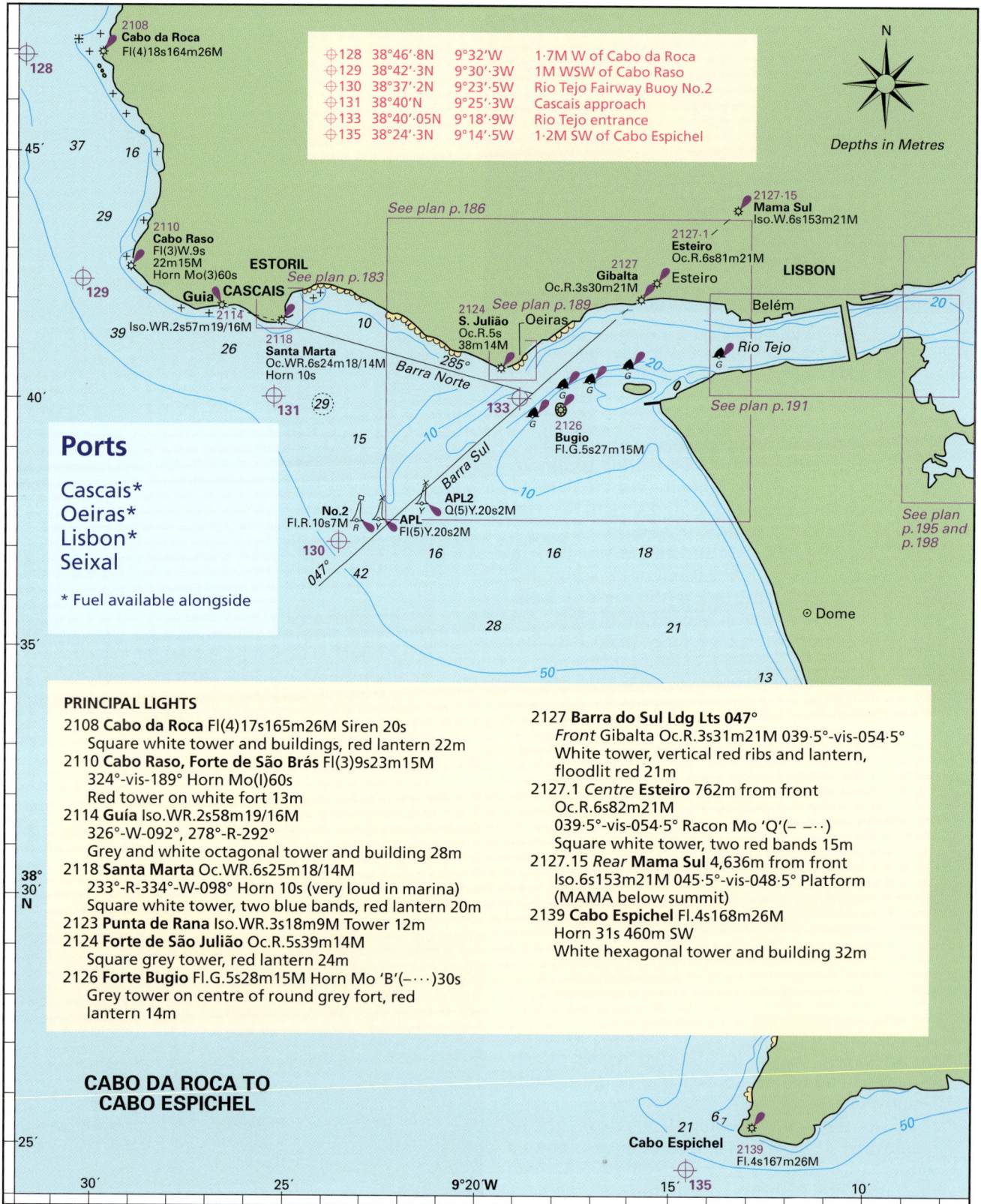

⊕128	38°46'·8N	9°32'W	1·7M W of Cabo da Roca
⊕129	38°42'·3N	9°30'·3W	1M WSW of Cabo Raso
⊕130	38°37'·2N	9°23'·5W	Rio Tejo Fairway Buoy No.2
⊕131	38°40'N	9°25'·3W	Cascais approach
⊕133	38°40'·05N	9°18'·9W	Rio Tejo entrance
⊕135	38°24'·3N	9°14'·5W	1·2M SW of Cabo Espichel

2108
Cabo da Roca
Fl(4)18s164m26M

128

45'   37   16

29

2110
Cabo Raso
Fl(3)W.9s
22m15M
Horn Mo(3)60s

ESTORIL

See plan p.183

129

Guia   **CASCAIS**

2114
39   Iso.WR.2s57m19/16M

285°

2118
Santa Marta
Oc.WR.6s24m18/14M
Horn 10s

26

Barra Norte

40'

131   29

15

Barra Sul

See plan p.186

2127·15
Mama Sul
Iso.W.6s153m21M

2127·1
Esteiro
Oc.R.6s81m21M

2127
Gibalta   Esteiro
Oc.R.3s30m21M

LISBON

Belém

2124   *See plan p.189*
S. Julião   Oeiras
Oc.R.5s
38m14M

Rio Tejo

20

133   G   G
G   G
G
2126
Bugio
Fl.G.5s27m15M

See plan p.191

See plan
p.195 and
p.198

10

Ports

Cascais*
Oeiras*
Lisbon*
Seixal

* Fuel available alongside

No.2
Fl.R.10s7M

APL2
Q(5)Y.20s2M

APL
Fl(5)Y.20s2M

130
047°   42

16   16   18

⊙ Dome

28   21

35'

50   13

PRINCIPAL LIGHTS

2108 Cabo da Roca Fl(4)17s165m26M Siren 20s
Square white tower and buildings, red lantern 22m

2110 Cabo Raso, Forte de São Brás Fl(3)9s23m15M
324°-vis-189° Horn Mo(I)60s
Red tower on white fort 13m

2114 Guía Iso.WR.2s58m19/16M
326°-W-092°, 278°-R-292°
Grey and white octagonal tower and building 28m

2118 Santa Marta Oc.WR.6s25m18/14M
233°-R-334°-W-098° Horn 10s (very loud in marina)
Square white tower, two blue bands, red lantern 20m

2123 Punta de Rana Iso.WR.3s18m9M Tower 12m

2124 Forte de São Julião Oc.R.5s39m14M
Square grey tower, red lantern 24m

2126 Forte Bugio Fl.G.5s28m15M Horn Mo 'B'(—···)30s
Grey tower on centre of round grey fort, red
lantern 14m

2127 Barra do Sul Ldg Lts 047°
Front Gibalta Oc.R.3s31m21M 039·5°-vis-054·5°
White tower, vertical red ribs and lantern,
floodlit red 21m

2127.1 *Centre* **Esteiro** 762m from front
Oc.R.6s82m21M
039·5°-vis-054·5° Racon Mo 'Q'(— —··)
Square white tower, two red bands 15m

2127.15 *Rear* **Mama Sul** 4,636m from front
Iso.6s153m21M 045·5°-vis-048·5° Platform
(MAMA below summit)

2139 Cabo Espichel Fl.4s168m26M
Horn 31s 460m SW
White hexagonal tower and building 32m

38°
30'
N

CABO DA ROCA TO
CABO ESPICHEL

21   6   7
Cabo Espichel   2139
Fl.4s167m26M

50

25'

30'   25'   9°20'W   15'   135   10'

The Rio Tejo estuary

Outer approaches to Cascais, Oeiras, Lisbon and the Rio Tejo

Waypoints
⊕100 – 38°45'N 10°05'W (27·7M W of Cabo da Roca)
⊕128 – 38°46'·8N 9°32'W (1·7M W of Cabo da Roca)
⊕129 – 38°42'·3N 9°30'·3W (1M WSW of Cabo Raso)
⊕130 – 38°37'·2N 9°23'·5W (Fairway Buoy No.2)
⊕133 – 38°40'·05N 9°18'·9W (Rio Tejo entrance)
⊕135 – 38°24'·3N 9°14'·5W (1·2M SW of Cabo Espichel)

Courses and distances
⊕123 (Peniche) – ⊕130 (via ⊕128 & ⊕129) = 45·2M,
  191° & 164° & 134° or 314° & 344° & 011°
⊕127 (Ericeira) – ⊕130 (via ⊕128 & ⊕129) = 24·2M,
  205° & 164° & 134° or 314° & 344° & 025°
⊕100 – ⊕130 = 33·4M, 103° or 283° (not advised due
  to the Traffic Separation Scheme off Cabo da Roca)
⊕130 – ⊕131 (Cascais) = 3·1M, 333° or 153°
⊕130 – ⊕133 = 4·6M, 052° or 332°
⊕130 – ⊕136 (Sesimbra, via ⊕135) = 21·6M, 151° & 089°
  or 269° & 331°
⊕130 – ⊕139 (Setúbal, via ⊕135) = 25·2M, 151° & 090°
  or 270° & 331°
⊕130 – ⊕142 (Sines, via ⊕135) = 48M, 151° & 152° or
  328° & 329°

Charts	Approach	Entrance
Admiralty	3635, 3636	3220
Imray	C19, C49	C19, C49
Portuguese	23203, 24203, 24204, (26406)	(26406), 26303, 26304

Navtex
Monsanto Identification letters 'R' and 'G'
Transmits on 518kHz in English; 490kHz in Portuguese
Weather bulletins and navigational warnings for
Galicia, Portugal and Andalucía: English – 0250, 0650,
1050, 1450, 1850, 2250 UT; Portuguese – 0100, 0500,
0900, 1300, 1700, 2100 UT

Weather bulletins and navigational warnings
Algés (38°44'N 9°11'W)
Weather bulletins in Portuguese and English for
Galicia, Portugal and Andalucía: 2657kHz and VHF
Ch11 at 0905, 2105 UT
Navigational warnings in Portuguese and English
within 200 miles offshore: 2657 kHz and VHF Ch 11 at
1905, 2105 UT

Maritime radio station
Lisbon (38°44'·1N 9°11'·3W) *Digital Selective Calling*
MMSI 002630100
MF Transmits on 2182, 2582, 2693, 2780kHz
Receives 2182kHz
VHF Manual – Ch 16, 23, 25, 26. *Autolink* – VHF Ch 83

Approach

From the north, keep 1M off the high cliffs of Cabo da Roca (⊕128) and the lower headland of Cabo Raso (⊕129) off which there is a Traffic Separation Zone 7M wide and approximately 10M from the headland.

From the south, Cabo Espichel is clear of offlying hazards, though all three headlands can produce nasty seas in wind over tide conditions.

See continuation into the Rio Tejo after Cascais page 186.

Cabo da Roca, with its prominent lighthouse and associated buildings, seen from the south

Approaching Cabo da Roca from the north *David Russell*

PORTUGAL – THE WEST COAST

Cascais

Waypoints
⊕131 – 38°40′N 9°25′·3W (approach)
⊕132 – 38°41′·65N 9°24′·75W (entrance)

Courses and distances
⊕123 (Peniche) – ⊕131 (via ⊕128 & ⊕129) = 42·4M,
91° & 164° & 120° or 300° & 344° & 011°
⊕130 (Rio Tejo Fairway Buoy No.2) – ⊕131 = 3·1M,
333° or 153°
⊕131 – ⊕132 =1·7 M, 015° or 095°
⊕132 – ⊕133 (Rio Tejo entrance) = 4·9M, 109°/289°
⊕131 – ⊕136 (Sesimbra, via ⊕135) = 24·7M, 152° & 089°
or 269° & 332°
⊕131 – ⊕139 (Setúbal, via ⊕135) = 32·3M, 152° & 046°
or 226° & 332°
⊕131 – ⊕142 (Sines, via ⊕135) = 51·1M, 152° & 152°
or 332° & 332°

Tides
Standard port Lisbon
Mean time differences
HW –0035 ±0010; LW –0010 ±0005
Heights in metres
MHWS MHWN MLWN MLWS
3·5   2·7   1·5   0·7
Or refer to EasyTide at www.ukho.gov.uk/easytide

Charts

	Approach	Harbour
Admiralty	3635	3220
Imray	C19, C49	C19, C49
Portuguese	23203, 24203, 24204, (26406)	26303

Principal lights
2118 **Santa Marta** Oc.WR.6s25m18/14M Horn 10s White
tower, blue bands, red cupola 233°-R-334°-W-098°
2121 **Praia da Ribeira** Oc.R.4s7m6M 251°-vis-309°
White metal column, red bands 4·5m
2122 **Albatroz** Oc.R.6s13m5M
Lantern on verandah of Hotel Albatroz 6m
2119 **Marina southeast breakwater** Fl(3)R.4s7m6M
Red post, white bands, on concrete base 3m
2119.1 **Marina north mole** Fl(2)G.5s5m3M
Green post, white bands 5m

Night entry
Should not present problems in any but the strongest
onshore conditions

Harbour communications
Marina de Cascais ☏ +351 214 824857
Fax +351 214 824860 *Email* info@marina-cascais.com
www.marina-cascais.com
VHF Ch 09, 16 (0900–1900 May to September inclusive,
otherwise 0900–1800)

Large marina with good facilities and shelter

A traditional fishing village, which flourished in the
14th century, when it was a port on the way into
Lisbon. In the second half of the 19th century, it
became a very fashionable summer resort when the
king of Portugal converted the Fortaleza da Cidadela
into the summer residence of the Portuguese
monarchy. The festival of Our Lady of Seafarers has
reproductions of saints carried through the town's
streets and onto fishing boats. There is also bull-
running, music, fireworks and lots of food.

It is a good 20 minutes' walk from the marina into
the town centre, though buses run regularly from the
main gate. Alternatively, a walkway has been
completed along the walls above the Clube Naval de
Cascais, giving excellent views and cutting the time
considerably. An unexpected bonus is the very
pleasant leafy park right opposite the marina's
landward gates, complete with children's
playground (a supervised indoor adventure play area
is provided in the marina itself). There is also a small
maritime museum nearby.

The bronze statue of Dom Diogo de Meneses beside Cascais citadel *Jane Russell*

The anchorage at Cascais looking south. Dinghy landing is not permitted on this beach *Jane Russell*

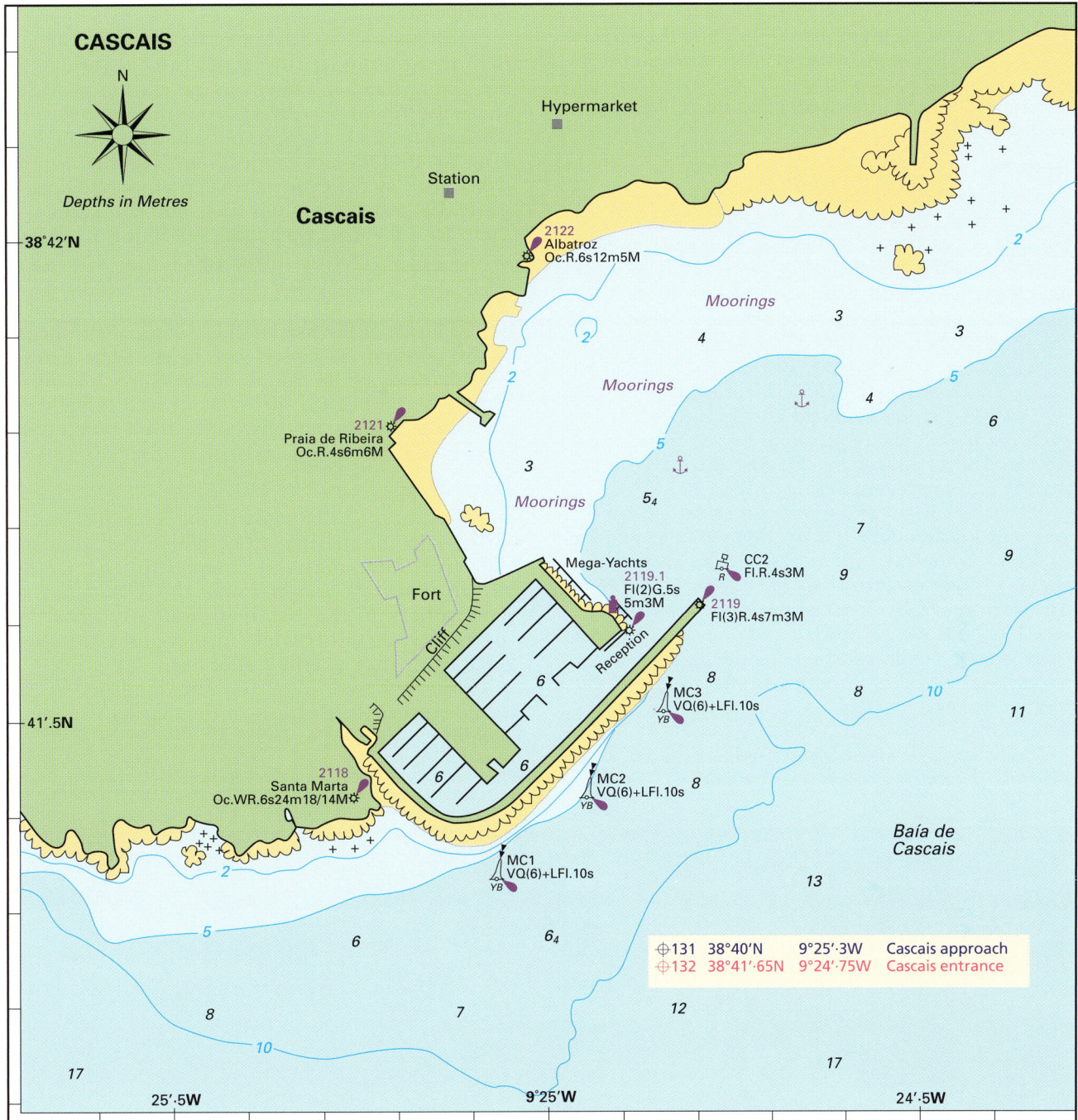

CASCAIS

N

Depths in Metres

38°42'N

Cascais

Hypermarket

Station

2122
Albatroz
Oc.R.6s12m5M

Moorings

2

3

3

Moorings

4

5

2121
Praia de Ribeira
Oc.R.4s6m6M

5

4

6

Moorings

3

5₄

7

Mega-Yachts
2119.1
Fl(2)G.5s
5m3M

CC2
Fl.R.4s3M

9

9

Fort

2119
Fl(3)R.4s7m3M

Cliff

Reception

8

41'.5N

6

MC3
VQ(6)+LFl.10s
YB

8

10

11

6

6

MC2
VQ(6)+LFl.10s
YB

8

2118
Santa Marta
Oc.WR.6s24m18/14M

Baía de
Cascais

2

MC1
VQ(6)+LFl.10s
YB

13

5

6

6₄

⊕131   38°40'N   9°25'.3W   Cascais approach
⊕132   38°41'.65N   9°24'.75W   Cascais entrance

8

7

12

17

10

17

25'.5W   9°25'W   24'.5W

PORTUGAL – THE WEST COAST

Approach

If coastal sailing from the north, between Cabo da Roca (⊕128) and Santa Marta there are steep rocky cliffs and fishing nets may be laid at least 0·5M offshore.

From the south, the track between Cabo Espichel and Cascais lies along 331°, leaving the Rio Tejo Fairway Buoy No.2 about 1M to port and thus crossing the Barra Sul at close to a right-angle. Considerable traffic should be anticipated at this point, and it is not a route to choose in poor visibility unless radar is carried. If approaching from the south at night, the light on São Julião will probably be picked up before that on Santa Marta.

The bright shore lights may mask fishing boats, another time when radar will be useful.

From offshore, ⊕131 lies 1·7M south-southwest of the entrance.

Entrance

The bay is entered between the Cidadela de Cascais, prominently situated on the headland 300m behind the Marina de Cascais, and the Forte de Santo António da Barra, 1·5M to the east. Three south cardinal buoys and a single red can buoy are positioned some 100m from the marina's main breakwater, supposedly keeping yachts off a second, submerged wall which lies some distance outside the visible one. The marina entrance faces northeast with a fetch of no more than 0·4M, and for a yacht with a reliable engine (there is little protection from strong south or southwest winds until inside) should remain feasible in almost all conditions. Towage is available if necessary.

Berthing

A reception berth will be found on the starboard hand on entry, immediately below the marina office. Hours are from 0900–2000 from May to September inclusive, 0900–1900 during the rest of the year. Mega-yachts – those over 40m or so – berth on a pontoon outside the north mole, west of the fuel pontoon, where they lie stern-to (with buoys provided) in a least depth of 7m. All 638 berths inside the marina are alongside finger pontoons (with thoughtfully rounded ends), with access to each main walkway controlled by the usual card-operated electronic gate. Depths throughout the marina are in excess of 6m.

On arrival, berth at the reception pontoon on the starboard side under the windows of the marina office to complete formalities and be allocated a berth. Visiting yachts of less than about 14m (46ft) LOA are generally directed to the southern basin, which is both well-protected and convenient to the main gate. It should be noted that the fog horn at the Santa Marta light just outside the south of the marina makes a noise of ear splitting intensity in fog conditions.

The office staff speak good English and are most helpful. The marina charges are expensive.

Anchorage

It is still possible to anchor in Cascais bay, though the area occupied by smallcraft moorings is increasing steadily. However, the marina provides some additional protection from the southwest to compensate. Pick any spot outside the moorings so long as it does not impede the fairway to the fishermen's quay or the marina entrance. Holding is generally good over sand and light mud (though there are a few rocky patches), but much of the bay is foul and a tripline is a wise precaution. The bay is frequently rolly and there may be downdraughts off the surrounding hills. Dinghies can normally be left on the inside of the marina fuel pontoon (the mega-yacht pontoon is closed off by security gates), though for shopping trips it may be more convenient to land on the slightly dirty town beach to the west of the pier. Dinghy landing on the main beach is no longer allowed.

Formalities

All formalities are handled in the reception block, initially in the marina office where the standard multipart form must be completed. The *GNR–Brigada Fiscal*, *Polícia Marítima* and *Alfândega* also have offices in the building, and may chose to inspect a yacht either while she lies at the reception pontoon or after a berth is allocated.

Those anchored in the bay should also visit the authorities at their offices in the marina reception building.

The Marina de Cascais looking north

Facilities

Boatyard PortFair Yacht Service ☎ 214 847025, *Fax* 214 847026, handles general maintenance and repairs in all materials including GRP, timber and metal, as well as antifouling etc.

Travel-lift 70-tonne capacity lift in the boatyard area, with pressure hoses, etc. – book at the marina office. Maximum beam is currently 6·5m, but there are plans to increase this.

Engineers, mechanics, electronic and radio repairs All available via PortFair, who are authorised dealers for a number of international suppliers. Alternatively try Enervolt, *Mobile* 91 4006 990, who sell and service solar panels, batteries, switch panels etc.

Sailmaker, sail repairs Vela Sailmaker Service, *Mobile* 91 7429 107 *Fax* 218 847490 *Email* info@oficinadavela.com, handles sail repairs and canvaswork. If considering a new purchase it might be worth going further afield – see page 195.

Chandlery There are three chandleries in the central block: NautiStar Lda ☎ +351 214 846 370/1 *Fax* +351 214 845 014 *Email* info@nautistar.pt www.nautistar.pt, stocks general chandlery, galleyware and some books. Advertised hours are 1000–1800 Monday to Saturday, but it is often open much later. The helpful staff will order from an impressive stack of catalogues. Good English is spoken; Mar Masters Lda, ☎ 214 847490 (open 0900–1300, 1400–1800) which carries hardware such as rope, anodes and paint; and Motor & Sail, ☎ 214 845656 (open 1030–1300, 1400–2100), with general chandlery and clothing. In addition there is a good hardware/tool shop in the town.

Charts Available in Lisbon – see page 196.

Water On all pontoons.

Showers Three shower blocks, two in the central part of the complex and one at the reception building.

Launderette In the reception building (a longish walk from the southern basin). A 24 hour service wash is available if required.

Electricity On all pontoons, with plugs etc available at the marina office (deposit required).

Fuel Fuel pontoon (diesel and petrol) outside the north mole. Open marina office hours, with credit cards accepted. Fuel can also be obtained out of hours by prior arrangement and on payment of a surcharge.

Bottled gas Camping Gaz cylinders can be exchanged at both the NautiStar chandlery and the fuel pontoon.

Clube naval The Clube Naval de Cascais has premises immediately north of the marina, but there is no direct access.

Weather forecast Posted daily in the marina office.

Banks At least one automatic card machine in the marina complex, with banks in Cascais.

Shops/provisioning Excellent grocery and other shopping can be found in Cascais itself.

Produce market In Cascais, plus fish sold on the beach in the late afternoon. A general market is held every Wednesday and every second Sunday.

Cafés, restaurants and hotels More than a dozen restaurants and cafés in the marina complex, with plenty more of all three in the town.

Medical services First aid centre at the marina office, with full medical facilities (including English-speaking doctors) in the town.

A yacht lies alongside the reception pontoon at the Marina de Cascais   *Anne Hammick*

Communications

Post office In Cascais.

Mailing address The marina office will hold mail for visiting yachts – c/o Marina de Cascais, Casa de S. Bernardo, 2750–800 Cascais, Portugal. It is important that the envelope carries the name of the yacht in addition to that of the addressee.

Public telephones Kiosks around the marina complex as well as in the town.

Internet access There is no longer a cybercafé in the marina complex but there are several in the town, including Net Phone & Fun which has branches on the corner of Rua Frederico Aronca and Rua das Flores, and on Rua Sebastião José de Carbalho e Melo. Rates (the same at both) are high.

Fax service At the marina office *Fax* 214 824899.

Car hire/taxis Can be arranged through the marina office.

Buses Buses into Cascais from outside the main entrance.

Trains Frequent trains from Cascais to Lisbon's Cais do Sodré station, close to the city centre. The journey, via Estoril and Belém, takes about 30 minutes.

Air services Lisbon International Airport is less than an hour away by train and taxi.

PORTUGAL – THE WEST COAST

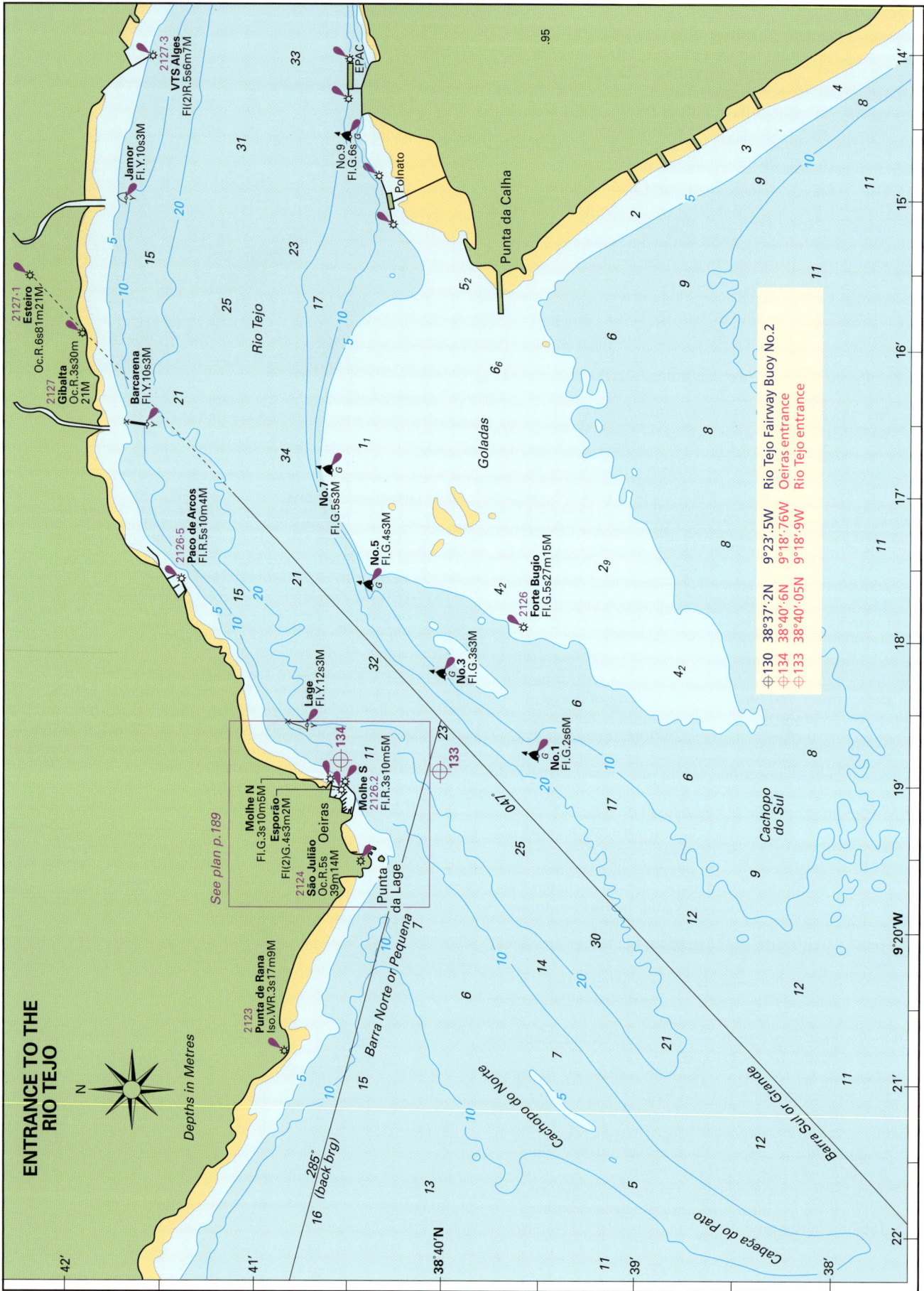

ENTRANCE TO THE RIO TEJO

Depths in Metres

N

2127.3
VTS Alges
Fl(2)R.5s6m7M

Jamor
Fl.Y.10s3M

EPAC

No.9
Fl.G.6s

Polnato

2127.1
Esteiro
Oc.R.6s81m21M.

2127
Gibalta
Oc.R.3s30m
21M

Barcarena
Fl.Y.10s3M

Punta da Calha

Rio Tejo

Goladas

2126.5
Paco de Arcos
Fl.R.5s10m4M

No.7
Fl.G.5s3M
G

No.5
Fl.G.4s3M
G

2126
Forte Bugio
Fl.G.5s27m15M

Lage
Fl.Y.12s3M

No.3
Fl.G.3s3M
G

See plan p.189

134

Molhe S 11
Fl.R.3s10m5M

23

133

No.1
Fl.G.2s6M
G

Molhe N
Fl.G.3s10m5M

Esporão
Fl(2)G.4s3m2M

Oeiras

2126.2

2124
São Julião
Oc.R.5s
39m14M

Punta
da Lage

Cachopo
do Sul

2123
Punta de Rana
Iso.WR.3s17m9M

Barra Norte or Pequena

047°

285°
(back brg)

Cachopo do Norte

Barra Sul or Grande

Cabeça do Pato

			Rio Tejo Fairway Buoy No.2
⊕130	38°37'.2N	9°23'.5W	
⊕134	38°40'.6N	9°18'.76W	Oeiras entrance
⊕133	38°40'.05N	9°18'.9W	Rio Tejo entrance

The Rio Tejo

Approach

If heading for Oeiras or Lisbon the choice is between the main Barra Sul (or Grande) and the shallower but less defined Barra Norte (or Pequena). Depths of the Cachope do Norte, which separates the two channels, shoal to less than 5m and seas may break even in low swell. As the greatest danger to a well-navigated yacht is probably from shipping, the northern route on 105° (or a back bearing of 285°) on Santa Marta and Guia lights may be the best choice, particularly in poor visibility if not equipped with radar (see plans opposite and on p.180). At night however, shore lights tend to hide fishing boats which often display inadequate navigation lights or sometimes none at all.

If approaching from offshore or from the south the Barra Sul will be more direct, joining near Fairway Buoy No.2 (⊕130) and following the leading line on 047° (see plan p.180). It is also the safest route if any swell is running. Note, however, that shipping may approach from any direction, joining the Barra Sul well inside Fairway Buoy No.2 or crossing en route to the designated ship anchorage which lies directly between Fairway Buoy No.2 and Cascais. Tidal streams in the Barra Sul can attain 3kn at springs – more on the ebb after heavy rain – creating heavy seas during strong southwesterlies.

Entrance

The Rio Tejo is entered between Punta de Lage (Fort de São Julião) on the northern shore and Fort Bugio to the southeast, and yachts are advised to remain on, or slightly north of, the leading line as traffic dictates (⊕133) until well up to Gibalta before turning upriver. Tidal streams reach 2 or 3kn either way at springs, not always running parallel to the shore, but are somewhat less powerful near the northern bank. This should be given an offing of at least 300m until the unmistakable Tôrre de Belém has been passed, but beyond that can be approached within 100m in good depths. The Ponte 25 de Abril suspension bridge has a clearance of 70m – unlikely to worry any yacht! – but spare a glance for the towering statue of Christ near its southern end.

Forte Bugio, on the south side of the mouth of the Rio Tejo. Not very long ago it was surrounded by drying banks at all states of the tide

Looking northeast into the wide mouth of the Rio Tejo. The marina at Oeiras can be seen on the left and Forte Bugio and its associated shoals at right of centre

Oeiras

Waypoints
⊕133 – 38°40'·05N 9°18'·9W (Rio Tejo entrance)
⊕134 – 38°40'·6N 9°18'·76W (Oeiras entrance)

Courses and distances
⊕130 (Rio Tejo Fairway Buoy No.2) – ⊕133 = 4·6M,
  052° or 332°
⊕132 (Cascais) – ⊕133 = 4·9M, 109° or 289°
⊕133 – ⊕134 = 0·6M, 011° or 191°

Tides
Standard port Lisbon
Mean time differences
HW –0020 ±0500; LW –0005 ±0500
Heights in metres

MHWS	MHWN	MLWN	MLWS
3·7	2·9	1·4	0·6

Charts

	Approach
Admiralty	3635, 3220
Imray	C19, C49
Portuguese	(26406), 26303

Principal lights
2126.2 **South mole** Fl.R.3s9m5M
  White tower, red bands, 5m
2126.25 **North mole** Fl.G.3s9m5M
  White tower, green bands, 4m
2126.3 **Inner mole** Fl(2)G.4s3m2M

Night entry
Feasible with care in light weather, but best avoided in stronger onshore winds

Harbour communications
Puerto de Recreio Oeiras ② +351 214 401510,
Fax +351 214 401515, *Email* precreio@oeirasviva.pt,
www.oeirasviva.pt (Google translate to English)
VHF Ch 09

A marina close west of Lisbon

While for many the chief attraction of Oeiras will undoubtedly be its proximity to Lisbon (door-to-door in 40 minutes or so, less if a taxi is taken to the station) the marina is flanked by an outstanding beach and large sports complex including swimming pools.

There are cafés and restaurants onsite, one owned by Peter Azevedo's son of Café Sport fame in Horta, Faial, Azores – it bears the same name. The Marina staff offer a free taxi service in their pick-up truck to the local supermarket and back.

The old town centre is pleasant, and there are several attractions in the vicinity, including the palace of Sebastião José de Carvalho e Melo, later Marquês de Pombal. It can get very crowded during the popular arts and music festival in July.

Approach

For outer approaches see The Rio Tejo estuary, pages 180 and 186.

If coastal sailing from Cascais, no more than 5M to the west, the Barra Norte (or Pequena) is the logical choice – see plan on page 186. Either continue until ⊕133 is reached before turning onto 011° for 0·6M to ⊕134 or, after rounding Punta de Lage and the prominent Fort de São Julião, steer by eye until the marina entrance is open before rounding to port.

Entrance

Beware of strong currents (3kns at springs) across the entrance. The marina entrance is narrow with a

Puerto de Recreio Oeiras looking west

pronounced dog-leg, difficult for less manœuvrable yachts and almost impossible under sail other than for the very skilled. The (well-fendered) reception/fuel berth is starboard-to on the west side of the inner mole. At least 5m will be found in the entrance and 3m at the reception berth.

The inner mole, it should be said, appears almost 100% efficient in preventing surge entering the marina, even in established easterlies.

Berthing

A marina official will often meet a yacht at the reception berth, otherwise walk up to the office near the root of the spur. It shares premises with a helpful turismo desk and is open 0800–2200 from 1/5 to 30/9 and 0800–1800 from 01/10 to 30/4, with security staff on duty at other times. All personnel speak some English, with those in the office near fluent. Security is via the usual card-operated gates – if arriving after hours be sure to leave someone inside to operate the gate (via a button 10m or so down the walkway) if no official is to be found.

Visitors are normally berthed on the westernmost two of the six pontoons, with larger yachts near the root of the inner mole. Twenty-three of the 274 slots are reserved for visitors (defined as a stay of less than 30 days), all able to accommodate 10m or more overall in a minimum of 2m. Four of the nine berths able to take yachts of 15–20m are also currently reserved for visitors. All berths are alongside finger pontoons.

Formalities

Visit the marina office equipped with passports, ship's papers and insurance documents. There are no forms to complete but copies of passports and boat's papers are taken. There is also no need to clear out from each port as details are kept in computer systems which most ports have access to. If a change of crew is made, however, the authorities need to be informed for safety reasons. Should any officials wish to visit the yacht, most probable if either boat or crew are of non-EU origin, it is their responsibility to make the first move.

Facilities

The Puerto de Recreio Oeiras does not aspire to provide shoreside facilities for a yacht with serious problems, but these are near at hand in Cascais, Lisbon and Seixal.

Boatyard/travel-lift Not provided although a small crane is available for dry stack storage of 100 places.

Engineers/electronics Contractors are believed to be on site.

Chandlery Available on site. Otherwise Lisbon's excellent chandleries are close at hand.

Water On the pontoons.

Showers In the reception block, with further toilets by the shops and cafés.

Launderette Available on site.

Electricity On the pontoons.

Fuel Diesel and petrol at the reception berth, nominally 24 hours per day. Credit cards are accepted.

Bottled gas Nothing nearby, though check at the chandlery.

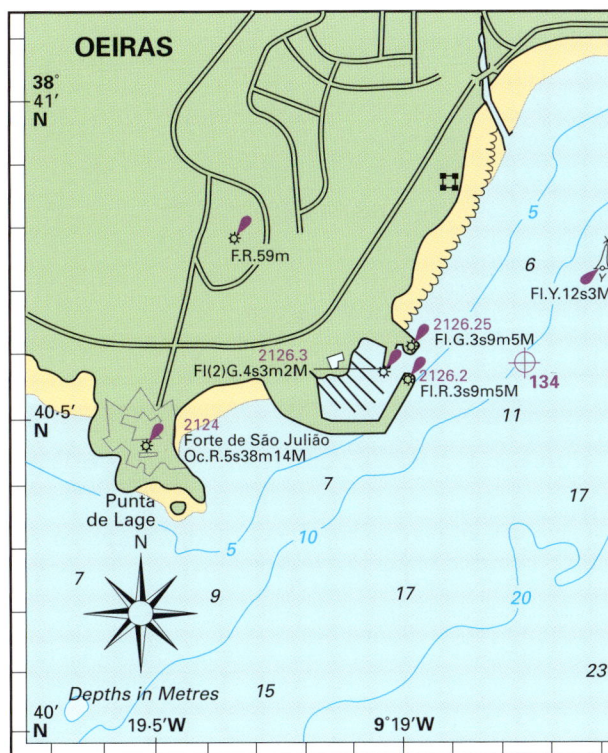

Weather forecast Posted daily at the marina office.

Banks In the town, about 20 minutes on foot.

Shops/provisioning A general store is available on site.

Cafés, restaurants, bars and hotels Several cafés, restaurants and bars are in the marina complex, and there are numerous hotels nearby. Overlooking the beach west of the marina is the unusual Carruagem Bar in an old (and very plush) railway carriage.

Medical services First aid centre in the sports complex, with full services in the town.

Communications

Post office In the town centre, about 20 minutes on foot.

Mailing address The marina office will hold mail for visiting yachts – c/o Puerto de Recreio de Oeiras, Estrada Marginal – Praia da Torre, 2780-267 Oeiras, Portugal. It is important that the envelope carries the name of the yacht in addition to that of the addressee.

Internet access There is a single (but fast) terminal at the tourist desk in the marina office, which visitors can use without charge for up to 20 minutes. Identification is required. Wireless broadband is available throughout the marina, but there is no shoreside phone socket through which laptops can be connected.

Public telephones In the sports complex.

Fax service At the marina office, *Fax* 214 401 515.

Car hire/taxis Can be arranged via the marina office.

Trains Frequent (and cheap) trains to Lisbon's Cais do Sodré station, close to the city centre. Closest station is Santo Amaro, about 15 minutes on foot – Oeiras station is a little further. Walk east beside the beach, crossing the busy road via the underpass, and the station is 100m or so north. The journey takes about 20 minutes.

Air services Lisbon International Airport is less than an hour away by train and taxi.

PORTUGAL – THE WEST COAST

Lisbon and the Rio Tejo

Waypoints
⊕133 – 38°40'·05N 9°18'·9W (Rio Tejo entrance)

Courses and distances
⊕130 (Rio Tejo Fairway Buoy No.2) – ⊕133 = 4·6M,
  052° or 332°
⊕132 (Cascais) – ⊕133 = 4·9M, 109° or 289°

Tides
Standard port Lisbon
Heights in metres

MHWS	MHWN	MLWN	MLWS
3·8	3·0	1·4	0·5

Or refer to EasyTide at www.ukho.gov.uk/easytide

Charts

Charts	Entrance	River
Admiralty	3220	3221, 3222
Imray	C49	C49
Portuguese	(26406), 26303, 26304,	(26406), 26305, 26306, 26307

Principal lights
2127.3 **VTS Algés** Fl(2)R.5s6m7M Red post, white bands
2127.4 **Doca de Pedroucos, west mole**
  Fl.R.6s12m2M Metal mast 7m
2127.6 **Doca de Pedroucos, east mole**
  F.G.12m4M Metal mast 7m
Note Although some publications give light details for both
  the Doca do Bom Sucesso and the Doca de Belém, neither
  have had functional lights for some years
2130.4/5 **Ponte 25 de Abril, north pillar**
NW and NE sides Fl(3)G.9s7m6M
  Green column, ▲ topmark, 2m
SW and SE sides Fl(3)R.9s7m6M Horn (2)25s
  Red column, ■ topmark, 2m
Top Fl.R.10s189m Summit of pillar
2130.6/7 **Ponte 25 de Abril, south pillar**
NW and NE sides Fl(3)G.9s7m6M Horn 25s
  Green column ▲ topmark, 2m
SW and SE sides Fl(3)R.9s7m6M Red column, ■ topmark, 2m
Top Iso.R.2s189m Summit of pillar
Both pillars NW and SW lights 000°-vis-180°
  NE and SE lights: 180°-vis-000°
2133.4 **Lisnave, Dolphin**, Fl.G.2s4m3M Column with red and
  white bands

2132 **Doca da Marinha**, W side F.R.10m2M Post 7m
2132.2 Doca da Marinha, E side F.G.10m2M Post 7m
2136.1 **Seca (Seixal), north bank** Fl.G.3s7m5M Green
  column 5m
2136 **Pilar (Seixal), south pillar** Fl.R.3s5m6M
  Red and white pillar on concrete plinth 2m
Plus many other lights throughout the harbour and
  further upriver

Night entry
Probably best avoided if new to the area, though
  perfectly feasible in all normal conditions. Tides run
  strongly at springs

Harbour communications
Lisboa Port Control ☎ +351 213 922026 (for leisure craft
  berthing instructions) *Fax* +351 213 922028
Email admin.junqueira@porto-de-lisboa.pt
VHF Watch: Ch 12, 13, 16, Working: 64 (call *Lisbon
  Control*) (24 hours)
Administração do Porto de Lisboa (APL) ☎ +351 213
  611000, *Fax* +351 213 611005,
Email geral@portodelisboa.pt
www.portodelisboa.com *(the same site as the above, in
  Portuguese only, and mainly about the commercial port)
VHF Ch 12 (0900–1300, 1400–1800 daily)
Tagus Yacht Center – see Seixal, page 199

Marinas
Doca de Bom Sucesso ☎ +351 213 013027 *Fax* +351 213
  020092 *Email* doca.bomsucesso@porto-de-lisboa.pt
Doca de Belém ☎ +351 213 631246 *Fax* +351 213 624578,
Email doca.belem@porto-de-lisboa.pt
Doca de Santo Amaro ☎ +351 213 922011/2, *Fax* +351
  213 922038, *Email* doca.stamaro@porto-de-lisboa.pt
Doca de Alcântara ☎ +351 213 922048, *Fax* +351 213
  922085 *Email* doca.alcantara@porto-de-lisboa.pt
A little surprisingly, the individual APL marinas above
  are not equipped with VHF
Pedestrian bridge *Ponte Móvel*, Doca de Alcântara VHF
  Ch 68. Marina Parque das Nações ☎ +351 218 949 066
Fax +351 218 919 067 www.marinaparquedasnacoes.pt
Email info@marinaparquedasnacoes.pt
VHF CH 09 (call sign *Marina Parque das Nações*).

A historic capital city with good (though crowded) facilities for yachts

An ancient city remarkable for its slightly dilapidated beauty and the reverberations of its maritime past – its people, its way of life and its architecture all show influences far removed from Europe. Its roots can be traced back to the Romans and very probably the Phoenicians and it has been the capital of Portugal since its very bloody reconquest by the Crusaders from the Moors in 1147. Throughout the Middle Ages it was one of Europe's busiest ports and it later owed its wealth to its trade in slaves. Much of the city was rebuilt after a serious earthquake and fire in November 1755 in which more than 40,000 people died.

There are enough sights to occupy a month, and a guidebook is a necessity. But perhaps the most memorable parts of Lisbon are in the Belém area to the west of the city. These include the fairytale Tôrre de Belém and the Museu de Marinha (maritime museum) housed in the western wing of the impressive Mosterio dos Jerónimos. The old Alfama district on its hill to the east, dominated by the Moorish Castelo de São Jorge is the other area not to

be missed. Much remains as it was before the district was recaptured from the Moors in 1147, and Moorish influences can still be heard in the haunting music which can be heard in the cafés.

The Jeronimos Monastery is symbolic of Portugal's power and wealth during the Age of Discovery. King Manuel I built it in 1502 on the site of a hermitage founded by Prince Henry the Navigator. Vasco da Gama and his crew spent their

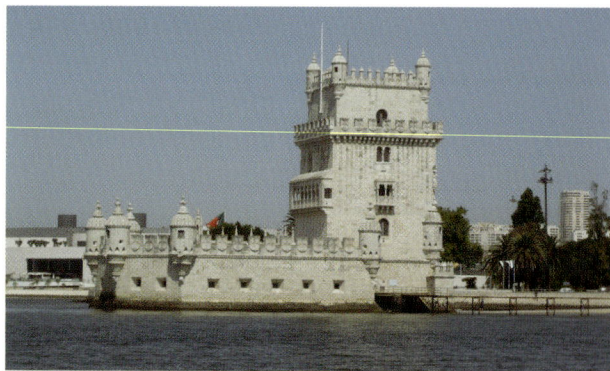

Tôrre de Belém, Lisbon *David Russell*

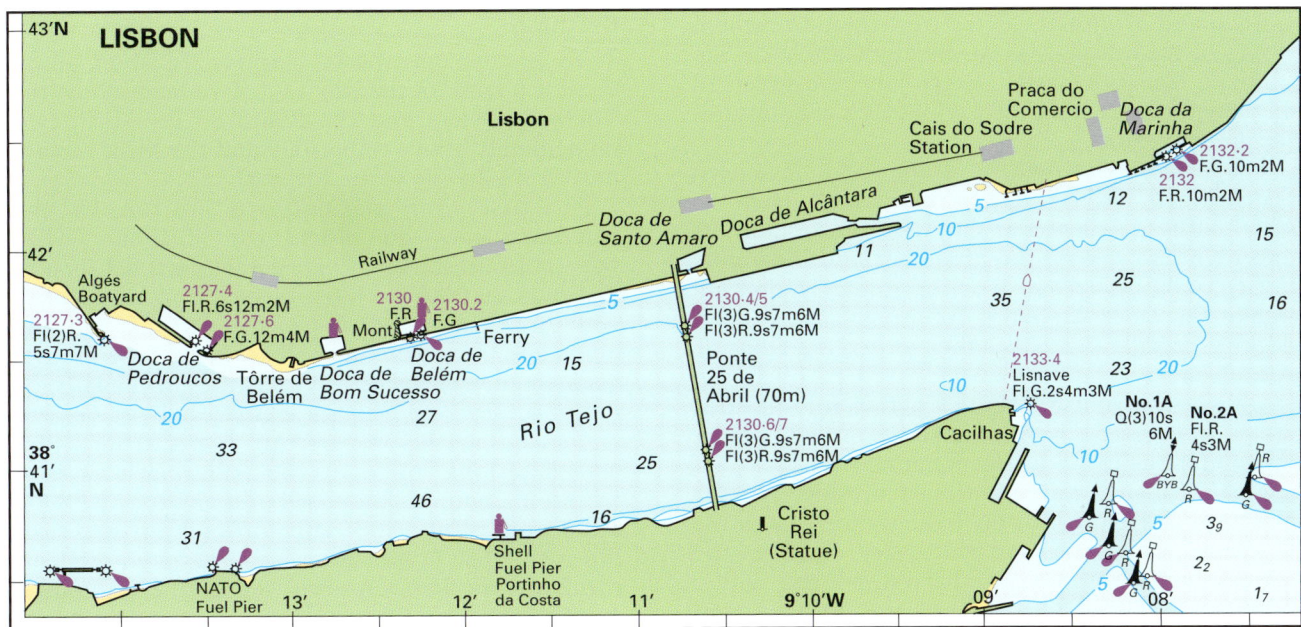

Algés boatyard to the west of Belém *Algés Boatyard*

last night in Portugal in prayer here before leaving for India and their historic voyage. Built to commemorate this voyage, Vasco da Gama's tomb is probably the most significant tomb in the monastery. A UNESCO World Heritage site, maritime motifs play a significant part in the design of the monastery.

Jeronimos monastery *David Russell*

The tomb of Vasco da Gama *David Russell*

While wandering around Lisbon, it is impossible not to be constantly reminded of and impressed by Portugal's pioneering role in the voyages of discovery. This can be traced back to the early part of the 13th century when King Diniz set out to improve Portugal's emerging navy. He invited a Genoese sea captain to Portugal and placed him in charge of developing the mercantile and naval fleets. He also ordered the Atlantic coastline to be planted with trees to provide timber for the ships. In 1341, three vessels sailed from Lisbon and explored the Canary Islands. Although the expedition showed no profit and Castile later gained control of the islands, this voyage was the first official expedition by a European state to discover the lands beyond Europe. Portuguese captains soon became the best in Europe, using what was then the latest maritime technology and cartography.

The Alfama is one of the oldest quarters in Lisbon. Since it largely survived the earthquake of 1755, the area still retains much of its original layout. Adjacent to the Alfama are the old quarters of

PORTUGAL – THE WEST COAST

Castelo and Mouraria, on the western and northern slopes of the hill that is crowned by Castelo de São Jorge (St George's Castle). Every June, the streets of all three quarters come alive with feasts in honour of the popular saints.

The newly revitalised Alcantara docks have been transformed from their commercial past as warehouses to new uses as shops, offices, restaurants and nightclubs, with the attendant and inevitable noise, and are buzzing. Work continues. However, unlike the Doca de Santo Amaro where wooden decking literally overhangs the marina, the Doca de Alcântara has a relatively wide paved area between buildings and basin. All the better for outdoor tables, of course. You will not starve or be bored by the food in the Doca de Alcantatara.

An impressive, air-conditioned produce market almost opposite the Cais do Sodré station east of the Doca de Alcântara (and thus very close to the Garraio and Godinho chandleries), is open 0600–1400 and 1500–1900. A vast area of fruit and vegetables is surrounded by flowers, eggs, meat and fish – all meticulously clean and with much ice in evidence. The large, two-storey building is decorated with beautiful azulejos (painted tiles) and surmounted by a distinctive dome, and is well worth a visit even if not buying.

The Lisbon Festival of the Seas in August each year is meant as a celebration of Portugal's sea-faring traditions. It does include some nautical events among the many other manifestations of the Portuguese way of life.

Cafés, restaurants and hotels are an essential part of life in Lisbon, but no visit to Lisbon is complete without sampling bars and restaurants featuring live fado singing.

Berthing

There are five operational marinas in Lisbon, all on the north bank of the Rio Tejo. Two lie between the Tôrre de Belém and the Ponte 25 de Abril, two immediately above the bridge and the fifth, further upriver on the site of the MarinaExpo.

The first four marinas are all run by the Administração do Porto de Lisboa (APL) www.portodelisboa.pt, *Email* geral@portodelisboa.pt and thus share characteristics such as good security with card-operated access gates, and similar working hours and price structure. All are popular with local yachtsmen, but space for a visitor can usually be found somewhere, though it is strongly advised to make contact before arrival. Apart from other considerations, none of the APL marinas have reception pontoons. Standard office hours are 0900–1300 and 1400–1800 daily throughout the year. Fluent English is spoken at both the main office at the Doca de Santo Amaro and at the individual marina offices.

The fifth marina, Marina Parque das Nações (ex MarinaExpo), is run by the Parque Expo Group with all the facilities of a modern marina. These are described in the following pages.

Note that the current in the river runs swiftly and that, with the possible exception of the Doca de Alcântara, all the marina entrances can have awkward crosscurrents at the entrance. Not only will these set the yacht sideways, they may also tend to slew her round during those seconds when the bow is in the stationary water of the entrance and the stern still in the moving river.

Formalities

At all the marinas it is only necessary to complete a standard form at the office, copies of which are distributed to the *GNR–Brigada Fiscal*, *Polícia Marítima* and *Alfândega* (customs). Whether any or all chose to visit will be based on the yacht and crew's nationalities and her last port of call.

The monument to the Discoveries, with the masts of yachts in the Doca de Belém behind *David Russell*

A section of the vast tiled map of the world set into the waterfront promenade near the Monument to the Discoveries. It shows that the Portuguese were in the Timor Sea in 1512 *Jane Russell*

Marinas

1. **Doca do Bom Sucesso** – a short distance upstream from the (floodlit) Tôrre de Belém. Once the marina to which foreign yachts were directed, it is now crowded with local yachts and unlikely to have space for a visitor unless a long-term berth-holder is known to be absent. The 163 berths (all with finger pontoons) are limited to 12m LOA, but dredging has increased depths to 3·5m. Fuel is available, the fuel pontoon being in the northeast corner of the basin with the office and showers nearby. However there is very little room to manoeuvre. The entrance is unlit.

2. **Doca de Belém** – 700m east of the Doca do Bom Sucesso and immediately beyond the prominent Padrão dos Descobrimentos (Monument to the Discoveries) which resembles a ship's prow. The entrance is not lit.

   Again, the 194 berths are reserved for residents and, as in the Doca do Bom Sucesso, there is unlikely to be room for a visiting yacht except on a very temporary basis. Previously rather shallow, dredging has now ensured depths of at least 3m throughout. The marina office lies at the northeast corner of the basin with showers etc in the same block, both adjacent to a thriving boatyard (see *Facilities*, below). A welcome and imaginative touch, when new workshops were being built for boatyard contractors, was to place a café/restaurant on their roofs ensuring both cool breezes and interesting views.

3. **Doca de Santo Amaro** – 150m beyond the suspension bridge and dredged to a nominal 4m, though reported to carry considerably less than this over a very soft bottom. Second largest of the four with 388 berths all equipped with finger pontoons, it is nevertheless crowded with local craft though a visiting yacht can sometimes be squeezed in. The entrance is narrow and unlit, but there is a convenient pontoon just inside on the port hand (though short on mooring cleats as it is not technically a reception pontoon but the property of the local rowing club). The marina office, labelled APL Docas de Recreio, is at the northeast end of the basin at the east end of the row of cafés and restaurants.

The only real drawback to the Doca de Santo Amaro – should space be available at all – is that it is not quiet. Traffic passing over the bridge sounds like a swarm of bees and could become irritating in time, but more importantly the area has become a popular centre for Lisbon nightlife with the bars and restaurants overlooking the basin remaining lively until 0400 or beyond. Of course more energetic crews may well consider this a plus.

The Doca de Santo Amaro close east of the Ponte de 25 Abril suspension bridge

Lisbon's Doca de Belém and Doca do Bom Sucesso looking a little north of west, with the Padrão dos Descobrimentos (Monument to the Discoveries) prominent in the centre. At far right is the Mosterio dos Jerónimos, which houses the extensive Museu de Marinha (maritime museum). Jutting out to sea at far left is the fairytale Tôrre de Belém

PORTUGAL – THE WEST COAST

Entry to the Doca de Alcântara at its east end is through a relatively narrow passage crossed by a pedestrian bridge

4. **Doca de Alcântara** – A much larger basin than any of the others, entered about 1M upstream of the suspension bridge via an entry channel which, rather surprisingly, is not lit. A pedestrian bridge, or Ponte Móvel, crosses the entrance. It is normally left open; closing being signalled by lights and a horn. The control booth (when manned) operates on VHF Ch 68. The bridge is positioned well inside the entrance proper, and though a waiting pontoon is not provided there are normally plenty of moored vessels alongside which a yacht could lie for a short time.

Originally concentrated at the west end of the 0·5M long basin, the marina has now grown to 442 berths on ten pontoons and is said to have spread as far east as it can. Space is most likely to be at a premium in the early autumn when many visitors are passing through, yet long-term berth-holders are also present. In summer many of the latter are away cruising. Yachts of up to 30m are normally berthed in the basin bow or stern-to with pick up lines, but the seriously large are expected to stay outside and will be treated as the ships they are. Depths throughout the entire basin are considerable.

The marina office and related services are situated about half way along the marina on the north side, inside a gated compound for which a security code is needed and which provides the only access to the pontoons.

The Doca de Alcântara is a peaceful spot and the distant hum from bridge traffic is not a problem.

The restored Portuguese East Indiaman D Fernando II e Glória (rebuilt Aveiro see page 157), is permanently berthed in the basin and is open to the public. In addition APORVELA, the Associação Portuguesa de Treino de Vela (sail training association), are in the process of moving from their old home at the Doca do Terreiro do Trigo and already keep several of their recreated caravels in the basin. It is possible that a small maritime museum will be added to the attractions.

5. **Marina Parque das Nações** – Redesigned with a lock entrance system and re-opened again in 2009 at the site of MarinaExpo, an area that had itself suffered from silting and other problems, the marina was once more subjected to a major dredging effort in June 2014. In July 2014 it was declared fully operational but it had continued at reduced capacity while the work took place. The best time to arrive, to avoid the strongest currents in the river and for negotiating the locks, is two hours either side of high water. Visiting yachtsmen have reported that the welcome here is outstanding, with a full information pack not only being provided but explained too. Discounts are offered to members of most of the better known cruising and sailing associations. If planning to stay for more than two weeks it is as cheap to stay for a month.

This is described as a good place to leave a yacht to overwinter, being very close to the airport, very secure and, of course, totally enclosed by the locks.

The facilities at *Marina Parque das Nações* are described on page 197.

Alternative anchorages and moorings

There are two areas where anchoring can be made:

1. The first of these is beyond the impressive Vasco da Gama motorway bridge to the north where the main channel carries 5m. This widens into the Mar de Palha (literally 'Sea of Straw', or reeds). Large-scale Portuguese charts or electronic charts will be required for this area. Alandra is the effective limit for yachts working up the Rio Tejo as the bridge above (De Xira on plan) has only 10m clearance.

Marina Parque das Nações looking north-northwest

2. The second area for anchoring is to the southeast of Lisbon in the Canal do Montijo, and to a very limited extent at Seixal in the Canal do Judeu. Space in the latter has been taken for visitor moorings and a short stay pontoon, but find the details in pages 198-201. There are high speed ferry links between Seixal and Lisbon.

APL Marinas – Facilities

Many harbours have their 'Mr Fixit', in this case a gentleman known as Carlos, *Mobile* +351 91 9868 807, has been consistently recommended as able to either handle or at least advise on almost anything. A yachtsman himself, he is well aware of what visitors may need. Carlos speaks several languages including fluent English.

Boatyard Next to the Doca de Belém and administered by APL, with all work carried out by sub-contractors who have to satisfy APL of their competence. There is a large area of secure hard-standing where owners can, if they wish, do their own work and are generally permitted to live on board while the boat is ashore (though this must be confirmed with APL on an individual basis). It would also be a possible venue for winter lay-up.

  If professional services are required the best place to start is undoubtedly Técniates Yacht Services, ☎ +351 213 623 362 *Fax* +351 213 649147. *Email* geral@tecniates.eu www.tecniates.eu (in Portuguese and English), who have premises near the east end of the row of office/workshops and have been highly praised by more than one visiting skipper. As well as being an agent for Volvo Penta they can also handle repairs in GRP and timber, painting, osmosis treatment etc. Where a job is outside their sphere they can generally recommend a suitable contractor. Good English is spoken.

  For details of the well-equipped Tagus Yacht Center near Seixal on the south bank of the Rio Tejo, see page 199.

Travel-lift The 20-tonne capacity lift at the Doca de Belém is operated by Técniates Yacht Services (see above) though owned by APL, and bookings must be made at the marina office. Due to depth restrictions it can operate only about six hours in twelve, but urgent cases are given priority. Yachts are generally placed in cradles backed up by additional props.

  A 70-tonne capacity hoist with about 7m width, operable at all states of the tide, is to be found at the Tagus Yacht Center – see page 199.

Engineers Técniates Yacht Services at the Doca de Belém (see above) are Volvo Penta agents/engineers and may be willing to tackle more general problems. Otherwise they will advise who best to contact. See also Tagus Yacht Center, page 199.

Electronic and radio repairs NautiRadar Lda, ☎ +351 213 005 050 (10 lines) *Fax* +351 213 005 059 *Email* geral@nautiradar.pt or tecnica@nautiradar.pt www.nautiradar.eu (in Portuguese only), at Gare Marítima da Rocha, Rocha Conde de Óbidos, 1350–352 Lisboa. They sell and repair radar, autopilots, GPS, generators etc and stock both whole units and spares for all the familiar names including Raytheon, Garmin, Mastervolt etc. Open 0900–1300 and 1400–1800 weekdays, closed weekends. They are to be found on the south side of the Doca de Alcântara close to its

RIO TEJO

N

Depths in Metres

De Xira

Marina Parque das Nações

Ponte Vasco de Gama Bridge

Doca do Poço do Bispo

LISBON

Rio Tejo

Doca do Terreiro do Trigo (closed)

10

10

See plan p.198

Lisnave

Seixal

eastern end and so quite a long walk, though a courtesy bus runs a shuttle service as far as the passenger terminal. They are willing to visit yachts in Cascais as well as in any of the Lisbon marinas, and can generally respond within 24 hours. See also Tagus Yacht Center, page 190.

Dimofel, on the first floor at Avenida de Liberdade 85, has been recommended as selling a good range of electronic components, with other shops in Rua São Jose, a block to the east.

Sailmaker/sail repairs Vela-Rio ☎/Fax 212 155994, at Rua D João de Castro, 15-B Santo André, 2830-186 Barreiro, Lisboa, makes and repairs sails and will also handle general canvaswork such as sprayhoods and awnings. The owner, Antonio Martines, speaks good English.

Chandleries Lisbon is well served for chandleries, with five in the Doca de Alcântara/Cais do Sodré area alone. All are short on display space with much more stock in store, so if you don't see what you want it is well worth asking – good English is spoken in all five. Listed alphabetically they are:

Contrafogo, SA ☎ 21 253 57 06 *Fax* 21 253 20 77 *Email* contrafogo@contrafogo.pt www.contrafogo.pt Qta. do Conde de Mascarenhas, Lote 8, Vale Fetal 2820-652 Charneca da Caparica

J Garraio & Ca Lda ☎ 213 473081 *Fax* 213 428950 *Email* info@jgarraio.pt www.jgarraio.pt opposite the Cais do Sodré station at Avenida 24 de Julho 2–1°, 1200–478 Lisboa, open 0900–1230 and 1400–1900 weekdays, 0900–1230 Saturday. Particularly strong on pilot books and charts (Admiralty and Imray) in both Portuguese and English, but also with some general stock.

Luíz Godinho Lda ☎ 213 421001 *Fax* 213 016 658 *Email* luizgodinho@iol.pt (note 'iol' not 'aol'), at Avenida 24 de Julho 1 F/G, 1200–478 Lisboa (in the next block to J Garraio), open 0900–1900 weekdays, 0900–1300 Saturday. A conventional yacht chandler with good stocks of rope, chain, rigging wire and terminals (plus a swage machine) and other hardware, but few electronics and no books.

Marítima ☎ 213 979598 *Fax* 213 979 572 *Email* raul@maritimaonline.com at Doca de Santo Amaro, 1350–353 Lisboa (at the west end of the Doca de Santo Amaro, right under the suspension bridge), open 1000–1930 Monday to Saturday, with a good range of clothing and boots, as well as hardware (including windlasses), teak fittings, paint, rope and galleyware.

NautiStar Lda ☎ +351 214 846 370/1 *Fax* +351 214 845 014 *Email* info@nautistar.pt www.nautistar.pt, have moved to Cascais marina. Advertised hours are 1000–1800 Monday to Saturday, but it is often open much later. The helpful staff will order from an impressive stack of catalogues. Good English is spoken.

Finally, sharing the Associação Naval de Lisboa clubhouse at the Doca de Belém is the tiny GeoNáutica ☎ 213 618761 *Email* geonautica@ geonautica.pt open 1300–1700 weekdays, 1000–1500 weekends, which appears to specialise in clothing, including oilskins and boots.

General hardware Rua da Boavista, which runs behind the main produce market, contains a number of small hardware shops and is a good bet for non-standard items. In particular, plugs for the Doca de Alcântara electricity supply are available there.

Charts Surprisingly, only one company on the Atlantic coast of Portugal is licensed to sell Portuguese charts –

J Garraio & Ca Lda. It may be worth noting that, whilst Admiralty charts are not cheap, Portuguese charts are even more expensive, even when bought in Lisbon (though there is some variation based on size and publication date) and are unlikely to be corrected to date. Charts can also be purchased directly from the Instituto Hidgrográfico in Lisbon.

Liferaft servicing Contrafogo SA and NautiStar can arrange for servicing of most makes. Alternatively contact Orey-Técnica Naval e Industrial Lda ☎ +351 21 361 08 90 *Fax* 21 364 0144 *Email* jose.ribeiro@orey.com, lisboa.tecnica@orey.com or orey-tecnica@orey.com, at Poligono Industrial Leziria Park, Armazem No2 EN 10 2625-445 Forte da Casa, Lisboa. They supply and service liferafts as well as other safety equipment including flares, lifebuoys etc.

Water On the pontoons in all the APL marinas.

Showers At all the APL marinas, though in busy periods the six provided at the Doca de Alcântara are hardly adequate for its size.

Launderette No machines at any of the APL marinas, but many in the surrounding city. Alternatively NautiStar Lda can arrange for laundry to be done, but check the price first.

Electricity On the pontoons in all the APL marinas.

Fuel Diesel and petrol pumps at both the Doca do Bom Sucesso and the Doca de Belém (the latter is more accessible, with depths of at least 3m), operational during office hours (0900–1300 and 1400–1800 daily). In summer they may stay open later, but this should be confirmed beforehand. Credit cards including VISA are accepted.

Bottled gas Camping Gaz exchanges at Marítima (see above) and elsewhere. Butane and propane refills can be organised by NautiStar (see above) as well as by Carlos (see head of section), who can also arrange for diving bottles to be recharged.

Clube naval The Associação Naval de Lisboa has premises next to the Doca de Belém, where visiting yachtsmen are made welcome.

Weather forecast Posted daily at all the marina offices.

Banks All over Lisbon, almost invariably with at least one cash dispenser outside. Banks are normally open 0830–1200 and 1345–1430, weekdays only.

Shops/provisioning Absolutely everything available, as befits a capital city. Most convenient for provisioning if in the Doca de Santo Amaro/Alcântara complex is the large Pingo Doce supermarket reached via a pedestrian tunnel under the road and railway (ask at the marina office for directions).

Produce market Impressive, air-conditioned produce market almost opposite the Cais do Sodré station east of the Doca de Alcântara (and thus very close to the Garraio and Godinho chandleries), open 0600–1400 and 1500–1900. A vast area of fruit and vegetables is surrounded by flowers, eggs, meat and fish – all meticulously clean and with much ice in evidence. The large, two-storey building is decorated with beautiful azulejos (painted tiles) and surmounted by a distinctive dome, and is well worth a visit even if not buying.

Cafés, restaurants and hotels Many and varied, at all prices. Some bars and restaurants feature live fado singing.

Medical services If berthed in an APL marina one has access to the Administração do Porto de Lisboa's own Medical Centre, close to the Doca de Santo Amaro/Alcântara complex. More extensive medical services of all kinds are available in the city.

Communications

Post office Large post office just west of the Praça Comerçio, plus many others.

Mailing address Mail for a yacht hoping to stay in one of APL's marinas is best sent to the head office: Administração do Porto de Lisboa SA, Rua da Junqueira, 94, 1349-026 Lisboa, Portugal. www.portodelisboa.pt. *Email* geral@portodelisboa.pt ✆ +351 21 361 10 00. It is important that the envelope carries the name of the yacht in addition to that of the addressee.

Internet access Many possibilities throughout the city – the Tourist Office on Praça dos Restauradores can supply a current list. Those closest to the Doca de Santo Amaro/Alcântara complex were Espaço Agora at Rua da Cintura do Porto de Lisboa, Armazém 1 Naves 3–5, open 0900–0330 Monday–Saturday, 0900–2200 Sunday; and Hiper Net in the Fundação das Comunicações (Communications Museum) at 22 Rua D Luis I, open 1000–1230 and 1400–1730 weekdays, closed weekends and holidays. The useful online Lisbon Guide at www. lisbon-guide.info also carries a listing in its Essential Information section.

Public telephones Kiosks handy to all marinas, plus many throughout the city.

Fax service At the APL marinas, *Fax* 213 922038 (actually the head office's number, but the best initial bet).

Car hire Many companies in the city, though APL receive a discount from AVIS which they passed on to the hirer. But be warned – the normally easygoing Portuguese appear to suffer a character change behind the wheel, and some city driving is manic. At the very least, pay the extra charge for collision damage waiver.

Taxis No shortage. Taxis can generally be ordered via the marina office.

Buses/trams The city's well-organised bus and tram service is particularly useful near the waterfront, linking all four APL marinas with the city centre. A ride in one of the small, pre-war trams is a Lisbon 'must', and most visitors also enjoy the various 'elevators' which give access to the city's different levels. For the Doca de Santo Amaro/Alcântara complex take the E15 or E18 tram from the Praça Comerçio, getting off at Infante Santo and walking over the brightly painted footbridge.

Tickets covering travel by bus, tram, elevador and *metro* (see below) can be bought individually, by the day, or for longer periods, the latter often representing a considerable saving.

Trains and Metro Regular and frequent rail service from the Cais do Sodré station to Cascais and other points west. Most other trains depart from Rossio station at the south end of the Avenida da Liberdade. Both stations are notorious for pickpockets and other non-violent crime – be warned!

Lisbon's *metro* was given a facelift for the 1998 Expo, making it the quickest way to reach city destinations away from the waterfront. However finding a city centre station can be a real challenge – they tend to be very poorly signed.

Ferries Frequent ferries across the Rio Tejo to Cacilhas, from which one can get a bus up to the prominent statue of Christ near the south end of the 25 de Abril suspension bridge, as well as to Seixal and Montijo.

Air services International airport in the northeast part of the city, with scheduled flights to all parts of the world.

Marina Parque das Nações – Facilities

The Marina Parque das Nações (ex MarinaExpo) situated at 38°45'·22N 09°05'·33W re-opened fully again after dredging in 2014. It is in the north margin of the Tagus estuary, about seven miles from the Tower of Belém, and approximately 1·5M downstream from the Vasco da Gama bridge. It has a total of 600 berths with some for boats of up to 25m in length. The dredged depth is 2·4m.

Office reception hours are 0900 to 2000 and the reception pontoon is just to the west of the entrance sluice gates controlled by traffic lights. These gates are 9·5m wide and will be operated every day from 0900 to 2000.

Contact details Marina Parque das Nações, Edificio da Capitania, Passeio de Neptuno, 1990-193 LISBOA. ✆ +351 218 949 066 *Fax* +351 218 919 067. www.marinaparquedasnacoes.pt. *Email* info@marinaparquedasnacoes.pt

Security 24h/day

Travel lift 35 tonne travel lift. Three tonne crane.

Fuel Fuel pontoon on the south side of the outer marina entrance. Open 0900 to 1800. Credit cards accepted.

Weather Posted every day at reception.

Electricity and Water At the pontoons.

Shops There is a large supermarket nearby which will deliver directly to the boat.

Other facilities in Lisbon
(See photo and chart page 191)

Boatyard CNA – Centro Náutico de Algés. (Sopromar group) www.cnalges.pt Passeio Marítimo Algés, Torre VTS 1495-165 Algés, Lisboa - Portugal GPS 38°41'·77N 9°14'·03'W Luís Fidalgo Director *Email* luis.fidalgo@cnalges.pt or geral@cnalges.pt ✆ +351 213032440 *Fax* +351 213017372

Services Hard stand/Travel lift 50tons.

Marine Services/Maintenance Chandlery, Rigging.

The 17km Ponte Vasco de Gama. The bridge at De Xira some 7km further north is the effective head of navigation for most yachts.

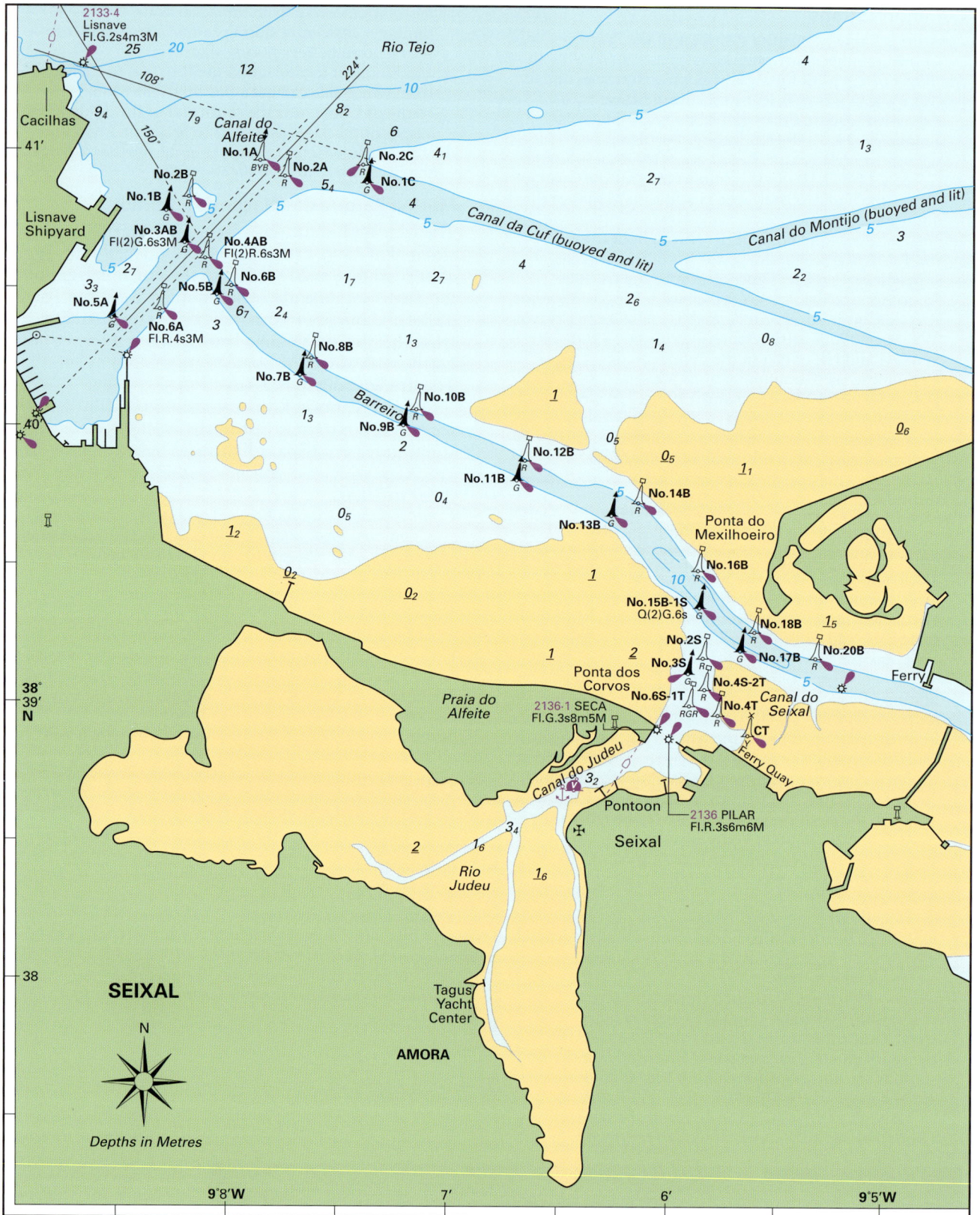

2133·4
Lisnave
Fl.G.2s4m3M
25
20
108°
9₄
12
Rio Tejo
10
4
Cacilhas
41'
7₉
Canal do
Alfeite
224°
8₂
6
No.2C
No.1A
BYB
No.2A
R
No.1C
G
4₁
5₄
1₃
2₇
No.2B
R
No.1B
G
No.3AB
Fl(2)G.6s3M
No.4AB
Fl(2)R.6s3M
5
Canal da Cuf (buoyed and lit)
5
Canal do Montijo (buoyed and lit)
5
3
Lisnave
Shipyard
5
2₇
No.6B
1₇
2₇
4
2₂
No.5B
6₇
2₄
2₆
No.5A
G
No.6A
Fl.R.4s3M
3₃
3
1₄
0₈
5
40'
No.8B
1₃
No.7B
G
Barreiro
No.10B
1₃
0₅
0₅
0₆
No.9B
2
1
1₁
No.12B
R
No.11B
G
5
No.14B
R
Ponta do
Mexilhoeiro
1₂
0₄
0₅
No.13B
G
1
10
No.16B
B
0₂
0₂
No.15B-1S
Q(2)G.6s
No.18B
G
1₅
1
2
No.2S
R
No.17B
No.20B
No.3S
R
Ponta dos
Corvos
No.4S-2T
R
5
Ferry
Praia do
Alfeite
No.6S-1T
R
No.4T
Y
Canal do
Seixal
2136·1 SECA
Fl.G.3s8m5M
RGR
CT
Ferry Quay
Canal do Judeu
3₂
Pontoon
2136 PILAR
Fl.R.3s6m6M
3₄
Seixal
2
1₆
1₆
SEIXAL
Rio
Judeu
N
Tagus
Yacht
Center
AMORA
Depths in Metres

38°
39'
N

38

9°8'W
7'
6'
9°5'W

Seixal

38°38'·9N 09°06'W (entrance)

Principal lights
2133.4 **Lisnave, Dolphin,** Fl.G.2s4m3M Column with red and white bands
Buoy No 3AB Fl(2)G.6s3M Reflector Radar
Buoy No 4AB Fl(2)R.6s3M Reflector Radar
Buoy No 15B-1S Q(2)G.6s3M Reflector Radar
2136.1 Seca **(Seixal), north bank** Fl.G.3s7m5M Green column 5m
2136 Pilar **(Seixal), south pillar** Fl.R.3s5m6M Red and white pillar on concrete plinth 2m

Harbour communications
 Tagus Yacht Center ☏ +351 212 276 400 *Fax* +351 212 224 811 *Mobile* +351 935 055 588
 Email info@ tagusyachtcenter.com
 www.tagusyachtcenter.com
 (note the spelling of 'center')

Quiet anchorage with impressive, full-service boatyard

There are two main reasons for visiting Seixal. One is to enjoy tranquil mooring, although limited pontoon and anchorage space, within easy reach of Lisbon by ferry; the other is to visit the Tagus Yacht Center, an enterprise which looks set to meet the maintenance needs of all but the very largest cruising yachts.

Approach (Canal do Barreiro)

Round Ponta de Cacilhas and the Lisnave Light, on the south bank of the Rio Tejo 1·5M east of the suspension bridge, and head 150° past the prominent Lisnave shipyard to cross the Canal do Alfeite near buoys No.3AB and No.4AB. Continue down the Canal do Barreiro, which is well buoyed but has quite heavy ferry traffic, some of it at high speeds. Buoy No.15B-1S marks the junction of the Canal do Seixal with the Canal do Barreiro, from

which can be seen the relatively narrow entrance to the Canal do Judeu.

Pass between buoys No.2S and No.3S, the Pilar (Seixal) red and white column on an old bridge support and Seca (Seixal) green post on the battlement, through the narrow entrance. At least 2·5m should be found throughout the approach and entrance.

Berthing and Mooring

A new pontoon is in position off the town beach, marked on the plan on page 198. The idea is for this to be a short stay pontoon for water and access to the town, mooring alongside. Water and electricity is hooked up to the new pontoon and (unconfirmed) charges are €14 a night.

There are a number of new 'visitor' moorings laid along the Canal do Judeu (charge €7 a night (2014) for a 10–12m boat), but they are apparently laid with only 1 ton blocks of concrete and are therefore inadequate for cruising boats of any reasonable size. Contact VHF Ch 09 or ☏ +351 919306580, and for more information on planned improvements for visiting yachts contact *email* rogerio.ferreira@cm-seixal.pt

A dinghy can still be secured on the old town quay ramp outside the pontoon security gates for no charge, but avoid landing a dinghy on their pontoon unless you want to use their facilities and pay.

Anchorage

It should be noted that NO ANCHORING is allowed anywhere in the apparently suitable area just inside the entrance to the lagoon. Large barges are towed in and turned to go to the shipyard at the southeast of that first basin. The advised anchorage is where marked, just beyond the trot of moorings on the north side of the channel, but the

The short stay pontoon at Seixal *Jane Russell*

Entrance to the Canal do Judeu at Seixal looking southwest.
The isolated block in the centre, an old bridge support, must be left to port on entry

anchoring space is much reduced as a result of the buoys being laid.

The area is surprisingly peaceful despite its proximity to the city and there is relatively little traffic (the ferry berth is outside the entrance). There is currently no charge for anchoring.

Facilities

Seixal has an attractive waterfront with a small sandy beach. All the usual shops will be found, as well as cafés, restaurants, a post office and public telephones.

There is a Tide Mill museum at the west end of the lagoon and a maritime museum on the east bank, south of the town. The beautiful local sailing barges are linked to the maritime museum.

A ferry connects the town with Lisbon's Cais Terreiro do Paço, running every 25 minutes between 0610 and 2330 and taking about 15 minutes for the trip.

Boatyard

Although worth a short visit on its merits alone, Seixal's attraction for yachts is enhanced by the Tagus Yacht Center. Office hours are normally 0800–1200 and 1300–1700 weekdays only.

Established in 2002 as an offshoot of the Vanamar shipyard – the two are headed by brothers Nuno and Rafael Venâncio. Tagus Yacht Center has impressive facilities including a 70-tonne capacity travel hoist with about 7m width, plus a 30-tonne capacity crane, both of which can operate at all states of the tide. A 300-tonne floating dock provides a third option for large yachts and multihulls.

Almost any yacht-related task can be tackled, from straightforward painting to creating unobtainable parts from scratch (for which the shipyard's extensive machine-shop is utilised). Repairs can be carried out in GRP, wood and all types of metal, a large team of engineers have experience of virtually all makes of engine, and electricians and electronics experts can be called in from the shipyard as required.

The short stay pontoon from the beach with the Canal do Judeu beyond and Lisbon in the far distance *Jane Russell*

Traditional vessel off Seixal *Jane Russell*

The yard is reached via a buoyed channel, approximately 40m wide and dredged to carry a minimum of 3m at all times. There is a small waiting pontoon – though most would probably prefer to wait at anchor, as described above – and although the yard expects to handle major work, owners are welcome to carry out other tasks while their boat is ashore and can live aboard if they wish (toilets and showers are provided). There are small shops nearby for daily needs, with a large supermarket a few kilometres away. If coming by land, the 113 bus from the Seixal ferry terminal passes close to the yard.

As a final bonus, the brothers are outstandingly pleasant and helpful and both speak excellent English.

Navegador, further upstream from the Tagus Yacht Center *Email* felisberto.carlos@navegador.com.pt ✆ +351 212 277 913, is reported to have good hardstanding and painting facilities. They do not, however, allow living onboard or DIY.

Canal do Montijo anchorages

Round Ponta de Cacilhas and the Lisnave Lt and head 108° into the buoyed Canal da CUF (Companhia União Fabril). The Canal do Montijo (also buoyed) leads off at 073° just over 1M from the entrance of the Canal da CUF. At high water it appears to be a large bay, but at low water mud and sandbanks define the channel accurately. The airfield on the low headland to the north is military, and landing is prohibited.

Montijo itself is not particularly attractive and has little room, but there are pleasant anchorages to be found by soundings along the channel or its southern offshoots. A current copy of either Admiralty 3222 or Portuguese 26305 is essential. There are no facilities.

Approaching Seixal looking SW down the Canal do Judeu with the town to port and moorings to starboard *Jane Russell*

II.5 Cabo Espichel to Cabo de São Vicente

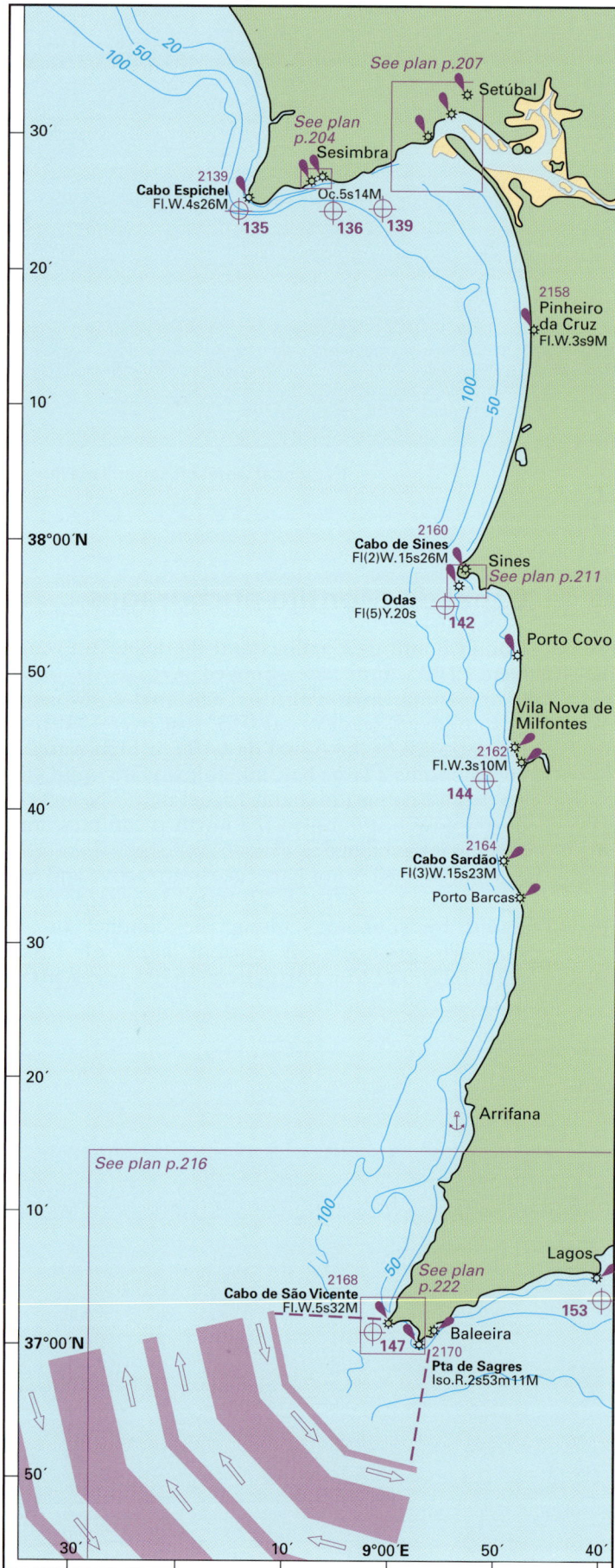

⊕135	38°24'·3N	9°14'·5W	1·2M SW of Cabo Espichel
⊕136	38°24'·4N	9°05'·7W	Sesimbra approach
⊕139	38°24'·3N	9°01'·1W	Setúbal & the Rio Sado approach
⊕142	37°54'·8N	8°54'·8W	Sines approach
⊕144	37°42'·2N	8°50'·5W	Vila Nova de Milfontes approach
⊕147	37°01'N	9°00'·7W	1M SW of Cabo de São Vicente
⊕153	37°03'·8N	8°39'·2W	1·1M SE of Ponta da Piedade (Lagos approach)

PRINCIPAL LIGHTS

2139 Cabo Espichel Fl.4s167m26M
 Horn 31s 460m SW
 White hexagonal tower and building 32m
2140 Forte do Cavalo Oc.5s34m14M
 Red tower 7m
2158 Pinheiro da Cruz Fl.3s66m9M
 White column, red bands
2160 Cabo de Sines Fl(2).15s55m26M
 001°-obscd-003° and 004°-obscd-007°
 White tower and building 28m
2162 Milfontes (Rio Mira) Fl.3s22m10M
 Turret on white building 5m
2164 Cabo Sardão Fl(3)15s67m23M
 Square white tower and red-roofed
 building 17m
2168 Cabo de São Vicente Fl.5s85m32M Horn(2)30s
 Off-white tower, red lantern, and building 28m
2170 Pta de Sagres Iso.R.2s53m11M
 Tower on a building mounted with a lantern
 and red cupola

Ports

Sesimbra*
Setúbal*
Sines*
Vila Nova de Milfontes

* Fuel available alongside

One of the few remaining double-ended trading
vessels which used to ply the Sado estuary under sail.
Most now take tourists on river trips *Anne Hammick*

Approaching Sesimbra from Cabo Espichel *Jane Russell*

Map labels

See plan p.207
Setúbal
See plan p.204
Sesimbra
2139
Cabo Espichel
Fl.W.4s26M
Oc.5s14M
135 136 139
2158
Pinheiro da Cruz
Fl.W.3s9M
2160
Cabo de Sines
Fl(2)W.15s26M
Sines
See plan p.211
Odas
Fl(5)Y.20s
142
Porto Covo
Vila Nova de Milfontes
2162
Fl.W.3s10M
144
2164
Cabo Sardão
Fl(3)W.15s23M
Porto Barcas
Arrifana
See plan p.216
Lagos
2168
Cabo de São Vicente
Fl.W.5s32M
See plan p.222
153
147
Baleeira
2170
Pta de Sagres
Iso.R.2s53m11M

Sesimbra

Waypoints

⊕135 – 38°24'·3N 9°14'·5W (1·2M SW of Cabo Espichel)
⊕136 – 38°24'·4N 9°05'·7W (approach)
⊕137 – 38°26'·3N 9°06'·2W (entrance)
⊕138 – 38°28'·6N 8°58'·7W (Portinho de Arrábida anchorage)

Courses and distances

⊕130 (Rio Tejo Fairway Buoy No.2) – ⊕136 (via ⊕135) = 21·6M, 151° & 089° or 269° & 331°
⊕131 (Cascais) – ⊕136 (via ⊕135) = 24·7M, 152° & 089° or 269° & 332°
⊕136 – ⊕137 = 1·9M, 348° or 168°
⊕136 – ⊕138 = 7M, 053° & by eye or by eye & 133°
⊕136 – ⊕139 (Setúbal) = 3·6M, 092° or 272°
⊕136 – ⊕142 (Sines) = 30·8M, 164° or 344°

Tides

Standard port Lisbon
Mean time differences
HW –0035 ±0010; LW –0015 ±0005

Heights in metres

MHWS	MHWN	MLWN	MLWS
3·4	2·6	1·4	0·6

Or refer to EasyTide at www.ukho.gov.uk/easytide

Charts

	Approach	Harbour
Admiralty	3635, 3636	
Imray	C19, C49	C49
Portuguese	23203, 24204, 26407	26407

Principal lights

2140 **Forte do Cavalo** Oc.5s34m14M Red tower 7m
2142 **Ldg Lts 003°** *Front* LFl.R.5s10m7M
Red lantern on SW turret of fortress 10m
2142.1 *Rear* 34m from front LFl.R.5s22m6M
Red lantern on NW turret of fortress 17m
Note These lights do NOT lead into the harbour but to a point on the shore about 0.5M to the east. Two sets of three lights in line (Fl.R and Fl.W), and one set of two lights in line (Fl.W) close east of Sesimbra mark a submarine cable area and again are NOT leading lights.
2144 **Breakwater head** Fl.R.3s12m8M
White tower, red bands 7m

Night entry

Straightforward in most conditions, though it would be wise to anchor until daylight rather than to attempt berthing alongside.

Harbour communications

Marina de Sesimbra (run by the Clube Naval de Sesimbra) ☎ +351 212 233 451, +351 212 281 039
Fax +351 212 281 668
Email secnaval.sesimbra@mail.telepac.pt
www.naval-sesimbra.pt (in Portuguese only)
VHF Ch 9, 12, 16, (0900–1200, 1400–1700)

Busy fishing harbour sheltering a small, club-run marina

The town of Sesimbra lies 2km from its harbour, which despite the growing numbers of visitors is still dominated by the fishing industry. On the hill behind the town, on the site of a Moorish fortress captured in 1165, is the restored medieval castle built in the 13th century. Its five towers and walls protect the 12th-century church of Santa Maria. There are wonderful views from here. The town has always been popular with Portuguese royalty; the diminutive 17th-century fortress of Sao Teodosio was built by Joao IV to protect the port from pirates.

The harbour is very much a working port, with brightly painted fishing boats clustered alongside a newly expanded unloading wharf. It is well protected by a 900m breakwater and, despite having limited space for visiting yachts, makes an interesting port of call for those not overly concerned about a lack of marina comforts.

Sesimbra harbour from the south

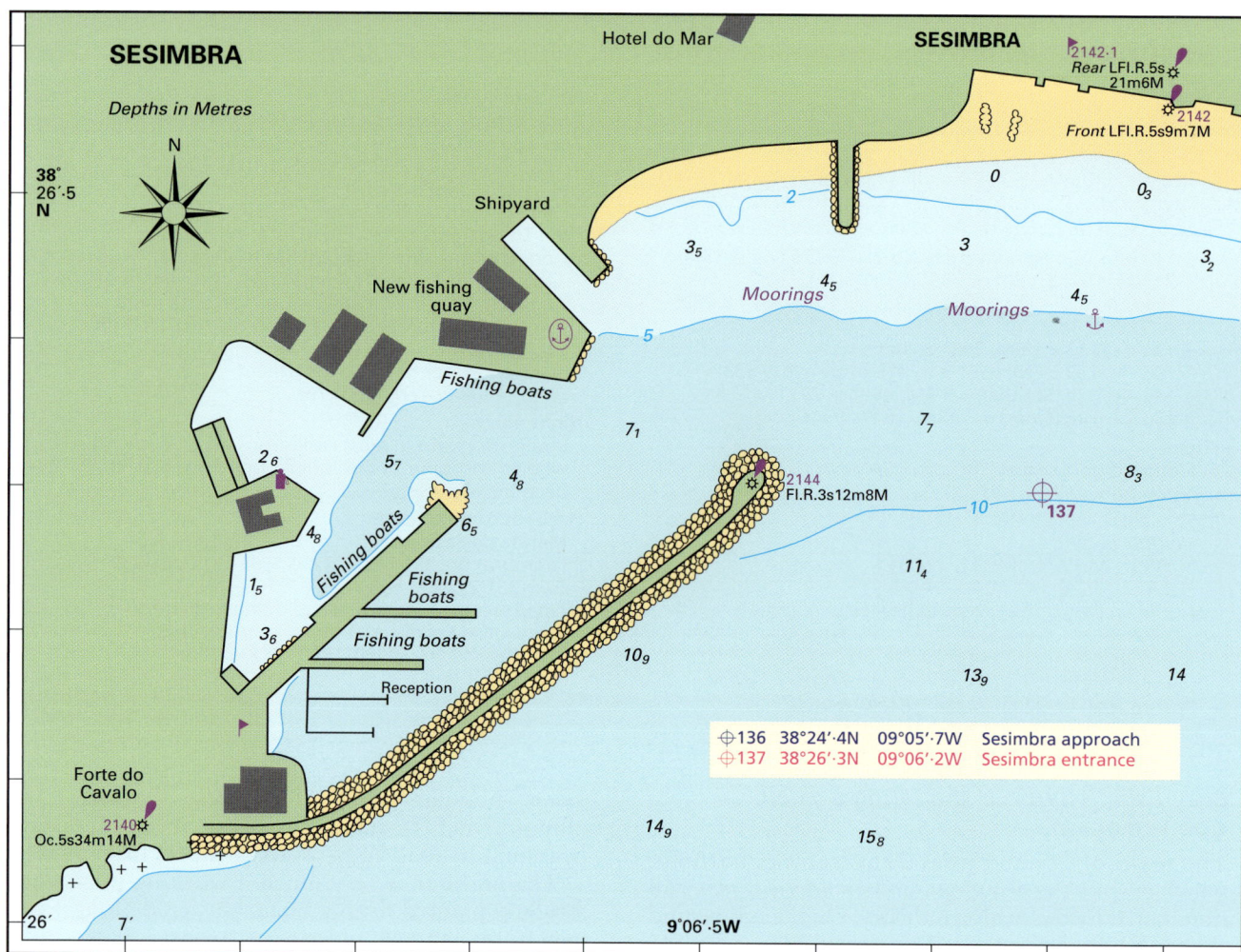

Approach

The major mark from north or south is Cabo Espichel. Forte do Cavalo, 6·5M east of Cabo Espichel, marks the landward end of the outer harbour mole. If coastal sailing, the coast between the two should be given an offing of at least 0·5M and after rounding Cabo Espichel there is still some southing to be made to get round Ponta da Pombeira.

The bluff trending east from Cabo Espichel rises from 160m near the cape to 500m towards Setúbal.

Note that the 'Leading Lights' at Sesimbra do NOT lead into the harbour but to a point on the shore about 0·5M to the east! Other Lights that can confuse a navigator are as follows:

Running up the hillside immediately east of Sesimbra are two sets of three lights in line: both sets flash 2·5s front, 3s centre, 3·5s rear, with a range of 2M; the western set on 030° flashes red and the eastern, on 000°, white. A third set of two white lights flashing 2·5s front and 3·5s rear, on 058°, are between the other two sets of three lights. They mark submarine cables and anchoring within their limits is prohibited. In addition, three outfalls lie within a 0·5M radius of the breakwater head to its southwest and southeast. Each is marked by a yellow post, × topmark on land, plus a nearby yellow spherical buoy, also × topmark. The pairs are

lit, Fl.Y.8s3M, Fl.Y.6s3M and Fl.Y.4s3M respectively. Finally, east of Cabo de Ares is a line of three yellow buoys with × topmarks (All Q(5)Y.10s2M). It would appear that they define the seaward extent of coastal water within which navigation is prohibited.

From offshore, ⊕136 lies 1·9M south-southeast of the entrance, a course of 348° leading to ⊕137, close outside the harbour mouth.

Entrance

The entrance is straightforward, though it would be unwise to cut the outer molehead too closely in case of fishing vessels exiting at speed.

Berthing

The small (130 berth) marina run by the Clube Naval de Sesimbra is full to capacity with local boats. If local yachts are away and berths are empty, perhaps room could be found but it would obviously be wise to make contact before arrival.

A clubhouse has been built at the extreme southwest end of the harbour, overlooking the marina.

Anchorage

Sesimbra is an extremely busy fishing port and there is nowhere inside the harbour that a visiting yacht can conveniently anchor. Local yachts and smallcraft lie on moorings off the beach between the shipyard and the short east mole, and the only possible anchorage is to the east of them in 5–6m, exposed to the south and southeast. Holding is variable over kelp and rock with sand patches – the excellent sandy beach fronting the harbour and town is at least partially man-made.

Sesimbra has a deserved reputation for strong local northerlies which get up in the late afternoon and die in the small hours – lay ground tackle accordingly.

Formalities

The *Polícia Marítima* have premises on the new fishing wharf and there is a *GNR–Brigada Fiscal* office in the town. In theory it is the skipper's duty to seek them out immediately on arrival, but in view of the walk involved it would be worth checking at the *Clube Naval* whether this is still considered necessary. Alternatively one or both may come to the yacht.

Facilities

Boatyard Fast Boats Repair Lda ① +351 212 686 540 or +351 917 519 360 *Email* fastboats@iol.pt www.fboatrepair.com in the Zona Técnica da Marina, Doca de Sesimbra, 2970 Sesimbra, advertise their services for all kinds of maintenance and repair to wood and GRP, including painting and antifouling.

Travel-lift Not as such, though there are several cranes in the fishing quay.

Engineers, mechanics, electronic and radio repairs Available, though more used to working on fishing vessels. Enquire at the *Clube Naval*.

Water On the pontoons, and from a tap near the fuel pumps.

Showers At the *clube naval*.

Electricity On the pontoons.

Fuel Diesel and petrol are available from pumps on the old fishing quay (see plan) via long hoses. However depths alongside have not been verified and it would be wise to check by dinghy first – in any case, the wall is high and a visit at high water would make good sense.

Bottled gas Camping Gaz exchanges at several hardware stores in the town (a longish walk), but no refills.

Weather forecast Displayed daily outside the *Clube Naval*.

Banks In the town.

Shops/provisioning/produce market In the town.

Cafés, restaurants and hotels No shortage. Many of the former specialise in seafood, including an outdoor café opposite the new fishing quay.

Medical services In Sesimbra.

Communications

Post office In the town.

Telephones There does not appear to be a kiosk in the harbour area though there are plenty in the town.

Internet access Several cybercafés in Sesimbra.

Car hire/taxis In the town.

Buses Bus station near the market (about an hour to Lisbon), with minibuses running a frequent service into town from a stop at the root of the fishing mole.

Adjacent anchorages

1. An unnamed bay 1·5M east of Cabo de Ares (3·5M east of Sesimbra), which has an offlying rock requiring at least 0·5M clearance, over sand off a pleasant beach. The bottom shoals steadily towards the shore at the west end of the beach. It was reported in 2007, however, that the cliffs had collapsed onto the beach so this spot may no longer be such an attractive place to anchor.

2. **Portinho de Arrábida** (⊕138 – 38°28'·6N 8°58'·7W – see plan on page 207), a wooded bay backed by high cliffs some 6M east of Sesimbra. While very scenic, and with good holding, in the evenings it is prone to very heavy downdrafts of wind from the mountains. There is sometimes 25–30kn of wind in the anchorage, whereas 3 miles offshore, there could be only 5–10kn! Some would say the anchorage is for lunchtime stops only, although being fully open to the south a surprising number of small craft lie on summer moorings in the western part of the bay.

   The approach from the west is complicated by a drying sandbank, the Baixo de Alpertuche, off Forte Arrábida. Keep 0·4M offshore until lightbeacon No.2 bears 090°, before altering to 033° to clear Forte Arrábida by 150–200m. This should give a least depth of 2·2m at low water springs but be careful as the bank may grow and/or move. Admiralty chart 3259 will be found useful and the water is crystal clear. Anchorage can be found in 5·5m just to seaward of the moorings, over weed and hard sand. There are rocks and a small offlying island, Anixa, at the east end of the bay.

   There are no facilities other than a telephone kiosk behind the beach, half a dozen waterfront restaurants, and an oceanographic museum in Forte Arrábida on the western headland. Much of the surrounding area, including Anixa island, is a nature reserve.

Portinho de Arrábida seen from the southeast, with Ilha Anixa on the right and the Baixo do Alpertuche clearly visible in the foreground

Setúbal, Tróia and the Rio Sado

Waypoints
⊕139 – 38°24'·3N 9°01'·1W (approach)
⊕140 – 38°26'·62N 8°58'·72W (leading line)
⊕141 – 38°29'·22N 8°55'·9W (entrance)

Courses and distances
⊕130 (Rio Tejo Fairway Buoy No.2) – ⊕139 (via F135) =
  25·2M, 151° & 090° or 270° & 331°
⊕131 (Cascais) – ⊕139 (via F135) = 32·3M, 152° & 046°
  or 226° & 332°
⊕136 (Sesimbra) – ⊕139 = 3·6M, 092° or 272°
⊕139 – ⊕140 = 3M, 039° or 219°
⊕140 – ⊕141 = 3·4M, 040° or 220°
⊕139 – ⊕142 (Sines) = 29·9M, 170° or 350°

Tides
Standard port Lisbon
Mean time differences
HW –0015 ±0005; LW 0000 ±0005
Heights in metres

MHWS	MHWN	MLWN	MLWS
3·4	2·7	1·3	0·5

Or refer to EasyTide at www.ukho.gov.uk/easytide

Charts

Charts	Approach	Entrance/estuary
Admiralty	3635, 3636	3259, 3260
Imray	C19, C49	C49
Portuguese	23203, 24204	26308, 26309

Principal entrance lights
2151 **Ldg Lts 040°** *Front* **Fishing harbour E jetty**
  Iso.Y.6s13m22M
  Red and white striped metal structure 9m
2151.1 *Rear* **Azêda** 1·7M from front Iso.Y.6s60m22M
  038·3°-vis-041·3° White tower, red bands 31m
Difficult to distinguish against the lights of the city
2150.22 **Lightbeacon No.2** Fl(2)R.10s13m9M
  Racon Mo 'B'(– · · ·)15M Red post, white lantern
2150.26 **Lightbeacon No.4** Fl.R.4s13m4M
  Red and white chequered column 5m

2150 **Forte de Outão** Oc.R.6s33m12M
  Red hexagonal tower and lantern 11m
2150.28 **Lightbeacon No.5** Fl.G.4s13m4M
  Black post and platform 5m
2150.4 **Forte de Albarquel** Iso.R.2s15m6M
  Red lantern on S corner of fort
2152.1 **Anunciada** Iso.R.4s22m15M Red lantern
2152 **Algarve Exportador** Oc.R.4s14m15M Red lantern

Night entry
While entrance to the estuary should present no
problems in light conditions and good visibility (when
the leading lights will come into their own), it would be
wise to await daylight before entering the marina

Harbour communications
Administração dos Portos de Sesimbra e Setúbal
☎ +351 265 542000, *Fax* +351 265 230992
Email geral@portodeSetubal.pt
www.portodesetubal.pt (mainly concerned with
commercial activity, and almost entirely in Portuguese)
VHF Ch 11, 16
Doca de Recreio das Fontainhas ☎ +351 265 542 076,
Fax +351 265 542 048
Email docadasfontainhas@portodesetubal.pt
www.portodesetubal.pt (in Portuguese and some
English).
VHF Ch 16 but prior contact by telephone to check
whether a berth is available is advised.
Tróia Marina communications ☎ +351 265 499 333
Fax +351 265 488 330
Email (General) marina@troiaresort.pt
Email (Booking) marinabooking@troiaresort.pt
www.troiaresort.net (in Portuguese and English, click on
Marina)
VHF Ch 9

The Península de Tróia and entrance to the Rio Sado seen from the south-southwest over some of the extensive offlying sandbanks. The Setúbal waterfront is clearly visible beyond. The new Tróia marina is behind the high-rise building near the end of the peninsula

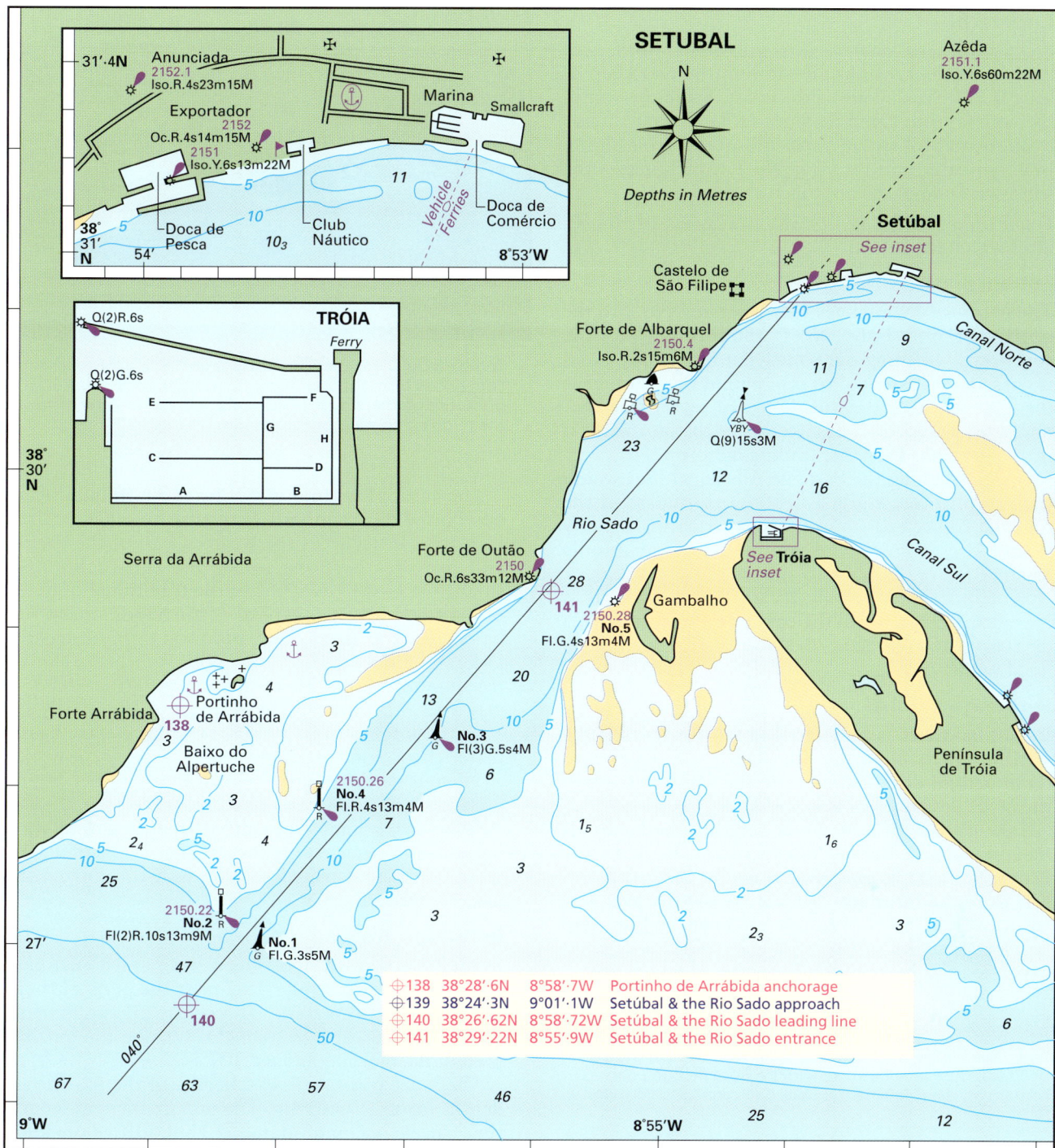

Chart labels

SETUBAL (inset)

- Anunciada — 2152.1 — Iso.R.4s23m15M — 31′.4N
- Exportador — 2152 — Oc.R.4s14m15M
- 2151 — Iso.Y.6s13m22M
- Doca de Pesca
- Club Náutico
- Marina
- Smallcraft
- Vehicle Ferries
- Doca de Comércio
- 38° 31′ N — 54′ — 8°53′W
- 11 — 5 — 10 — 10₃ — 5

TRÓIA (inset)

- Q(2)R.6s
- Q(2)G.6s
- Ferry
- E — F
- G
- C — H
- A — D — B
- 38° 30′ N

Main chart:

- **SETUBAL** — N — Depths in Metres
- Azêda — 2151.1 — Iso.Y.6s60m22M
- Setúbal — See inset
- Canal Norte
- Castelo de São Filipe
- Forte de Albarquel — 2150.4 — Iso.R.2s15m6M
- YBY — Q(9)15s3M
- See Tróia inset
- Canal Sul
- Rio Sado
- Gambalho
- Forte de Outão — 2150 — Oc.R.6s33m12M
- 141
- No.5 — 2150.28 — Fl.G.4s13m4M
- 28
- Serra da Arrábida
- Forte Arrábida
- 138
- Portinho de Arrábida
- Baixo do Alpertuche
- No.3 — Fl(3)G.5s4M
- No.4 — 2150.26 — Fl.R.4s13m4M
- No.2 — 2150.22 — Fl(2)R.10s13m9M
- No.1 — Fl.G.3s5M
- 140
- Península de Tróia
- 27′
- 040°
- 9°W — 8°55′W

Depth figures (selection): 5, 10, 9, 11, 7, 23, 12, 16, 20, 13, 6, 3, 2, 4, 25, 47, 67, 63, 57, 46, 50, 25, 12, 6, 1₅, 1₆, 2₃, 2₄

Waypoint table:

⊕138	38°28′·6N	8°58′·7W	Portinho de Arrábida anchorage
⊕139	38°24′·3N	9°01′·1W	Setúbal & the Rio Sado approach
⊕140	38°26′·62N	8°58′·72W	Setúbal & the Rio Sado leading line
⊕141	38°29′·22N	8°55′·9W	Setúbal & the Rio Sado entrance

Rio Sado with improved space at the new marina at Tróia

Setúbal marina lies 3M from the entrance to the Rio Sado (⊕141), and Tróia marina just 1·5M to starboard near the end of the Tróia peninsula. The commercial port of Setúbal is the country's third largest and cannot claim to be attractive, though areas of the city have some charm. The beautifully sited pousada to the west of Setúbal lies within the walls of the Castelo de São Filipe built by Philip II of Spain to cow the local inhabitants and repel English pirates. The entrance channel into the Rio Sado is narrow but well marked, although yachts are advised not to attempt it other than in fine weather and on the flood. The spring ebb can run at more than 3kns and with onshore winds of any strength should not be contemplated.

Of all the basins in Setúbal only the Doca de Comércio (commercial dock) containing the Doca de Recreio das Fontaínhas may have room for a visiting yacht. The new Tróia marina on the peninsula is a better bet. It is possible to anchor throughout much of the estuary, and although large areas dry there is a navigable channel as far as Alcacer do Sal, 24M upstream, or at least to the railway bridge below it.

Approach

If coastal sailing from the direction of Sesimbra, note that Cabo de Ares has an offlying rock so keep at least 0·5M clear all along the coast. From the south, the course from Cabo de Sines of 353° stands away from the unbroken low sand hills of the Tróia shore. In either case head for buoy No.2, which marks the southwest end of the approach channel.

From offshore ⊕139 lies 3M southwest of ⊕140, after which see below.

Entrance

The entrance channel lies between buoy No.2 to the northwest and buoy No.1 about 600m to the southeast, widening out somewhat after buoy No.3 is passed. It is essential to stay within the channel as there are shoals and drying banks on either side and, once past buoy No.3, best to favour the north side if traffic permits. There are leading lights on 040°.

Before reaching the Forte de Albarquel the estuary opens up to the southeast. 800m southeast of the fort the Cabeça do João Farto west cardinal buoy marks the western end of an extensive middle ground. Leave the buoy to starboard for Setúbal, or well to port and turning to starboard into Tróia marina or to run down the east side of the Península de Tróia. Most of the north shore west of the town is lined with moorings.

Berthing – Setúbal

In Setúbal there is only one basin of interest to the visiting yachtsman at the Doca de Comércio (commercial dock) containing the small marina of the Doca de Recreio das Fontaínhas.

Take particular care when entering the basin, as meeting any of the car ferries plying between the Península de Tróia and Setúbal would be unpleasant. The port-hand turn into the basin is swiftly followed by a second turn through an even tighter gap between the end of the west wall and a very solid concrete ferry berth dolphin, neither of which are lit.

The three basins at Setúbal are, from west to east, the Doca de Pesca, the Clube Nautico, and the Doca de Comércio containing the small marina Doca de Recreio das Fontainhas

Setúbal's Doca de Comércio or Doca de Recreio das Fontaínhas from the south-southeast, with the marina pontoons on the left, the Península de Tróia ferry terminal in the middle and smallcraft moorings on the right

The Setúbal marina is run by the Administração dos Portos de Sesimbra e Setúbal whose head office is nearby. It occupies the western half of the basin, and provides berthing for about 150 yachts and smallcraft as well as a few of the traditional double-ended trading vessels typical of the Sado estuary. All berths on the three long pontoons are alongside fingers and depths are said to be 3–3·5m throughout. Only three berths are reserved for visitors, and though one of these is nominally of 15m, if space is tight a smaller yacht clearly has a better chance of being squeezed in.

There is no designated arrivals berth. Office hours are 0900–2100 daily from May to October, 0900–1900 at other times. The staff are reported to be very helpful and security in the marina is particularly good, with uniformed guards in addition to the usual electronic gate.

Berthing – Tróia

Enter from the west between both starboard and port hand lights (range 3M) near the ends of their respective breakwaters. The centre of the marina entrance is 38°29'·652N 008°54'·173W. See the outline plan of the marina on page 207.

There are a total of 184 berths in the marina in depths from 2·5m to 4m. The maximum boat length that can be accommodated is 18m. Office opening hours are 0830–2100 May to September, and 0900 to 1800 October to April.

Formalities – Setúbal and Tróia

The *GNR–Brigada Fiscal* have a desk in the marinas' office buildings, with the *Alfândega* and *Polícia Marítima* nearby. Copies of the marina paperwork are circulated to all three, and it is no longer necessary for most skippers to visit them in person. The marina manager will advise if this is required – most probably due to non-EU yacht registration or crew.

Facilities – Setúbal

Boatyard The somewhat ramshackle boatyard at the west end of the town waterfront may be able to work on a yacht, but its marine railways would be unsuitable for hauling a deep-keeled yacht.

Travel-lift No travel-lift, though a mobile crane capable of lifting up to 40 tonnes is situated at the Doca de Recreio das Fontaínhas. There are no boatyard facilities on site and it should only be regarded as an emergency measure. The Clube Náutico de Setúbal (see below) has a 5-tonne crane.

Chandlery A branch of Contrafogo is at Rua da Saúde, 80, 2900-572 Setúbal. ☎ +351 265 534 014 *Fax* +351 265 509 753 www.contrafogo.pt *Email* contrafogo.setebul@contrafogo.pt. Anything not in stock can be ordered from Lisbon.

Water On the marina pontoons.

Showers Shower block near the marina office, with card access (for which a deposit is required).

Launderette In the city.

Electricity On the marina pontoons.

Fuel Diesel and petrol pumps will be found on a pontoon in the eastern end of the basin beyond the ferry berths, open 0900–1200 and 1400–1800 in season. Payment must be made in cash. Small amounts of fuel can be bought from a filling station opposite the marina.

Bottled Gas The filling station above sells only Portuguese gas cylinders, though Camping Gaz is understood to be available elsewhere in the city.

Clube Náutico The Clube Náutico de Setúbal has premises overlooking the small basin west of the marina, with the usual bar and restaurant.

Weather forecast Displayed daily at the marina office.

Banks In the city.

Shops/provisioning Large supermarket one road inland from the Clube Náutico, and doubtless many others, as well as good general shopping in the city proper.

Produce market Fish and produce market adjacent to the supermarket above.

Cafés, restaurants and hotels Many throughout the city, including several waterside restaurants in the nearby public gardens.

Medical services In the city.

Facilities – Tróia

There is electricity and water on the pontoons, fuel, laundry service, showers and toilets, internet facilities and several restaurants. There is a supermarket within four minutes' walk of the marina. There is no travel-lift and probably no repair facilities or chandlery available.

The ferry terminal to Setúbal is adjacent to the marina.

Communications – Setúbal

Post office In the city.

Mailing address The marina office will hold mail for visiting yachts – c/o Administração do Porto de Setúbal, Doca de Recreio das Fontaínhas, Praça da República, 2904–508 Setúbal, Portugal. It is important that the envelope carries the name of the yacht in addition to that of the addressee.

Internet access At least one cybercafé in the city, but at some distance from the marina.

Public telephones On the rear wall of the marina office.

Fax service The marina office can receive faxes but cannot send them.

Car hire/taxis In the city.

Buses and trains Services to Lisbon and elsewhere.

Ferries Shuttle service for foot passengers and vehicles to the Península de Tróia from inside the Doca de Recreio das Fontaínhas.

Air services Lisbon airport is some 35km distant.

Communications – Tróia

WiFi, phone, fax and photocopiers are available in a 'business centre'.

Ferries Shuttle service for foot passengers and vehicles to the inside the Doca de Recreio das Fontaínhas from the Península de Tróia.

Tróia Marina looking west-southwest

Adjacent anchorages

1. There is a designated fishing and smallcraft anchorage southeast of the conspicuous Castelo de São Felipe in 10–12m, but it is some distance from all facilities. Alternatively it is possible to anchor off the Clube Náutico basin, convenient for shopping and where a dinghy can be left.

2. In the shallow bay west of Forte de Albarquel, if space can be found amongst the moorings. Beware the double rock, Arflor, to the west, though this is now buoyed.

3. Along the eastern shore of the Península de Tróia, the northern 3M of which is quite steep-to.

4. Among the rice fields on the upper Rio Sado, well beyond the commercial wharves and shipyards. A large-scale Portuguese chart, a reliable echo sounder and plenty of time are all essentials.

Sines

Waypoints
⊕142 – 37°54'·8N 8°54'·8W (approach)
⊕143 – 37°55'·98N 8°52'·74W (entrance)

Courses and distances
⊕130 (Rio Tejo Fairway Buoy No.2) – ⊕142 (via ⊕135) = 48M, 151°&152° or 328°&329°
⊕131 (Cascais) – ⊕142 (via ⊕135) = 51·1M, 152° & 152° or 332° & 332°
⊕136 (Sesimbra) – ⊕142 = 30·8M, 164° or 344°
⊕139 (Setúbal) – ⊕142 =29·9M, 170° or 350°
⊕142 – ⊕143 = 2M, 054° or 234°
⊕142 – ⊕144 (Vila Nova de Milfontes) = 13M, 165° or 345°
⊕142 – ⊕147 (Cabo de São Vicente) = 54M, 185° or 005°

Tides
Standard port Lisbon
Mean time differences
HW –0040 ±0010; LW –0015 ±0005
Heights in metres

MHWS	MHWN	MLWN	MLWS
3·3	2·6	1·3	0·6

Or refer to EasyTide at www.ukho.gov.uk/easytide

Charts

	Approach	Harbour
Admiralty	3636	3224
Imray	C19, C49, C50	C19, C49, C50
Portuguese	23203, 24204, 24205	26408

Principal harbour lights
2160 **Cabo de Sines** Fl(2).15s55m26M
001°-obscd-003° and 004°-obscd-007°
White tower and building 28m
Note Numerous nearby red lights mark chimneys, radio masts etc

2160.16 **West breakwater** Fl.3s20m12M
White tower, red bands 8m
Note Lies about 500m SHORT of the breakwater end, which is marked by a buoy
2160.3 **Terminal Ldg Lts 358°**
Front Iso.G.6s18m10M Post 6m
2160.31 *Rear* 579m from front Oc.G.6s29m10M Post 20m
2160.36 **Fishing harbour (NW) mole** Fl.R.6s6M
White tower, red bands 4m
2160.37 **Marina (SE) mole** Fl.G.4s4M
White tower, green bands 5m
2160.08 **Southeast breakwater, NW corner** LFl.G.8s16m6M
White column, green bands 7m
Other lights exist within the commercial harbour

Night entry
Well-lit and straightforward, with the option to anchor off the beach until daylight if desired

Maritime radio station
Atalaia (38°10'·3N 8°38'·6W)
Remotely controlled from Lisbon
Manual – VHF Ch 16, 23, 24, 25. *Autolink* – VHF Ch 85

Harbour communications
Administração do Porto do Sines ☎ +351 269 860 600
Fax +351 269 860 690 *Email* geral@portodesines.pt
www.portodesines.pt
VHF Ch 12, 16 call *Sines Port Control* (24 hours)
Marina de Sines ☎ +351 269 860 612
Fax +351 269 860 714
Email portoderecreio@portodesines.pt
Website as above, VHF Ch 09.

Small but highly-praised marina in large commercial harbour complex

The town's history can be traced back to Roman times when it was called Sinus, and over the years it established good trading relations in the Mediterranean and thrived. Vasco da Gama was born in the castle here, and although until 1971 it was a relatively quiet fishing port, Sines (pronounced *cinch*) can now handle 500,000-tonne tankers and has heavy industry as well as petrochemicals supporting its economy. However, although it can be identified from well offshore by its many chimneys, many either lit or smoking, once in the anchorage or marina the industrial areas are masked behind the attractive old town and are soon forgotten. The location is quite pleasant, sitting on a cliff overlooking a small sandy bay and there are still traces of its heritage in a reasonably pleasant town centre. The only trace of da Gama in Sines these days is a statue in front of the Parish church.

The Marina de Sines, which lies behind a substantial stone mole southeast of the fishing harbour, has received a unanimous thumbs up from all who have reported on it since it opened in 1996 – an almost unique accolade.

Approach

Sines is most conveniently placed, being the only all-weather harbour between Lisbon, some 50M to the north, and Cabo de São Vicente, nearly 60M to the south.

For 35M north of Cabo de Sines the coast is an unbroken line of low sand hills – one long beach.

The theoretical ranges of Cabo Espichel and Cabo de Sines lights overlap, but there are no other major lights in between. Cabo de Sines has offlying rocks and islands but 0·5M provides safe clearance.

From the south, the last major light is Cabo Sardão 13M distant, with a less powerful light Vila Nova de Milfontes. The coast between Cabo Sardão and Sines is rocky with cliffs, though there are sandy beaches around Vila Nova de Milfontes and Porto Covo (the latter about 7M southeast of Sines and identifiable by its water tower).

From offshore, ⊕142 lies 2M southwest of the main breakwater, a course of 054° leading to ⊕143 in the centre of the wide harbour mouth. A considerable amount of commercial and fishing traffic should be anticipated on closing the coast, and watch kept accordingly.

The approaches are littered with pot buoys. Also keep a good lookout for commercial shipping entering and leaving the harbour.

Entrance

The entrance to the main harbour lies 1·5M south of Cabo de Sines and is protected by a long breakwater, the southern end of which has been in ruins for some years and is partially submerged – note that the breakwater light is situated almost 500m SHORT of the breakwater end, which is marked by a (lit) red pillar buoy. DO NOT CUT INSIDE this buoy.

From the south the entrance is wide and should present no problems, though ships *en route* to the commercial terminals in the southeastern part of the harbour must be given ample space to manoeuvre.

SINES

SINES

Depths in Metres

| ⊕142 | 37°54'·8N | 08°54'·8W | Sines approach |
| ⊕143 | 37°55'·98N | 08°52'·74W | Sines entrance |

Cabo de Sines
2160
Fl(2)W.15s
55m26M

Cabo de Sines

◇ Market

◇ Castle

Praia Vasco da Gama

Porto de Pesca

2160·31
Oc.G.6s
29m10M

Oil Terminal

2160·36
Fl.R.6s6M

2160·37
Fl.G.4s4M

2160·3
Iso.G.6s18m10M

Cargo Terminal

2160·42
Fl.G.2s3M

2160·41
Fl.R.2s3M

2160·16
Fl.3s
21m12M

2160·08
LFl.G.8s
16m6M

Coal Terminal

Fl.R.3s6M
R

37°
56'
N

8°53'W

143

52'

51'

57'

10

19

24

25

21

10

34

48

33

25

18

N

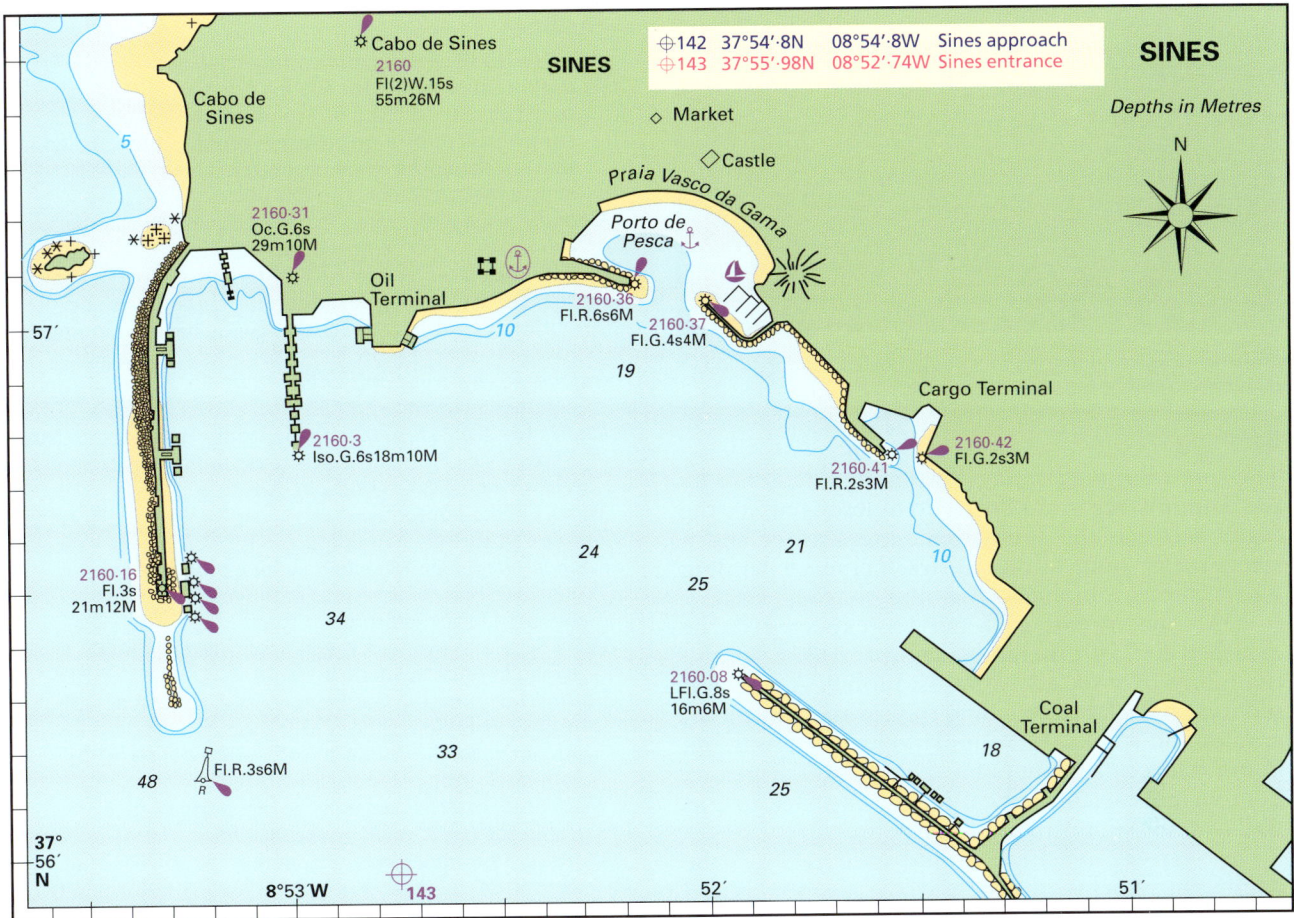

The inner harbour at Sines looking north. The Marina de Sines is on the right

PORTUGAL – THE WEST COAST

The anchorage and marina at Sines in one of the fogs common to this coast *Jane Russell*

Berthing

The small but welcoming Marina de Sines, run by the Administração do Porto do Sines, occupies the bight between the south inner breakwater and a steep rocky outcrop. Facilities include a hauling wharf, slipway, mobile crane, pontoons and fingers. It has capacity for 230 berths (expected to be enlarged to 250), including two or three for more than 20m overall, and a hardstanding. A range of services is available including fresh water, electricity, cradles and stocks, fuel supply, refuse disposal and liquid waste collection, public phone, cash dispenser, boat watch, meteorological reports, a snack bar, as well as some support on yacht repairs.

On arrival yachts should secure to the hammerhead below the rock, which also serves as a fuelling pontoon.

The smart marina office is manned around the clock by notably helpful and friendly staff, all of whom speak English. Reception is upstairs and showers, WC and laundry are downstairs. In place of the more usual gated pontoons the entire marina area is fenced off, with security guards making regular patrols.

Twenty eight berths are reserved for yachts in transit, normally on the northwestern pontoon (the approach to which can be exciting when the *Nortada* is blowing). This is the first part of the marina to be affected by swell and storm surge, when visitors will be moved further in if space allows. Depths vary from 3–8m, with 5m or more throughout the visitors' area, and all berths are alongside finger pontoons.

Anchorage

Yachts are still permitted to anchor off the Praia Vasco da Gama, in 3–5m over sand and a little weed, provided they keep well clear of both fishing vessels and the marina approach. Being open to the southwest the anchorage is seldom without a slight roll, but the marina could not be closer should the wind shift onshore. Dinghies can be landed on the beach, which is cleaned and raked daily and is very popular with local residents.

There are charges for anchoring but only if marina facilities are used. Facilities include showers, launderette and the internet. Payment should be made at the marina office.

Facilities

Boatyard In the fishing and commercial areas, but as yet nothing specifically for yachts.

Cranes The marina has a 6·3-tonne static crane, supplemented by a much larger mobile crane brought in from the docks when necessary. There is also a slipway where yachts can dry out.

Chandlery Chandlery and marine business are on the ground floor of the new office building. Sinaútica ✆ +351 269 635 670, on Rua Teófila Braga, sells some chandlery in addition to inflatables and outboards. Also one near the fishing harbour, though naturally more geared towards commercial needs.

Engineers, electronic and radio repairs In the fishing and commercial areas – enquire at the marina office.

Charts Local charts are available from Nautisines on Rua Marquês de Pombal, which also offers internet access. The owner speaks good English.

Water On the pontoons.

Showers In the office building.

Launderette Single washing machine plus dryer at the marina office, plus several in the town.

Electricity On the pontoons.

Fuel Diesel and petrol at the hammerhead pontoon. Payment must be made in cash.

Bottled gas Camping Gaz exchanges in the town, with refills available via the GALP shop on Rua Pero de Alenquer. GALP claims to refill any cylinder with butane or propane, but allow three days.

Weather forecast Posted daily at the marina office.

Banks In the town. ATM in the marina.

Shops/provisioning Good selection in the town, about 2km from the marina (though a lot less if the dinghy is used, when nearly all the carrying will be downhill). No shops at all near the marina, though see Berthing, above.

Produce market Small but good open market in the old town.

Cafés, restaurants and hotels A snack bar next to the marina office, which may eventually expand. In the meantime the old town is well supplied with restaurants and hotels.

Medical services In the town.

Communications

Post office In the town.

Mailing address The marina office will hold mail for visiting yachts – c/o Administração do Porto do Sines, Porto de Recreio, Apartado 16, 7520–953 Sines, Portugal. It is important that the envelope carries the name of the yacht in addition to that of the addressee.

Internet access Those berthed in the marina or paying to anchor can use one of the office computers for a small fee. Alternatively try Nautisines (see *Charts* above), open 1730–1900, or the pay-as-you-go terminal in the main post office on Praça Tomás Ribeiro. Wireless broadband is reported to be available throughout the marina, but this has not been verified.

Public telephones At the marina office and in the town.

Fax service Faxes can be received at the marina office, but not sent.

Car hire/taxis In the town, or can be arranged via the marina office.

Buses Local buses, with long distance services to Lisbon (just under three hours) and elsewhere from the bus station in the eastern part of the old town.

Trains Sines no longer has a passenger rail service.

Vila Nova de Milfontes

Waypoints
⊕144 – 37°42'·2N 8°50'·5W (approach)
⊕145 – 37°42'·7N 8°48'·2W (entrance)
⊕146 – 37°17'·56N 8°52'·17W (Arrifana anchorage)

Courses and distances
⊕142 (Sines) – ⊕144 = 13M, 165° or 345°
⊕144 – ⊕145 = 1·9M, 075° or 255°
⊕142 – ⊕146 = 37·7M, 180° & by eye or by eye & 000°
⊕144 – ⊕146 = 25M, (186°) & by eye or by eye & (006°)
⊕144 – ⊕147 (Cabo de São Vicente) = 42M, 191° or 001°
⊕146 – ⊕147 (Cabo de São Vicente) = 17·8M, (202° or 002°)

Tides
Standard port Lisbon
Mean time differences Milfontes
HW –0035 ±0005; LW No data
Heights in metres Milfontes

MHWS	MHWN	MLWN	MLWS
3·7	2·9	1·5	0·7

Or refer to EasyTide at www.ukho.gov.uk/easytide

Charts

Charts	Approach	River
Admiralty	3636	
Imray	C19, C50	
Portuguese	23203, 24205	(27501)

Principal lights
2162 **Milfontes (Rio Mira)** Fl.3s22m10M
Turret on white building 5m

Night entry
Not possible under any circumstances – the bar calls for eyeball pilotage in good overhead light.

Beautiful, unspoilt river with challenging entrance

Reputedly used by Hannibal and once rich enough to be sacked by Algerian pirates, pretty little Vila Nova de Milfontes on the Rio Mira shows scant evidence of its former importance. Despite much recent holiday development, the white and tile village on the north bank has retained much of its character, and mercifully escaped the high-rise blocks which mar so many Portuguese resorts. There are superb beaches both inside and outside the entrance and the area's peace and tranquillity are a real treat – but first you must pick your way in.

Though viable for a keelboat in the right conditions the Rio Mira is shallow and, in common with many other Portuguese rivers, has a bar with a reported depth of no more than 1m at datum – considerably less if any swell is running. Once inside protection is excellent but flat weather, and particularly an absence of swell, are essential for both entry and departure. About a mile from the entrance there is a road bridge with a clearance of some 12m, but it is possible to explore the river by dinghy for many kilometres beyond.

The shallow bar at Vila Nova de Milfontes, seen from the southwest. The challenge of entering the Rio Mira is exacerbated by the fact that no reliable chart is available

A panoramic shot taken from near the Rio Mira light, looking up upstream towards the town and bridge. Again, the V-shaped middle ground shows up as a pale, sandy shadow   *Anne Hammick*

Approach

The coast between Cabo de Sines to the north and Cabo Sardão to the south consists of rocky cliffs. There is a sandy beach at Porto Covo about 8M to the north, identifiable by its water tower.

From offshore ⊕144 lies 1·9M west-southwest of the rivermouth, a course of 075° leading to ⊕145 on the 10m line, about 0·7M from the entrance. This is the time to decide whether it is viable to investigate further or whether, perhaps regretfully, to alter course for the next destination.

Entrance

Since Vila Nova de Milfontes calls for careful eyeball pilotage, enter only in calm weather on a rising tide, preferably in the afternoon with the sun behind the boat. The entrance is marked by the Rio Mira light, shown from the corner of a square white building with a tiled roof on the north side of the entrance.

Approach to about 600m with the light bearing 050° and, with luck, a local fisherman will lead the way across the bar (though this is considerably less likely now that most of the local smallcraft have moved the mile north to Portinho do Canal). Failing this, turn east and keep the reef which extends southwards from the light about 60m off on the port hand. Although part is exposed it extends for some distance underwater as a brownish–purple area – be guided by the colour of the water.

Just inside the entrance best water is found relatively close under the light, but further upstream there is an unmarked middle ground, drying at low water springs, below and downstream from the fort. Its shape – a wide V with the apex pointing downstream – makes it particularly dangerous and it would be only too easy to find oneself in a blind alley. It appears that a deep channel leads south of the middle ground (see photo), but minimum depths in this have not been ascertained. Fishing nets suspended from buoys are sometimes laid inside the river.

Anchorage

There is plenty of room to anchor in the river, either in the northwest bight just inside the mouth (depths are shallow), or further upstream off the fishermen's quay in 4m or more. The ebb tide runs at up to 3kn with the spring flood only marginally less, and it may be wise to set two anchors.

Formalities

The arrival of a foreign yacht in the river is a sufficiently rare event that it would almost certainly attract a visit from the authorities. Failing that there is a *GNR–Brigada Fiscal* office up the steps at the downstream end of the quay and, supposedly, a *Polícia Marítima* office in the building supporting the single light.

Facilities

Quay with steps for dinghy landing, with a café/restaurant ashore and a public tap opposite. The town contains a range of shops from supermarkets to souvenirs, as well as banks, restaurants, a post office and several telephone kiosks. Buses run to Sines and elsewhere.

Looking out to sea from the Rio Mira light structure, with all kinds of rocks and reefs in the foreground   *Anne Hammick*

Adjacent harbours and anchorages

1. **Porto Corvo, Portinho do Canal and Porto das Barcas** – if coastal sailing, the sharp-eyed may spot Porto Corvo at 37°51′N, Portinho do Canal at 37°44′·4N and/or Porto das Barcas at 37°33′·2N. Though all three are lit, to call any of them a 'port' is highly misleading and none could be entered by even the smallest yacht. Neither are there viable anchorages in their offings – sail on by.

2. **Arrifana**, this is a lovely anchorage in quiet, stable weather. The bay is surrounded by dramatic cliffs giving shelter from north and east, and lies 26M south of Vila Nova de Milfontes and 18M north of Cabo de São Vicente. The anchoring waypoint is at ⊕146. Though isolated and remote it can be a useful passage anchorage, particularly if beating into the prevailing nortada. However, with any swell rolling in, the surfing community arrive in force – and they know where to find waves.

   The coast is rocky and steep-to with offlying stacks and islands. The ruins of an old fort stand on the cliff to the north with a cairn, Pedra da Agulha, to the south. Beneath both are rocky islets – those under the fort are lumpy while those under the cairn have needle-like angularity. Approaching from the southwest, the islets off the fort stand out from the land and the white cottages behind the sandy beach become plain. Anchor off the beach in 7m over sand, avoiding the northern area which is peppered with rocky shoals. Pots or net floats may be encountered anywhere in the bay.

   A miniature harbour, home to half-a-dozen small fishing boats, nestles amongst the rocks at the north end of the beach. However it has nothing to offer in terms of facilities – not even a water tap – and is considerably further from the village by road than is the beach. A café/restaurant overlooks the latter, with a public telephone about 50m up the steep cobbled road to the village. Other than dramatic views and a few more restaurants there is little to justify the climb.

3. **Carrapateira** (37°11′·3N 8°54′·8W), lying 6·5M south of Arrifana and 11M north of Cabo de São Vicente, may also suggest itself as a possible anchorage in northeasterly winds. However shelter is considerably poorer than at Arrifana and there are numerous rocks both in the approach and off the beach.

Arrifana: Looking NNW from the anchorage at 37°17′·56N 008°52·17W.
Note the fishing boat mooring buoys at approximately 37°17′·5N 8°52′·3W *Henry Buchanan*

The wide bay at Arrifana offers potential anchorage on the long haul between Sines and Cabo de São Vicente. Fully open to the west, however, it is also a popular spot with surfers *Anne Hammick*

PORTUGAL – THE WEST COAST

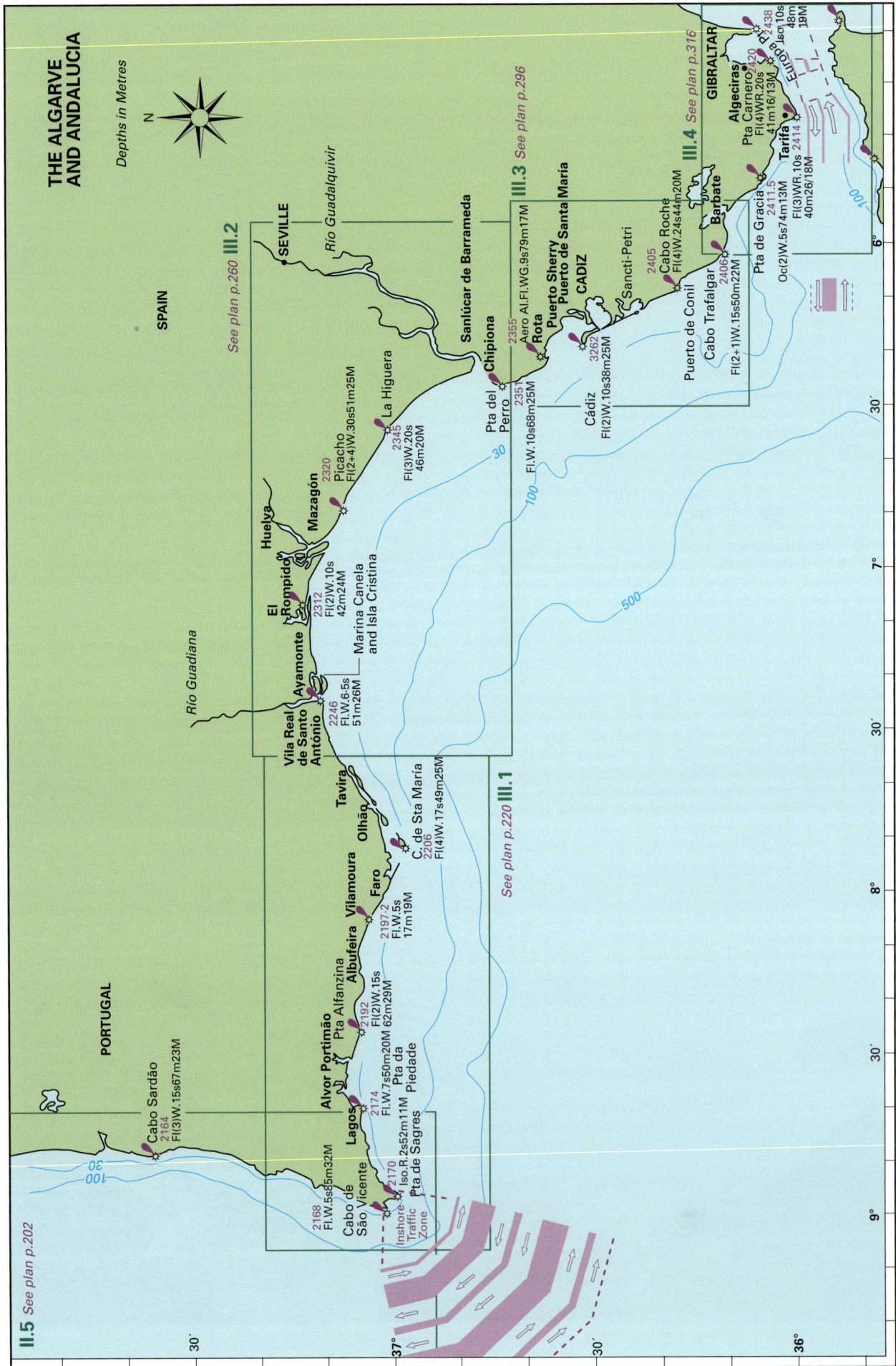

PORTUGAL

SPAIN

Río Guadiana

Río Guadalquivir

SEVILLE

II.5 *See plan p.202*

See plan p.260 III.2

See plan p.220 III.1

III.3 *See plan p.296*

III.4 *See plan p.316*

Cabo Sardão
2164
Fl(3)W.15s67m23M

Lagos
2168
Fl.W.5s85m32M

Alvor Portimão
Albufeira Vilamoura
Pta Alfanzina
2192
Fl(2)W.15s
62m29M

Faro
2197.2
Fl.W.5s
17m19M

2174
Fl.W.7s50m20M
Pta da
Piedade

2170
Iso.R.2s52m11M
Pta de Sagres
**Cabo de
São Vicente**

Inshore
Traffic
Zone

**Vila Real
de Santo
António**

Ayamonte
2246
Fl.W.6.5s
51m26M

**El
Rompido**
2312
Fl(2)W.10s
42m24M

Marina Canela
and Isla Cristina

Huelva

Mazagón
2320
Picacho
Fl(2+4)W.30s51m25M

La Higuera
2345
Fl(3)W.20s
46m20M

Tavira

Olhão

C. de Sta Maria
2206
Fl(4)W.17s49m25M

Sanlúcar de Barrameda

Chipiona
2355
Fl.W.10s68m25M

Pta del
Perro
2351

Rota
Aero Al.Fl.WG.9s79m17M

**Puerto Sherry
Puerto de Santa Maria**

CADIZ

Cádiz
3262
Fl(2)W.10s38m25M

Sancti-Petri
2405

Cabo Roche
Fl(4)W.24s44m20M

Puerto de Conil

Cabo Trafalgar
2406
Fl(2+1)W.15s50m22M

Barbate

Pta de Gracia
2411.5
Oc(2)W.5s74m13M

Tarifa 2414
Fl(3)W.10s
40m26/18M

GIBRALTAR

Algeciras
Pta Carnero
2420
Fl(4)WR.20s
41m16/13M

2438
Euro... Iso... 10s
48m
19M

30

100

500

30

100

30

III. The Algarve and Andalucía

Cabo de São Vicente to Gibraltar

Cabo de São Vicente from the southeast, early morning
Henry Buchanan

Isla de Tarifa from the southeast
Henry Buchanan

Gibraltar 'The Rock' looking north, with Europa Point lighthouse at bottom right, and nearer it –
very distinctive from the sea – the white-painted mosque with its tall minaret

THE ALGARVE & ANDALUCIA

Cabo de São Vicente to Gibraltar

Both ends of this stretch offer spectacular scenery with impressive cliffs. In the middle, these give way to sandy beaches often backed by lagoons – staging posts for migrant birds – including the Parque Natural de Ría Formosa around Faro and Olhão and the Parque Nacional de Doñana west of the Río Guadalquivir. The western Algarve has been intensively developed for the tourist and in places the shoreline is littered with high-rise blocks and time-share estates, though these decrease as one approaches the border. In Spain, the stretch east of Cádiz is the least developed piece of coast between Portugal and France. Human activity can be traced back for millennia, with Faro, Seville, Cádiz and other settlements dating back to Phoenician or Roman times. While on the Algarve see if you find any traces of the fish paste developed by the Phoenicians. This was a delicacy throughout the classical world and was major source of income for the people of the ancient Algarve.

In contrast to the west coast there are a number of good estuary and river anchorages, generally over good holding. From São Vicente to the Guadalquivir the bottom is sand. From Cádiz onwards it is usually mud, often glutinous, providing good holding but needing a deck pump (or mop and bucket) when the anchor is brought in. Anchoring off any beach is possible in fine, settled weather when there is no swell.

Hazards – tunny nets, fish cages and artificial reefs

Between March and early autumn *almadrabas* or tunny (tuna) nets tough enough to foul the screw of a freighter can be a considerable hazard, and may stretch several miles offshore. It is not advisable to sail over one, and officially vessels should not pass between the inner end of a net and the shore (though local fishermen habitually do so). Tunny nets can be found as far west as Fuzeta but are concentrated mainly in the 30M between Puerto de Conil and Tarifa. Further details of dates, locations and buoyage will be found under the notes for the nearest harbour, and annual positions are often displayed on marina notice boards. Note that the cardinal buoys used to mark the nets are frequently very undersized – sometimes less than 2m in height, including topmark – and should not be relied upon, particularly at night.

More prevalent though less worrying are the nets laid for other fish – less worrying because they generally lie too far beneath the surface to bother a yacht. When first laid they are inspected and must be correctly marked – two red or orange flags at the western end (anywhere from south-southwest to north) and a single green flag at the eastern end (north to south-southeast). In addition, white flags should be set at 1M intervals. At night each flag should be replaced by a yellow light (so two lights at the western end). However with the passage of time both lights and flags may disappear, to be replaced at random if at all.

In a few places floating fish cages may be encountered, and again details are included in the text. Most are indicated by yellow buoys and lights, and positions are indicated on current Admiralty and other charts. Finally, a number of artificial reefs have been constructed off the coast to provide fish havens, reducing the charted depth by up to 2·5m. However since these seldom lie in less than 10m and more often straddle the 20m line – and assuming that while yachtsmen may fish by line they seldom tow a trawl – they can safely be ignored.

Swell

Though less of a problem than along the west-facing coast, heavy swell can be produced either by an Atlantic disturbance or by a *levanter* blowing through the Strait of Gibraltar, and the shallower entrances should be avoided in such conditions.

Winds

In summer north and northeast winds predominate in the west, but the further offshore the more variable they become. Further east, the influence of the Portuguese trade winds gradually dies away. Like the Atlantic coast, the Algarve is also subject to stiff afternoon sea breezes. From early summer onwards these start to blow at around 1400, regularly reaching Force 6 and occasionally Force 7 (25 or 30kn) within an hour and continuing until sundown. Typically they pick up from the southwest, moving through west to west-northwest or northwest by evening.

East of Cádiz, the effect of the Strait becomes increasingly marked with 80% of winds in the Strait from either west (*poniente*) or east-northeast (*levante*). Gales are unlikely in the height of summer but *levanters* with winds of 50–60kn are not unknown, visibility dropping to 1M or less. They are not seasonal, generally last for two to three days, and blow up with little or no warning from the barometer – though sometimes a deep purple bank of haze in the morning or a sudden fast steep swell may give a clue. The *poniente* is generally less strong than the *levanter* but may last five days or more. Squalls can occur at any time in the Bay of Gibraltar if the wind is between northeast and southeast.

Visibility

Poor visibility, less than 2M, is more common (2–5%) in summer than in winter. Fog is infrequent but not unknown in the Algarve, while the Cádiz area has a reputation for fog in certain conditions associated with a *levanter*.

Shelter

In a *levanter* (easterly) shelter in the Strait is limited to the Cádiz complex, west of the Tarifa causeway, and Gibraltar. In a *poniente* (westerly) it is limited to the Cádiz complex, Tarifa itself, and Gibraltar.

Currents

Along the Algarve coast the set is predominantly east of southeast, running at about 0·5 knot. By the time it reaches the Strait it is running east at 1–1·5kn, compensating for water lost from the Mediterranean through evaporation. However this pattern can be upset by the wind – a southeasterly gale in the south of the area can produce a west-going stream along the coast as far as Cabo de São Vicente, while persistent strong westerlies, coupled with the regular current, can produce an easterly set of 4kn.

Tides

Tidal predictions for the Algarve use Lisbon as the Standard Port; those for Andalucía use either Lisbon, Cádiz or Gibraltar. When calculating Spanish tides using Lisbon data, note that allowance has already been made for the difference in time zones (Spanish time being UT+1, Portuguese time UT, both advanced one hour in summer – see page 4.) Volume 2 of the Admiralty *Tide Tables: The Atlantic and Indian Oceans including tidal stream predictions (NP 202)*, published annually, covers the entire coastline. Alternatively consult the UK Hydrographic Office's *EasyTide* programme at www.ukho.gov.uk/easytide which gives daily tidal data for all major harbours.

Tidal range decreases eastward, from 2·8m at springs and 1·2m at neaps at Lagos, to 0·9m and 0·4m respectively at Gibraltar – see individual harbours. There is no reliable information about tidal streams along the coast, though 2–3kn has been reported in some places, notably around Faro and Olhão. In the centre of the Straits the east-going stream starts shortly after HW Gibraltar and the west-going stream about six hours later, though the closer inshore, the earlier the change takes place – see diagrams pages 316–318.

Cruising the Algarve is much more pleasant if it can be timed to coincide with morning and evening high tides (in practice a few days before neaps). Otherwise the typically shallow river entrances – which in many cases are dependant on at least half flood and good daylight – can complicate departure and arrival times.

Climate

Most rain falls between the end of October and the beginning of April with virtually none in July and August. Cool in winter, hot in summer, Lagos has a mean of 36°C in July with Gibraltar capable of 40°C in a *levanter*. Sea temperatures at Gibraltar range from 21°C in summer to 14°C in winter.

Maritime radio stations and weather/navigational services

Many Portuguese Maritime radio stations and those broadcasting weather and navigational information are situated between, rather than at, ports or harbours. Details will be found under the nearest harbour to the station. All are remotely controlled from Lisbon. In Andalucía, all Maritime radio stations are remotely controlled from Málaga. Broadcast times are quoted in UT, but all other times (office hours etc) are given in LT.

One of the hazards to navigation on this coast (see page 218) – the large fish conservation and tuna net area south of Fuzeta now marked by six large cardinal buoys (see page 256) *Martin Northey*

III.1 Cabo de São Vicente to Tavira

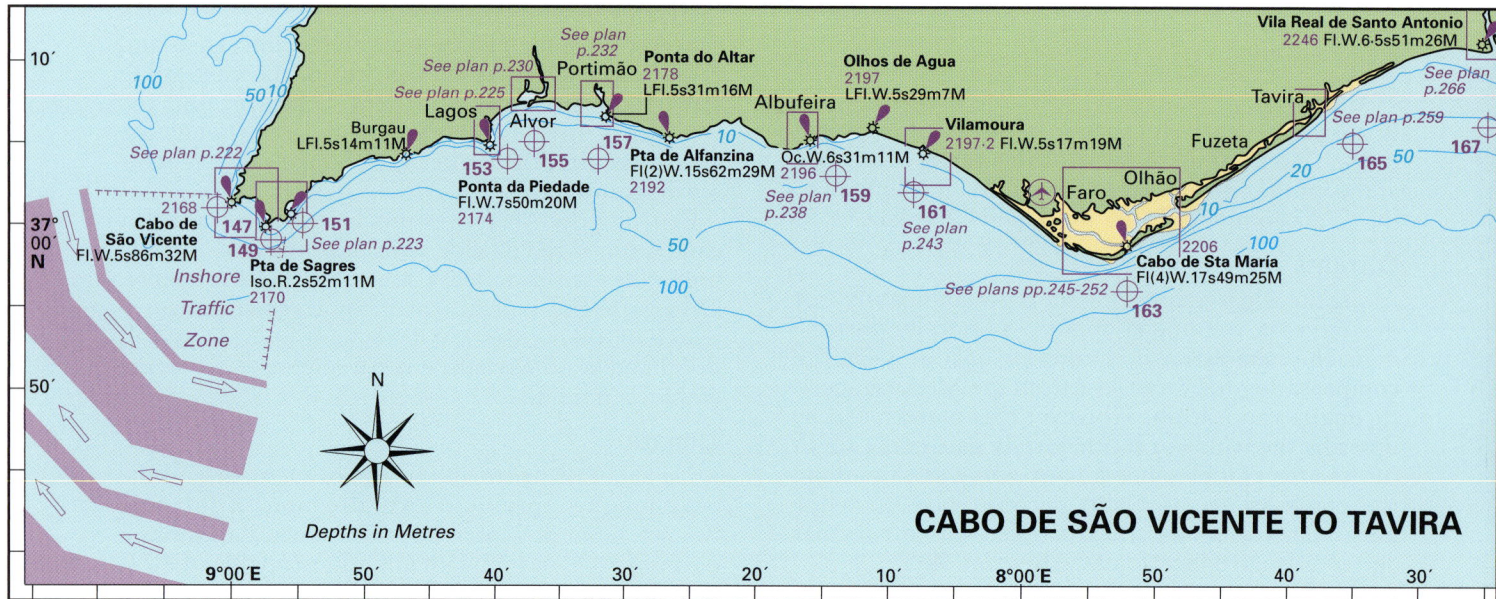

Map labels:

- 10′
- 37° 00′ N
- 50′
- 100 50 10
- Cabo de São Vicente Fl.W.5s86m32M
- 2168
- 147
- 151
- 149
- 2170
- Pta de Sagres Iso.R.2s52m11M
- See plan p.222
- Inshore
- Traffic
- Zone
- Depths in Metres
- N
- Burgau LFl.5s14m11M
- 153
- 155
- 157
- See plan p.225
- Lagos
- See plan p.223
- Alvor
- Ponta da Piedade Fl.W.7s50m20M 2174
- Pta de Alfanzina Fl(2)W.15s62m29M 2192
- See plan p.230
- Portimão
- See plan p.232
- Ponta do Altar 2178 LFl.5s31m16M
- Albufeira
- Oc.W.6s31m11M 2196
- 159
- See plan p.238
- Olhos de Agua 2197 LFl.W.5s29m7M
- Vilamoura 2197·2 Fl.W.5s17m19M
- 161
- See plan p.243
- 50
- 10
- 100
- Faro
- Olhão
- See plans pp.245-252
- 163
- Cabo de Sta María Fl(4)W.17s49m25M 2206
- Tavira
- Fuzeta
- See plan p.259
- 165
- 20 50
- 167
- Vila Real de Santo Antonio 2246 Fl.W.6·5s51m26M
- See plan p.266
- CABO DE SÃO VICENTE TO TAVIRA
- 9°00′E 50′ 40′ 30′ 20′ 10′ 8°00′E 50′ 40′ 30′

⊕147	37°01′N	9°00′·7W	1M SW of Cabo de São Vicente
⊕149	36°58′·8N	8°56′·9W	0·9M S of Ponta de Sagres
⊕151	37°00′N	8°54′·6W	Baleeira approach
⊕153	37°03′·8N	8°39′·2W	1·1M SE of Ponta da Piedade (Lagos approach)
⊕155	37°04·9N	8°36′·9W	Alvor approach
⊕157	37°04′·4N	8°31′·9W	Portimão approach
⊕159	37°03′·4N	8°13′·5W	Albufeira approach
⊕161	37°02′N	8°07′·8W	Vilamoura approach
⊕163	36°55′·6N	7°51′·9W	2·2M S of Cabo de Santa María
⊕165	37°04′·6N	7°35′·4W	Tavira approach
⊕167	37°06′·2N	7°24′·2W	Río Guadiana approach

Ports

Baleeira
Lagos*
Alvor
Portimão*
Albufeira*
Vilamoura*
Faro and Olhão
Tavira

* Fuel available alongside

PRINCIPAL LIGHTS

2168 **Cabo de São Vicente** Fl.5s86m32M Horn (2)30s
   Off-white tower, red lantern, and building 28m
2170 **Ponta de Sagres** Iso.R.2s52m11M
   Square white tower and building 13m
2174 **Ponta da Piedade** Fl.7s50m20M
   Square yellow tower on building 5m
2178 **Ponta do Altar** LFl.5s31m16M 290°-vis-170°
   Square white tower and building 10m
2192 **Ponta de Alfanzina** Fl(2)15s62m29M
   Square white tower and building 23m
2196 **Albufeira** Oc.6s31m11M White column, red bands
2197 **Olhos de Agua** LFl.5s29m7M
   White column, red bands
2206 **Cabo de Santa María** Fl(4)17s49m25M
   White tower and building 46m
2246 **Vila Real de Santo António** Fl.6·5s51m26M
   White tower, narrow black rings, red lantern 46m

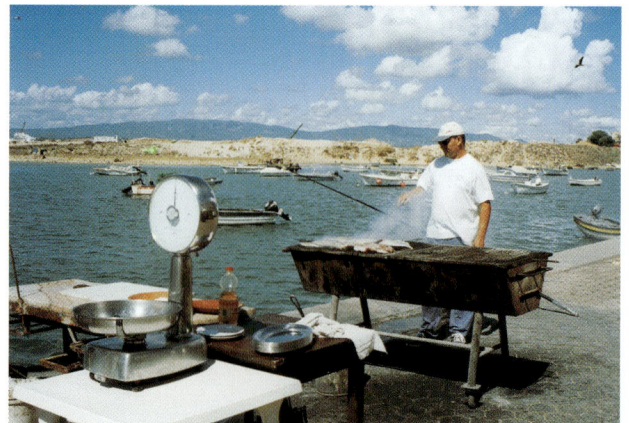

Fish are landed, cleaned, cooked and eaten on the quayside at Ferragudo, across the river from Portimão

Cabo de São Vicente, Ponta de Sagres and Baleeira

Waypoints
⊕147 – 37°01'N 9°00'·7W (1M SW of Cabo de São Vicente)
⊕148 – 37°01'·5N 8°59'W (Enseada de Belixe anchorage)
⊕149 – 36°58'·8N 8°56'·9W (0·9M S of Ponta de Sagres)
⊕150 – 37°00'·143N 8°56'·218W (Enseada de Sagres anchorage)
⊕151 – 37°00'·4N 8°54'·6W (Baleeira, approach)
⊕152 – 37°00'·71N 8°55'·15W (Baleeira entrance)

Courses and distances
⊕142 (Sines) – ⊕147 = 54M, 185° or 005°
⊕147 – ⊕149 = 3·8M, 126° or 306°
⊕147 – ⊕153 (Lagos, via ⊕149) = 18·8M, 126° & 071° or 251° & 306°
⊕149 – ⊕152 = 2·4M, 036° or 216°
⊕151 – ⊕152 = 2M, 328° or 148°
⊕151 – ⊕153 (Lagos) = 12·7M, 068° or 248°

Tides
Standard port Lisbon
Mean time differences (at Enseada de Belixe)
HW –0040 ±0010; LW –0015 ±0005
Heights in metres

MHWS	MHWN	MLWN	MLWS
4·1	3·2	1·7	0·8

Or refer to EasyTide at www.ukho.gov.uk/easytide

Charts

	Approach	*Anchorages*
Admiralty	3636, 91, 89	
Imray	C19, C50	
Portuguese	23203, 23204, 24205, 24206	27502

Principal lights
2168 **Cabo de São Vicente** Fl.5s86m32M Horn (2)30s
  Off-white tower, red lantern, and building 28m
2170 **Ponta de Sagres** Iso.R.2s52m11M
  Square white tower and building 13m
2171 **Baleeira breakwater**
  Fl.WR.4s12m14/11M 254°-W-355°-R-254°
  White tower, red bands 6m

Warning
Long surface nets, lit or unlit, may be laid throughout the area and particularly in the vicinity of Baleeira, in addition to shorter nets and individual fish pots

Night entry
  All three anchorages can be approached after dark in the right conditions, but very careful watch must be kept for the nets mentioned above

Maritime radio station
  Sagres – *Digital Selective Calling* (MF)
  MMSI 002630400 (planned)
  Foia (37°18'·9N 8°36'·3W)
  Remotely controlled from Lisbon
  Manual – VHF Ch 16, 23, 24, 28. *Autolink* – VHF Ch 27.

Cabo de São Vicente and Sagres – the sacred promontory

Once the end of the known world and a springboard for the great Portuguese Discoveries, Cabo de São Vicente and Ponta de Sagres make a formidable pair, wild and windswept, sometimes seen for miles but, even in summer, sometimes heard before seen.

A few miles east of the headlands lies Baleeira, a relatively undeveloped harbour overlooked by a growing tourist resort. Its origins as a whaling centre are given away by its name and today a small fishing fleet still operates from the quay, along with a number of tourist boats. The beach close north of the harbour can be dirty, but Praia do Martinhal a little further east is well up to the Algarve's usual high standard.

Cabo de São Vicente and Ponta de Sagres – Approach

When coastal sailing from the north the last major light is Cabo Sardão and from the east it is Ponta de Piedade south of Lagos.

On passage southwards in the prevailing *nortada* both wind and waves are likely to increase noticeably on approaching Cabo de São Vicente, a combination of gusts off the cliffs and reflected swell. Both Cabo de São Vicente and Ponta de Sagres should be allowed a generous 2M clearance in these conditions, though much flatter water will generally be found east of Ponta de Baleeira. Equally, yachts heading west and north may expect to encounter rapidly deteriorating conditions on rounding Ponta de Baleeira, and should prepare accordingly. It may be necessary to stay 2M or more offshore until 5–6M north of Cabo de São Vicente in order to avoid the worst. By far the best time to make the passage is early in the morning before the *nortada* reaches its full strength, especially if heading north.

If making landfall from offshore, particular care must be taken whilst crossing the Traffic Separation Zone which rounds Cabo de São Vicente and Ponta de Sagres – in fact there is much to be said for avoiding it altogether. The zone is up to 22M in width, its inshore edge nowhere less than 14M from the coast. On closing the headlands, ⊕147 lies 1M southwest of Cabo de São Vicente, ⊕149 about 0·9M south of Ponta de Sagres. The distance between the two is 3·8M on a course of 126°/306°.

Anchorages

Three anchorages can be useful if waiting for the usual strong afternoon *nortada* to die before heading north around Cabo de São Vicente, and though none give much protection from the south in these conditions most crews will, in any case, be wanting to press on.

Cabo de São Vicente from almost due south, with the lighthouse on the left and the Enseada de Belixe anchorage beneath the pale cliffs at centre right

THE ALGARVE & ANDALUCIA

ENSEADA DE BELIXE

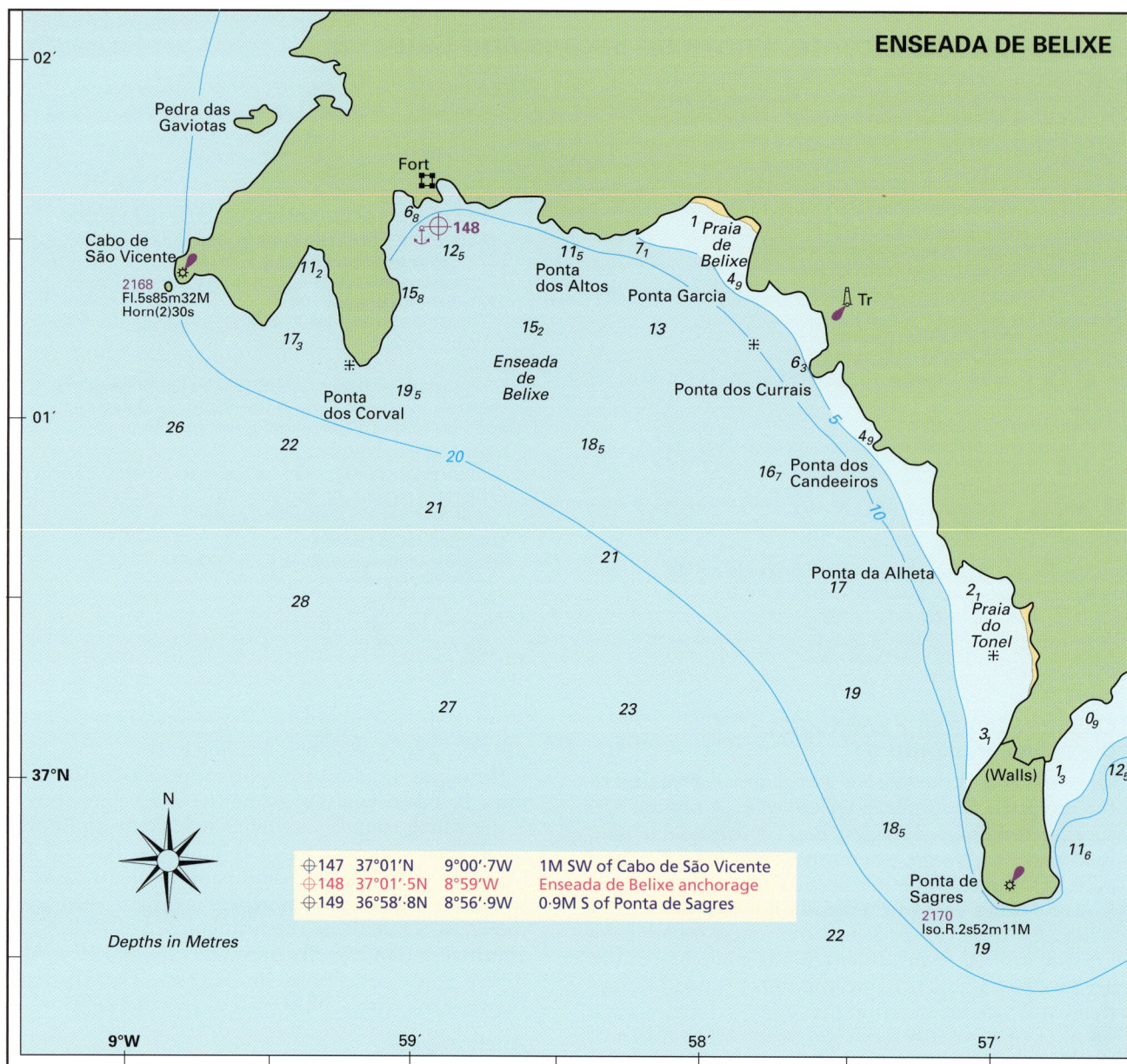

Chart labels (depths in metres):

- 02′
- Pedra das Gaviotas
- Fort
- 6₈
- ⚓ ⊕ **148**
- 12₅
- 11₅
- 7₁
- 1
- Praia de Belixe
- Cabo de São Vicente
- 2168 Fl.5s85m32M Horn(2)30s
- 11₂
- 15₈
- Ponta dos Altos
- Ponta Garcia
- 4₉
- ⬩ Tr
- 17₃
- 15₂
- 13
- 6₃
- Ponta dos Corval
- 19₅
- Enseada de Belixe
- Ponta dos Currais
- 01′
- 26
- 22
- 20
- 18₅
- 4₉
- 5
- 21
- 16₇ Ponta dos Candeeiros
- 10
- 21
- Ponta da Alheta
- 17
- 2₁
- Praia do Tonel
- 28
- 19
- 27
- 23
- 3₁
- 0₉
- (Walls) 1₃ 12₅
- 37°N
- N
- 18₅
- 11₆
- Ponta de Sagres
- 2170 Iso.R.2s52m11M
- 22
- 19
- Depths in Metres

⊕147	37°01′N	9°00′·7W	1M SW of Cabo de São Vicente
⊕148	37°01′·5N	8°59′W	Enseada de Belixe anchorage
⊕149	36°58′·8N	8°56′·9W	0·9M S of Ponta de Sagres

- 9°W
- 59′
- 58′
- 57′

Cabo de São Vicente and Ponta de Sagres – adjacent anchorages

1. **Enseada de Belixe** (⊕148 – 37°01′·5N 8°59′W) is wide open to the southwest and south, with straightforward entry day or night using the loom of Cabo de São Vicente light. If coming from the north, pass outside the tall rock off the headland and continue beyond the first, small, wedge-shaped bay until Enseada de Belixe opens up round Pontal dos Corval.

   Anchor in the northwestern part of the Enseada de Belixe in 14m, or off the Praia de Belixe. Beware the rock some 200m south of the east end of the Praia de Belixe, which rises almost sheer out of 9m to show only at low water. The only realistic dinghy landing is on the beach at Praia de Belixe.

2. **Enseada de Sagres** (⊕150 – 37°00′·143N 008°56′·218W) is open to the southeast, with easy entry and excellent shelter from west through north to northeast. Anchor off the Praia da Marela or the Prainha Das Poças just north of the wall of the fort in 3·5m. There is good holding over sand at both positions. In Sagres at the top of the hill there are hotels (including Pousada), supermarkets, shops, banks and restaurants.

Baleeira – approach

Two fish farms lie northeast of Baleeira, a potential hazard if on passage to or from Lagos or beyond. One is marked by four yellow can buoys, all Fl.Y.14s4M, and is centred on 37°01′·1N 8°53′·5W, the other by four spherical yellow buoys, all Fl.Y.5s3M, and is centred on 37°01′·5N 8°52′·6W. In addition long nets may be set at an angle to the shore, normally indicated by lit yellow buoys (powered by solar panels) and supported by yellow floats. These nets are not connected to the shore and, with due care, yachts can pass on either side.

SAGRES & BALEEIRA

Depths in Metres

N

Praia do Martinhal

Ilhotes do Martinhal

Enseada da Baleeira

Moorings

BALEEIRA

⊙ Mast

SAGRES

2171
Fl.WR.4s12m14/11M

Ponta de Baleeira

Praia do Tonel

Praia da Marela

Prainha das Poças

(Walls)

Enseada de Sagres

Ponta da Atalaia

37°N

Ponta de Sagres
2170
Iso.R.2s52m11M

⊕149	36°58'·8N	8°56'·9W	0·9M S of Ponta de Sagres
⊕150	37°00'·14N	8°56'·22W	Enseada de Sagres anchorage
⊕151	37°00'·4N	8°54'·6W	Baleeira approach
⊕152	37°00'·71N	8°55'·15W	Baleeira entrance

8°55'W

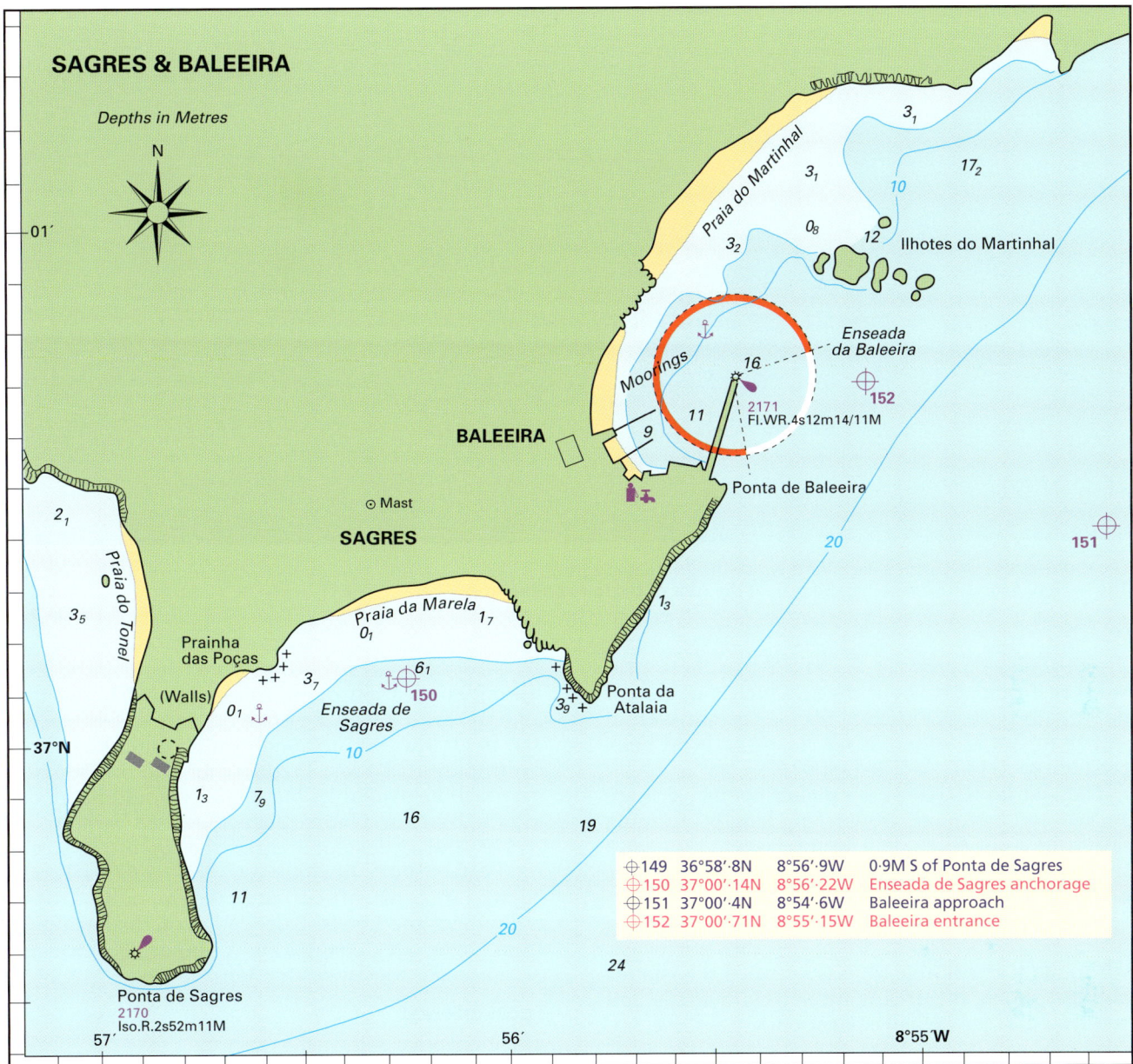

Anchorage at Enseada de Sagres from Sagres fortress
Henry Buchanan

Baleeira harbour looking northeast
Henry Buchanan

Looking west across Baleeira harbour towards the Ponta de Sagres.
The walls of Sagres fortress can be seen near the root of the long promontory

From offshore make for ⊕151, 2M to the south-southeast of the harbour, from which a course of 328° leads in to ⊕152 close off the entrance. From ⊕149 to ⊕152 – there is no reason to head back offshore to ⊕151 – is 2·4M on 036°.

The harbour itself is sheltered by a high breakwater around 400m in length running northeast from Ponta de Baleeira, leaving it open to the east and with a fetch of nearly 1M to the northeast. The breakwater light is sectored, with its red area covering the Ilhotes do Martinhal, a group of large rocks about 500m to the northeast. Although it is possible to pass between the islands and the shore, the area is littered with rocks and strictly a case for eyeball navigation.

Baleeira – harbour and anchorage

The Baleeira anchorage gains some protection from the breakwater and is open only to the east. Anchor outside the moorings, northwest or north of the breakwater head, in 6–10m. Holding is patchy and the bottom is reported to be very foul – a tripline is recommended.

There are several ladders and a ramp convenient for landing, but if possible avoid going ashore at low water as the bottoms of the ladders are seriously dilapidated and the lower part of the ramp lethally slippery. The *Polícia Marítima* have an office in the Doca de Pesca building and may well intercept the skipper and crew as they come ashore – bring ship's papers and passports, in case. The *GNR–Brigada Fiscal* are also likely to check on any foreign flag yacht.

Facilities in the harbour are limited to diesel and water on the fishermen's quay, and a telephone kiosk at the top of the steps up from the harbour. There is an old-style boatyard just north of the jetties where fishing boats are brought ashore for work, but the (elderly) cradle would not suit a deep-keeled yacht and in all but sinking condition it would be worth continuing to Lagos. Engineering and other skills may well be available, but again it would be much safer to head for a more yacht-orientated harbour.

The tourist development at the top of the steep road offers shops (including several supermarkets), banks, a post office and innumerable cafés, restaurants and hotels. Baleeira lies on the bus route from Lagos out to Sagres and Cabo de São Vicente, both popular tourist destinations.

Local interest

The inquisitive will wish to visit the site of the Sagres fortress on the peninsula at Ponta de Sagres. Although Henry the Navigator founded the town of Sagres to support ships sheltering in the bay, and built his Vila do Infante there, it is a myth that a school of navigation ever existed. There is what may be a 15th-century *rosa dos ventos* (wind compass) in the courtyard of the fortress, but with the exception of a small chapel and the northern wall, little else remains. Sir Francis Drake must take a share of the blame, although the final havoc was wrought by the 1755 earthquake which devastated much of the Algarve. An 'interpretative centre' has been set up within the vast Fortaleza, but inevitably the information presented (in several languages) is aimed at a very broad public and sadly the buildings are ugly and do not add to the general ambience.

Lagos

⊕153 37°03'·8N 8°39'·2W 1·1M SE of Ponta da Piedade/Lagos approach
⊕154 37°05'·86N 8°39'·68W Lagos entrance

Waypoints
⊕153 – 37°03'·8N 8°39'·2W (1·1M SE of Ponta da Piedade or Lagos approach)
⊕154 – 37°05'·86N 8°39'·68W (entrance)

Courses and distances
⊕147 (Cabo de São Vicente) – ⊕153 (via ⊕149) = 18·8M, 126° & 071° or 251° & 306°
⊕151 (Baleeira) – ⊕153 = 12·7M, 068° or 248°
⊕153 – ⊕154 = 2·1M, 349° or 169°
⊕154 – ⊕156 (Alvor entrance) = 2·3M, 064° or 244°
⊕154 – ⊕158 (Portimão entrance) = 6·4M, 085° or 265°

Tides
Standard port Lisbon
Mean time differences
HW –0025 ±0010; LW –0030 ±0005
Heights in metres

MHWS	MHWN	MLWN	MLWS
3·3	2·6	1·3	0·6

Or refer to EasyTide at www.ukho.gov.uk/easytide

Charts

	Approach	Harbour
Admiralty	3636, 91, 89	
Imray	C19, C50	C19, C50
Portuguese	23203, 23204, 24205, 24206	27502

Principal lights
2175 **West breakwater** Fl(2)R.6s5·5M
White tower, red bands 7m
2176 **East breakwater** Fl(2)G.6s6·5M
White tower, green bands 6m

Warning
Long surface nets, lit or unlit, may be laid in the bay near the entrance to the harbour, in addition to shorter nets and individual fish pots

Night entry
Straightforward other than in strong onshore winds. The reception pontoon is not lit, but there is sufficient ambient light for all practical purposes

Harbour communications
Port Authority ☎ +351 282 762826
Marina de Lagos ☎ +351 282 770210 *Fax* +351 282 770219
Email marina@marlagos.pt
www.marinadelagos.pt
VHF 09, 16 (0800–2200 1/6–15/9, otherwise 0900–1800)
Weather information VHF Ch 12 at 1000 and 1600 daily from 16/7–31/8.

A historic town with a large established marina

Lagos, a town of Roman origin situated on the banks of the Rio Bensafrim, was once the capital of Portugal. Together with Tavira, Lagos was coveted by Spain when it ruled Portugal. The two Atlantic ports were a major source of conflict between the two nations before Portugal finally gained its independence in the mid-17th century. It is a crowded and active trading, tourist and fishing town. The expedition to capture Ceuta set out from here in 1415. It was later favoured by Henry the Navigator, who founded a company here to trade with the newly discovered regions of Africa. The merchants of Lagos were assiduous in the search for gold and slaves and it was these merchants who played a major role in Portuguese economic expansion during the late medieval period. Under the arches of the old Custom House, there was once the only slave market in Portugal. Within the 5th-century walls the churches of São Sebastião, Santa Maria of Misericórdia, Santo António and the very old São João Hermitage (8th–9th centuries) are all worth a visit. There are many other notable buildings as well as an interesting museum and good nightlife. Its fairs, held in mid-August and mid-October, are lively events, especially Festa dos Descobrimentos, (Festival of the Discoveries) celebrating the town's links with Portugal's maritime history. It is notable for the processions in period costume through the town's streets.

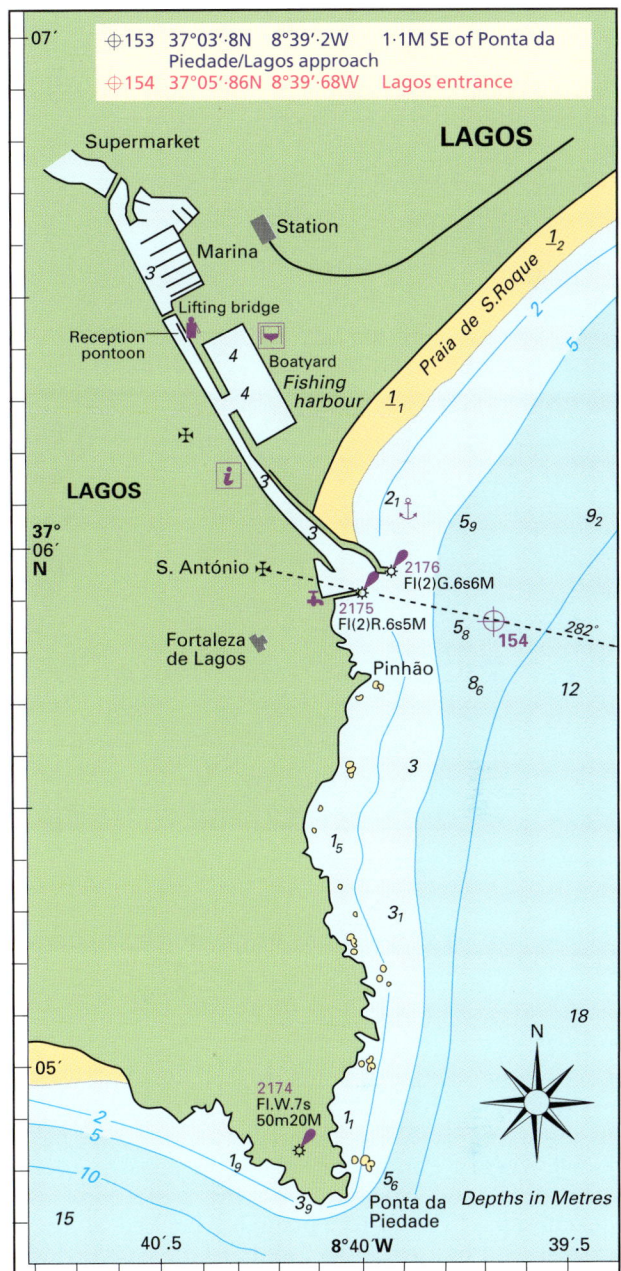

Approach

There is a fish farm (2013) to be avoided between Baleeira and Lagos. It is in a box shaped area orientated N/S E/W, 0·75nm square with four yellow buoys at the corners, all with x topmark and a light.

The entrance to Lagos harbour, looking north

The approximate positions of the northerly buoys are:

NE buoy: 37°04'·362N 008°41'·036W
NW buoy: 37 04·223'N 008 41'·7W

Lagos lies in the lee of Ponta da Piedade, itself at the east end of a stretch of dramatic coastline noted for its cliffs and caves (see Adjacent anchorages, page 228). West of Ponta da Piedade the coast is rocky with cliffs and caves, but to the east, there are beaches past Alvor to Portimão, backed at their eastern end by low cliffs. Lights to the east include Ponta do Altar and Ponta de Alfanzina. If approaching Lagos from the east and on the wind (as is likely), the transit formed by the end of the west breakwater and the church of Santo António on 282° is useful.

From offshore ⊕153 lies 2·1M south of the entrance and a good mile from the rocks of Ponta da Piedade, a course of 349° leading to ⊕154 outside the harbour mouth.

Entrance

Entrance between the twin breakwaters is straightforward, and though a bar periodically builds up southeast of the breakwater heads there is seldom less than 2·5m above datum. Even so, seas can build up in onshore winds. Once through the entrance the channel has a least depth of 3m, as does the marina. There is a 3kn speed limit in the entrance channel and throughout the marina.

Berthing

The marina lies about 0·7M inside the entrance. Secure to the 80m reception pontoon, close downstream of the lifting pedestrian bridge, to arrange a berth and complete formalities. Otherwise the bridge normally opens on demand (VHF Ch 09) during office hours (see page 225), seven days a week. When a train is due to depart or arrive – the station lies just behind the marina – the bridge remains closed for 15 minutes before or after, respectively. Multihull owners should note that the bridge has a limiting width of 11m.

The marina can take 462 yachts of up to 30m LOA, with room always found for visitors. All berths are alongside finger pontoons, with exceptionally large yachts occupying the seven hammerheads. The marina has been popular with British yachtsmen ever since it opened, and has a small but growing (and very loyal) band of long-term residents. It is also a frequent choice for owners wishing to over-winter in the Algarve, whether living aboard or returning home with occasional visits when the northern climate becomes too unpleasant.

Anchorage

Anchor northeast of the east breakwater in 5–6m over good holding in hard sand. The corridor off the beach a little further east, indicated by a number of small yellow buoys, serves the local windsurfing centre and should be left clear. The anchorage is very exposed to south and east, and a southwesterly swell may also work its way around Ponta da Piedade. Land on the beach near the Clube de Vela de Lagos or in the small harbour overlooked by the turretted Fortaleza. There is no possible anchorage inside the harbour itself – the large fishing boat basin may look tempting, but the authorities would not agree.

Formalities

The *GNR–Brigada Fiscal, Polícia Marítima* and *Alfândega* all have offices in the marina reception building – enquire on first arrival whether or not it is necessary to visit them. If anchored off, the skipper should call at all three offices with ship's papers, passports etc.

Facilities

Boatyards Yachtsmen are now well provided for by Sopromar Centro Nautico Lda, Estrada Sopromar , Estaleiro No 1, Lagos 37° 06'·00N 08° 40'·00W (① +351 282 763 889 Fax +351 282 792 135 *Email* geral@sopromar.com www.sopromar.com Opening hours 0830-1200, 1300-1800 Mon-Sat, closed Sunday.

This is a family-run concern which has been highly praised by numerous owners. Yard hours are officially 0830–1200 and 1300–1800 Monday to Saturday, closed Sunday, but in practice at least one member of the Pereira family is nearly always onsite. English, French, German and Spanish are all spoken in addition to Portuguese. Many of the services offered – engineering, electronics, osmosis treatment with the Hotvac system, painting, rigging etc – are detailed below, but there is a very good chance that even if a particular service is not mentioned, Sopromar will be able to handle it.

Other services, including regular checking of unattended yachts left afloat in the marina, are offered by various long-term marina residents and local people – consult the noticeboard in marina reception.

Travel-lift 50-tonne capacity lift at Sopromar, with two waiting pontoons, a wide slipway and a scrubbing grid. The approach through the fishing boat harbour is said to carry adequate depths at all states of the tide and a 30m crane is available for mast removal.

Ashore there is secure lay-up space for at least 140 yachts plus 2,000m² of undercover workshops and storage. The hardstanding is well provided with water and electricity points, and ladders (or substantial steps for the less agile) can be borrowed. Owners are welcome to live aboard (there are immaculate toilets and showers on site), and to do their own work. 15 CCTV cameras monitor the area day and night.

Engineers Sopromar has an extensive engine repair shop, handles welding in all materials and is agent for Volvo Penta, Yanmar and Mercruiser. Pedragosa Engineering ① 282 688056, *Mobile*s 96 7965 481 and 96 9018 894 *Email* mgsnook@bigfoot.com advertise their services for all types of work in stainless-steel and aluminium, including making one-off fittings from scratch. Finally Bluewater Yacht Services (though based mainly in Portimão, see page 234), still have engineers in Lagos who are happy to visit yachts in the marina. Their Lagos office, handling mainly brokerage, will be found on the first floor of the main commercial block.

Electronic and radio repairs At both Sopromar and Bluewater Yacht Services. In addition John Holloway, *Mobile* 91 4902 538 *Email* nojfairchild@hotmail.com handles all kinds of electrical and electronic work including radar etc.

Diver Francisco, *Mobile* 91 8287 551, will change anodes etc.

Sailmaker/sail repairs Fofovelas, ① 282 799425, *Mobile* 91 7550 960, *Email* fofovelas@sapo.pt, fofovelas@mail.pt, make and repair sails, as well as being agent for several well-known names.

Rigging Sopromar has a swage machine and stocks wire of all sizes.

Chandleries The chandlery at Sopromar – open 0900–1200 and 1430–1800 weekdays, 0900–1200 Saturdays – is one of the largest in Portugal, and items not in stock can generally be ordered within 48 hours. AlaRede, ①/*Fax* 282 792238 *Email* alarede@sapo.pt at the north end of the fishing boat basin carries some general chandlery in addition to fishing and diving equipment. There are several good ironmongery and hardware stores in the town.

The Marina de Lagos looking northeast

THE ALGARVE & ANDALUCIA

Charts Local charts are available from both the marina office and AlaRede (see above). The latter will order Portuguese charts from Lisbon if required.

Water At all berths. Yachts anchored off may be able to get water in the small western harbour (but check depths in advance).

Pump Out Available next to the fuel pontoon for black water only.

Showers Single block – but large and very well kept – at the north end of the marina's café/shops complex. Crews of yachts anchored off may be able to shower at the *clube de vela* (see below).

Launderette At the north end of the marina's café/shops complex. Tokens are available at the marina office.

Electricity At all berths, with a variety of voltages available.

Fuel Petrol and diesel pumps on the reception pontoon below the bridge, run by the marina and available during office hours only. Credit cards are not accepted.

Bottled gas Camping Gaz cylinders can be exchanged either at Sopromar or at a hardware shop near the bus station in town. Sopromar can also arrange for other cylinders to be refilled with either propane or butane. A third possibility is the PB service station about 1km along the Portimão road, on the north side, where American yachtsmen have had propane cylinders refilled.

Clube náutico The Clube de Vela de Lagos ① +351 282 762 256 *Fax* +351 282 764 277 www.cvlagos.org *Email* mail@cvlagos.org has premises near the root of the west breakwater.

Weather forecast Posted daily at the marina reception and, during the high season, broadcast on VHF Ch 12 at 1000 and 1600.

Banks Several in the town, plus two cash dispensers in the marina complex.

Shops/provisioning Several large supermarkets, including an enormous Pingo Doce near the road bridge north of the marina (trolleys can be wheeled back and left at one of several designated 'trolley areas' for collection). Good general shopping in the older town on the west bank (direct access over the pedestrian bridge). Limited shopping in the marina complex – mostly tourist items and newspapers, including one supplying UK titles on day of issue.

Produce market Large produce and fish market on the west bank of the river (with great views from the roof terrace).

Cafés, restaurants and hotels Dozens if not hundreds, including several overlooking the marina itself.

Medical services LuzDoc ① 282 780700, a private medical clinic which also handles dental problems, has an office in the marina at Núcleo Gil Eanes 13 and a larger facility in the town, where there is also a public hospital.

Communications

Post office In the town.

Mailing address The marina office will hold mail for visiting yachts – c/o Marina de Lagos, Edifício da Administração, Sítio da Ponte, 8600–780 Lagos, Portugal. It is important that the envelope carries the name of the yacht in addition to that of the addressee.

Public telephones Several around the marina complex.

Internet access Owners can connect their own laptop at the marina office, or use wireless broadband from on board (the necessary cards are on sale at reception). Alternatively there are public terminals at the Regatta Club Bar

Fax service At the marina office *Fax* +351 282 770 219.

Car hire/taxis Can be arranged via the marina office or in the town.

Trains Brand new station just behind the marina complex, the western end of the (distinctly slow) Algarve coastal line.

Air services Faro international airport is about 50 minutes by taxi or, at a fraction of the taxi fare, 90 minutes by train (though a taxi will still be needed between the station and the airport).

Adjacent anchorage

Off the beach at Praia da Luz (37°04'·82N 008°43'·61W), 3·5M west of Ponta da Piedade. Reported to be a pleasant anchorage in settled conditions off a small slipway, but fully exposed to the south.

Right and below Ponta de Piedade on the approach to Lagos. The limestone rocks have been sculpted into caves, arches and pillars and are a popular lunch stop *Jane Russell*

Alvor

Waypoints
⊕155 – 37°'04·9N 8°36'·9W (approach)
⊕156 – 37°06'·87N 8°37'·06W (entrance)

Courses and distances
⊕154 (Lagos entrance) – ⊕156 = 2·3M, 064° or 244°
⊕155 – ⊕156 = 2M, 356° or 176°
⊕156 – ⊕158 (Portimão entrance) = 4·3M, 097° or 277°

Tides
See Lagos, page 233

Charts

Charts	Approach	Harbour
Admiralty	3636, 91, 89	
Imray	C19, C50	
Portuguese	23203, 23204, 24205, 24206	27502

Principal lights
2176.2 **West breakwater** Fl.R.4s8m7M
  White tower, red bands 4m
2176.4 **East breakwater** Fl.G.4s8m7M
  White tower, green bands 4m

Night entry
Not feasible due to shifting shoals which call for eyeball navigation. Any buoys encountered are likely to be unlit.

The Alvor breakwaters and entrance from the south-southeast

Attractive, windswept anchorage flanked by some tourist development

Although until relatively recently Alvor was little more than a small fishing village, it has a significant history, and its formidable fortress attracted the Crusaders in 1189. It is believed the Carthaginians founded Alvor, it was considered an important port by the Romans and it was allowed to issue its own money. Its importance is confirmed by the ruins of a wealthy Roman villa located slightly inland from the present village. After conquest by the Moors, it was finally recovered in 1250. Most of the original village and the castle were destroyed in the earthquakes of 1532 and 1755. Construction of twin breakwaters at the entrance during the early 1990s, allied to extensive dredging within, has opened the Rio Alvor to the cruising yachtsman. Even so, care is still required and the entrance should not be attempted at low water, when swell is running, in onshore winds, on the ebb tide or at night.

The town is touristy but attractive, with good shops, restaurants and cafés, and the anchorage a pleasant change from fishing harbours and marinas – and a paradise for birdwatchers.

Continuing pride in the area's maritime heritage is confirmed by the flawless condition in which the village's old rowing and sailing lifeboat is

THE ALGARVE & ANDALUCIA

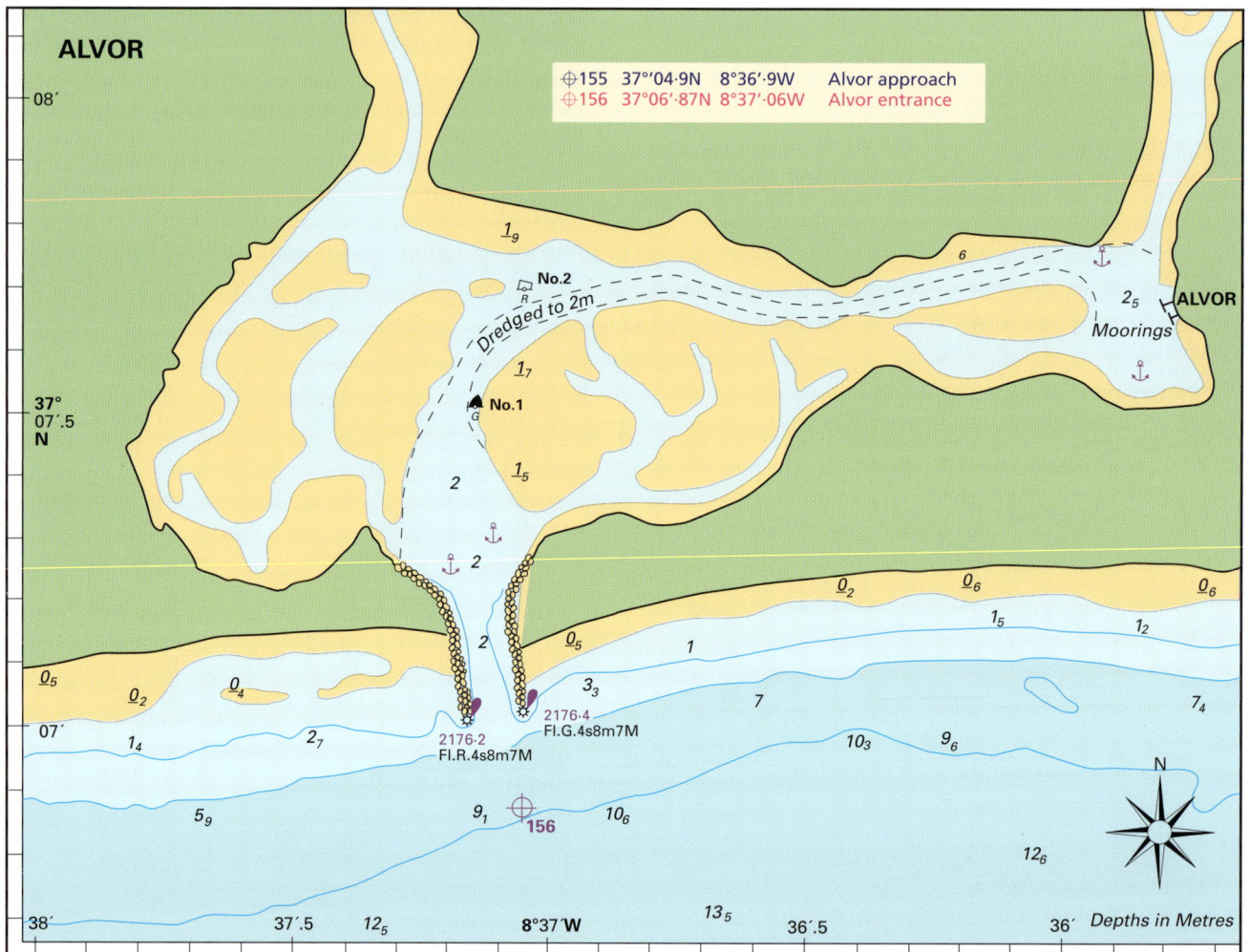

ALVOR

| ⊕155 | 37°'04·9N | 8°36'·9W | Alvor approach |
| ⊕156 | 37°06'·87N | 8°37'·06W | Alvor entrance |

Dredged to 2m

No.2

No.1

ALVOR

Moorings

2176·4 Fl.G.4s8m7M

2176·2 Fl.R.4s8m7M

156

Depths in Metres

maintained. The red doors to her boathouse can hardly be missed, and now feature a glass panel through which she can be admired when they are closed.

Approach

If coastal sailing, Alvor lies 2·3M east of Lagos and 4·3M west of Portimão, surrounded by sandy beaches – the Meia Praia, one of the Algarve's finest, stretches between Lagos and Alvor. The nearest major lights are Ponta da Piedade west of Lagos, and Ponta de Altar, close east of Portimão – Alvor no longer has a major light of its own, though both breakwaters are lit. High man-made sand dunes (created from dredged material) stand close each side of the entrance with conspicuous high-rise apartments further east.

From offshore ⊕155 lies 2M south of the entrance, a course of 356° leading to ⊕156, close outside the harbour mouth.

Entrance

Parallel breakwaters bracket the entrance channel which, in common with other Rio estuaries, needs to be regularly dredged. Although dredged to a nominal 4m this can be reduced to 2m in some years. Enter on the half flood keeping to the middle of the narrow channel on a bearing of approximately 352°.

Once inside, the estuary opens out and it is possible to anchor in the pool just inside the entrance, where at least 2m should be found at all times.

An added complication is that buoy positions inside in the Rio Alvor have been reported to be out of position on occasions over the years. Local advice should be sought.

The narrow, dredged channel leading up to the basin off the town is most easily followed below half tide when the fringing sandbanks are uncovered. Both channel and basin carry a nominal 2m at MLWS, but if in doubt the dinghy could be sent ahead to recce.

Anchorage

Anchor near the entrance, as described above, or off the village to the north of the moorings, an area which, in summer, may become very crowded. It is understood that holding in the river in the approach to the town, which is where visiting yachts have been seen anchored, is not good. Shelter in the basin is excellent and holding good over muddy sand. A small charge is sometimes made. The fairway leading to the fishermen's quay is no longer clearly defined by small craft moorings but must still not be impeded.

There are two pontoons with floating hammerheads, and though both are adorned with

Looking northeast over the shallow lagoon at Alvor, backed by the channel leading to the anchorage off the town

notices stating that it is 'Forbidden to place arts of fishing and to park any kind of boats', both are colonised by flotillas of dinghies. A long painter would clearly be an advantage.

A tidal lagoon just off the bottom left of the photo has been created for the conservation of the local wildlife habitat.

Facilities

Water by can from one of the waterfront cafés, with supermarkets, general shopping and a vast choice of restaurants in the town (the local shell fish is reputed to be particularly good). Services include a post office, public telephones, taxis and buses (at the roundabout), and Portimão station about 5·5km away.

The anchorage off Alvor town looking northwest

THE ALGARVE & ANDALUCIA

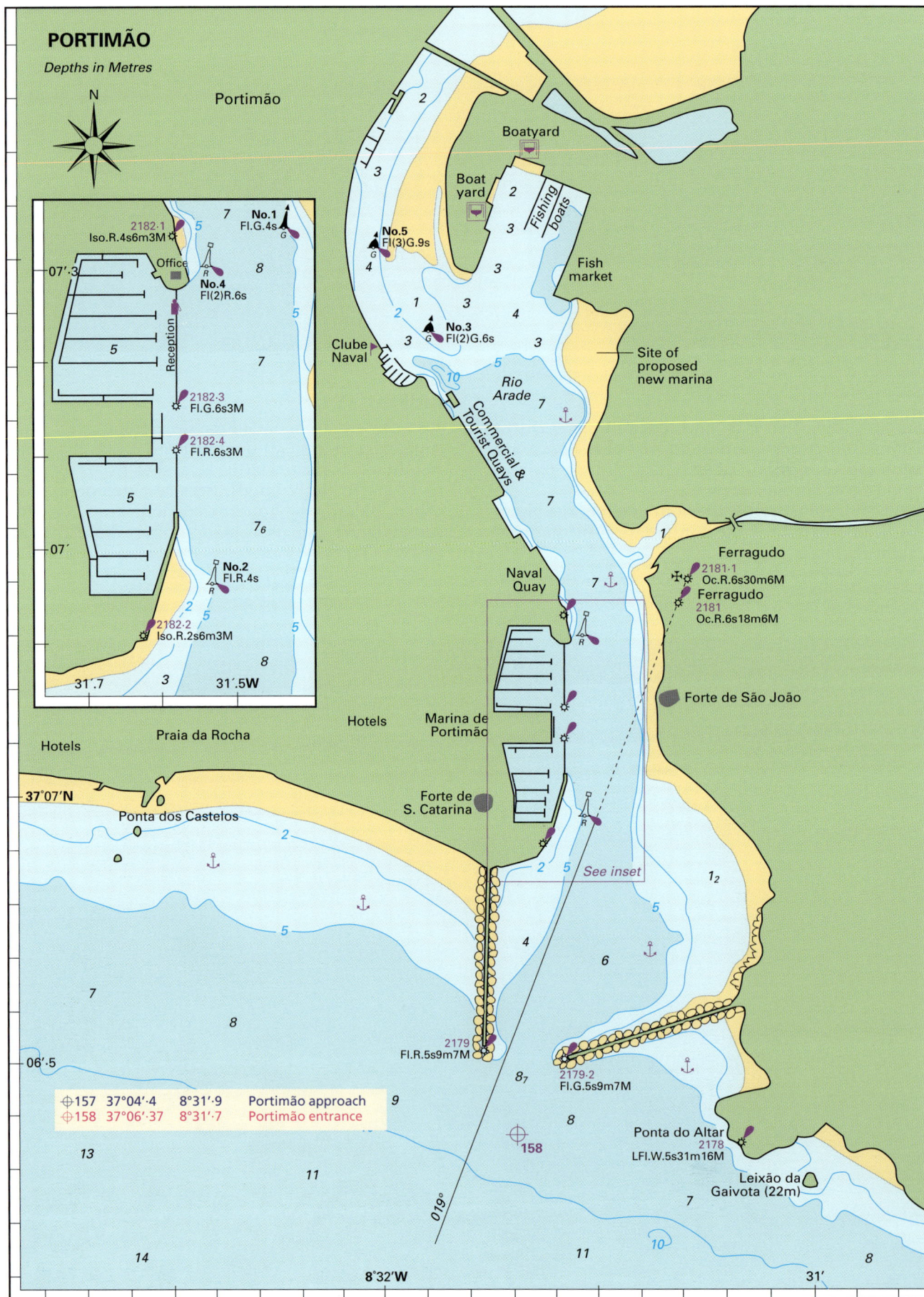

PORTIMÃO

Depths in Metres

N

Portimão

2182·1
Iso.R.4s6m3M

7 **No.1**
Fl.G.4s
G
5

Office
R
No.4
Fl(2)R.6s
8

07'·3

Reception

5

5

7

2182·3
Fl.G.6s3M

2182·4
Fl.R.6s3M

07'

5
5

7 6

No.2
Fl.R.4s
R

2
5

2182·2
Iso.R.2s6m3M

8

5

31'·7   3   31'·5W

Boatyard

Boat
yard   2

Fishing boats

No.5
Fl(3)G.9s
G
4   3

Fish
market

3

2   1   3   4

3   **No.3**
Fl(2)G.6s
G   3

Clube
Naval

10   5

*Rio
Arade*

7

Site of
proposed
new marina

Commercial &
Tourist Quays

7

1

Ferragudo
2181·1
Oc.R.6s30m6M
Ferragudo
2181
Oc.R.6s18m6M

Naval
Quay   7

R

See inset

Marina de
Portimão

Forte de
S. Catarina

R

Forte de São João

1 2

2   5

5

Hotels
Hotels

Praia da Rocha

Hotels

37°07'N

Ponta dos Castelos

2

5

5

4   6

2179
Fl.R.5s9m7M

8 7

2179·2
Fl.G.5s9m7M

8

7
8

06'·5

⊕ 157	37°04'·4	8°31'·9	Portimão approach
⊕ 158	37°06'·37	8°31'·7	Portimão entrance

9

13   11

019°

⊕
158

Ponta do Altar
2178
LFl.W.5s31m16M

Leixão da
Gaivota (22m)

7

14   11   10   8

8°32'W   31'

Portimão

Waypoints
⊕157 – 37°04'·4N 8°31'·9W (approach)
⊕158 – 37°06'·37N 8°31'·7W (entrance)

Courses and distances
⊕154 (Lagos entrance) – ⊕158 = 6·4M, 085° or 265°
⊕156 (Alvor entrance) – ⊕158 = 4·3M, 097° or 277°
⊕157 – ⊕158 = 2M, 005° or 185°
⊕157 – ⊕159 (Albufeira) = 14M, 096° or 276°
⊕157 – ⊕161 (Vilamoura) = 19·5M, 097° or 277°

Tides
Standard port Lisbon
Mean time differences
HW –0025 ±0010; LW –0030 ±0005
Heights in metres

MHWS	MHWN	MLWN	MLWS
3·3	2·6	1·4	0·7

Or refer to EasyTide at www.ukho.gov.uk/easytide

Charts

	Approach	Harbour
Admiralty	3636, 91, 89	83
Imray	C19, C50	C50
Portuguese	23203, 23204, 24206	26310

Principal lights
2178 **Ponta do Altar** LFl.5s31m16M 290°-vis-170°
  Square white tower and building 10m
2181 **Ldg Lts 019°** *Front* **Ferragudo** Iso.R.6s18m6M
  White tower, red bands 4m

2181.1 *Rear* 54m from front Iso.R.6s30m6M
  White tower, red bands 5m
2179 **West breakwater** Fl.R.5s9m7M
  White tower, red bands 7m
2179.2 **East breakwater** Fl.G.5s9m7M
  White tower, green bands 7m
2182.2 **Marina, southeast**
  Iso.R.2s6m3M White column, red bands
2182.4 **Marina south pontoon head**
  Fl.R.6s3M White column, red bands
2182.3 **Marina north pontoon head**
  Fl.G.6s3M White column, green bands
2182.1 **Marina, northeast**
  Iso.R.4s 6m3M White column, red bands

Night entry
No problem – spacious, well lit and with generous depths.

Harbour communications
Marina de Portimão ☎ +351 282 400 680 *Fax* +351 282 400 681 *Email* info@marinaportimao.com.pt
www.marinadeportimao.com.pt
VHF Ch 09, 16 (0830–2100 1 July to 31 August, otherwise 0900–1800).
Weather information in Portuguese and English VHF Ch 09 at 1000 daily from 1 July to 31 August

Portimão from the south. The anchorage can be seen inside the east breakwater

All-weather entrance leading to a large, modern marina

Portimão on the Rio Arade has long been a busy fishing harbour, also handling small naval and commercial vessels. Since 2000, however, the waterfront on the west side near the entrance has been transformed with the opening of the large Marina de Portimão. Almost overnight Portimão began to rival Lagos and Vilamoura in its provision of berths and other services for visiting yachts. The marina staff speak English and their attitude is helpful and friendly.

The town of Portimão, on the west bank nearly 2M from the harbour mouth, is old and agreeable, but the beach resort of Praia da Rocha is somewhat brash. The region's undoubted gem is the waterside village of Ferragudo on the east side of the estuary. If settled in the marina, make the effort to launch the dinghy, cross the river, and enjoy a lunch of *sardinhas* grilled on a charcoal brazier on the tiny quay with seagulls wheeling overhead. A stroll through the village's steep cobbled alleys (mostly impassable to cars) will work off any resulting somnolence.

Approach

If inshore sailing, from Lagos to Portimão the coast consists of sandy beaches with a backdrop of hills. East of Portimão there are a few small sandy beaches but the shore is mainly rocky with cliffs. There are no off-lying hazards.

From offshore ⊕157 lies 2M south of the entrance, a course of 005° leading to ⊕158 close outside the harbour mouth.

The anchorage and moorings off Ferragudo looking W towards the Naval Quay *Jane Russell*

Entrance

Entrance is safe in all but the heaviest onshore conditions, and should present no problems by day or night. The ends of the breakwaters are lit – these lights line up on 097° for those coming from Lagos. The charted leading line to enter the harbour itself is 019° (two red and white striped posts close east of Ferragudo church). However this leads close to a growing shoal around the head of the west breakwater, and about equidistant between the two heads offers better depths. From there leave buoy No.2 close to port before ducking through the marina entrance (both sides of which are lit) and securing to the inner side of the north pontoon.

If venturing further upstream, the buoyage is straightforward with a pair of lit buoys and then two unlit starboard hand buoys. The channel as far as Ponta São Francisco has a least depth of around 7m, but soundings shoal rapidly outside the buoyed channel.

Berthing

Nearly all the inner side of the marina's north pontoon is used for reception, though during office hours a yacht which makes contact via VHF or mobile phone may well be routed directly to a berth in the marina proper. Even when the tide is running at spring ebb it is claimed that the marina remains

Looking across the river towards the Forte de São João, with port hand buoy No.4 in the foreground *Anne Hammick*

The anchorage inside the breakwater at Portimao looking SSW towards the entrance *Jane Russell*

With little unused space near the marina, a sizeable boatyard has been established upriver in the old fishing harbour. The old centre of Portimão can be seen across the river at right, with the Clube Naval de Portimão and smallcraft basin (not open to visitors) at left

unaffected and securing is never a problem, though it has been reported that swell works into the north basin in southerly winds. Reception is housed in the circular orange building overlooking the pontoon and operates 0830–2030 from 1 July to 31 August and 0900–1800 at other times.

Although having a total capacity of 620 berths including one 50m slot, nearly all in 5m or more depths, the marina has become crowded with the larger berths being particularly popular. Its only real downside, however, is its sheer size. Those berthed centrally face a lengthy walk to shops, toilets and showers (a bicycle would quickly prove its worth), while those in the south basin, though conveniently near most of the facilities, may be kept awake far into the night by music from the bars and karaoke joints. In compensation, there is an excellent beach nearby and swimming pool for hotel and marina users. Security throughout the marina is excellent, with two guards patrolling at all times in addition to card access gates and facilities.

There are no other visitors' berthing option on the Rio Arade. The upstream basin near the new Clube Naval building is reserved for local smallcraft, and visitors are no longer welcome on the old yacht pontoon just below the bridge. Rumours of a 'new marina' beyond the bridge relate to a private leisure club with a single, equally private, pontoon for small motorboats, limited by an air height of 5m beneath the old road bridge.

It is understood that plans to build a second yacht marina on the east side of the river just upstream of Ferragudo remain a pipe dream. A website exists with an artist's impression at www.marinasdeferragudo.com (℡ +351 282 414 480 *Fax* +351 213 841 666). If this comes to fruition a further 330 berths for vessels of up to 50m and 5m draught would become available.

Anchorage

The anchorage inside the east breakwater is secure with good holding in sand, though sometimes affected by swell and/or wash. It would be a safe choice if arriving by night, but note that the bottom shelves steeply between the 5m and 2m contours. Alternatively, anchor off Ferragudo near the fishing boat moorings, in 3–4m over mud, but note that available space is very variable. Be sure to leave the marked channel clear as the fishing fleet appears to leave en masse in the hours before daybreak (if the throb of their engines does not wake you, their wash will).

To go ashore at Ferragudo, land your dinghy at the steps on the quay on top of which there is a stout iron ring. At low water, you will need a long line to reach the ring on the top of the quay. Also note that numerous taxi/ferry boats land passengers at the steps, so you should do your best to leave the dinghy out of their way.

No charge is made for anchoring in either spot.

A dinghy can safely be left at the marina, for a charge, but note that this can be substantial! A marina landing also involves a long walk into the town. Upstream possibilities are limited, though it would certainly be worth asking both at the smallcraft basin and at the *Clube Naval* de Portimão (where, if permission is granted, it would clearly be tactful to patronise the bar).

Formalities

All paperwork is carried out in the marina office with copies passed to the usual officials. None need to be seen, but non-EU registered yachts, or those carrying non-EU citizens, may be visited by one or more sets of officials in the days after arrival.

Facilities

Boatyard The marina's boatyard is some distance away in the old fishing harbour just short of the old road bridge (see plan p.232), with the compensation of almost unlimited lay-up area. Security is good, with high fences, gates locked overnight and regular patrols. Lockerage can be rented if required.

While lifting, pressure-hosing and chocking-up are carried out by marina employees, all other work is done by specialist contractors – see below. DIY is permitted, and owners may live aboard whilst ashore (the yacht area is provided with a single, rather basic, shower and toilet). There is a supermarket within walking distance.

Travel-lift Choice of two at the boatyard, of 50-tonne and 300-tonne capacity respectively. The latter is believed to be the largest travel-hoist in mainland Portugal. Book at the marina office.

Engineers, electronics, and general maintenance Amongst the four or five contractors who regularly work in the yard, Bluewater Yacht Services, ☎ +351 282 432 405 *Fax* +351 282 432 406 *Email* info@bluewateralgarve.com www.bluewateralgarve.com, who also have an office near the marina's northern basin, appear to offer by far the widest range of services. Owner Paul Mallett is an engineer (as well as an Ocean Yachtmaster) and other members of the eight permanent staff can handle electrical work and electronics (installation and repair of water-makers and refrigeration are specialities), repairs in all materials, osmosis treatment (including slurry blasting and peeling), painting, in fact all disciplines necessary to keep yachts of up to 20m or so in good working order. Unattended yachts can be collected from and returned to the marina, and finally all work, or damage, should one be so unlucky, can be overseen/assessed by a fully qualified surveyor, recognised by Lloyds. Languages spoken currently include English, Portuguese, Spanish, German, Dutch and some French, and Paul and his team are happy to travel throughout southern Portugal and Spain to carry out work on boats in situ.

Sailmaker/sail repairs Marine Canvas, ☎ 967 084 927 *Email* marinecanvas@sapo.pt, in the boatyard area make covers, awnings etc, and can handle minor sail repairs. While not sailmakers themselves, Bluewater Yacht Services have contacts throughout the Algarve and can arrange for sails of almost any size to be made or repaired.

Rigging Bluewater Yacht Services can supply and fit all sizes of rigging, and have in the past replaced entire rigs on yachts in the 20m range.

Chandlery Good selection at Aradenáutica Lda in the boatyard area. Failing that, the resources of Lagos and Vilamoura are both within reach by train.

Charts A stock of local charts is held by the marina office, while Portuguese charts for more distant waters can be ordered overnight from Lisbon.

Liferaft servicing Another item in the Bluewater Yacht Services portfolio

Water Throughout the marina, and in the boatyard.

Showers Two blocks in the marina complex, with card access, but quite a long walk from some berths.

Launderette Next to the marina office, with six washers and three dryers all token-operated, open 0900–1800. Again, a long walk from some berths.

Electricity Throughout the marina, and in the boatyard.

Fuel Two diesel and petrol pumps near the root of the north pontoon, operational during office hours. Fuel should be paid for in cash – though a credit card will be accepted in an emergency, a surcharge will be imposed (and note that it is a long walk from the fuel berth to the marina's single cash dispenser).

There is a second yacht fuelling berth just upstream of the *clube naval*, but operating times and other details are not known.

Bottled gas Camping Gaz is available in the town, and it has been reported that other cylinders can be refilled at the BP service station (ask for directions at the marina desk). Allow several days for the latter.

Weather forecast Posted daily at the marina office and during the high season, broadcast on VHF Ch 09 at 1000.

Clube naval The Clube Naval de Portimão has smart new premises complete with their own pontoon on the Quai Vasco da Gama, just upriver of the smallcraft basin.

Banks In Praia da Rocha and Portimão, with a cash dispenser near the southwest corner of the marina's south basin.

Shops/provisioning In Praia da Rocha and Portimão, though considerably better (and cheaper) in the latter. See also under Buses, below.

There is a mini-market near the southwest corner of the marina, opposite the cash dispenser. Nearby are the usual range of tourist shops and newsagents. Limited shopping in Ferragudo.

Produce markets In Portimão and Ferragudo.

Cafés, restaurants and hotels Every second building in Praia da Rocha, if not even more, with a large hotel fronting much of the marina. The waterfront restaurant on the end of the central spur is said to be good.

Medical services In Praia da Rocha and Portimão – contact is best made via the marina office.

Communications

Post offices In Praia da Rocha and Portimão.

Mailing address The marina office will hold mail for visiting yachts – c/o Marina de Portimão, Edificio Administrativo, 8500 Portimão, Portugal. It is important that the envelope carries the name of the yacht in addition to that of the addressee.

Telephones Several kiosks around the marina complex, and in the town.

Internet access Wireless broadband has been installed throughout the marina, and there is a desk in the reception building with telephone points to which laptops can be connected. Failing this there is free internet access at the library in the old town, plus several cybercafés in nearby Praia da Rocha.

Fax service At the marina – ☎/*Fax* +351 282 400 681.

Car hire/taxis No shortage. Both can be ordered via marina reception.

Buses Frequent if slow. A minibus runs daily from the reception area to the Modelo supermarket and the old town – enquire at the marina office for times.

Trains Station north of Portimão, and a convenient way to reach Faro airport.

Air services Faro International Airport is about 55km away.

Adjacent anchorage

Good anchorage in 5m is to be found 1·6M west of the west breakwater at Portimao at the west end of Praia da Rocha beach. It is well sheltered from a strong northwest wind and landing can be made on a small beach amid rocks and stacks before walking to the main beach. Beware a shoal patch carrying less than 2m extending 70m southeast from the southernmost of the two rocks off Ponta dos Castelos, itself 0·7M west of the breakwater. The anchorage is probably suitable for daytime use only, and open to the south.

Albufeira

Waypoints
⊕159 – 37°03'N 8°14'·5W approach
⊕160 – 37°04'·82N 8°15'·24W (entrance)

Courses and distances
⊕157 (Portimão) – ⊕159 = 14M, 096° or 276°
⊕159 – ⊕160 = 1·9M, 342° or 162°
⊕159 – ⊕161 (Vilamoura) = 5·5M, 101° or 287°

Tides
Standard port Lisbon
Mean time differences
HW –0010 ±0025; LW 0000 ±0005
Heights in metres

MHWS	MHWN	MLWN	MLWS
3·6	2·8	1·5	0·7

Charts

	Approach	Harbour
Admiralty	91, 89	
Imray	C19, C50	
Portuguese	(90), 23203, 23204, 24206	(27503)

Principal lights
2196 **Albufeira** Oc.6s31m11M White column, red bands
2196.02 **North breakwater** Fl(2)G.5s9m4M
White column, three green bands 3m
2196.01 **South breakwater** Fl(2)R.5s9m4M
White column, two red bands 3m
Marina E Inner channel, north side Fl.G.2s5m1·5M
White column, three green bands 3m
Marina W Inner channel, south side Fl.R.2s5m1·5M
White column, three red bands 3m

Night entry
Though narrow, the entrance is well lit and should
present no problems in normal conditions. However
swells may build up outside in strong southerlies, making
close approach in darkness unwise

Harbour communications
Marina de Albufeira ☎ +351 289 510 180 *Fax* +351 289
510 189 *Email* info@marinaalbufeira.com
www.marinaalbufeira.com
(0900–2100 1/6–15/9, 0900–1800 1/11–31/3, 0900–1900 at
other times)
VHF Ch 09

The harbour and marina at Albufeira looking west-northwest

THE ALGARVE & ANDALUCIA

ALBUFEIRA

Depths in Metres

Praia do Peneco

N

37° 05' N

2 5

3 3

3 3

Reception

4

4 Boatyard

4

Fl.G.2s

Fl.R.2s

Moorings Fl.G

Fl.R.2s

G

R

Smallcraft Moorings Fl.G

Fl(2)G.5s9m4M
2196·02

Fl.R.2s
R

Albufeira
Oc.6s31m11M
2196

Fl(2)R.5s9m4M
2196·01

Dredged to 5m

160

04'·6 N

8°16'W

15'·5W

| ⊕159 | 37°03'N | 8°14'·5W | Albufeira approach |
| ⊕160 | 37°04'·82N | 8°15'·24W | Albufeira entrance |

A marina distant from the main tourist centre

Berthed in the Marina de Albufeira it is hard to believe that the somewhat brash tourist resort of the same name is less than 2km away. Due at least in part to its position in a natural amphitheatre, the complex forms its own enclosed world, subtly emphasised by the quirky architecture and unusual colours of the surrounding buildings.

The inner basin is overlooked by apartments, villas, shops restaurants and bars, and is a lively spot.

Approach

The marina lies just under 15M east of Portimão and 5M west of Vilamoura. The approach is straightforward and without hazards, marked by Ponta Baleeira light on the cliffs close south in addition to the two breakwater lights. However by day the stone breakwaters may be difficult to pick out against the cliffs behind, particularly with an afternoon sun. Currently the marina lies at the

southwest end of the considerable Albufeira conurbation, but it can only be a matter of time before this leapfrogs onto the ochre cliffs to the southwest. Several fishing floats were observed in the approach, a potential hazard to a yacht's propeller, particularly after dark.

From offshore ⊕159 lies 2M southeast of the entrance, a course of 316° leading to ⊕160, close outside the harbour mouth.

Entrance

The marina's outer entrance is just over 100m wide and faces almost due east. Although this may well make entry in southerly winds more feasible than is the case with some of its neighbours, it should still be approached with caution in these conditions. The slightly angled channel through the outer harbour is indicated by four good-sized buoys, all of which are lit, and is dredged to 5m. Smallcraft lie to moorings on either side of the channel.

The long, relatively narrow cutting which gives access to the inner basin carries 4m along its length, as does the small intermediate basin where larger yachts are berthed. The long reception pontoon lies on the starboard hand near the far end of this passage, with the marina office behind. Surge may affect the reception pontoon even in relatively light conditions making generous fendering wise.

Berthing

The Marina de Albufeira contains 475 berths, including one for a yacht of 30m or more, all alongside finger pontoons. Around 80 berths are reserved for visiting yachts in depths which decrease from 4m near the entrance to 2·5m in the western part of the basin. Once inside, shelter is excellent, though some surge may penetrate as far as the larger yacht berths. Security is also taken seriously, with CCTV and security patrols in addition to card access to the pontoon gates (most of which are, thoughtfully, provided with a small plan of the marina with essential services marked).

The office staff speak Spanish and some French in addition to English. Most unusually there is no weekly or monthly berthing rate, the shortest 'long term' it is possible to book for being nine months.

Formalities

None of the usual triumvirate of officials, the *GNR–Brigada Fiscal, Polícia Marítima* and *Alfândega*, have offices on site, though copies of the paperwork are circulated to them electronically. For skippers of EU-registered vessels with EU crews arriving from within Portugal, that is the end of the matter. Others might receive a visit from *Imigração* (immigration) or perhaps *Alfândega* (customs), though the onus was on the officials to visit the yacht rather than vice versa. Marina officials will advise.

Anchorage

Anchoring in the outer harbour is not permitted – in any case there would be no room to swing between the moored smallcraft – and though in theory one could drop a hook outside in the wide bay running east to Albufeira resort there is little protection.

Facilities

Boatyard Contractors operate within the boatyard area to the south of the intermediate basin. For services see below.

Travel-lift 70-tonne capacity lift plus 6·3-tonne crane – book at reception. The marina does not provide props, which are currently available only from boatyard contractors.

Engineers, electronics and maintenance Although PowerCool *Mobile* 91 7866 373 *Fax* 289 324 857 *Email* info@powercoolmarine.com www.powercool.org, specialises in generators and air-conditioning (Kohler and Dometic respectively), British owner Michael Killeen is cheerfully flexible and happy to handle anything from engineering (he spent 10 years working on large aircraft engines) through electronics to antifouling and polishing. They are also a Volvo Penta agent and service centre. Some spares are held in stock, while others can be ordered direct from the manufacturer or, failing that, fabricated locally. Should a task be outside PowerCool's scope, Michael will almost certainly 'know a man who can'.

The marina basin at Albufeira. The reception pontoon can just be seen at the head of the narrow approach channel on the right

Looking across the approach channel towards the reception pontoon, with a large ketch tucked in behind it *Anne Hammick*

Ben Smith (see *Chandlery*, below) is also an experienced marine engineer, formerly based in Vilamoura.

General maintenance Riominho Náutica *Mobile* 96 8492 215 *Email* albufeira@riominho.com www.riominho.com handles yacht valeting and straightforward maintenance including painting/antifouling and minor GRP repairs. Alternatively Peter Heitman, *Mobile* 91 7262 359, offers carpentry services.

Diver Available via the marina office.

Sailmaker The boatyard buildings contain a purpose-built sail loft, but may not be operational. However Vilamoura is not far up the road…

Chandlery Tudo Marine Services Lda, *Mobile* 91 8608 809 and 91 2556 134, *Email* tudomarine@yahoo.co.uk, run by Ben Smith and Gavin Hawkins has premises in the boatyard area. Stock focuses on general chandlery and engine spares.

Nearby is Santa María Artigos Náuticos, whose other shop overlooks the smallcraft marina at Faro. General chandlery, lifejackets and some clothes are likely to feature, with good English spoken.

Water At all berths.

Showers Temporarily housed in portacabins on the central spur, with two permanent shower blocks planned for the north side of the basin.

Launderette A launderette is likely to be built in due course, but in the meantime laundry can be left at the marina office to be done elsewhere.

Electricity At all berths.

Fuel Diesel and petrol pumps on a pontoon on the port side, opposite and slightly beyond the reception pontoon, open during office hours. Credit cards are accepted.

Holding tank pump-out At the fuel pontoon.

Bottled gas Camping Gaz exchanges at a filling station in the town, but no refills. It would also be worth enquiring at the chandlery.

Weather forecast Posted daily at the marina office.

Clube náutico Planned for the central spur.

Bank A cash dispenser is in the marina complex.

Shops, provisioning Mini-market in the marina complex, with other shops about 400m (most of it uphill) to the northeast.

Cafés, restaurants and hotels Several cafés and restaurants in the buildings overlooking the inner basin (some of which offer discounts to berth-holders and/or will deliver to yachts). A hotel is to be included in the second phase of the development.

Medical services First aid clinic in Albufeira and hospital in Faro – the office will be happy to advise.

Communications

Post office Planned, but not a priority. Several in Albufeira.

Mailing address The marina office will hold mail for visiting yachts – c/o Marina de Albufeira, Sítio da Orada, 8201-918 Albufeira, Portugal. Envelopes should give both the name of the yacht and that of the addressee.

Telephones Numerous kiosks dotted around the marina complex.

Internet access Visitors can either use one of the office computers to check Email, or bring their own laptop to the reception building. Wireless broadband may be installed in the longer term.

Fax service At the marina office, *Fax* 289 514292.

Car hire/taxis Can be ordered via the marina office.

Buses Bus stop at the roundabout not far from the reception building.

Trains Station at Ferreiras, about 6km distant.

Air services Faro airport is 30km away – about 30 minutes by taxi.

Vilamoura

Waypoints
⊕161 – 37°02′N 8°07′·8W (approach)
⊕162 – 37°04′N 8°07′·35W (entrance)

Courses and distances
⊕157 (Portimão) – ⊕161 = 19·5M, 097° or 277°
⊕159 (Albufeira) – ⊕161 = 5·5M, 101° or 287°
⊕161 – ⊕162 = 2M, 010° or 190°
⊕161 – ⊕163 (Cabo de Santa María) = 14·3M, 117°
   or 297°
⊕161 – ⊕165 (Tavira, via ⊕163) = 30·3M, 117° & 056°
   or 236° & 297°
⊕161 – ⊕167 (Río Guadiana, via ⊕163) = 38·9M,
   117° & 064° or 244° & 297°

Tides
Standard port Lisbon
Mean time differences (at Albufeira)
HW –0010 ±0025; LW 0000 ±0005
Heights in metres

MHWS	MHWN	MLWN	MLWS
3·6	2·8	1·5	0·7

Charts	Approach	Harbour
Admiralty	91, 89, 93	
Imray	C19, C50	C50
Portuguese	23203, 23204, 24206	(27503)

Principal lights
2197.2 **Vilamoura** Fl.5s17m19M
   Red framework on cream and red control tower 16m
Vilamoura marina
2197.3 **West breakwater** Fl.R.4s13m5M
   White tower, red bands 7m
2197.4 **East breakwater** Fl.G.4s13m5M
   White tower, green bands 7m
Quarteira (fishing) harbour
2198.1 **West mole** Fl.R.3s12m6M
   Red tower, white bands 6m
2198.2 **West mole spur** Fl(2)R.4s9m3M
   Red tower, white bands 4m
2198.3 **East mole** Fl.G.3s12m6M
   Green tower, white bands 6m

Night entry
Straightforward other than in strong southerlies.

Harbour communications
Port Authority ☎ +351 289 313 214
Fax +351 289 310 580
Marina de Vilamoura ☎ +351 289 310 560 *Fax* +351 289
310 580 *Email* marinavilamoura@lusort.com
www.marinadevilamoura.com
VHF Ch 09, 16 call *Vilamoura Radio* (24 hours)
Weather information in Portuguese and English:
VHF Ch 12 at 1000 daily.

The approach to Vilamoura Marina with the reception pontoon in the centre, the boatyard on the left and the large basin behind

THE ALGARVE & ANDALUCIA

Large, well-established marina backed by vast tourist complex

The marina and its adjacent boatyard are surrounded by a large tourist complex which includes four golf courses, a casino and countless hotels, and offers a wide choice of open-air cafés, boutiques, souvenir shops etc. In contrast, a serious effort is being made to establish a 200 hectare Environmental Park just west of the marina to preserve the wetland home of many species of birds. There are also Roman ruins close by, together with a small museum or, for the less culturally inclined, an excellent beach within a short dinghy ride, or in walking distance if berthed on the west side of the basin.

Vilamoura is a popular and secure place to leave a yacht, either long-term or for a few months – perhaps between a summer passage southwards and the late autumn passage to Madeira, the Canaries and beyond – in which case its proximity to Faro airport is an obvious advantage.

Approach

The coast on both sides of Vilamoura is low and rocky and the breakwaters may be difficult to pick out, but the marina is surrounded by conspicuous tower blocks, particularly to the east where a large pale pink hotel stands close to the entrance. A small fishing harbour lies a few hundred metres east of the entrance, with the tower blocks of Quarteira beyond. There is no excuse for confusing the two entrances. Vilamoura to the west is considerably larger, and though the light characteristics of each breakwater pair are surprisingly similar the marina has its own major light close to the reception quay. Nevertheless more than one arriving yacht has managed to end up in the wrong place.

From offshore ⊕161 lies 2M south of the entrance, a course of 010° leading to ⊕162, on the 5m line close to the harbour mouth.

Entrance

The entrance is about 100m wide, between breakwaters which stretch a good 500m from the shore, and can be dangerous in strong southerly winds (true of most Algarve harbours). Previously congested with moored fishing boats the outer basin remains empty, but anchoring is not permitted.

Head for the 60m wide channel leading to the inner basin and secure to the long reception pontoon beneath the control tower and offices. Depths in the outer harbour are approximately 4m, decreasing to 3·3m off the reception pontoon and in the southern part of the basin and 2m in the northeast section. Although silting is an ongoing problem, particularly in the outer basin, periodic dredging has largely kept it at bay.

Berthing

The Marina de Vilamoura contains around 1,000 berths (the exact number appears to be flexible) and can take vessels of 60m or more. On arrival secure to

The inner basin at Vilamoura Marina seen from the southwest

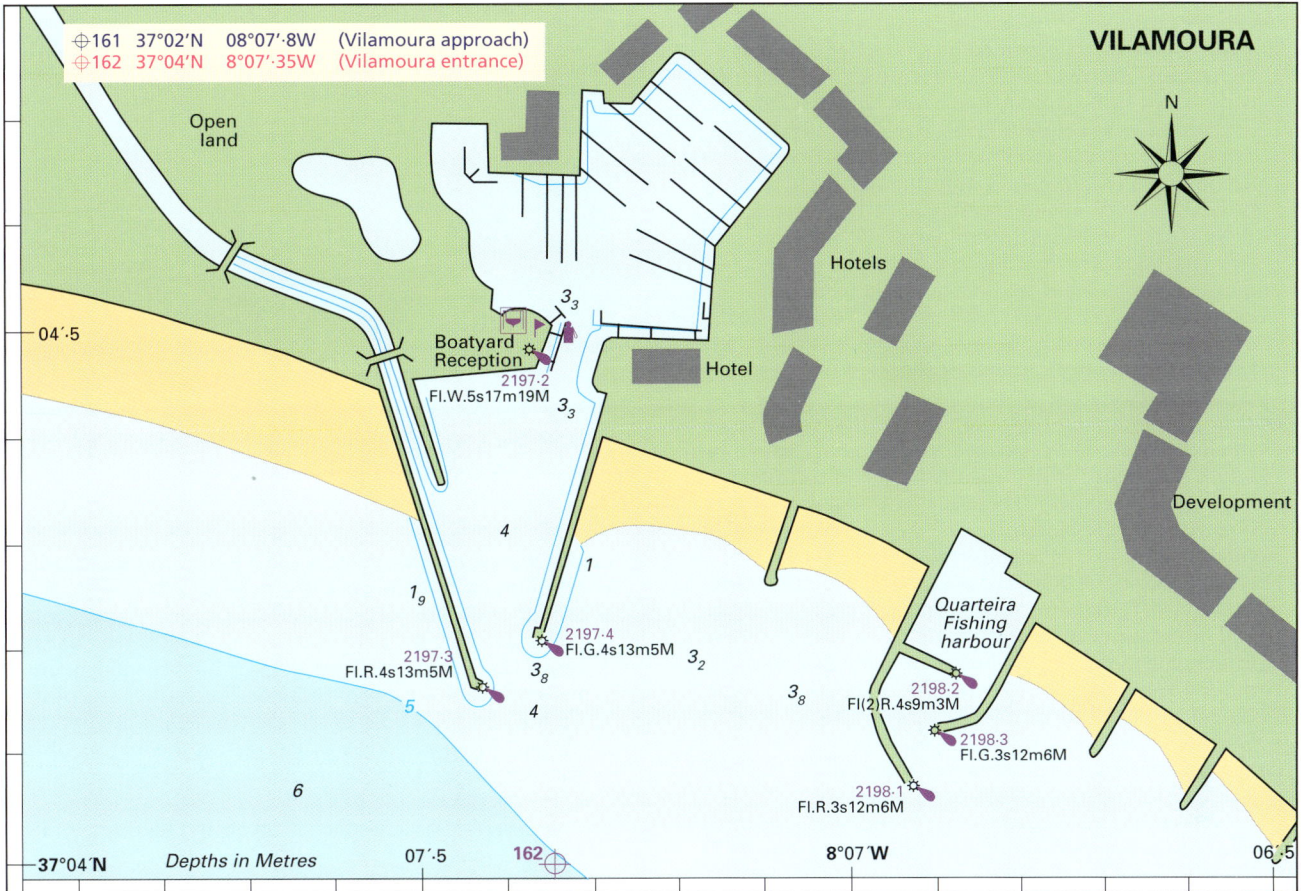

⊕161 37°02'N   08°07'·8W   (Vilamoura approach)
⊕162 37°04'N   8°07'·35W   (Vilamoura entrance)

VILAMOURA

Open land

Hotels

Hotel

Boatyard Reception
2197·2
Fl.W.5s17m19M

Development

Quarteira Fishing harbour

2197·4
Fl.G.4s13m5M

2197·3
Fl.R.4s13m5M

2198·2
Fl(2)R.4s9m3M

2198·3
Fl.G.3s12m6M

2198·1
Fl.R.3s12m6M

37°04'N   *Depths in Metres*   07'·5   162   8°07'W   06'·5

the reception pontoon until clearance procedures have been completed and a berth allocated. Office hours all year are from 0830 to 1930 (1/4–31/5), to 2130 (1/6–15/9), to 1930 (16/9–3/10), and to 1830 (1/11– 31/3). If arriving outside these times it will be necessary to remain at the reception pontoon until the offices open at 0830 in the morning. Water and electricity are both available on the reception pontoon. Security throughout the marina is assured by CCTV, frequent patrols and pontoon gates operated by electronic cards.

Formalities

All paperwork (for which ship's papers, passports and evidence of insurance are required) is carried out in the marina office overlooking the reception pontoon. Where non-EU nationals and/or yachts are involved it is still necessary for the skipper to visit *Imigração*, while the *Alfândega* are most interested in yachts which have arrived from outside Portugal, and particularly from outside the EU. Both offices open seven days a week, maintaining the same hours as the marina office itself.

The outer breakwaters of Vilamoura Marina seen from the southwest with Quarteira fishing harbour in the background

THE ALGARVE & ANDALUCIA

Facilities

Boatyard Services are provided by a range of different contractors, or owners can do their own work. Largest is probably BEB Carpentry Services, ☎ +351 289 302 797 *Mobile* +351 96 9097 580 *Fax* +351 289 302 721 *Email* bebcarpentry@hotmail.com run by Brian Brennan which can handle almost anything in timber or GRP. Others include Heitmann Yacht Services, ☎ +351 289 360 610; Technimarine, ☎ +351 289 301 070 *Fax* +351 289 322 347 *Email* tecni-marine@mail.telepac.pt; Lacomar Lda (osmosis experts), ☎ +351 289 312 470 *Mobile* 96 5089 867; and Emmanuel Bosch, *Mobile* +351 96 8959 359, who between them offer carpentry services, painting and GRP repairs.

Travel-lifts 30- and 60-tonne capacity hoists, plus two smaller cranes. The concreted hardstanding, which can take a maximum of 200 yachts, has good security, and DIY is not a problem. There is also a tidal grid for boats drawing less than 2m.

Engineers A number of engineering workshops are established in the boatyard area, including agents for Volvo and Yanmar and others specialising in welding and fabrication. A full list, including contact numbers, is included in the marina brochure (available on request from mid February onwards).

Electrical, electronic and radio repairs Janusz Oszczepalski, ☎ +351 289 322 615

Sailmaker/sail repairs The JP Velas-Doyle loft ☎ +351 289 314 827 *Fax* +351 289 321 159 *Email* j.p.velas@mail.telepac.pt will be found on the second floor of the reception building. Peter and Joanne Keeping, who together with their team speak seven languages, will build new sails from scratch, repair old ones, and handle canvaswork including spray hoods and biminis. They also supply roller furling gears and running rigging.

Chandlery A branch of Náutica Capitalcar, ☎ +351 289 314 764, overlooks the boatyard area – well-stocked and carrying a good range of maintenance materials. Open 0900–1200 and 1400–1800 weekdays, 0900–1230 Saturday. Other chandleries exist around the marina basin, but tending towards the decorative rather than the practical.

Charts Both Admiralty and Portuguese charts can be ordered from Lisbon via the marina office.

Water At all berths and the reception/fuel pontoon.

Showers Behind the marina office (effectively in the boatyard compound) plus two other blocks around the marina basin, all with card access.

Holding tank pump-out A very useful free service, though almost unique in this area, is the provision of a pump-out barge to empty a yacht's holding tank without the need for her to leave the berth. Arrange via marina reception.

Launderettes One on each side of the marina basin.

Electricity At all berths and the reception/fuel pontoon.

Fuel Diesel and petrol pumps will be found at the north end of the reception pontoon, open marina office hours and with credit cards accepted.

Bottled gas Camping Gaz cylinders can be exchanged at the chandlery, where it may also be possible to get other bottles refilled.

Clube náutico The Clube Náutico de Vilamoura has premises next to the marina office, overlooking the reception pontoon. Crews of visiting yachts are made welcome.

Weather forecast Posted daily at the marina office and broadcast on VHF Ch 12 at 1000.

Alongside the reception / fuel berth in the entrance to Vilamoura Marina *Anne Hammick*

Banks Several cash dispensers (ATMs) around the marina complex, with banks in the tourist area.

Shops/provisioning Several small supermarkets, mostly a street or two back from the marina, which meet daily needs (and will sometimes deliver) but are inadequate for serious passage provisioning. For serious stocking-up the best bet would be the big Modelo supermarket about 15 minutes away by car (ask at the marina office for directions). Dozens of tourist and general shops overlook the marina basin.

Produce market Well-stocked markets in Quarteira and Lidl.

Cafés, restaurants and hotels Dozens of the former right beside the marina (including one at the *clube náutico*), with lots more, plus several luxury hotels, within walking distance.

Medical services Medical centre (including dentists) in the tourist area, best contacted with the assistance of marina reception. Hospital in Faro.

Communications

Post Office In the tourist complex behind the marina.

Mailing address The marina office will hold mail for visiting yachts – c/o Marina de Vilamoura, 8125–409 Quarteira, Algarve, Portugal. It is important that the envelope carries the name of the yacht in addition to that of the addressee.

Public telephones Several around the marina complex, including one beside the reception quay and another in the boatyard compound.

Fax service At the marina office *Fax* 289 310580.

Internet Free access via a computer in the marina office, plus a phone socket to which laptops can be connected. There is free WiFi in all marina berths for which the internet code/password will be given when checking-in at marina reception. Lastly, there are several cybercafés in the tourist resort.

Taxis/car hire In the commercial area, or via the marina office. Note that sign-posting within the tourist complex is poor – allow for a few wrong turnings if hiring a car to catch or meet a plane etc.

Buses Bus service to Faro (about 40 minutes) and elsewhere, from stops in the tourist complex. Ask at the marina office for directions.

Air services Faro international airport is about 20 minutes by taxi, 40 minutes by bus (though a taxi will be needed from town to airport).

Faro and Olhão

Faro and Olhão

Waypoints
⊕163 – 36°55'·6N 7°51'·9W (2·2M S of
  Cabo de Santa María)
⊕164 – 36°57'·55N 7°52'·25W
  (Cabo de Santa María, entrance)

Courses and distances
⊕161 (Vilamoura) – ⊕163 = 14·3M, 117° or 297°
⊕163 – ⊕164 = 2M, 352° or 172°
⊕163 – ⊕165 (Tavira) = 16M, 056° or 236°
⊕163 – ⊕167 (Río Guadiana) = 24·6M, 064° or 244°

Tides
Standard port Lisbon
Mean time differences (at Cabo de Santa María)
HW –0040 ±0010; LW –0010 ±0005
Heights in metres

MHWS	MHWN	MLWN	MLWS
3·4	2·6	1·3	0·6

Or refer to EasyTide at www.ukho.gov.uk/easytide

Charts

	Approach	Channels
Admiralty	91, 89, 93	83
Imray	C19, C50	
Portuguese	23204, 24206	26311

Principal lights
2206 **Cabo de Santa María**
  Fl(4)17s49m25M
  White tower and building 46m
2208 **West breakwater** Fl.R.4s9m6M
  White tower, three red bands 5m
2209 **East breakwater** Fl.G.4s9m6M
  White tower, three green bands 5m
2206.1 **Ldg Lts on 021°** *Front* Barra Nova Oc.4s8m6M
  White column, red stripes
2206 *Rear* 512m from front **Cabo de Santa María** (above)
2211 **Ilha de Cultra**, training wall
  Oc.G.5s6m3M Metal column on building 6m
Canal de Faro
2212 **First Ldg Lts 099°** (a back bearing if entering)
  Front **Mar Santo** Oc.R.5s9m5M
  White column, red bands 5m
2206 *Rear* 244m from front **Cabo de Santa María** (above)
2214 **Second Ldg Lts 328°**
  Front **Casa Cubica (Fabrica Fritz)** Fl.R.3s11m6M
  Lantern on south wall of building 5m
2214.1 *Rear* 731m from front Oc.R.6s63m6M
  Lantern on church tower 21m
Canal de Olhão
2222 **Cais Farol** Fl.G.3s7m6M Green metal column 5m
2221 **First Ldg Lts 220°** (a back bearing if entering)
  Front **Golada** LFl.R.5s6m6M
  White over red cylinder on three white columns 6m
2221.1 *Rear* 447m from front Oc.R.5s8m7M
  White over red cylinder on three white columns 7m
2218 **Ponte do Carvão, Ilha de Culatra**
  Fl.5.5s6m6M Green column 4m
2219 **Ponte Cais, Ilha de Culatra**
  Oc.G.4s6m5M Green column

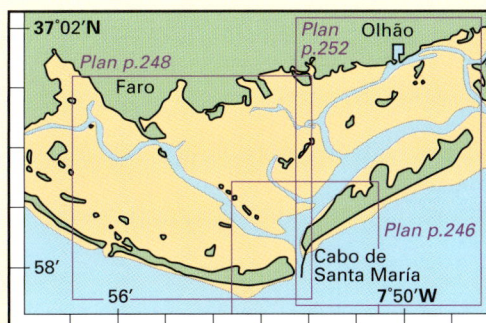

2224 **Second Ldg Lts 125°** (back bearing if entering)
  Front Arraiais Iso.G.1·5s7m5M
  Black and white striped column, ▲ topmark 5m
2224.1 *Rear* 226m from front Oc.G.3s13m5M
  Black and white striped column, ▲ topmark 8m
2225 **Third Ldg Lts on 352°** *Front* Murtinas
  LFl.R.5s7m7M White column, red bands
2225.1 *Rear* 301m from front Oc.R.5s13m7M
  White column, red bands
2226 **Fourth Ldg Lts 044°** *Front* **Cais de Olhão**
  Iso.R.6s8m7M White column, red bands 7m
2226.1 *Rear* **Igreja** 360m from front Oc.R.4s20m6M
  Church tower 12m
2226.3 **Doca de Olhao** – west of dock entrance Fl.R.6s6M
  Post 5m
Many other lit buoys and beacons exist in the Canal de
Faro, Canal de Olhão and Canal da Assetia. However
none should be relied upon implicitly, and any or all may
be moved if the channels shift

Night entry
  The entrance is well lit, but tidal currents – and eddies –
  can be powerful. If unfamiliar with the channels it
  would be wise to anchor at the first opportunity and
  await daylight

Maritime radio station
  Estoi (37°06'·1N 7°49'·8W)
  Remotely controlled from Lisbon
  Manual – VHF Ch 16, 24, 27, 28. *Autolink* – VHF Ch 86
  Weather bulletins and navigational warnings
  Weather bulletins in Portuguese and English for Cabo
  Carvoerio to the Rio Guadiana within 20 miles offshore
  VHF Ch 11 at 0805, 2005 UT
  Navigational warnings in Portuguese and English
  within 200 miles offshore: VHF Ch 11at 0805, 2005 UT

Harbour communications
  Faro – Port Authority ☎ +351 289 803601 *Fax* +351 289
  860666 *Email* portfaro@mail.telepac.pt
  VHF Ch 11, 16 (call *Postradfaro*) (24 hours)
  Olhão – Port Authority ☎ +351 289 703160
  VHF Ch 11, 16 (call *Capimarolhão*) (0900–1230, 1400–
  1730 weekdays only)
  Olhão – Marina ☎ +351 962 095 793
  www.villagemarinaolhao.com
  Email enquiries@villagemarinaolhao.com

*A single entrance leading to many anchorages
and a marina at Olhão*

Both Faro and Olhão (pronounced '*Oh-le-ow*') are
sizeable towns, but for many the greater appeal lies
with the tidal lagoons which run along the coast for
some 30M between the mainland and the sea. The
offlying islands, together with the coastal fringes,
form the Parque Natural de Ría Formosa. Certain
restrictions apply but the bird life, including storks
and various waders, is abundant. To take full
advantage of the geography a sailing dinghy or a
shoal-draught boat able to take the ground is

preferable, but there is water enough in the main
channels for deep-draught yachts.

The entrance at Cabo de Santa María is well
marked and the way through the sand defined by
breakwaters. A stream of fishing boats may give a
useful lead when they return with their catch in the
early morning, but the bar, which is dredged from
time to time, presents few problems in fine weather.
Once inside, the channels are well buoyed, but if
going to Olhão beware the wash of passing fishing
boats. The ferries, too, are not over-considerate.
Another potential problem throughout the area is

THE ALGARVE & ANDALUCIA

Chart

CABO DE SANTA MARIA

Marsh

7_7

59'

2_7

No.7
Fl.G.6s

No.10
Fl.R.3s

No.8
Fl.R.6s

No.5
Fl.G.3s

0_9

10

5

9

5_8

0_2

0_6

No.3
Fl.G.6s

099°

Mar Santo

2_1

58'·5

36°
58'
N

Marsh

No.6
Fl.R.6s

No.1
Fl.G.3s

3_1

10

10

9_6

No.4
Fl.R.6s

LFl.R.5s
6m6M
2221

No.2
Fl.R.3s

Golada
Beacons

Oc.R.5s8m7M
2221.1

Ilha da
Barreta

Praia de Santa María

See plan p.248

57'·5

0_1

3_4

2

0_6

4_6

11

1_9

2_4

0_3

0_2

220°

No.6-0
Fl.R.4s

1_2

2_8

Cais Farol
Fl.G.3s7m6M
2222

Oc.R.5s9m5M
2212

Cabo de Santa María
Fl(4)17s49m25M 2206

Oc.G.5s6m3M
2211

0_4

Barra Nova
Oc.W.4s8m6M
2206.1

3_7

4

021° Barra Nova

0_4

Fl.G.4s9m6M
2209

3_4

6_9

36

164

20

10 20

10

352°

Ponte do
Carvão
Fl.W.5.5s6m6M
2218

Ilha da
Culatra

0_3

0_4

2

5_6

See plan p. 252

⊕163   36°55'·6N   7°51'·9W   2·2M S of Cabo de Santa María
⊕164   36°57'·55N 7°52'·25W Cabo de Santa María, Faro &
                                        Olhão entrance

53'·5   53'   52'·5   7°52'W   51'·5   51'

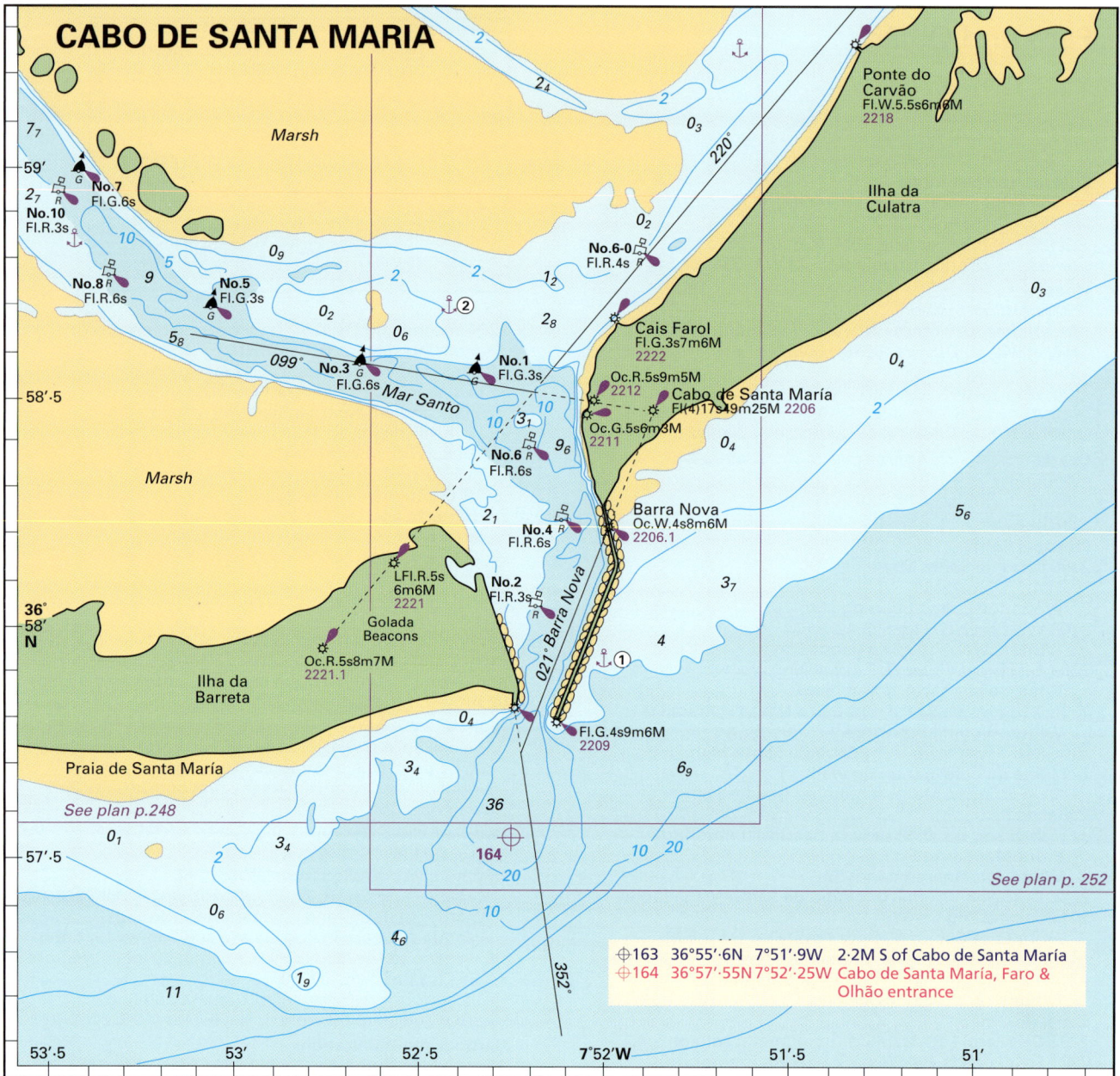

the prevalence of floating weed, which tends to clog engine water filters, and small crustaceans which take up residence in log impellers. Both will need clearing regularly.

Approach

The coast is very low-lying and currents of up to 3kn may set along it. The 50m contour runs at 1M offshore at the point, further away on either side. The major light of Cabo de Santa María is on the sandspit about 1·3M northeast of the most southerly point of the cape and 0·7M north-northeast of the breakwaters. From a distance it looks like a needle on a sandy island.

Coming along the shore from the west, the beach starts a few miles east of Vilamoura and is backed by tourist villages. It becomes deserted to the southeast and 8M west from Santa María the lagoon starts, with an occasional shallow entrance across the sand,

and Faro airport behind. The 5m line runs 600–700m offshore, except southwest of the entrance where it turns south to a point, very steep-to (shoaling from 30m down to 5m within 50m or less) more than 0·5M offshore. A short distance further west the 2m contour does much the same, forming a southwest facing bank over which the water shoals from 15m to 2m in little more than 100m. Either of these may cause a southwesterly swell to break. Remain at least 0·7M offshore until the west breakwater bears 352°.

Caution

There is an area of tuna nets south of Cabo de St Maria that is marked with a total of four special mark buoys and one south cardinal buoy as follows:

Special Mark No.1: 36°56'·05N 007°56'·94W
Special Mark No.2: 36°56'·90N 007°56'·63W
Special Mark No.3: 36°56'·93N 007°55'·52W

On the Barra Nova transit 1 hour before HW *Jane Russell*

Special Mark No.4: 36°56'·08N 007°55'·17W

South Cardinal Buoy marked as S. Maria Sul near 36°55'·58N 007°55'·97W

All five buoys are large (about 3m high) and lit and all are powered with solar panels.

To the east, the lagoon and its protecting banks extend 20M with some wide, but generally shallow, gaps. Opposite Fuzeta, 5M east of Olhão and identified by a distinctive church, the 50m line runs about 2M offshore. There is a network of tunny nets south of Fuzeta centered on 37°01'·20N 007°42'·80W that extends to a radius of ½M round that point. They are unusual, in that the nets are not in a long line extending for several miles, but instead are a complicated system of channels all in this one mile diameter. This area is well buoyed and lit and marked on all Portuguese charts as 'Armacoes do Atum'.

Looking north through the entrance to the Ria Formosa at Cabo de Santa Maria. Ilha da Barreta to port, Ilha da Culatra to starboard

From offshore ⊕163 lies 2M south of the entrance, a course of 352° down the leading line linking with ⊕164, 500m south of the entrance.

Entrance

From a point at least 0·7M south of the entrance, steer 352° until the end of the east breakwater just opens to the east of a line with Santa María light. There can be a marked set across the entrance and it is important to remain on the leading line. Although there is adequate depth to enter at any state of the tide the spring ebb may run at 7kn through the entrance. In these circumstances hug the west mole – there is good water within 15m of it and the ebb will be reduced to about 4kn – but be ready for powerful eddies and keep a careful watch for fish-traps (often marked by black flags). There are three port-hand buoys before the channels to Faro and Olhão divide. Local yachtsmen frequently cut inside these, not least to escape the tide, but new arrivals may feel happier leaving them close to port.

Both channels are buoyed, and though in the past buoys were frequently reported to be out of position this is no longer common, particularly during the summer. A corrected copy of either Portuguese chart 26311 or Admiralty chart 83 is almost essential, but even so the banks shift continually and yachts have reported grounding well within the marked channel. As always, best water is to be found on the outsides of bends.

Note Vessels drawing more than 2·5m may not use the channel at night (not recommended for the visitor, in any case), and vessels are forbidden to cross each other's bows at the junction of the channels – those outward bound should remain outside the channel and let inward bound vessels pass.

Anchorages near Cabo de Santa María

There are several possibilities in this area, most of them weather dependent and all requiring an anchor light to be displayed if remaining after dark. (Several yachts have been fined in this area in recent years for not displaying either an anchor ball or a light, as appropriate).

In settled northerlies yachts occasionally anchor outside, east of the east breakwater and south of Santa María light (1).

A useful anchorage for timing your entrance or exit will be found north-northwest of buoy No.1 (2) (see plans on pages 246 and below).

The lagoon on Ilha de Culatra, a popular wintering hole for bilge-keelers and multihulls *Anne Hammick*

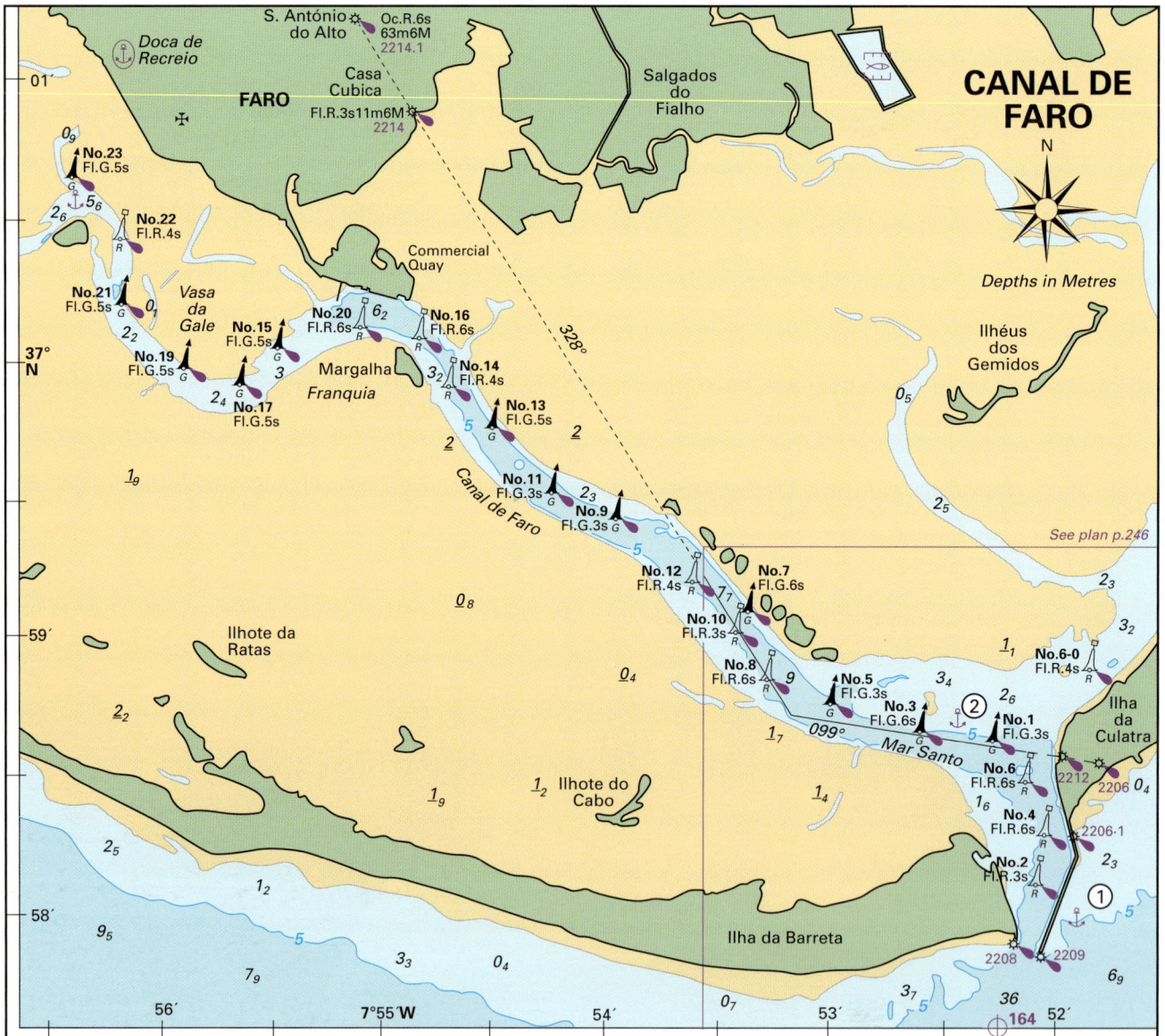

| ⊕163 | 36°55'·6 | 7°51'·9 | 2·2M S of Cabo de Santa María |
| ⊕164 | 36°57'·55 | 7°52'·25 | Cabo de Santa María, Faro & Olhão entrance |

Faro

37°00'·8N 7°56'·2W

This is a small marina for local fishing boats about 100m east of Ponte Cais pier.

Not to be confused with the tourist sprawl behind the beaches to the west of the city, Faro's walled Cidade Velha (old town) right next to the small Doca de Recreio should not be missed, providing welcome shade on a hot day and superb views over the estuary and town from the belltower of the Sé (cathedral). Pause to watch the storks on their untidy nests on the cathedral tower, above the Cidade Velha's neo-classical Arco de Vila, on lamp posts overhanging the city's streets...everywhere. Until recently they flew south to Morocco for the winter, but it seems that global warming has encouraged them to stay year-round.

Approach and anchorage

Again there is no option but to anchor, the favoured spot being the pool formed at the junction of the creeks in 3–4m, with the railway bridge covering the entrance to the Doca de Recreio bearing about 040°. Although now largely occupied by moorings it may be possible to find space in the channel leading southwest, where there is at least one deep pool, though two anchors (both from the bow and laid upstream and downstream respectively) may be required to limit swinging space.

When approaching the junction, favour the port side of the channel past buoys No.17 and No.21, switching to the starboard hand when the latter is 100m or so astern to avoid an extensive sand spit running out from the port bank (visible until mid-tide and marked by port hand buoy No.22). The deep channel here carries 4m or more depth but is a bare 15m wide.

Land either at the Doca de Recreio, passing under the railway bridge (about 1m clearance at high

Faro is famous for its storks – this pair have set up home on neo-classical Arco de Vila which gives access to the old city *Anne Hammick*

A single-track railway links Faro in the west to Vila Real de Santo António in the east, looping around the old city of Faro only feet from the water's edge *Anne Hammick*

water), or at one of the three jetties outside (the northernmost is probably the best bet). If landing in the basin note that the pontoons are closed off by individual security gates, and that the entire east side is reserved for fishermen. The office of the Capitania – where the *Policía Marítima* are often to be found – overlooks the north end of the basin, sharing its premises with a small maritime museum (open 1430–1630). A weather forecast is posted outside.

Facilities and communications

Facilities include water from taps beside the slipway on the quay between the basin and the marshes, and the possibility of showers at the Ginásio Clube Navale next door (which also has a snack-bar and upstairs restaurant – the only thing it does not appear to have is much to do with sailing!). In the same building is Nautifaro, previously a chandlery but now specialising mainly in outboard engines and their needs. Santa María Artigos Náuticos ☏ +351 289 804 805 *Fax* +351 289 882 559 www.santamarianautica.com

Email info@santamarianautica.com (open 0900–1300 and 1500–1800 weekdays, 1000–1300 Saturday) a little way down the same quay has filled the gap. Good English is spoken and the helpful owner, a local yachtsman, is happy to order as

THE ALGARVE & ANDALUCIA

Perhaps the most aristocratic of the Faro storks are the pair which nest on the belltower of the Sé (cathedral) *Anne Hammick*

Yachts wintering at Faro, seen from a rooftop in the city centre *Anne Hammick*

necessary. Diesel is available by can from a filling station on the landward side of the basin, though there is nowhere that a yacht can fill tanks directly. Camping Gaz bottles can be exchanged at several hardware stores in the city, but it is not possible to get other cylinders refilled.

Faro is the regional capital and has facilities to match, including banks, shops of all kinds, wining and dining spots, and medical services. Communications include a post office and numerous telephone kiosks, several internet cafés (including three terminals and two phone booths with jack plugs at the Western Union office directly opposite the smallcraft basin, plus a cybercafé on the nearby Praça Ferreira de Almeida), taxis, car hire, buses, trains (the station is close north of the smallcraft basin) and of course Faro International Airport, a couple of kilometres northwest as the egret flies, though rather more by road. Perhaps surprisingly, the aircraft noise is not intrusive and there appears to be little flying at night. In any case, any problems are more than offset by the proximity of the airport for crew changes and visiting friends.

Boatyard and storage ashore

If wishing to haul out for work or dry storage it would be well worth investigating the friendly Quinta do Progresso boatyard.
Mobile +351 919 317 171 *Fax* +351 289 822506
Email jbotas@vodaphone.pt

Looking east-southeast towards the Doca de Recreio at Faro and the yacht anchorage off to the right. The boatyard can be seen on the left

This is an unpretentious but well-run concern some distance north northwest (approach channel approximately 37°01'·213N 007°56'·74W) of the Doca de Recreio. 'Bruce', the helpful Portuguese owner/manager, speaks English, French, Spanish and some German and Dutch, while engineer John grew up in the United States. There are onsite workshops

Looking north-northeast over the anchorage at Faro to the Doca de Recreio and the boatyard beyond

for engineering, electronics, spars and rigging, GRP work and painting, though owners are welcome to do their own work, and stout metal cradles are available. Owners of yachts ashore are welcome to live aboard if they wish, with water and electricity throughout the yard and showers provided. Supermarkets and other shops are within walking distance.

Due to environmental concerns, as it is on the northern fringes of the Parque Natural de Ría Formosa, it took many years to obtain permission to dredge a channel up to the yard, but there should be at least 1·6m found at LWS and up to 4·4m at HWS. At the same time a massive 100-tonne capacity travel-lift should have replaced the slightly elderly 24-tonne lift of old.

There is a possibility of a small marina being built here with around 180 berths in 2m or so.

Anchorage at Ilha da Culatra

(3) – see plan on page 252

A very popular anchorage (more than 100 yachts in holiday periods) can be found along the length of Praça Larga north of Ilha da Culatra. Holding in both areas is good over sand, though wind against tide conditions can set up quite a chop and also cause yachts on single anchors to yaw considerably. Two anchors (both from the bow) may be wise if planning to stay for any length of time but take into account how yachts around you are anchored.

It is possible to enter or leave the Praça Larga from the east, via the Barra Grande (also known as the Barra Velha), but the shifting banks are not reliably buoyed and this route is not recommended without local knowledge.

There are reckoned to be around 3,000 permanent residents on Isla de Culatra, mostly in Culatra village though the village close to Cabo de Santa María (referred to locally as Farol, literally, 'lighthouse'), is also growing at speed. There are no roads, and no cars, though a few tractors plough their way through the loose sand. But Ponte Cais is a popular holiday spot, particularly during the music festival held in August, so it has several shops including a small but surprisingly well-stocked supermarket, a cash point, numerous restaurants and bars, and both post and telephone offices.

Yachts anchored at the eastern end of Praca Larga. Olhao is beyond to the NNW *Jane Russell*

There are shallow channels marked with withies across the sands between Praca Larga and the Olhao channel, but even these will dry out on you if you become too distracted in Olhao market! *Jane Russell*

Ferries run between Ponte Cais, Farol and Olhão – two or three a day in winter and far more in summer.

Close east of Ponte Cais is a tidal lagoon, a favourite wintering spot with both locals and liveaboard owners of multihulls and bilge-keelers, some of whom have been there more than a decade. There are no facilities as such, but no charges either, and daily needs can easily be met in Culatra village. However local people naturally feel they should have first rights to the limited foreshore space, and there may be little room to spare. If interested, anchor off and prospect first by dinghy, both to check depths in the northeast-facing entrance and to ensure that space will be available, either on the beach or at anchor.

There is a small marina for local fishing boats about 100m east of Ponte Cais pier.

Praca Larga anchorage Ilha da Culatra looking NE from the marina breakwater *Jane Russell*

THE ALGARVE & ANDALUCIA

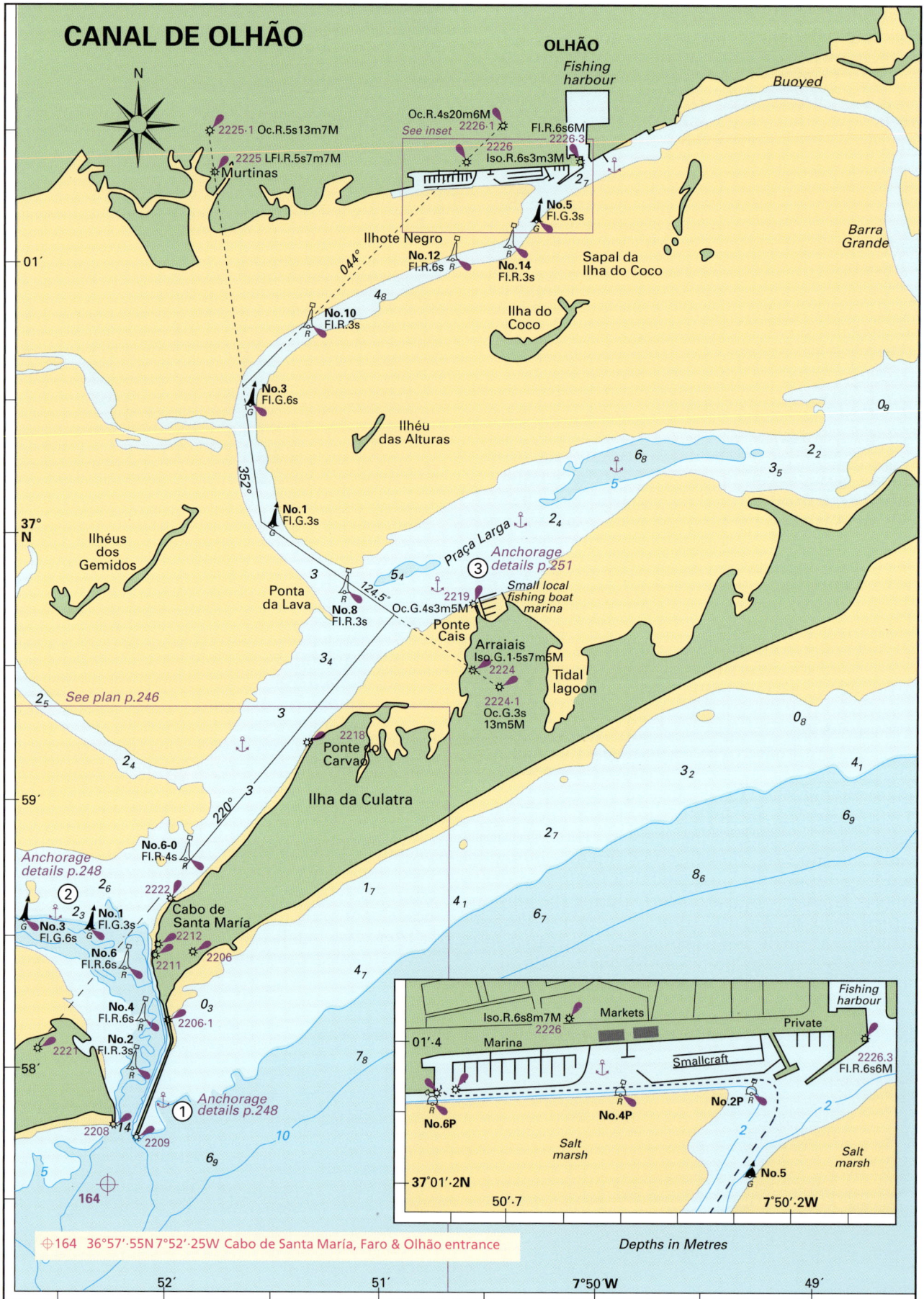

CANAL DE OLHÃO

OLHÃO

Fishing harbour

Buoyed

N

2225·1 Oc.R.5s13m7M

2225 LFl.R.5s7m7M
Murtinas

Oc.R.4s20m6M
2226·1

2226
Iso.R.6s3m3M

Fl.R.6s6M
2226·3

See inset

No.5
Fl.G.3s

Barra Grande

044°

Ilhote Negro
No.12
Fl.R.6s

No.14
Fl.R.3s

Sapal da Ilha do Coco

4₈

No.10
Fl.R.3s

Ilha do Coco

No.3
Fl.G.6s

352°

Ilhéu das Alturas

0₉

6₈
5

3₅

2₂

No.1
Fl.G.3s

2₄

Praça Larga

Anchorage
details p.251

③

37°
N

Ilhéus dos Gemidos

3

5₄

2219
Oc.G.4s3m5M

Small local fishing boat marina

Ponta da Lava

124.5°

No.8
Fl.R.3s

Ponte Cais

Arraiais
Iso.G.1·5s7m5M

2224

Tidal lagoon

3₄

2224·1
Oc.G.3s
13m5M

0₈

See plan p.246

2₅

3

2218

Ponte Carvao

Ilha da Culatra

3₂

4₁

2₄

220° 3

6₉

59′

No.6-0
Fl.R.4s

1₇

2₇

8₆

Anchorage details p.248

②

2₆

2222

2₃ No.1
Fl.G.3s

Cabo de Santa María

4₁

6₇

No.3
Fl.G.6s

No.6
Fl.R.6s

2212

2211

2206

4₇

No.4
Fl.R.6s

0₃

2206·1

No.2
Fl.R.3s

2221

58′

7₈

Anchorage
details p.248

①

2208

14

2209

6₉

10

5

164

Inset (lower right):

Fishing harbour

Iso.R.6s8m7M
2226

Markets

Private

01′·4   Marina

Smallcraft

2226.3
Fl.R.6s6M

No.6P

No.4P

No.2P

Salt marsh

2

Salt marsh

37°01′·2N

No.5

50′·7

7°50′·2W

⊕164 36°57′·55N 7°52′·25W Cabo de Santa María, Faro & Olhão entrance

Depths in Metres

52′   51′   7°50′W   49′

Olhão's marina and small craft harbour looking northwest, with the Grupo Naval's small basin and the much larger fishing dock on the right

Olhão

37°01'·3N 07°50'·5W

There is reported to be little space for visitors at Olhão marina, and the minimum length of stay is one month. If intending to arrive by yacht, there is much to be said for first anchoring off Ponte Cais and taking the ferry over to Olhão to assess the current situation.

Olhão itself is a pleasant, non-touristy town with superb markets on the waterfront surrounded by public gardens and a small children's play area.

Saturday morning market in Olhão is full of entertaining distractions *Jane Russell*

Approach

Although it is perfectly possible to negotiate the channel (marked with withies) up to Olhão at low water, most skippers will feel happier at around half flood. From the Praça Larga turn northwest leaving Ponta da Lava and buoy No.8 to port, and either steer the courses indicated on the plan opposite or follow the buoyage as far as starboard hand No.5. Almost continuous dredging is required to keep this channel clear and yachts must not, under any circumstances, anchor in the fairway.

From a position close west of buoy No.5 steer directly for the hammer-head ferry pier, swinging west only just short of it to skirt the smallcraft pontoons and leave buoy No.2P well to port. Beyond it will be seen No.4P and, in the distance, No.6P. All are spherical red buoys with topmarks and are lit, though this is no place to be on the move after dark. Continue west, staying as close to the smallcraft pontoon as conditions allow, repeating the process past the marina proper. On no account err to the south, as the edge of the dredged channel is too steep to give any warning before impact (though too soft to do much damage). The marina is entered at its western end, as indicated on the inset plan.

Berthing

The marina comprises two separate sections, the eastern berthing local smallcraft on two long east/west pontoons, the western providing around 270 berths for yachts of up to 17m, in 3m depths. 250 of these berths are on the 11 inner pontoons, which run on a north/south axis from a single pontoon which parallels the shore. The remaining berths, and the only ones which may be accessible to a visitor, lie inside the long 'shelter' pontoon. It seems likely that this pontoon was never intended to provide more than short-term berthing as it is not provided with water and electricity points, though cleats are provided on the inner side. It is reported that, during strong southerlies, it becomes distinctly lively as soon as the rising tide covers the mudbanks to the south. A full-scale southerly gale has yet to be experienced.

On arrival, unless allocated a berth in advance, the best bet will probably be to raft alongside a yacht of suitable size on the inside of the long south pontoon. However this is frowned on by the authorities and the boat should not be left unattended even with the consent of those on the inside yacht. Security is via the usual card, and more necessary than in some areas, due to the traveller encampment to the west of the town.

Anchorage

It may be possible for two or three yachts to anchor in the western part of the gap between the two parts of the marina, though space is tight due to moored smallcraft. Holding is good in about 3m over mud.

Formalities

All formalities are currently handled at the office of the Instituto Portuário e dos Transportes Marítimos do Sul (IPTM), which overlooks the west side of the large fishing boat basin, open 0800–1200 and 1300–1630 weekdays. The *Capitania* and *Polícia Marítima* share an office on the corner opposite the Grupo

Naval, easily distinguished by its array of radio aerials, with the *GNR–Brigada Fiscal* between the two.

Facilities

Boatyard The nearest boatyard to Olhão is the Marina Formosa located just up channel past the fishing harbour (37°01'·518N 007°49'·670W). Contact Dias and Sabino, Lda. Doca Nova de Pesca – Apartado 63 – 8700909 Olhão. ☎/*Fax* +351 289 703 364. There is neither a website nor an email address for the boatyard. This is a working boat yard which carries out one-off and annual maintenance and repair work including lifting and craneage, boat cleaning, storage, polishing and antifouling and have specialists in mechanical and electrical engineering. There are also GRP services, yacht painting and traditional shipwright skills for the building and repair of all types of boats.

Also provided are dry berthing arrangements, a public slipway, drying out facilities, storage ashore and winter lay up, electricity ashore, shower and toilet facilities, and towing services within the Ría Formosa. The hydraulic trolley for lifting out, however, is really only suitable for fairly small boats (see photo opposite).

Engineers, mechanics, radio repairs At the fishing harbour.

Chandlery Sulcampo on the seafront road sells some general chandlery and electronics in addition to fishing tackle and diving equipment. Cabrita Lda, opposite the market buildings, is similar. The larger Sulnáutica, on the road behind the IPTM office, stocks outboards, batteries, inflatables, some chandlery and the inevitable fishing gear.

Looking north-northwest over the Olhão marina

The narrow approach to Olhão marina, seen from the ferry pier to the east. It is essential to leave all three buoys to port *Anne Hammick*

Hydraulic trolley at Marina Formosa boatyard Olhão

Water No access to water on the outer pontoon of the marina, though supplied to the inner berths. Several public taps and water fountains nearby, however.

Showers Nothing at the marina, but several local *residencials* are willing to let yachtsmen use showers for a small fee.

Launderette Several in the town.

Electricity Not available on the outer pontoon.

Fuel By can from a filling station near the root of the ferry jetty.

Bottled gas Camping Gaz exchanges at the Casa Jóvale hardware store close northwest of the market buildings, and at Cabrita Lda (see above) but no refills.

Clube naval The Grupo Naval de Olhão has its own basin east of the ferry pier, but there is no space for visitors.

Banks In the town, with a cash dispenser almost opposite the market buildings.

Shops, provisioning Small supermarket up the road opposite the market buildings, plus a large Pingo Doce supermarket five minutes walk to the north of the pier at Olhão. Good general shopping in the town.

Produce market Excellent – and spotlessly clean – produce and fish markets virtually overlooking the marina. As always, at their best in the early morning.

Cafés, restaurants and hotels The usual wide variety, with some particularly good fish restaurants on the road behind the market buildings.

Medical services In the town.

Communications

Post office In the town, close to the church.

Telephones Several public kiosks near the market buildings with others in the town.

Internet access Provided by the town authorities on a street one back from the waterfront (go down the wide road opposite the market buildings, turn left and then left again), open 1000–2200 Monday–Thursday, 1000–1300 and 1500–1800 Thursday–Friday, 1000–2000 Saturday, closed Sunday. The first half hour is free, but there are likely to be long queues outside school hours.

Car hire In the town, or from Faro airport.

Taxis A few in the town.

Buses & trains To Faro, Tavira and beyond.

Ferries Regular ferries to Ilha Armona and Ilha de Culatra

Air services Major airport at Faro, about 10km to the west as the gull flies, though considerably further by land.

THE ALGARVE & ANDALUCIA

Fuzeta

Entrance centre at 37°03'·03N 007°43'·75W

The small inlet at Fuzeta off the lagoon east of Olhão looking north-northwest. It can only be approached by shoal-draught yachts or multihulls, or perhaps by dinghy from larger yachts anchored further west

The inlet of Fuzeta, 15M east of Cabo de Santa María, might be described as a smaller version of Olhão, tucked behind broadly similar banks.

In February 2010 a storm caused a breach in the sand bank to the west of the original entrance to the tidal lagoon off Fuzeta. A new entrance was created to the west of the original entrance while the breach in the sandbank and the original entrance have been

The eastern entrance to the lagoon off Fuzeta should not be tackled without local knowledge – and this is why...

blocked with a very large quantity of sand. The centre of the new entrance to Fuzeta is at 37°03'·03N 007°43'·75W. Approach to this position should be made on a course of 282° and, for the deepest water, continue on this course toward a radio antenna and water tower in the centre of Fuzeta. Even this new entrance is extremely shallow and there is reported to be not much more than 1·5m at half tide. Approach with caution!

Though very appealing, it is feasible only for shoal-draught yachts or multihulls able to enlist local assistance for the approach. The inner banks appear to be largely of sand, rather than the mixture of mud and sand encountered further west, making drying out much more pleasant. The small town has all the usual facilities, including fuel at the fishermen's quay (up the narrow inlet, marked by prominent red/white and green/white banded towers), and nearby shops and produce market. A small and somewhat ramshackle boatyard lies near the head of the creek.

There is a large fish conservation and tunny net area south of Fuzeta marked by no less than six large (3m) cardinal buoys as follows:

1. North	NCB	037°01'·00N	007°44'·48W
2. Northeast	NCB	037°01'·94N	007°42'·20W
3. East	ECB	037°00'·88N	007°41'·57W
4. Southeast	SCB	037°00'·00N	007°44'·00W
5. South	SCB	036°59'·30N	007°46'·22W
6. West	WCB	037°00'·38N	007°45'·94W

There is a network of tunny nets within this area centred on 037°01·20N 007°42'·80W that extends to a radius of about ½M around that point.

In 2012 additional tuna nets were laid a little to the east of the nets mentioned above, marked by a south cardinal buoy at 37°01'·85N 007°39'·10W. About one mile to the north, the northern limit of the nets are marked by three special marks.

Tavira

Waypoints
⊕165 – 37°04'·6N 7°35'·4W (approach)
⊕166 – 37°06'·38N 7°36'·63W (entrance)

Courses and distances
⊕161 (Vilamoura) – ⊕165 (via ⊕163) = 30·3M,
117°&056° or 236°&297°
⊕163 (Cabo de Santa María) – ⊕165 = 16M, 056° or
236°
⊕165 – ⊕166 = 2M, 331° or 151°
⊕165 – ⊕167 (Río Guadiana) = 9·1M, 080° or 260°

Tides
See Vila Real de Santo António, Río Guadiana,
page 261

Charts

	Approach	Harbour
Admiralty	91, 89, 93	
Imray	C19, C50	
Portuguese	23204, 24206	(27503)

Principal lights
2234 **Ldg Lts 326°** *Front* Armação Fl.R.3s10m4M
White post, red bands 5m
2234.1 *Rear* 132m from front Iso.R.6s11m5M
White post, red bands 5m
2235 **West breakwater** Fl.R.2·5s8m6M
White column, red bands 4m
2235.2 **East breakwater** Fl.G.2·5s6m6M
White column, green bands 4m

Night entry
Though perfectly feasible, entry in darkness calls for
settled conditions, a rising tide (half-flood or more)
and considerable confidence.

Attractive and unspoilt river anchorage with limited facilities

A very old town, one of its bridges claims Roman origins, and the only Greek inscription to be found in Portugal was discovered in nearby Santa Luzia, Tavira is still heavily dependant on fishing and in spite of an ever-growing tourist trade has managed to retain much of its character. Some of its old walls and many of its tiled houses remain, with wrought iron balconies and original decoration, overlooked by floodlit churches and a ruined castle.

The anchorage is connected to the town by a 2km causeway flanked by salt pans and parking areas, and by the Rio Gilão which at high tide is navigable by dinghy. Once in the anchorage there is good protection from the sea, though little from the wind, and the current runs strongly. The area is part of the Parque Natural de Ría Formosa and the birdwatching possibilities are endless.

Approach

Between Cabo de Santa María and Tavira the coast comprises a low sandbank, broken east of Olhão and again off Fuzeta. A floating fish cage is positioned south of Fuzeta – see page 256 – and at certain times of year tunny nets may be laid up to 1·5M offshore, but otherwise there are no natural hazards.

The entrance is dredged every few years, when 4m can be found along the leading line. It is not known, however, when this was last done and it would be prudent to assume some silting has taken place. The leading marks, a pair of red and white banded poles, can be difficult to identify – if in doubt err to the east, as a shoal extends beyond the end of the west breakwater.

From offshore ⊕165 lies 2M south-southeast of the entrance, a course of 331° leading to ⊕166 on the 10m line outside the harbour mouth.

Entrance

Do not enter before half flood or at all if the swell is heavy – if wind and/or swell are onshore conditions become rougher on the ebb. The best time for either entering or for leaving is about one hour before high water. When taking the sharp turn to port into the

Looking northwest into the Ría Formosa entrance at Tavira

THE ALGARVE & ANDALUCIA

Yachts anchored off the Quatro Aguas ferry jetty in the Ria Formosa.
The main channel – though not the ferry passage – is indicated by pairs of stout, lit posts

anchorage give the (unlit) tourist ferry quay and its off-lying post a generous berth (floating lines may trail from it), and keep a sharp lookout for the small ferries, some of which move at surprising speed.

Anchorage

The channel west past Quatro Aguas ('four waters') towards Santa Lucia is indicated by pairs of very solid posts, all nominally lit, and though some local boats remain moored in what appears to be the fairway it would be most unwise to anchor in it. At the very least one would regularly be disturbed by wash from passing fishing boats. In summer it may be difficult to find sufficient space for a larger yacht to swing, in which case (and for all yachts at spring tides) it would be prudent to set two anchors, both from the bow and laid upstream and downstream respectively. The bottom is foul in places and a tripline is advised. Holding is good over sand, but the current runs strongly enough at springs for most yachts to remain tide-rode even in contrary winds of 20kn.

A local fishing boat heads out to sea past the breakwaters at Tavira *Anne Hammick*

Shallow-draught vessels have the option of continuing southwest along the Ría Tavira towards Santa Lucia, again anchoring well clear of the fairway which is used by fishing boats day and night. The lower reaches are marked by lit posts.

Formalities

There is a manned *GNR–Brigada Fiscal* office next to the ferry jetty, but Tavira is not a port of entry/exit and passports cannot be stamped for departure (which in any case should only be necessary in the case of non-EU citizens). The Capitania is located in the town, close west of the fishing quay.

Facilities and communications

At the anchorage water by can from the Clube Náutico de Tavira, which also has showers and a small bar (seek permission before helping oneself to either of the former, as a small fee may be charged), plus several other bars and restaurants but no shops. Fresh shellfish can be bought from a counter at the rear of wholesaler Tomé Mariscos, housed in a large yellow building west of the *clube náutico*.

A square concrete barge against which it is possible to dry out lies on the beach immediately opposite the ferry jetty. However it appears to be settling into the sand and now covers at high water springs. The smallcraft harbour on the west bank just inside the Rio Gilão is too small, shallow and crowded to be feasible for a visiting yacht, and landing by dinghy at the single pontoon is impractical due to a locked security gate. There is a lay-up area for local yachts (maximum about 8m) behind the *clube náutico*, and though there is no possibility of hauling a larger keel-yacht this would undoubtedly be the place to start enquiries if faced with a major problem.

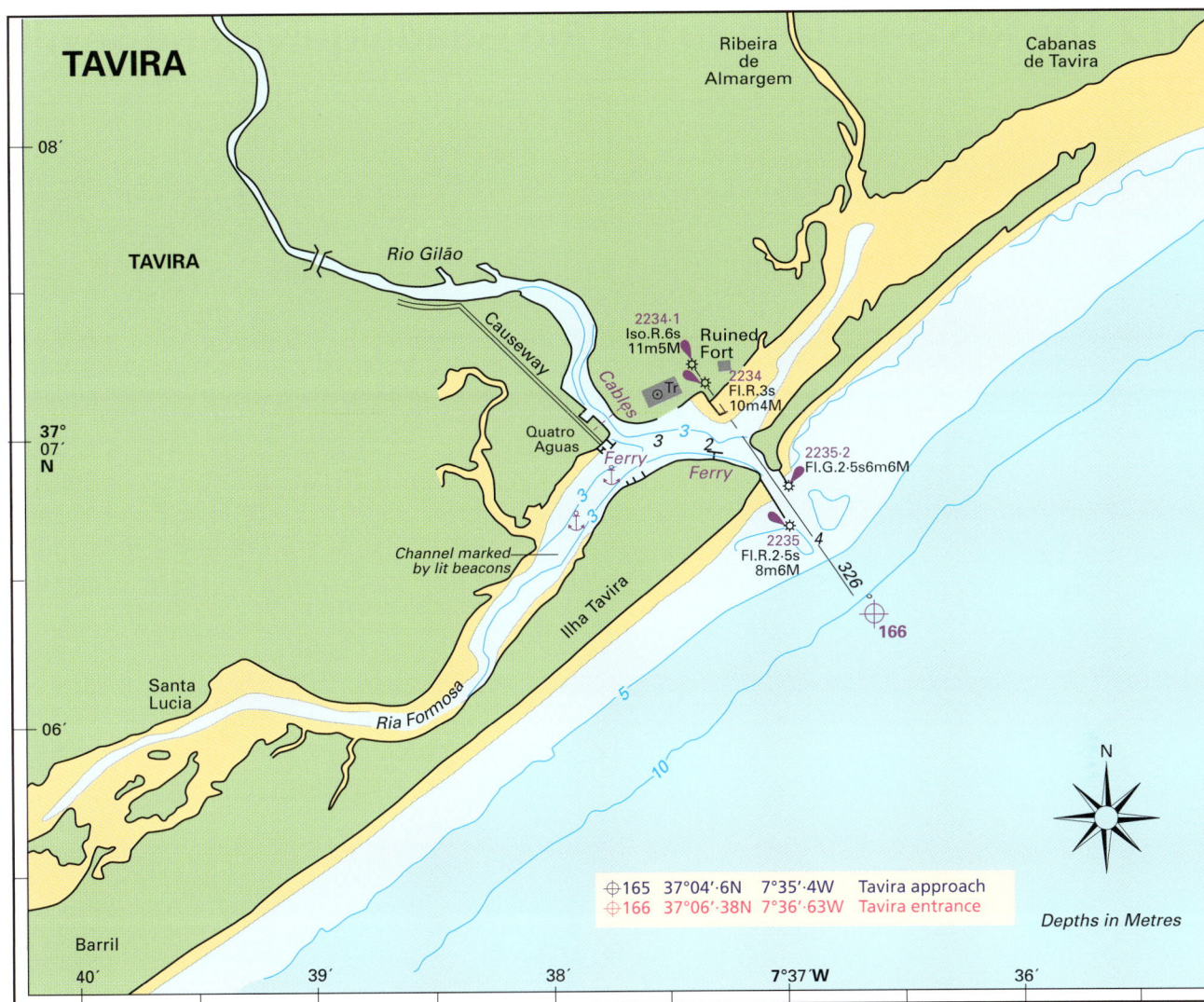

TAVIRA

Rio Gilão

Causeway

Cables

2234·1
Iso.R.6s
11m5M

Ruined
Fort

2234
Fl.R.3s
10m4M

Ribeira
de
Almargem

Cabanas
de Tavira

Tr

Quatro
Aguas

Ferry

Ferry

2235·2
Fl.G.2·5s6m6M

Channel marked
by lit beacons

2235
Fl.R.2·5s
8m6M

Ilha Tavira

326°

166

Santa
Lucia

Ria Formosa

5

10

Barril

⊕165   37°04'·6N   7°35'·4W   Tavira approach
⊕166   37°06'·38N   7°36'·63W   Tavira entrance

Depths in Metres

N

There is a phone kiosk near the ferry jetty and the area is served by Tavira's 'land train' – popular with younger crewmembers as well as older ones encumbered with shopping. Heading in the other direction there is a passenger ferry to Ilha Tavira which operates on demand.

On Ilha Tavira campsite with several cafés and restaurants, a phone kiosk and a cash dispenser but, rather surprisingly, no shop.

In the town good shopping (including a vast Pingo Doce on the east bank near the new bridge), banks with cash dispensers, restaurants, hotels etc. Diesel can be transported by can from a waterside filling station just upstream of the new bridge (accessible by dinghy). There are several hardware stores at which Camping Gaz bottles can be exchanged (but not refilled), plus one near the east end of the cast-iron bridge which sells limited chandlery. Runabouts, outboards and inflatables are displayed in a showroom on the west bank near the filling station.

A post office, telephones and several cybercafés will be found (the latter including one on the east bank of the river between the two old bridges, which

Dos and don'ts in the Parque Natural de Ria Formosa
Anne Hammick

has 10 or 12 computers plus multiple sockets for laptop users). Transport options include taxis, buses (including the road train mentioned previously) and a station just north of the town. Faro airport is about 30km down the coast.

III. 2 The Río Guadiana to the Río Guadalquivir and Seville

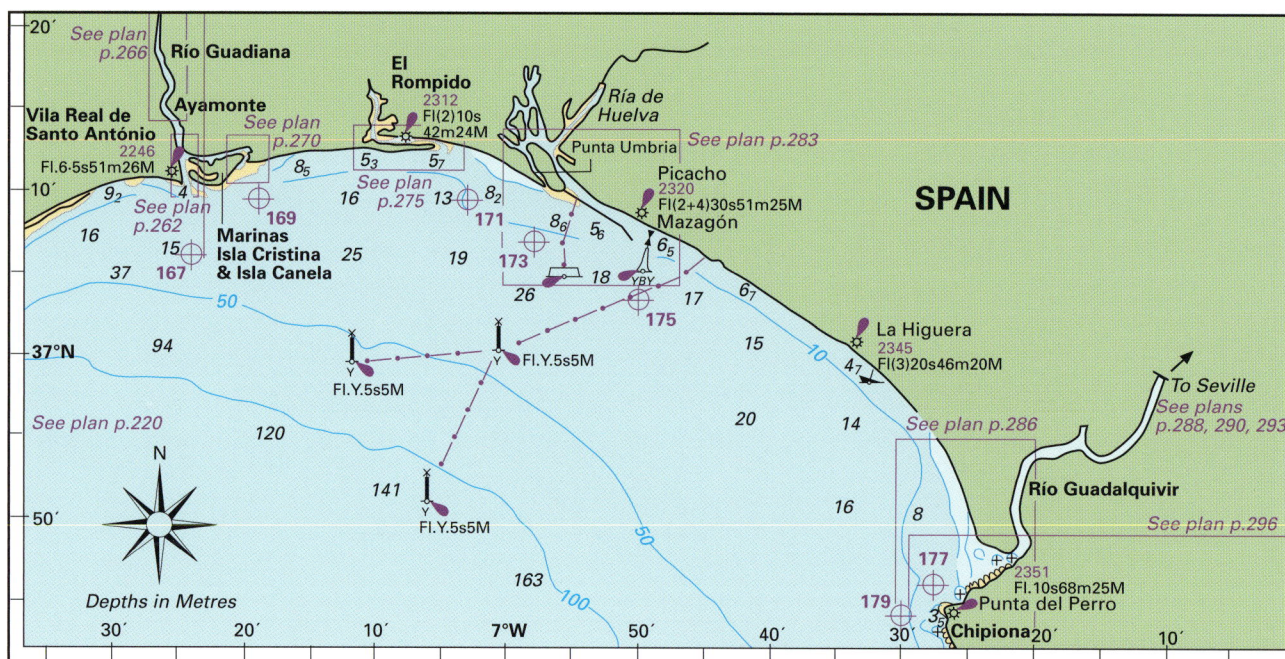

(Chart showing the coast from Río Guadiana to Río Guadalquivir, with the following labels)

See plan p.266
Río Guadiana
Ayamonte
Vila Real de Santo António
2246
Fl.6·5s51m26M
See plan p.262
See plan p.270
Marinas Isla Cristina & Isla Canela
169
167
El Rompido
2312
Fl(2)10s 42m24M
See plan p.275
171
173
175
Ría de Huelva
Punta Umbria
See plan p.283
Picacho
2320
Fl(2+4)30s51m25M
Mazagón
SPAIN
La Higuera
2345
Fl(3)20s46m20M
To Seville
See plans p.288, 290, 293
See plan p.286
Río Guadalquivir
See plan p.296
177
179
2351
Fl.10s68m25M
Punta del Perro
Chipiona
See plan p.220
Fl.Y.5s5M
Fl.Y.5s5M
Fl.Y.5s5M
YBY
N
Depths in Metres
Y

(Depth figures on chart): 20′, 10′, 9₂, 16, 15, 37, 94, 120, 141, 163, 50, 100, 8₅, 16, 25, 19, 13, 8₂, 8₆, 5₆, 6₅, 26, 18, 17, 6₇, 15, 47, 20, 14, 16, 8, 4, 50, 5₃, 5₇

37°N
37′
50′
30′ 20′ 10′ 7′W 50′ 40′ 30′ 20′ 10′

⊕167 37°06′·2N 7°24′·2W Río Guadiana approach
⊕169 37°08′·6N 7°18′·6W Marina Canela & Isla Cristina approach
⊕171 37°09′·2N 7°03′·3W El Rompido approach
⊕173 37°06′·7N 6°57′·7W Punta Umbría approach
⊕175 37°03′·3N 6°49′·7W Mazagón approach
⊕177 36°46′N 6°28′W Chipiona & the Río Guadalquivir approach
⊕179 36°44′N 6°30′·3W 3·1M W of Punta del Perro

PRINCIPAL LIGHTS

2246 **Vila Real de Santo António** Fl.6·5s51m26M
White tower, narrow black rings, red lantern 46m
2312 **El Rompido** Fl(2)10s42m24M
White tower, single red band 29m
2320 **Picacho** Fl(2+4)30s51m25M
White tower with brick corners, as has building, 25m
2345 **Higuera** Fl(3)20s46m20M
White tower and lantern 24m
2351 **Punta del Perro (Chipiona)** Fl.10s68m25M
Stone tower on building 62m

Ports

Vila Real de Santo António*
and Ayamonte (Río Guadiana)
Islas Canela* and Cristina*
(Ría de la Higuerita)
El Rompido*
Punta Umbría
Mazagón*
Chipiona*
The Río Guadalquivir and Seville*

* Fuel available alongside

The long west breakwater at the mouth of the Río Guadiana looking north-northwest. Vila Real de Santo António (Portuguese) and Ayamonte (Spanish) lie on either bank, with the tall suspension bridge visible in the distance

The Agencia Pública de Puertos de Andalucía marinas

One cannot cruise for very long on the Andalucían coast without encountering the string of yacht marinas and sport fishing harbours financed, built and run by the Agencia Pública de Puertos de Andalucía. www.puertosdeandalucia.es

They run nine yacht harbours to the west of Gibraltar as well as several in the Mediterranean. From west to east these comprise: Ayamonte, Isla Canela, Isla Cristina, Punta Umbría, Mazagón, Chipiona, Rota, Puerto América (Cádiz), Sancti Petri and Barbate, only 35M west of Gibraltar.

A leaflet, available in several languages, covers all nine, featuring an aerial photograph of each marina together with a plan showing the location of facilities such as fuel, travel lift, showers etc. In addition, there are leaflets issued for each individual harbour. There is much the same information available in the revamped (2013) website at www.puertosdeandalucia.es that has much of the most useful information in both Spanish and English.

Prices are standard for the entire chain, despite widely differing facilities and appeal, but it appears that some discretion is allowed when it comes to charging for use of water and electricity. Multihulls are subject to a 50% surcharge. If a berth of the correct length is not available and a yacht is forced to occupy a larger berth this is charged for, irrespective of the actual length of the boat.

A 10% discount is available for a stay of a month or more, 15% for three months and 30% for six months (the latter not including July or August). All payment must be made in advance, with most major credit cards accepted. Evidence of insurance may be required, but does not need to be translated into Spanish.

All the marinas appear well maintained and nearly all offices include at least one English-speaker, often fluent. The office attitude is nearly always helpful, though not always as flexible as might be the case with a privately-run concern. Where facilities include a travel-lift and hardstanding these also appear to be well-maintained and efficiently handled, with boats ashore normally placed in robust cradles with additional props. However, while owners are welcome to work on their own boats while ashore, living aboard – even for a single night – is totally forbidden. Rumour has it that an inhabited yacht blew over during a gale in 2003, and though no one was injured it led to an existing rule being taken out, dusted down, and strictly enforced. Security gates are locked at night (usually 2200–0700) and in some harbours there may be no access at weekends. Check when booking.

The Río Guadiana,
Vila Real de Santo António (Portugal) and Ayamonte (Spain)

Waypoints
⊕167 – 37°06'·2N 7°24'·2W (approach)
⊕168 – 37°08'·15N 7°23'·83W (entrance)

Courses and distances
⊕161 (Vilamoura) – ⊕167 (via ⊕163) = 38·9M, 117° & 064° or 244° & 297°
⊕163 (Cabo de Santa María) – F167 = 24·6M, 064° or 244°
⊕165 (Tavira) – ⊕167 = 9·1M, 080° or 260°
⊕167 – ⊕168 = 2M, 009° or 189°
⊕167 – ⊕169 (Islas Canela & Cristina) = 5·1M, 062° or 242°
⊕167 – ⊕175 (Mazagón) = 27·8M, 096° or 276°

Tides
Standard port Lisbon
Mean time differences (Portuguese time zone)
HW –0035 ±0020; LW –0020 ±0020
Heights in metres

MHWS	MHWN	MLWN	MLWS
3·2	2·5	1·3	0·5

Or refer to EasyTide at www.ukho.gov.ukeasytide
Both Vila Real and Ayamonte are listed, on the Portuguese and Spanish pages respectively

Charts	Approach	River
Admiralty	91, 89, 93	
Imray	C19, C50	C50
Portuguese	23204, 24206	26312
Spanish	44B, 440	440A

Principal lights
Entrance
2246 **Vila Real de Santo António** Fl.6.5s51m26M
    White tower, narrow black rings, red lantern 46m
2249 **West breakwater** Fl.R.3s7m4M
    White post, red bands 5m
2250 **East (submerged) training wall** Fl(3)G.9s3M
    Green tripod on concrete tower
Vila Real de Santo António (Portugal)
2247 **Marina south mole, angle** Fl.R.3s2M Grey post 2m
2247.1 **Marina south mole, head** Fl.R.3s2M Grey post 2m
2247.2 **Marina north mole, head** Fl.G.3s2M Grey post 2m
2247.3 **Marina north mole, root** Fl.R.3s2M Grey post 2m
2249.5 **Fishermen's quay** Fl.Y.3s5m2M Yellow x on yellow post 2m
Ayamonte (Spain)
Marina basin south side
2300 Q.G.1s1M Green truncated conical tower
Marina basin north side
2300.1 Q.R.1M Red column
2305 **Baluarte** Fl(2)G.5s2m1M Green tower

Night entry
Perfectly feasible in light conditions on a flood tide, but nevertheless not advised unless familiar with the area. See also the warning regarding the ferry jetty on page 261

Harbour communications
VHF Ch 09
(See also individual marinas, pages 261and 263).

Scenic river with two small marinas, yacht pontoons and anchorages upstream

The Río Guadiana forms part of the border between Portugal and Spain. A suspension bridge spans the river about 2M north of the twin towns of Vila Real de Santo António and Ayamonte, though a diminutive car ferry (which at first glance looks more like a fishing boat) still carries local traffic between the two. The river, which has strong currents, is navigable to Pomarão some 25M upstream and can make a pleasant change to seafaring. It has been reported that the upper valley of the Río Guadiana remains noticeably cooler than the surrounding areas even during the height of summer, possibly due to the chill of the river water which comes straight off the mountains inland.

THE ALGARVE & ANDALUCIA

There are small marinas at Vila Real de Santo Antónío and Ayamonte (the latter run by the Agencia Pública de Puertos de Andalucía (see page 261). Some provision for yachts is also in place upriver, primarily at Alcoutim (Portuguese) and Sanlúcar de Guadiana (Spanish).

Approach

Either side of the Río Guadiana the coast consists of a low sandbank broken by gaps giving access to the lagoons which run from west of Cabo de Santa María to 2M east of the Río Guadiana. Further east the sand continues unbroken for another 12M. If coastal sailing, note that depths between the Río Guadiana and the Ría de la Higuerita are very shoal, with drying patches up to 1M offshore. The 5m line generally runs more than 1·5M offshore, making 2M a safe distance off. Fishing nets may be laid several miles offshore.

Approaching from the west, two conspicuous marks are the high-rise buildings of Monte Gordo 2M west of the entrance and the tall Vila Real light (white with narrow black bands). From the east, the tower blocks of Isla Cristina stand out. The twin pillars of the suspension bridge can also be seen for many miles.

From offshore ⊕167 lies 2M south of the entrance, a course of 009° leading to ⊕168, about 0·6M southwest of the outer entrance buoys.

Entrance

Do not attempt to enter other than at half flood or above and be especially careful if there is any swell. If making for the marina (Porto de Recreio do Guadiana) at Vila Real de Santo Antónío be aware that manoeuvring there is least traumatic at slack water.

The river is canalised between a breakwater and a submerged training wall running 335°, their ends 550m apart and lit. Seaward of the walls are two pairs of port and starboard hand buoys, all lit (though the starboard hand buoys in particular have a reputation for unreliability and long periods off station).

Pass between the buoys and then head for the west breakwater, keeping it slightly open on the port bow. The east training wall is almost totally submerged, with a concrete tower marking its seaward end. Keep about 50m off the breakwater, remaining on

Looking upstream towards the suspension bridge, with one of the diminutive car ferries in the foreground
Anne Hammick

the west side until off the town of Vila Real de Santo Antónío.

The bar can be rough on the ebb, particularly if there is any swell running, and is hazardous in onshore weather. When planning departure, allow time to reach the bar before the ebb gathers speed.

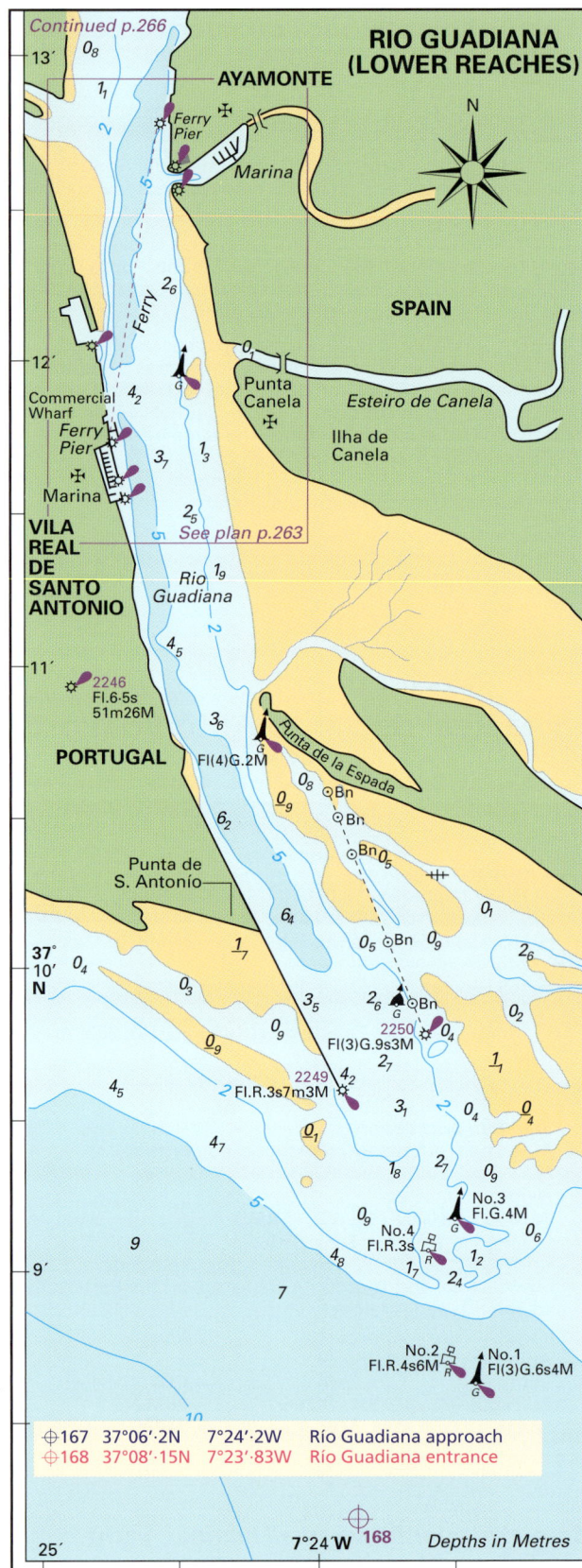

RIO GUADIANA (LOWER REACHES)

Continued p.266

AYAMONTE
Ferry Pier
Marina
SPAIN
Punta Canela
Esteiro de Canela
Ilha de Canela

Commercial Wharf
Ferry Pier
Marina

VILA REAL DE SANTO ANTONIO
See plan p.263
Rio Guadiana

2246 Fl.6·5s 51m26M

PORTUGAL
Fl(4)G.2M
Punta de la Espada
Bn
Bn
Bn

Punta de S. Antonío

37° 10' N

2250 Fl(3)G.9s3M
2249 Fl.R.3s7m3M

No.3 Fl.G.4M
No.4 Fl.R.3s

No.2 Fl.R.4s6M
No.1 Fl(3)G.6s4M

| ⊕167 | 37°06'·2N | 7°24'·2W | Río Guadiana approach |
| ⊕168 | 37°08'·15N | 7°23'·83W | Río Guadiana entrance |

7°24'W 168 Depths in Metres

Vila Real de Santo António (Portugal)

Port Authority
☎ +351 281 512035/513769 *Fax* +351 281 511140
Email anguadiana@mail.telepac.pt
VHF Ch 11, 16 call *Capimarvireal* (24 hours)
Porto de Recreio do Guadiana
☎ +351 281 541 571 /+351 281 513 769 *Fax* +351 281
511 140 *Email* anguadiana@mail.telepac.pt
www.anguadiana.com VHF Ch 09, 12

The town of Vila Real de Santo António was largely rebuilt in the 18th century, following destruction in the 1755 earthquake and tidal wave which decimated Lisbon as well as much of the Algarve. It follows a strict grid plan of wide avenues and open squares, often paved with black and white cobbles in intricate patterns. Even the much newer suburbs follow these lines – less interesting perhaps than the winding lanes of the older villages, but with considerably less scope for getting lost. A large part of the centre is a pedestrian area, making Vila Real de Santo António a very pleasant town in which to wander. As a final bonus it has, for some inexplicable but happy reason, been very largely overlooked by foreign tourists.

The Porto de Recreio do Guadiana contains about 360 berths for yachts of up to 20m, all against finger pontoons. A high proportion of these are nominally reserved for visitors, but the definition of 'visitor' is necessarily vague and the marina is frequently full in the high season. It is claimed that space will nearly always be found for new arrivals, but sometimes only for a single night. Even when the marina is full, yachts are not permitted to berth in the old Doca de Pesca about 0·5M upstream.

Entrance and berthing

The narrow marina entrance, which is less than 20m wide, is situated at its downstream end, with reception berths on the starboard hand alongside the

Porto de Recreio do Guadiana at Vila Real de Santo Antonio looking northwest

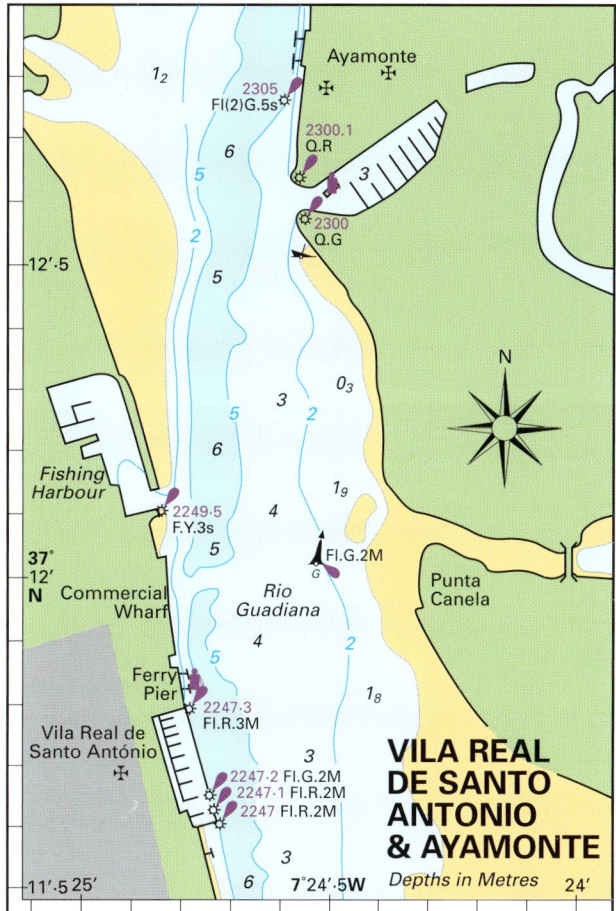

inside of the long pontoon protecting the marina on its east flank. When this is occupied, the fuel pontoon, between the marina and the ferry pier to the north, may be pressed into service as a reception berth. At other times arriving yachts may be directed straight to a berth by marina staff. The staff cannot, of course, allow for the handling characteristics of individual craft, and at periods of strong tide it may occasionally be necessary to be deaf to directions and secure wherever possible until the flow diminishes. If planning to leave other than at slack water it would also be wise to turn the yacht in her berth in advance.

If manoeuvring in the river at night in the vicinity of the ferry jetty, note that although the pylons to which the ferry jetty is secured both carry lights, the jetty itself, which is painted matt black and projects a further 10m out into the stream, is totally unlit.

Both entrance and marina are subject to strong cross-currents. Flow in the river itself can reach 3kn on the ebb and 2kn on the flood making slack water by far the best time to manoeuvre. Once inside space is tight. Both sides of the entrance, as well as the upstream end of the fuel pontoon, are lit but movement at night is to be avoided as it will be difficult to estimate and allow for the cross-current. When new, the marina carried 4m or more in the southern part of the basin, decreasing slightly to the north, but silting has been an ongoing problem.

THE ALGARVE & ANDALUCIA

Fishing in the traditional way – azulejos (painted tiles) on the wall of the *Capitania* at Vila Real de Santo António
Anne Hammick

Dredging took place in 2005 and it was stated that this would provide 10m beside the river, 8m down the middle and 6m next to the street. Even allowing for the silting which must have followed, depths should remain adequate for a few years yet.

The marina office, open 0900–1230 and 1430 to 1800 (October–March), to 1900 (April–June) and to 2000 (July–August), occupies a smart portacabin at the north end of the basin with the services alongside. Both services and pontoons are secured by locked gates with the usual card access.

Formalities

If the yacht is registered in the EU, and all her crew are EU nationals, completion of the usual multi-part form in the marina office is sufficient. Otherwise it may be necessary to visit the offices of the *Polícia Marítima* and *Imigração* at the *Capitania*, about 50m south of the marina.

Facilities

Boatyard There is a newish (2006) boatyard, the Marina Guadiana, downstream from the marina at 37°10'·9N 007°24'·7W adjacent to the north side of the lifeboat station. *Address* Marina Guadiana Seca, Punta de Areia, Vila Real de Santo Antonio ☎ +351 281 542 069 *Email* info@marinaguadiana.com www.marinaguadiana.com. The Spanish owner, Enrique Garcia Tomé, is supported by the Portugese Edmundo Almeida who is the yard's electrician (*Email* Emundo@marinaguadiana.com). There is a large shed/workshop and tarmac yard with 40 boat spaces.

Boat owners can live aboard. WC and shower block are open to all hours. Water and 230v power points available for a small charge. Good security with residents given a key to the gate. Own work is not allowed on the hull outside of the boat.

The yard will arrange taxi to a supermarket, the largest of which is Intermarche, ½ mile north of the centre, close to the railway station.

There is a good restaurant just south on the road (the second restaurant) and plenty more in town (20–25 minute walk).

This is a friendly and helpful yard with an expert travel-lift and particularly good chocking up of boats.
Travel-lift A 70-tonne travel-lift uses a concrete ramp into the river at high water.
General repairs can be carried out in most materials including GRP. Some engineering work, antifouling, and sand/shot blasting is available for yachts, fishing boats, and government craft.

Chandlery Nautiguadiana, opposite the marina, carries fishing tackle and some general chandlery. Marinautica, a little further down the road, stocks the above plus some electronics, stainless steel fittings, paint etc. The Boutique Náutica at the *clube naval* sells some chandlery in addition to clothing.
Water On the pontoons.
Showers In well-kept portacabins next to the marina office.
Launderette In the town – ask at the office for directions.
Electricity On the pontoons.
Fuel Diesel from a fuelling berth extending upstream from the marina, with petrol available by can from a pump ashore. Payment must be made in cash.
Bottled gas Gas bottles can be filled 400m out from the centre of town roundabout towards Faro. Look out for the blue elephant sign.
Weather forecast Posted daily outside the marina office and in the window overlooking the slipway.
Clube naval The Associação Naval do Guadiana, which now occupies a blue-tiled building at the south end of the marina basin, has a terrace bar and restaurant open to non-members.
Banks In the town, with a cash dispenser directly opposite the marina.
Shops/provisioning/produce market Good shopping of all kinds in the town, including a supermarket four blocks directly inland from the marina.
Cafés, restaurants and hotels An abundance of the former nearby, a good restaurant on the quay (2010) and a comfortable if somewhat traditional hotel right opposite.
Medical services In the town.

Communications

Post office In the town.
Mailing address The marina office will hold mail for visiting yachts – c/o Associação Naval do Guadiana, Doca de Recreio, Apartado 40 Avenida da República, 8901-909 Vila Real de Santo António, Algarve, Portugal. It is important that the envelope carries the name of the yacht in addition to that of the addressee.
Public telephones Several nearby.
Internet access Directly opposite the marina in the foyer of the Hotel Guadiana (small fee payable), at the public library (free, but often busy) and elsewhere.
Fax service At the marina office *Fax* +351 281 511140.
Car hire/taxis In the town or via the marina office.
Buses Bus station beyond the ferry pier, itself next to the marina. Ten minutes ride northward is the attractive riverside village of Castro Marim, with two castles and a unusually imaginative children's playground.
Trains Vila Real is the eastern terminus of the Algarve coastal line, with a sleepy station close to the fishing harbour in the northern part of the town.
Ferries The diminutive passenger and car ferry departs every hour for Ayamonte, returning on the half hour.
Air services Faro International Airport is some 60km by road or rail.

Ayamonte (Spain)

Puerto Deportivo del Ayamonte
Ayamonte, 21400 Huelva
☎ +34 959 034 498 - 600 149 140 *Fax* +34 959 077 531
Email ayamonted@eppa.es www.puertosdeandalucia.es
VHF Ch 09

Ayamonte, a village of Greek origin, is, in its way, just as attractive as its Portuguese rival and certainly as historic. The parador here has extensive views of the town and river. Parts of the original 16th-century walls are still visible, there are several old and interesting churches, and all the generations gather for the evening *paseo* in the exuberantly tiled squares. With fewer tourists than the Algarve, the shops are better stocked with practical, everyday items and the cafés are thronged with local people.

This old fishermen's basin contains the westernmost of the string of yacht marinas and sport fishing harbours run by the Agencia Pública de Puertos de Andalucía – see page 261. There are now nine pontoons with finger berths in the marina with a reported capacity of around 317 berths (mostly for yachts 18–20m in length), 25% of which are nominally reserved for yachts in transit. It is believed that the entire basin has been dredged to a minimum of 3m.

Entrance and berthing

The entrance to the basin is some 60m wide and subject to strong cross-currents, but complete protection is gained once inside. Both sides are lit, and night arrival is feasible, but preferably call on VHF Ch 09 before entering the basin. Failing the quick allocation of a berth, secure to the westernmost hammerhead or, failing that, choose a suitable berth on the westernmost pontoon.

Puerto Deportivo de Ayamonte looking south   *APPA*

Weekdays office hours are 0930–1330 and 1600–1700, closed Saturday and Sunday afternoons in winter. There is 24 hour security in addition to electronic pontoon access gates, toilets/showers, water, electricity, and used oil disposal.

Formalities

As is usual in Spain, formalities are very relaxed. After completing the usual paperwork in the marina office it is possible that an official may visit the yacht, though this is unlikely in the case of an EU yacht and crew.

Facilities

Boatyard Fishermen's yard near the ferry pier, but nothing for yachts.
Engineers Some mechanical skills available – enquire at the marina office.
Chandlery AYAMAR yacht chandlers opposite the marina run by John and Diane Poer. Well-stocked and a laundry service ☎ +34 959 470 814 *Email* centronautico@aol.com
Water On the pontoons.
Showers In a portacabin next to the marina office.
Electricity On the pontoons
Fuel A 'fuel pontoon' has been in position near the entrance to the basin on the port side for many years completely bereft of pumps or even shore access. It is a real hazard to yachts entering after dark being grey, low-lying, and totally unlit.
Bottled gas Camping Gaz exchanges in the town, but no refills.
Weather forecast Posted daily outside the marina office.
Banks In the town.
Shops/provisioning Good shopping in the town, plus a supermarket one block to the east of the marina basin.
Produce market In the town.
Cafés, restaurants and hotels Plenty in the town, but nothing at the marina itself.
Medical services In the town.

Communications

Post office In the town.
Mailing address The marina office will hold mail for visiting yachts – c/o Puerto Deportivo Ayamonte, 21400 Ayamonte, Huelva, España. It is important that the envelope carries the name of the yacht in addition to that of the addressee.
Public telephones Beside the marina office and elsewhere.
Internet access At Todoapc on the north side of the basin near the entrance, which also advertises computer maintenance and repairs.
Fax service At the marina office, ☎/*Fax* +34 959 321694.
Car hire/taxis/buses In the town.
Ferries Small but frequent passenger and car ferry to Vila Real de Santo António.
Air services Faro International Airport is some 65km distant by road, Seville approximately twice as far.

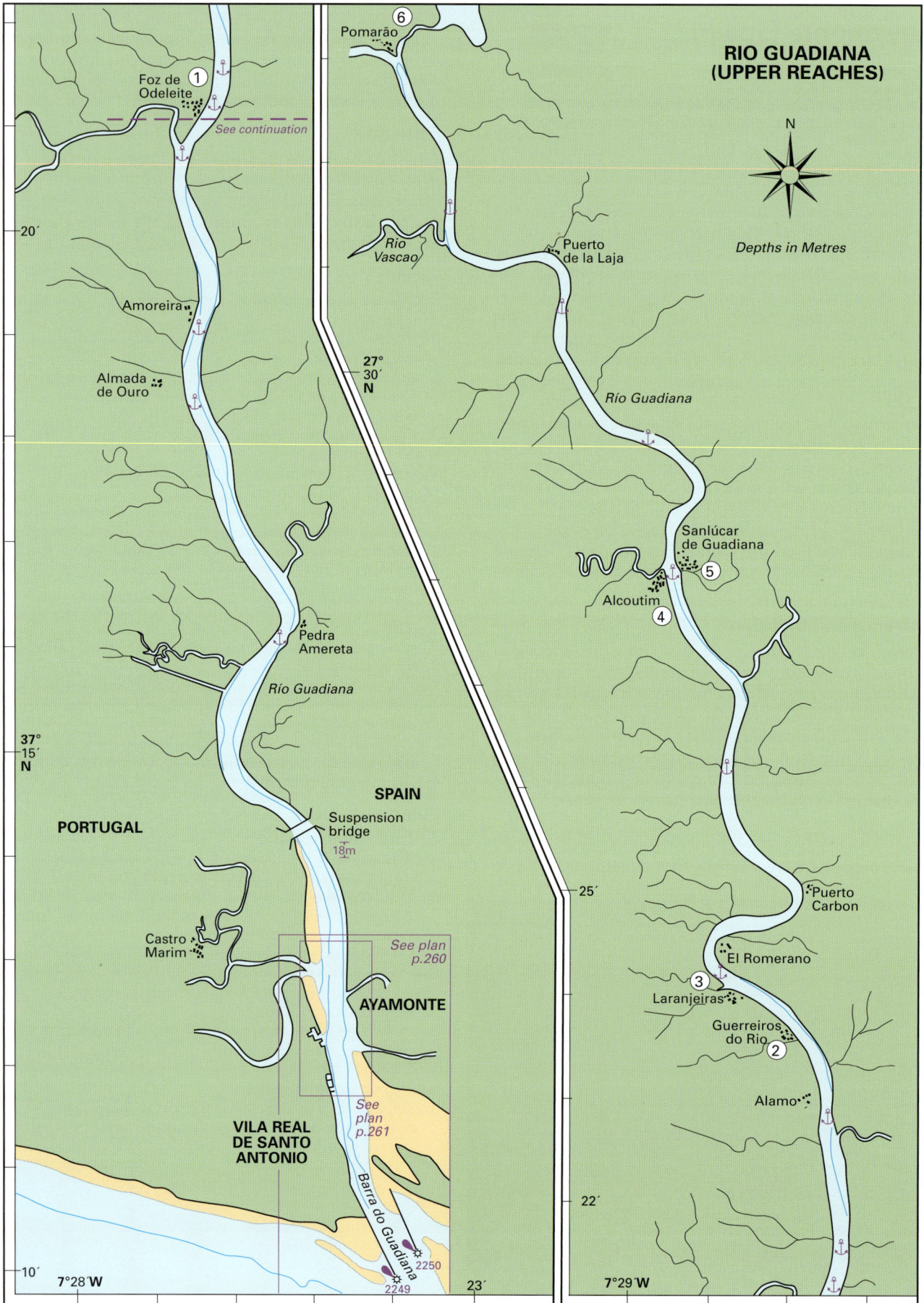

RIO GUADIANA (UPPER REACHES)

N

Depths in Metres

Pomarão ⑥

Foz de Odeleite ①

See continuation

20′

Río Vascao

Puerto de la Laja

Amoreira

27° 30′ N

Almada de Ouro

Río Guadiana

Sanlúcar de Guadiana

Alcoutim ④ ⑤

Pedra Amereta

Río Guadiana

37° 15′ N

SPAIN

PORTUGAL

Suspension bridge 18m

25′

Puerto Carbon

Castro Marim

El Romerano

See plan p.260

AYAMONTE

③

Laranjeiras

Guerreiros do Rio ②

See plan p.261

VILA REAL DE SANTO ANTONIO

Alamo

22′

Barra do Guadiana

2250

10′

2249

7°28′W

23′

7°29′W

Upriver

There is general agreement that the upper reaches of the Río Guadiana are not to be missed, particularly by birdwatchers. White storks can often be seen on the lower reaches of the river above Ayamonte, along with other interesting birds. These include cattle egrets, black-winged stilts and kingfishers. Red-rumped swallows, hoopoes, golden orioles and bee-eaters may be seen further upriver, and a flock of azure-winged magpies live close upstream of Alcoutim/Sanlúcar (the home of manzanilla wine).

If heading upriver, leave at low water, favouring the starboard side while passing Ayamonte to avoid the muddy shoal which extends nearly halfway across the river north of Vila Real. There is relatively little traffic other than regular ferries, excursion boats in summer and a few fishing vessels.

After passing under the rather elegant suspension bridge (note that the clearance given on Portuguese charts is 18m but that this is referenced to Mean Sea Level.) the Río Guadiana is quiet, pretty and deep but has a current to be reckoned with – approaching 2kn on the flood and 3kn on the ebb. With the aid of the former it is possible to make the 20M or so up to Portuguese Alcoutim and Spanish Sanlúcar de Guadiana on one tide. The river is not buoyed, other than a single red can marking shallows just downstream from the bridge, and the channel is not always obvious. However, with a little care, a minimum of 3·5m, and a maximum of 20m, may to be found as far as Alcoutim/Sanlúcar even at dead low water. The channel generally runs deepest on the outside of bends, often only 20–50m from the bank, but shoals may be found off the mouths of many tributaries.

Anchorages

Straight stretches usually offer the best anchorages, with 6–8m depths and good holding over mud. Boats anchor on both sides of the river, but experience has shown that wind against tide make

The pontoon at Foz de Odeleite (1), the first settlement one passes when venturing up the Río Guadiana *Anne Hammick*

The second pontoon lies off the Portuguese village of Guerreiros do Rio (2), where there is a small river museum *Anne Hammick*

for an uncomfortable berth. Also, there have been instances of local fishermen setting nets around anchored boats. In one case this led to a light ramming and demands for money to repair nets. Others simply reported torrents of abuse.

High water at Alcoutim/Sanlúcar occurs about 2hrs after Vila Real, high water at Pomarão about 2·5 hours later. In both cases tidal range is marginally reduced compared to the entrance.

Avoid venturing upstream immediately after heavy rain further inland which, as well as adding to the already strong current, can send large items of floating debris such as branches, bamboo canes etc careering downstream.

The Spanish side is sparsely inhabited as far as Sanlúcar, but there are several small villages on the Portuguese bank, including Foz de Odeleite (37°21'·22N 7°26'·46W), Guerreiros do Río (37°23'·85N 7°26'·8W) and Laranjeiras (37°24'·23N 7°27'·48W). All three have short pontoons, also used by tourist boats running day excursions up the river from Vila Real, to which yachts can secure for no more than three nights. All three pontoons are nominally equipped with water and electricity but may not be operational. Depths alongside have not been verified, but appear generous. Although it was reported some years ago that visitors moorings were

The third Portuguese village to have its own pontoon is Laranjeiras (3), where there is also a good anchorage *Anne Hammick*

The town of Alcoutim (4) on the Portuguese bank, which has three pontoons (one reserved for commercial craft) and is a favourite spot for over-wintering *Anne Hammick*

to be laid off the villages, there is little evidence of this. None has much in the way of shoreside facilities beyond a bar or two, though a van selling bread and basic foodstuffs makes regular visits, but all are served by the bus which runs north from Vila Real to Alcoutim and beyond. A 'river museum' can be visited at Guerreiros do Río, while a Roman villa is being excavated near Laranjeiras (yachts too large for the pontoon will find good anchorage opposite the village in 4–5m).

Portuguese Alcoutim (37°28′·29N 7°28′·25W) and Spanish Sanlúcar de Guadiana (37°28′·37N 7°28′·11W), linked by pedestrian ferry, are an entirely different matter to the villages downstream. Both have good pontoons, three on the Portuguese side and a single long one on the Spanish, all with functioning water and electricity (though Alcoutim's central pontoon is intended for tourist boats rather than yachts). Adjacent to the Sanlúcar pontoon are purpose-built showers and toilets for the use of berth-holders (key from the nearby Capitania). There is a small flat fee for all yachts lying alongside overnight, though lying to a buoy is understood to be free, as is anchoring. In common with the other Portuguese villages,

Alcoutim has a three night berthing rule throughout the year. Although sometimes relaxed out of season it is rigorously enforced during the summer. Sanlúcar nominally allows a maximum of two weeks alongside, but this is seldom enforced.

Both towns have cafés, restaurants, limited shopping (including pharmacies), banks with cash dispensers and public telephones, while Alcoutim also has a small hospital and internet access in the public library (booking advised). Squat stone castles peer at each other across the river, but most would agree that the Castelo de San Marcos on the Spanish side, with origins dating back to the 13th century, has the visual edge over its Portuguese rival, though the latter contains a small museum. Younger crew members will enjoy the praia fluvial (river beach) on a narrow tributary just north of Alcoutim, complete with sand, safe paddling/swimming, and a nearby play area. On the Portuguese side buses run to south to Vila Real and north (twice weekly) as far as Mértola, an old walled town complete with obligatory castle and museums.

At least two dozen visitors of all nationalities choose to winter at Alcoutim/Sanlúcar, five or six alongside, a few on moorings and the majority at anchor. If planning to stay at anchor for any length of time it would be wise to lay two, the heaviest upstream and a second, more than a kedge, downstream, secured together at a point deep enough for the yacht to swing).

Upper reaches of the river

Hand drawn charts of the upper reaches of the river can be obtained from the library in Alcoutim for a minimal copying fee. They are obviously only basic aids, but seem reasonably accurate, and might be useful to anyone going up as far as Pomarao.

During May there is a fishery for spawning fish in the upper reaches. The fish is only taken for its roe,

Opposite Alcoutim is the Spanish town of Spanish Sanlúcar de Guadiana (5), dominated by its hilltop castle. A pedestrian ferry plies between the two towns *Anne Hammick*

Pomarão (6), on the Portuguese bank, is as far up the Río Guadiana as most yachts can penetrate, though care is needed on the approach *Anne Hammick*

the carcase being ditched, but overfishing has led to licensing of the fisherman. This has led to 'gentlemen of the night' taking the law into their own hands and several illegal nets being set at night, some very close to established anchorages (e.g. just around the corner above Alcoutim). Nets have appeared after dark and sunken nets have fouled anchors. Apparently the fishermen simply drop the net at dawn so they are not evident, and recover them again after dark with the aid of grapnel.

There are a number of sizeable boats that look to be abandoned up the river anchored with considerable amounts of chain veered. They are a menace in squally weather, taking up most of the swinging room around them.

A muddy shoal runs out from the west bank just north of Alcoutim and local advice is to keep well to starboard of the line of mooring buoys if heading upriver. With persistence most yachts can get as far as Pomarão (37°33'·28N 7°31'·57W), on the Portuguese side about 7M upstream of Alcoutim. This takes one past disused mine workings and derelict piers once used by sizeable ore-carriers, but the river narrows and has silted in places (the best water will generally be found on the eastern side). Particular caution should be exercised in the approach to Pomarão, which has numerous offlying rocks and boulders. Two short pontoons, both provided with water and electricity, lie beneath the village, which has a seasonal café but little else. There is a short pontoon on the south side but nothing whatsoever ashore. Some road maps show a bridge at Pomarão, but it has long gone if it ever existed at all, and there is no sign of supports or other remains. If anchoring in the vicinity of Pomarão it is best to avoid the area off the old ore-loading jetty immediately west of the pontoons, which is reported to be fouled with chains, and to continue about 200m upstream before dropping. Even so a trip line would be adviseable.

Intrepid explorers may wish to continue beyond Pomarão towards Mertola, a sizeable Portuguese town, though currently a sand and shingle bar halts yachts a few miles downstream of the town, not even allowing sufficient depth to proceed by dinghy. This last stretch of the river runs between stony cliffs and is totally undeveloped. However rocks and sandbanks abound, the latter most often around the mouths of small tributary creeks, and navigation is strictly visual. The water comes straight off the mountains and is clear but very cold.

THE ALGARVE & ANDALUCIA

Islas Canela and Cristina (Ría de la Higuerita)

Waypoints
⊕169 – 37°08'·6N 7°18'·6W (approach)
⊕170 – 37°10'·45N 7°18'·93W (entrance)

Courses and distances
⊕167 (Río Guadiana) – ⊕169 = 5·1M, 062° or 242°
⊕169 – ⊕170 = 1·9M, 352° or 172°
⊕169 – ⊕171 (El Rompido) = 12·3M, 087° or 267°
⊕169 – ⊕173 (Punta Umbría) = 17M, 096° or 276°
⊕169 – ⊕175 (Mazagón) = 23·7M, 103° or 283°

Tides
See Río Guadiana, page 261

Charts

	Approach	River
Admiralty	91, 89, 93	
Imray	C19, C50	C50
Spanish	44B, 440	440A

Principal entrance lights
2308 **Ldg Lts 313°** *Front* Q.8m5M
Aluminium framework tower 7m
2308.1 *Rear* 100m from front Fl.4s13m5M
Aluminium framework tower 12m
2307 **West breakwater** VQ(2)R.5s8m4M
Red framework tower 4m
2309 **Pantalán del Moral, head** F.W
Note The tall white building on Punta del Caimán
is NOT a light structure but an apartment block

Night entry
As with the (much wider) Río Guadiana, while night entry is perfectly
possible in the right conditions it is best avoided by those unfamiliar
with the area

Harbour communications
VHF Ch 09 (see also marinas, pages 272 and 273).

Dredger off Isla Cristina

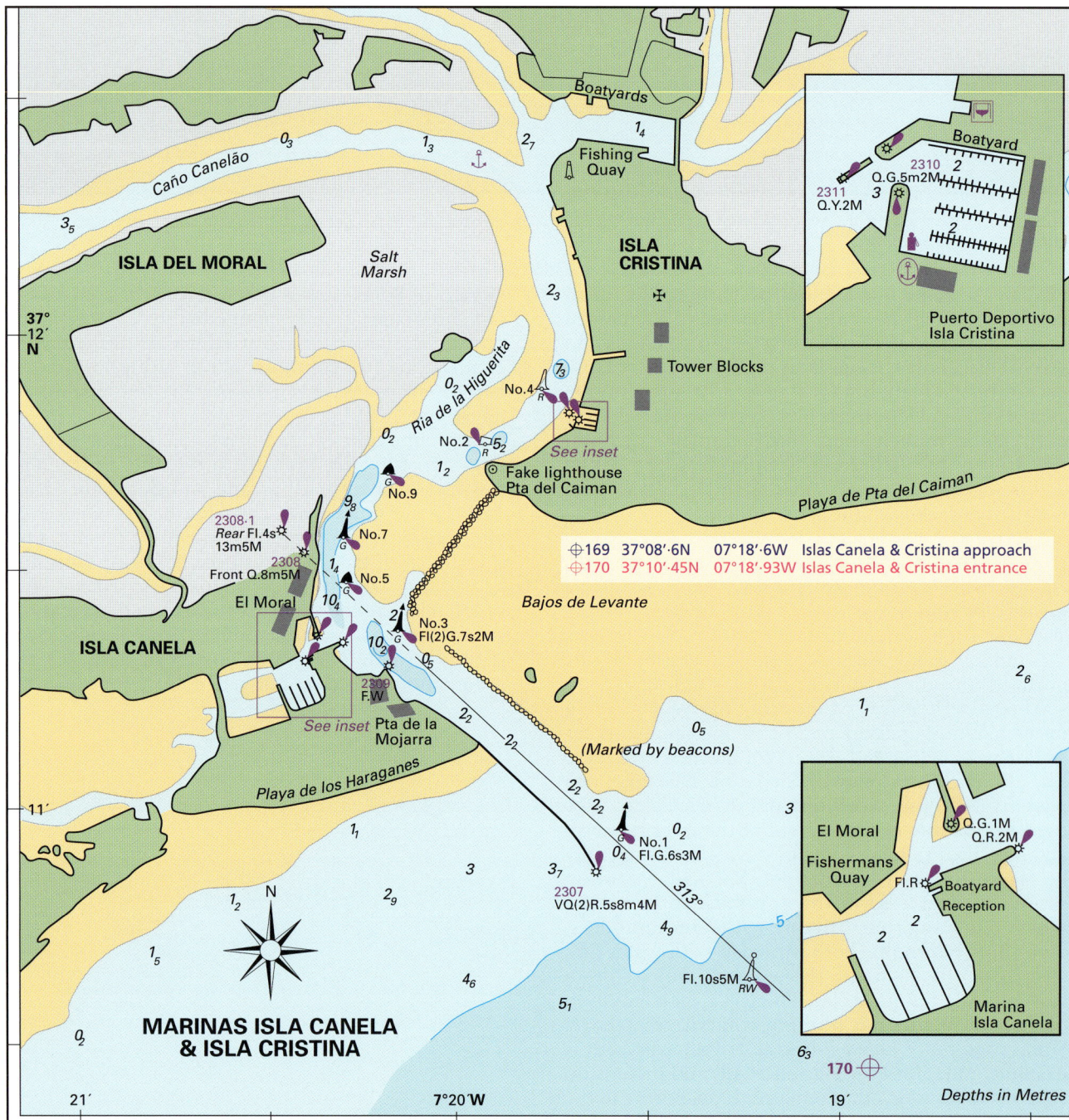

| ⊕169 | 37°08'·6N | 07°18'·6W | Islas Canela & Cristina approach |
| ⊕170 | 37°10'·45N | 07°18'·93W | Islas Canela & Cristina entrance |

**MARINAS ISLA CANELA
& ISLA CRISTINA**

Depths in Metres

Two well-run marinas surrounded by windswept salt marsh

Marina Isla Canela and the Puerto Deportivo Isla Cristina represent very contrasting styles of Spanish marina development. The former, opened in 2001, is of the 'marina village' style and while quiet and secure lacks any shoreside atmosphere. The old fishermen's quarter at Punta del Moral on the north side of the basin is being swallowed up by new development, while much of the area to the south, while rather attractive with its moorish architecture, some of it atop old castle walls and in well-kept grounds, is emphatically private. It is only a short walk to a superb beach, however.

In contrast Isla Cristina, on its long sandspit to the east of the Ría de la Higuerita, is one of the most important fishing ports in Andalucía. Although tourism – much of it Spanish – is a growing industry, the old town a short walk away is attractive and the waterfront north of the marina interesting, particularly the thriving fishing harbour with its bustling market. An illustrated notice in three languages gives some explanation for the visitor. The Puerto Deportivo Isla Cristina was one of the first built by the Agencia Pública de Puertos de Andalucía (see page 261) and is best suited to smaller yachts, being relatively shallow and with few berths able to accommodate more than 10m overall.

Approach

If coastal sailing, note that depths between the Río Guadiana and the the Ría de la Higuerita are very shoal, with drying patches up to 1M offshore. The 5m line generally runs more than 1·5M offshore, making 2M a safe distance off.

From offshore ⊕169 lies 1·9M south of the entrance, a course of 352° leading to ⊕170 on the leading line and about 0·7M from the west breakwater head. A fish haven lies 2M offshore, and the chart still shows a fish farm marked by two yellow pillar buoys with x topmarks, both lit Q.Y, centred on 37°08'·12N 7°17'·53W.

Looking SW into Marina Isla Canela entrance from main channel *Jane Russell*

Although the shore on either side of the entrance is low-lying, the new development at Punta de la Mojarra (generally referred to as Isla Canela, though correctly this is the island close north) and long, pale buildings at Isla Cristina show up well from seaward. Near the southwest corner of Punta del Caimán will be seen a tall beige building complete with domed superstructure, looking for all the world like a rather fancy lighthouse. In fact it is yet another apartment block, but a fine daymark. An older tower, the Torre Catalán, lies halfway between Isla Cristina and Rompido.

Entrance

Approach from the south, preferably at between half and three-quarter flood, and turn in to run parallel with the west breakwater. The deeper water is on the western side of the channel. Follow the leading marks on 313°. The grey framework towers resemble electricity pylons and can be difficult to distinguish from offshore.

Upriver

Above the marinas and fishing wharves the channel becomes sinuous and shoal, flanked by salt marsh and ancient, abandoned hulks. The Caño Canelão is marked on the north side with withies and then two prominent wrecks. It is possible to anchor in the entrance to the Caño Canelão (though rolly from fishing boat wash), but otherwise this is an area to be explored by dinghy, and with an eye to the tide-tables.

The mouth of the Ría de la Higuerita looking northwest, with Marina Isla Canela and its associated development on the left and Isla Cristina further upstream on the right. The distinctive 'fake lighthouse' stands just to the right of centre

Marina Isla Canela

Principal lights
2309 **Pantalán del Moral, head** F.W
2308.2 **South mole** Q.R.2M Red post 2m
2308.3 **North mole** Q.G.1M Green post
2308.4 **Travel-hoist dock** Fl.R.1M Red post
Communications
☎ +34 959 479000 *Fax* +34 959 479020
Email marina@islacanel.es
www.marina-islacanela.com
VHF Ch 09

Marina Isla Canela is of the 'marina village' type. The surrounding buildings have a distinctly north African character – perhaps related to the fact that *canela* means cinnamon. The initial phase contains 231 berths in minimum depths of 2·5m. Only 24 of these can take yachts of more than 11m overall including three hammerheads, each rated for 24m. But there is room for expansion to the west, where dredging will one day create space for a further 305 berths.

Entrance and berthing

The entrance is well marked and is lit to port, but the triangular green base on the starboard hand has been reported without lens or light. The reception berth requires a second turn to port, lying just beyond the travel-lift and crane and below the blue and white marina office. The four pontoons lie beyond, well sheltered from fishing boat wash and other disturbance, with the largest yachts to the southwest and smallest to the northeast. Access requires the usual electronic card. Office hours are 0900–1400, 1600–2000 from June to September and 0900–1400, 1500–1800 throughout the rest of the year, Monday to Saturday only. The staff are helpful and efficient, and excellent English is spoken.

Multihulls pay a 50% surcharge, water is included but electricity is metred and charged in addition. Discounts are available for longer stays if paid in advance. Most major credit cards are accepted.

Formalities

Whether arriving from Spain or Portugal a single-sheet form is completed at the marina office, a copy of which is automatically passed to the authorities.

Facilities

Boatyard Generous (if slightly exposed) area of secure, concreted hardstanding on which yachts are propped but not in cradles. Several contractors operate workshops in the area, including Náutica Avante, ☎ +34 959 479013, *Fax* +34 959 479530. DIY work is permitted, but this is restricted to office hours (so no work on Sunday) and owners are not allowed to live aboard a yacht while ashore.
Travel-lift 32-tonne capacity lift in the boatyard.
Engineers, electronic and radio repairs In the boatyard (or visit Náutica Levante SYS at Puerto Deportivo Isla Cristina, see opposite).
Chandlery Náutica Avante (see above) operate a small chandlery in the commercial centre but it is almost totally given over to fishing tackle.

Marina Isla Canela looking northeast *APPA*

Water On the pontoons.
Showers In the blue and white reception building.
Launderette Neither available nor planned.
Electricity On the pontoons.
Fuel Diesel and petrol available 24 hours a day from pumps near the office.
Bottled gas Not available.
Weather forecast Posted daily at the marina office.
Club náutico Already established in the reception building, though how much it is a true club and how much a commercial organisation is difficult to say.
Bank No bank, but at least one cash dispenser in the commercial area.
Shops, provisioning Two small supermarkets in the commercial area. For more serious shopping it would be necessary to visit either Ayamonte or Isla Cristina.
Cafés, restaurants and hotels A wide choice in the commercial centre, with a few more in the old town to the north.
Medical services Can be summoned from Ayamonte via the marina office.

Communications

Post office Not as such – not even a post box! – but the supermarket sells stamps and mail for despatch can be left at the marina office.
Mailing address The marina office will hold mail for visiting yachts – c/o Marina Isla Canela, 21409 Isla Canela, Ayamonte, Huelva, España. It is important that the envelope carries the name of the yacht in addition to that of the addressee.
Telephones In the marina office and commercial centre.
Internet access Cybercafé in the commercial centre.
Fax service At the marina office, *Fax* +34 959 479020.
Car hire At least one agency in the commercial centre.
Taxis Order via the marina office.
Buses Bus stop a little way down the road.
Air services International airports at Faro (Portugal) and Seville (Spain).

Puerto Deportivo Isla Cristina

Principal lights
2310 **South mole** Q.G.5m2M Green column 2m
2311 **Wavebreak pontoon** Q.Y.2M Post 2m
Communications
☎ +34 959 077613 - 600 149 130 *Fax* +34 959 998003
Email islacristinad@eppa.es
www.puertosdeandalucia.es
VHF Ch 09

Shortly after passing the entrance to Marina Isla Canela the channel bends to starboard around a drying middle ground marked by several starboard hand buoys (do not be tempted to emulate local craft which may take a short cut across the shallows). A port-hand buoy opposite the 'lighthouse' and a second almost opposite the marina entrance mark a second shoal. A 90m wavebreak pontoon has been laid off the marina entrance in a partially successful attempt to deflect the considerable wash from passing fishing boats, few of which take any notice of the 4kn speed limit.

Entrance and berthing

The relatively narrow entrance to Puerto Deportivo Isla Cristina lies inside the shelter pontoon described above. Although the latter is lit, particular care should be taken if entering after dark. Depth in the entrance is 2·5m, decreasing to 2m inside. Secure to the reception/fuel pontoon immediately to starboard to be allocated a berth, preferably having already called up on VHF Ch 09 – a wise precaution in any case, since only 20 of the marina's 203 berths are able to take yachts of more than 10m overall. These are all on the northernmost pontoon, with all berths now alongside finger pontoons.

Office hours vary from summer to winter, being 0800–2000 daily in summer, 0930–1330 and 1600–1730 in winter, closed weekend afternoons. Berthing staff are on duty from 0700–2200 and there is 24 hour security, as well as electronic gates to individual pontoons and the boatyard area. All the staff on duty are exceptionally helpful and friendly, and several speak good English.

Formalities

Whether arriving from Spain or Portugal a single-sheet form is completed at the marina office, a copy of which is automatically passed to the authorities. Nothing further needs to be done, even if arriving from outside the EU, though occasionally the *Guardia Civil* may visit the yacht in her berth.

Facilities

Boatyard An area of gated hardstanding near the travel-lift enables owners to do their own maintenance or to call in one of the contractors in the area. By far the largest, and longest established, is Náutica Levante SYS, ☎ +34 959 332730 *Mobile* +34 60 9508 204 *Fax* +34 959 332797 *Email* info@nauticalevante.com www.nauticalevante.com (Spanish only), which handles repairs and maintenance in all materials, osmosis treatment, painting etc. Norwegian owner Rino Johansen speaks fluent English as well as several other languages.

Puerto Deportivo Isla Cristina looking south *APPA*

Travel-lift 32-tonne capacity lift. Yachts are placed in cradles with additional shores.
Engineers, electronics and radio repairs Náutica Levante SYS, as above.
Sail repairs Can be arranged via Náutica Levante SYS, though an entire new sail would have to be ordered from further afield.
Chandlery Well-stocked chandlery in the commercial block – another Náutica Levante SYS enterprise. Items not available can be ordered, usually within 24 hours.
Liferaft servicing Náutica Levante are an agent/service centre for Zodiac, but will also handle other makes.
Water On the pontoons.
Showers At the rear of the commercial block.
Launderette At the rear of the commercial block.
Electricity On the pontoons.
Fuel Diesel and petrol available at the fuel/reception berth, open 0700–1900 daily. Exact payment must be made in cash – no change is given.
Bottled gas Camping Gaz available in the town, but no refills.
Weather forecast Posted daily at the marina office.
Banks In the town.
Shops/provisioning All usual shops in the town, a short walk from the marina, but no food shops on site.
Cafés, restaurants and hotels Small café overlooking the marina, but no restaurant. However both are to be found in the older part of the town, with hotels mainly centred in the newer beachside areas.
Medical services In the town.

Communications

Post office In the town.
Mailing address The marina office will hold mail for visiting yachts – c/o Puerto Deportivo Isla Cristina, Officina del Puerto, Bda Punta del Caiman s/n, 21410 Isla Cristina, Huelva, España. It is important that the envelope carries the name of the yacht in addition to that of the addressee.
Public telephones Kiosk near the marina office, with others in the town.
Internet access Several places in the town, including a cybercafé on the ground floor of the 'lighthouse' building.
Fax service At the marina office, *Fax* +34 959 345501.
Car hire/taxis Available in the town or via the marina office.
Buses To Ayamonte, Huelva and beyond.
Air services International airports at Faro (Portugal) and Seville (Spain).

THE ALGARVE & ANDALUCIA

El Rompido

Waypoints
⊕171 – 37°09'·2N 7°03'·3W (approach)
⊕172 – 37°11'·32N 7°02'·73W (entrance)

Bearings and distance
⊕169 (Islas Canela and Cristina) – ⊕171 = 12·3M, 087° or 267°
⊕171 – ⊕172 = 2·2M, 012° or 192°
⊕171 – ⊕173 (Punta Umbría) = 5·1M, 119° or 299°
⊕171 – ⊕175 (Mazagón) = 12·4M, 118° or 298°

Tides
See Mazagón, page 282

Charts

Charts	Approach	River
Admiralty	91, 89, 93	
Imray	C19, C50	
Spanish	44B, 440	441A

Principal lights
2312 **El Rompido** Fl(2)10s42m24M
White tower, red band 29m
buoy **Fairway No.1** LFl.10s5M
Red and white vertical striped pillar buoy, • topmark
Note At least a dozen further buoys should indicate the channel (see plan).

Warning
Both the position of the bar and the depths over it alter frequently, and local yachtsmen are now responsible for relocating the buoyage in response to these changes. Current positions of the first ten buoys are listed on the marina website (recalada translates as fairway or landfall buoy), and referenced to the WGS84 datum. All in all it appears wisest to trust current local knowledge as reflected in the buoys themselves.

Night entry
Unsuitable for night entry by a keel yacht under any circumstances.

Harbour communications
Puerto Marina El Rompido ☎ +34 959 399614
Fax +34 959 399 082 *Email* info@puertoelrompido.com
www.puertoelrompido.com VHF Ch 71
Varadero Río Piedras SA ☎ +34 959 399026
Fax +34 959 399034 *Email* varadero@vianwe.com
VHF Ch 09
Club Náutico Río Piedras ☎/*Fax* +34 959 399349
VHF Ch 09

Shallow, challenging entrance leading to windswept coastal lagoon

Most cruising yachtsmen would agree that El Rompido is one of the most attractive spots along this stretch of the coast, but before gaining its tranquil interior the difficult, twisting bar must be negotiated – see *Entrance*, below. That it has been inhabited since pre-Roman times comes as no surprise, the long sandspit of the Punta del Gato (*rompeolas* = breakwater) making the protected waters of the Río Piedras seem more like a lagoon than a river.

However, after millennia with few changes, development has been rapid since 1994 when El Rompido was a small, picturesque, riverside village with limited facilities other than an excellent boatyard. Then visiting yachts, once safely over the bar, could anchor or perhaps rent a mooring. It has since become a popular holiday destination for Spaniards from Seville and elsewhere, backed by a

The shallow bar at the mouth of the Río Piedras, looking west-northwest. The positions of the numerous buoys change frequently

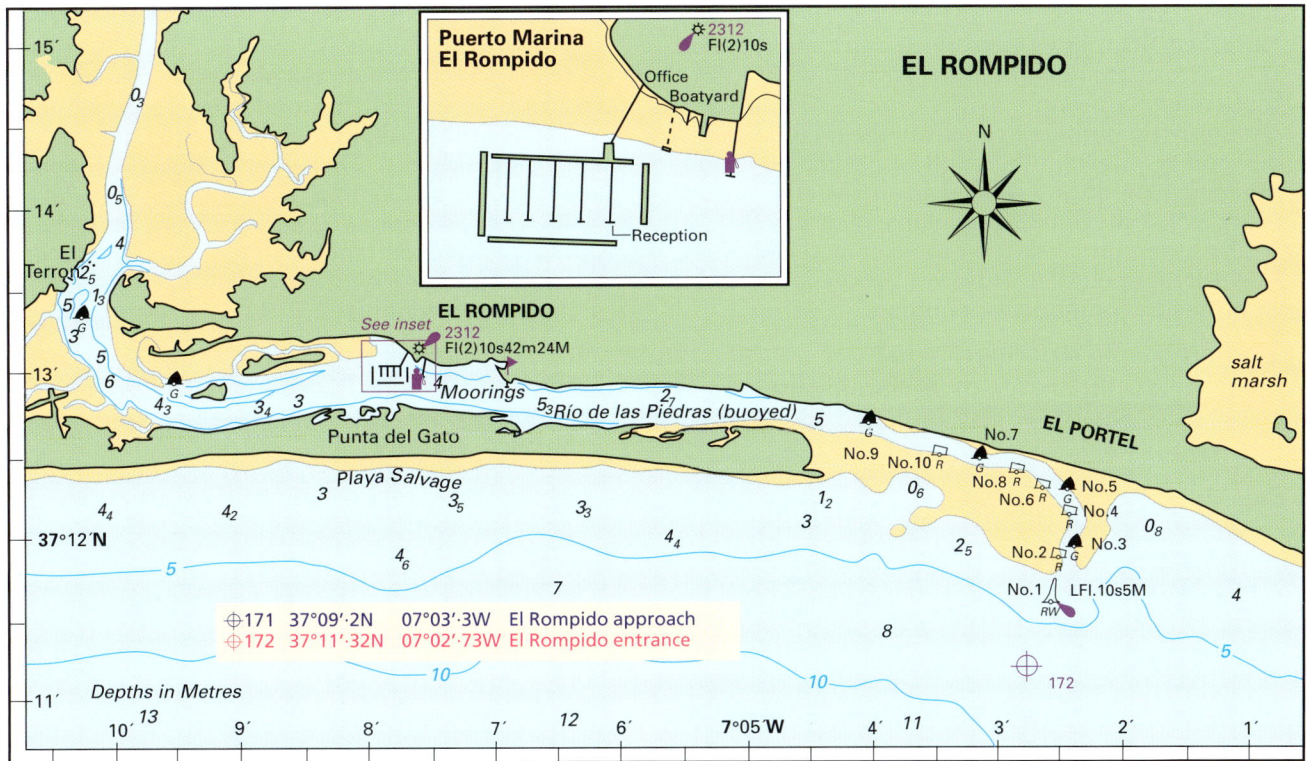

Puerto Marina
El Rompido

Office
Boatyard

☼2312
Fl(2)10s

Reception

EL ROMPIDO

N

EL ROMPIDO
See inset ☼2312
Fl(2)10s42m24M

Moorings

salt
marsh

El
Terron

Punta del Gato

Río de las Piedras (buoyed)

EL PORTEL

Playa Salvage

No.9
No.10
No.8
No.6
No.7
No.5
No.4
No.2
No.3
No.1 LFl.10s5M
RW

37°12′N

⊕171 37°09′·2N 07°03′·3W El Rompido approach
⊕172 37°11′·32N 07°02′·73W El Rompido entrance

Depths in Metres

172

large new hotel to serve the 36 hole golf course and is crowded with moored yachts and smallcraft. There is little space left for anchoring, but the latest innovation is the construction of a 331 berth marina, close to the long-established Varadero Río Piedras SA boatyard and some 4·5M from the river entrance.

Approach

From the west, the shoreline is unbroken between Isla Cristina and El Rompido with a daymark, the Torre Catalán, on the higher dunes west of the point where the Río de las Piedras turns inland. From this tower to the entrance – some 7·5M – the river runs parallel to the shore behind the Punta del Gato and Playa Salvage. To the east the beach is backed by dunes rising up to 40m and topped by umbrella pines.

From offshore ⊕171 lies 2·2M south-southwest of the entrance, a course of 012° leading to ⊕172, nearly 0·5M south of the fairway buoy but already in depths of less than 5m. This is the time to decide whether it is safe to press on, or whether conditions are less than perfect and it would be more prudent to turn west for Portugal or east for Mazagón and beyond.

A fish haven centred on a spot about 1M south of the entrance and measuring a good 1M² is shown on Admiralty Charts 89, 90 and 92, but as clearance over is at least 5m it should not concern many yachts.

Entrance

Note the *Caution* opposite. The bar alters continuously in both shape and depth, but local knowledge claims about 1m at MLWS. With a spring range of 2·5m (and neap range of 1·3m) most cruising yachts should be able to enter with reasonable care, particularly if local assistance is forthcoming. In exceptional situations there may be currents of more than 2kn in the river. Yachtsmen are strongly recommended to contact marina manager Wolfgang Michalsky (who speaks fluent English) for up-to-date information prior to arrival. With sufficient notice it may even be possible to arrange to be 'talked in' via mobile phone by an English-speaking assistant dispatched to the entrance by car. Marina staff can assist with berthing and have a workboat, but if conditions are particularly adverse there are moorings available to wait until suitable conditions pertain.

It should be noted that strong northwesterly winds in the Strait of Gibraltar may reduce predicted sea levels.

Berthing

The marina is fully open and contains 331 berths, 40% of them reserved for yachts in transit and half of these for short-stay visitors. Although long-term berths are limited to yachts of 14m or less, a few 30m visitor berths are available. Depths are limited at 2–3m, but in practice any yacht able to negotiate the bar will be able to berth in the marina.

The structure is unusual, with a single pontoon secured by piles projecting some distance into the river and giving access to the marina's five projecting fingers. All berths are against finger pontoons. Detached floating wavebreaks made from recycled tyres are secured up and downstream, with a third (concrete) pontoon to the south. These will obviously do nothing to decrease the tidal flow, and newcomers would be well advised to avoid manoeuvring during the height of the ebb or, to a lesser extent the flood, particularly at springs.

The reception berth is on the hammerhead of the downstream pontoon. However the office is ashore, near the head of the access pontoon.

Anchorage and moorings

There is now little room to anchor downstream of the marina but space may be found immediately upstream.

Multihulls and other shoal draught vessels may be able to work upstream as far as El Terrón, where

there is a busy fishermen's quay and a shallow pontoon for local smallcraft. Holding is said to be good over mud. Water, telephones, restaurants and basic shopping will be found ashore, and fuel is available at the quay (though depths alongside have not been verified). There are information boards about the *Paraje Natural 'Marismas del Río Piedras y Flecha de El Rompido'*, an area covering the Punta del Gato sandspit and much of the Río Piedras estuary. For those with yachts already on a secure mooring it would make an interesting dinghy excursion.

Facilities

Boatyard, engineers, electronic and radio repairs The Varadero Río Piedras SA ☎ +34 959 399026 *Fax* 959 399034 *Email* varadero@vianwe.com, is tucked between the long hammerhead jetty and the new marina, almost directly below the lighthouse. After 25

The Marina El Rompido has 331 berths. All situated in the grain of tidal currents

The highly-praised Varadero Río Piedras at El Rompido *Anne Hammick*

Puerto Marina El Rompido looking North *APPA*

years, founder owner Wolfgang Michalsky has recently sold up in order to become marina manager. New owners are Christian and Borja, a German/Spanish couple who have every intention of continuing the yard's excellent reputation for helpfulness and efficiency.

Employees or subcontractors can handle repairs in timber, GRP and metals including stainless steel and aluminium. Alternatively owners can do their own work. There are on-site mechanical and electronics workshops, plus an agency for Volvo, Nautech and Lewmar. The yard would be an excellent place for winter lay-up, though space is limited.

Travel-lift The boatyard's marine railway can handle vessels of up to 100 tonnes and 6m beam.

Sailmaker Olivier Plisson of Vop Sails, ☎/*Fax* +34 959 399025 *Email* info@vopsails.com www.vopsails.com who has premises just outside the Varadero Río Piedras, makes and repairs sails and will handle canvaswork of all kinds.

Chandlery Small chandlery at the boatyard, with further items ordered as required.

Water Available on the marina pontoons, or by can from the boatyard or the Club Náutico Río Piedras (where there is a coin-operated tap on the pontoon).

Showers At the marina. Otherwise at the boatyard or the *club náutico*, both of which make a small charge.

Launderette To be installed at the marina. In the meantime, there is a washing machine at the boatyard (timing and fee negotiable).

Electricity On the marina pontoons.

Fuel At the hammerhead jetty east of the boatyard, open 0900–1530 Tuesday to Thursday, 0900–1500, 1600–1900 Friday and Saturday, 0900–1500 Sunday, closed Monday. ☎ +34 62 0922 969.

Club náutico The Club Náutico Río Piedras ☎ +34 959 399349 *Fax* +34 959 399217 occupies a slightly isolated site some distance downstream from the town and has its own hammerhead pontoon, plus a very pleasant terrace bar/restaurant.

Weather forecast At the marina office. May also be

The 42m lighthouse at El Rompido stands in attractive surroundings some distance from the shoreline, but is nevertheless an important light *Anne Hammick*

Nets – and some oversize blocks – cover the fishermen's wharf at El Terrón on the Río Piedras *Anne Hammick*

available at the boatyard on request.

Bank In the town, including a cash machine at the west end of the old quarter.

Shops/provisioning Several small supermarkets, including one near the church. A small supermarket is planned for the marina.

Produce market On the main square.

Cafés, restaurants A profusion in the old part of the town, including restaurants serving excellent seafood. Hotels are mostly to be found in the newer area to the east. Cafés, restaurants etc are planned for the new marina complex.

Medical services Clinic and pharmacy in the town, but no hospital.

Communications

Post office Backing onto the church.

Mailing address The marina office will hold mail for visiting yachts – c/o Puerto El Rompido, E 21459 El Rompido, Cartaya/Huelva, España. It is important that the envelope carries the name of the yacht in addition to that of the addressee.

Public telephones Several throughout the town.

Internet access Wireless broadband is available throughout the marina, with additional connection facilities in the office.

Fax service At the boatyard, *Fax* +34 959 399034, by arrangement.

Taxis Best ordered by phone.

Buses To Huelva, for connection with trains to Seville etc.

Air services International airports at Faro and Seville.

Punta Umbría

Waypoints
⊕173 – 37°06'·7N 6°57'·7W (approach)
⊕174 – 37°08'·71N 6°56'·91W (entrance)

Courses and distances
⊕169 (Islas Canela & Cristina) – ⊕173 = 17M, 096° or 276°
⊕171 (El Rompido) – ⊕173 = 5·1M, 119° or 299°
⊕173 – ⊕174 = 2·1M, 017° or 197°
⊕173 – ⊕175 (Mazagón) = 7·3M, 118° or 298°

Tides
See Mazagón, page 282

Charts

	Approach	River
Admiralty	91, 93	73
Imray	C19, C50	
Spanish	44B, 441	4411

Principal lights
2315 **Breakwater head** VQ(6)+LFl.10s9m5M
Black tower, yellow top 4m

Night entry
Though well lit, in view of depths at the bar night entry is not recommended for those unfamiliar with the area

Harbour communications
Real Club Marítimo y Tennis de Punta Umbría
☎ +34 959 311899 or +34 959 315 677
Fax +34 959 312 125
www.rcmtpu.es
VHF Ch 09, 16
Puerto Deportivo de Punta Umbría
☎ +34 959 314 298 *Fax* +34 959 314 706
Email puntaumbriad@eppa.es
www.eppa.es
VHF Ch 09
Club Deportivo Náutico Punta Umbría
☎ +34 959 071 081 *Fax* +34 959 071 022
Email puntaumbriad@eppa.es
www.puertosdeandalucia.es
VHF Ch 09

Attractive river inside a shallow entrance

Once a small fishing village, of which there are still traces to be found upstream from the busy fishing quay, and with some elegant houses lining the riverbank, Punta Umbría is a growing tourist resort, thanks largely to its excellent beaches. The town is now said to be one of the fastest-growing in Andalucía.

Many British people settled in Punta Umbría during the 19th and early 20th century and this is reflected in the architecture of the houses, some of which are still referred to as the English's homes. The marshlands and the natural park of Las Marismas de Odiel are the other major attractions with the World Biosphere Reserve providing a habitat for over 200 species of birds.

It was on the beach at La Bota that the corpse of *The Man Who Never Was* and the disinformation contained with the body was found by local fishermen. It had been launched from the submarine HMS *Seraph* and the 'intelligence' reached the Punta Umbría police, found its way to Berlin and formed the first stage of the plot to deceive Hitler over Allied intentions for the landings on Sicily later in 1943.

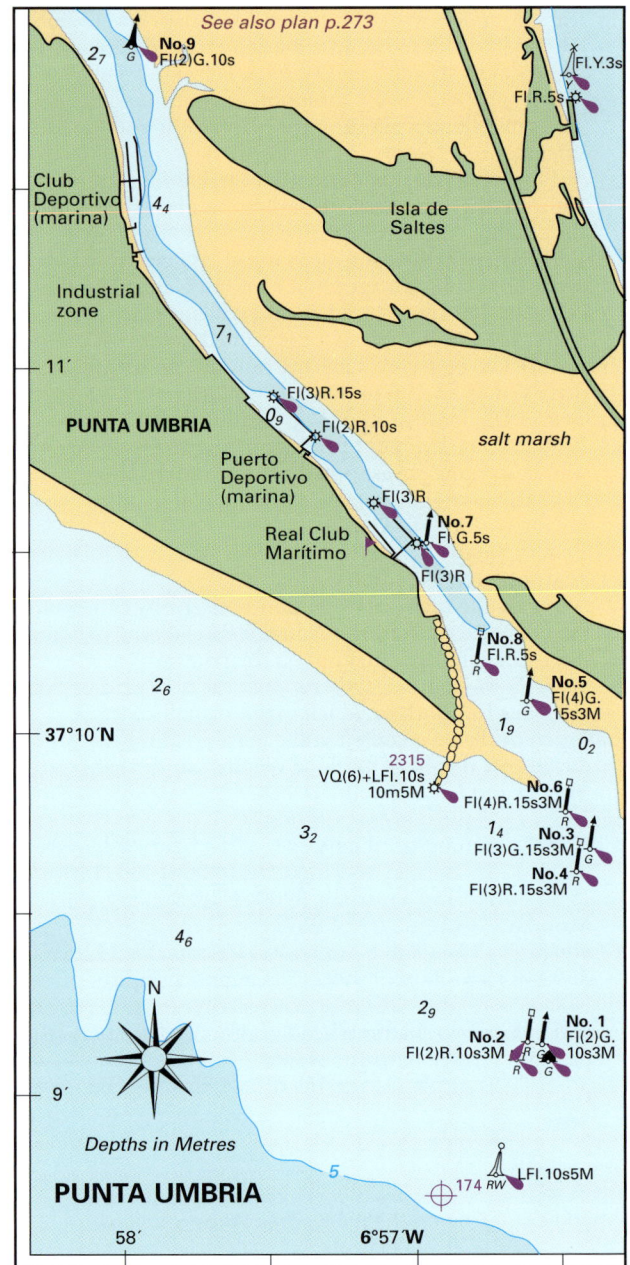

⊕173	37°06'·7N	6°57'·7W	Punta Umbría approach
⊕174	37°08'·71N	6°56'·91W	Punta Umbría entrance

The body of Glyndwr Michael is now buried in the cemetery of Nuestra Senora de la Soledad in Huelva (Grave No. 1886).

Advantages for the visiting yachtsman include convenient food shopping, with at least one large supermarket close to the river. Following the reconstruction of the Real Club Marítimo y Tennis de Punta Umbría there is space for larger yachts to berth in the river. The channel is too narrow and full of moorings to anchor opposite the town and the lower reaches may not prove as peaceful as expected as the fishing fleet start leaving soon after 0400 and keep passing until dawn.

Approaching Punta Umbría from south-southeast, with the shoal which runs out from the western promontory just visible beneath the surface

Approach

Approaching from the west, low, sandy, pine-topped cliffs stretch from the lighthouse at El Rompido all the way to Punta Umbría. The most prominent coastal feature is the refinery on the Huelva channel. Because of the narrow strip of low land between the Huelva channel and Punta Umbría, the refinery appears to be just east of the Punta Umbría entrance. There is a line of tower blocks to the west of Punta Umbría. From the east, the coast from Matalascañas as far as Mazagón is backed by sand dunes, while the final 7M from Mazagón is formed almost entirely of the impressive Juan Carlos I breakwater, against which a low-lying sandy beach – the Playa de Espigón – has built up. A restricted area containing a tanker loading berth and associated pipeline extends almost 5M offshore about 2M east of the entrance. Anchoring and fishing are banned in its vicinity, but vessels may pass inside or between the buoys.

From offshore ⊕173 lies 2·1M south-southwest of the entrance, a course of 017° leading to ⊕174, close to the red and white landfall buoy.

Entrance

The breakwater is about 0·5M in length, though much of this is masked from the west by an accretion of sand. Entering Punta Umbría, both the position and depth of the channel is unpredictable and care must be taken. Depths at the bar are no more than 1m at chart datum (4·2m at MHWS or 3·5m at MHWN), with eight buoys indicating the channel.

With so much river traffic there would be an excellent chance of following a local vessel in, though allowance must be made for the probable difference in draught.

Once past the root of the mole the channel begins to deepen, after which 5m or more should be found about 100m from the western bank.

Berthing and moorings

There are three berthing possibilities:
1. The **Real Club Marítimo y Tennis de Punta Umbría** has been reconstructed and became fully operational in 2009. The original reservations over space, shelter and fishing boat wash should have been overcome. The marina has been much enlarged with 260 berths, of which 25% are

Real Club Marítimo y Tennis de Punta Umbría looking north
APPA

THE ALGARVE & ANDALUCIA

Columbus Ships Museum
La Rabida

Huelva channel

Looking northeast at Punta Umbría showing the marinas from left to right –
Club Deportivo Náutico Punta Umbría, Puerto Deportivo de Punta Umbría and Real Club Marítimo y Tennis de Punta Umbría.
The Huelva channel is beyond.

reserved for transit yachts, and can take yachts up to 15m it is believed. A breakwater system pioneered in Spain should allow a reduction of noise and movement caused by wash.

Available services include electricity, water and 24 hour assistance and security. In addition there is WiFi covering the entire marina area.

Half a mile up the river there is a CAMPSA service station for diesel and petrol.

2. The **Puerto Deportivo de Punta Umbría** is one of APPA's smallest in all senses of the word. It also lacks many of the shoreside facilities found at its larger peers. Even though depth is not an issue, there is a minimum of 2·5m throughout, only a dozen of the 197 berths can take vessels of more than 10m and the vast majority are occupied by diminutive runabouts. At first glance the long outer pontoon appears spacious and tempting, but any direction to secure to it should be resisted strenuously. A detached wave-break pontoon is positioned downstream of the marina, but the outer pontoon receives no protection whatsoever from the wash of speeding fishing boats. The entire marina heaves and groans alarmingly as each one passes, and few fishermen appear to pay even lip service to the 5kn speed limit. When several boats follow each other in close succession and their washes combine, damage may occur.

The marina office is open from 1000–1330 and 1630–2000 daily in summer, closing at 1730 during the winter (when it is also shut on weekend afternoons). Water and electricity are available on the pontoons, with showers ashore (but no launderette). A weather forecast is posted daily, and fuel is available nearby (see *Facilities*, below), but little else appears to be on offer. Surprisingly, despite jutting much further into the channel than any of the other jetties, the southeast corner of the marina appears to be unlit.

Club Deportivo Náutico Punta Umbría looking south *APPA*

3. The **Club Deportivo Náutico Punta Umbría**, formed in 1995, now operates the only true marina on the river. Being upstream of the fishermen's quay it is also by far the most peaceful. Although private and normally full of members' boats, space for a visiting yacht of up to 10m can usually be found alongside the long outer pontoon in depths of 5–6m, if only for a night or two. The club also controls a number of moorings able to take up to 12m. In both cases it would be wise to make contact before arrival.

The club has extensive grounds and a sizeable clubhouse featuring the usual bar and restaurant. The secretary's office will be found upstairs, having entered at the rear of the building, and is open 1100–1400 and 1600–2000 Monday to Saturday inclusive. There appears to be no fixed price structure for visiting yachts, another thing to enquire about when booking. Water and electricity are available on the pontoons, including the outer one, and there are doubtless showers in the clubhouse, but there are no other facilities on site. However it is only a short walk into the town, and even shorter to the supermarket in the industrial zone (see *Facilities* opposite).

Anchorage

The channel is largely occupied by moorings, with very little space left in which to anchor anywhere near the town. Continue past the Club Deportivo Náutico, beyond the moorings. Anchor either side of the channel where depth allows. Though most fishing boats go no further than the wharf just upstream of the APPA-run Puerto Deportivo, tripper boats ply to and fro to Huelva via the connecting channels and the fairway must be left clear. An anchor light should be displayed at night. In all cases allow for the strength of the ebb tide, which may reach 4–5kn at springs even close in to the shore.

Facilities

Boatyard Náuticas Punta Umbría SA ☎ +34 959 310 700 operate a large, gated boatyard in the industrial area north of the Puerto Deportivo and the fishing wharf, where many local yachts are wintered ashore. Although served by a good-sized marine railway, the maximum size appears to be around 10m.

Nauti-Ría SL, ☎ +34 959 315590 *Fax* +34 959 312107 *Email* nautiria@yahoo.es handle repairs to smaller vessels, with an anonymous GRP fabricator opposite. Other yards build and repair tugs and small military/official vessels, mostly in steel, with yet another building sizeable timber fishing boats. All are on the well-named 'Calle Veraderos' (shipyard road) between the industrial area and the river.

Travel-lift None (though see above).

Engineers, electronics Náuticas Punta Umbría SA is able to handle most types of yacht and engine maintenance.

Sailmaker/sail repairs Shanty Sails, ☎ +34 959 310700, *Fax* +34 959 310696, close to Náuticas Punta Umbría in the industrial zone, make and repair sails and handle general canvaswork.

Chandlery Náuticas Punta Umbría SA (open 1000–1330, 1630–2030, closed Saturday afternoon and all day Sunday) has a well-stocked chandlery adjacent to its boatyard.

Puerto Deportivo de Punta Umbría looking west *APPA*

Water On all three pontoons.

Showers At all three clubhouses/offices.

Launderette In the town.

Electricity On all three pontoons.

Fuel Diesel and petrol from a pontoon between the Puerto Deportivo and the fishermen's quay. Hours are not specified.

Bottled gas Camping Gaz exchanges available in the town, but no refills.

Weather forecast At the Puerto Deportivo office.

Club náutico The long-established Real Club Marítimo y Tennis de Punta Umbría and the much newer Club Deportivo Náutico Punta Umbría. See under Berthing, above.

Banks In the town, with cash dispensers.

Shops/provisioning Large and cavernous supermarket (the Spanish equivalent of a Cash and Carry) one block in from the boatyards mentioned above. General shopping of all kinds in the town.

Cafés, restaurants and hotels At the two clubs, with dozens more throughout the town.

Medical services In the town.

Communications

Post office In the town.

Mailing address Both the Puerto Deportivo (Puerto Deportivo de Punta Umbría, Plaza Pérez Pastor Punta Umbría, 21100 Huelva, España) and the Club Deportivo Náutico (Club Deportivo Náutico Punta Umbría, Prolongación Avenida de la Marina s/n, Apartado de Correos No 78, 21100 Huelva, España) will hold mail for visiting yachts, by prior arrangement only. In both cases it is important that the envelope carries the name of the yacht in addition to that of the addressee.

Telephones Close to the Puerto Deportivo office and elsewhere.

Car hire Several offices in the town.

Taxis In the town, or order via the berthing office.

Buses In the town, connecting with trains at Huelva.

Dinghies It is possible to take the dinghy through the east arm of the channel under a causeway bridge to the main Huelva channel. This comes out opposite the power station and Columbus statue with La Rabida opposite, beyond another causeway bridge, to secure the dinghy.

Air services About equidistant between Faro (Portugal) and Seville (Spain).

THE ALGARVE & ANDALUCIA

Mazagón

Waypoints
⊕175 – 37°03'·3N 6°49'·7W (approach)
⊕176 – 37°05'·25N 6°49'W (entrance)

Courses and distances
⊕167 (Río Guadiana) – ⊕175 = 27·8M, 096° or 276°
⊕169 (Islas Canela & Cristina) – ⊕175 = 23·7M, 103° or 283°
⊕171 (El Rompido) – ⊕175 = 12·4M, 118° or 298°
⊕173 (Punta Umbría) – ⊕175 = 7·3M, 118° or 298°
⊕175 – ⊕176 = 2M, 016° or 196°
⊕175 – ⊕177 (Chipiona and the Río Guadalquivir) = 24·6M, 135° or 315°

Tides
Standard port Lisbon
Mean time differences (at Huelva bar)
HW +0010 ±0010; LW +0035 ±0005
(allowing for one hour difference in time zones)
Heights in metres

MHWS	MHWN	MLWN	MLWS
3·2	2·5	1·2	0·4

Or refer to EasyTide at www.ukho.gov.uk/easytide

Charts	Approach	Harbour
Admiralty	91, 93	73
Imray	C19, C50	C50
Spanish	44B, 441	4411

Principal lights
River entrance
2321 **Breakwater head** Fl(3+1)WR.20s30m12/9M
165°-W-100°-R-125° Racon Mo 'K'(−·−)12M
White tower, red band 27m
2324.05 **Dir Lt 339.2°** DirWRG.60m8M
337.5°-G-338°-R-338·6°-Oc.G-339·1°-W-339·3°-Oc.R-339·8°-R-340·4°-R-340·9° White tower 15m
Note The deep channel shifts from time to time and buoys are moved accordingly.
Marina
2325 **Southwest breakwater head** Q.G.8m2M
Grey framework on green base 4m
2325.2 **Northeast breakwater head** Q.R.6m2M
Grey framework on red base 4m
2325.5 **Southwest breakwater spur** Fl.G.5s4m1M
Grey framework on green base 4m
2325.7 **Reception quay** Fl.R.5s4m1M
Grey framework on red base 3m

Night entry
The approach to Mazagón and Huelva is buoyed and lit for large commercial vessels – a yacht should have no trouble in any but the worst conditions.

Coast radio station
Huelva *Digital Selective Calling*
MMSI 002241012
VHF Ch 10, 16, 26
Weather bulletins and navigational warnings
Weather bulletins and navigational warnings in Spanish and English: VHF Ch 10 at 0415, 0815, 1215, 1615, 2015 UT

Harbour communications
Puerto Deportivo de Mazagón
☎ +34 959 070 071 - 671 539 702 *Fax* +34 959 101 006
Email mazagon@eppa.es www.puertosdeandalucia.es
VHF Ch 09, 16

Modern, purpose-built yacht marina with good facilities, little character but local interest

Another of the new harbours built and run by the Agencia Pública de Puertos de Andalucía, Puerto Deportivo Mazagón is somewhat larger than most. It contains 647 berths, including 25 reserved for visiting yachts. The marina is also home to various 'official'

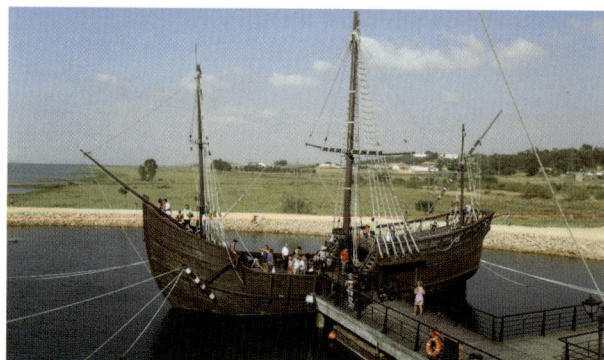
One of the Columbus Ships at La Rabida *Jane Russell*

craft including the smaller Huelva pilot boats, fishery protection vessels and a Guardia Civil RIB.

There is an excellent beach right next to the marina, with the quiet and leafy town a steepish walk up the road, worth the effort for some friendly local colour and good restaurants.

Mazagón is a good base for exploring links with Columbus at Palos de la Frontera and La Rábida monastery. The pronouncement that the voyage would go ahead was made in the church of St George at Palos de la Frontera. Many of the crew for the ships came from here, and it was from here that Columbus finally set sail. The replica Columbus Ships at La Rabida are worth the walk down from the monastery.

Approach and entrance

Approaching from the west, low, sandy, pine-topped cliffs stretch from the lighthouse at El Rompido to the tower blocks at Punta Umbría. From this point, the last 7M of very low shore is backed by Juan Carlos I breakwater – one of the longest in Europe. A restricted area containing a tanker loading berth and associated pipeline extends almost 5M offshore about 4·5M west of the rivermouth. Anchoring and fishing are banned in its vicinity, but vessels may pass inside or between the buoys.

To the east, for some 16M the shore is backed by sand dunes ending at the resort town of Matalascañas which has prominent radio aerials. A firing range – which is not marked on the Admiralty chart – exists inshore from about 5M southeast of Mazagón almost as far as Matalascañas. When active, a Range Safety Vessel will call up any craft straying into the area on VHF Ch 16 with instructions to keep clear.

A gas pipeline nearly 25M in length and fed by at least two production wells comes ashore about 4M southeast of Mazagón. Two yellow buoys with topmarks, both Fl.Y.5s5M, indicate its western and southern extremes at 36°59'·5N 7°11'·4W and 36°51'N 7°05'·3W respectively. A further two buoys, identical to the above, mark the junction at 37°09'·9N 6°59'·7W. Anchoring and mooring are prohibited in the vicinity, but there are no restrictions on sailing over it.

From offshore ⊕175 lies about 2·5M south-southwest of the entrance, a course of 016° leading to ⊕176, itself some 750m from the (west cardinal) fairway buoy and on the 339° leading line for the main channel.

Chart: APPROACHES TO PUNTA UMBRIA, MAZAGON & HUELVA

MAZAGON MARINA (inset)

- 2325·2 Q.R.1s6m2M
- 2320 Fl(2+4)30s 52m25M
- 2325 Q.G.1s 8m2M
- 2325·7 F.R.5s 4m1M
- 2325·5 Fl.G.5s 4m1M
- Fishing Boats

⊕173	37°06'·7N	6°57'·7W	Punta Umbría approach
⊕174	37°08'·71N	6°56'·91W	Punta Umbría entrance
⊕175	37°03'·3N	6°49'·7W	Mazagón approach
⊕176	37°05'·25N	6°49'W	Mazagón entrance

Chart labels:

- HUELVA
- Power Station
- Río Tinto
- Br.
- La Rabida
- Causeway
- Punta Umbría
- Pta Umbría
- Oil refineries and tanks
- 2328·51 Fl(3)G.15s11m3M
- Muelle de Reina Sofia
- 2328·5 Fl(3)G.15s
- Channel marked by lit buoys
- LFl.10s5M BW
- See plan p.278 174
- No.5 Fl(4)Y.20s
- No.4 Fl(4)Y.20s
- No.3 Fl(4)Y.20s5M
- Juan Carlos I Breakwater
- Pilot Station
- 2324·05 Dir.WRG.60m8M See inset
- Mazagón
- Picacho
- 2320 Fl(2+4)30s52m25M
- No.9 Fl.G.5s
- No.10 Fl.R.5s
- No.7 Fl(2+1)G.12s
- Fl(4)R.20s No.8
- No.6 Fl(3)R.15s
- No.5 Fl(3)G.15s
- No.2 Fl(4)Y.20s5M
- No.4 Fl.R.11s
- 2321 Fl(3+1)WR.20s30m12/9M
- No.3 Fl(2)G.10s
- No.1 Fl.G.5s4M
- No.2 Fl.R.5s4M
- 173
- No.1 Fl(4)Y.20s5M
- 339°
- Q(9)15s5M AIS YBY
- 176
- 2319 Fl(4)Y.20s8M Siren30s
- Depths in Metres
- **APPROACHES TO PUNTA UMBRIA, MAZAGON & HUELVA**

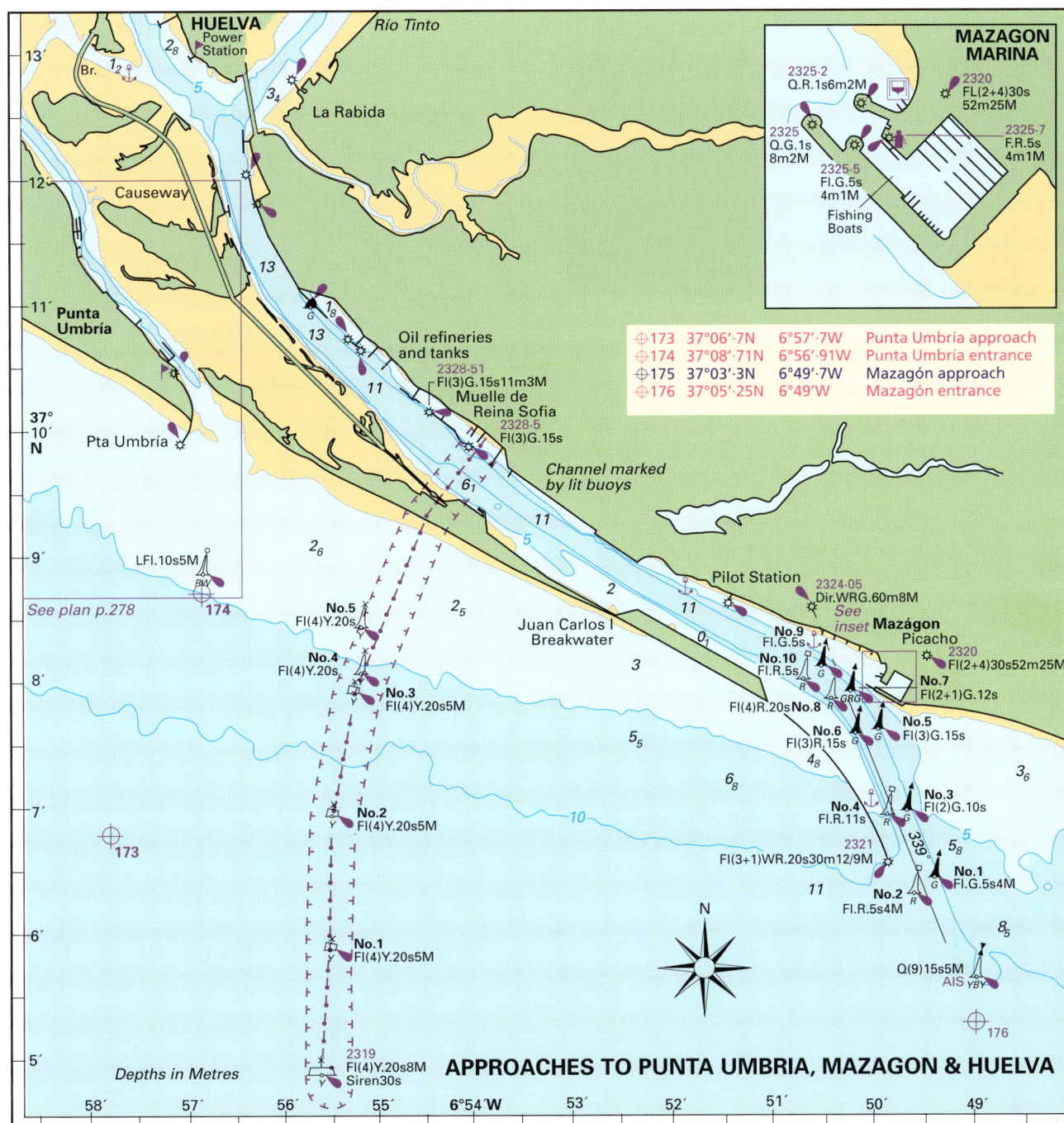

Once in the channel, Mazagón marina will be seen on the starboard hand about 1·5M inside the breakwater end. The entrance, which is lit, carries at least 4·5m as far as the reception pontoon, which is on the port hand below the prominent tower housing the marina office.

Berthing

Secure to the long reception pontoon, which doubles as a fuelling berth (avoid securing in the centre for this reason). If arriving outside office hours (1000–1300, 1600–1730 daily in winter, rather longer in summer), security staff will allocate a berth, or leave the yacht where she is if no berth is available. A total of 11 pontoons (all with fingers) take yachts of up to 20m in 4m depths throughout. Yachts of more than 20m are normally berthed alongside the southwest breakwater. Visitors over 12m are put on pontoons in the southeast corner. Wind funnelling through the harbour entrance can make it uncomfortable here.

Anchorages

Anchoring in the Ría de Huelva is possible but not encouraged. The tide runs strongly, heavy ground tackle is required, and it is essential to display a riding light as there is considerable fishing boat traffic at night as well as large freighters which pass each other in the channel.

In southwesterly winds yachts have successfully anchored close north of the breakwater, about 400m in from the end. Considerable wash from passing traffic should be anticipated and this is a distinctly short-term solution. In all but strong southerlies, a better bet would be either off the beach northwest of

Puerto Deportivo Mazagón seen from southwest beyond the long and elegant curve of the Juan Carlos I breakwater

the marina (taking care to avoid the sewage outfall, marked by an unlit yellow post with an × topmark), or about 1M further up the channel beyond the pilot station. Both offer good holding over sand, but again may be uncomfortable due to wash. It is essential to keep well clear of the channel itself.

Finally, yachts occasionally venture up the Huelva channel and anchor off the port side of the channel. The best spot is southwest of the main channel port hand marker to the west of the power station and prominent Columbus statue. This anchorage is in the side channel which connects, under a causeway bridge, to the Punta Umbría channels (see above). The connecting channels are used by local boats, so find a spot to one side of this channel, below the causeway bridge, as depth allows. There is a local marina and mooring area on the east side of the main channel, adjacent to the power station. Wind against tide in the river generates noticeable waves which may make the marina berths on the outer pontoon very uncomfortable.

Facilities

Boatyard Not as such, though there is a large area of rather windswept hardstanding and several workshops run as individual enterprises, with more currently being built. Alternatively owners are welcome to do their own work, but cannot live aboard whilst ashore. The gates are locked from 2100 until 0900, with card access at other times.

Travel-lift 32-tonne capacity hoist.

Engineers In addition to selling chandlery, Náutica Raggio, *Mobile* 609 814805, handles engine and other mechanical repairs.

Electronic and radio repairs Alfamar, ① +34 959 377825, who have premises in the commercial block near the marina office, is agent for Simrad, Furuno, Trepat, Raymarine etc, and also handles repairs.

Sailmaker/sail repairs The marina office will contact Shanty Sails, ① +34 959 310700, in Punta Umbría.

Chandlery An unexpected variety, all in the commercial block on the northwest side of the marina and all quite small. In alphabetical order: Broker de Servicios Náuticos SL ① +34 959 376221, sells general chandlery and clothes in addition to yacht brokerage. Idamar Náutica ① +34 959 536160, *Email* nautica@grupo-idamar.com stocks general chandlery and fishing equipment. A branch of the much larger Idamar Group, they are also agents for Bénéteau and for RFD inflatables (see also *liferaft servicing*, below).

Titulaciones Náuticas, ① +34 959 376292, is a Jeanneau agent and also stocks some chandlery, clothing and shoes. Náutica Raggio (see above) sells fishing equipment and some chandlery.

Charts Spanish charts are available in Huelva from Valnáutica SL–Idamar SA ① +34 959 250999 *Fax* +34 959 250214 at Avenida Enlace 16, and from the Instituto Geográfico Nacional ① +34 959 281967 at Vázquez López 12.

Liferaft servicing Idamar Náutica is agent for RFD but will repair and service all makes of liferaft and inflatable dinghy.

Water On the pontoons.

Showers At the rear of the commercial block, and on the southeast mole.

Launderette In a block on the southeast mole, so a long walk for those berthed near the marina office. Access by electronic card.

Electricity On the pontoons.

Fuel Diesel and petrol at the reception/fuel berth during office hours.

Club náutico The blue and white tiled Club Náutico de Mazagón looks strangely like an up-ended swimming pool (which it has, plus a tennis court, both available to visitors for a nominal fee). It also offers the more usual restaurant etc.

Weather forecast Posted daily at the marina office.

Banks Cash dispenser in the commercial block, with banks in the town.

Shops/provisioning No food shop in the marina complex, but one close outside the gates and plenty more in the town (though some distance away).

Cafés, restaurants and hotels Several cafés and restaurants in the marina complex, with more in the town.

Medical services In the town.

Communications

Post office In the town.

Mailing address The marina office will hold mail for visiting yachts – c/o Oficina del Puerto, Puerto Deportivo Mazagón, Avda. de los Conquistadores, s/n, Mazagón, Palos de la Frontera, 21130 Huelva, España. It is important that the envelope carries the name of the yacht in addition to that of the addressee.

Public telephone Single phone in the commercial block with many more in the town.

Internet access Cybercafé at the Amena phoneshop in the town (up the hill and turn right beyond the park).

Fax service At the marina office, *Fax* +34 959 376237.

Car hire/taxis Can be arranged via the marina office.

Buses In the town, connecting with trains at Huelva.

Air services About equidistant between Faro and Seville.

Looking northeast over Mazagón Marina *APPA*

Chipiona

Waypoints
⊕177 – 36°46'N 6°28'W (approach – also for the Río Guadalquivir)
⊕178 – 36°45'·2N 6°26'·2W (entrance)
⊕179 – 36°44'N 6°30'·3W (3·1M W of Punta del Perro)

Courses and distances
⊕175 (Mazagón) – ⊕177 = 24·6M, 135° or 315°
⊕177 – ⊕178 = 1·7M, 119° or 299°
⊕177 – ⊕181 (Rota, via ⊕179 & ⊕180) = 14·3M,
223° & 149° & 107° or 287° & 329° & 043°
⊕177 – ⊕183 (Cádiz, via ⊕179 & ⊕180) = 16M,
223° & 149° & 121° or 301° & 329° & 043°

Tides
Standard port Lisbon
Mean time differences (at Río Guadalquivir bar)
HW 0000 ±0005; LW +0025 ±0005
(allowing for one hour difference in time zones)
Heights in metres

MHWS	MHWN	MLWN	MLWS
3·2	2·5	1·3	0·4

Or refer to EasyTide at www.ukho.gov.uk/easytide

Charts	*Approach*	*Harbour*
Admiralty	91, 93	85
Imray	C19, C50	C50
Spanish	44B, 44C, 442, 443	4422-II

Principal lights
2351 **Punta del Perro (Chipiona)** Fl.10s68m25M
Stone tower on building 62m
2352 **Breakwater head** Fl(2)G.10s5m5M Green tower 5m
2354 **East mole** Fl(4)R.11s3m3M Red tower 3m
2354·5 **Breakwater spur** Fl(3)G.9s3m1M Green tower 3m

Night entry
Not recommended for those unfamiliar with the area, due to shoals near the entrance.

Harbour communications
Puerto Deportivo Chipiona
☎ +34 856 109 711 - 600 143 522
Fax +34 856 109 334
Email chipiona@eppa.es
www.puertosdeandalucia.es
VHF Ch 09

A well-run marina backed by a pleasant holiday town

The north basin is largely occupied by larger yachts and those in transit, with local boats in the south basin and fishing vessels along the breakwater. Facilities are good and Chipiona is an obvious place to wait for a fair tide up the Río Guadalquivir, as well as to top up with fuel.

The town is pleasant and shady with many restaurants, supermarkets and shopping precincts, and is well worth exploring. Punta del Perro lighthouse, built in 1867, is particularly worth a visit as the lower floors are sometimes open to the public, despite apparently still having several keepers in residence. The low cliffs between the two feature a number of restaurants and cafés, nearly all with local seafood on the menu.

If intending to venture up the Río Guadalquivir, note the paragraph on page 289 regarding Ricardo Franco's *La Navegación de Recreo por el Río de Sevilla* (Leisure Navigation on the River of Seville). Though now out of print, a copy of this impressive work can be consulted at the marina office.

Looking northeast into the mouth of the Río Guadalquivir. Punta del Perro lighthouse is in the foreground, with the Puerto Deportivo Chipiona directly behind

CHIPIONA AND THE LOWER RIO GUADALQUIVIR

⊕177	36°46'N 6°28'W	Chipiona & the Río Guadalquivir approach
⊕178	36°45'·2N 6°26'·2W	Chipiona entrance
⊕179	36°44'N 6°30'·3W	3·1M W of Punta del Perro

Coto de Doñana

BnNo.4

See continuation p.278

Bn No.5
Pta de S.Carlos

Bn No.2

Placer de San Jacinto

Pta de Malandar

No.2 **Picacho**
Q(9)15s5M
YBY

No.20
No.18
No.17
2346
2348.51
Iso.4s 61m10M
2348.5
Q.28m10M

Bonanza

No.16
No.14
No.15
No.13
No.12
No.11
No.10
No.9
No.8
No.7
No.6
No.5
No.4
No.3

Sanlúcar de Barrameda

Broa de Sanlúcar

Ldg Lts 069°

El Perro
No.1
LFl.10s5M
Racon(M)
RW

177

178

Pta Montijo

Chipiona

2350.4
Q(9)15s9m5M
Bajo Salmedina

2351
Fl.10s68m25M
Pta del Perro

CHIPIONA MARINA

2352
Fl(2)G.10s 6m5M
2354.5
Fl(3)G.9s 7m1M
2354
Fl(4)R.11s3m3M
Boatyard

36° 45' N
44'.8
25'.8
6°25'.6W

6°20'W

Approach – Chipiona and the Río Guadalquivir

If coastal sailing towards the Río Guadalquivir from Mazagón the first 20M is backed by sand dunes, but southeast of Matalascañas the coastline flattens. A firing range exists inshore from about 5M southeast of Mazagón almost as far as Matalascañas. When active, a Range Safety Vessel will call up any craft straying into the area on VHF Ch 16 with instructions to keep clear.

In good visibility a course can be shaped directly for No.2 buoy, a west cardinal guarding Bajo Pichaco rock. Though the buoy is sometimes difficult to see against the land, the wreck which has lain on the rock for more than a decade is still prominent. At half tide and above it is possible for a yacht to cut inside the wreck, but without large-scale charts this is not recommended. In poor visibility it would be wise to stand on for ⊕177, see below.

Approaching from Bahía de Cádiz or other points south, the 10m line lies up to 1·75M from the coast between Rota and Punta del Perro. Off the latter lies the dangerous Bajo Salmedina, extending almost 1·6M offshore and marked by a west cardinal tower – plus several wrecks. If in doubt head for ⊕179, some 3M offshore. Having rounded Bajo Salmedina, remain a minimum of 0·5M offshore while working northeast for Chipiona as multiple obstructions – some natural, some artificial – extend at least 600m out from the shore for most of the distance. Do not turn in for Chipiona until the marina entrance bears at least 110°.

Reception and Fuel pontoon looking southeast. Office behind *Henry Buchanan*

Several new fish havens have recently been established off Punta del Perro and in the approaches to Bahía de Cádiz, but as all lie outside the 10m contour they pose no danger to yachts.

From offshore head for ⊕177, just under 1M west-northwest of El Perro No.1 buoy, a large red and white pillar. From ⊕177 a course of 119° for 1·7M leads to ⊕178, 0·5M from the Chipiona breakwater. Alternatively, 081° for 2·2M places one directly between channel buoys Nos.3 and 4 and on the 069° leading line for Bonanza and, eventually, Seville.

Entrance – Chipiona

If approaching from any point west of north the entrance is hidden until very close in. Make for the breakwater head with its bright green tower, leaving the two smallish red pillar buoys to port, finally swinging southwest to enter. Following dredging a minimum of 3·5m should be found at all times.

Berthing

Secure to the long reception pontoon at the head of the central mole – the Muelle de Espera – directly beneath the marina office. Visitors are usually berthed in the northeast basin (now dredged to 4m), convenient for the shops and restaurants, with finger pontoons throughout. One or two seriously large yachts – up to 40m – can lie alongside the west side of the outer pontoon, but it is essential to contact the marina office well in advance. All the marina's 412 berths are often full in the high season, though a smaller visitor may be found space in the south basin among the locals in 2·5–3m depths.

Weekdays office hours are 1000–1330 and 1600–1730 in winter, closed Saturday and Sunday afternoons, but remaining open later in summer with no weekend closing. As in most of the APPA marinas there is 24 hour security, with card-operated gates to the pontoons.

Anchorage

An anchorage can be found to the east of the marina entrance, but it is exposed to the northwest.

Facilities

Boatyard On the northeast arm, with a generous area of concreted hardstanding behind a high security fence. Yachts from several nations over-winter there, all generously propped, essential when there is so little protection from the wind. The gates are locked from 2200 until 0700 and living aboard is forbidden. The contractors' premises onsite were reported closed in June 2012.

Travel-lift 50-tonne capacity lift in the boatyard area – book at the marina office.

Engineers, electronic and radio repairs Volvo/Honda at Servicios Nauticos J.A Moreta. www.jamoreta.es Email info@jamoreta.es ① +34 956 371514 *Fax* +34 956 373 207 *Mobile* +34 670 211941. Also, Nautica Gusty (Yamaha) www.nauticagusty.com Email info@nauticagusty.com ① +34 956 371802 *Fax* +34 650 226255. Carretera Chipiona, Sanlucar km. 2,700, Pista Montijo Nave 2, CP: 11550. Chipiona (Cádiz)

Chandleries Fernando Medina Náutica, ① +34 956 374772, *Mobile* +34 670 594451 and +34 607 833237 opposite the southeast corner of the south basin, open 0930–1400 and 1630–1900 weekdays, closed Saturday afternoon and Sunday.

Water On the pontoons.

Showers New (2012) shower block on the south side of the basin, with access via electronic card.

Launderette Near the marina office.

Electricity On the pontoons.

Fuel Diesel and petrol at the reception pontoon, 0800–1300 and 1630–1930 weekdays, 0830–1400 weekends.

Looking north over Chipiona Marina *APPA*

THE ALGARVE & ANDALUCIA

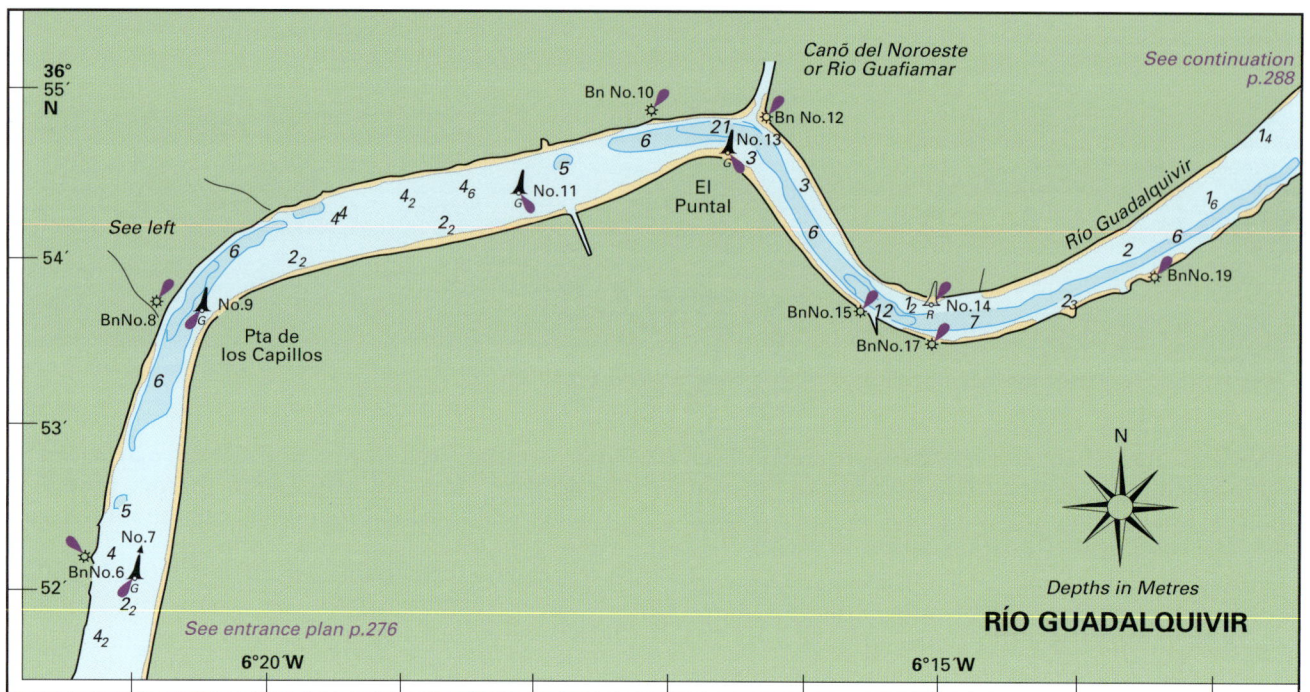

Chart labels:
Canõ del Noroeste or Rio Guafiamar
See continuation p.288
36° 55′ N
Bn No.10
Bn No.12
21
No.13
Bn No.13
6
5
No.11
El Puntal
3
3
Río Guadalquivir
1₄
4₂
4₆
2₂
1₆
See left
54′
4₄
6
2
6
BnNo.8
No.9
6
2₂
2
BnNo.19
Pta de los Capillos
BnNo.15
12
1₂
No.14
2₃
6
BnNo.17
7
53′
6
5
N
No.7
4
BnNo.6
52′
2₂
Depths in Metres
4₂
See entrance plan p.276
RÍO GUADALQUIVIR
6°20′W
6°15′W

Bottled gas Camping Gaz exchanges are available in the town, but no refills.

Weather forecast Posted daily at the marina office.

Banks In the town, but no cash dispenser at the marina.

Shops/provisioning Small general shop in the block overlooking the north basin, otherwise the nearest food shop is a supermarket some 300m distant, with plenty more in the town proper. The lonja (fish market) at the southwest corner of the basin also sells retail, and is well worth a visit.

Cafés, restaurants and hotels A good range – Chipiona has long been a popular holiday resort among Spaniards – with several small café/restaurants overlooking the north basin.

Medical services In the town.

Communications

Post office In the town.

Mailing address The marina office will hold mail for visiting yachts – c/o Oficina del Puerto, Puerto Deportivo Chipiona, Avda Rocío Jurado s/n, 11550 Chipiona, Cádiz, España. It is important that the envelope carries the name of the yacht in addition to that of the addressee.

Internet There is WiFi in the bar but not in the marina.

Public telephones Two in the marina complex, plus many in the town.

Fax service At the marina office, *Fax* +34 956 370037.

Car hire/taxis Best organised via the marina office.

Buses To Rota, Seville (about 2 hours) etc.

Air services International airport at Seville, national airport at Jerez for connections to Madrid etc.

The wide mouth of the Río Guadalquivir looking northeast, with several pairs of channel buoys clearly visible. Sanlúcar de Barrameda is on the right, with the long breakwater off Bonanza in the distance

The Río Guadalquivir and Seville

Waypoints
As for Chipiona, page 285

Tides
Standard port Lisbon
Mean time differences (at Río Guadalquivir bar)
(allowing for one hour difference in time zones)
HW 0000 ±005; LW +0025 ±0005
Heights in metres

MHWS	MHWN	MLWN	MLWS
3·2	2·5	1·3	0·4

Mean time differences (at Bonanza)
HW +0030 ±0010; LW +0070 ±0010
(allowing for one hour difference in time zones)
Heights in metres

MHWS	MHWN	MLWN	MLWS
3·0	2·4	1·1	0·5

Mean time differences (at Seville)
HW +0415 ±0015; LW +0530 ±0020
(allowing for one hour difference in time zones)
Heights in metres

MHWS	MHWN	MLWN	MLWS
2·1	1·8	0·9	0·5

Or refer to EasyTide at www.ukho.gov.uk/easytide

Charts	Approach	River
Admiralty	91, 93	85
Imray	C19, C50	
Spanish	44B, 44C, 442	4421, 4422, 4423, 4424, 4425

Principal lights
Entrance
2348.5 **Ldg Lts 069°** *Front* Q.1s27m10M
  Yellow ■ on metal tower
2348.51 *Rear* Iso.4s60m10M Yellow ■ on metal tower
Eight pairs of lit pillar buoys, plus one extra port-hand buoy, mark the channel as far as Bonanza
Bonanza
2346 **Bonanza** Fl.5s21m7M
  Red tower, cupola and building 20m
2349 **Detached breakwater, S end** Fl(2+1)G.14·5s5m5M
  Green column, red band, 2m
2349.1 **Detached breakwater, N end** Fl.G.5s5m5M
  Green post 2m
  Many other lit buoys and beacons mark the Río Guadalquivir up to Seville – see plans opposite, and on pages 286, 288 and 290
Night entry
  The river is well buoyed and lit as far as Bonanza, making a pre-dawn start upstream entirely feasible
Harbour communications
  Port Authority ① +34 954 247 300 *Fax* +34 954 247 343
  Email sevilla@apsevilla.com
  www.apsevilla.com
  VHF Ch 12 (24 hours)
  Puerto Gelves ① +34 955 761212 *Fax* +34 955 761583
  Email info@puertogelves.com
  www.puertogelves.com
  VHF Ch 09, 16
  Marina Yachting Seville ① +34 954 230326
  Fax +34 954 230172
  Club Náutico Sevilla ① +34 954 454777
  Fax +34 954 284693
  Email nauticosevilla@nauticosevilla.com
  www.nauticosevilla.com
  VHF Ch 09
  Seville lock ① +34 954 247 332 VHF Ch 12
  Puente de las Delicias lifting bridge
  ① +34 954 454 984 VHF Ch 12

Historic city with a lengthy river approach

Seville is one of the foremost cities of Spain, steeped in history and with something unexpected around every corner. The old part appears to have far more than its fair share of monuments and historic buildings, including a stunning cathedral and several royal palaces. A guide book and street plan are almost necessities. A yacht provides a most convenient base for exploration, but as summer temperatures can rise above 40°C (102°F) the best time to visit is in spring or autumn, though Seville is also becoming an increasingly popular place to winter on board for many nationalities. Highlights of the year are the Easter processions of *Semana Santa* and the vast *feria* which is held two weeks later on a site adjacent to the Club Náutico Sevilla.

In common with most large cities Seville has a reputation for petty crime, including pickpockets, but a purposeful air, valuables tucked away out of sight and avoidance of secluded areas after dark should give reasonable protection. It is not a place to hire a car as traffic is frequently grid-locked and parking next to impossible. Several (brave) yachtsmen and women have recommended bicycles as a practical means of transport. A stout chain is recommended.

The approach up the Río Guadalquivir (from the Arabic *Wadi-al-Kabir* or 'big river'), while tedious at times, is not without interest. In particular, the *Parque Nacional de Doñana* on the west bank is world famous for its birds and other wildlife and it is usually possible to spot some of its residents. In 1998 the park suffered an ecological disaster when the failure of a major dam upstream released nearly seven million cubic metres of lead-zinc slurry into the river system, killing most of the fish and many of the birds which depended on them. It has been estimated that it will take up to 50 years for the region to recover fully, but in the meantime much of the wildlife has already made a remarkable comeback.

If spending a few days in Chipiona prior to tackling the river, ask marina officials for a chance to study their copy of *La Navegación de Recreo por el Río de Sevilla* (Leisure Navigation on the River of Seville). This fascinating volume, first published in 1981 and revised in 1998 by master mariner and Guadalquivir pilot Ricardo Franco, is already out of print but a copy can be obtained from: *Flores Imprenta y Papeleria*, Avda. De la Raza S/N, Ed. Elcano 41012 – Sevilla ① +34 954 617257 *Email* floresdesantis@telefonica.net. It is beautifully presented in a dark blue box cover, profusely illustrated by aerial photographs and detailed charts, and with detailed and authoritative text in English as well as Spanish, it would well repay study with a notebook and the current chart to hand. While in the marina office it would also be worth confirming that the lock and bridge-opening times given over the next few pages are still current. The helpful Chipiona staff should have all the details to hand.

THE ALGARVE & ANDALUCIA

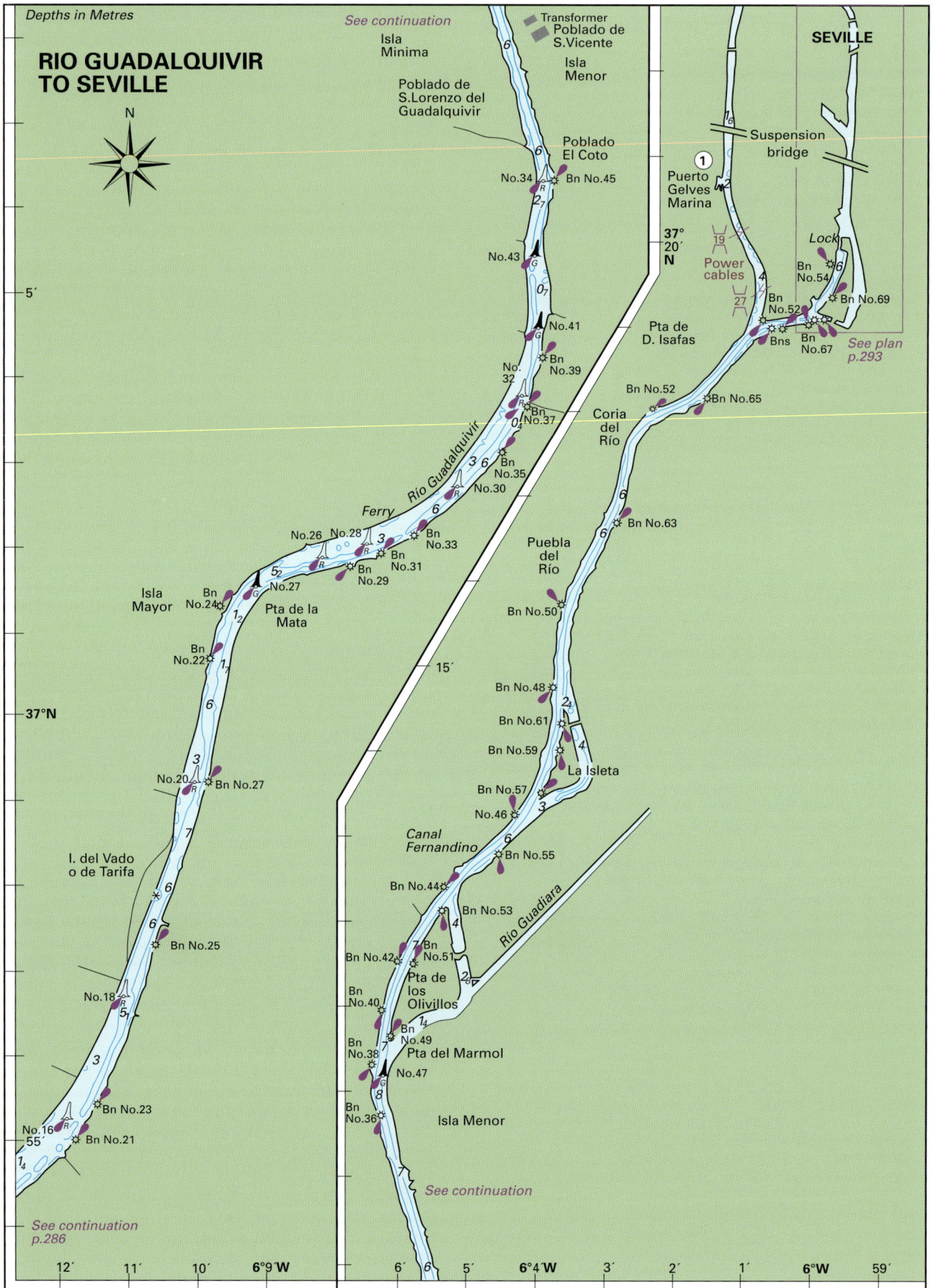

Depths in Metres

RIO GUADALQUIVIR TO SEVILLE

N

See continuation

Isla Minima

Transformer
Poblado de S.Vicente

Isla Menor

SEVILLE

Poblado de S.Lorenzo del Guadalquivir

Poblado El Coto

Suspension bridge

No.34

Bn No.45

Puerto Gelves Marina

No.43

37° 20' N

Lock

Power cables

Bn No.54

Bn No.69

No.41

Pta de D. Isafas

Bn No.52

Bns

Bn No.67

See plan p.293

No. 32

Bn No.39

Bn No.37

Bn No.52

Bn No.65

Río Guadalquivir

Coria del Río

Bn No.35

No.30

Ferry

Bn No.33

No.26 No.28

Bn No.63

Bn No.31

Puebla del Río

No.27

Bn No.29

Isla Mayor

Bn No.24

Pta de la Mata

Bn No.50

Bn No.22

Bn No.48

37°N

Bn No.61

Bn No.59

La Isleta

No.20

Bn No.27

Bn No.57

No.46

I. del Vado o de Tarifa

Canal Fernandino

Bn No.55

Bn No.25

Bn No.44

Bn No.53

Río Guadiara

No.18

Bn No.42

Bn No.51

Pta de los Olivillos

Bn No.40

Bn No.49

Bn No.38

Pta del Marmol

No.47

Bn No.23

Bn No.36

Isla Menor

No.16

Bn No.21

See continuation

See continuation p.286

12' 11' 10' 6°9'W 6' 5' 6°4'W 3' 2' 1' 6°W 59'

Approach
As for Chipiona – see page 286.

Entrance (see plan on page 286)
The channel close to the mouth is wide and very well buoyed, but can become dangerously rough when strong west or southwest winds oppose the spring ebb and cause short steep seas to build. The 'service centre' for the Río Guadalquivir's buoyage is at Bonanza and, perhaps as a result, maintenance is generally excellent.

The river

It is about 55M from the mouth to Seville. Starting an hour or so before the beginning of the flood (which a yacht can ride upriver for at least 9hrs – see *Tides* above) most yachts will be able to make it on one tide. To catch one's breath before heading upriver and to top up with fuel, a stop in the marina at Chipiona (page 286) would be convenient. Alternatively in light weather it is possible to anchor off Sanlúcar de Barrameda, where there is a large and stylish yacht club, a superb beach and, perhaps of greatest interest, the visitors' centre for the *Parque Nacional de Doñana* housed in the old ice factory – itself worth a visit for its imaginative tilework. In 1519 Sanlúcar was the departure point for Magellan's fleet and the port to which, three years later, the 18 survivors returned.

Little more than 1M further upriver lies Bonanza, where a yacht may be able to secure temporarily to the inside of the long detached concrete breakwater – quite unmistakable with its downstream end painted in diagonal red and green stripes – while the fishing fleet is at sea. Other possibilities are to anchor north of the moorings well out of the powerful current, or on the west bank around the corner 1M above Bonanza, again well out of both the fairway and the current. Even at neaps the ebb may run at 3kn in the centre of the channel, and is considerably stronger at springs. The flood never attains anything like the same rates. It is said that owners of wooden vessels should avoid Bonanza due to its reputation for shipworm, said to breed in the old hulks which litter the surrounding shores. Thefts of dinghies, oars and outboards have also been reported.

Above Bonanza
After passing the tall, shining heaps of locally-produced salt just upstream of Bonanza the river winds through flat and somewhat featureless countryside – a passage described with feeling as 'very long and boring' – until close to Seville, progress best being marked by simply ticking off the buoys and beacons as they are passed. There is good water the whole way – 6,000-tonne freighters visit the city – but the channel is not always in the centre of the river. Where beacons run down one side they indicate the main channel, seldom less than 5m

though down to 4m on the reach north of Bonanza (where the channel follows the west side) and above the first starboard turn (where the channel is to the north). A few red and green buoys also give guidance. The river carries such a heavy load of silt that echo-sounders are generally unable to cope – typical performance is to give no sensible reading for tens of minutes, then briefly read the correct depth for a minute or two, and then go haywire again. Probably of more concern is the commercial traffic, with ships apparently maintaining full speed both day and night.

There are several possible anchorages to be found out of the fairway, but none are very convenient and the current can be strong.

Returning downstream, unless one can make at least 7kn the passage will take more than one tide – low water at Bonanza occurs nearly 4·5 hours earlier than at Seville, so for every mile made downstream the ebb will finish that much earlier. Leave Seville about three hours before local high water, and after about two hours of foul tide pick up the ebb. If unable to make 7kn it will be necessary either to push against the flood – though this seldom exceeds 2kn even at springs – or to anchor en route.

Seville Cathedral *Henry Buchanan*

Columbus' tomb, Seville *Henry Buchanan*

THE ALGARVE & ANDALUCIA

Seville

Refer to page 289 for marina, lock and bridge communications

The Río Guadalquivir divides on the southern outskirts of the city to form an island, the two branches rejoining some 6M further upstream. The tidal western branch which contains the Puerto Gelves marina is in fact artificial, and was created to enable the eastern, commercial branch to be canalised. The latter, the Canal de Alfonso XIII, offers yachts a choice of two very contrasting places to berth, in addition to containing the city's surprisingly extensive cargo-handling wharves. These are the modest Marina Yachting Sevilla and, further up, the far more upmarket Club Náutico Sevilla.

Air height to both branches is determined by power cables. The single set which cross the eastern arm carry 44m so are unlikely to trouble any yacht, but the northern of the two sets which cross the western channel carry only 19m at high water (Admiralty chart 85 shows 16·5m, but the Spanish authorities confirm the slightly higher figure, as does an indicator board on the western bank). This has on occasion inconvenienced larger yachts, which may have to pass under at low water and then anchor before catching the ebb downstream, but this is rare. The cables encountered about 0·6M further downstream on the same channel carry a more generous 27m.

Canal de Alfonso XIII

Water levels in the Canal de Alfonso XIII are controlled by lock gates. The lock, which displays a green light when it is clear to enter, opens at 0100, 0400, 0700, 1000, 1100, 1300, 1600, 1900 and

Puerto Gelves marina from the north. The amount of suspended silt in the river water is very apparent

Approaching the lock which controls water levels in the Canal de Alfonso XIII, with the Marina Yachting Seville on the right. The Puente V Centenario suspension bridge crosses the canal at upper left

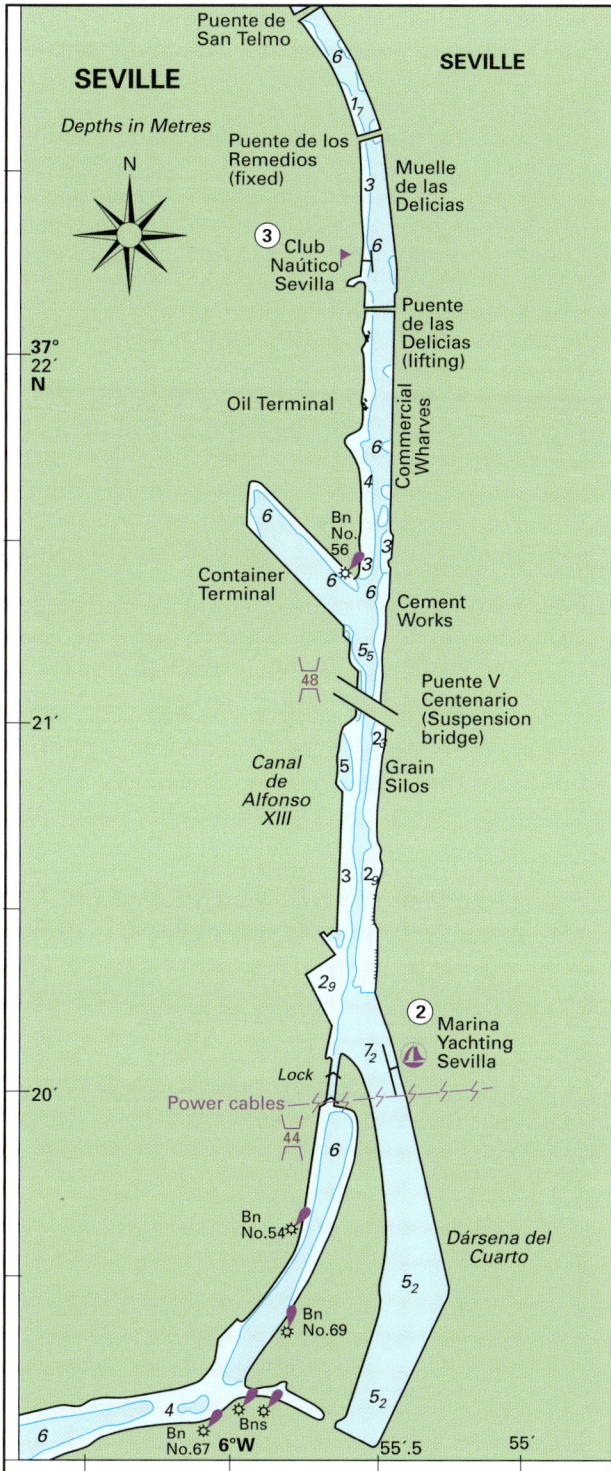

The view upstream from the Canal de Alfonso XIII lock is dominated by the Puente V Centenario suspension bridge (48m clearance), with the Puente de las Delicias lifting bridge beyond *Anne Hammick*

except very close to the banks, but the marina is effectively the limit of navigation for sailing yachts as several low road and rail bridges cross the river less than a mile upstream.

It is sad to report that in recent years (2013) the marina, which nominally contains 133 pontoon berths for yachts of up to 16m plus many more smallcraft 'dry-sailed' from the boatyard area, has suffered from chronic silting which has reduced low water depths in the basin to less than 2m (though the underlying mud is extremely soft). Boats of any size have decamped to a long pontoon (with power and water) on the riverbank outside the marina. There is no reception pontoon as such but the *marineros* are quick off the mark to spot new arrivals. However, four out of six of them were laid off in 2013 and security has suffered. The mooring fees have increased dramatically. The office is open weekdays only 0900–1400.

A haul out here was reported to have been carried out very professionally. Owners can work on their own boats.

Normally, one would secure to the reception pontoon on the starboard side of the entrance and call at the portacabin office at the root of the north wall. The entrance is lit, with appropriately painted beacons on either side, but navigating in the river after dark would be unwise.

Facilities at and around Puerto Gelves are listed on page 294.

Adjacent anchorage It is possible to anchor in the river just upstream of the marina entrance, where maximum tidal range is 1·6m and holding generally good in soft mud – but note that after heavy rain inland the current has been known to attain 8kn! On payment of a small fee, those at anchor can use the marina's showers, launderette, etc.

2. **Marina Yachting Sevilla** (37°20′N 5°59′·5W) is situated hard round to starboard from the lock, amidst rural if somewhat bleak surroundings. Although established in the early 1990s, it does not appear to have developed much in that time and facilities remain poor. Noise from the nearby

2100 daily throughout the year. When tidal heights permit, both gates are left open for considerable periods though entry is still controlled by the lights. The lock-keepers monitor VHF Ch 12 and speak some English. There are no bollards inside the lock, though some loops of rope are provided at the upstream end or yachts may secure to the ladders. Reports of fuel pumps at the lock are unfounded.

1. **Puerto Gelves** 37°20′·4N 6°01′·4W (plan page 288) is the centrepiece of a small marina village, planned in conjunction with EXPO '92 but not completed for a further two years. The river carries 4–5m

THE ALGARVE & ANDALUCIA

Map labels:

SEVILLE

Depths in Metres

N

Puente de San Telmo

SEVILLE

Puente de los Remedios (fixed)

Muelle de las Delicias

③ Club Naútico Sevilla

37° 22′ N

Puente de las Delicias (lifting)

Oil Terminal

Commercial Wharves

Container Terminal

Bn No. 56

Cement Works

21′

Puente V Centenario (Suspension bridge)

Canal de Alfonso XIII

Grain Silos

② Marina Yachting Sevilla

Lock

20′

Power cables

Bn No.54

Dársena del Cuarto

Bn No.69

Bn No.67 6°W

Bns

55′.5   55′

shipyard, combined with the lock loudspeaker, can also be a problem. Its final disadvantage for visitors is that it is some 3·5km from the city centre, tucked behind an industrial area and far from either shops or public transport – though there is no reason why the enterprising crew should not commute into the city by dinghy.

The marina comprises a single pontoon with yachts berthed alongside. Depths range from 3–6m. Secure in any available space, and if an attendant does not appear call at the small office, open 0930–1900 weekdays, closed weekends (though with 24 hour security). Charges are calculated on a length x breadth basis and do not alter throughout the year. Water and electricity are included. Facilities at and around Marina Yachting Sevilla are listed in the following pages.

3. **The Club Náutico Sevilla** (37°22'·2N 5°59'·6W) This Club unquestionably offers by far the most convenient berthing in the city as well as excellent shoreside facilities. It lies on the west bank just upstream of a lifting bridge, backed by extensive and well-kept grounds containing tennis courts, mini-golf and several swimming pools, all of which may be used by visiting crews. It is freely admitted that only a small percentage of the 8,000 or so members own, or have any real interest in, boats.

To reach the club it is necessary to negotiate not only the lock but also the Puente de las Delicias lifting bridge (which replaces the now demolished Puente Alfonso XIII, though still shown on Admiralty chart 85). The previous twice-daily opening was cut back drastically a few years ago, and it now opens only on Monday, Wednesday and Friday at 2000, and on Saturdays and

The Club Nautico Sevilla looking upstream from the Puente de las Delicias   *Henry Buchanan*

holidays at 0830 and 2000 (substituting 1730 for 2000 between November and March). It remains closed throughout the day on Sunday, Tuesday and Thursday. There are several jetties below the bridge where it may be possible to secure whilst waiting.

The majority of berthing is stern-to off one of two long pontoons (haul-off lines are provided, tailed to the pontoon). That furthest upriver is reserved for club members, the lower one is mainly used for visitors and can take 27 yachts of 12m or less, including a few against its inner side. Further downstream again is a section of wall against which can be fitted a maximum of 14 yachts of between 12m and 24m overall (fewer if a high proportion are very beamy), lying to their own bower anchors. At least 4m is found throughout. Perhaps surprisingly, space is nearly always available other than during the April *Feria*, when for a few days the prices treble, but even so it is wise to make contact in advance, either by phone from downriver or at the very least on VHF before passing through the bridge.

The club office is to be found upstairs in the main building, open 0900–1900 weekdays, 0900–1300 Saturday, closed Sunday. Many of the notices throughout the club's premises are in English as well as Spanish. Charges are calculated on a length x breadth basis and do not alter throughout the year, other than at the time of Seville's great April *Feria*. Water, electricity, IVA and 'port tax' (which comprises nearly ⅓ of the total) are all included.

Facilities at and around the Club Náutico Sevilla are listed in the following pages.

Facilities

Boatyard It has been reported (2013) that Astilleros Magallanes ☎/*Fax* +34 955 760545 *Mobile* +34 610 829297, at Puerto Gelves, has been shut down on the death of the owner.

Travel-lift 25-tonne capacity hoist at Puerto Gelves, booked via the marina office, backed by a generous area of hardstanding where owners are welcome to do their own work.

Engineers, electronics and radio repairs Náutica Vergara and Didier Boat Broker (see Chandlery, below) have workshops either on site or nearby. Albea, a short distance up the road, deals mainly with cars but will handle boat electrics and is a good source for 12 volt batteries. Ask at the marina office if in search of less usual items or services – eg they can recommend a company to re-galvanise anchor chain.

There is a well-equipped engineering workshop at Marina Yachting Sevilla, workshop ☎ +34 954 230208, while the office at the Club Náutico Sevilla will call in mechanics and other specialists as necessary.

Sail repairs and canvaswork Sun Sails has premises near Puerto Gelves, but has concentrated on diving work with little interest in anything else. Opening hours are irregular and initial contact is best made via the marina office.

Chandlery Náutica Vergara at Puerto Gelves ☎ +34 955 761063 *Fax* +34 955 761053 *Email* nauticavergara@vianwe.com, holds limited

Below the Canal de Alfonso XIII lock the Río Guadalquivir
is almost entirely rural   *Anne Hammick*

stock and recommends local DIY/household stores
which are excellent.

Resident French yachtsman Benjamin Ponroy is
based at Puerto Gelves. He speaks English and Spanish
and does carpentry and other work. He will work for
or alongside owners and has excellent knowledge of
who to approach for services and materials in the area.
Also based at Puerto Gelves is Didier Boat Broker,
☎/*Fax* +34 955 761792
Mobile +34 654 800 256 whose range tends towards
spares and hardware.
Email info@didierboatbroker.com
www.didierboatbroker.com

NáutiSevilla SL (see *Charts*, below) occupies
premises in the city itself where limited stocks are held.
Hours are 1000–1330, 1630–2000 weekdays, 1000–
1330 Saturday.

Charts NáutiSevilla SL, ☎ +34 954 414832 *Fax* +34 954
422056 at Calle Recaredo 14, and the Instituto
Geográfico Nacional ☎ 955 569324 at Avenida San
Francisco Javier 9, No.8, mod 7, both stock Spanish
charts.

Water On the pontoons at all three marinas. The Club
Náutico Sevilla has separate taps for drinking water
and for boat washing – do not confuse them!

Showers At all three marinas.

Launderette Washing machines next to the shower block
at Puerto Gelves, but no laundry facilities at the Club
Náutico Sevilla (though the office can arrange for it to
be done elsewhere). The latter does not appear to have
a washing line ban, however…

Electricity On the pontoons at all three marinas.

Fuel Diesel and petrol pumps at Puerto Gelves, on the port
side on entry, the only convenient source of yacht fuel
in the entire city.

Bottled gas Camping Gaz exchanges at most hardware
stores, including one almost opposite the Puerto Gelves
entrance, but little chance of getting other cylinders
refilled.

Club náutico The Club Náutico Sevilla is worth a visit
even if not staying on its pontoons. A reasonable
standard of dress is expected in the clubhouse.

Weather forecast Posted at the Puerto Gelves office at
weekends – during the week it is necessary to ask, and
daily at the Club Náutico Sevilla.

Banks Throughout the city and at Gelves.

Shops/provisioning Excellent in the city, as one would
expect, but no shops anywhere near Marina Yachting
Sevilla, and some distance to walk from the Club
Náutico Sevilla (fortunately, several of the larger city
supermarkets have delivery services). Puerto Gelves
boasts a handy mini-market just around the corner
from the marina bar, with more shops within walking
distance.

Produce markets Near the river north of the bullring and
on Calle Alfarería in the Triana district (about 20
minutes' walk from the Club Náutico Sevilla), plus a
weekly market at Gelves.

Cafés, restaurants and hotels Thousands, at all price
levels, with only the Marina Yachting Sevilla
apparently lacking. The Club Náutico Sevilla has a
particularly pleasant terrace bar overlooking its yacht
pontoons.

Medical services All aspects including major hospitals.
Doctor and dentist at Gelves.

Communications

Post office Throughout the city and at Gelves.

Mailing address All three marina offices will hold mail for
visiting yachts – c/o Puerto Gelves, Autovía
Sevilla–Coria, km 3.5, 41120 Gelves, Sevilla, España;
c/o Marina Yachting Sevilla SA, Carretara del Copero
s/n, Punta del Verde, 41012 Sevilla, España; or c/o
Club Náutico Sevilla, Avda Sanlúcar de Barrameda s/n,
Apartado de Correos 1003, 41011 Sevilla, España. It is
important that the envelope carries the name of the
yacht in addition to that of the addressee.

Public telephones Next to the chandlery at Puerto Gelves,
and several in the grounds of the Club Náutico Sevilla.
There is no longer a public telephone at Marina
Yachting Sevilla.

Internet access Numerous possibilities throughout the city,
with Sevilla@Internet almost opposite the Cathedral
particularly recommended – fast computers,
reasonably quiet and, being on the first floor, generally
quite cool and airy.

Compustation, near Puerto Gelves, does not offer
internet access but does handle computer repairs as
well as selling consumables such as inkjets.

Fax service At Puerto Gelves, *Fax* +34 955 761583, and
the Club Náutico Sevilla, *Fax* +34 954 284693.

Car hire/taxis Readily available in the city (though the
rush hour is even worse than most). The office staff at
all three marinas are happy to telephone for taxis.

Buses Run every 20 minutes from just outside Puerto
Gelves into the centre of Seville (about 15 minutes),
and from near the Club Náutico Sevilla.

Trains Good services throughout Spain (eg 2·5 hours to
Madrid). Seville's new metro line features a stop little
more than 1km from Puerto Gelves which will provide
a handy link with the city centre.

Air services International airport just outside the city,
served by Iberia, BA and Ryanair.

III.3 The Río Guadalquivir to Cabo Trafalgar

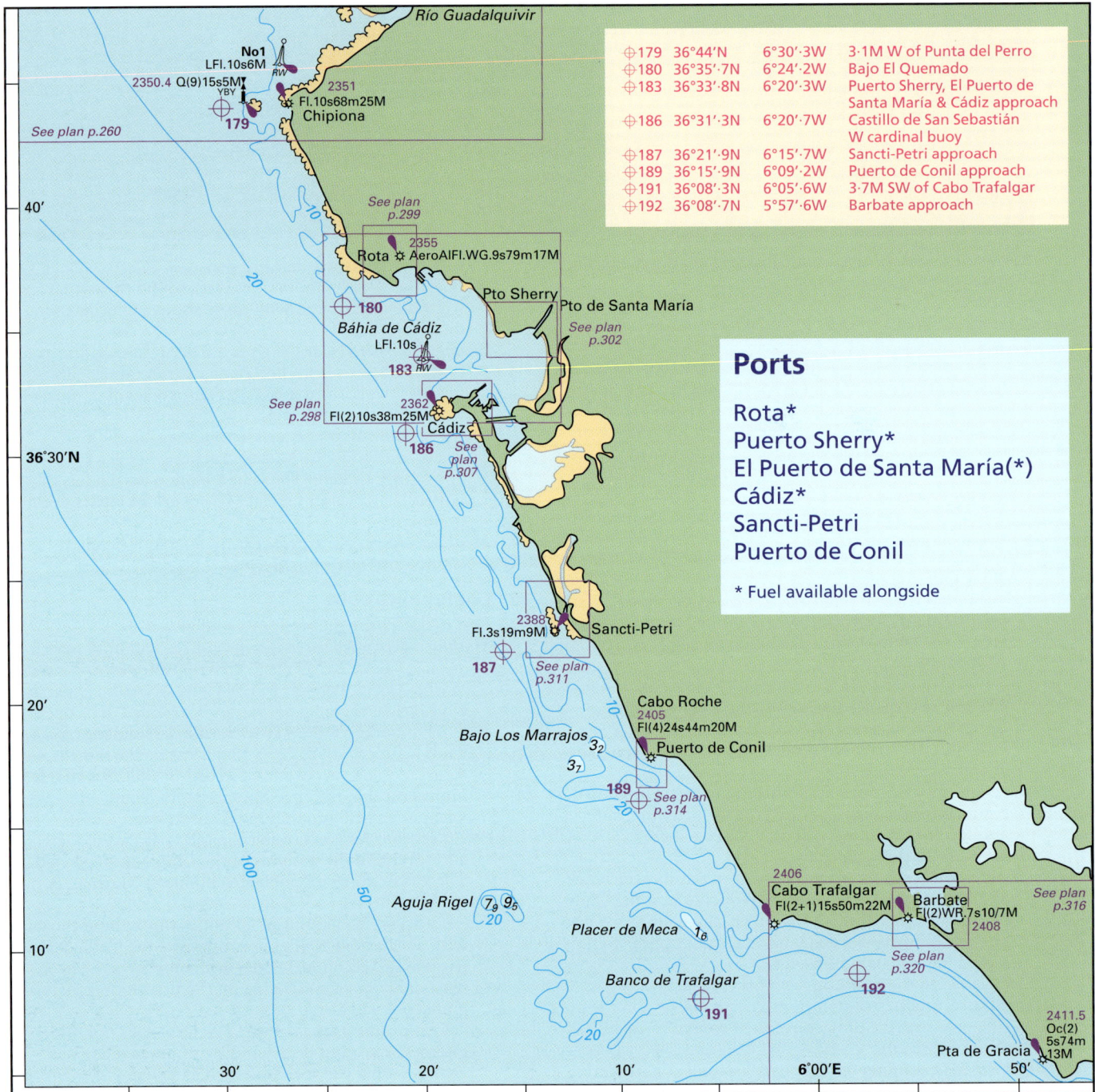

Río Guadalquivir

No1
LFl.10s6M

2350.4 Q(9)15s5M
YBY

179

See plan p.260

2351
Fl.10s68m25M
Chipiona

40'

See plan
p.299

2355
Rota ☆ AeroAlFl.WG.9s79m17M

Pto Sherry

Pto de Santa María

See plan
p.302

180

Báhia de Cádiz
LFl.10s

183 RW

See plan
p.298

2362
Fl(2)10s38m25M

Cádiz

186

See
plan
p.307

36°30'N

⊕179	36°44'N	6°30'·3W	3·1M W of Punta del Perro
⊕180	36°35'·7N	6°24'·2W	Bajo El Quemado
⊕183	36°33'·8N	6°20'·3W	Puerto Sherry, El Puerto de Santa María & Cádiz approach
⊕186	36°31'·3N	6°20'·7W	Castillo de San Sebastián W cardinal buoy
⊕187	36°21'·9N	6°15'·7W	Sancti-Petri approach
⊕189	36°15'·9N	6°09'·2W	Puerto de Conil approach
⊕191	36°08'·3N	6°05'·6W	3·7M SW of Cabo Trafalgar
⊕192	36°08'·7N	5°57'·6W	Barbate approach

Ports

Rota*
Puerto Sherry*
El Puerto de Santa María(*)
Cádiz*
Sancti-Petri
Puerto de Conil

* Fuel available alongside

2388
Fl.3s19m9M
Sancti-Petri

187

See plan
p.311

Cabo Roche
2405
Fl(4)24s44m20M
☆ Puerto de Conil

Bajo Los Marrajos 3₂

3₇

189
See plan
p.314

20

2406
Cabo Trafalgar
Fl(2+1)15s50m22M
☆

Barbate
Fl(2)WR.7s10/7M
☆ 2408

See plan
p.316

See plan
p.320

Aguja Rigel 7₉ 9₅
20

Placer de Meca 1₆

192

Banco de Trafalgar
⊕
191

20

2411.5
Oc(2)
5s74m
13M
Pta de Gracia ☆

30' 20' 10' 6°00'E 50'

PRINCIPAL LIGHTS

2351 **Punta del Perro (Chipiona)** Fl.10s68m25M
Stone tower on building 62m
2350.4 **Bajo Salmedina** Q(9)15s9m5M
West cardinal tower, ⊻ topmark
2355 **Rota Aeromarine Aero** AlFl.WG.9s79m17M
Red and white chequered spherical tank 49m
2362 **Cádiz, Castillo de San Sebastián** Fl(2)10s38m25M
Horn Mo 'N'(—·)20s Aluminium tower on castle 37m

2388 **Castillo de Sancti-Petri** Fl.3s19m9M
Square tower 16m
2405 **Cabo Roche** Fl(4)24s44m20M
Square pale yellow tower, silver lantern 20m
2406 **Cabo Trafalgar** Fl(2+1)15s50m22M
White conical tower and building 34

Bahía de Cádiz (Cádiz Bay)
Approaches to Rota, Puerto Sherry, Santa María and Cádiz

Waypoints
⊕180 – 36°35'·7N 6°24'·2W (Bajo El Quemado)
⊕181 – 36°35'·1N 6°21'·8W (Rota, approach)
⊕183 – 36°33'·8N 6°20'·3W (Puerto Sherry, El Puerto de Santa María and Cádiz, approach)
⊕186 – 36°31'·3N 6°20'·7W (Castillo de San Sebastián west cardinal buoy)

Courses and distances
⊕177 (Chipiona & Río Guadalquivir) – ⊕181 (via ⊕178 & ⊕179) = 14·3M, 223° & 149°&107° or 287° & 329° & 043°
⊕177 (Chipiona & Río Guadalquivir) – ⊕183 (via ⊕178 & ⊕179) = 16M, 223° & 149° & 121° or 301° & 329° & 043°
⊕181 – ⊕183 = 1·8M, 137° or 317°
⊕181 – ⊕187 (Sancti-Petri, via ⊕186) = 14·1M, 167° & 157° or 337° & 347°
⊕181 – ⊕191 (Cabo Trafalgar, via ⊕186) = 29·9M, 167° & 152° or 332° & 347°
⊕183 – ⊕187 (Sancti-Petri, via ⊕186) = 12·7M, 187° & 157° or 337° & 007°
⊕183 – ⊕191 (Cabo Trafalgar, via ⊕186) = 28·5M, 187° & 152° or 332° & 007°
⊕183 – ⊕192 (Barbate, via ⊕186 & ⊕191) = 35M, 187° & 152° & 086° or 266° & 332° & 007°

Charts

	Approach	Bay
Admiralty	91, 93	86
Imray	C19, C50	C19, C50
Spanish	44B, 44C, 443, 443A, 443B	

Principal lights
2355.2 **Rota old lighthouse** Oc.4s33m13M
Off-white tower, red band 28m
2355 **Rota Aeromarine Aero** AlFl.WG.9s79m17M
Red and white chequered spherical tank 49m
2362 **Cádiz, Castillo de San Sebastián** Fl(2)10s38m25M
Horn Mo 'N'(–·)20s Aluminium tower on castle 37m
Harbours and marinas – listed individually.

Coast radio station
Cádiz (remotely controlled from Mâlaga)
Digital Selective Calling MMSI 002241011
VHF Ch 16, 26, 74
Weather bulletins and navigational warnings
Weather bulletins in Spanish and English: VHF Ch 74 at 0315, 0715, 1115, 1515, 1915, 2315 UT
Navigational warnings in Spanish and English: on receipt

Although it is difficult to find any local references to it, **Part III.3** covers an area which witnessed one of the most significant naval battles ever fought. At the beginning of the 19th century, Napoleon's ambitions to invade Britain depended on his navy being able to protect his Grande Army as they crossed the English Channel. The English fleet under Admiral Nelson, charged to prevent this, attempted to blockade the French and then followed their fleet across to the Caribbean and back to Europe. By October 1805 the combined fleet of French (Admiral Villeneuve) and Spanish ships (Admiral Gravina) were anchored under the protection of the forts of Cádiz.

On 20th October the combined fleet under Admiral Villeneuve sailed from Cádiz heading in line to the southeast in a light wind. He was unaware that the watching English frigate HMS *Sirius* acted, through a line of relay ships, as eyes for Nelson's force, which gave chase. Nelson briefed his captains on his unconventional plan of attack. On the morning of the 21st Villeneuve turned his fleet back north towards Cádiz. Nelson made his memorable flag signal 'England expects every man will do his duty', and at 1215 gave his final message to the Fleet – 'Engage the enemy more closely'.

Nelson's 27 ships attacked the combined fleet of 33 ships in two columns. His Flagship HMS *Victory* (Captain Hardy) led the weather column, HMS Royal *Sovereign* (Captain Collingwood) the lee. By late afternoon the battle was over, the combined fleet was destroyed or scattered without loss of a single English ship, and Nelson had been shot by a French marine from the fighting top of the *Redoubtable*. Napolean's invasion plans were thwarted and Britain controlled the seas – 'Trafalgar' shaped the course of European history for 100 years.

Nelson, a national hero, was buried in St Paul's Cathedral. His famous statue on its column overlooks Trafalgar Square. The second ship in line behind HMS *Victory* at Trafalgar remains immortalised as *The Fighting Temeraire* – the most popular work by JWM Turner who painted her in 1838 as she was towed upriver to be broken up.

Two hundred years after the battle, French and Spanish vessels formed a substantial part of an international naval fleet which joined the Royal Navy in a Fleet Review and festival in the Solent off Portsmouth in summer 2005. On 21st October 2005, members of several yacht clubs laid wreaths off Cabo Trafalgar and gathered on the beach to honour the heroism, and the loss of life, on all sides in this greatest of sea battles.

Martin Walker

HMS *Victory*, launched in 1765 and the only surviving 18th-century ship of the line in the world, remains in service in Portsmouth Dockyard with her masts towering above the modern navy *Martin Walker*

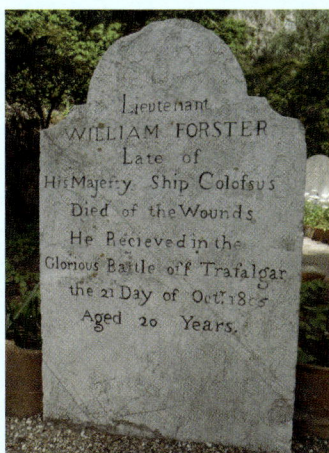

The graves in the Trafalgar Cemetery in Gibraltar are a personal and poignant reminder of the loss of life on all sides in the battle *Jane Russell*

THE ALGARVE & ANDALUCIA

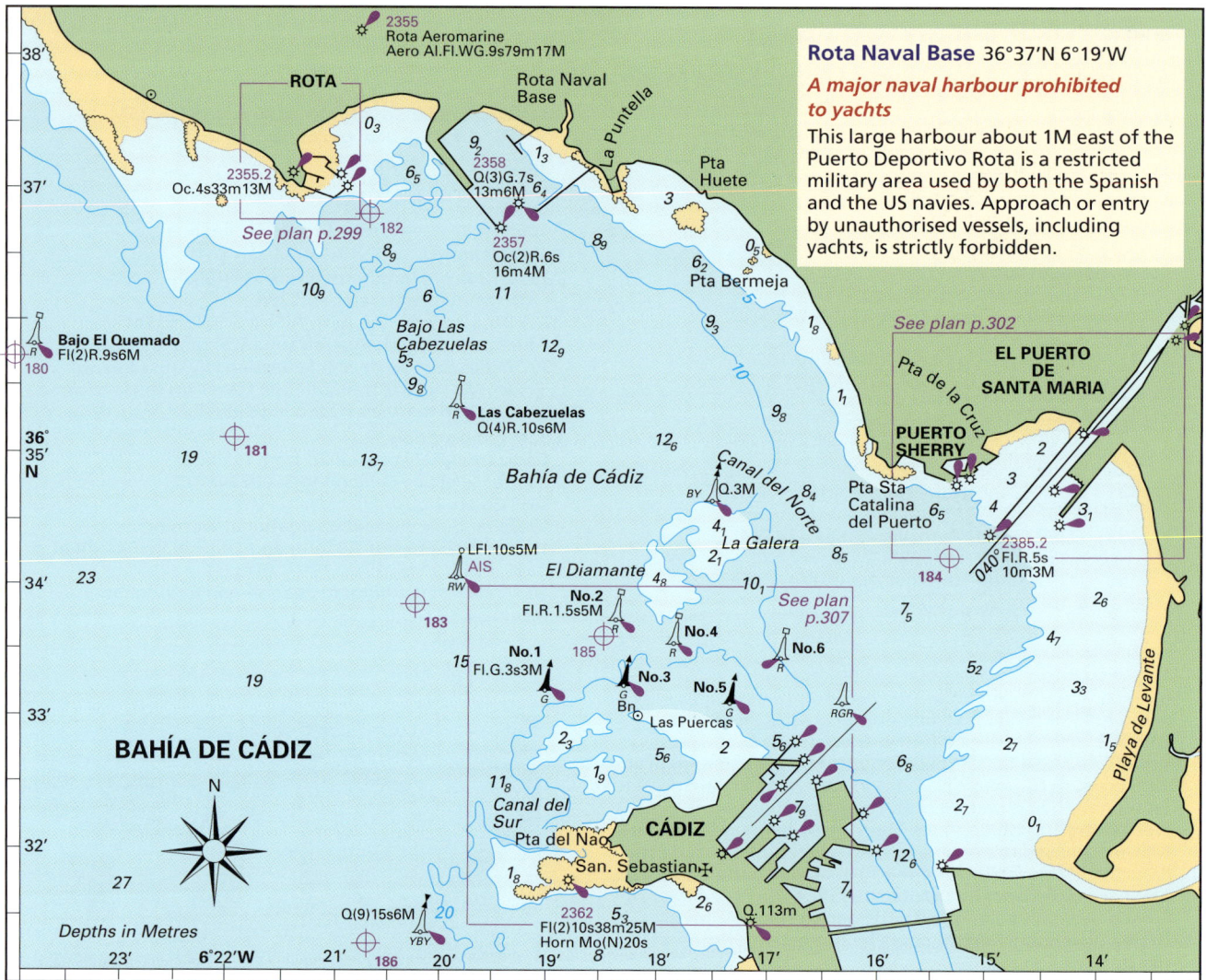

Chart labels:

2355
Rota Aeromarine
Aero Al.Fl.WG.9s79m17M

ROTA

Rota Naval
Base

La Puntella

Pta
Huete

Rota Naval Base 36°37'N 6°19'W
A major naval harbour prohibited to yachts
This large harbour about 1M east of the Puerto Deportivo Rota is a restricted military area used by both the Spanish and the US navies. Approach or entry by unauthorised vessels, including yachts, is strictly forbidden.

2355.2
Oc.4s33m13M

See plan p.299

2358
Q(3)G.7s
13m6M

2357
Oc(2)R.6s
16m4M

Pta Bermeja

See plan p.302

Bajo El Quemado
Fl(2)R.9s6M
180

Bajo Las Cabezuelas

EL PUERTO DE SANTA MARIA

Pta de la Cruz

PUERTO SHERRY

Las Cabezuelas
Q(4)R.10s6M

Pta Sta
Catalina
del Puerto

181

Bahía de Cádiz

Canal del Norte

BY Q.3M

2385.2
Fl.R.5s
10m3M

184

LFl.10s5M
AIS
RW

El Diamante

La Galera

183

No.2
Fl.R.1.5s5M

See plan p.307

No.4

No.6

No.1
Fl.G.3s3M
G

185

No.3
Bn
Las Puercas

No.5
G

RGR

BAHÍA DE CÁDIZ

N

Canal del Sur
Pta del Nao

CÁDIZ

San Sebastian

Q.113m

Depths in Metres

Q(9)15s6M
20
YBY
186

2362
Fl(2)10s38m25M
Horn Mo(N)20s

6°22'W

Approach

It should be noted that fishing nets can be found as far out as the 100m line which is 10–12M from Cadiz.

The Bahía de Cádiz is more than 5M wide across at its mouth and gives access to the harbours of Rota, Puerto Sherry and El Puerto de Santa María as well as to Cádiz itself.

From the northwest, the 10m line lies up to 1·75M from the coast between Punta del Perro and Rota. Off the former lies the dangerous Bajo Salmedina, extending almost 1·6M offshore and marked by a west cardinal tower. If in doubt, ⊕179 lies some 3M offshore. Having rounded Bajo Salmedina remain a minimum of 1·3M offshore until south of 36°36'N. In poor weather head for ⊕180, Bajo El Quemado, and follow the waypoints as above.

From the south, an offing of at least 2M is necessary to clear the various offshore hazards. In particular, do not be tempted to take any short cuts around the peninsula of Cádiz itself – the reefs and shoals running westwards from the Castillo de San Sebastián have claimed many vessels over the years.

⊕180	36°35'·7N	6°24'·2W	Bajo El Quemado
⊕181	36°35'·1N	6°21'·8W	Rota approach
⊕182	36°36'·78N	6°20'·76W	Rota entrance
⊕183	36°33'·8N	6°20'·3W	Puerto Sherry, El Puerto de Santa María & Cádiz approach
⊕184	36°34'·2N	6°15'·3W	Puerto Sherry & El Puerto de Santa María entrance
⊕185	36°33'·57N	6°18'·42W	Cádiz entrance
⊕186	36°31'·3N	6°20'·7W	Castillo de San Sebastián W cardinal buoy

Unless very confident it would be wise to come in on the west cardinal buoy about 1M southwest of the Castillo, from there shaping a course of 030° for Los Cochinos buoy No.1 and so entering the Canal Principal. Alternatively a course of 332° from ⊕191 (Cabo Trafalgar) to ⊕186, followed by 007° to ⊕183 takes one well clear of all hazards en route to any of the bay's three southeastern harbours.

From offshore the approach to both ⊕181 and ⊕183 is straightforward.

Further information on the final approaches to each harbour will be found in that harbour's notes.

Rota

Waypoints
⊕180 – 36°35'·7N 6°24'·2W (Bajo El Quemado)
⊕181 – 36°35'·1N 6°21'·8W (approach)
⊕182 – 36°36'·78N 6°20'·76W (entrance)

Courses and distances
⊕177 (Chipiona & Río Guadalquivir) – ⊕181 (via ⊕179
& ⊕180) = 14·3M, 223° & 149° & 107° or
287° & 329° & 043°
⊕181 – ⊕182 = 1·9M, 027° or 207°
⊕181 – ⊕183 = 1·8M, 137° or 317°
⊕181 – ⊕187 (Sancti-Petri, via ⊕186) = 14·1M,
167° & 157° or 337° & 347°
⊕181 – ⊕191 (Cabo Trafalgar, via ⊕186) = 29·9M,
167° & 152° or 332° & 347°

Tides
Standard port Cádiz
Mean time differences
HW –0010; LW –0015 ±0005
Heights in metres

MHWS	MHWN	MLWN	MLWS
3·1	2·4	1·1	0·4

Or refer to EasyTide at www.ukho.gov.uk/easytide

Charts	*Harbour*
Admiralty	86
Imray	C19, C50
Spanish	4431

Principal lights
2355.2 **Rota old lighthouse** Oc.4s33m13M
Off-white tower, red band 28m
2355.4 **Southwest breakwater** Fl(3)R.10s8m3M Red post on
towered hut 3m
2355.5 **Northeast breakwater** Q(6)G.12s3M Green metal
post (Close to floodlit statue of the Virgin and Child)

Night entry
Without problem provided no corners are cut – literally. Although the entrance is relatively narrow it is well lit, with the reception berth directly opposite.

Harbour communications
Puerto Deportivo Rota Puerto Deportivo Rota, Nave 1,
11520 ROTA (Cadiz) ☎+34 856 104011
and +34 600 141558 *Fax* +34 856 587581
Email rota@eppa.es www.puertosdeandalucia.es
VHF Ch 09
Club Nautico de Rota ☎ +34 956 813 821 *Fax* +34 956 813
821 *Email* clubnauticorota@telefonica.net
www.clubnauticorota.com

A well-kept, expanding marina close to an interesting old town

The northwesternmost of the Bahía de Cádiz harbours, Rota is an attractive old town with strong Moorish influences, not least in the massive stone archways which span its narrow streets. Like many Spanish towns it is best explored on foot. Excellent beaches fringe its harbour on both sides, and the tall slim lighthouse with its single red band which stands near the root of the south breakwater makes identification certain by day or night. Rota is becoming an increasingly popular place for liveaboards to winter afloat.

The Corrales de Rota reserve extends along the beach to the northwest from the old town. The corrales are a system of fish pens dating back to Roman times. Fish, cuttlefish and octopi were brought into the pens by the tide and then harvested. The dune system backing the beach is part of the reserve, accessed by a wooden walkway, and is home

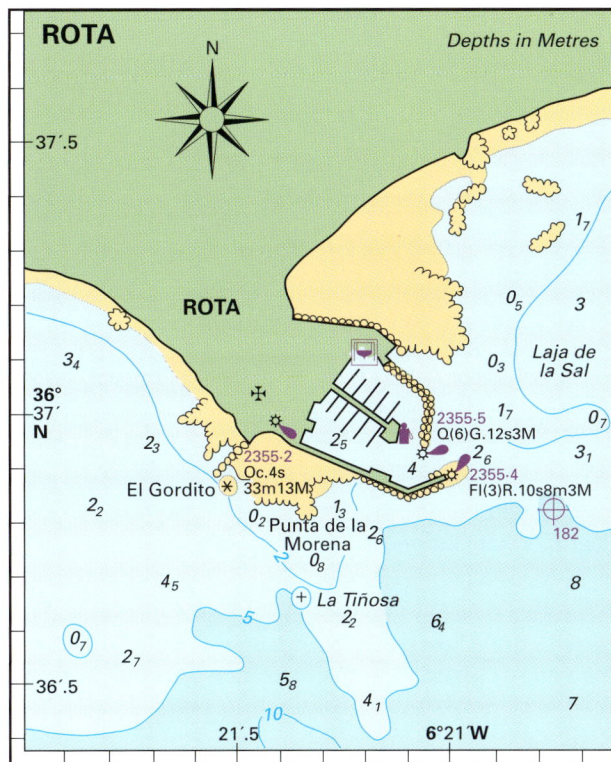

⊕181 36°35'·1N 6°21'·8W Rota approach
⊕182 36°36'·78N 6°20'·76W Rota entrance

This tiny chamaeleon is one of the residents of the reserve *David Russell*

to Spain's largest population of chamaeleons. Spot one if you can!

Like a number of other harbours run by the Agencia Pública de Puertos de Andalucía, Rota combines the functions of yacht and fishing harbour, though the latter have now been banished to the southwest breakwater. It is occasionally referred to as Puerto Astaroth, but is more normally known by the less romantic but much more descriptive title of Puerto Deportivo Rota. It should on no account be confused with the much larger Rota Naval Base which lies about 1M further east.

Major construction work has been taking place ashore to provide restaurants, bars and shops, including the new *club náutico* de Rota. There are ferries from the marina across the bay to Cadiz.

Approach and entrance

For outer approaches from the northwest and southeast refer to Bahía de Cádiz.

Once ⊕180 is reached – or when south of 36°36'N if sailing closer inshore – head due east until the southwest breakwater head bears 030° or less before altering course to round its end. Allow generous

Puerto de Rota looking east of north *APPA*

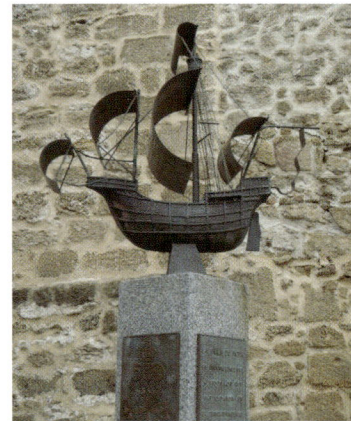

A caravel statue in old Rota
Jane Russell

clearance as sand has built up beyond the light. The north breakwater will open up behind – for maximum protection the entrance was built facing northeast – with the prominent white statue of the Virgin and Child close to its end. From the south or southeast the breakwater head can be approached direct. The entrance forms a dogleg and is relatively narrow, but otherwise presents no problems.

From offshore ⊕181 lies 1·9M south-southwest of the entrance, a course of 027° leading to ⊕182 close outside the harbour mouth.

Berthing

The reception/fuel pontoon lies directly opposite the entrance against the end of the diamond-shaped hammerhead, with the marina office close by. With a total of 509 berths on eleven pontoons, 144 of them able to take yachts of 12m or more, space for a visitor can nearly always be found, if only for a couple of nights (though note APPA's policy that if a berth of the correct length is not available and a yacht occupies a larger berth this will be charged for, irrespective of the actual length of the boat). If staying long-term and offered a choice, the northeast basin is considerably more protected than that to the southwest which, during gales, suffers both from surf breaking over the breakwater and swell from the entrance. Depths shoal gradually from 4m near the hammerhead to 2·5m along the northwest perimeter.

Weekdays in winter, office hours are 1000–1330 and 1600–1730, closed Saturday and Sunday afternoons. The office remains open later in summer with no weekend closing. The staff are particularly helpful, and there is 24 hour security with card-operated gates to the pontoons.

Facilities

Boatyard On the north side of the marina, with a large area of secure (but somewhat windy) hard standing. All larger occupy cradles, with additional shores. Laying-up ashore in Rota is becoming increasingly popular.
Travel-lift 50-tonne capacity lift at the boatyard.

Engineers, electronic and radio repairs Available at or via the boatyard. For more major jobs specialists may be called in from Puerto Sherry.
Chandlery Nautica Pepito has shut down. There is Nautica Vergara (Yamaha) ☎ +34 956 846362. *Email* nauticavergararota@hotmail.com
Water On the pontoons.
Showers On the hammerhead (in the building which also houses the fuel berth office), and in an anonymous cream building with grey doors near the root of the central mole, both well-kept.
Launderette In the anonymous cream building.
Electricity On the pontoons.
Fuel Diesel and petrol at the reception pontoon on the central hammerhead, 0800–1400 and 1500–1900.
Bottled gas Camping Gaz in the town, but no refills.
Weather forecast Posted daily outside the marina office.
Club náutico Now in new premises overlooking the marina.
Banks In the town, with cash dispensers.
Shops/provisioning Good shopping in the town only a short walk from the marina.
Produce market Directly opposite the marina.
Cafés, restaurants and hotels Mina Street is a lively, fun area at night with several reasonable restaurants.
Medical services In the town.

Communications

Post office In the town.
Mailing address The marina office will hold mail for visiting yachts – c/o Oficina del Puerto, Puerto Deportivo Rota, Calle Higuereta 1, 11520 Rota, Cádiz, España. It is important that the envelope carries the name of the yacht in addition to that of the addressee.
Public telephones Around the marina with more in town.
Internet access There is one internet pay terminal in the café at the root of the central jetty. There are other places in town, and free access in the library.
Fax service At the marina office, Fax +34 956 813811.
Car hire/taxis Can be organised via the marina office.
Ferry There is a small ferry terminal in the same building as the marina office. Ferries ply across to Cadiz.
Buses To Chipiona, El Puerto de Santa María, Seville etc.
Air services Airports at Seville and Jerez, both served by Ryanair among others.

Puerto Sherry

Waypoints
- 183 – 36°33'·8N 6°20'·3W (approach, also for El Puerto de Santa María and Cádiz)
- 184 – 36°34'·2N 6°15'·3W (entrance, also for El Puerto de Santa María)
- 185 – 36°33'·57 6°18'·42 (Cádiz entrance)

Courses and distances
- 177 (Chipiona & Río Guadalquivir) – 183 (via 179 & 180) = 16M, 223° & 149°&121° or 301° & 329° & 043°
- 183 – 184 (via 185) = 4·1M, 099° & 076° or 256° & 279°
- 183 – 187 (Sancti-Petri, via 186) = 12·7M, 187° & 157° or 337° & 007°
- 183 – 191 (Cabo Trafalgar, via 186) = 28·5M, 187° & 152° or 332° & 007°

Tides
See El Puerto de Santa María, page 304

Charts

	Harbour
Admiralty	86
Imray	C19, C50
Spanish	4431

Principal lights
2385.2 **Santa María, West training wall, head**
　Fl.R.5s9m3M Red metal tower 4m
2382 **South breakwater** Oc.R.4s5M
　White truncated conical tower
2382.3 **East mole, SE corner** Oc.G.5s3M Green tower
2382.5 **Inner harbour, W side** Q.R.1M
　Squat red tower 2m
2382.4 **Inner harbour, E side** Q.G.1M
　Squat Green tower 2m

Night entry
　Straightforward but narrow. Swing wide and head up the centre to avoid shallows to port and an unlit concrete spur opposite

Harbour communications
Puerto Sherry ☎ +34 956 870 103 and +34 956 850 202
Fax +34 956 873 902
Email puertosherry@puertosherry.com
www.puertosherry.com (in English and Spanish)
VHF Ch 09 (24 hours)

Large, purpose-built marina with a good onsite boatyard but lack-lustre surroundings

Puerto Sherry is by far the largest, oldest and, in some ways, best equipped marina on the Atlantic coast of Andalucía. Planned as a true 'marina village' with construction begun in 1985, many of the buildings still remain unfinished 29 years on, although 33 apartments and a hotel have been completed. There is no true village ashore, the marina complex being backed by carefully landscaped villas and golf courses.

The overall impression is still that of a building site, with some of the completed buildings already beginning to peel. It would be fair to say that few cruising yachtsmen spend time in Puerto Sherry for pleasure, but more than one has found its well-equipped boatyard and concentration of specialised skills to be a veritable lifesaver in time of need.

To visit Cadiz it is necessary to take a taxi, or walk (45 minutes), to the ferry terminal at Santa Maria (see plan page 302) and take the ferry from there.

Approach

For outer approaches from the northwest and southeast refer to Bahía de Cádiz, page 298.

Once in the bay, from north of west approach via Las Cabezuelas buoy and the Canal del Norte, passing no more than 1M off Punta Santa Catalina del Puerto in order to avoid the La Galera and El Diamante banks which shoal to 2–1m. From south of west, follow the directions for Cádiz – page 307 – diverging from the Canal Principal after passing El Diamante port hand buoy No.4. From there a direct course of 063° leads to the marina entrance.

From offshore, on reaching 183 (also the approach waypoint for Puerto Sherry and Cádiz) either continue on 099° to 185 before altering to 076° for 184 or, in flat conditions and with due care, sail the direct course of 084° for 4·1M, crossing the edge of the El Diamante shoal en route. 184 lies about 800m south of the south breakwater head – on no account steer directly for the south breakwater from 183, unless happy to cross the La Galera shoal which carries 2·1m at datum.

From all directions the cream 'lighthouse' building at the end of the south breakwater, which houses the marina office, makes a conspicuous daymark.

Entrance

The 100m wide entrance faces slightly south of east and is well sheltered, but care must be taken of a shoal, at one time described as extensive, around and inside the end of the south breakwater. This has been marked by pink buoys, some in clusters, none of which are lit. A concrete spur, also unlit, juts out from the wall opposite. In 2012 the stated intention was to dredge around and inside the end of the south breakwater, and, looking further ahead, to build a training wall between Rota and Puerto Sherry.

Rounding the south breakwater light enter the harbour on a course of 289°. A minimum of 3m at low water is claimed in the centre of the entrance.

The reception pontoon is on the inside of the south breakwater close to the marina control tower.

Berthing

Puerto Sherry contains nearly 800 berths for craft of up to 60m (provided they can cope with the 3m depths) in totally sheltered conditions, and it would be rare for space not to be available for a visitor. All pontoons are equipped with fingers – those immediately overlooked by the two hotels are somewhat public, those to the south are quieter but entail a longer walk. In fact the size of the complex is such that, if berthed on one of the western pontoons and needing to visit the boatyard area, it might well be worth launching the dinghy.

The marina staff are efficient, welcoming, speak English and have been seen helping to moor a boat at the reception pontoon at 0200 in the morning. Security is excellent with gates to each pontoon and CCTV monitoring. The office is open 0800–2100 from 1/6-30/9 otherwise 0800-2000. Most major credit cards are accepted.

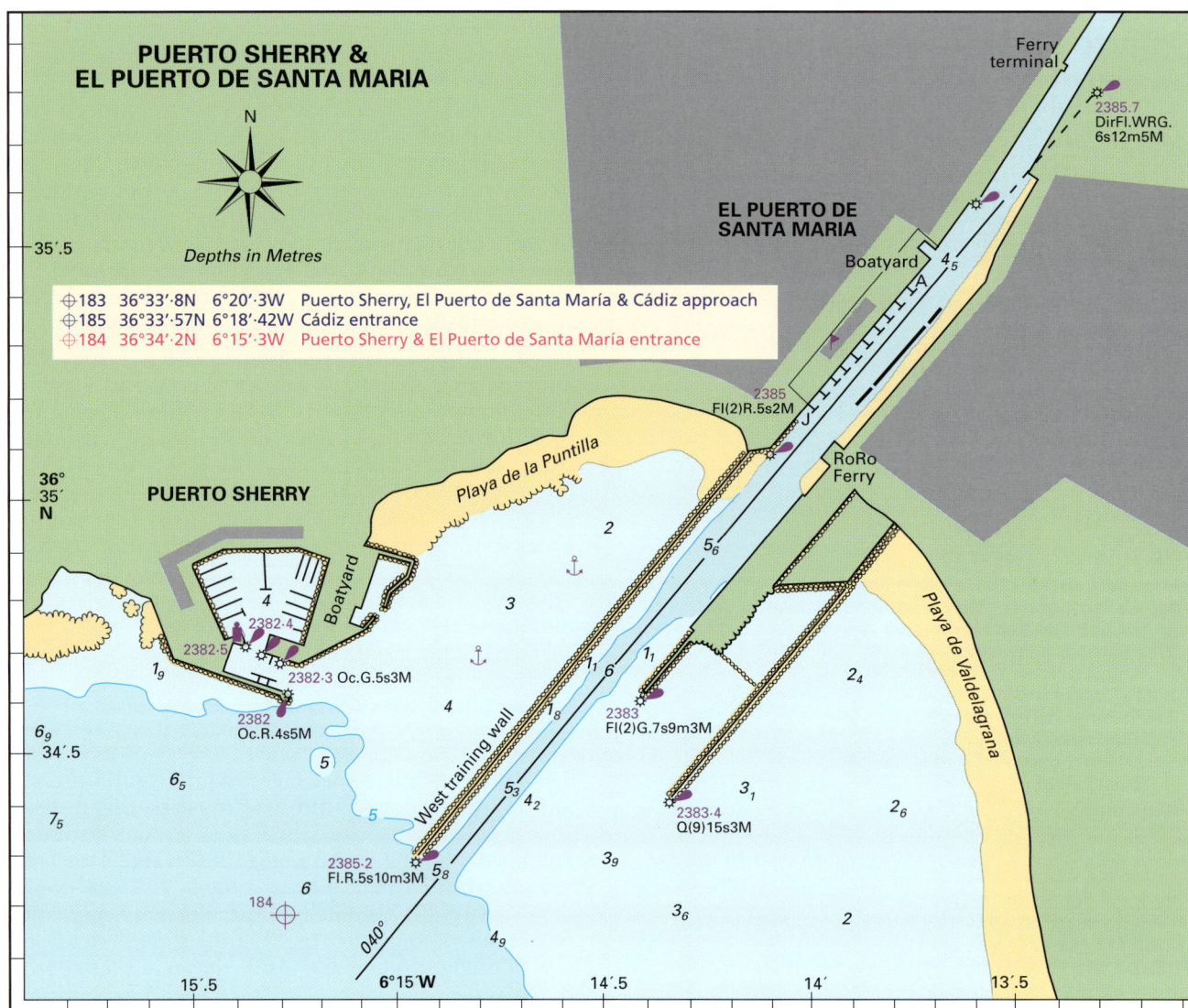

**PUERTO SHERRY &
EL PUERTO DE SANTA MARIA**

N

Depths in Metres

Ferry terminal

2385.7
DirFl.WRG.
6s12m5M

EL PUERTO DE
SANTA MARIA

Boatyard

35′.5

⊕183 36°33′·8N 6°20′·3W Puerto Sherry, El Puerto de Santa María & Cádiz approach
⊕185 36°33′·57N 6°18′·42W Cádiz entrance
⊕184 36°34′·2N 6°15′·3W Puerto Sherry & El Puerto de Santa María entrance

2385
Fl(2)R.5s2M

RoRo
Ferry

Playa de la Puntilla

36°
35′
N

PUERTO SHERRY

Boatyard

Playa de Valdelagrana

2382·4
2382·5
2382·3 Oc.G.5s3M

2382
Oc.R.4s5M

2383
Fl(2)G.7s9m3M

West training wall

2383·4
Q(9)15s3M

34′.5

2385·2
Fl.R.5s10m3M

184

040°

6°15′W   14′.5   14′   13′.5

Facilities

Boatyard There is a large area of gated hardstanding on the wide east mole, with work carried out by a number of companies – see below. Security is relaxed during the day but doubtless better at night. DIY work is permitted, but owners cannot live aboard yachts which are ashore.

Travel-lift 160-tonne capacity lift for which bookings must be made at the marina office. No shortage of shores and some cradles.

Engineers, electronic and radio repairs, chandlery Several companies share the workload in the boatyard, and each appears to have its own chandlery. As a result the range is good, prices are competitive, and all will order items not in stock. Taken alphabetically they are: Industria Náutica del Sur SL ☎ +34 956 874 001 *Fax* 34 956 874 001, www.inauticadelsur.com which handles hull and engine maintenance and repairs, osmosis treatment, painting etc; Náutica Sherry, ☎ +34 956 861 416 *Fax* +34 956 861 417 www.nauticasherry.com *Email* nauticasherry@yahoo.es which again handles mechanical repairs and general maintenance and has a well-stocked chandlery (English-speaking staff are more likely to be on duty in the morning); and Puerto Náutica SL, ☎ +34 956 540 878, which focuses largely on mechanical and electrical work, with less general chandlery stocked (they have a second outlet on the road into Santa María, mostly selling nautical nicknacks but with some galleyware and clothes).

Julio Romero Náutica ☎/*Fax* +34 956 870 392, which operates from a portacabin near the northeast corner of the inner basin, is a much smaller concern specialising in outboard repair.

Sailmaker/sail repairs Velas Climent SL, ☎/*Fax* +34 956 870 539, occupies a rather anonymous white building with blue trim in the boatyard area. They are experienced sailmakers, as well as handling repairs and general canvaswork.

Rigging Industria Náutica del Sur handles rigging, with a specialist brought in from Valencia if necessary.

Chandleries See above.

Water On the pontoons.

Showers Several shower blocks around the marina complex reported to be kept impeccably clean.

Launderette On the west quay of the marina.

Electricity On the pontoons. However large, non-standard adapter plugs are necessary and the marina office does not always have enough to lend or rent to visitors.

Fuel Petrol and diesel pumps on the west side of the entrance to the inner harbour. In theory fuel can be bought at any time of the day or night, and credit cards are accepted.

Puerto Sherry marina control tower
and reception pontoon
Puerto Sherry Marina

Looking northeast over Puerto
Sherry Marina *APPA*

Entrance to Puerto Sherry marina from the welcome
pontoon *Jane Russell*

Bottled gas Not available.
Weather forecast Posted daily at the marina office.
Bank Not only no bank, but no card machine in the entire
complex. Berthing can be paid for by credit card, but
not an ice-cream or a cup of coffee.
Shops/provisioning Small supermarket on the west side of
the inner basin, though it would be necessary to go into
El Puerto de Santa María (and take a taxi back) for
serious storing up.

Cafés, restaurants and hotels Several cafés and restaurants
along the west side of the inner basin, with a large
hotel to the north, but no longer a café in the boatyard
area.
Medical services First aid point in the marina, with more
serious facilities in nearby Puerto de Santa María.

Communications

Post office In El Puerto de Santa María.
Mailing address The marina office will hold mail for
visiting yachts – c/o Puerto Sherry, Marina Puerto de
Santa María SA, Apartado de Correos 106, El Puerto
de Santa María, Cádiz, España. It is important that the
envelope carries the name of the yacht in addition to
that of the addressee.
Public telephones A generous number dotted around the
marina complex.
Internet access WiFi elpuertowifi is free but described as
tortuous to use. Laptops can be connected via a
metered socket in the hotel.
Fax service At the marina office, *Fax* +34 956 873 902.
Car hire/taxis Can be arranged via the marina office. The
walk along the beach to El Puerto de Santa María takes
about half an hour.
Air services Airports at Seville and Jerez, both served by
Ryanair among others.

The anchoring area outside Puerto Sherry is this side of the
long breakwater and can become quite crowded at weekends. This is looking S from Playa Puntilla at low water
Jane Russell

Adjacent anchorage

Yachts of modest draught can anchor off Playa de la
Puntilla, east of Puerto Sherry marina and north of
the Puerto de Santa María training wall, sheltered
from all directions other than southwest when a
nasty swell can roll in from the bay to the anchorage.
The beach shoals gently and fairly evenly, though
there are a few shallower patches, with holding good
over sand and mud.

THE ALGARVE & ANDALUCIA

El Puerto de Santa María

See plan on page 302

Waypoints
⊕183 – 36°33'·8N 6°20'·3W (approach, also for Puerto Sherry and Cádiz)
⊕184 – 36°34'·2N 6°15'·3W (entrance, also Puerto Sherry)
⊕185 – 36°33'·57 6°18'·42 (Cádiz entrance)

Courses and distances
⊕177 (Chipiona & Río Guadalquivir) – ⊕183 (via ⊕179 & ⊕180) = 16M, 223° & 149° & 121° or 301° & 329° & 043°
⊕183 – ⊕184 (via ⊕185) = 4·1M, 099° & 076° or 256° & 279°
⊕183 – ⊕187 (Sancti-Petri, via ⊕186) = 12·7M, 187° & 157° or 337° & 007°
⊕183 – ⊕191 (Cabo Trafalgar, via ⊕186) = 28·5M, 187° & 152° or 332° & 007°

Tides
Standard port Cádiz
Mean time differences
HW –0005 ±0010; LW –0005 ±0010
Heights in metres

MHWS	MHWN	MLWN	MLWS
3·2	2·6	1·1	0·4

Or refer to EasyTide at www.ukho.gov.ukeasytide

Charts

	Harbour
Admiralty	86
Imray	C19, C50
Spanish	4431

Principal lights
2385.7 **Ldg Line 040°** Dir.Fl.WRG.6s12m5M Round metal tower
2385.2 **West training wall, head** Fl.R.5s10m3M Red tower 6m
2383.4 **East outer breakwater** Q(9)15s3M West cardinal tower 3m
2383 **East inner breakwater** Fl(2)G.7s9m3M Green tower 4m
2385 **West training wall, root** Q.R.5m2M Red tower 3m

Night entry
Not recommended in a strong southwesterly, otherwise well lit and without hazards

Harbour communications
Real Club Náutico de Santa María
☎ +34 956 852527 *Fax* +34 956 874400
Email rcnpuerto@ono.com
www.rcnpsm.com
VHF Ch 09 (0830–2130, not Sunday).

Small, club-run marina on a busy river

El Puerto de Santa María is a pleasant town and a very old port which formerly handled all the produce of Jerez, brought down the Río Guadalete on barges. Whitewashed sherry *bodegas* (warehouses) still line parts of the river and most producers offer tours – check with the tourist office. In Elizabethan times, at least one planned attack on Cádiz went awry when English sailors on forays ashore discovered the stored liquor and drank themselves to a standstill.

The Real Club Náutico de El Puerto de Santa María prides itself on its friendly atmosphere for members, but they take priority when busy at the height of the season when visitors can be treated as a nuisance. In common with many Spanish yacht clubs

it has a small but attractive garden and sports facilities including a gymnasium, tennis courts and open-air swimming pool, which visiting yachtsmen are welcome to use for a small fee.

The river, which is relatively narrow, still carries some commercial traffic as well as fishing and ferry boats, and there is no space to anchor.

Approach and entrance

For outer approaches from the northwest and southeast refer to Bahía de Cádiz, page 298.

Once in the bay, from north of west approach via Las Cabezuelas buoy and the Canal del Norte, passing no more than 1M off Punta Santa Catalina del Puerto in order to avoid the La Galera and El Diamante banks which shoal to 2·1m. From south of west, follow the directions for Cádiz – page 307 – diverging from the Canal Principal after passing El Diamante port hand buoy No.4. From there a direct course of 073° leads into the entrance channel, which itself runs 040°, parallel to the training west wall.

From offshore, on reaching ⊕183 (also the approach waypoint for Puerto Sherry and Cádiz) either continue on 099° to ⊕185 before altering to 076° for ⊕184 or, in flat conditions and with due care, sail the direct course of 084° for 4·1M, crossing the edge of the El Diamante shoal en route. ⊕184 lies about 500m from the end of the west training wall.

Berthing

The Real Club Náutico, founded in 1920, administers an ageing marina facility in need of a refit. It is capable of berthing around 175 yachts and smallcraft, including a few vessels of up to 25m. Other than at the innermost berths, depths are generous at 5m or more. Shelter from wind and waves is good, but wash from fishing boats and ferry boats that do not respect the 3kn speed limit are a problem and currents in the river can reach 2·5kn at springs. Think twice before leaving a boat here, especially on a hammerhead. About 20 berths are normally reserved for visitors, all of them on the 10 hammerhead pontoons approached from the northwest bank. The three detached pontoons on the southeast side of the channel are reserved for club members. Regattas are held during August, at which time the pontoons are likely to be full and visitors given a low priority. A visiting yacht can nearly always be found space at other times.

It is highly recommended that contact is made 24 to 48 hours before arrival to secure a berth. Otherwise call on VHF Ch 09 on the approach and hope for the best. It has been reported that communications can be difficult depending on who is on duty in the office (at least one of the office staff speaks excellent English), in which case secure to any hammerhead and enquire at the white control tower or the office (near the road gate and turnstile) for a berth. The office is open 0830–2130 Monday to Saturday and does not close for siesta. Security is good, with a uniformed guard when the office is closed and card-operated turnstiles into the grounds. The club's *marineros* will keep an eye on any unattended yacht.

The Real Club Náutico de Santa María looking southeast *APPA*

Looking down the Río Guadalete over the pontoons of the
Real Club Náutico de El Puerto de Santa María
Anne Hammick

Facilities

Boatyard Small boatyard at the upstream end of the
premises with limited hardstanding mostly occupied by
members' yachts.

Travel-lift There is a 25-tonne travel-lift in the Club
Nautico enclosure but rather typical of the marina
infrastructure it was in need of maintenance (2009).

Engineers Some mechanical capabilities at the boatyard.
For serious problems it may be necessary to go to
Puerto Sherry.

Chandlery There are no chandlers in Santa Maria but they
can be found in Puerto Sherry or Cádiz.

Water On the pontoons.

Showers In the Real Club Náutico building next to the
tennis court.

Laundry/launderette Available in the Club Nautico
building, otherwise there are launderettes in the town.

Electricity On the pontoons but cabinets in poor
condition and earth leakage significant (2009).

Fuel The planned installation had not materialised (2009),
and fuel is still not available.

Bottled gas Camping Gaz available at hardware stores in
the town, but no refills.

Weather forecast Available at the office on request.

Banks In the town, with cash dispensers.

Shops/provisioning/produce market Good shopping of all
kinds in the town 15 minutes away, with a busy market
a few blocks west of the Real Club Náutico.

Cafés, restaurants and hotels Very pleasant restaurants at
the Real Club Náutico, both terrace and indoor (the
latter more formal), with plenty more in the town and
along the beach.

Medical services In the town.

Communications

Post office In the town.

Mailing address The Real Club Náutico will hold mail for
visiting yachts – c/o Real Club Náutico de El Puerto de
Santa María, Avenida de la Bajamar 13, 11500 – El
Puerto de Santa María, Cádiz, España. It is important
that the envelope carries the name of the yacht in
addition to that of the addressee.

Public telephones Several on the Real Club Náutico
premises.

Internet access There are reported to be several cybercafés
in the town, as well as free connection at the library.
Great choice of hardware and (Spanish) software at the
enormous PC City computer superstore a few km out
of town on the road to Jerez.

Fax service At the Real Club Náutico office, *Fax* +34 956
874 400.

Car hire/taxis In the town, or can be arranged via the
office.

Buses and trains To Cádiz, Jerez, Seville (about an hour)
and elsewhere.

Ferries Passenger ferries to Cádiz (and not a bad way to
visit that city).

Air services Airports at Seville and Jerez, both served by
Ryanair among others.

THE ALGARVE & ANDALUCIA

Cádiz

Waypoints
- ⊕183 – 36°33'·8N 6°20'·3W (approach, also for Puerto Sherry and El Puerto de Santa María)
- ⊕185 – 36°33'·57N 6°18'·42W (entrance)
- ⊕186 – 36°31'·3N 6°20'·7W (Castillo de San Sebastián west cardinal buoy)

Courses and distances
- ⊕177 (Chipiona & Río Guadalquivir) – ⊕183 (via ⊕179 & ⊕180) = 16M, 223° & 149° & 121° or 301° & 329° & 043°
- ⊕183 – ⊕185 = 1·5M, 099° or 279°
- ⊕183 – ⊕187 (Sancti-Petri, via ⊕186) = 12·7M, 187° & 157° or 337° & 007°
- ⊕183 – ⊕191 (Cabo Trafalgar, via ⊕186) = 28·5M, 187° & 152° or 332° & 007°
- ⊕183 – ⊕192 (Barbate, via ⊕186 & ⊕191) = 35M, 187° & 152° & 086° or 266° & 332° & 007°

Tides
Standard port Cádiz
Heights in metres

MHWS	MHWN	MLWN	MLWS
3·3	2·5	1·2	0·5

Or refer to EasyTide at www.ukho.gov.uk/easytide

Charts

	Harbour
Admiralty	86, 88
Imray	C19, C50
Spanish	4430

Principal lights
2362 **Cádiz, Castillo de San Sebastián** Fl(2)10s37m25M
  Round metal tower on castle 37m

2367.2 **Dique Mar de Levante** Fl(4)G.10s10m3M
  Green post suspended from semicircular structure
2367 **North breakwater** Fl.G.3s9m5M
  Green triangular column 6m
2368 **East breakwater** Fl.R.2s10m5M
  Red triangular column 5m
2370 **Marina southeast breakwater** Fl(4)G.16s1M
  Green post 2m
2370.2 **Marina northwest mole** Fl(4)R.16s1M Red post 2m
Plus many other lights in the commercial harbour

Night entry
The Canal Principal is very well lit, and used by ferries and other large vessels day and night. Care should be taken on approaching the marina until all work is finished

Harbour communications
Port Authority ☎ +34 956 240400 *Fax* +34 956 240476
Email cadiz@puertocadiz.com
www.puertocadiz.com
VHF Ch 16, 74
Marina Puerto América ☎ +34 856 580 002 - 600 148 523
Fax +34 956 101 032
Email puertoamerica@eppa.es www.puertosdeandalucia.es
VHF Ch 09
Real Club Náutico de Cádiz ☎ +34 956 213 262
Fax +34 956 221 040
nautico-cadiz@rcncadiz.e.telefonica.net
VHF Ch 09
Centro Náutico Elcano ☎ +34 956 290 012 - 956 264 008
Fax +34 956 290 099,
Email secretariacnelcano@deportedecadiz.com
VHF Ch 09
Puerto de Gallineras ☎ +34 956 486 626.

The Cádiz peninsula looking northeast. In the foreground are the Castillo de San Sebastián, lighthouse and surrounding reefs, with the old city and harbour beyond. The Marina Puerto América can be seen in the middle distance to the left of the dockside cranes. Puerto Sherry Marina and the Santa Maria breakwater are visible top left.

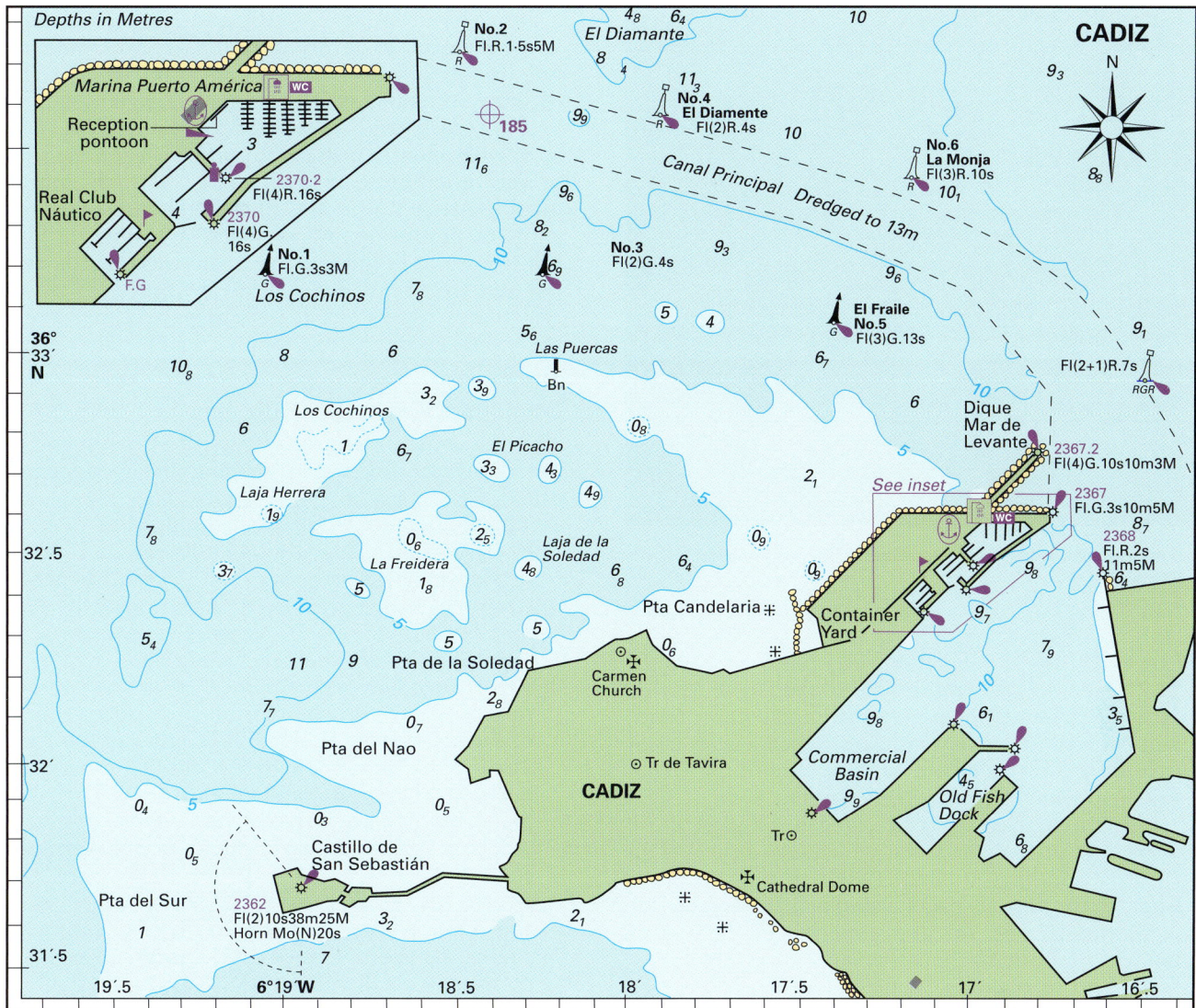

Chart labels:
Depths in Metres

CADIZ

N

Marina Puerto América

Reception pontoon

Real Club Náutico

F.G

No.2 Fl.R.1·5s5M

El Diamante

4₈ 6₄ 10

8

No.4 El Diamente Fl(2)R.4s

11₃ 10

No.6 La Monja Fl(3)R.10s 10₁

9₃

8₈

2370·2 Fl(4)R.16s

2370 Fl(4)G.16s

No.1 Fl.G.3s3M

Los Cochinos

185

11₆

9₉

9₆

9₃

9₆

No.3 Fl(2)G.4s

7₈

8₂

6₉

5

4

El Fraile No.5 Fl(3)G.13s

6₇

9₁

Fl(2+1)R.7s RGR

36° 33′ N

10₈

8

6

5₆

Las Puercas Bn

0₈

6

Dique Mar de Levante

2367.2 Fl(4)G.10s10m3M

See inset

2367 Fl.G.3s10m5M

6

Los Cochinos

1

6

6₇

El Picacho

3₃ 4₃

4₉

2₁

8₇

2368 Fl.R.2s 11m5M

32′.5

7₈

Laja Herrera

1₉

0₆

2₅

La Freidera 1₈

4₈

Laja de la Soledad

6₈

0₉

9₈

6₄

9₇

7₉

3₇

5

5

5

0₆

Pta Candelaria

Container Yard

WC

5₄

11

9

Pta de la Soledad

2₈

Carmen Church

0₆

9₈

6₁

3₅

32′

7₇

0₇

Pta del Nao

Tr de Tavira

CADIZ

Commercial Basin

9₉

Old Fish Dock

4₅

0₄

5

0₃

0₅

Castillo de San Sebastián

Cathedral Dome

Tr

6₈

31′.5

0₅

Pta del Sur

2362 Fl(2)10s38m25M Horn Mo(N)20s

1

3₂

7

2₁

19′.5 6°19′W 18′.5 18′ 17′.5 17 16′.5

A well-run marina (Puerto América) within walking distance of one of Spain's oldest cities

Cádiz is an ancient and fascinating city, founded by the Phoenicians over 3,000 years ago, settled by Romans and Moors, and today discovering its archeological heritage and presenting it to the world. It has long been a major port, with a fine defensive position and good shelter, and for many years handled nearly all the lucrative trade with the New World. This led to great wealth, the results of which can still be seen in the scale of its public and private buildings, many of which date back to the 18th century. The commercial area extends along the peninsula to the southeast, less impressive architecturally but containing good shopping, restaurants and hotels.

Until the early 1990s Cádiz was a difficult city to visit by yacht, the docks devoted to fishing and commercial use and the pontoons in the Real Club Náutico de Cádiz basin packed with local craft. The opening of the Marina Puerto América overcame this problem, and though set amidst bleak surroundings nearly a kilometre from the old city walls it offers good shelter and security for the yacht whilst the crew explore elsewhere.

⊕183	36°33′·8N	6°20′·3W	Puerto Sherry, El Puerto de Santa María & Cádiz approach
⊕185	36°33′·57N	6°18′·42W	Cádiz entrance
⊕186	36°31′·3N	6°20′·7W	Castillo de San Sebastián W cardinal buoy

Approach

For outer approaches from the northwest and southeast refer to Bahía de Cádiz, page 298.

From offshore ⊕183 (also the approach waypoint for Puerto Sherry and El Puerto de Santa María) lies 1·5M to the west, a course of 099° leading to ⊕185 in the entrance to the Canal Principal.

The final approach is best made via the Canal Principal, which is well buoyed and lit and may safely be used by day or night. After identifying Los Cochinos buoy No.1, in normal weather it is safe to make direct for buoy No.5 (starboard hand) on 094°, passing close south of buoy No.3 in a least depth of 5m. Do not, however, be tempted to cut much south of buoy No.1 for fear of the unmarked

THE ALGARVE & ANDALUCIA

Looking west-northwest over Marina Puerto América at Cádiz *APPA*

Los Cochinos shoal. From buoy No.5 a course of 115° leads well clear of the end of the Dique Mar de Levante, around which the north breakwater head, will be seen. In heavy weather, or when a large swell is running, it would be wise to remain in the Canal Principal which has a dredged depth of 13m.

Fishermen may be seen using a passage close northwest of the peninsula, which uses bearings on various buildings in Cádiz itself to plot a course between the various rocks and shoals. However, this is definitely one for the experienced navigator possessing both fair weather and a current large-scale chart or, of course, detailed local knowledge.

Entrance

On rounding the north breakwater, the marina entrance will be seen to starboard about 500m to the southwest. The marina's outer breakwater has been extended southwest and a short, low lying wave breaker has been laid from the southwest corner of the marina to form a narrow entrance between the ends of them (see photo). This provides greatly improved protection in the marina, which previously suffered from both swell and wash. The reception pontoon is tucked away in the northwest corner of the marina (see photo on page 309 and plan on page 307) reached by passing the inner mole to port and weaving past the pontoons in the north basin.

Berthing

The marina's capacity is now 175 berths with many of the new slots able to take yachts of 12m or more up to a maximum of 15m. All berths are alongside individual fingers. The marina is becoming popular so it is best to make contact by phone in advance, calling on VHF Ch 09 on closer approach.

Office hours are 0930–1300 and 1700–2000 daily in summer, 1000–1330 and 1600–1730 in winter, remaining closed in the afternoon on Wednesday, Saturday and Sunday. The marina manager is helpful and pleasant and speaks excellent English. His somewhat elderly portacabin office is near the root of the inner mole. Security is good with guards outside office hours and individual card-operated gates to pontoons and services. In common with other marinas in the area, the night time guards may not take over immediately after the office closes but are friendly and helpful if ships papers, passports etc. are taken to them as soon as possible after a late arrival.

Other berthing in the Cádiz area

The following are included largely for interest and to dispel any possible hopes, since none have much to offer a visiting yacht.

1. **The Real Club Náutico de Cádiz** lies next to Puerto América (though threatened with displacement to make way for a container park), where it has a 182-berth basin packed with member's own vessels. Visitors are welcome to visit the bar and waterside restaurant.

2. **The Centro Náutico Elcano** (36°30'·1N 6°15'·3W) is a relatively new, private marina situated just north of the main (bascule) bridge. Depths are less than 2m and maximum length 9m, though most craft berthed there are considerably smaller. No provision is made for visitors and it is doubtful whether space could be found for an overnight stay.

3. **Puerto de Gallineras** (36°26'·2N 6°12'·1W) is a somewhat ambitious name for the single pontoon run by the Club Náutico de Gallineras to which a number of smallcraft are secured. On the shallow waterway which links Cádiz with Sancti-Petri, controlling depths are no more than 1m and there are several bridges if approached from the north.

Puerto America – From the inner mole looking southwest showing a yacht entering the marina *Henry Buchanan*

A climb to one of the bell towers of Cádiz Cathedral gives panoramic views over the old city and beyond *Jane Russell*

Facilities

Boatyard There is a large gated area of hardstanding, but no boatyard as such.

Travel-lift There is not thought to be a travel-lift in situ although a large ramp has been built in the north basin facing the reception pontoon. There is a 10-tonne crane onsite, and in an emergency a mobile crane can be brought in from the commercial docks which is a very expensive process.

Engineers, mechanics, general maintenance Náutica Benítez ✆ +34 956 220244 *Fax* +34 956 227821 *Email* nautica@nautica.benitez.com www.nauticabenitez.es has premises overlooking the south basin where mechanical and other repairs are carried out.

An outfit calling itself Marina Puerto América ✆/*Fax* +34 956 211 091 *Mobile* +34 638 082 528 www.marinapuertoamerica.com *Email* marina@puertoamerica.com operates in the marina. This appears to be a brokerage but claims to have repair, engineering and electrical expertise.

Chandlery Some chandlery, mostly of a practical nature and including an impressive range of engine spares, at Náutica Benítez.

Charts The Spanish Instituto Hidrográfico de la Marina has its national headquarters in Cádiz, but does not sell direct to the public. Instead try either Libreria 'Alfa 2' (also known as Papelería Manuel Pereira González, open 0930–1330 and 1730–2030, closed Saturday afternoon and Sunday) at Calle Pelota 14, in a pedestrian area close to the cathedral; or JL Gándara y Cia SA ✆ +34 956 270443 *Fax* +34 956 272207 *Email* cadiz@gandara-sa.com at Calle La Línea de la Concepción 11 in the Zona Franca industrial area.

Water On the pontoons.

Showers A smart shower block is on the main breakwater overlooking the north basin.

Launderette Adjacent to the shower block.

Electricity On the pontoons.

Fuel Diesel and petrol pumps on the end of the inner mole.

Bottled gas Camping Gaz available in the city, but no refills.

Club náutico The Real Club Náutico de Cádiz, close south of the marina, welcomes reasonably tidy visitors to its terrace bar and restaurant.

Weather forecast Posted daily in the marina office, as are warnings of firing exercises.

Banks Many in the city, but no cash dispenser at the marina.

Shops/provisioning/market Excellent shopping and a good produce market in the city, but all at some distance from the marina. It is hoped that in due course a supermarket and other shops will open on the large empty space nearby.

Cafés, restaurants and hotels Snack bar next to the marina office plus a small restaurant at the Real Club Náutico. For those with transport (or happy to walk) there is a wide choice in the old city.

Medical services In the city.

Communications

Post office In the city. Stamped mail can be left at the office for posting.

Mailing address The marina office will hold mail for visiting yachts – c/o Puerto América, Punta de San Felipe s/n, 11004 - Cádiz, España. It is important that the envelope carries the name of the yacht in addition to that of the addressee.

Public telephone Next to the marina office, otherwise a booth at the Real Club Náutico plus many in the city.

Internet access At the Real Club Náutico, plus several cybercafés in the city – ask for directions at the office. Informática Gaditana SA on the road behind the ferry basin sells computers and consumables such as inkjets.

Fax service At the marina office, *Fax* +34 956 224220.

Car hire/taxis There is a car hire/taxi office in the marina.

Buses and trains Links to Jerez, Seville etc from the city, but no public transport near the marina.

Ferries Passenger ferries to El Puerto de Santa María – and to the Canaries!

Air services Airports at Seville and Jerez, both served by Ryanair among others.

Slipway and reception pontoon looking northeast. Shower block centre right. Marina office centre left *Henry Buchanan*

The star shaped fortaleza overlooks La Caleta *Jane Russell*

Sancti-Petri

Waypoints
⊕187 – 36°21'·9N 6°15'·7W (approach)
⊕188 – 36°22'·3N 6°13·16W (entrance)

Courses and distances
⊕181 (Rota) – ⊕187 (via ⊕186) = 14·1M, 167° & 157° or 337° & 347°
⊕183 (Cádiz) – ⊕187 (via ⊕186) = 12·7M, 187° & 157° or 337° & 007°
⊕187 – ⊕188 = 2·1M, 079° or 249°
⊕187 – ⊕189 (Puerto de Conil) = 8M, 139° or 319°
⊕187 – ⊕192 (Barbate, via ⊕191) = 22·4M, 149° & 086° or 266° & 329°

Tides
See Cádiz, page 306

Charts

Charts	Approach	River
Admiralty	91, 93	
Imray	C19, C50	C50
Spanish	44B, 44C, 443, 443B	4438

Principal lights
2387 **Punta del Arrecife** Q(9)15s8m3M
  West cardinal beacon, ⊻ topmark
2388 **Castillo de Sancti-Petri** Fl.3s19m9M
  Square tower 16m
2398 **Ldg Lts 050°** *Front* Fl.5s13m6M
  Aluminium framework tower 10m
2398.1 *Rear* 45m from front Oc(2)6s17m6M
  Aluminium framework tower 10m
2404 **Ldg Lts 346°** *Front* Punta del Boquerón
  Fl.5s12m6M Aluminium framework tower 6m
2404.1 *Rear* 60m from front Oc(2)6s22m6M
  Aluminium framework tower 10m
2404.4 **Bajo de Poniente** Fl.R.5s8m2M Red pillar
2404.5 **Piedra Larga** Fl.G.5s8m2M Green pillar

Night entry
Not recommended under any circumstances. However in light conditions it would be possible to anchor close south of the outer buoys and await daylight

Harbour communications
Puerto Deportivo Sancti-Petri ☎ +34 856 101 096 and 600 141 564 *Fax* +34 956 100 302
Email sanctipetri@eppa.es www.puertosdeandalucia.es
VHF Ch 09
Club Náutico de Sancti-Petri ☎ +34 956 495 434 and 956 494 565 *Fax* +34 956 495434
Email clubnauticosanctipetri@gmail.com
VHF Ch 09.

Attractive, windswept anchorage with local boating facilities

The sandy and windswept lagoon at Sancti-Petri provides a peaceful port of call for those confident of their pilotage. The peninsula to the east has become a recreational boating centre with an active club náutico, small APPA marina and cafés. The old village buildings have either fallen into ruin or been demolished, but the little church has been restored. Street lamps run down the cobbled streets and benches recline in the shade of palm trees around the square. A *paseo* and fishermen's quay has been constructed along the southeast side of the peninsula.

History is divided as to whether Sancti-Petri died after the tunny fishing company which provided nearly all its employment closed down, or whether it was forcibly emptied during the Franco years for use as a military training area.

Facilities for yachts are improving, though it is highly unlikely that a cruising yacht will be able to find a slot in either of the marinas. A mooring is a possibility, though many visitors prefer to lie to their own anchors. The stone quay is used by fishing vessels and ferries out to the tiny, rocky Isla de Sancti-Petri, which has been inhabited since prehistoric times. It is claimed that the remains of a temple to Hercules can still be seen, along with more recent fortifications and the square-sided lighthouse. Alternatively explore further up the estuary where the bird life is superb, particularly during the winter when large flocks of flamingoes are to be seen.

Approach

Coastal sailing towards Sancti-Petri from Cádiz or other points north the coastline appears low and somewhat featureless, consisting of marshes and saltpans. Remain outside the 10m line in order to avoid a small, unmarked, isolated rock about 2M north of Punta del Arrecife, at the north end of the reef which extends more than 1M north from the Isla de Sancti-Petri. Punta del Arrecife is marked by a lit west cardinal column with topmark – on no account attempt to cut inside it, but instead give the island generous clearance until able to pick up either the outer pair of buoys or the outer leading marks on 050° as detailed below.

Coming from the south, beware the long, rocky shoal which runs southwest from Cabo Trafalgar, culminating in the dangerous Bajo Aceitera more than 1·5M offshore. In heavy weather the Placer de Meca bank, 3·2M to the west, may break and should also be avoided. A race can form up to 8M offshore in these conditions, particularly when east-going current and tidal stream oppose the *levanter*. North of the cape a direct course for Sancti-Petri takes one uncomfortably close to the 1·2m shoal of Lajas de Conil – keep a good 2·5M offshore until approaching Cabo Roche. Once past the headland with its square lighthouse there are no hazards other than the isolated Laja Bermeja about 1M south of the entrance. Remain outside the 10m line until able to pick up either the outer pair of buoys or the outer leading marks on 050° as detailed below.

From offshore care must be taken to avoid the Hazte Afuera/Cabezo de la Pasada bank, a long narrow ledge which shoals to 3·1m in places. The bank, which lies parallel to the coast about 2·5M off, extends for more than 3M from end to end. ⊕187 lies off the northern end of the bank, a course of 079° for 2·1M leading to ⊕188 and the outer entrance buoys.

In onshore swell the offshore banks may break, in which case any thoughts of entering Sancti-Petri should be forgotten.

Entrance

Though protection once inside is good, the entrance should only be attempted on a rising tide, in fair weather and in good visibility. If in doubt wait for a local vessel to give a lead in. The bar is believed to

SANCTI-PETRI

N

⊕187 36°21'·9N   06°15'·7W   Sancti-Petri approach
⊕188 36°22'·3N   6°13'·16W   Sancti-Petri entrance

Punta del
Arrecife

2387
Q(9)15s8m3M
YBY

Canal de Boquerón

Bateria de
Urrutia

2404·1
Oc(2)6s22m6M

2404
Fl.5s12m6M

No.8
Fl(3)R.9s
R   G

No.9
Fl(3)G.9s

SANCTI
PETRI

No.6
Fl(2)R.7s

Punta del
Boquerón

No.7
Fl(2)G.7s
R   G

El Arrecife

011°

Punta de la Piedras

Placer de
Punta
del Boqueron

2404·5
Fl.G.5s8m2M
G

2404·4
Fl.R.5s
8m2M
R

346.5°

Coto de San José

2398·1
Oc(2)6s
17m6M
2398
Fl.5s13m6M

2388
Fl.3s
19m9M

Castillo de
Sancti-
Petri

Los
Farallones

No.4
Fl(4)R.11s3M
R

No.3
Fl(4)11s3M
G

Bajo de Fuera

050°

Laja de la
Duquesa

No.2
Fl(3)R.9s5M
R

No.1
Fl(3)G.9s5M
G

188

6°13'W

Depths in Metres

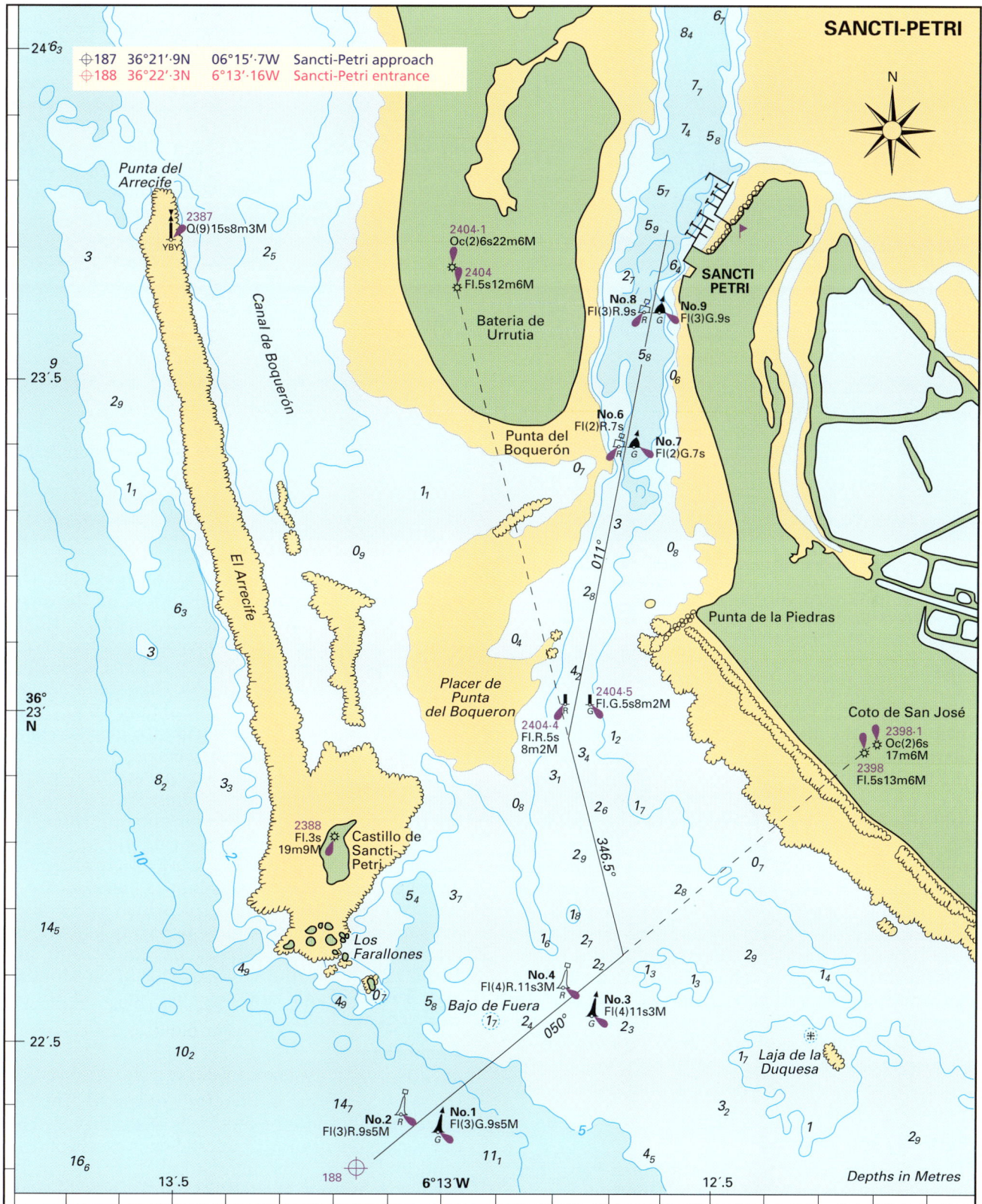

carry at least 2m at MLWS, but an onshore swell can create very dangerous conditions and the surrounding sandbanks shift with every gale. The current runs strongly, with a good 2kn on the flood and more on the ebb. Night approach should not be contemplated, even though the entrance is lit.

Having made a position southwest of the Castillo de Sancti-Petri as described above, pass between the outer pair of buoys, at the same time picking up the Coto de San José outer leading marks on 050° – the aluminium framework towers are not conspicuous and tend to blend in with the vegetation. After

Sancti-Petri entrance from south-southwest. The island castle stands on the left, from which the Los Farallones reef runs out towards the pair of entrance buoys. At near low water the Placer de Punta del Boqueron sandbank shows clearly, with Sancti-Petri village behind

passing between the inner buoys alter course onto 346° when the Batería de Urrutia inner leading marks (also aluminium towers) come into line. The channel shifts from time to time, and if the buoys do not agree exactly with the leading marks it is probably best to trust the former. Although all four buoys are officially listed as being pillars with topmarks (and shown as such on the plan on page 311), they have been reported as being much smaller and without topmarks, though of the correct colour.

Continue on 346° until about 100m short of the gate formed by Bajo de Poniente and Piedra Larga (identical red and green columns with lattice baskets surrounding their lights), turning slightly to starboard through the gap. Continue upriver on 011°, favouring the starboard side. Two extra sets of port/starboard hand buoys have been laid in the final approach channel where a minimum of 3m should be found.

Berthing and mooring

There are two sets of pontoons at Sancti-Petri. The downstream set form the Puerto Deportivo Sancti-Petri, and the upstream set, together with the many moorings, are administered by the Club Náutico de Sancti-Petri.

The Puerto Deportivo Sancti-Petri contains 87 berths for boats of up to 12m, but of the 25 nominally reserved for visitors only one can take a yacht of more than 10m. Depths of 5m are claimed for the three hammerheads, where it may be possible

to lie for a short period to fill water tanks etc. The marina office is located in a building on the quay, open 1000–1330 and 1600–1830 weekdays, 1000–1330 weekends, and some English is spoken. Access to the marina is via an electronic gate, making it unsuitable for landing by dinghy. However it may be possible for crews at anchor to obtain, on payment of a small fee, a card which will also give access to the immaculate toilets and showers.

The Club Náutico de Sancti-Petri no longer accepts visiting yachts on its pontoons, which are full to capacity with locally-owned boats, though it may be possible to rent a mooring out of season. Again, pontoon access is via an electronic gate, limiting dinghy landing possibilities unless a card is forthcoming. The *club náutico*, which also houses the bar/café, occupies the only two story building on the waterfront. Office hours are 0900–1400 and 1600–1930 daily, but closing at 1900 on Monday and Tuesday and not opening until 0930 on weekends and holidays.

Anchorage

Many moorings have been laid in the estuary and space for anchoring is, therefore, restricted. There is more room beyond the moorings. Note that the ebb can run at 3kn or more, but holding is excellent over sand and mud. It is understood that 2m can be carried right up to the jetty at San Fernando, some 3M into the lagoon. It may be necessary to pick a buoy for which a charge will be made.

In the absence of a card to give access to one of the pontoons, the best prospect for dinghy landing is on the muddy beach at the head of the peninsula, also used by local fishermen. Watch out for numerous underwater obstructions if coming in using an outboard motor.

Facilities
Boatyard The *club náutico* has a walled compound near the quay where members lay up yachts to 11m or so. However a crane must be brought in for the purpose as there is no travel-lift or marine railway.

Engineers Enquire at the *club náutico* .

Chandlery Nautime Jet ① +34 956 495975, has premises on the quay, mainly concerned with jet skis but also selling a limited range of general chandlery, clothes and electronics.

Water On both sets of pontoons – yachts on moorings may be able to lie alongside briefly to fill tanks.

Showers On the quay for *puerto deportivo* users, or in the *club náutico* .

Electricity On both sets of pontoons.

Fuel The diesel pump previously on the club náutico jetty was removed in 2005 and has not been reinstated.

Club náutico Small and friendly club, with few facilities but helpful members.

Weather forecast Posted daily outside both offices.

Banks Several in Chiclana de la Frontera about 7km inland, and at least one cash dispenser in Costa Sancti-Petri about 2km away.

Shops/provisioning/market Other than a kiosk selling cold drinks and ice-creams there is no shop in Sancti-Petri of any kind. The nearest serious shopping is in Chiclana de la Frontera, though basic needs can be met in Costa Sancti–Petri.

Cafés, restaurants and hotels Bar/café at the *club náutico* with restaurants on either side, plus other cafés and restaurants on the east side of the peninsula.

Medical services Red Cross post operational in summer only, otherwise in Chiclana de la Frontera.

Communications
Post office In Chiclana de la Frontera. No box either, though harbour staff may be willing to post stamped mail for visitors. Alternatively hand to the postman on his daily visit.

Mailing address Both offices will hold mail for visiting yachts – c/o Oficina del Puerto, Puerto Deportivo Sancti-Petri, Poblado de Sancti-Petri, 11139 Chiclana de la Frontera, Cádiz, España; or Club Náutico de Sancti-Petri, Apdo de Correos 118, Chiclana de la Frontera, Cádiz, España. It is important that the envelope carries the name of the yacht in addition to that of the addressee.

Public telephones On the quay and in the *club náutico*.

Internet access In Chiclana de la Frontera and understood to be available in Costa Sancti–Petri, though this has not been verified.

Fax service At the *puerto deportivo* office, ①/Fax +34 956 496169, or the *club náutico* , ①/Fax +34 956 495434.

Taxis Organise via either office.

Buses About every two hours from a stop near the quay (check the return timetable before departure).

Looking southeast over Sancti-Petri. Most visitors must anchor, as both the APPA-run Puerto Deportivo Sancti-Petri and the pontoons of the Club Náutico de Sancti-Petri are generally full

THE ALGARVE & ANDALUCIA

Puerto de Conil

Waypoints
⊕189 – 36°15'·9N 6°09'·2W (approach)
⊕190 – 36°17'·5N 6°08'W (entrance)
⊕191 – 36°08'·3N 6°05'·6W (3·7M SW of Cabo Trafalgar)

Courses and distances
⊕183 (Cádiz) – ⊕189 (via F186) = 20·2M, 187° & 149° or 329° & 007°
⊕187 (Sancti-Petri) – ⊕189 = 8M, 139° or 319°
⊕189 – ⊕190 = 1·9M, 031° or 211°
⊕189 – ⊕192 (Barbate, via ⊕191) = 14·6M, 159° & 086° or 266° & 339°

Tides
Standard port Cádiz
Mean time differences (at Cabo Trafalgar)
HW +0015 ±0010; LW −0005 ±0010
Heights in metres

MHWS	MHWN	MLWN	MLWS
2·4	1·9	0·9	0·4

Charts

	Approach
Admiralty	91, 93
Imray	C19, C50
Spanish	44B, 44C, 105, 444

Principal lights
2405 **Cabo Roche** Fl(4)24s44m20M
  Brown square tower, silver lantern 20m
2405.4 **Southwest breakwater** Fl(2)R.8s9m5M
  Red round tower 6m
2405.6 **Northeast mole** LFl.G.7s6m3M
  Green round tower 3m
2405.8 **Inner mole** Fl(2)R.8s7m2M Red round tower 4m

Night entry
  In light conditions it would be possible to anchor east of the harbour, having noted the CAUTION detailed on the next page.

Harbour communications
  nauticoconil@gmail.com www.puertosdeandalucia.es

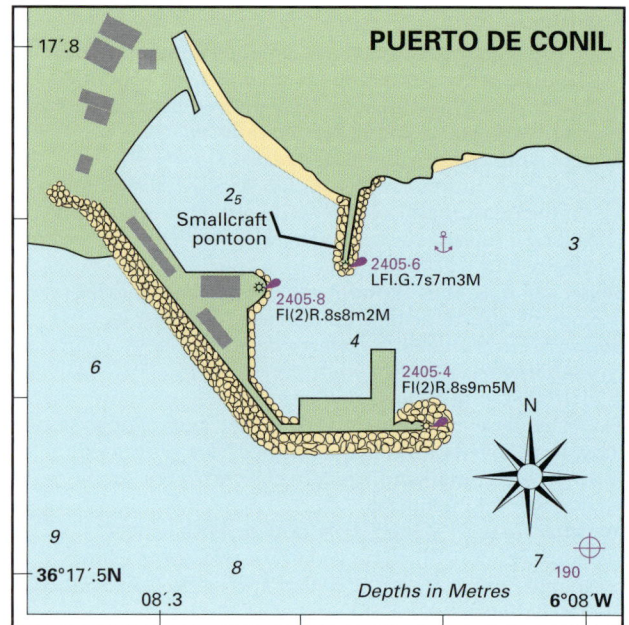

| ⊕189 | 36°15'·9N | 06°09'·2W | Puerto de Conil approach |
| ⊕190 | 36°17'·5N | 06°08'W | Puerto de Conil entrance |

Busy fishing harbour with anchorage outside

Puerto de Conil lies tucked behind the headland of Cabo Roche, almost midway between the Isla de Sancti-Petri and Cabo Trafalgar. It is a colourful, busy and thriving fishing harbour with all the associated smells and interest, but with few facilities on site. The harbour is situated several kilometres from the town of the same name, and there is

Puerto de Conil looking north. The small harbour has nowhere for a visiting yacht to lie alongside, but there is a good anchorage outside

literally nothing outside the harbour gates other than miles of open heathland.

Hundreds of rusty fisherman anchors are stored behind the harbour, to be used when the tunny (tuna) nets are set (see page 218) There is a major fossil bank near the root of the east mole.

Approach

If coastal sailing, approaching Cabo Roche from northwards presents no particular hazards in fair weather, though in any swell the 3·4m and 3·7m offshore banks may well break. In such conditions it would be wise to stay well outside the 20m line and continue for Barbate or beyond. Coming from the south, rocky shoals run southwest from Cabo Trafalgar culminating in the dangerous Bajo Aceitera more than 1·5M offshore. In heavy weather the Placer de Meca bank, 3·2M to the west, may break and should also be avoided. A race can form up to 8M offshore in these conditions, particularly when east-going current and tidal stream oppose the *levanter*. An inside passage is used by fishermen, but it should not be attempted without local knowledge. Careful pilotage remains necessary after rounding the cape to pass either inside or outside the 1·2m Lajas de Conil. The inside passage is more than a mile wide and carries 8m or more, but see the *Caution* about other hazards below.

From offshore ⊕189 lies 1·9M south-southwest of the entrance, a course of 031° leading to ⊕190, about 200m from the breakwater head.

Caution

A large marine farm has been established just over 4M west of Puerto de Conil, centred on 36°17'·5N 6°13'·3W but covering an area almost 5M square. Its perimeter is marked by six yellow buoys with × topmarks, all lit Fl.Y.1·2s3M.

In early 2002 a 48m cable, supported by buoys and lying 2m below the surface, was laid in a northeasterly direction from 36°17'·1N 6°08'·2W (about 0·7M south of Cabo Roche).

Also, an *almadraba* or tunny (tuna) net known as *El Palmar* is laid from March to August/September each year between Cabo Roche and Cabo Trafalgar. It remains in much the same position, and is marked by four lit cardinal buoys:

North Cardinal buoy 36°15'·07N 6°06'·87W
Q.3M

East Cardinal buoy 36°15'·03 N 6°05'·37W
Q(3)10s3M

South Cardinal buoy 36°14'·17N 6°08'·04W
Q(6)+LFl.15s3M

West Cardinal buoy 36°14'·40N 6°08'·73W
Q(9)15s3M

Berthing and anchorage

Until the late 1990s Puerto de Conil consisted only of a single short breakwater, but the addition of an angled extension plus a short opposing mole has much increased its size. Even so all the inner walls other than the fishing quay are rubble-fronted

Fishing boats rafted four and five abreast in Puerto de Conil on a quiet Sunday afternoon *Anne Hammick*

(dinghies and other smallcraft lie on haul-out moorings), and a yacht would almost certainly have to remain outside the entrance. The Club Náutico de Conil's smallcraft pontoon just inside the north mole is already full to capacity with no possible space for even the smallest cruising yacht, while security gates limit its practicality for dinghy landing.

Anchor east of the short northeast mole in 3–5m over sand, protected from southwest through north to east but fully exposed to south and southeast. There is a reported 2·5m inside the harbour.

Facilities

Little more than a small bar and several water taps, though it might be possible to take on diesel from the fishermen's pump. There is a 10-tonne capacity travel-lift, but propping up a deep-keeled yacht would pose a challenge.

A traditional wooden fishing vessel in build at Puerto de Conil *Anne Hammick*

III.4 Cabo Trafalgar to Gibraltar

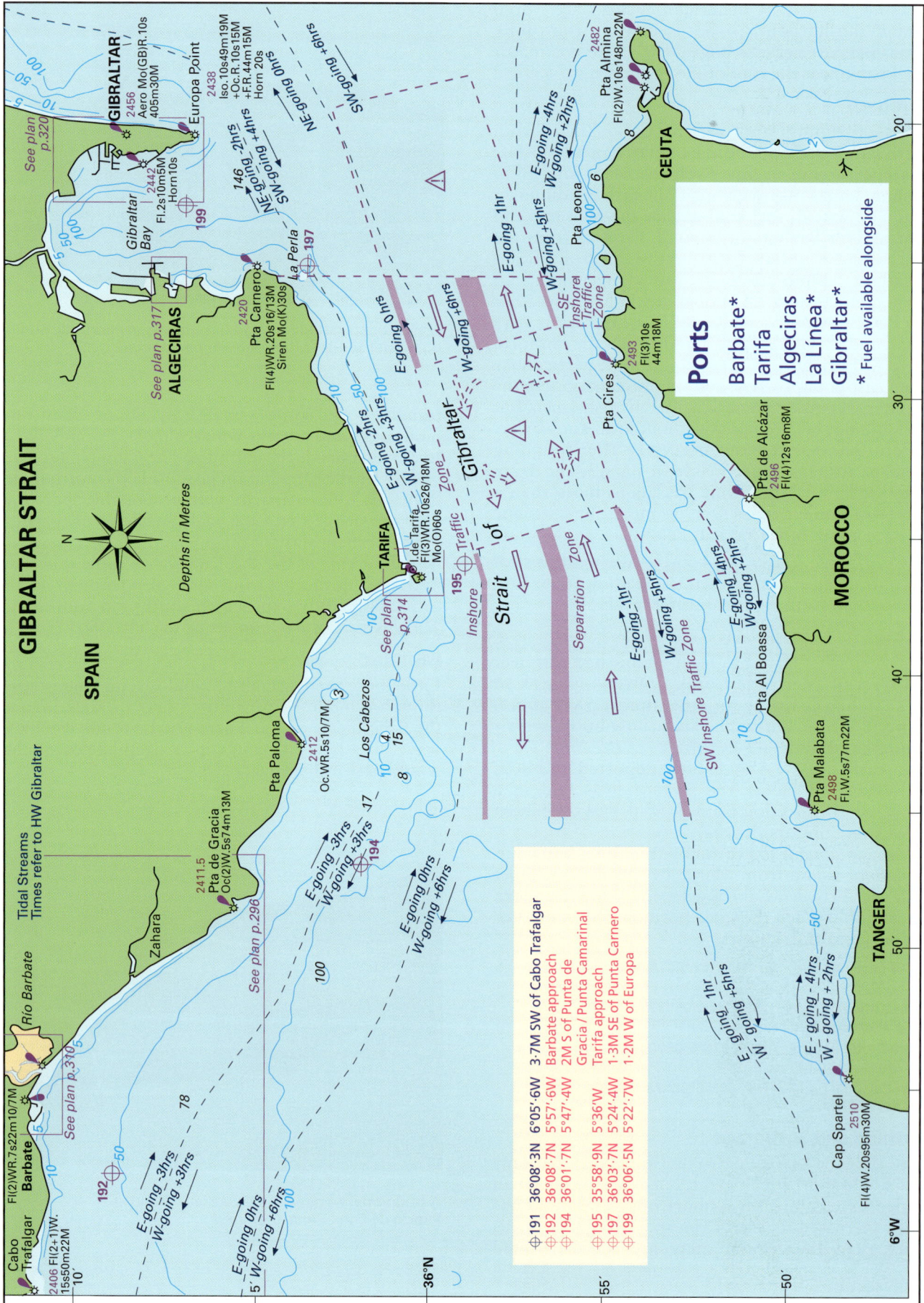

GIBRALTAR

2456 Aero Mo(GB)R.10s 405m30M

Europa Point

2438 Iso.10s49m19M +Oc.R.10s15M +F.R.44m15M Horn 20s

146 -2hrs NE-going +4hrs SW-going 0hrs

See plan p.320

Gibraltar Bay

2442 Fl.2s10m5M Horn10s

199

See plan p.317

ALGECIRAS

2420 Pta Carnero Fl(4)WR.20s16/13M Siren Mo(K)30s

La Perla

197

NE-going 0hrs SW-going +6hrs

SW-going 0hrs

E-going 0hrs

E-going -2hrs W-going +3hrs

E-going +3hrs

E-going -1hr

E-going -4hrs W-going +2hrs

W-going +5hrs

Pta Leona

SE- Inshore Traffic Zone

2482 Pta Almina Fl(2)W.10s148m22M

CEUTA

20'

Ports

Barbate*
Tarifa
Algeciras
La Línea*
Gibraltar*

* Fuel available alongside

2493 Fl(3)10s 44m18M

Pta Cires

Pta de Alcázar 2496 Fl(4)12s16m8M

30'

GIBRALTAR STRAIT

SPAIN

N

Depths in Metres

I.de Tarifa Fl(3)WR.10s26/18M Mo(O)60s

TARIFA

195

See plan p.314

Inshore Traffic Zone

Strait of Gibraltar

Traffic Separation Zone

E-going -1hr W-going +5hrs

SW Inshore Traffic Zone

E-going -4hrs W-going +2hrs

Pta Al Boassa

MOROCCO

40'

Tidal Streams
Times refer to HW Gibraltar

Pta Paloma

2412 Oc.WR.5s10/7M

Los Cabezos 3 15 4 10 8 17

E-going -3hrs W-going +3hrs

194

E-going 0hrs W-going +6hrs

Pta Malabata 2498 Fl.W.5s77m22M

2411.5 Pta de Gracia Oc(2)W.5s74m13M

See plan p.296

Zahara

100

78

See plan p.310

Río Barbate

E-going -3hrs W-going +3hrs

192

E-going 0hrs W-going +6hrs

E-going -1hr W-going +5hrs

E-going -4hrs W-going +2hrs

Cap Spartel 2510 Fl(4)W.20s95m30M

TANGER

50'

Cabo Trafalgar Fl(2+1)W. 15s50m22M

Barbate Fl(2)WR.7s22m10/7M

2406 Fl(2+1)W. 15s50m22M

10'

⊕191	36°08'.3N	6°05'.6W	3.7M SW of Cabo Trafalgar
⊕192	36°08'.7N	5°57'.6W	Barbate approach
⊕194	36°01'.7N	5°47'.4W	2M S of Punta de Gracia / Punta Camarinal
⊕195	35°58'.9N	5°36'.W	Tarifa approach
⊕197	36°03'.7N	5°24'.4W	1.3M SE of Punta Carnero
⊕199	36°06'.5N	5°22'.7W	1.2M W of Europa

55'

36°N

50'

6°W

PRINCIPAL LIGHTS

Europe

2406 Cabo Trafalgar Fl(2+1)15s50m22M White conical
tower and building 34m

2411.5 Punta de Gracia (Punta Camarinal)
Oc(2)5s74m13M Round masonry tower 20m

2412 Punta Paloma Oc.WR.5s44m10/7M
010°-W-340°-R-010° (over Bajo de Los Cabezos)
Two-storey building 5m

2414 Tarifa Fl(3)WR.10s40m26/18M
089°-R-113°-W-089° (over Bajo de Los Cabezos)
Racon Mo 'C'(–·–··)20M AIS White round tower 33m

2420 Punta Carnero Fl(4)WR.20s41m16/13M
018°-W-325°-R-018° (Red sector covers La Perla and
Las Bajas shoals)
Round masonry tower and white building 19m

2438 Europa Point, Gibraltar
Iso.10s49m19M 197°-vis-042°, 067°-vis-125°
Oc.R.10s19M and F.R.15M 042°-vis-067°
(Red sector covers La Perla and Las Bajas shoals) Horn
20s White tower, red band 19m

2442 South mole Gibraltar Fl.W.2s10m5M
White column 7m

Africa

2510 Cabo Espartel Fl(4)20s95m30M
Yellow square stone tower

2498 Pta Malabata Fl.5s76m22M
White square tower on white dwelling

2496 Ksar es Srhir Fl(4)12s16m8M
Column on metal framework tower

2493 Pta Cires Fl(3)10s44m18M
Brown truncated conical tower

2482 Pta Almina Fl(2)10s148m22M
White round tower on white building

Traffic Separation Zone

There is a Traffic Separation Zone in the Strait of
Gibraltar between 5°25'·5W and 5°45'W – see plan
opposite. The Inshore Traffic Zone to the north is
nowhere less than 1·7M wide (off the Isla de Tarifa)
and generally more than 2M. Tarifa Traffic monitors
VHF Ch 16 and 10 and vessels are advised to maintain a
listening watch whilst in the area. Weather and
visibility information for an area including the Traffic
Separation Zone is broadcast on VHF Ch 10 and 67 as
detailed over.

Cabo Trafalgar – one of the most famous headlands in the
world – seen from the southeast. The 50m lighthouse can be
seen 22M away

Surface flow in the Strait

Surface water flow through the Strait is the product of a
combination of current and tidal stream, the former
dominant for at least eight hours out of the twelve.

A permanent, east-going current sets through the Strait,
compensating for water lost from the Mediterranean
through evaporation. Strength varies from 1kn close to the
northern shore to approaching 2kn in the centre and
southern part of the channel, with a decrease to 1·5kn or
less near the Moroccan shore. However this pattern can be
upset by the wind, and persistent strong westerlies,
coupled with the regular current, can produce an easterly
set of up to 4kn. Conversely, the entire flow may reverse
after prolonged easterly winds, though in practice this
seldom happens.

Tidal streams, though capable of exceeding 3kn at springs
and more off the major headlands, must be worked
carefully if attempting to make progress westwards – riding
the stream eastwards is generally not a problem unless
faced with a strong *levanter*. Streams turn earlier near the
coast – see plan opposite – but bear in mind that even then
the current may prove stronger than the tide for a
considerable part of the cycle. In the middle, the tidal
stream runs directly through the Strait, but inshore it tends
to follow the coastline. Where the boundary between east
and west-moving water lies with a west-going tide depends
on the relative strengths of the two forces, and in stronger
winds may be readily detectable by the sea state. Tidal
races may form off Cabo Trafalgar, the Bajo de Los Cabezos
west of Tarifa, and Isla de Tarifa itself, typically when east-
going current and tidal stream oppose the *levanter*.

Over the course of the passage, particularly in a slower
yacht or if beating, it may be possible to extend the
duration of favourable tide available by moving from one
tidal band into another. For example: leaving Gibraltar at
HW+0300 to head west, using the west-going stream
inshore until it turns east at HW–0300, then moving
offshore to gain a further three hours of west-going stream
until HW Gibraltar (though it should be noted that this
tactic will take a yacht from the Inshore Traffic Zone into
the main west-going shipping channel). *See also overleaf.*

Warning If enjoying a fine spinnaker run into the
Straits from the west be aware that winds in excess
of 30kn are said to blow at Tarifa for 300 days of the
year.

THE ALGARVE & ANDALUCIA

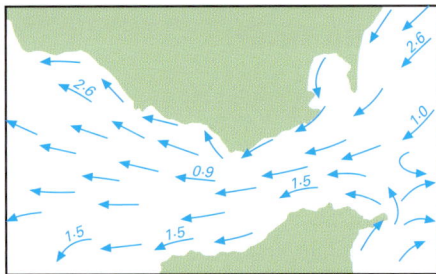
5 HOURS BEFORE HW GIBRALTAR

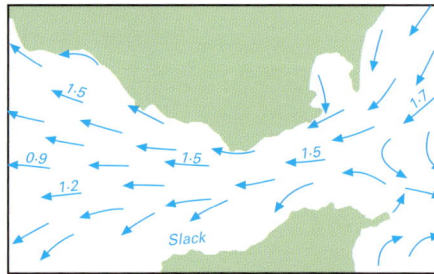
4 HOURS BEFORE HW GIBRALTAR

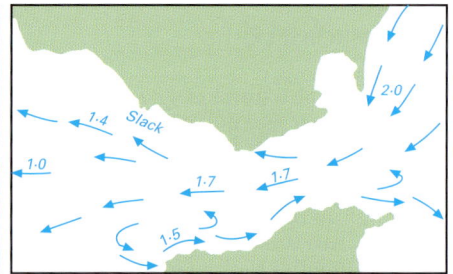
3 HOURS BEFORE HW GIBRALTAR

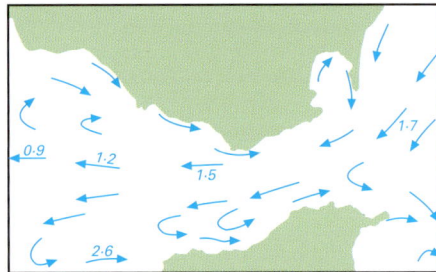
2 HOURS BEFORE HW GIBRALTAR

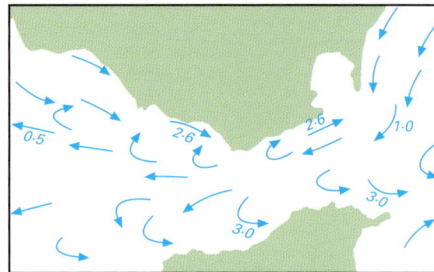
1 HOUR BEFORE HW GIBRALTAR

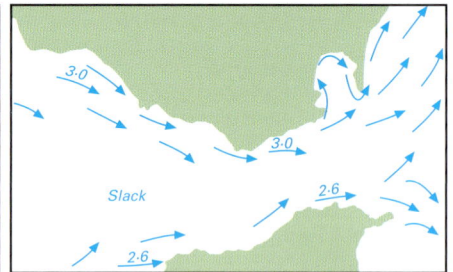
HW GIBRALTAR

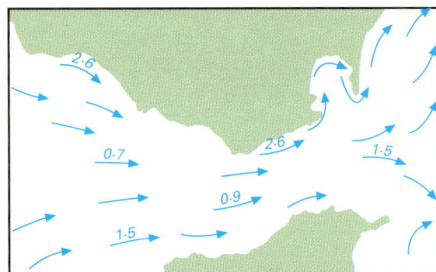
1 HOUR AFTER HW GIBRALTAR

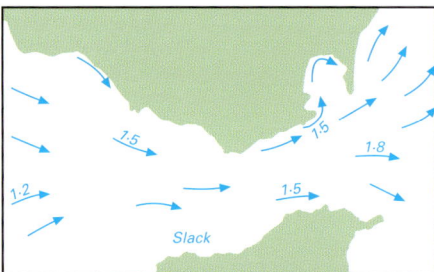
2 HOURS AFTER HW GIBRALTAR

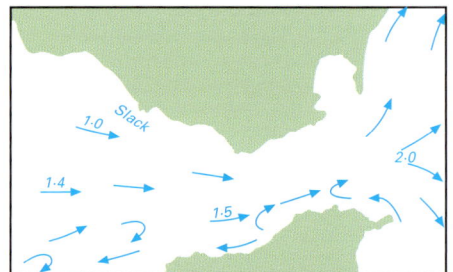
3 HOURS AFTER HW GIBRALTAR

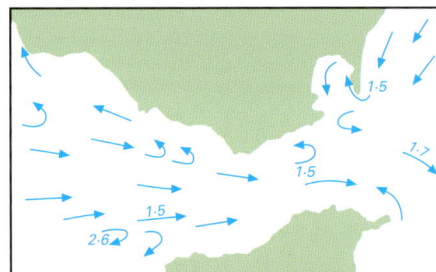
4 HOURS AFTER HW GIBRALTAR

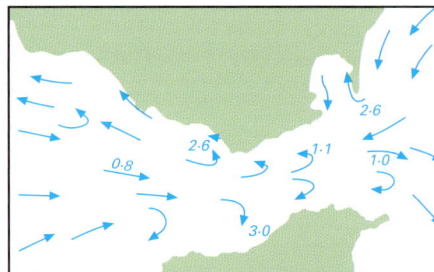
5 HOURS AFTER HW GIBRALTAR

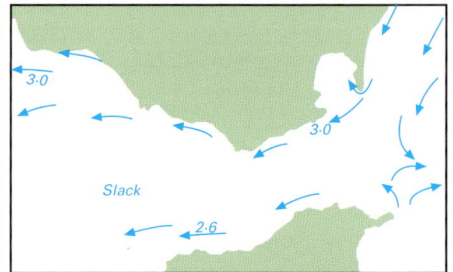
6 HOURS AFTER HW GIBRALTAR

These diagrams are published with the kind permission of Dr M Sloma, editor of *Yacht Scene*. Under no circumstances will *Yacht Scene* or the RCC Pilotage Foundation be liable for any accident or injury which may occur to vessels or persons whilst using the above current predictions.

Graham Hutt, author of RCCPF *North Africa*, who knows the Strait well, offers the following strategy:

Eastbound vessels

For yachts entering the Strait from the west, there is no real problem going eastwards, unless there is a strong easterly wind, in which case passage will be rough, especially around Tarifa, where winds often reach 40kn. If strong winds are forecast, stay in Barbate (or Tanger) until it drops or anchor in the lee of Tarifa or Cabo de Gracia if strong east winds are encountered once on passage. The best time to depart for the trip east is soon after LW.

Westbound vessels

In strong westerlies it is almost impossible to make progress west, due to the combined east-going current that can, with unfavourable tide, reach 6kn or more – with steep swell and overfalls off Tarifa, Ceuta Point and Punta Malabata.

In good conditions, to make use of the favourable current, set off from Gibraltar two hours after HW. Keeping close inshore, a foul current of around a knot will be experienced off Punta Carnero. A favourable west-going current four hours after HW will assist passage during springs, although this is weak and east-going at neaps. If heading south out of Gibraltar for Tanger, it is usually wise to use the engine to cross from Tarifa making a fast passage to counter the increasing east-going current – or anchor in the shelter of Tarifa and wait for the next favourable tide, around LW, to make the crossing.

Barbate

Waypoints
⊕192 – 36°08'·7N 5°57'·6W (approach)
⊕193 – 36°10'·56N 5°55'·8W (entrance)
⊕194 – 36°01'·7N 5°47'·4W (2M S of Punta de Gracia or Punta Camariñal)

Courses and distances
⊕183 (Cádiz) – ⊕192 (via ⊕186 & ⊕191) = 35M, 187° & 152° & 086° or 266° & 332° & 007°
⊕187 (Sancti-Petri) – ⊕192 (via ⊕191) = 22·4M, 149° & 086° or 266° & 329°
⊕191 (Cabo Trafalgar) – ⊕192 = 6·5M, 086° or 266°
⊕192 – ⊕193 = 2·4M, 038° or 218°
⊕192 – ⊕195 (Tarifa, via ⊕194) = 20·5M, 130° & 107° or 287° & 310°
⊕192 – ⊕200 (Queensway Quay, Gibraltar, via ⊕194, ⊕195 & ⊕197) = 35·7M, 130° & 107° & 063° & 022° or 202° & 243° & 287° & 310°
⊕192 – ⊕201 (Marina Bay, Gibraltar, via ⊕194, ⊕195 & ⊕197) = 36·6M, 130° & 107° & 063° & 017° or 197° & 243° & 287° & 310°

Tides
Standard port Cádiz
Mean time differences
HW +0005 ±0000; LW +0015 ±0000
Heights in metres

MHWS	MHWN	MLWN	MLWS
1·9	1·5	1·0	0·6

Or refer to EasyTide at www.ukho.gov.uk/easytide

Charts

	Approach	*Harbour*
Admiralty	91, 773, 142	
Imray	C19, C50	C50
Spanish	44C, 105, 444	4441

Principal lights
2408 **Barbate** Fl(2)WR.7s23m10/7M 281°-W-015°-R-095° White round tower, dark red bands 18m
2409 **Outer south breakwater** Fl.R.4s12m5M Red truncated conical tower 2m
2410 **Inner breakwater** FlG.3s8m2M Green truncated conical tower 2m
2410.5 **Wave barrier SE end** Fl(2+1)R.21s2M Red post, green bands
2411.25 **Marina, south mole** Fl.R.4s2M Red column 3m
2411.2 **Marina, north mole** Fl(2)G.2M Green post 3m

Night entry
Straightforward in normal conditions, taking care to avoid both the tunny nets detailed below and the low-lying anti-swell barrier inside the harbour itself (see plan)

Harbour communications
Puerto Deportivo Barbate ☎ +34 856 108 399 and +34 600 140 312
Fax +34 956 066 851 *Email* barbated@eppa.es
www.puertosdeandalucia.es
VHF Ch 09.

The large harbour at Barbate looking east-northeast. The marina basins are at the lower left of the photograph

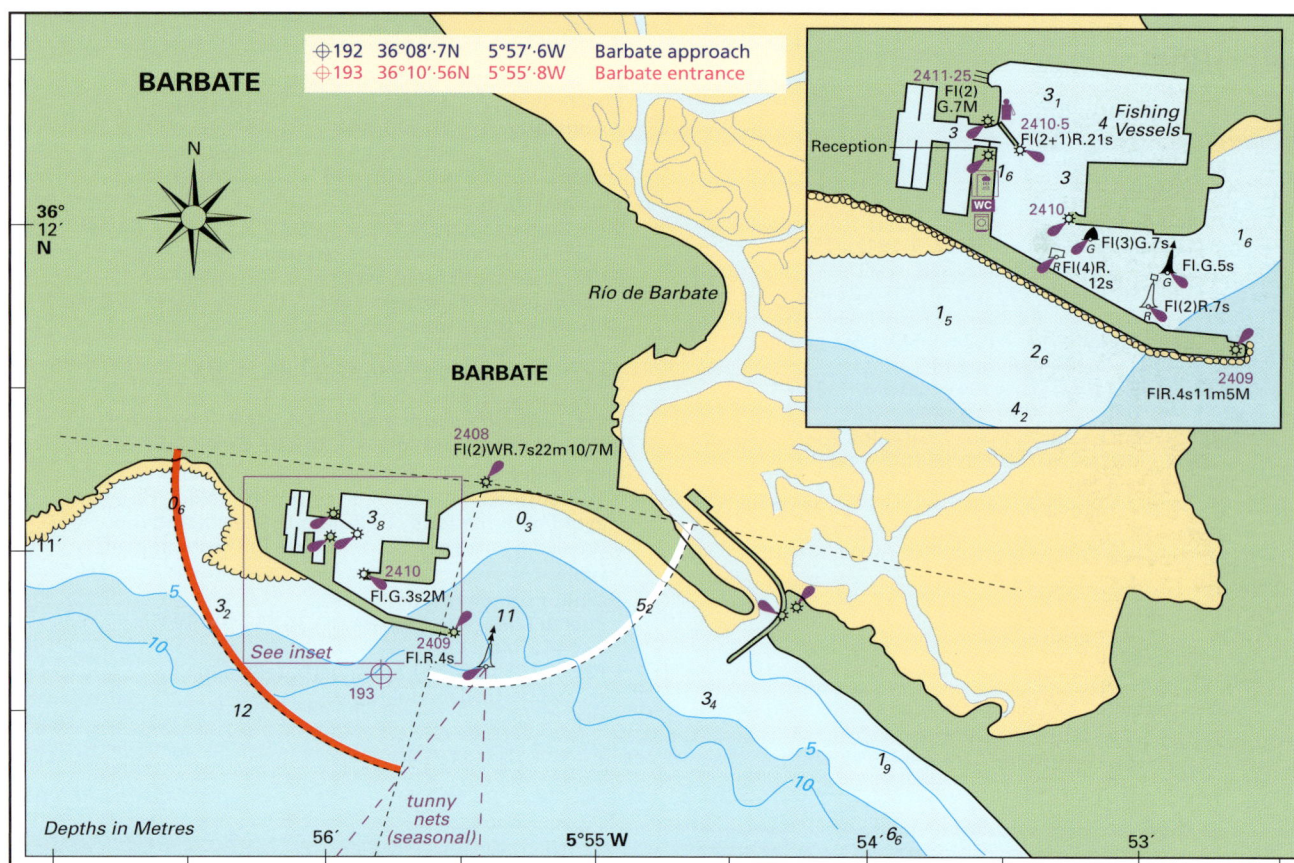

Chart legend:
- ⊕192 36°08'·7N 5°57'·6W Barbate approach
- ⊕193 36°10'·56N 5°55'·8W Barbate entrance

BARBATE

Río de Barbate

BARBATE

2408 Fl(2)WR.7s22m10/7M

2410 Fl.G.3s2M

2409 Fl.R.4s

See inset

193

Depths in Metres

tunny nets (seasonal)

Inset:
- 2411·25 Fl(2)G.7M
- 2410·5 Fl(2+1)R.21s
- Reception
- Fishing Vessels
- WC
- 2410
- Fl(3)G.7s
- Fl(4)R.12s
- Fl.G.5s
- Fl(2)R.7s
- 2409 FlR.4s11m5M

The nearest marina west of the Gibraltar Straits. Very useful, if rather soulless

Formerly known as Barbate de Franco (pronounced 'Barbartay', with the 'de Franco' now dropped), the old town has been swallowed up by new development and has no great appeal, though the marina is useful as a refuge from the strong winds characteristic of the Straits. The harbour, in which fishing boats berth to the east and yachts to the west, covers a large area and is the easternmost (in the Atlantic) of the string of harbours and marinas financed, built and run by the Agencia Pública de Puertos de Andalucía in Seville – see page 261.

The shallow Río Barbate about 0·4M to the east is used by local boats, but the entrance is difficult and depths within are less than 2·5m.

Approach and entrance

If inshore sailing from the west, swing wide around Cabo Trafalgar to clear the dangerous rocky shoal which runs southwest from the Cape to Bajo Aceitera more than 1·5M offshore. Cabo Trafalgar, only about 20m high, appears low-lying compared to the hills 2km to the northeast. In heavy weather the Placer de Meca bank, 3·2M to the west, may break and should also be avoided. A race can form up to 8M offshore in these conditions, particularly when east-going current and tidal stream oppose the *levanter*. An inside passage is used by fishermen, but it should not be attempted without local knowledge.

From the southeast, Punta Camariñal cuts the direct line from Tarifa (off which a race may also form). Note also the dangerous Bajo de Los Cabezos shoal, 5M west of Tarifa and 2M south of Punta Paloma, on which waves break even in calm weather. Between Punta Camariñal and Barbate the coast is relatively steep-to. In either case take care to avoid the two tunny nets laid in the area each year – see below.

From offshore ⊕192 lies 2·4M southwest of the entrance, a course of 038° leading to ⊕193, close outside the harbour mouth. This course clears the western edge of tunny nets referred to below.

Caution

Three *almadrabas* or tunny (tuna) nets are laid annually in the vicinity of Barbate.

The Ensenada de Barbate net is laid from March to September each year very close to the harbour entrance – it is stated that vessels should not pass between the inner end of the net and the shore, but local fishermen habitually do so. It remains in roughly the same position each year and is marked by four lit cardinal buoys:

North Cardinal buoy 36°10'·75N 5°55'·4W
(about 200m SE of the south breakwater head)
Q.3M
West Cardinal buoy 36°09'·18N 5°56'·00W
V.Q(9)10s3M
South Cardinal buoys
36°08'·85N 5°57'·09W (March to June)
36°08'·08N 5°55'·08W (June to September)
V.Q(6)(1)+LFl.12s3M
East Cardinal buoy 36°09'·90N 5°55'·39W
Q(3)10s3M

Puerto Deportivo Barbate lies at the west end of the harbour, seen here looking northwest. *APPA*

Between September and February the Ensenada de Barbate net is replaced by a floating fish cage some 270m by 60m, marked by two lit buoys:

West Cardinal buoy 36°09'·18N 5°56'·00W
   V.Q(9)10s3M
East Cardinal buoy 36°09'·90N 5°55'·39W
   Q(3)10s3M

The Cabo Plato tunny net is laid from March to August each year off the small village of Zahara some 4·5M southeast of Barbate. Again it appears to maintain much the same position, and is marked by three lit cardinal buoys:

West Cardinal buoy 36°07'·53N 5°52'·07W
   Q(9)15s3M
West Cardinal buoy 36°06'·38N 5°52'·07W
   Q(9)15s3M
South Cardinal buoy 36°06'·33N 5°50'·58W
   Q(6)(1)+LFl.15s3M

Finally, and a more recent addition, the Ensenada de Bolonia net is laid about halfway between Barbate and Tarifa off the village of that name (worth visiting for its Roman ruins). It is also marked by three lit cardinal buoys:

West Cardinal buoy 36°04'·15N 5°46'·29W
   Q(9)15s3M
South Cardinal buoy 36°03'·73N 5°47'·05W
   V.Q(6)+LFl.15s3M
East Cardinal buoy 36°04'·07N 5°45'·76W
   Q(3)10s3M

Entrance

The entrance is straightforward although a shoal can build up around the head of the south breakwater which must be given a generous clearance. Two pairs of lateral buoys should then be seen, though the starboard hand inner buoy is seldom on station. A minimum of 2m should be found in the channel at MLWS.

Berthing

The marina is reached through a narrow entrance leading almost due west from the main harbour, with a reception pontoon on the port hand under the office building and a fuel facility opposite. A low yellow and black anti-swell barrier runs out from the northern side – see plan. The weakish red light on its end is said to be unreliable so particular care must be taken at night.

The marina consists of two separate and almost completely enclosed basins, one leading out of the other, with pontoons laid around their perimeters and down the centre of the larger, western basin. There is at least 3m depth throughout. There are 314 berths in total, 120 of them able to take yachts of more than 11m and 18 for more than 15m. There is always room for visitors, who are usually berthed near the marina office. Hours are 0800-1430 and 1530-2130 from 1/6-30/9, and 0830-1430 and 1530-1900 from 1/10-31/5.

Facilities

Boatyard, engineers, electronic and radio repairs Talleres Gonzalez-Guerra, ☎+34 956 431903, *Fax* +34 956 434 659, *Mobile* +34 666 400 677 *Email* gonzalez.guerra@enterpyme.com, handle general and mechanical repairs from their premises just outside the boatyard on the north side of the marina, and also fabricate in stainless steel.

Also Nautica Trafalgar, ☎+34 956 434265 *Fax*+34 956 432403, *Email* nautica@trafalgar.e.telefonica.net, for engines' servicing and some chandlery.

Travel-lift 45 tonne and 150 tonne capacity lifts handling both yachts and fishing boats, with a large area of fenced (but windy) hardstanding. Book at the marina office.

Chandlery A good range of general chandlery at Talleres Gonzalez-Guerra, open 0900–1400 and 1530–1830 weekdays, 0900–1330 Saturday. They are happy to order if necessary, and some English is spoken.

Water On the pontoons.

Showers In the office building.

Launderette In the office building.

Electricity On the pontoons (but using non-standard plugs which are available from the marina office).

Fuel Available during office hours at the fuelling pontoon on the north side of the entrance.

Bottled gas Camping Gaz available in the town about 2km distant.

Club náutico Near the fishing harbour.

Weather forecast Posted daily at the marina office.

Bank In the town.

Shops/provisioning Good supermarket on the road behind the harbour, with more in the town.

Produce market In the town.

Cafés, restaurants and hotels In 2012 the café and restaurant in the harbour were closed as was the Fairplay Beach and Yacht Club. Victims of the 2008 financial crisis. The town offers alternatives.

Medical services In the town.

Communications

Post office In the town.

Mailing address The marina office will hold mail for visiting yachts – c/o Puerto Deportivo Barbate, Oficina del Puerto, Avda del Generalisimo s/n, 11160 Barbate, Cádiz, España. It is important that the envelope carries the name of the yacht in addition to that of the addressee.

Public telephones Several kiosks around the marina.

Internet access WiFi at the café/bar in the marina (but closed 2012). At least one cybercafé in the town.

Fax service At the marina office, *Fax* +34 956 431918.

Car hire/taxis Book via the office.

Buses Bus service to Cádiz, Algeciras and La Línea.

Air services International airport at Gibraltar, a short walk across the border from La Línea. Alternatively Jerez or Seville.

Looking north across the narrow entrance to the Puerto Deportivo Barbate, with the fuel pontoon opposite and the yellow and black anti-swell barrier on the right
Anne Hammick

Tarifa

Waypoints
⊕195 – 35°58'·9N 5°36'W (approach)
⊕196 – 36°00'·24N 5°36'·14W (entrance)

Courses and distances
⊕192 (Barbate) – ⊕195 (via F194) = 20·5M, 130° & 107°
or 287° & 310°
⊕195 – ⊕196 = 1·3M, 355° or 175°
⊕195 – ⊕198 (Algeciras, via ⊕197) = 14M, 063° & 346°
or 166° & 243°
⊕195 – ⊕200 (Queensway Quay, Gibraltar,
via ⊕197) = 15·2M, 063° & 022° or 202° & 243°
⊕195 – ⊕201 (Marina Bay, Gibraltar,
via ⊕197) = 16·1M, 063° & 017° or 197° & 243°

Tides
Standard port Gibraltar
Mean time differences
HW –0040; LW –0040
Heights in metres

MHWS	MHWN	MLWN	MLWS
1·4	1·0	0·6	0·3

Or refer to EasyTide at www.ukho.gov.uk/easytide

Charts

	Approach	Harbour
Admiralty	91, 773, 142	142
Imray	C19, C50	C50
Spanish	44C, 105, 445, 445B	4450

Principal lights
2414 **Isla de Tarifa** Fl(3)WR.10s41m26/18M
089°-R-113°-W-089° (over Bajo de Los Cabezos)
Racon Mo 'C'(─·─·)20M AIS White round tower 33m
2415 **Isla de Tarifa East side** Fl.R.5s12m5M
Red ■ on red 4-sided tower 2m
2416 **East breakwater** Fl.G.5s11m5M 249°-vis-045°
Green ▲ on green metal framework tower
(Dwarfed by square stone pillar surmounted by
statue of man, approximately 55m)

2417 **Breakwater elbow** Q(3)10s11m3M
255°-vis-045° Easterly cardinal column,
east topmark, 2M
2418 **Inner Mole east end** Fl(2)R.7s7m1M
Red ■ on corner of white hut 4m

Night entry
Not advised, at least until an area in the harbour is
designated for visiting yachts.

Navtex
Tarifa Identification letters 'G' and 'T'
Transmits 518kHz in English; 490 in Spanish
Weather bulletins for Cabo de São Vicente to Gibraltar
and the Western Mediterranean within 450 miles of
the coast: English – 0900, 2100; Spanish – 0710, 1910
Navigational warnings for the Rio Guadiana to
Gibraltar: English – 0100, 0500, 1300, 1700; Spanish –
0310, 0710, 1110, 1510, 1910, 2310

Coast radio station
Tarifa (remotely controlled from Málaga)
Digital Selective Calling MMSI 002240994
MF Transmits/receives: 2182kHz
VHF Ch 10, 16, 67, 74
Weather bulletins and navigational warnings
Weather bulletins and visibility (fog) warnings in
Spanish and English for Bahía de Cádiz, Strait of
Gibraltar and Alborán: VHF Ch 10, 67 at 0015, 0215,
0415, 0615, 0815, 1015, 1215, 1415, 1615, 1815, 2015,
2215 UT
Navigational warnings in Spanish and English for the
Strait of Gibraltar: VHF Ch 10, 67 on receipt

Commercial and fishing harbour with little provision for yachts

Tarifa is the most southerly city of mainland Europe and, at barely 8M distant, considerably closer to North Africa than is Gibraltar. It is famous for its frequent strong winds, which together with excellent beaches have made it the boardsailing capital of Europe.

It is reputedly where the Moors landed on their European invasion, and the older part of the town still shows a strong North African influence, particularly in the well preserved streets around the harbour. It has an active tourist industry and consequently is well provided with shops, restaurants and hotels. Unfortunately the Isla de

Looking north over Isla de Tarifa, with the busy fishing and ferry harbour on the right

Chart / Map labels

⊕195 35°58'·9N 5°36'W Tarifa approach
⊕196 36°00'·24N 5°36'·14W Tarifa entrance

TARIFA

Torre de Guzman

walls

walls

Boatyard

Ferry
Terminal

Car
park

Ferries

2419
Fl(2)G.5s
4m1M

2419.5
Fl(2+1)G.
11s5m1M

Castillo de
Santa Catalina

Ferries

Ferries

Fish
market

Fishing boats

2418
Fl(2)R.7s
6m1M

2417
Q(3)10s

Commercial & cargo

2416
Fl.G.5s10m5M

(Statue)

vis

Isla de Tarifa

2415
Fl.R.5s11m5M

2414
Fl(3)WR.10s40m26/18M
AIS

36°00'·5N

36°N

36'·5

TARIFA

N

Depths in Metres

5°36'W

W

Approach

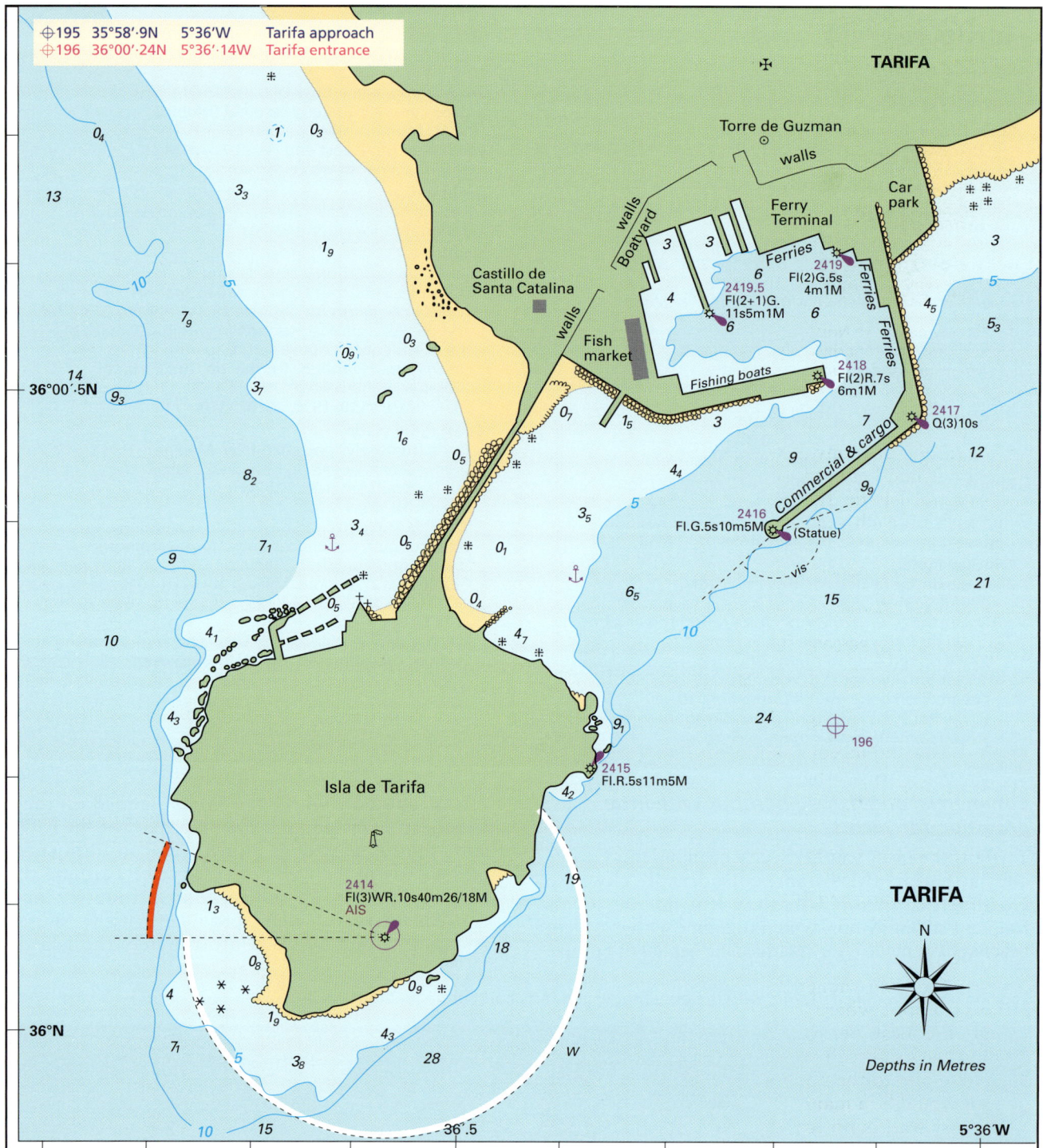

Tarifa is a military area and closed to the public, as is the handsome old Castillo de Santa Catalina to the northwest, but the road between Tarifa and Algeciras is worth traversing if possible for its dramatic views of both Gibraltar and the Strait.

Approach

If coastal sailing from the west, Tarifa light stands high on its promontory clear of the land. Chief danger is the Bajo de los Cabezos, 5M west of Tarifa and 3M south of Punta Paloma. The bank is marked by broken water even in calm weather, and several wrecks are reputed to lie close to the surface. From the east, there are dangers up to 1M offshore between Punta Carnero and Punta de Cala Arenas, but once west of the latter the shore is generally steep to. There is a prominent wind farm on the hills northeast of the town.

There is no true offshore approach due to the busy Traffic Separation Zone – see page 314 – but if coasting further out ⊕195 lies 1·3M almost due south of the entrance, a course of 355° leading up the east side of the Isla de Tarifa to ⊕196, close off the entrance.

A race may form off Isla de Tarifa when east-going current and tidal stream oppose the *levanter*.

Considerably nearer to North Africa than Algeciras or Gibraltar, Tarifa is primarily a commercial harbour with, as yet, no provision for yachts

Caution

An *almadraba* or tunny (tuna) net known as *Lances de Tarifa* is laid between March and July each year northwest of Isla de Tarifa. It remains in much the same position each year, and is marked by three lit cardinal buoys:

Northwest – West Cardinal buoy 36°01'·15N 5°38'·26W
 Q(9)15s3M
Southwest – West Cardinal buoy 36°00'·90N 5°38'·11W
 Q(9)5s3M
South Cardinal buoy 36°00'·70N 5°37'·61W
 Q(6)+LFl.15s3M

Entrance

The harbour entrance faces southwest towards the Isla de Tarifa and its connecting causeway. Head for the conspicuous statue at the end of the east breakwater, before making the dogleg into the harbour.

Note In a *levanter* this approach becomes a lee shore and it may be wiser to use the second of the anchorages mentioned below – or to press on for Barbate or beyond.

Berthing

Tarifa is far from yacht-orientated and there is no designated spot where visiting yachts may berth, though the best bet would almost certainly be amongst the local craft which lie bow or stern-to the concrete moles to the northwest. Some command of Spanish would be a major advantage.

The east wall is no longer viable, being entirely taken up with ferries and small cargo vessels.

Constant comings and goings by the fishing fleet make for almost continuous movement.

Formalities

The *Policía* and *Inmigración* both have offices in the ferry terminal (*Estación Maritima*) at the root of the east breakwater and should be visited if arriving from outside Spain. Foreign yachts are also a sufficient rarity that the Capitania is likely to visit. A charge is levied for an overnight visit despite the almost total lack of facilities.

Facilities

Virtually nothing, other than a few water taps. There is no yacht fuel and no possibility of getting electricity aboard. The small boatyard (with marine railway) in the northwest corner of the harbour is geared to fishing boats but could doubtless carry out minor yacht repairs if necessary.

A café/bar will be found on the southwest arm, otherwise the town has shops of all kinds, a produce market, banks, restaurants and hotels.

Communications

Post office in the old part of town, with telephones around the harbour etc. Several internet cafés, one (slightly northwest of the harbour) combining operations with a launderette! Taxis in surprising numbers. Buses to Cádiz, Algeciras and La Línea, from which it is a short walk to the international airport at Gibraltar.

Adjacent anchorages

A *Parque Natural* has been established along the coast between Punta de Gracia in the west and Punta Carnero in the east, extending more than 1M offshore. However although some fishing and diving activities are prohibited there appears to be no ban on anchoring in the area.

1. In the clean sandy bay northeast of Isla de Tarifa, between the causeway and the harbour entrance, in 4–5m over sand. The area is popular with both divers and boardsailors. Anchor well inside the track of the frequent high speed ferries.
2. Just north of a derelict mole on the northwest side of Isla de Tarifa, with shelter from easterly seas (though not the wind) given by the causeway. Good holding over sand in 3–4m.

Looking NE from Tarifa anchorage (1) towards the harbour. Anchor well inside the track of the regular high speed ferries *Jane Russell*

Algeciras

Waypoints
⊕197 – 36°03'·7N, 5°24'·4W (1·3M SE of Punta Carnero)
⊕198 – 36°06'·95N 5°25'·43W (entrance)

Courses and distances
⊕195 (Tarifa) – ⊕198 (via ⊕197) = 14M, 063° & 346° or
    166° & 243°
⊕197 – ⊕198 = 3·4M, 346° or 166°
⊕198 – ⊕200 (Queensway Quay, Gibraltar) = 2·7M,
    068° or 248°
⊕198 – ⊕201 (Marina Bay, Gibraltar) = 3·2M, 051° or
    231°

Tides
Standard port Gibraltar
Mean time differences
HW –0010; LW –0010
Heights in metres

MHWS	MHWN	MLWN	MLWS
1·1	0·9	0·4	0·2

Or refer to EasyTide at www.ukho.gov.uk/easytide

Charts

	Approach	Harbour
Admiralty	91, 773, 142, 3578, 1448	1455
Imray	C19, C50	
Spanish	44C, 45A, 105, 445, 445A	4451

Principal lights
Commercial Harbour
2425 NE breakwater Fl.R.5s11m7M
    Red round tower 6m
Dársena del Saladillo (yacht basin)
2423 South breakwater Fl(3)R.9s4m3M but reported
    replaced by Light Buoy(?)(2013)

Night entry
Not advised, since all three marinas in the Dársena del
Saladillo are private and anchoring is forbidden.

Coast radio station
Algeciras *Digital Selective Calling*
MMSI 002241001 VHF Ch 16, 74
Weather bulletins and navigational warnings
Weather bulletins in Spanish and English: VHF Ch 74 at
0315, 0515, 0715, 1115, 1515, 1915, 2315 UT
Navigational warnings in Spanish and English: on request

Harbour communications
Port Authority ☎ +34 956 585400
Fax +34 956 585445
Email apba@apba.es www.apba.es
VHF Ch 08, 13, 16, 68, 74 (call *Algeciras Tráfico*)
Club Náutico Deportivo el Saladillo ☎ +34 856 020 041
info@cdnauticosaladillo.es www.cdnauticosaladillo.es

Major commercial harbour, with three private marinas in a separate basin

Algeciras is primarily an industrial and ferry port,
through which passes many of the guest-workers
returning to Africa with roof racks bending under
their loads.

Yachts have their own basin – the Dársena del
Saladillo – south of the main harbour, where three
separate clubs run three separate marinas. Sadly
none welcome visiting yachts (See *Berthing*). The
following approach and entrance instructions are
given for the Dársena del Saladillo in the hope that
this situation may one day change.

Approach

The approaches to Algeciras are extremely busy with
commercial traffic of all sizes. In particular, a sharp
watch needs to be kept for the many high-speed
ferries, including hydrofoils, which run between
Algeciras and Morocco. These are notorious for
maintaining their course and speed at all times,
presumably adhering to the 'might is right' principle.

Coming from the west, there are dangers up to 1M
offshore between Punta de Cala Arenas and Punta
Carnero. On rounding this headland the city and
harbour will be seen some 3M to the north behind a
mile-long breakwater terminating with a light.
Various ledges run out from the headlands between
Punta Carnero and the entrance to the Dársena del
Saladillo (also lit).

If approaching from Gibraltar or other points east,
the entrance to the Dársena del Saladillo should be
easily seen south of the oil tanks on the commercial
quay and it can be approached directly.

If approaching from the south, possibly from
Ceuta or elsewhere in Morocco, ⊕197 lies in clear
water southeast of Punta Carnero, a course of 346°
for 3·4M leading to ⊕198 in the approaches to the
Dársena del Saladillo, passing close to a spherical
yellow ODAS buoy off Punta Calero en route.

Yachts can safely cut inside the east cardinal buoy
placed nearly a mile offshore, though an offing of at
least 0·5M should be maintained. Further ledges lie
both north and south of the entrance, and the three
buoys marking the approach should under no
circumstances be ignored. Major infilling work is
taking place to the north of the Saladillo entrance,
outside of which a new breakwater is under
construction, marked by additional east cardinal
light buoys. Keep well clear.

Entrance

The dogleg entrance to the Dársena del Saladillo has
been very well designed, such that when visited in a
30 knot easterly wind no swell at all was entering.
As noted above, three buoys mark the final
approach, after which the entrance itself is
straightforward.

Berthing

As stated above none of the three marinas in the
Dársena del Saladillo accept visitors. Taken
clockwise on entry these are the Real Club Náutico
de Algeciras, which previously had premises in the
main harbour, the Club Náutico Saladillo and the
Club Deportivo El Pargo. The first (southern)
marina is also the largest by a considerable margin,
and would undoubtedly be the best one to try in an
emergency. It is also the club where some English is
most likely to be spoken, and visitors are also
welcome to dine in the Real Club Náutico's
restaurant.

Facilities

The Real Club Náutico marina is provided with all
the usual facilities, including a fuel berth on the end
of the breakwater which forms its eastern limit.

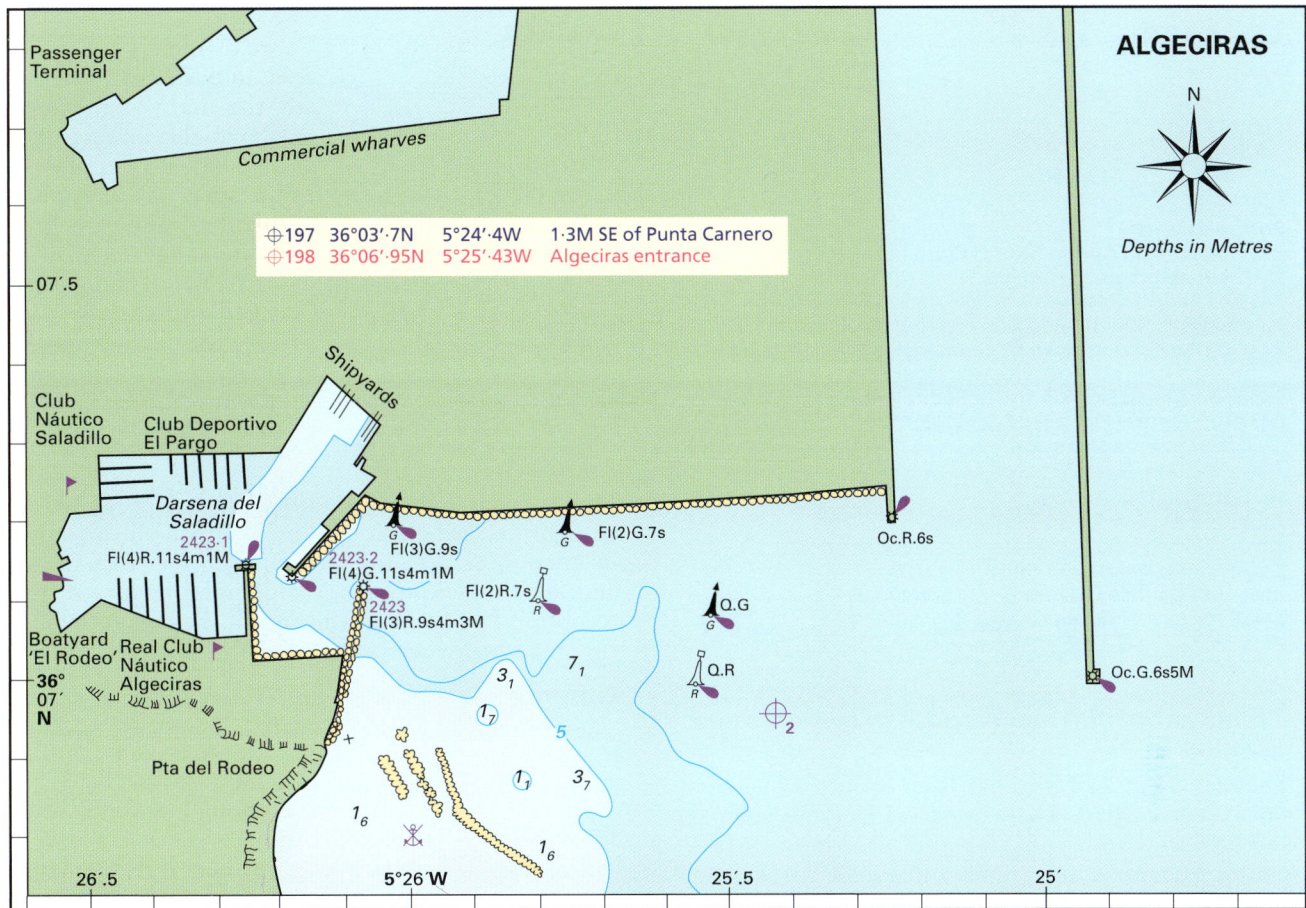

ALGECIRAS

N

Depths in Metres

Passenger Terminal

Commercial wharves

⊕197 36°03'·7N 5°24'·4W 1·3M SE of Punta Carnero
⊕198 36°06'·95N 5°25'·43W Algeciras entrance

07'.5

Shipyards

Club Náutico Saladillo

Club Deportivo El Pargo

Darsena del Saladillo
2423·1
Fl(4)R.11s4m1M

2423·2
Fl(4)G.11s4m1M

2423
Fl(3)R.9s4m3M

G
Fl(3)G.9s

G
Fl(2)G.7s

Oc.R.6s

Fl(2)R.7s
R

Q.G
G

Q.R
R

Oc.G.6s5M

Boatyard 'El Rodeo'

Real Club Náutico Algeciras

36°
07'
N

Pta del Rodeo

3₁

7₁

5

1₇

1₇

3₁

1₆

1₆

⊕2

26'.5

5°26'W

25'.5

25'

The Dársena del Saladillo at Algeciras, seen from east-southeast. Although the Real Club Náutico de Algeciras, the Club Náutico Saladillo and the Club Deportivo El Pargo all have pontoons in the harbour, none currently accept visitors

The west side of the basin is home to Astilleros y Varaderos 'El Rodeo', ☎ +34 956 600511, a shipyard primarily engaged with work on steel fishing vessels and other commercial craft, although a steel yacht ashore has been seen there. Almost opposite, across the busy harbourside road, will be found Náutica Iberia, where a limited range of chandlery is on sale in addition to smallcraft and jet-skis. Spanish charts may be obtained either from SUISCA SL ☎ +34 902 220007, *Email* admiraltycharts@suiscasl.com or in the Centro Blas Infante; or from Valnáutica SL ☎ +34 956 570677 at Avenida 28 de Febrero 33.

All the usual shops, banks, restaurants and hotels are to be found in the city, but at some distance, together with a post office, telephones, car hire and taxis. Trains run to many destinations including Madrid, and buses to La Línea, from which it is a short walk to the international airport at Gibraltar.

La Línea

Waypoints
⊕202 – 36°09'·5N 05°22'·2W

Charts
Admiralty	1455
Imray	C19, C50
Spanish	4451

Principal lights
2436.8 **Dique de Abrigo head** Fl.G.5s8m5M
   Green ▲ on green post 3m
2436.81 **Puerto Chico Jetty Muelle de San Felipe south**
   head Fl.R.5s5m3M Red ■ on red round column 3m
2437.05 **Puerto Deportivo de La Alcaidesa N Pier N head**
   Fl(4)G.11s5m1M Green round column 3m
2437.055 **S head** Fl(2)R.7s5m1M Red column 3m
2437.075 **Central Pier head** Fl(3)G.9s5m1M
   Green round column 2m
2437.08 Fl(2)G.7s5m3M Green post 3m

Harbour communications
Alcaidesa Marina ☎ +34 956 021 660,
Fax +34 956 021 661 www.alcaidesamarina.com
Email marina@alcaidesa.com VHF Ch 09
Real Club Nautico La Línea ☎ +34 956 171 017
Email contacto@rcnlalinea.es

A modern Spanish marina close to overcrowded Gibraltar

The marina at La Línea has been open for business since August 2010. There are good facilities such as showers and toilets, water and electricity on the pontoons, with security gates and patrols.

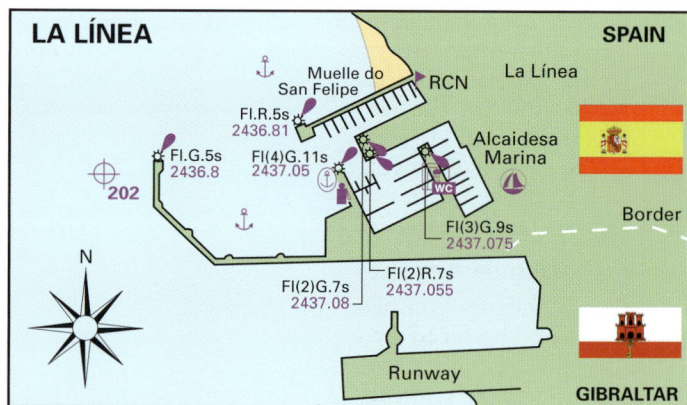

Approach

The approach through Gibraltar Bay to ⊕202 is straightforward, although many anchored ships will be encountered to the west of the rock. Round the end of the Dique de Abrigo and head for the reception/fuel berth at the end of the concrete quay running northwest/southeast.

Entrance

The entrance to the marina is immediately beyond the reception/fuel berth leaving the hardstanding area and boatyard to port.

Berthing

The reception/fuel berth is at the end of the concrete quay with large bollards that are rather a long distance apart, so be prepared with long warps. The marina office is just behind this.

Looking southeast over the Alcaidesa marina at La Línea *APPA*

The Marina has 624 moorings for boats of 8–50m in length, and approximately 170 in dry stack storage for lengths of 6–8m. For yachts of less than 30m in length, the jetties are floating with finger pontoons. For larger yachts the jetties are fixed concrete jetties with vehicular access. It can be a long walk from the furthest pontoons to the marina office but a golf cart service is available.

Anchoring east of the Dique de Abrigo

The anchorage immediately outside the marina entrance, sheltered by the Dique de Abrigo, is not controlled by the marina. Many of the yachts using this anchorage use the RCN La Línea and dinghy ashore. The yacht club make a €5 charge per day for their facilities including showers, WiFi, etc. as well as safe dinghy dockage. The understanding is that the anchorage area is under local authority/port authority control. It's possible that at some point the authorities will decide that they don't want yachts to anchor, but so far there seems to have been no problem in this area.

Facilities

Showers and WC These are in the northeast corner of the marina.

Laundry A coin operated laundry service (washing machine and tumble drier) is located in the same building as the showers and WC.

Water and Electricity Supplied to all berths.

Boatyard The boatyard has a 75-tonne boat hoist and storage areas. There is a hard standing of 17,000m² for the repair of every kind of vessel. ☎ +34 956 021660 *Email* tovaradero@alcaidesa.com. A full workshop facility is operated by Elias Blanco S.L. (Volvo agent) ☎ +34 956 90 90 49.

Dry Dock Storage For boats from 6–8m on a rental basis for winter usage.

Chandlers In town or in Gibraltar.

Parking Facilities More than 1,000 parking bays are provided, both in the area reserved for marina clients, for whom access is available through a security checkpoint, and in the recreational and leisure areas.

Security Closed circuit television system and security surveillance and control. Access to the jetties is through automatic gates.

Fuel There is fuel at the reception berth and Calor gas is available.

A misty Gibraltar from Alcaidesa Marina *Henry Buchanan*

RCN La Línea The RCN yacht club is near the root of the Muelle do San Felipe (Puerto Chico jetty) at the north side of the marina area. This has 11 pontoons but it is strictly private with no space for visitors. The restaurant is open for visiting yachtsmen.

Shops/Provisioning There is good shopping, including a large supermarket and an excellent produce market in La Línea. Gibraltar is well within walking distance but passports are necessary to cross the border.

Cafés, restaurants and hotels The original concept of bars, shops and restaurants has not yet been realised in the wake of the 2008 financial crisis. However, the marina did announce the opening of the first cafeteria/snack bar 'Alcaidesa Lounge' in August 2012. The cafeteria is situated near the entrance to the marina adjoining Pontoon 9 where Sergio the landlord offers his speciality tapas.

Communications

WiFi In the marina but it is expensive.

Post office In town.

Mailing Address Alcaidesa Marina, Marina office, Avda. Príncipe de Asturias s/n,11.300 La Línea, Cádiz, Spain.

Transport Gibraltar airport a short distance away across the border. Bicycle hire available in the marina. Buses into Gibraltar from the Gibraltar side of the border. Taxi offices close by in La Línea.

La Línea tourist train During the summer months the train includes the Alcaidesa Marina on its route. It makes stops outside the Alcaidesa Lounge Bar for those who wish to make use of the service provided.

Looking north to La Linea from the Rock, Gibraltar
Henry Buchanan

THE ALGARVE & ANDALUCIA

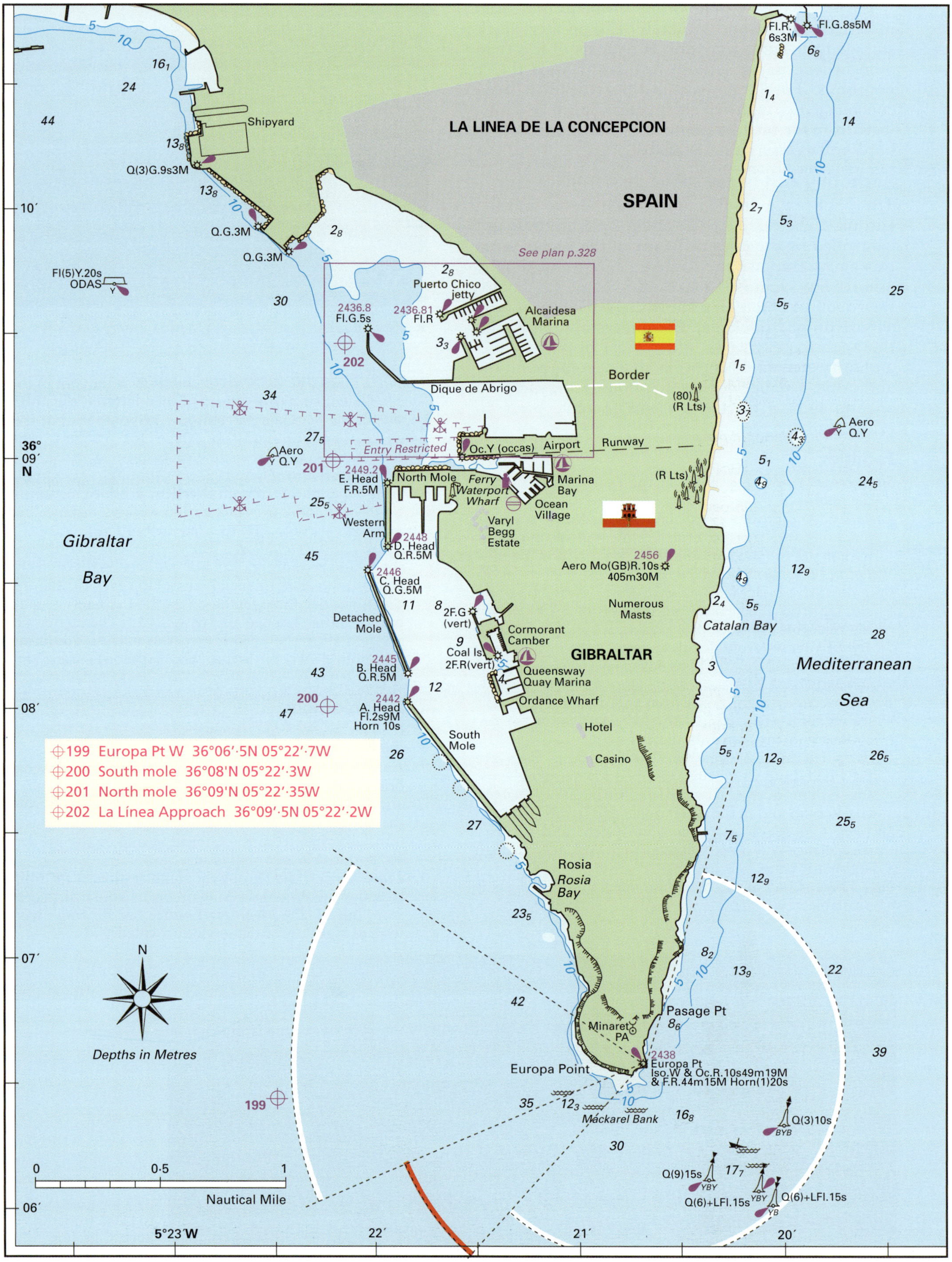

Shipyard

LA LINEA DE LA CONCEPCION

SPAIN

Q(3)G.9s3M

Q.G.3M

Q.G.3M

Fl(5)Y.20s
ODAS

16₁
24
44
13₈
13₈
2₈
30

2₈
Puerto Chico jetty
2436.8
Fl.G.5s
2436.81
Fl.R
202
Alcaidesa Marina
3₃

See plan p.328

Dique de Abrigo

Border

34
27₅
Aero
Y Q.Y
201
Entry Restricted
Oc.Y (occas) Airport
Runway

2449.2
E. Head
F.R.5M
North Mole
25₅
Ferry
Waterport
Wharf
Marina Bay
Ocean Village

Gibraltar
Bay

Western Arm
D. Head
Q.R.5M
2448
45
Varyl Begg Estate

2456
Aero Mo(GB)R.10s
405m30M

2446
C. Head
Q.G.5M
Detached Mole
11
8 2F.G (vert)
9 Coal Is
2F.R(vert)
Cormorant Camber
GIBRALTAR
Numerous Masts

2445
B. Head
Q.R.5M
43
47
12
Queensway Quay Marina
Ordance Wharf

2442
A. Head
Fl.2s9M
Horn 10s
200
26
South Mole
Hotel
Casino

Catalan Bay

Mediterranean
Sea

⊕199 Europa Pt W 36°06'·5N 05°22'·7W
⊕200 South mole 36°08'N 05°22'·3W
⊕201 North mole 36°09'N 05°22'·35W
⊕202 La Línea Approach 36°09'·5N 05°22'·2W

27
Rosia
Rosia Bay
23₅

N

Depths in Metres

42
Minaret
PA
Pasage Pt
8₆

Europa Point
2438
Europa Pt
Iso.W & Oc.R.10s49m19M
& F.R.44m15M Horn(1)20s

35
12₃
Mackarel Bank
16₈
30

Q(3)10s
BYB

0   0.5   1
Nautical Mile

199

Q(9)15s
YBY
17₇
Q(6)+LFl.15s
YBY
Q(6)+LFl.15s
YB

5°23'W   22'   21'   20'

Gibraltar

Waypoints
⊕199 – 36°06'·5N 5°22'·7W (Gibraltar Bay, SE)
⊕200 – 36°08'N 5°22'·3W (South Gap, for Queensway Quay)
⊕201 – 36°08'·98N 5°22'·35W (North mole, for Marina Bay)

Bearings and distance
⊕192 (Barbate) – ⊕200 (via ⊕194, ⊕195 & ⊕197) = 35·7M, 130°, 107°, 063° & 022° or 202°, 243°, 287° & 310°
⊕192 (Barbate) – ⊕201 (via ⊕194, ⊕195 and ⊕197) = 36·6M, 130°, 107°, 063° & 017° or 197°, 243°, 287° & 310°
⊕195 (Tarifa) – ⊕200 (via ⊕197) = 15·2M, 063° & 022° or 202° & 243°
⊕195 (Tarifa) – ⊕201 (via ⊕197) = 16·1M, 063° & 017° or 197° & 243°
⊕198 (Algeciras) – ⊕200 = 2·7M, 068° or 248°
⊕198 (Algeciras) – ⊕201 = 3·2M, 051° or 231°
⊕199 – ⊕200 = 1·5M, 012° or 198°
⊕199 – ⊕201 = 2·5M, 007° or 187°

Tides
Gibraltar is a standard port.
Heights in metres

MHWS	MHWN	MLWN	MLWS
1·0	0·7	0·3	0·1

Charts	Approach	Harbour
British Admiralty	91, 142	145
	773, 3578	144
Spanish	445, 445A	4452
French	7042, 7300	7026
Imray	M11, C19	M11
	C50	C50

Principal Lights
Approach
2420 **Punta Carnero** Fl(4)WR.20s41m16/13M
018°-W-325°-R-018°
(Red sector covers La Perla and Las Bajas shoals)
Round masonry tower and white building 19m
2456 **Gibraltar Aeromarine** 36°08'·6N 05°20'·6W
Mo(GB)R.I0s405m30M
Obscured on westerly bearings within 2M

2438 **Europa Point, Gibraltar** Iso.10s49m19M
197°-vis-042°, 067°-vis-125°
Oc.R.10s19M and F.R.15M 042°-vis-067°
(Red sector covers La Perla and Las Bajas shoals)
Horn 20s White tower, red band 19m

Harbour
2442 **South mole, north end** (A head) Fl.W.2s10m5M
Horn 10s White column 7m
2445 **Detached mole, south end** (B head) Q.R.9m5M
Metal structure on concrete building 11m
2446 **Detached mole, north end** (C head) Q.G.10m5M
Metal structure on concrete building 11m
2448 **North mole, western arm** (D head) Q.R.18m5M
Black 8-sided metal framework tower 17m
2449.2 **North breakwater, northwest elbow** (E head) F.R.28m5M Tower Plus other lights in the interior of the harbour and to the north

Port communications
Radio
Gibraltar Port Control VHF Ch 16, 6, 12, 13, 14 (24 hours)
Lloyds radio VHF Ch 8, 12, 14, 16 (24 hours)
Queens Harbourmaster VHF Ch 8 (0800–1600 Monday to Friday) All marinas VHF Ch 71 (0830–2030, later in summer)

Telephone and email
Port Captain ☎ +350 200772 54
Port Operations Room ☎ +350 20078134/ 20077004
Queensway Quay ☎ +350 20044700,
Fax +350 20044699
Email qqmarina@gibnet.gi
Marina Bay Office ☎ +350 20073300,
Fax +350 20042656
Email pieroffice@marinabay.gi www.marinabay.gi
Sheppards Marina Repair facilities
☎ +350 200768 95, Chandlery ☎ +350 200771 83
Ocean Village ☎ +350 200400 48
Email info@oceanvillage.gi www.oceanvillage.gi

Gibraltar: Rounding Europa Point. Note the mosque behind the light
Graham Hutt

The 'gateway to the Mediterranean', with excellent facilities for yachts but very crowded

Gibraltar is a safe and convenient stopping point for yachts entering or leaving the Mediterranean, as well as being a duty-free port. All facilities are available for repairs and general maintenance, and both general and ship's stores of every kind can be obtained in Gibraltar or by air from England (for some items it may be cheaper, if more effort, to arrange for delivery from England marked 'For Yacht – in Transit' and therefore duty free, rather than to buy off the shelf once there). Both the pound sterling and the Gibraltar pound (at parity) are legal tender.

There are three marinas on the eastern side of the Bay of Gibraltar (known as the Bay of Algeciras to the Spanish). The existing Queensway Quay Marina, the new Ocean Village Marina that is to combine with the existing Marina Bay Marina, and a third marina in La Línea, Spain, across the border to the north (page 328). There has been something of a hiatus as new marina construction has taken place and the 7-deck cruise liner *Sunborn* sunk in position between Ocean Village Marina and Marina Bay. This has exacerbated the cronic shortage of available yacht berths in Gibraltar making it essential to book ahead.

A tour of the Rock itself is recommended, as is a visit to the museum, with displays of Gibraltar in prehistoric, Phoenician and Roman times. The WWII tunnels are testament to the most extraordinary feats of mining and engineering. Crossing the border into Spain is quick and easy on foot, though a passport should be carried. Making the crossing by car is another matter entirely. It is normal to queue in either direction, but while the wait to come in seldom exceeds 10 minutes it is not unusual to queue for an hour or more to leave – considerably longer during the rush hour. A phonecall ☎ 42777 will give the current outward waiting time. If telephoning from Spain, or by mobile phone in either country, include the Spanish access code ☎ 9567.

Approach

By day Gibraltar Rock, rising to 406m, is clearly visible except in fog, which is rare, though more frequent in summer, It is safe to enter the Bay of Gibraltar (Algeciras Bay) in almost any conditions but beware of squalls near the Rock once in the bay, particularly during strong easterlies, when strong downdraughts occur off the Rock. From the south and east, Europa point is prominent, with its lighthouse at the end. A short distance further up the point, the minaret of a new mosque will be observed. Strong currents and overfalls occur around the tip of the point when wind is against tide. From the west, Punta Carnero light lies at the southwest entrance to the bay, near an old whaling station. The coast is fringed with wrecks from all eras, many popular as dive sites – any vessel flying International Code Flag 'A' (white with a blue swallowtail) should be given a generous clearance. Yachts must also give way to naval and commercial vessels at all times.

By night The west side of the Rock is well illuminated by the town; and to the east by the bright red lights marking the radio antennas on the north face; which is itself illuminated by spotlights. This can be confusing even in good visibility and makes lights difficult to identify. The most conspicuous are likely to be those on the south mole's A head and north mole's D head. To the south is the lighthouse on Europa Point, easily seen from north-northeast clockwise to north-northwest, with a small red sector indicating the dangerous rocky shoreline to the west between Punta del Acebuche and Punta Carnero, which must be given a wide berth. If approaching in poor visibility beware the amount of traffic in the vicinity. From ⊕199 in the southeast part of the Bay a course of 012° for 1·5M leads to ⊕200 for approach to Queensway Quay, 007° for 2·5M to ⊕201 for approach to the Ocean Village Marina (incorporating Marina Bay Marina), and 008° for 3·0M to ⊕202 for the approach to La Línea Marina.

Gibraltar weather forecasts

Radio Gibraltar (GBC) and British Forces Radio (BFBS) broadcast local weather forecasts (see table below). The marinas post weather faxes on their notice boards daily. See also www.bbc.co.uk/weather/coast/pressure/ and http://meteonet.nl/aktueel/brackall.htm for five day forecasts. Sites www.sto-p.com/atol and www.accuweather.com give complete hour-by-hour predictions over 16 hours and general forecasts up to 15 days.

Tarifa Radio broadcasts area weather on Channel 16 at regular intervals, in Spanish and English.

Gibraltar weather forecasts

LT	BFBS 1			BFBS2	Gibraltar BC		
	Mon-Fri	Sat	Sun	Mon-Fri	Mon-Fri	Sat	Sun
0530					X	X	
0630					X	X	X
0730					X	X	X
0745	X						
0845	X	X	X				
0945		X	X				
1005	X						
1030					X		
1200				X			
1202		X	X				
1230					X	X	X
1602			X				
1605	X						

Also storm warnings on receipt		1438 AM
	93·5 FM 89·4 FM	91·3 FM
	97·8 FM 99·5 FM	92·6 FM
Includes high and low water times		100·5 FM

Entry formalities

Whereas in the past all yachts calling at Gibraltar first proceeded to the customs and immigration offices opposite Marina Bay, this no longer applies. Proceed to any marina where paper formalities are part of the check-in process carried out by marina staff.

Gibraltar, like the UK, is not party to the Shengen agreement, which has different visa requirements to

Queensway Quay (centre) with Coaling Island (right) and the military base (left) *Graham Hutt*

Spain. Check for latest information from the Gibraltar government website www.gibraltar.gov,gi or contact the immigration department ☏ +350 20046411 *Email* rgpimm@gibynex.gi.

Crew intending to remain ashore, or obtain work in Gibraltar should inform Immigration Authorities of their intention and supply an address.

Anchoring in the Bay

Anchorage is possible (although not encouraged) north of the runway in 4–6m sand, with good holding. As this area is British territory it is first necessary to clear Customs and Immigration, which may create a problem now that these are handled only by the Gibraltar marinas.

Otherwise, there continues to be considerable uncertainty as to what is allowed and what is not allowed concerning anchoring in the Bay. Sometimes the Spanish Guardia come around and clear out the yachts, telling them to go into the Alcaidesa marina. At other times they leave them alone. Most of the time, they are just taking notes of who is there for future reference. As these yachts are clearly in Spanish waters, there is a theoretical tax liability after six months if the owners are living aboard. This is of course in addition to VAT if unpaid. Most yachtsmen think that because they are not tied up in a marina, they are considered as being at sea. Not so according to the tax authorities!

For safety reasons yachts are prohibited from anchoring close to the runway or on the flight path anywhere west of the runway.

Queensway Quay Marina

Location 36°08'·1N 05°21'·3W

The Marina

This is the closest marina to Europa Point, but was reconstructed during 2005/2006 due to initial design faults which allowed unacceptable surging, with resulting damage to yachts. The Queensway Quay Development includes luxury apartments, a restaurant and many business enterprises around the marina. Queensway Quay Marina has the advantage of being some distance from the airport, with all the noise, and is close to the largest supermarket, Morrisons, and Main Street, which is also within walking distance. It provides 150 berths. Some of which will have been allocated to the owners of the houses built on the new 'island' that forms the western breakwater of the marina.

Entry formalities

Both marina and entry formalitles are now completed at the marina office.

Approach

The marina is approached through the main harbour via either of the two entrances, continuing towards the gap between Coaling Island and the new 'island' which forms the western breakwater of the marina. On passing through this gap the entrance lies immediately to starboard. The buildings overlooking the marina are floodlit.

Berthing

Visitors' berths are few and it's best to call ahead on VHF Ch 71 to ask if one is available. Mooring is stern, or bows-to, on floating pontoons. A limited number of deepwater berths varying from 3–7m in depth at LWS, with power points and metered water, are available along the southern wall of the marina. Berth at the reception pontoon on the east side of the new entrance on first arrival. The marina office is to be relocated to overlook the area but in the meantime is situated near the root of the north mole. Hours are 0830–2200 daily in summer. 0830–2100 in winter. During the renovations the marina was dredged to 4m throughout.

Facilities

Berth Services Every berth has access to a Service Module, with electricity, water, intercom and telephone.

Security Access to the floating pontoons is by coded lockable gates and security is excellent.

Car park By the Marina Control Centre (MCC).

Office facilities Available in the MCC include Fax and photocopying, book swap and restaurant.

Repairs Only available at Sheppard's ☎ +350 20076895, Fax +350 20071780.

Showers and WC Situated in the MCC. Facilities available for the disabled. Bath available for a charge. These amenities close 30 minutes earlier than the rest of the establishment.

Toilets For after-hours use can be found along the Main Quayside to the rear of the large anchor. Lock code available from Reception.

Laundry Incorporating a dry cleaners in the MCC. Others in the town.

Weather Daily reports are posted in the office. A weather station is on view at the MCC.

Transport Local buses from the bus station. No.3 bus to the frontier from Line Wall Road.

Ocean Village Marina

This marina complex is on the site of Sheppard's old piers, just south of Marina Bay Marina with which it is going to combine. With a depth of 4·5m and over 200 berths, Ocean Village Marina can accommodate most vessels including super yachts. Each berth has new facility points for water, power, telephone, fax and satellite TV. New shower and toilet facilities, including those for the disabled, are available at the pier office building. Ocean Village is a vibrant new waterfront area with a variety of international stores and a range of restaurants and bars to suit all tastes. The Leisure Island complex will feature a casino, nightclub, champagne bar and much more. An artist's impression of the development can be seen at www.oceanvillage.gi

Ship Hotel *Sunborn*

A huge 7-deck cruise liner, the *Sunborn*, which is a luxury hotel, has been moved into the 'slot' between the Ocean Village Marina and Marina Bay. The ship is a permanent fixture, being sunk in position alongside the casino. It has meant the removal of many yacht pontoons, greatly reducing the capacity for yachts in a country where there are no spare visitors' berths available in the summer months. Fortunately for the yachting community, the Alcaidesa Marina (see above) less than a mile away has plenty of room and is an attractive and cheaper alternative to Gibraltar.

Looking east-southeast over the Marina Bay (left) and Ocean Village Marinas.
The ship hotel *Sunborn* is positioned in the 'slot' between the two marinas

Looking eastwards, the entrance to Marina Bay is just S (to the right) of the airport runway. Note the restricted navigation zone off the end of the runway (shown on plan p.330)

The Rock from Marina Bay *Jane Russell*

Marina Bay

Location 36°08'·9N 05°21'·4W

The Marina

Just south of the runway, Marina Bay is an excellent location from which to visit Gibraltar or Spain if they have berths available. The ground tackle which fell into disrepair has been replaced and facilities are excellent. The marina can take over 200 yachts up to 70m or 4·5m draught. The nearby bars and restaurants along the quay and in Neptune House provide excellent food and a good social atmosphere, as well as providing protection form the east winds.

Approach

The marina is 0·5M east of the north mole, and is approached by rounding the north mole's northwest corner. At night a row of red lights at the end of the airport runway mark the north side of the channel. Note that yachts may not move in the vicinity while the runway lights are flashing, There is also a height restriction of 23m.

Berthing

Call the marina office on Ch 71 for berth allocation. Note: Depths in the marina are around 4·5m but some areas are less. Make sure the berthing master knows your draft to ensure the correct location in the marina. If staff are not around, berth alongside the office, towards the outer end of the main pier or find an empty mooring. Hours are 0820–2200 daily in summer, 0830–2030 in winter. Berthing is Mediterranean-style – bow or stern-to with a buoy and lazy-line provided to the pontoon.

Facilities

Water Available at every berth charged at 1p per litre.
Electricity Available at every berth charged at 15p/Kwh.
Repairs Mechanics can be brought to the yacht.
Showers and WC On ground floor under Pier Office building. Facilities for the handicapped.
Launderette In the marina.
Dentist Mr C. Linale, Neptune House Marina Bay.
Security Security guards 24hr ☎ +350 20040477.
Weather Daily bulletins are posted at the Pier Office, BFBS Radio ☎ +350 20053416.
Eating out Enjoy the relaxed atmosphere of the waterfront restaurants within the marina complexes or the many restaurants, pubs and fastfood houses in the town, particularly in Main Street. A full list may be obtained from the tourist board.
Transport The No. 9 bus from the frontier to the bus station stops in Winston Churchill Avenue in front of the tower blocks at the northern end of Glacis Road, but it is only a 10 minute walk to the bus station and city centre.

General facilities

Gas Camping gaz can only be obtained from Sheppard's (closes 1300 on Saturdays). It is not stocked by the fuel stations in Marina Bay. Otherwise gas is available from the 'New Harbours' commercial area ☎ +350 2007026.
Fuel Diesel (and water) is obtainable at the Shell or BP stations opposite Marina Bay. Shell ☎ +350 20048232, BP ☎ +350 20072261.

Provisions Morrisons supermarket is a short walk from Queensway Quay and not far from Marina Bay. It is on the No. 4 and 10 bus route (see below), fresh fruit and vegetables are best obtained from La Línea market, just across the border in Spain, on Wednesday mornings, Duty-free stores are available via Albor Ltd ☎/*Fax* +350 20073283, at Marina Bay – which doubles as a newsagent, bookshop and cybercafe – where almost anything in almost any quantity for a yacht in transit can be purchased.

Charts Available from the Gibraltar Chart Agency, Irish Town ☎ +350 20076293.

Chandlery Most items available at Sheppard's (temporarily at the old marina site ☎ +350 20077183 *Fax* +350 20042535 www.sheppard.gi which has the best range of yacht chandlery here. **However**, do be aware that with all the changes – including a move of the Sheppard's chandlery shop – several yachtsmen have complained that availability of 'just about anything' no longer applies. There are also smaller chandlers located at Marina Bay.

Repair facilities Sheppard's boatyard and repair facilities are currently reduced because of the closure of the yard for the Ocean Village development and move to new premises. However, they are operating a 40-tonne travel-hoist and crane and engineering facilities from temporary premises near Queensway Quay, (Coaling Island) ☎ +35020076895.

Engineers Sheppard's can handle light engineering, welding, engine servicing and repairs to most makes and are Volvo Penta agents. Also-Marine Maintenance Ltd ☎ +350 20078954 *Fax* +350 20074754 *Email* fred@gibnet.gi (Perkins and Yanmar) at Marina Bay, and Medmarine Ltd ☎ +350 20048888 *Fax* +350 20048889, (Yamaha) at Queensway Quay, Tempco Marine Engineering ☎ +350 20074657 *Fax* 2007617, specialise in refrigeration.

Electronics and radio repairs Sheppard's workshops (as above) or Electromed ☎ +350 20077077 *Fax* +350 20072051 *email* mail@electro-med.com www.eletro-med.com at Queensway Quay, who can supply and repair equipment from most major manufacturers.

Sailmaker/sail repairs Sail makers, ☎ +350 20041469 in South Pavilion Road, who also handle general canvaswork and upholstery. Alternatively Magnusson Sails ☎/*Fax* +350 952 791241, about 35 miles away in Estepona, who may be willing to deliver/collect. Canvas work and sprayhood (but not true sailmaking) is also undertaken by ME Balloqui & Sons ☎ +350 20078105, *Fax* +350 20042510, at 3941 City Mill Lane.

Rigging Sheppard's workshops, as above.

Liferaft servicing GV Undery & Son +350 20073107 *Fax* +350 20046489 *Email* compass@gibtelecom.net (who are also compass adjusters). Note: Currently with the old Sheppard's boatyard and repair facilities in a temporary location, facilities in Gibraltar are limited. A crane can lift yachts, which are then placed on the hard and moved by travel lift. The process is expensive and not suited to larger displacement yachts. The plan to move the boatyard and haul-out facility to the N side of the runway has been abandoned. The nearest boatyard and travel hoist is currently Sotogrande Marina, 10M N of Gibraltar. Other possibilities for larger vessels are the old Naval shipyards S of Queensway quay.

Money The UK Pound Sterling is legal tender, along with the Gibraltar pound and of equal value, but only in Gibraltar. Beware of trying to exchange excess Gibraltar currency in the UK, as it is worth very little there. Euros can also be used in most shops but not in the Post Office where only sterling is accepted. There are several Bureaux de Change agencies in Main Street. Visa, Switch, American Express, Mastercard etc, are accepted almost everywhere, though not the post office and some government offices. ATMs at Barclays Bank in Main Street and Morrisons supermarket.

Banks Gibraltar has well established banking services for both offshore and local customers with a full range of international banks, including several UK institutions, Banking hours are generally between 0900–1530 Monday to Friday.

Crossing the Border Crossing the border into Spain is quick and easy on foot but another matter by car. In both cases a passport must be carried. By car, it is normal to queue in either direction, but while the queue to come into Gibraltar seldom exceeds ten minutes, it is not unusual to queue for up to an hour to leave during rush hour. Long queues also result when planes take off and land. There is a very reasonably priced airport carpark opposite the airport, near the border which charges about 50p an hour short term and £4 for 24 hour parking.

International travel Gibraltar airport is located close to the frontier for daily flights to the UK and onward connections ☎ +350 20073026. Málaga airport is a little an over an hour's drive up the coast (A7 or AP7 *peaje* toll road) for more destinations. Taxis are expensive.

Approaching the Rock from the northeast *Henry Buchanan*

Lords of all they survey! Do not approach the Barbary apes too closely *David Russell*

Appendix

I. Charts and books

Obtaining charts

Up-to-date information on British Admiralty chart coverage for North Africa is available at
www.ukho.gov.uk
where full details of chart schemes, titles and scales are given.

The catalogue of Spanish charts may be seen at
www.armada.mde.es

Up-to-date lists of sales agents for Portugal and IHM (Spain) are available on the websites.

The catalogue of Portuguese charts may be seen at
www.hidrografico.pt

Imray Laurie Norie and Wilson are sales agents for UKHO charts and publications which may be ordered through **www.imray.com**

Imrays are able to help with enquiries and supply Spanish and Portuguese charts.

Chart agents

Before departure

British Admiralty and Spanish charts from
Imray Laurie Norie & Wilson Ltd,
Wych House, The Broadway, St Ives,
Cambs PE27 5BT
℡ 01480 462114, *Fax* 01480 496109
www.imray.com.
However in the case of Spanish charts, stocks held are limited and it may take some time to fill an order. It may be simpler to order directly with a credit card from
Instituto Hidrográfico de la Marina,
Pl. San Severiano, 3, DP 11007 Cádiz
℡ (956) 59 94 12, *Fax* (956) 25 85 48

Gibraltar

Gibraltar Chart Agency,
4th Floor, Leon House I
℡ +350-200-76293
Email gibchartag@gibtelecom.net
www.gibraltarchartagency.com

Spain (Algeciras)

SUISCA SL
Avda. Blas Infante, Centro Blas Local 1, 11201
Algeciras, Cádiz
℡ +34 902 220007 *Fax* +34 902 220 008
Email barcelona@suiscasl.com
www.suiscasl.com

Portugal

J. Garraio & C.ª, Lda
Avenida 24 de Julho, 2, 1200-478 Lisboa,
Portugal
℡ +351 213473081, *Fax* +351 213428950
www.jgarraio.pt

Imray charts

Chart	Title	Scale
C18	**Western Approaches to the English Channel and Biscay** WGS 84	1:1,000,000
C19	**Portuguese Coast Passage Chart Cabo Finisterre to Gibraltar** WGS 84 *Plans* Bayona, Viana do Castelo, Figueira da Foz, Approaches to Lisbon, Lagos, Bahía de Cádiz, Strait of Gibraltar, Gibraltar	758,800
C48	**La Coruña to Porto** WGS 84 *Plans* Ría de Vivero, Ría de Cedeira, Rías de Ares and Betanzos, La Coruña, Ría de Camariñas, Ríia de Muros, Ría de Arousa Ría de Vigo, Viana do Castelo, Rías de Corme and Lage, Ría de Pontevedra, Póvoa de Varzim, Leixões	1:350,000
C49	**Ría de Aveiro to Sines** WGS 84 *Plans* Figuera da Foz, Nazaré, Cascais, Lisboa, Sines, Porto de Peniche, Setúbal, Rio Sado, Sesimbra	1:350,000
C50	**Sines to Gibraltar** WGS 84 *Plans* Sines, Portimão, Vilamoura, Vila Real de St António, Lagos, Isla Christina, Mazagón, Chipiona, Puerto Sherry, Sancti-Petri, Barbate, Tarifa, Rota, Bahía de Cadiz, Gibraltar, Strait of Gibraltar	1:350,000
M10	**Western Mediterranean – Gibraltar to the Ionian Sea** WGS 84 WGS 84	1:2,750,000
M11	**Mediterranean Spain – Gibraltar to Cabo de Gata & Morocco** WGS 84 *Plans* Strait of Gibraltar, Gibraltar, Ceuta, Almeria, Estepona, Puerto de Almerimar	1:440,000

II. Waypoints

Waypoints are listed by part sections. Users are reminded that they are offered as an aid to navigation. Whilst every effort has been made to ensure their accuracy none has been proved at sea, no assumption may be made that direct passage is possible between any two (unless the text specifically states that it may) and all should be used in conjunction with visual or other observation.

Positions

Although a few official charts of this area have yet to be converted from Datum ED50, skippers should note that all positions in this book are to WGS84. All were derived using C-Map electronic charts and Admiralty charts, and in some cases handheld GPS ashore.

III. Useful addresses

Spanish embassies and consulates

London (Embassy) 39 Chesham Place, London SW1X 8SB
 www.spain.embassyhomepage.com
  ☎ +4420 7235 5555 - *Fax* +4420 7259 5392
London (Consulate) 20 Draycott Place
 London SW3 2RZ. ☎ 020 7589 8989
 Fax 020 7581 7888
Manchester (Consulate) Brook House,
 64-72 Spring Gardens, Manchester M2 2BQ
  ☎ +44907 018 0023
Edinburgh (Consulate) 57 Castle Street
 Edinburgh, EH2 3HT ☎ +44131 220 1843
Washington DC (Embassy) 2375 Pennsylvania Ave,
 NW Washington DC 20037
  ☎ +1 202 452 0100 & +1 202 728 2340
 Fax +1 202 833 56 70
 Email emb.washington@maec.es
New York (Consulate) 150 East 58th St, 30th Floor
 NY 10155, New York, USA
  ☎ +1 212 355 40480 *Fax* +1 212 644 3751
 Email cog.nuevayork@maec.es

Portuguese embassies

London 11 Belgrave Square, London SW1X 8PP
  ☎ +4420 7235531 *Fax* +4420 72350739
 Email londres@mne.pt
 www.portuguese-embassy.co.uk
Washington DC 2310 2012 Massachusetts Ave
 NW Washington DC 20036
  ☎ +1 202 328 8610
 Email embassyportugal-us.org

British and American embassies and consulates

In Spain
British Embassy Madrid Torre Espacio, Paseo de la
 Castellana 259D 28046 Madrid, Spain
  *Email (*Consular enquiries): Info.consulate@fco.gov.uk
  ☎ +34 917 146 300 *Fax* +34 917 146 301
British Consulate General Madrid Torre Espacio,
 Paseo de la Castellana 259D, 28046 Madrid
  ☎ +34 91 334 2194 *Fax* +34 91 714 6401
 Email enquiries.madrid@fco.gov.uk
Embassy of the United States Spain
 Serrano 75 28006 Madrid, Spain
  ☎ +34 91 587 2200 *Fax* +34 91 587 2303
United States Consulate General Barcelona Paseo Reina
 Elisenda de Montcada, 23 08034 Barcelona, España
  ☎ +34 93 280 22 27 *Fax* +34 93 280 61 75
 Email barcelonaacs@state.gov

In Portugal
British Embassy Lisbon Rua de São Bernardo 33,
 1249-082 Lisbon , Portugal
 Email ppa.lisbon@fco.gov.uk
  ☎ +351 21 392 40 00 *Fax* +351 21 392 40 21
 portugal.consulate@fco.gov.uk
British Consulate Lisbon Rua de São Bernardo 33,
 1249-082 Lisboa, Portugal
 Email portugal.consulate@fco.gov.uk
  ☎ 808 20 35 37 *(if calling from Portugal)*
  ☎ +351 21 392 4082 *(if calling from overseas)*
 Fax +351 21 392 41 53
United States Embassy Lisbon Avenida das Forças
 Armadas, 1600-081 Lisboa
 or Apartado 43033 1601-301 Lisboa
  ☎ + 351-21-727-3300 or +351-21-094-2000
 Fax +351-21-726-9109
 Email lisbonweb@state.gov

Spanish national tourist offices

London 6th Floor 64 North Row, London W1K 7DE
  ☎ +442073172011 *Fax* +44 2073172048
 www.spain.info/en_gb/
New York 60 East 42nd Street-Suite 5300 (53rd Floor),
 New York NY 10165-0039
 www.spain.info/en_us

Portuguese national tourist offices

London 11, Belgrave Square, London, SW1X 8PP
  ☎ 020 7201 6666 *Fax* 020 7201 6633
 Email tourism.london@portugalglobal.pt
 www.visitportugal.com
New York 590 Fifth Avenue, 4th Floor, New York,
 NY 10036-4704
  ☎ +1 212 354 4403 *Fax* +1 212 764 6137

IV. Regulations, tax and VAT

(The information below should not be considered definitive. Skippers of non-VAT paid boats and those planning to stay for more than 183 days in a years are strongly advised to verify the regulations which will be applicable to them.)

Personal documentation

Spain – Currently EU nationals – including UK citizens – may visit for up to 90 days, for which a national identity card or passport is required but no visa. American, Canadian and New Zealand citizens may also stay for up to 90 days without a visa, though Australians need one for more than 30 days. EU citizens wishing to remain in Spain may apply for a *permiso de residencia* once in the country; non-EU nationals can apply for a single 90-day extension, or otherwise obtain a long-term visa from a Spanish embassy or consulate before leaving home. The website www.graysworld.co.uk/spanish-property/resident-tourist provides advice on this matter.

Certificate of competence
1. Given below is a transcription of a statement made by the Counsellor for Transport at the Spanish Embassy, London in March 1996. It is directed towards citizens of the UK but doubtless the principles apply to other EU citizens. One implication is that in a particular circumstance (paragraph 2a below) a UK citizen does not need a Certificate of Competence during the first 90 days of his visit.
2. a. British citizens visiting Spain in charge of a UK registered pleasure boat flying the UK flag need only fulfil UK law.

b. British citizens visiting Spain in charge of a Spanish registered pleasure boat flying the Spanish flag have one of two options:

i. To obtain a Certificate of Competence issued by the Spanish authorities. See *Normas reguladore para la obtención de titulos para el gobierno de embarcaciones de recreo* issued by the Ministerio de Obras Publicas, Transportes y Medio Ambiente.

ii. To have the Spanish equivalent of a UK certificate issued. The following equivalencies are used by the Spanish Maritime Administration:
Yachtmaster Ocean *Capitan de Yate*
Yachtmaster Offshore *Patron de Yate de altura*
Coastal Skipper *Patron de Yate*
Day Skipper *Patron de Yate embarcaciones de recreo*
Helmsman Overseas* *Patron de embarcaciones de recreo restringido a motor*

*The Spanish authorities have been informed that this certificate has been replaced by the International Certificate of Competence.

3. The catch to para 2(a) above is that, in common with other EU citizens, after 90 days a UK citizen is technically no longer a visitor, must apply for a *permiso de residencia* and must equip his boat to Spanish rules and licensing requirements.

In practice the requirement to apply for a *permiso de residencia* does not appear to be enforced in the case of cruising yachtsmen who live aboard rather than ashore and are frequently on the move. By the same token, the requirement for a British skipper in charge of a UK registered pleasure boat flying the UK flag to carry a Certificate of Competence after their first 90 days in Spanish waters also appears to be waived. Many yachtsmen have reported cruising Spanish waters for extended periods with no documentation beyond that normally carried in the UK.

4. The RYA suggests the following technique to obtain an equivalent Spanish certificate:

a. Obtain two photocopies of your passport
b. Have them notarised by a Spanish notary
c. Obtain a copy of the UK Certificate of Competence and send it to the Consular Department, The Foreign and Commonwealth Office, Clive House, Petty France, London SW1H 9DH, with a request that it be stamped with the Hague Stamp (this apparently validates the document). The FCO will probably charge a fee so it would be best to call the office first ✆ 020 7270 3000.
d. Have the stamped copy notarized by a UK notary.
e. Send the lot to the Spanish Merchant Marine for the issue of the Spanish equivalent.

It may be both quicker and easier to take the Spanish examination.

Tax

Although the tax rules appear not to be applied evenly across Spain the following is offered as general advice to help individuals consider whether to seek more formal advice regarding their particular situation. The Spanish operate a self assessment system and can reclaim tax back for five years. Three types of taxes may apply specifically to yacht owners:

Tarifa G-5 This is broadly a port tax levied to help maintain the port. Its application appears to vary from harbour to harbour and province to province. It is likely to form part of a marina fee for short stays. If staying for long periods or over-wintering it would be wise to ensure that a contract with the marina is inclusive of all taxes,

Wealth tax This is a national tax but may be applied differently from region to region. A person staying in Spain for less than 6 months is not liable to wealth tax. However, if the 183 day limit is exceeded the rules of residency may apply and trigger a demand for the tax. It is the individual's time in Spain which is relevant, not the location of the boat.

Other taxes If staying beyond 183 days the full Spanish Legislation and tax rules apply – and could include such matters as income tax, property tax, local town tax.

Portugal Currently EU nationals need only a national identity card or passport to enter Portugal and can then stay indefinitely. American and Canadian citizens can remain for up to 60 days without a visa, Australians and New Zealanders for up to 90 days. Extensions are issued by the Sevico de Estrangeiros which has a branch in most major towns, or failing that by the local police. At least one week's notice is required.

VAT and temporary import

A boat registered in the EU and on which VAT has been paid in an EU country, or which was launched before 1 January 1985 and is therefore exempt on the grounds of age (and has the documents to prove it), can stay indefinitely in any other EU country without further VAT liability.

The time limit for which relief from customs duty and VAT is available to non-EU registered yachts visiting the EU is 18 months. The period for which a yacht must remain outside the EU before starting another 18 month period is not specified. Those affected are recommended to check current regulations which may be found on HM Customs and Excise website www.hmce.gov.uk Search under the words 'Pleasure craft'.

Spain A VAT paid (exempt) yacht may normally remain in the country almost indefinitely provided a '*Permiso Aduanero*' is first obtained, but may not be used commercially (i.e. for chartering).

Portugal There is no limitation on length of stay for a VAT paid or exempt yacht. An annual tax is levied on all yachts kept for long periods (over 183 days) in Portuguese waters irrespective of their VAT status, see page 122.

Gibraltar As Gibraltar is not a part of the EU, VAT does not apply.

V. Portugal and Andalucía on the net

Portugal

www.algarvenet.com – covers all of southern Portugal (though slightly dated in places) with pages for the Algarve Resident and Região Sul newspapers (the latter with English translation).

www.ana-aeroportos.pt – ANA Aeroportos de Portugal SA runs Portugal's three mainland airports. Daily arrival / departure times, and much more.

www.cp.pt – website of Comboios de Portugal (the national railway system), in Portuguese and English. Routes, timetables, fares and online booking in an impressively user-friendly layout.

www.flytap.com – website of the national airline, TAP Portugal. In most major languages with schedules, fares and online booking. Fast and user-friendly.

www.hidrografico.pt – website of the Portuguese Hydrographic Institute, with full chart catalogue. In

Portuguese only, but easy enough to follow. No online sales, but links to two Lisbon chart agents

www.portugal.org – website of ICEP (Investment, Trade and Tourism Portugal) but a long way from the dry-as-dust site which might be expected. Vast amounts of useful information in several languages including English plus dozens (possibly hundreds) of relevant links. A great place to start.

www.portugal-info.net – a well-organised site carrying information on and/or links to pretty well every town of any size in the entire country. Useful maps, current weather conditions, telephone numbers etc. English language only.

www.portugalvirtual.pt – another general site worth investigating. A little more commercially-orientated than some, but if you want a plan of the Lisbon metro or opening times for the Palácio Nacional de Ajuda, it's all here. In Portuguese and English.

www.the-news.net – online edition of The Portugal News, an English-language national daily paper.

www.travel-images.com – thousands of downloadable pictures of the entire world, including Portugal and Spain, but with little accompanying text. Check the Utilities section for some quirky lists.

www.visitportugal.com – Portugal's official tourism website, in six languages including English. Well constructed and illustrated, and updated regularly with details of forthcoming events. Several short video clips. Recommended.

Andalucia

www.andalucia.com – commercial (and some might say superficial) site mainly slanted towards the Mediterranean part of the province.

www.andalucia.org – official website of the Andalucían Tourist Office, covering all the usual aspects plus (via the Sports Activities button) an unusually full and accurate list of the province's marinas and yacht harbours. In good English, with a useful search facility.

www.andalucia2.com – a very busy site with lots of facts, figures and useful phone numbers, but lacking any great appeal.

www.armada.mde.es – website of the Spanish Hydrographic Institute, with full chart catalogue as well as Avisos a los Navegants (Notices to Mariners). In Spanish only, but relatively easy to follow.

www.puertosdeandalucia.es – website of the the Agencia Pública de Puertos de Andalucía which runs the majority of marinas in Andalucía. Other, non-APPA marinas are also included. In Spanish and English, though not all pages are fully translated.

www.iberia.com – the Iberia website, in numerous languages (the United Kingdom is Reino Unido) and with all the usual bells and whistles.

www.idealspain.com – perhaps the most appealing of the Andalucían tourist sites, with maps and well-illustrated notes about many places of interest. Includes an image library and message board. English only.

www.renfe.es – fast but slightly forbidding site of RENFE, the Spanish rail network, in four languages including English.

VI. Glossary

A more complete glossary is given in the *Yachtsman's Ten Language Dictionary* compiled by Barbara Webb and Michael Manton with the Cruising Association (Adlard Coles Nautical). Terms related to meteorology and sea state follow at the end of each section.

General and chartwork terms

English	Spanish	Portuguese
anchor, to	fondear	fundear
anchorage	fondeadero, ancladero	fundeadouro, ancoradouro
basin, dock	dársena	doca
bay	bahía, ensenada	baía, enseada
beach	playa	praia
beacon	baliza	baliza
beam	manga	largura, boca
berth	atracar	atracar
black	negro	preto
blue	azul	azul
boatbuilder	astillero	estaleiro
bottled gas	cilindro de gas, carga de gas	cilindro de gás, bilha de gás
breakwater	rompeolas, muelle	quebra-mar, molhe
buoy	boya	bóia
bus	autobús	autocarro
cape	cabo	cabo
car hire	aquilar coche	alugar automóvel
chandlery (shop)	efectos navales, apetrachamento	fornecedor de barcos, aprestos
channel	canal	canal
charts	cartas náuticas	cartas hidrográficas
church	iglesia	igreja
crane	grua	guindaste
creek	estero	esteiro
Customs	Aduana	Alfândega
deep	profundo	profundo
depth	sonda, profundidad	profundidade
diesel	gasoil	gasoleo
draught	calado	calado
dredged	dragado	dragado
dyke, pier	dique	dique
east	este	este
eastern	levante, oriental	levante, do este
electricity	electricidad	electricidade
engineer, mechanic	ingeniero, mecánico	engenheiro, técnico
entrance	boca, entrada	bôca, entrada
factory	fábrica	fábrica
foul, dirty	sucio	sujo
gravel	cascajo	burgau
green	verde	verde
harbourmaster	diretor do porto	capitán de puerto
height, clearance	altura	altura
high tide	pleamar, marea alta	preia-mar, maré alta
high	alto/a	alto/a
ice	hielo	gelo
inlet, cove	ensenada	enseada
island	isla	ilha, ilhéu
islet, skerry	islote	ilhota
isthmus	istmo	istmo
jetty, pier	malecón	quebra-mar

English	Spanish	Portuguese
knots	nudos	nós
lake	lago	lago
laundry,	lavandería,	lavanderia,
launderette	automática	automática
leading line, transit	enfilación	enfiamento
leeward	sotavento	sotavento
length overall	eslora total	comprimento
lighthouse	faro	farol
lock	esclusa	esclusa
low tide	bajamar,	baixa-mar,
	marea baja	maré baixa
mailing address	dirección de	endereço para
	correo	correio
marina,	puerto deportivo,	porto desportivo,
yacht harbour	dársena de yates	doca de recreio
medical services	servicios	serviços médicas
	médiocos	
mud	fango	lôdo
mussel rafts	viveros	viveiros
narrows	estrecho	estreito
north	norte	norte
orange	anaranjado	alaranjado
owner	propietario	propietário
paraffin	parafina	petróleo para
		iluminãçao
petrol	gasolina	gasolina
pier, quay, dock	muelle	molhe
point	punta	ponta
pontoon	pantalán	pontão
port (side)	babor	bombordo
Port of Registry	Puerto de	Porto de Registo
	Matrícula	
port office	capitanía	capitania
post office	oficina de correos	agência do
		correio
quay	muelle	molhe, cais
ramp	rampa	rampa
range (tidal)	repunte	amplitude
red	rojo	vermelho
reef	arrecife	recife
reef, spit	restinga	restinga
registration number	matricula	número registo
repairs	reparacións	reparações
rock, stone	roca, piedra	laxe, pedra
root (eg. of mole)	raíz	raiz
sailing boat	barca de vela	barco à vela
sailmaker,	velero,	veleiro,
sail repairs	reparacións velas	reparações velas
saltpans	salinas	salinas
sand	arena	areia
sea	mar	mar
seal, to	precintar	fechar
shoal, low	bajo	baixo
shops	tiendas, almacéns	lojas
shore, edge	orilla	margem
showers (washing)	duchas	duches
slab, flat rock	laja	laje
slack water,	repunte	águas paradas
tidal stand		
slipway	varadero	rampa
small	pequeño	pequeno
south	sur	sul
southern	meridional	do sul
starboard	estribor	estibordo
strait	estrecho	estreito
supermarket	supermercado	supermercado
tower	torre	tôrre
travel-lift	grua giratoria,	e pórtico, pórtico

English	Spanish	Portuguese
pórtico elevador	elevador, içar	
water (drinking)	agua potable	água potável
weather forecast	previsión/boletin	previsão de
	metereológico	tempo, boletim
		meteorológico
weed	alga	alga
weight	peso	pêso
west	oeste	oeste
western	occidental	do oeste
white	blanco	branco
windward	barlovento	barlavento
works (building)	obras	obras
yacht (sailing)	barca de vela	barco à vela
yacht club	club náutico	clube náutico,
		clube naval
yellow	amarillo	amarelo

Meteorology and sea state

English	Spanish	Portuguese
calm	calma	calma
(Force 0, 0–1kns)		
light airs	ventolina	aragem
(Force 1, 1–3kns)		
light breeze	flojito	vento fraco, brisa
(Force 2, 4–6kns)		
gentle breeze	flojo	vento bonançoso,
(Force 3, 7–10kns)		brisa suave
moderate breeze	bonancible	vento moderado,
(Force 4, 11–16kns)		brisa moderado
fresh breeze	fresquito	vento fresco,
(Force 5, 17–21kns)		brisa fresca
strong breeze	fresco	vento muito
(Force 6, 22–27kns)		fresco,
		brisa forte
near gale	frescachón	vento forte,
(Force 7, 28–33kns)	ventania moderada	
gale	duro	vento muito
(Force 8, 34–40kns)		forte,
		ventania fresca
severe gale	muy duro	vento
(Force 9, 41–47kns)		tempestuoso,
		ventania forte
storm	temporal	temporal,
(Force 10, 48–55kns)		ventania total
violent storm	borrasca,	temporal
(Force 11, 56–63kns)	tempestad	desfieto,
		tempestade
hurricane	huracán	furacão, ciclone
(Force 12, +64kns)		
breakers	rompientes	arrebentação
cloudy	nubloso	nublado
depression (low)	depresión	depressão
fog	niebla	nevoeiro
gust	racha	rajada
hail	granizada	saraiva
mist	neblina	neblina
overfalls, tide race	escarceos	bailadeiras
rain	lluvia	chuva
ridge (high)	dorsal	crista
rough sea	mar gruesa	mar bravo
short, steep sea	mar corta	mar cavado
shower	aguacero	aguaceiro
slight sea	marejadilla	mar chão
squall	turbonada	borrasca
swell	mar de leva	ondulação
thunderstorm	tempestad	trovoada

Appendix

General and chartwork terms

Spanish	English	Portuguese
Aduana	Customs	Alfândega
agua potable	water (drinking)	água potável
alga	weed	alga
almacéns	shops	lojas
alto/a	high	alto/a
altura	height, clearance	altura
amarillo	yellow	amarelo
anaranjado	orange	alaranjado
ancladero	anchorage	fundeadouro, ancoradouro
apetrachamento	chandlery (shop)	fornecedore de barcos, aprestos
aquilar coche	car hire	alugar automóvel
arena	sand	areia
arrecife	reef	recife
astillero	boatbuilder	estaleiro
atracar	berth	atracar
autobús	bus	autocarro
azul	blue	azul
babor	port (side)	bombordo
bahía	bay	baía, enseada
bajamar	low tide	baixa-mar, maré baixa
bajo	shoal, low	baixo
baliza	beacon	baliza
barca de vela	sailing boat, yacht	barco à vela
barlovento	windward	barlavento
blanco	white	branco
boca	entrance	bôca, entrada
boya	buoy	bóia
cabo	cape	cabo
calado	draught	calado
canal	channel	canal
capitanía	port office	capitania
carga de gas	bottled gas	cilindro de gás, bilha de gás
cartas náuticas	charts	cartas hidrográficas
cascajo	gravel	burgau
cilindro de gas	bottled gas	cilindro de gás, bilha de gás
club náutico	yacht club	clube náutico, clube naval
dársena de yates	marina, yacht harbour	porto desportivo, doca de recreio
dársena	basin, dock	doca
dique	dyke, pier	dique
dirección de correo	mailing address	endereço para correio
diretor do porto	harbourmaster	capitán de puerto
dragado	dredged	dragado
duchas	showers (washing)	duches
efectos navales	chandlery (shop)	fornecedore de barcos, aprestos
electricidad	electricity	electricidade
enfilación	leading line, transit	enfiamento
ensenada	bay, inlet, cove	baía, enseada
entrada	entrance	bôca, entrada
esclusa	lock	esclusa
eslora total	length overall	comprimento
este	east	este
estero	creek	esteiro
estrecho	narrows, strait	estreito
estribor	starboard	estibordo
fábrica	factory	fábrica
fango	mud	lôdo
faro	lighthouse	farol
fondeadero	anchorage	fundeadouro, ancoradouro
fondear	anchor, to	fundear
gasoil	diesel	gasoleo
gasolina	petrol	gasolina
grua giratoria	travel-lift	e pórtico, pórtico elevador, içar
grua	crane	guindaste
hielo	ice	gelo
iglesia	church	igreja
ingeniero, mecánico	engineer, mechanic	engenheiro, técnico
isla	island	ilha, ilhéu
islote	islet, skerry	ilhota
istmo	isthmus	istmo
lago	lake	lago
laja	slab, flat rock	laje
lavandería, l. automática	laundry, launderette	lavanderia, l.automática
levante	eastern	levante, do este
malecón	jetty, pier	quebra-mar
manga	beam	largura, boca
mar	sea	mar
marea alta	high tide	preia-mar, maré alta
marea baja	low tide	baixa-mar, maré baixa
matricula	registration number	número registo
meridional	southern	do sul
muelle	breakwater, pier,	quebra-mar,
molhe,	quay, dock	cais
negro	black	preto
norte	north	norte
nudos	knots	nós
obras	works (building)	obras
occidental	western	do oeste
oeste	west	oeste
oficina de correos	post office	agência do correio
oriental	eastern	levante, do este
orilla	shore, edge	margem
pantalán	pontoon	pontáo
parafina	paraffin	petróleo para iluminaçao
pequeño	small	pequeno
peso	weight	pêso
piedra	rock, stone	pedra
playa	beach	praia
pleamar	high tide	preia-mar, maré alta
pórtico elevador	travel-lift	e pórtico, pórtico elevador, içar
precintar	seal, to	fechar
previsión/boletin metereológico	weather forecast	previsão de tempo, boletim meteorológico
profundidad	depth	profundidade
profundo	deep	profundo
propietario	owner	propietário
Puerto de Matrícula	Port of Registry	Porto de Registo
puerto deportivo	marina, yacht harbour	porto desportivo, doca de recreio

Spanish	English	Portuguese
punta	point	ponta
raíz	root (eg. of mole)	raiz
rampa	ramp	rampa
reparacións	repairs	reparações
repunte	tidal range, stand, slack water	águas paradas, amplitude
restinga	reef, spit	restinga
roca	rock	laxe
rojo	red	vermelho
rompeolas	breakwater	quebra-mar, molhe
salinas	saltpans	salinas
servicios médicos	medical services	serviços médicas
sonda	depth	profundidade
sotavento	leeward	sotavento
sucio	foul, dirty	sujo
supermercado	supermarket	supermercado
sur	south	sul
tiendas	shops	lojas
torre	tower	tôrre
varadero	slipway	rampa
velero, reparacións velas	sailmaker, sail repairs	veleiro, reparações velas
verde	green	verde
viveros	mussel rafts	viveiros

Meteorology and sea state

Spanish	English	Portuguese
calma	calm (Force 0, 0–1kns)	calma
ventolina	light airs (Force 1, 1–3kns)	aragem
flojito	light breeze (Force 2, 4–6kns)	vento fraco, brisa
flojo	gentle breeze (Force 3, 7–10kns)	vento bonançoso, brisa suave
bonancible	moderate breeze (Force 4, 11–16kns)	vento moderado, brisa moderado
fresquito	fresh breeze (Force 5, 17–21kns)	vento frêsco, brisa fresca
frêsco	strong breeze (Force 6, 22–27kns)	vento muito fresco, brisa forte
frescachón	near gale (Force 7, 28–33kns)	vento forte, ventania moderada
duro	gale (Force 8, 34–40kns)	vento muito forte, ventania fresca
muy duro	severe gale (Force 9, 41–47kns)	vento tempestuoso, ventania forte
temporal	storm (Force 10, 48–55kns)	temporal, ventania total
borrasca, tempestad	violent storm (Force 11, 56–63kns)	temporal desfieto, tempestade
huracán	hurricane (Force 12, 64+kns)	furacão, ciclone
aguacero	shower	aguaceiro
depresión	depression (low)	depressão
dorsal	ridge (high)	crista
escarceos	overfalls, tiderace	bailadeiras
granizada	hail	saraiva
lluvia	rain	chuva
mar corta	short, steep sea	mar cavado
mar de leva	swell	ondulação
mar gruesa	rough sea	mar bravo
marejadilla	slight sea	mar chão
neblina	mist	neblina

Spanish	English	Portuguese
niebla	fog	nevoeiro
nubloso	cloudy	nublado
racha	gust	rajada
rompientes	breakers	arrebentação
tempestad	thunderstorm	trovoada
turbonada	squall	borrasca

General and chartwork terms

Portuguese	English	Spanish
agência do correio	post office	oficina de correos
água potável	water (drinking)	agua potable
águas paradas, amplitude	tidal range, stand, slack water	repunte, repute
alaranjado	orange	anaranjado
alfândega	customs	aduana
alga	weed	alga
alto/a	high	alto/a
altura	height, clearance	altura
alugar automóvel	car hire	aquilar coche
amarelo	yellow	amarillo
areia	sand	arena
atracar	berth	atracar
autocarro	bus	autobús
azul	blue	azul
baía, enseada	bay, inlet, cove	bahía, ensenada
baixa-mar, maré baixa	low tide	bajamar, marea baja
baixo	shoal, low	bajo
baliza	beacon	baliza
barco à vela	sailing boat, yacht	barca de vela
barlavento	windward	barlovento
bôca, entrada	entrance	boca, entrada
bóia	buoy	boya
bombordo	port (side)	babor
branco	white	blanco
burgau	gravel	cascajo
cabo	cape	cabo
calado	draught	calado
canal	channel	canal
capitán de puerto	harbourmaster	diretor do porto
capitania	port office	capitanía
cartas hidrográficas	charts	cartas náuticas
cilindro de gás, bilha de gás	bottled gas	carga de gas, cilindro de gas
clube náutico, clube naval	yacht club	club náutico
comprimento	length overall	eslora total
dique	dyke, pier	dique
do oeste	western	occidental
do sul	southern	meridional
doca	basin, dock	dársena
dragado	dredged	dragado
duches	showers (washing)	duchas
e pórtico, pórtico elevador, içar	travel-lift	grua giratoria, pórtico elevador
electricidade	electricity	electricidad
endereço para correio	mailing address	dirección de correio
enfiamento	leading line, transit	enfilación
engenheiro, técnico	engineer, mechanic	ingeniero, mecánico
esclusa	lock	esclusa
estaleiro	boatbuilder	astillero

Appendix

Portuguese	English	Spanish
este	east	este
esteiro	creek	estero
estibordo	starboard	estribor
estreito	narrows, strait	estrecho
fábrica	factory	fábrica
farol	lighthouse	faro
fechar	seal, to	precintar
fornecedore de barcos, aprestos	chandlery (shop)	apetrachamento, efectos navales
fundeadouro, ancoradouro	anchorage	fondeadero, ancladero
fundear	anchor, to	fondear
gasoleo	diesel	gasoil
gasolina	petrol	gasolina
gelo	ice	hielo
guindaste	crane	grua
igreja	church	iglesia
ilha, ilhéu	island	isla
ilhota	islet, skerry	islote
istmo	isthmus	istmo
lago	lake	lago
laje	slab, flat rock	laja
largura, boca	beam	manga
lavanderia, l. automática	laundry, launderette	lavandería, l. automática
laxe	rock	roca
levante, do este	eastern	levante, oriental
lôdo	mud	fango
lojas	shops	almacéns, tiendas
mar	sea	mar
margem	shore, edge	orilla
norte	north	norte
nós	knots	nudos
número registo	registration number	matricula
obras	works (building)	obras
oeste	west	oeste
pedra	rock, stone	piedra
pequeno	small	pequeño
pêso	weight	peso
petróleo para iluminãçao	paraffin	parafina
ponta	point	punta
pontáo	pontoon	pantalán
Porto de Registo	Port of Registry	Puerto de Matrícula
porto desportivo, doca de recreio	marina, yacht harbour	puerto deportivo, dársena de yates
praia	beach	playa
preia-mar, maré alta	high tide	pleamar, marea alta
preto	black	negro
previsão de tempo, boletim meteorológico	weather forecast	previsión/boletin metereológico
profundidade	depth	profundidad, sonda
profundo	deep	profundo
propietário	owner	propietario
quebra-mar	jetty, pier	malecón
quebra-mar, molhe, cais	breakwater, pier, quay, dock	muelle, rompeolas
raiz	root (eg. of mole)	raíz
rampa	ramp, slipway	rampa, varadero
recife	reef	arrecife
reparações	repairs	reparacións
restinga	reef, spit	restinga

Portuguese	English	Spanish
salinas	saltpans	salinas
serviços médicas	medical services	servicios médicos
sotavento	leeward	sotavento
sujo	foul, dirty	sucio
sul	south	sur
supermercado	supermarket	supermercado
tôrre	tower	torre
veleiro, reparações velas	sailmaker, sail repairs	velero, reparacións velas
verde	green	verde
vermelho	red	rojo
viveiros	mussel rafts	viveros

Meteorology and sea state

Portuguese	English	Spanish
calma	calm (Force 0, 0–1kns)	calma
aragem	light airs (Force 1, 1–3kns)	ventolina
vento fraco, brisa	light breeze (Force 2, 4–6kns)	flojito
vento bonançoso, brisa suave	gentle breeze (Force 3, 7–10kns)	flojo
vento moderado, brisa moderado	moderate breeze (Force 4, 11–16kns)	bonancible
vento fresco, brisa fresca	fresh breeze (Force 5, 17–21kns)	fresquito
vento muito fresco, brisa forte	strong breeze (Force 6, 22–27kns)	fresco
vento forte, ventania moderada	near gale (Force 7, 28–33kns)	frescachón
vento muito forte, ventania fresca	gale (Force 8, 34–40kns)	duro
vento tempestuoso, ventania forte	severe gale (Force 9, 41–47kns)	muy duro
temporal, ventania total	storm (Force 10, 48–55kns)	temporal
temporal desfieto, tempestade	violent storm (Force 11, 56–63kns)	borrasca, tempestad
furacão, ciclone	hurricane (Force 12, 64+kns)	huracán
aguaceiro	shower	aguacero
arrebentação	breakers	rompientes
bailadeiras	overfalls, tide race	escarceos
borrasca	squall	turbonada
chuva	rain	lluvia
crista	ridge (high)	dorsal
depressão	depression (low)	depresión
mar bravo	rough sea	mar gruesa
mar cavado	short, steep sea	mar corta
mar chão	slight sea	marejadilla
neblina	mist	neblina
nevoeiro	fog	niebla
nublado	cloudy	nubloso
ondulação	swell	mar de leva
rajada	gust	racha
saraiva	hail	granizada
trovoada	thunderstorm	tempestad

VII. Abbreviations used on charts

Spanish	Portuguese	Meaning
F.	F.	Fixed
D.	Rl.	Flashing
Gp.D.	Rl.Agr.	Group flashing
F.D.	F.Rl.	Fixed and flashing
F.Gp.D.	F.Rl.Agr.	Fixed and group flashing
Ct.	Ct	Quick flashing
Gp.Ct. flashing	Ct int	Interrupted quick
Oc.	Oc.	Occulting
Gp.Oc.	Oc.Agr.	Group occulting
Iso	Is.	Isophase
Mo.	Morse	Morse

Colours

am.	am.	Yellow
az.	azul	Blue
b.	br.	White
n.	pr.	Black
r.	vm.	Red
v.	vd.	Green

Seabed

A	A.	Sand
Al	Alg	Weed
R.	R.	Rock
F	L.	Mud
Co.	B.	Gravel

Index

Index

Index